The TUDOR
YEARS

Edited by John Lotherington

Contributing authors
David Grossel, Henry Jefferies, John Lotherington,
Malcolm Saxon, Peter Servini, Roy Sloan, Edward Towne.

Hodder & Stoughton

A MEMBER OF THE HODDER HEADLINE GROUP

British Library Cataloguing in Publication Data

Tudor Years
  I. Lotherington, John
  942.05

ISBN 0 340 53794 9

First published 1994
Impression number   10 9 8 7 6 5 4
Year   1998 1997 1996

Typeset by Wearset, Boldon, Tyne and Wear
Printed in Great Britain for Hodder & Stoughton Educational, a division of Hodder Headline
Plc, 338 Euston Road, London NW1 3BH by Redwood Books, Trowbridge, Wiltshire.

CONTENTS

LIST OF ILLUSTRATIONS

LIST OF MAPS

LIST OF DIAGRAMS

ACKNOWLEDGEMENTS

The maps were drawn by Alison Ryder. Thanks are due to her for her care and expertise, and to Jennifer Page and Stephen McEvoy for their assistance in typing and indexing. And throughout the preparation of this book the guidance and support offered by David Lea and Mandy Hill have been much appreciated.

The Publishers would like to thank the following for permission to reproduce copyright material:

Barrie & Jenkins for extracts from *The King's Cardinal* by Peter Gwyn, 1990; Cambridge University Press for extracts from *Elizabeth I* by G Regan and *The Tudor Constitution* by G R Elton; Cambridge University Press and Professor G R Elton for extracts from *The Parliament of England 1559–1581* by G R Elton, 1986; Jonathan Cape for extracts from *Essays in Elizabethan History* (1958) and *Elizabeth and her Parliaments* (1953, 1957) by J E Neale; Chatto & Windus for extract from *The Elizabethan World Picture* by E M W Tillyard; Eyre & Spottiswood Ltd for extracts from the following *Edward IV* by Charles Ross, 1974, *Henry VII* by S B Chrimes, 1988 and *Henry VIII* by Professor J J Scarisbrick, 1968; Professor R A Griffiths for extract from *The Reign of Henry VI* by R Griffiths, 1981; The Historical Association for extracts from the following *English Puritanism* by P Collinson, 1983, 'William Cecil and the British Dimension of Early Elizabethan Foreign Policy' by Jane Dawson, *History* 74, 241, 1989 and 'Faction at the Court of Henry VIII; the Fall of Anne Boleyn' by E W Ives, *History*, June 1972; HarperCollins Publishers for extract from *Peace, Print and Protestantism 1450–1558* by C S L Davies, 1977; Longman Group UK for extracts from the following *Elizabethan Parliaments 1559–1601* by M Graves, *Elizabeth I* by C Haigh, *The Age of Elizabeth* by D M Palliser, 1983, *Henry VII* by A F Pollard, *Poverty and Vagrancy in Tudor England* by Dr J Pound, 1978, *The English Court* by D Starkey, 1987, *The Reign of Mary Tudor* by Tittler, 1983 and *The Making of Elizabethan Foreign Policy 1558–1603* by R B Wernham, 1987; Oxford University Press for extracts from the following *Tudor England* by John Guy, 1988, *Hospitality in Early Modern England* by F Heal, 1990, *The Nobility of Later Medieval England* by K B MacFarlane (edited by J Campbell), 1973 and *The Tudor Regime* by Penny Williams, 1979; Random House UK Limited for extracts from *Before the Armada* by R B Wernham (Cape), 1966; Thames and Hudson Ltd for extract from *Robin Hood* by J C Holt, 1989, rev.; Weidenfeld & Nicholson Ltd for extract from *Religion and the Decline of Magic* by Keith Thomas, 1971.

The Publishers would also like to thank the following for permission to reproduce copyright illustrations in this volume:

By courtesy of the Board of Trustees of the Victoria and Albert Museum – cover.
The National Portrait Gallery, London p.1; p.32; p.55; p.61; p.122; p.160; p.182; p.208; p.400; p.403; p.404; p.405; p.409.
The British Museum p.107.
The Mansell Collection p.197.
By Courtesy of the Marquess of Salisbury p.410.
By permission of Sudeley Castle, Gloucestershire p.406.
Douce.D. Subt.30, Bodleian Library p.407.
Siena, Pinacoteca Nazionale/SCALA p.408

Every effort has been made to trace and acknowledge ownership of copyright. The Publishers will be glad to make suitable arrangements with any copyright holders whom it has not been possible to contact.

PREFACE: APPROACH TO STUDY

—

1 USING THE TEXT

TEXTBOOKS are dangerous. They can encourage a passive approach to learning if all that is thought necessary is the mechanical absorption of the facts on the page. An active approach is always more interesting and more successful – the purpose of this book is to provide the structure and stimulus for individual thought and for further enquiry.

Each chapter is divided into subsections to make the material more manageable, and to help you focus on what is most important there is a section of discussion points at the end of each chapter. They may be used for class debate or to guide note-taking. Answering them in sequence could be one way of structuring your notes as well as stimulating some of your own interpretation.

The views and disagreements of historians are mentioned in the introduction to each chapter and throughout the text. Brief references or summaries cannot do them justice and their books need to be consulted at first hand whenever possible. There is also a bibliography at the end of each chapter which suggests the next steps for further reading.

Major historical works can sometimes seem daunting. If this is the case, the best approach may be to allot a specific amount of time and then, with a clear idea in your mind of the question at issue, you can use chapter headings and the index to find out as efficiently as possible what you need to know.

2 USING THE DOCUMENTS

There are short documentary extracts interspersed in the text and longer documentary exercises at the ends of several chapters.

The documents within the text are there as reminders of what is the basis for everything the historian says. It is important to answer the questions that follow each document so that its significance becomes clear and the points being made in the text are linked, supported – or amended according to your own interpretation.

The longer documentary exercises give you an opportunity to approach a specific historical problem in greater depth. The extracts are longer than those normally used at G.C.S.E., so it is necessary to read them two or three times before answering the questions. It is also advisable to review the relevant section of the preceding chapter, and to follow up references to other historians' views which you may want to support or criticise in the light of your own source-based findings.

3 ASSESSING AND ANSWERING ESSAY QUESTIONS

At the end of every chapter there is a list of essay questions. Before starting on one you need to check whether you have sufficient infor-mation and, if not, where to go to gather more. But, more importantly, you should choose a question which will give full scope to your own thoughts rather than just an opportunity to report the basic facts and historians' viewpoints. You need to be sure you have something to say, a particular line to take. And before you make a final choice, think through carefully what a question demands – there can be pitfalls in what, at first sight, appears easy.

It is essential to plan an essay. Write down an outline of your argu-ment so that when you write the final version it will be coherent. List paragraph headings and number them so that you have a sequence which will allow the argument to unfold neatly. Check that your plan includes, as appropriate: references to primary sources, any relevant historical debates, comparative points, context in time (what was going on before and after) and space (larger European or global develop-ments).

As well as choosing and practising on an individual question, you should note the range and types of essay questions. Try framing an argument for as many questions as possible – it helps you to establish different perspectives on a topic and, to be strictly practical, it prepares you for whatever type of question the examiner decides to set you at the end of your course. There are also essay writing exercises to illus-trate some of the approaches which may be called for.

Finally, there are other end of chapter exercises which are compara-tive or historiographical, or relate to the use of historical categories. It would be worth incorporating the insights and information these exer-cises yield into the main body of your notes along with an indication of which essay questions they should help to answer.

THE WARS OF THE ROSES

—

Richard III, anon.

1 INTRODUCTION

The appeal of the Tudors

Thou elvish – marked, abortive and rooting hog! . . .,
Thou slander of thy heavy mother's womb!
Thou loathed issue of thy father's loins!
Thou rag of honour! . . .

(*William Shakespeare*, Richard III Act 1, Scene III)

THE reputation of certain English kings is so notorious that they are familiar even to those with no serious interest in history. One such figure is Richard III. His image as the evil hunchback who murdered his nephews, seized the throne and was then killed at Bosworth Field in 1485, is secure in our national mythology. Richard's notoriety seems strange. Many kings have been accused of murder and died violent deaths and they are not widely remembered.

It is not in fact difficult to establish why such controversy surrounds Richard III. First of all, William Shakespeare drew an unforgettable portrait of him as a tormented hunchback, which may not bear much resemblance to his looks or deeds, but is familiar to countless people who have never read a serious history book. The quotation with which this book opens illustrates the venom constantly directed at Richard III by Shakespeare.

Richard's overthrow led to the establishment of the Tudor dynasty, which ruled the country until 1603. Henry Tudor, who became Henry VII, had a very questionable claim to the throne and his family needed to have the legitimacy of their right to rule established. One obvious way was to blacken Richard III's name and reputation. Tudor historians, such as Polydore Vergil and Sir Thomas More, were not paid government propagandists, but they certainly understood the need to justify the current regime.

For different reasons, historians of the nineteenth and early twentieth centuries continued to attach great importance to 1485. It came to be seen as the turning point between the medieval and modern worlds. In particular, it was in the sixteenth century that the English Church became free from control by the Pope. Moreover, the Tudors were an unusually talented dynasty. Henry VIII and Elizabeth I are amongst England's best known rulers. Events such as the defeat of the Spanish Armada in 1588 have associated the Tudors with some of the more stirring episodes in English history. More recently historians have become interested in the extent to which policies and practices of the Tudors were based on their Yorkist and Lancastrian predecessors.

The problem of the fifteenth century

Traditionally historians have neglected the fifteenth century in favour of the sixteenth century. Until the 1950s it was usually portrayed as a dark period of endless civil war – the so called 'Wars of the Roses', which followed the humiliating loss of the Hundred Years War against France. In contrast, it was argued that Henry VII established a 'new monarchy' in England which brought stable and effective government to the country. Historians were further put off by the lack of good contemporary sources. The century did not produce many historians and this leads to excessive reliance on official documents which are dry and often difficult to use.

Over the last thirty years, however, professional historians have shown a growing interest in the fifteenth century. J R Lander challenged existing assumptions after a close examination of the official records. Amongst his 'revisionist' arguments was that the amount of fighting in the Wars of the Roses was actually very small and that in this supposedly barbaric century the English peasantry achieved a degree of prosperity not to be equalled for another three centuries.

It has also become common to view Edward IV, who ruled the country for nearly twenty-five years, and Henry VII as men with similar aims and methods. The fall of the house of York and the establishment of the Tudor dynasty after 1485 can, on the basis of this view, be seen as no more than a change of personnel. By extension it becomes difficult to see 1485 as the beginning of some ill-defined 'modern' age.

Many of the revisionist arguments of historians, such as Lander, are now accepted. No historian would now deny the limited effect of the Wars of the Roses on much of the population. The relative prosperity of the peasantry is also accepted and the Church is certainly no longer seen as decadent and in desperate need of reform. This does not mean that the debate is over; it has simply become more refined and sophisticated.

For example, Charles Ross, the author of the standard modern biography of Edward IV, argues that Edward's reputation has risen too far. He may have been far superior to the inept Henry VI, but he was impulsive and over-confident. For Ross, Edward was neither as ingenious, nor as ruthless, nor as consistent as Henry VII.

Other recent historians such as Alexander Grant and A J Pollard agree that there is now too much stress on the continuity between the fifteenth and sixteenth centuries. They argue that between the 1450s and 1480s the monarchy was weaker than at any time since 1066. Henry VI, Edward V and Richard III all lost the throne during this period, while Edward IV was temporarily dethroned. After 1485 there may have been many rebellions, but all of them failed. Henry VII's great achievement, therefore, was to restore dynastic and governmental stability after a period of chaos. In this sense 1485 was to be a turning point.

Outline of the Wars of the Roses

The Wars of the Roses lasted from the early 1450s until 1487. There was only sporadic violence and the symbolism of the White Rose of York and the Red Rose of Lancaster, which Shakespeare utilised so effectively, would not have been familiar to contemporaries.

Indeed, there is a case for arguing that there were four very distinct episodes, each of which had its own causes and did not necessarily directly relate to previous events. In 1455, there was a skirmish at St Albans. Between 1459–61, there was serious fighting leading to the bloody battle of Towton and the overthrow of Henry VI by Edward IV. Further conflict between 1469–71 saw the temporary return of Henry VI and the eventual triumph of Edward IV. In 1485, Henry Tudor defeated Richard III at Bosworth Field and then survived the final military challenge to his throne at Stoke in 1487.

May 1455: St Albans – Yorkist victory

September 1459: Blore Heath – Indecisive
October 1459: Ludford Bridge – Lancastrian victory
July 1460: Northampton – Yorkist victory
December 1460: Wakefield – Lancastrian victory
February 1461: Mortimer's Cross – Yorkist victory
February 1461: St Albans – Lancastrian victory
March 1461: Towton – Yorkist Victory
(Edward IV wins the throne)

July 1469: Edgecote – Lancastrian/Neville victory

March 1470: 'Lose-Coat' Field – Yorkist victory
(*October 1470:* Re-adeption of Henry VI)

April 1471: Barnet – Yorkist victory
May 1471: Tewkesbury – Yorkist victory
(Return of Edward IV)

August 1485: Bosworth Field – Tudor/Lancastrian victory
(Henry VII wins the throne)

June 1487: Stoke – Tudor victory

Two separate issues need to be examined. First of all the events that brought about the overthrow of Henry VI, Edward IV and Richard III. Second any general causes that underlay the instability of this period must be established.

2 HENRY VI AND THE CRISIS OF THE 1450S

Henry VI was one of the most unfortunate and unsuccessful of English monarchs. The circumstances of his birth suggested otherwise. His father, Henry V, had destroyed the French army at Agincourt in 1415 and established a huge English empire in France. The Treaty of Troyes (1420) made Henry V heir to the French throne and the French King's daughter became his wife.

Henry VI inherited this vast empire in 1422, but within thirty-five years Lancastrian power in France was confined to the port of Calais and English rule was never to return. It would be easy simply to blame

Henry VI for these catastrophic disasters. It certainly did not help the English that Henry V's death (31 August 1422) followed the birth of his son (6 December 1421) by only a few months. However, the government of the country during Henry VI's childhood was relatively stable and competent and the English were able to maintain their grip in France.

France was a much more populous and wealthy country than England and English influence was always likely to decline if a stronger and more capable French government emerged. Despite the coronation of Henry VI as King of France at Paris in 1431, the French claimant to the throne, Charles VII, began to consolidate his position in the 1430s. The English had always depended for their success on alliance with the Dukes of Brittany and Burgundy. The Dukes of Burgundy were wealthy and powerful rulers, who controlled much of eastern France and the Low Countries. In 1435, the French and Burgundians allied. The destruction of the Lancastrian empire in France was now simply a matter of time.

Nonetheless, Henry VI's reaction to these events was inept. By 1437, he had taken personal control of the government of the country. His marriage, in 1445, to Margaret of Anjou, was a typical error. She brought with her no dowry (land or money) and, therefore, no political benefit to the English Crown. Despite the lingering reputation of military invincibility, by August 1450 Normandy was lost to the King of France.

Even more devasting was the collapse of English power in Gascony in the south-west of France. This had belonged to the English monarchy for 300 years, but in July 1451 Bordeaux fell to the French. Dissident Gascons invited the English back the next year and an army was sent under the veteran Sir John Talbot, Earl of Shrewsbury, the most able and feared English General. In July 1453 his army was utterly defeated at Castillion and he was killed. The Hundred Years War had ended in ignominious defeat. Only Calais remained of the English possessions in France.

It would be absurd to blame Henry VI entirely for this. It might even be argued that the campaigns of his father had been foolish and ill-conceived and that it was unrealistic for England to challenge France. But Henry VI can possibly be blamed for the devasting rapidity and finality of the French victory. Traditionally war with France had been a popular policy in England, which was invariably supported by Parliament. The completeness of the English defeat was a devasting blow. With the exception of Calais, the coastline facing England was now in enemy hands and there was growing fear of French raids. To compound the problem in the summer of 1453 Henry suffered a complete nervous breakdown, possibly caused by defeat at Castillion.

Defeat in France was not Henry's only problem. Another major source of complaint was his method of governing the country. It was essential that any monarch should attempt to gain support and popularity from all sections of the aristocracy, on whom he was so dependent for assistance in governing the country. There were few paid royal servants and the aristocracy was the main agent of government in the provinces. The main technique for gaining their support was the use of patronage. This meant no more than the distribution of titles, land, and government office to the great landowners of the realm. In return, they would enforce royal authority in the shires and provide manpower for the king.

It was essential that patronage should be distributed evenly and fairly. It was in this task that Henry proved singularly inept. In the 1440s he came to rely on a small group of favourites attached to the Royal Household. In particular, he favoured the Beaufort family. They were of royal blood and descended from John of Gaunt, Edward III's third son. Originally, their line was illegitimate, but the family was legitimised in 1397 and quickly became prominent. By the 1440s the Beaufort family, who became Dukes of Somerset, had accumulated vast amounts of patronage and influence. Even more important was the Duke of Suffolk. He owed his ascendancy to his influence over the King. He and his close allies, Adam Moleyns and Lord Saye and Sele were given land, money and office by the King in a thoughtless and extravagant fashion. They became particularly prominent in East Anglia and the South-East. It seemed that the only criterion for gaining royal patronage was to be a member of the King's Household.

This might not have mattered if these had been men of ability, but they were mostly closely associated with the disastrous events in France. In particular, Edmund Beaufort, Duke of Somerset, was – with some justice – held responsible for the defeats in Normandy. At home there was further strong criticism of these men. The support of the aristocracy was vital if law and order was to be maintained in the shires. Quite often rival families would contest for power and influence. A growing number of people began to believe that the King's Household was unduly favoured and that royal justice was being manipulated in the interests of a faction. Lord Saye and Sele, for example, was entrusted with vast amounts of land and influence in Kent by the King. He became Constable of Dover Castle and Warden of the Cinque Ports. The county, however, was notorious for its disorder and Henry was blamed for this. Ralph Griffiths summarises Henry's failings excellently in his biography:

> To ensure social stability and public order, a circumspect
> government needed to avoid antagonising prominent magnates
> . . . Wise, and as far as politics allowed, impartial patronage was
> the key to regional control. This is precisely what Suffolk's
> regime did not appreciate.

Rival Royal Houses

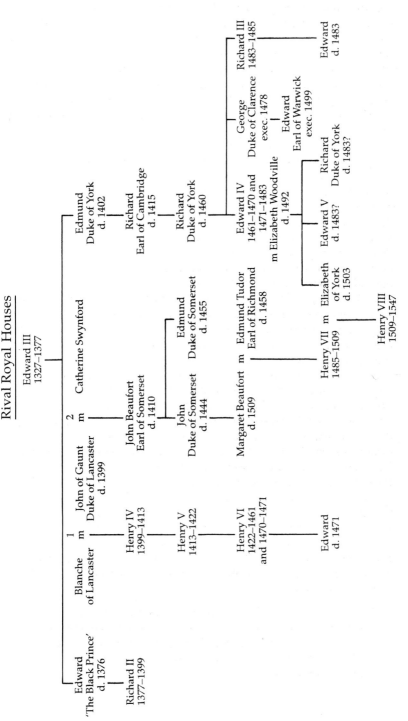

3 OPPOSITION TO THE GOVERNMENT 1450–53

The great favours granted to the house of Beaufort were bound to offend other families of royal blood. By far the most important was the family of Richard, Duke of York. He was descended from the second son of Edward III and was one of the greatest landowners in the country. His estates were widely scattered throughout England and also in Ireland. He was particularly well endowed with land on the Welsh borders.

Richard was ten years older than Henry and there seems always to have been some mutual antagonism. In July 1440, he was appointed Lieutenant-Governor of Normandy for five years. There is no evidence that he made much of what was admittedly a very difficult position. It is clear that Henry favoured the Beauforts over him and that Richard left his position owed a large amount of money by the Crown. He was then sent to Ireland for ten years to recover lands lost to the Irish, further emphasising his isolation from the centre of affairs. It seemed likely that Henry would choose a Beaufort in preference to him as his successor should he remain childless.

As for Parliament at this time it was the King's servant and generally very obedient. The King could summon and dismiss Parliament entirely at his own convenience and parliamentary (or statute) law gave authority to royal policies. However, under normal circumstances, the King was expected to 'live of his own' on the revenues of his own estates and customs dues which were traditionally granted for life. Additional taxation had to be approved by Parliament and this was rarely possible, except for a popular military campaign.

The Parliament which assembled in November 1449 was not compliant. The disastrous situation in France was becoming clear, while foreign trade was at a standstill thanks to an embargo by Philip, Duke of Burgundy. This reduced cloth exports to the Low Countries, which were the basis of English wealth, by one-third.

Parliament blamed these disasters on the clique which surrounded Henry VI. The Duke of Suffolk was sent to the Tower. He was released in May 1450 and then murdered as he went into exile. His close supporter, Adam Moleyns, had already been murdered the previous January by unpaid and mutinous soldiers at Portsmouth.

Finally, a genuinely popular rebellion broke out in Kent. Disaffection was understandable in this part of England; there was a growing fear of French invasion and trade with the Low Countries had virtually ceased. Kent was a county with a large number of independent farmers, who were not closely dependent on a particular lord, and there was resentment at the patronage granted to Lord Saye and Sele, one of Henry's most unpopular supporters.

The rebellion broke out in May 1450 under the leadership of Jack Cade who claimed to be connected with the family of Richard of York.

The rebels' demands were very specific: first of all that the King's Council should include all the great aristocrats of the country and second they supported Parliament in demanding Acts of Resumption. Acts of Resumption would return to the King all lands that he had granted to his supporters. In this way he would be able to live of his own and would require no parliamentary taxation. A first Act of Resumption was passed in May 1450, but a mob still executed Lord Saye and Sele in July after Henry had fled from London.

There is no evidence that the Duke of York inspired Jack Cade's rebellion. Moreover, despite the King's weakness, his wife, Margaret of Anjou, proved a formidable figure and helped to organise the dispersal of the rebels. But Richard of York did return in September 1450 from Ireland. He was not seeking the Crown, but he wanted to consolidate his position as heir to the throne. He also resented Henry's continued favouritism towards his rival, the Duke of Somerset.

Despite its problems, Henry's regime survived. In part this reflects the power of the monarchy in the fifteenth century. A man like Richard of York may have associated himself with popular discontent, but was clearly essentially a self-interested and disappointed intriguer. Henry also now asserted himself more effectively than ever before in his reign. Parliamentary grievances were responded to by a second and more effective Act of Resumption later in 1450. Henry also made a concerted effort to deal with problems of law and order at a time when, throughout the country, violence was believed to be increasing dramatically. In 1451, he toured Kent and in 1452/3 there were further tours to other areas in which he acted as judge and used his power and influence to enforce the law.

Richard of York did mount a half hearted conspiracy, but was forced to back down in March 1452. By 1453, the restoration of royal authority was so complete that a Parliament at Reading voted sufficient funds to raise 20 000 men to re-conquer France.

4 ROYAL MADNESS AND THE DRIFT TO CIVIL WAR 1453–59

The events of 1449–53 demonstrated the weaknesses of Henry's government. The war in France, the favouritism towards a small circle of courtiers, the irresponsible distribution of land and office, and the failure to maintain order had caused a sustained challenge to royal authority. But, by early 1453 it seemed not inconceivable that Sir John Talbot would re-conquer Gascony, the most unpopular royal servants were dead, and Richard of York could be seen as no less selfish than his aristocratic rivals. Acts of Resumption had been passed and the King had toured the south of England in a fairly successful attempt to restore order.

Two events shattered this progress. In August 1453, news arrived of the disaster at Castillion, which destroyed for ever the chance of re-establishing an English empire in France. At the same time, and possibly as a direct result, Henry VI suffered a complete breakdown which lasted for eighteen months. Certain diagnosis of his condition is of course impossible, but it seems likely that it was some form of schizophrenia. For the rest of his life, his mental health was always fragile.

The incapacity of the King meant that government of the country had to be re-organised with some urgency. A further complicating factor was the birth of an heir to the thone, Prince Edward, in October 1453. Margaret of Anjou possessed the energy and strength of character that her husband increasingly lacked. Her determination to ensure that their son succeeded Henry as king was to be at the centre of the struggle for power over the next two decades.

Richard of York was an obvious candidate to become Protector, but there were other claimants, such as the Duke of Exeter and Edmund Beaufort, Duke of Somerset. Success in the struggle for power would depend on the attitude of the other great aristocrats. Most important of these was Richard Neville, who became Earl of Warwick in 1449. The Nevilles had risen to prominence largely by virtue of their ability to produce children and make successful marriages to great heiresses. Originally their power was concentrated in the north of England. The North was thinly populated and economically backward compared with the South. The need, however, to defend the border against the raids of the Scots created a warlike atmosphere and a large number of experienced fighting men. It was the policy of the government to give responsibility for defence of the border to the local aristocratic families.

Traditionally the Percy family had been dominant, but they had rebelled against Henry IV and by 1450 the Nevilles surpassed their influence, especially in Yorkshire. The Nevilles' great castle at Middleham in north Yorkshire and their possession of large estates gave them a loyal following. In particular, many 'retainers' attached themselves to the Nevilles. A retainer agreed a contract, or indenture, with a great lord and agreed to serve him in return for his patronage and protection.

Richard Neville's marriage to Anne Beauchamp, heiress to the Earl of Warwick, brought him great estates throughout England. In 1453, he was disputing possession of the lordship of Glamorgan with the Duke of Somerset, to whom it had been granted by Henry.

Neville's grievances against Somerset and Henry ensured that he would support Richard of York. In November 1453, Somerset was sent to the Tower and on 27 March 1454 Richard of York was finally appointed 'Protector and Defender of the Kingdom of England and Chief Councillor of the King'.

York did not govern the country badly, but he could not pretend to have the support of all the great aristocrats. In particular, the Duke of Somerset and Henry Percy, Earl of Northumberland, were bound to be foes of a Yorkist/Neville alliance and Margaret of Anjou would be suspicious that Richard of York sought the throne.

Everything was thrown into confusion by the recovery of Henry by Christmas 1454. Somerset was released from prison and restored to the vital position of Captain of Calais which gave him control of a garrison of 1000 men. York and Warwick (Richard Neville) fled to the North and were then summoned to a Great Council at Leicester in May 1455. The estates of the house of Lancaster were concentrated in this area of the Midlands, which increasingly became the centre of royal power.

The reaction of York and Warwick was to raise an army and the two sides met at St Albans on 22 May 1455. This was a skirmish rather than a battle with only a few casualties. But two of the dead were Somerset and Northumberland.

St Albans may have seemed a triumph for Richard of York and some benefits were gained. The Earl of Warwick became Captain of Calais and turned it into a Yorkist stronghold. For a few months between November 1455 and February 1456 Richard again acted as Protector as Henry, presumably, relapsed into insanity.

But there is no evidence of widespread support for the Yorkists and Nevilles. Indeed, they had shed blood and earned the hostility of many other peers. Moreover, Henry may have been in serious decline, but Margaret of Anjou was a formidable and determined antagonist, anxious to protect her son's right to the throne.

The years between 1455 and the outbreak of serious fighting in 1459 are not well documented by contemporary historians and the pattern is not always clear. Some attempts were made to reconcile the opposing factions. In March 1458, there was a 'Loveday' when the victors of the Battle of St Albans met the sons of the men who had been killed and performed a public act of reconciliation.

This seems to have been an isolated incident. More important was the exclusion of the Yorkists and Nevilles from government. The Earl of Warwick used his base at Calais to raise funds by piracy, while York withdrew to his estates. Meanwhile, Margaret of Anjou increasingly governed the country from the Midlands, where there was the greatest concentration of Lancastrian estates. The city of Coventry was her main base. Coventry was a centre of clothmaking and the fourth largest city in the country; its population was loyal to the King. The move to Coventry suggested a lack of confidence amongst the Lancastrians that they could be sure of the loyalty of the people of London and of those aristocrats who were not their personal followers.

In the summer of 1459, a Lancastrian council at Coventry finally decided to accuse the Yorkists and Nevilles of treason. Their response was to raise armies. Richard of York raised a force in the Welsh

Marches while the Nevilles drew on their strength in north Yorkshire and Calais. After a skirmish at Blore Heath, they moved to Ludlow shadowed by a larger royal army. The troops from Calais were led by Andrew Trollope, an able veteran of the wars in France. They were shocked to discover that they were expected to fight the King and changed sides. York and Warwick had no option but to abandon the struggle. On the night of 12 October with the armies drawn up at Ludford they decided to flee; York escaped to Ireland and Warwick returned to Calais.

The rebels had attracted very little support, but their resources were so vast that this had not really mattered. Understandably Margaret of Anjou was determined to follow up the Lancastrian triumph. A Parliament was summoned to Coventry known to Yorkists as the 'Parliament of Devils'. Acts of Attainder were passed against the rebels. This legal procedure effectively combined an accusation of treason with the loss of civil rights. The Yorkists and Nevilles were faced with permanent legal condemnation and the confiscation of their estates. Inevitably they would try to reverse this situation.

5 THE FIRST WARS 1459–61

These two years saw the most sustained fighting of the Wars of the Roses. In June 1460 after consulting with Richard of York in Dublin, Warwick landed in Kent. Accompanied by York's son, the Earl of March (the future Edward IV), he marched to Northampton where the Lancastrian army was defeated and the hapless King captured. The Yorkists then marched to London and summoned a Parliament to meet in October. Its main purpose, of course, would be to reverse the Acts of Attainder.

However, when Richard of York returned to England for the first time he laid claim to the throne. There is no evidence that this had always been his aim. Indeed, he seems to have surprised his closest supporters. It was agreed that he should succeed Henry VI on the latter's death.

This was an unworkable compromise and particularly unacceptable to Margaret of Anjou whose son would be denied the throne. Further fighting was inevitable. In December at Wakefield Richard of York and Warwick's father, the Earl of Salisbury, were killed. In February 1461 there was a Yorkist victory under the leadership of Edward (now Duke of York) at Mortimer's Cross but it was cancelled out by defeat for Warwick at the second Battle of St Albans and the recovery of Henry VI by his supporters.

Margaret of Anjou now had Henry as her figurehead and a clear road to London. She failed to seize this outstanding opportunity and withdrew to the North. This seems an inexplicable decision, but her army had mainly been recruited in the North and Yorkist propaganda had convinced the population of London that a band of uncontrollable barbarians was approaching the city. It was, therefore, likely that the Lancastrians would be resisted.

This hesitancy enabled Warwick and Edward of York to seize London and in March 1461 Edward was proclaimed King. Edward IV was a formidable opponent for the Lancastrians. His energy and appearance – he was a notably handsome man and well over 6 feet tall – contrasted starkly with the enfeebled Henry VI. He quickly raised an army and marched to meet the Lancastrians.

By far the bloodiest battle of the Wars of the Roses took place at Towton near Pontefract in south Yorkshire on 28/9 March 1461. Estimates of the numbers involved in battles of this period are notoriously unreliable, but the armies at Towton were certainly huge by the standards of the day and may have reached 25 000. The battle was fought in a blizzard and brought complete victory to Edward IV. Margaret of Anjou and Prince Edward fled to Scotland.

Until his capture and imprisonment by the Yorkists in 1465, Henry VI wandered as a fugitive in northern England. He has been treated harshly by historians. There is no evidence of mental instability before 1453, but he did govern the country through a coterie of favourites and showed no sensitivity in his dealings with the Yorkists and Nevilles. Great aristocrats expected great influence, especially if they had royal blood, and this was repeatedly denied Richard of York. After 1453 it was Margaret of Anjou who was the effective leader of the Lancastrian cause and Henry became a mere figurehead. The degree of Henry's personal responsibility for the outbreak of war has been much debated. How far others were to blame and how far the wars reflected weaknesses in the social and political system will be discussed later in this chapter.

6 EDWARD IV: THE EARLY YEARS 1461–69

Edward had the appearance and physical dynamism of a true king. His record has been much debated. He undoubtedly made serious mistakes leading to the loss of the throne between 1469–71. His methods of government, especially after 1471, anticipate the vigorous and effective approach of Henry VII. On the other hand much of his success appears to be the result of good luck rather than wise policies and his failure to secure the peaceful accession to the throne of his son after his death must be accounted a great failure.

Edward started his reign facing major problems. In the words of his biographer, Charles Ross, 'Towton had discredited but not destroyed the Lancastrian cause'. Margaret of Anjou and Prince Edward would be invaluable figureheads for any foreign power or discontented aristocrat who wished to challenge the King. There were still Lancastrian strongholds in remote corners of the kingdom. In Northumberland Lancastrians retained control of Alnwick, Bamburgh and Dunstanburgh castles. Twice they were driven out only to return until their final defeat in the summer of 1464. Harlech Castle remained in Lancastrian hands until 1468.

In order to retain the throne, Edward needed broad based aristocratic support. The Earl of Warwick's reputation as the 'Kingmaker' is something of an exaggeration; he was less successful in battle than Edward. But his influence was still vast. In the South, he was Captain of Calais, Constable of Dover Castle, and Warden of the Cinque Ports. In the North, Warwick now held the Wardenships of both the eastern and western Marches on the Scottish border for the Neville family and so had sole responsibility for the defence of northern England against the Scots. The gentry of north Yorkshire provided a strongly loyal band of personal retainers with a tradition of violence.

During the 1460s, Warwick became estranged from Edward IV. This was partly a consequence of his arrogance and ambition and dislike of other councillors, such as Sir William (later Lord) Hastings who was Edward IV's most loyal supporter. Edward was, however, the sole author of some of his difficulties. In particular, his marriage was a crucial and avoidable error. Romantic considerations played no part in the marriages of fifteenth-century kings and aristocrats. A well chosen bride could bring a beneficial foreign alliance, or valuable land and wealth. The power of the Nevilles was based above all on their marriages to wealthy heiresses. In April 1464, Edward IV married Elizabeth Woodville. He was an impulsive and sensual man and it does seem that romantic considerations determined his decision.

Although Elizabeth Woodville's mother, Jacquetta of Luxemburg, came from a great European aristocratic family, her father, the first Earl Rivers, was a minor aristocrat, and the new Queen with her family were disdained as upstarts.

The marriage was to bring Edward no political or economic benefits. The great magnates of the realm had not been consulted at a time when Warwick was actively negotiating a French marriage alliance and he was entitled to feel aggrieved. A further cause of grievance was the huge Woodville family. Elizabeth had two sons, five brothers and seven sisters. The simplest way to advance their position was to find wealthy marriage partners for them. This cut across the Earl of Warwick's own ambitions. He had two daughters, Isabel and Ann, and wanted suitable husbands for them. Edward IV seems to have opposed Warwick's plan for Isabel to marry his younger brother, the Duke of Clarence.

There was also a growing division over foreign policy between the King and Warwick. Warwick favoured an alliance with France, while Edward IV and the Woodvilles looked to Burgundy. The Low Countries, ruled by the Dukes of Burgundy, were the most important market for English cloth and economically crucial. Anti-French policies were universally popular and it does seem that Edward's strategy was sounder than Warwick's. In 1467 a trade treaty was signed with Burgundy and Edward's sister, Margaret of York, married Charles of Burgundy. Warwick's own negotiations with Louis XI of France failed completely and his brother George Neville, the Archbishop of York, was dismissed as Chancellor.

Warwick retreated to the North and used his influence amongst his retainers to foment uprisings against Edward. Meanwhile, his daughter, Isabel was married to the Duke of Clarence, Edward's volatile and untrustworthy younger brother.

7 POLITICAL CRISIS 1469–71

The next two years saw a return to political chaos. Warwick and Clarence initially used Calais as a base. On their return to England they quickly gathered support; many were attracted by Warwick's habitual and calculated generosity. Victory at Edgecote (26 July 1469) was followed by the capture of Edward IV and the ruthless execution of two Woodvilles, Lord Rivers and Sir John Woodville.

Warwick's lack of widespread aristocratic and popular support was soon exposed. He was forced to release Edward from Middleham Castle. Edward took steps to counter Warwick's influence in the North by restoring Henry Percy to the Earldom of Northumberland and returning many of his family estates lost after rebellion fifty years previously. Edward next returned to London in October 1469. Neither side was strong enough to defeat the other and uneasy stalemate ensued.

Warwick now proclaimed the Duke of Clarence as his candidate for the throne. They inspired a rising in Lincolnshire in March 1470, but it was easily suppressed by Edward at 'Lose-Coat' Field and in May 1470 they fled to France.

Louis XI of France was nicknamed 'the universal spider' and was a cunning and unprincipled intriguer. It was he who inspired a most unlikely alliance between Warwick and Margaret of Anjou at Angers in July 1470. They agreed to restore Henry VI and marry Prince Edward (Henry's son) to Ann, Warwick's younger daughter.

In September 1470, Warwick landed in Devon. He was joined by Clarence and Jasper Tudor, who was the staunchest supporter of the Lancastrian cause. Edward IV has been accused of complacency in the face of these events, but he was unavoidably detained by continued disaffection in Yorkshire. What is strange is the speed with which his authority collapsed. This can be partially explained by the defection of John, Marquis of Montagu, who was Warwick's brother and had lost both land and influence as a result of the restoration of the Percies.

In October, Edward was forced to flee virtually penniless to the Low Countries. In the legal phraseology of the day the 'Re-adeption' of Henry VI followed. Henry's new regime was always unstable. The Lancastrians and Nevilles were only united in their opposition to Edward IV, while the Duke of Clarence had gained little power and patronage from his selfish actions. In order to survive, Henry needed a vigour and unity which he was unlikely to find. He also needed an effective foreign policy for it was only with foreign help that Edward could return.

Charles the Bold of Burgundy was a wealthy and ambitious ruler married to Edward IV's sister. He was naturally worried by Warwick's links with France and the political debts that the Lancastrians owed to Louis XI. In 1471, Henry VI's government made a treaty with France and looked set to fight Burgundy. This was neither a popular, nor a sensible policy. Burgundy was England's greatest trading partner and popular opinion was always anti French. Charles of Burgundy's response was to give Edward 50 000 florins and some ships.

On 14 March 1471, Edward landed at Ravenspur on the Yorkshire coast. Initially he found little support, but at least Henry Percy remained neutral and did not hinder him. Edward now displayed his undisputed qualities of boldness and energy. He claimed to be only concerned with recovering his duchy and built up a following from the vast estates of his close ally Lord Hastings in the Midlands. He was joined by the unreliable Clarence who had gained little from Warwick and the Lancastrians.

Edward marched straight to London. If he gained control of London, it would be hard to dislodge him and it is significant that the citizens, who consistently seemed to have favoured Edward over Henry, admitted him without a struggle. On Easter Sunday (14 April) Edward's forces joined battle with Warwick's at Barnet. In a confused encounter in fog Warwick and Montagu were killed and the power of the Nevilles was broken.

Meanwhile, a Lancastrian army landed at Weymouth and, hearing of Warwick's defeat, began to march to Wales where the Lancastrians had a strong following. Edward IV again showed his decisiveness as a military leader and marched rapidly west. At Tewkesbury on 4 May the Lancastrians were crushed and Prince Edward, the real hope of the Lancastrian dynasty, was killed. On Edward's return to London Henry VI was almost certainly murdered in the Tower.

Edward's recovery of the throne owed something to good luck, but he must be given great credit for seizing the initiative and taking well-calculated risks. Although there was some sporadic activity by Lancastrians over the next two years, there was now no really convincing Lancastrian claimant to the throne. Henry Tudor who became the most active Lancastrian leader had only a remote claim and there seemed no reason why the Yorkist line should not establish itself permanently.

8 THE RULE OF EDWARD IV 1471–83

Edward IV was still a young and vigorous man in 1471. He quickly adopted a conciliatory policy towards his former opponents. There were only thirteen Acts of Attainder, six of which applied to the estates of dead men. Twenty-three earlier attainders were reversed. Able men, who had served the Lancastrian cause, entered Edward's service. A good example was John Morton. He had followed Margaret of Anjou into exile, but by 1478 was both Master of the Rolls (a leading judge) and Bishop of Ely; he later became one of Henry VII's most trusted servants. Special favour was given to Edward's younger brother, Richard of Gloucester. He succeeded Warwick as Great Chamberlain of England (controller of state occasions) and in 1471 was given Warwick's estates in the North. Richard's marriage to Warwick's daughter, Ann Neville, confirmed him as the King's representative in the North and the inheritor of Warwick's great influence.

Edward's government of the country in these years has been closely scrutinised by historians. Many of his actions have been seen as the precursors of the so called 'new monarchy' of Henry VII so that continuity of aims, methods, and personnel between the two men is now often stressed. It is perhaps hardly surprising that two men with similar problems adopted similar policies. It is also clear that no grand strategy lay behind Edward's methods of government. He had no conscious political philosophy, but simply a desire to govern more efficiently.

Wales

Although the government of England was relatively centralised compared to that of many European countries, effective government of the more remote regions remained difficult. (This is dealt with in depth in Chapter XII 'The Frontier Regions'.) The whole of Wales had been conquered by the English only relatively recently and its administration was particularly confused. The remote north and west had been divided into shires, but the border between Wales and England was still ruled by the Marcher Lords. 'March' simply means border and in this traditionally violent region, all powers of law and administration had been delegated to the Marcher Lords and the King's authority was only nominal.

Edward IV was himself a great Marcher Lord and in 1471 he created the Council in the Marches primarily to administer his own estates. But it was also necessary to combat the lawlessness of an area where no single authority responsible for law and order existed. In 1473, it was decided that the Prince of Wales should live in Ludlow in the heart of the Marches and his council became the centre of royal authority. Power was gradually consolidated in the hands of this council in

Ludlow. In 1476, the Prince of Wales was given extensive legal powers in Wales and the Marches by what was known as a General Commission of Oyer and Terminer. In 1477 he was given direct control of the Earldom of March and in 1479 of the Earldom of Pembroke.

Edward's policy was no more than a series of improvisations dictated as much by the need to find a role for his son as by any desire to improve the administration of the area. He was not prepared to abolish the Marcher lordships and create new shires as eventually happened in the reign of Henry VIII. The Prince's household was run by a Woodville, Anthony, Earl Rivers, which created suspicion amongst many other great aristocrats. On the other hand, a serious attempt had been made to co-ordinate and improve the administration of a notably violent region.

The North

Northern England presented special problems to any monarch at this time. There was a continued threat from Scotland and traditionally the local aristocrats had been given the task of organising the defence of the border. Many of the gentry felt a stronger loyalty to local magnates, such as the Nevilles and Percies, than to the King. Any great aristocrat in the North was guaranteed a large retinue of retainers.

Edward's policy in the North was conservative and arguably short-sighted. First of all, Henry Percy was restored to the Earldom of Northumberland in 1470. The Percies had a great following and he effectively became the King's Lieutenant in Northumberland and an influential figure in Yorkshire.

Even more important was the role given to Richard of Gloucester. All the estates, offices, and influence of the Earl of Warwick passed into his hands. The wardenship of the West March, for example, was to be hereditary in his family. Effectively, Edward was not extending royal power, but creating an over-mighty subject and concentrating a vast amount of power in the hands of Richard of Gloucester. Richard had his own private council and a vast following inherited from the Nevilles. It was this regional influence that enabled him to seize power on Edward's death. It might also be argued that the favouritism given to Richard was one factor in the continued disaffection of Edward's other brother, the Duke of Clarence, which led to his execution in 1478.

Administration and law and order

Edward's government was intensely personal. He aimed to improve efficiency not through a visionary programme of reform, but by improving the vigour and quality of the government's personnel.

One important example of this was the growing number of letters and warrants issued under the signet, which was the seal carried by the King's secretary. This meant that there was a growing amount of administration carried out by the King and his personal servants. Government was becoming increasingly centred on the King's Household and less use was made of the inefficient bureaucracy.

The King's Council retained its importance and its functions changed little. There is no doubt that many of Edward's personal servants were capable and effective, but he did lack a strong personal following in the provinces, such as that built up by Richard of Gloucester in the North, and there was always suspicion and jealousy of the Woodvilles. Edward made no consistent effort to restrain the power of the aristocracy. He still relied on the support of great families in the shires, such as the Stanleys in Lancashire and Cheshire. His failure to restrain aristocratic power can be contrasted unfavourably with the far more assertive Henry VII. If the country was not as lawless as in the reign of Henry VI, this simply reflected Edward's more powerful personality. No legal checks were placed on the aristocracy and their followings of retainers. In particular, nothing was done to control livery (the practice of wearing some badge of loyalty to a great lord), or maintenance (the intimidation of juries by aristocratic retainers). These practices are often seen as examples of excessive noble power used irresponsibly in the provinces.

There is a shortage of good primary source material for this period to illustrate the unchecked power of the aristocracy. However, the 'Paston Letters' are a series of documents written by members of an important gentry family in East Anglia. They are amongst the earliest surviving family letters in English and give an unrivalled insight into the problems and preoccupations of a gentry family of this period.

The Pastons became involved in a complicated legal dispute over property which brought them into conflict with the Duke of Suffolk, who was one of the most powerful men in East Anglia. In 1465, he sent a force of armed men against their property. Margaret Paston reported the incident in a letter a few days later.

1465, 27 October.
I was at Hellesdon upon Thursday last past and saw the place there, and in good faith there will be no creature think how foul and horribly it is arrayed but if they saw it. There cometh much people daily to wonder thereupon, both of Norwich and of   5
other places, and they speak shamefully thereof . . .
    The Duke [of Suffolk]'s men ransacked the church and bare away all the good that was left there, both of ours and of the tenants, and left not so much but that they stood on the high altar and ransacked the images, and took away such as they   10
might find, and put away the parson out of the church till they had done, and ransacked every man's house in the town five or

six times . . . If it might be, I would some men of worship might be sent from the King to see how it is, both there and at the lodge, ere than any snows come, that they may make report of   15
the truth . . .

And at the reverence of God, speed your matters now, for it is too horrible a cost and trouble that we now have daily, and must have till it be otherwise; and your men dare not go about to gather up your livelihood, and we keep here daily more than   20
three hundred persons for salvation of us and the place . . .

It is thought here that if my Lord of Norfolk would take upon him for you, and that he may have a commission for to inquire of such riots and robberies as hath be done to you and others in this country, then all the country will await upon him   25
and serve your intent, for the people love and dread him more than any lord except the King and my Lord of Warwick.

1 *When Margaret Paston uses the term 'country' (line 25), what does she mean?*

2 *Why do you think that the Duke of Suffolk was able to organise such extensive acts of violence?*

3 *To whom did the Pastons look for assistance? What is the significance of this?*

4 *The letter makes direct reference to the power of the Earl of Warwick. With whom is his power compared and to whom was it passed on?*

5 *Why do you think that the 'Paston Letters' are so valued by historians of the fifteenth century?*

Parliament and finance

Because disputes between monarchs and Parliament eventually came to assume such significance in English history, it is easy to misunderstand the role of Parliament. There is no evidence that Parliament either increased or decreased in importance in the reign of Edward IV. Parliament met six times in twenty-three years for a total of eighty-four and a half weeks. Its major task was to carry out the King's business. For example, a Parliament was summoned to secure the attainder of Clarence in 1478. Fifty-four parliamentary statutes were passed in Edward's reign, mostly concerned with economic matters. In 1463, he was granted tunnage and poundage (customs revenues) for life. Apart from this he was expected to 'live of his own' on the revenues of his estates and only ask for further taxes if war threatened.

The kings of England possessed limited resources compared with their continental rivals. Edward IV was the first king for 200 years to die solvent, which was an impressive achievement possibly owing more to good luck rather than good judgement.

Edward inherited a financial crisis. Henry VI's irresponsible distribution of royal lands and patronage had been a major cause of his unpopularity. A trade recession worsened matters in the middle of the century and greatly reduced customs revenues. Henry VI's annual revenues eventually dropped to £24 000 compared with £90 000 in the reign of Henry IV.

Edward IV boosted revenue by a series of practical measures. Better foreign relations created a better climate, for trade and customs revenues increased from an average of £25 000 at the start of his reign to £34 000 at the close. After the Treaty of Picquigny with France in 1475 (*see next section*) a valuable pension of 50 000 gold crowns was paid annually by the French King. A commercial treaty with Burgundy in 1478, which smoothed relations with England's most important trading partner, was only one of many successful trading agreements with foreign powers.

Another important source of revenue was the royal estates. Edward's own estates were extensive. Acts of Attainder added the estates of two dukes, five earls, one viscount and six barons. Edward also made money from the profits of wardships. Wardship gave the king the revenues of great estates when the heir was a minor. Early in Edward's reign, this included the lands of the Duchy of Buckingham and the Earldom of Shrewsbury.

The most significant development in financial policy lay in the use of the King's Chamber rather than the Exchequer in the administration of the royal estates. The Exchequer traditionally ran the finances of the government, but its methods had become inefficient and cumbersome. The Chamber was the main state room at Court and housed the Lord Chamberlain's department within the Royal Household. Edward adopted a system that had been used on the Yorkist estates. Receivers and surveyors were appointed and made directly responsible to the King's Chamber. This meant that money now went directly to the King and not through an inefficient bureaucracy.

Again matters were improved by a more direct and personal approach, which anticipated methods adopted by the Tudors. By 1475 Edward was solvent and did not need financial help from Parliament.

He can, however, be criticised for distributing rather than keeping forfeited estates. Although the French pension was valuable, it did cost him his freedom of action in foreign policy. Moreover, not all the administrative improvements were effective. On royal estates, such as the Duchy of Lancaster, it proved particularly difficult to implement new ideas. Henry VII was a far more efficient and vigorous administrator.

As a financier Edward was outstanding in comparison with Henry VI. Annual revenue rose from £25 000 to more than £65 000, but it is interesting to note that it reached more than £104 000 in the last year of Henry VII. It was, nonetheless, an impressive achievement to attain solvency and to establish many of the procedures later adopted by Henry VII.

Foreign policy

There was an intimate connection between foreign policy and financial stability throughout the fifteenth and sixteenth centuries. No monarch in any country was able to finance a war without borrowing vast sums and acquiring huge debts. One of the chief reasons for Edward's solvency was his avoidance of major foreign wars. However, luck and chance seem to have played a greater part in this than planning and foresight.

Edward was born at Rouen in Normandy and his father played a major role in the wars with France. He remained attached to the idea of military success in France. Throughout the fifteenth century France increased in power. Its population and resources greatly exceeded England's and Louis XI was a formidable ruler. Traditionally England had allied with Burgundy and Brittany against France, while Louis harboured territorial ambitions against both these states.

In 1472, Edward negotiated the Treaty of Châteaugiron with Brittany and promised to invade France, but the Bretons were defeated before any English invasion could take place. Despite the traditional popularity of war with France, Parliament was notably unenthusiastic about financing the war and in many ways Edward had a lucky escape.

This did not prevent further diplomatic and military planning. The Treaty of London (25 July 1474) united England and Burgundy in a plan to repeat Henry V's destruction of the French monarchy; Brittany then joined the alliance and even Scotland – so often a useful ally for France – was neutralised. Parliament provided substantial financial support and an army of over 11 000 was raised. This would be the largest force ever sent from England to France and by July 1475 Edward was established in Calais.

The seriousness of Edward's invasion plans has been questioned. He may simply have been trying to intimidate the French. Again, he was possibly saved by the lack of commitment of his allies. Charles the Bold of Burgundy had territorial ambitions to the east of his duchy and was reluctant to invade France. Edward's army lacked the experience of previous expeditions and was unlikely to have won great victories.

When the French offered a truce it was quickly accepted. In 1475, the Treaty of Picquigny followed the truce. In many ways this was very favourable to Edward; it gave him 75 000 crowns to be followed by an annual pension of 50 000 crowns and freedom of trade with France. In return there was to be a seven-year truce and Louis' son was to marry Edward's daughter. This French pension ensured that Edward no longer needed substantial grants from Parliament and contributed significantly to his solvency.

On the other hand it does seem that Edward had actively been seeking war and was only saved by good fortune. The death in battle of Charles the Bold at Nancy in 1477 enabled Louis XI to capture territory in Artois and Picardy in northern France. This directly threatened the vital English base of Calais and English trade with the Low Countries. Edward decided not to intervene and it can be argued that Louis' combination of cunning diplomacy and bribery had completely neutralised England. It was felt that Edward now cared too much for money and a life of ease and luxury.

In his last years Edward further limited his freedom of action on the continent by his decision to invade Scotland. There had been a series of Scottish raids possibly encouraged by the French, to which Edward responded by sending an army to Edinburgh in 1482. Apart from the recovery of Berwick, little was gained. Meanwhile at Arras in 1482, Burgundy and France made peace. One result of this was that Louis stopped paying Edward his annual pension. In addition, French possession of Artois was confirmed and the threat to Calais made real. The marriage alliance with France never took place. Things did not in fact turn out as badly as it seemed they might; Louis died in 1483 and Burgundy had not collapsed completely. On the other hand, there is no sign of coherence or effectiveness in Edward's foreign policy.

The end of the reign

Edward IV died on 25 August 1483 at the age of 41. The cause of his death was probably a stroke and an increasingly self indulgent private life may have contributed to this. In many ways he can be regarded as a capable ruler. In his youth he had proved daring and decisive and his audacious recovery of the throne after the 'Re-adeption' of Henry VI was a remarkable personal achievement.

Much has been made of his financial success, but his major concern seems to have been personal extravagance at the expense of the country as a whole. On the other hand, despite his generally unimpressive conduct of foreign policy, he did understand the importance of developing overseas trade.

There was an attractive side to his character. He was the first English king to possess a library and Court circles encouraged the Caxton printing press. His physical presence and youthful dynamism enhanced the prestige of the monarchy. But he must be blamed for the consequences of his marriage and the succession crisis that followed his death. One major task for any king was to ensure a peaceful succession. The unpopularity of the Woodvilles and Edward's own lack of support amongst the aristocracy as a whole ensured that this would not happen.

9 THE REIGN OF RICHARD III

The period between Edward's death and the Battle of Bosworth Field (August 1485) exemplifies the political instability of fifteenth-century England. Edward's brother, Richard of Gloucester, was able to seize the throne and declare himself King Richard III only to be defeated in battle by Henry Tudor, a remote and virtually unconsidered claimant to the throne.

Richard had been well rewarded for his support by Edward IV. He had married the Earl of Warwick's daughter Ann and taken control of the vast Neville estates in the north of England. Richard resided in Warwick's castle at Middleham in north Yorkshire and Edward made him the effective governor of the whole of the North. Contemporary historians were not kind to Richard, but they were mostly southerners; he was undoubtedly popular in the North with a strong personal following. He could offer much patronage and draw on a reservoir of experienced fighting men. Edward had created an exceptionally 'over-mighty' subject with a strong regional base. After 1478, Richard rarely came to London and he established his military reputation in the campaign against Scotland.

It is not difficult to explain why Richard III was able to seize the throne. Edward V was still a child and had lived in Ludlow on the Welsh border under the protection of his Woodville relation, Earl Rivers. The unpopularity of the Woodvilles cannot be overstated. They were regarded as ambitious upstarts and would clearly dominate the young King. Virtually all the great aristocrats disliked them and even Edward IV's most loyal supporter, Lord Hastings, had a grievance against them.

Richard's seizure of Edward V on 30 April and appointment as Protector on 4 May should not be seen as unpopular moves. It is not certain that he initially intended to declare himself King, but it is worth remembering that Edward IV had overthrown his predecessor and was responsible for the deaths of Henry VI and his own brother the Duke of Clarence. Politics in fifteenth-century England was cruel and violent.

The executions of Lord Hastings (13 June) and Earl Rivers (25 June) suggest that by this time Richard was undoubtedly aiming for the throne. His coronation swiftly followed on 6 July. He could count on fervent support in the north of England and the passivity of many of the great nobility, who had learned to avoid political commitment after thirty years of instability.

It was not Richard's seizure of the throne that shocked contemporaries, but his murder of Edward's two sons. Despite the persistent attempts to acquit Richard of this crime that still continue today, the evidence points to his guilt. Richard had a motive and custody of the children. His responsibility was widely believed at the time and it is surely significant that he could not produce the children during the rebellions of the autumn of 1483. Their mother, Elizabeth Woodville, supported Henry Tudor on condition that he married her daughter and her behaviour makes most sense as revenge against the murderer of her sons.

Dominic Mancini was a distinguished Italian scholar who spent some time in England in the early 1480s probably working for the French. His account of the background to the usurpation of the throne by Richard III is an attempt by an intelligent outsider to make sense of these complex events.

> By reason of his marriage some of the nobility had renewed
> hostilities against Edward, and revived hope amongst King
> Henry's party of regaining the crown, but after their defeat and
> the complete overthrow likewise of King Henry [VI] and his
> faction, Edward's power in the kingdom was re-affirmed. The   5
> queen then remembered the insults to her family and the
> calumnies with which she was reproached, namely that
> according to established usage she was not the legitimate wife
> of the king. Thus she concluded that her offspring by the king
> would never come to the throne, unless the Duke of Clarence   10
> were removed; and of this she easily persuaded the king . . .
> Accordingly whether the charge was fabricated, or a real plot
> revealed, the Duke of Clarence was accused of conspiring the
> king's death by means of spells and magicians. When this
> charge had been considered before a court, he was condemned   15
> and put to death. The mode of execution preferred in this case
> was, that he should die by being plunged into a jar of sweet
> wine. At that time Richard of Gloucester was so overcome by
> grief for his brother, that he could not dissimulate so well, but
> that he was overheard to say that he would one day avenge his   20
> brother's death. Thenceforth he came very rarely to Court. He
> kept himself within his own lands and set out to acquire the
> loyalty of his people through favours and justice. The good
> reputation of his private life and public activities powerfully
> attracted the esteem of strangers. Such was his renown in   25
> warfare, that, whenever a difficult and dangerous policy had to
> be undertaken, it would be entrusted to his discretion and his
> generalship. By these arts Richard acquired the favour of the
> people, and avoided the jealousy of the queen, from whom he
> lived far separated.   30

1   *Why might Elizabeth Woodville not have been regarded as Edward's legitimate wife (line 8)?*

2   *What does this passage suggest about Edward IV's character and personality?*

3   *How convincing is the explanation of Richard's behaviour? (lines 18–19)*
4   *What are Mancini's weaknesses as a source for this period?*

For all his crimes, Richard was an energetic and capable ruler, but his position was never secure. In late 1483, rebellion broke out in southern England. Its ostensible leader, the Duke of Buckingham, proved ineffectual and was executed, but the antagonism towards Richard in southern England was made plain. The appointment of northerners, such as Sir Richard Ratcliffe, to positions in the South was bitterly resented. English society was intensely parochial and outsiders were always unpopular.

Despite lavish distribution of office and land and tours of the country, Richard was not able to broaden his political base. The deaths of his son and his wife were further blows. A handful of great men could dramatically shift the political balance. In particular, he could not rely on the Percies in Yorkshire and Northumberland and the Stanleys in Lancashire and Cheshire. The Percies were traditional rivals of the Nevilles and Thomas, Lord Stanley, was married to Margaret Beaufort, Henry Tudor's mother.

There was a surprising continuity of personnel in government. Of Richard's 54 councillors, 24 had served Edward IV and 9 were to serve Henry VII. The one innovation of Richard's reign was forced upon him. He had had his own council in the North, but on his assumption of the throne, a separate Council of the North was created as a branch of the Royal Council in 1484. This met four times each year in York and was to last until 1641. Richard did not choose a local grandee as its head, but John de la Pole, Earl of Lincoln, who was an outsider.

Richard also needed to neutralise the threat of Henry Tudor, who at Rennes Cathedral in Brittany on Christmas Day in 1483 pledged to marry Elizabeth of York. The rise of the Tudor dynasty is one of the more unlikely events of the fifteenth century. The family were originally minor Welsh gentry at a time when to be Welsh was to be considered a foreigner. Henry's grandfather, Owen Tudor, married Katherine, Henry V's widow. One of their sons, Jasper, became Earl of Pembroke. The other, Edmund, became Earl of Richmond and married Margaret Beaufort, whose father was Duke of Somerset. She was descended from Edward III's son, John of Gaunt. Henry Tudor was their son and inherited his claim to the throne from his mother.

The Tudors became important Lancastrians mainly because Henry VI had few close relatives. Jasper was amongst the most tenacious and loyal Lancastrians. Edmund Tudor died in 1456 and Henry was born in early 1457. Jasper acted as Henry's guide and protector. For most of the next twenty years, Jasper and Henry were landless exiles, whose estates had been confiscated by Edward IV. Jasper intrigued actively in Wales, where the Tudor name was an advantage.

It would have been impossible for these exiles to have recovered the throne without foreign help. Throughout the 1470s, they depended on the protection of Duke Francis of Brittany. After the execution of Buckingham in 1483, Henry was the only other claimant to the throne of royal blood and he did have support in England. The Woodville family saw a marriage alliance with Henry as their only means of recovering influence. A final link was Henry's mother, Margaret Beaufort. Her second husband Thomas, Lord Stanley, was probably aware that a conspiracy was being hatched. After his pledge to marry Elizabeth of York, Henry could present himself as the unifier of Lancaster and York.

The Duke of Brittany abandoned Henry in 1484 and he was forced to flee to France. France was in some disarray after the death of Louis XI. Charles VIII was only 13 years old and his court was divided. But the French were aware that an invasion of England would preoccupy Richard III and prevent English assistance being sent to Francis of Brittany, whose duchy was coveted by the French Crown.

French money enabled Henry to raise 4000 troops, only 400 of whom were English. On 7 August 1485, they landed at Milford Haven in the west of Wales.

As is often the case with decisive battles, it is by no means clear why Richard was defeated. His northern following largely supported him and, while it is true that many great peers did not fight, it may simply be that they did not have time to get to Bosworth. The turning point at Bosworth was Richard's own death. It seems that he recklessly charged Henry and was killed as a result. Almost as important was the desertion of the Stanleys, whose influence in the north-west was vast and whose family links with Henry have been explained. The Percies also did not fight. This may have been because of the cramped battlefield, but might also suggest an element of disloyalty.

Richard's death robbed the country of an effective, but cruel monarch. He was not the uniquely evil figure of Tudor propaganda, but in the words of Charles Ross, his biographer, 'a violent man in a violent age'.

10 CONCLUSION: THE WARS OF THE ROSES

No-one would now suggest that the Wars of the Roses were marked by unprecedented violence and disorder. Revisionist historians have rightly drawn attention to the disappearance of town walls, the growing aristocratic practice of building houses rather than castles, the prosperity of the peasantry, and the outstanding quality of the churches of this period.

Despite this, historians, such as Charles Ross and A J Pollard are right to stress the excessive instability of this period. Two kings were murdered and there were constant complaints about aristocratic disorder. The traditional explanation for this was the existence of a following of liveried retainers attached to great aristocrats known to historians as 'bastard feudalism'. These 'retainers' provided an armed following loyal to their lord and not to the Crown. The greatest twentieth-century historian of the fifteenth century, K B MacFarlane, rejected this view. He argued that the number of retainers rarely exceeded eighty and that they were 'an expression of the Lord's need for service in peace rather than in war'. Rather than promoting instability, retaining created loyalty and helped to organise the social, political, and administrative life of the counties. In his own words: 'On the whole, hierarchical bonds of loyalty and service which bound kings, lords, and retainers, made for social and political stability.'

For MacFarlane the cause of the civil strife was simply the incompetence of Henry VI. Only an under-mighty king had anything to fear from over-mighty subjects. Henry VI allowed dynastic struggle, factional conflict, and private vendettas to develop.

Many of MacFarlane's views are still accepted, but the degree of civil strife is not now seen as derisory. In 1965, J R Lander estimated that there had been only thirteen weeks of fighting in thirty-two years; A J Pollard in the most recent study of the Wars of the Roses raises the figure to nearly two years, while conceding that continental wars were far more destructive.

Pollard sees the root cause of the wars as the excessive influence of the upper nobility, whose wealth and power increased from the fourteenth century onwards as many married into the royal family. This did not matter when the war with France was going well, but after 1340, Edward III 'allowed the gap in power and influence [between the King and aristocracy] to narrow'. He argues that this made the government of the country much more difficult unless the monarch was unusually able. It is certainly true that at crucial times, the Nevilles, Stanleys and even Woodvilles determined the course of events.

11 BIBLIOGRAPHY

John Gillingham *The Wars of the Roses* (Weidenfeld & Nicolson, 1988).
A Goodman *The Wars of the Roses. Military activity and English society, 1452–97* (Routledge, 1990).
R Griffiths *The Reign of Henry VI* (Benn, 1981).
J R Lander *Government and Community: England 1450–1509* (Edward Arnold, 1980).
A J Pollard *The Wars of the Roses* (Macmillan, 1983).
C D Ross *Edward IV* (Methuen, 1974).
C D Ross *Richard III* (Methuen, 1981).
B P Wolffe *Henry VI* (Methuen, 1983).

12 DISCUSSION POINTS AND EXERCISES

A *This section consists of questions or points that might be used for discussion (or written answers) as a way of expanding on the chapter and testing understanding of it:*

1 What are the arguments for and against 1485 as a turning point?

2 How far was defeat in France the fault of Henry VI?

3 Why did faction become a particular problem under Henry VI?

4 Why was Parliament not as compliant as normal in 1449?

5 What was the significance of Jack Cade's rebellion?

6 How did Henry VI restore his authority by 1453?

7 What were the most important consequences of the royal madness?

8 'The responsibility for the outbreak of war must lie firmly with Margaret of Anjou.' Do you agree?

9 Why were the Lancastrians defeated by 1461?

10 How did Warwick become so great a threat to Edward IV by 1469?

11 Why was the 'Re-adeption' of Henry VI a failure?

12 What were the strengths and weaknesses of Edward IV's government of Wales and the North?

13 In what ways was the aristocracy a threat to law and order?

14 What lay behind Edward IV's financial success?

15 'Edward IV was just lucky that his foreign policy was not a disaster.' Do you agree?

16 What made Richard of Gloucester's usurpation of the throne so easy?

17 Why did Richard III lose his throne?

18 'Over-mighty subjects' or 'under-mighty kings': which was the greater cause of instability in the years 1450–85?

B *Essay questions*

1 Is the 'Wars of the Roses' an appropriate term for the years 1455–71?

2 Account for the deposition of Henry VI in 1461.

3 How successfully did Edward IV re-invigorate royal authority during his reign?

4 'His only real achievement was solvency.' Discuss this view of Edward IV.

5 Why was Richard Neville, Earl of Warwick so important?

6 Why did Richard III take the throne in 1483 and why did he lose it in 1485?

13 ESSAY WRITING – ORGANISATION

Historians of this period are mainly concerned with trying to understand its political instability, particularly for the period between 1450–85.

A typical essay question might ask a student to explain the weakness of the English monarchy between 1450–85. Such a question demands concentration on the relevant material and careful selection and organisation. There is a vast amount of material available and it is easy to miss the point of the question.

Since specific reference is made to the monarchy, it would certainly make sense initially to focus on the character and abilities of the three monarchs in question: Henry VI, Edward IV, and Richard III. A first step might be to consider their personal weaknesses and political errors. At some time in their reign, all three of them lost the throne. How far were they personally to blame for this?

/A second stage might be to consider the problems facing the English monarchy that were beyond the control of these men. What was the relationship between the Crown and the aristocracy? How far was royal authority weakened by the power of 'over-mighty subjects' and financial weakness?

Any answer should also make reference to foreign policy and the attitude of neighbouring powers. What was the role of the Kings of France and the Dukes of Burgundy and Brittany?

We now have a structure involving examination of the personal weaknesses of the three kings, their relationship with the aristocracy and the attitude of key foreign powers. This is by no means the only approach that could be followed. It simply serves to suggest that any good essay must be planned to take close account of the question.

The problem that faced the English
monarchy on the 15 & 16 Century England
was truly out of the Control of the throne.
The relationship between Catholic &
the reformation of the religion protestantism
was due to King Henry VIII reign of
supremacy & break ties with the pope
in rome.

II

THE REIGN OF HENRY VII

—

Henry VII, attributed to Michael Sittow

1 INTRODUCTION

HENRY VII founded the most colourful and best known dynasty in English history. He, however, is the least familiar of the Tudors to modern eyes. He was as unfamiliar to contemporaries in 1485. His paternal grandfather, Owen Tudor, was a minor Welsh gentleman, who had the good luck to marry Katherine, the widow of Henry V. Owen's son, Edmund Tudor, married Margaret Beaufort, a descendent of Edward III's son, John of Gaunt. The Beaufort children were born before John of Gaunt's marriage to their mother Catherine Swynford. Although Richard II granted them legitimacy, Henry IV specifically denied them any claim to the throne.

The Tudor Dynasty

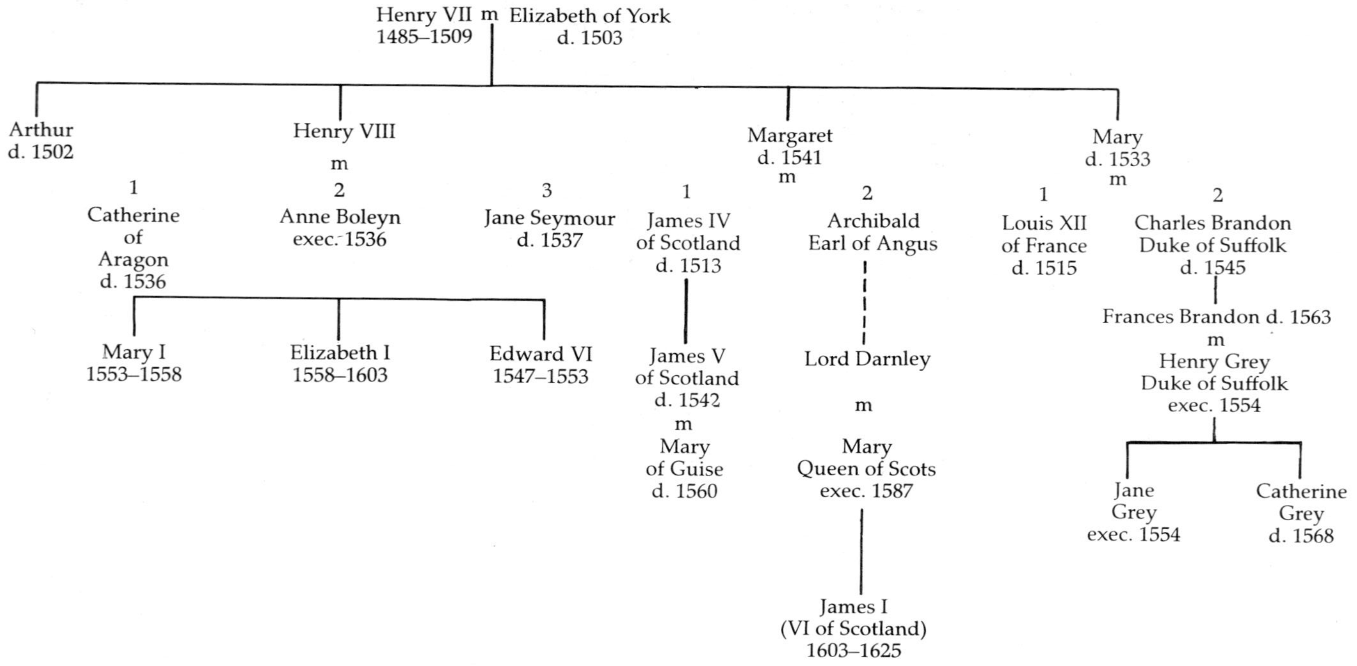

Henry VII m Elizabeth of York
1485–1509   d. 1503

Arthur
d. 1502

Henry VIII
m
2
Anne Boleyn
exec. 1536

1
Catherine
of
Aragon
d. 1536

3
Jane Seymour
d. 1537

Margaret
d. 1541
m
1
James IV
of Scotland
d. 1513

2
Archibald
Earl of Angus

Mary
d. 1533
m
1
Louis XII
of France
d. 1515

2
Charles Brandon
Duke of Suffolk
d. 1545

Mary I
1553–1558

Elizabeth I
1558–1603

Edward VI
1547–1553

James V
of Scotland
d. 1542
m
Mary
of Guise
d. 1560

Lord Darnley
m
Mary
Queen of Scots
exec. 1587

Frances Brandon d. 1563
m
Henry Grey
Duke of Suffolk
exec. 1554

Jane
Grey
exec. 1554

Catherine
Grey
d. 1568

James I
(VI of Scotland)
1603–1625

32

Henry VII did spend the first fourteen years of his life (1457–71) in Wales, but there is no evidence that he spoke Welsh, nor that his Welsh background was of any significance to him. After the final overthrow of Henry VI in 1471, he spent fourteen years in exile in Brittany and France. It was his good fortune that the French King was willing to support his expedition to England in 1485 after the Bretons had abandoned him.

His knowledge of England was inevitably very limited. He had been a refugee for fourteen years and had probably paid only one short visit to London. He had possessed neither land nor money in exile and had none of the training or experience an heir to the throne would normally enjoy. He had no experience of government and administration and no close contacts with leading members of the aristocracy.

If his disadvantages seem formidable, his advantages were not inconsiderable. One problem that had faced Edward IV was the feuding within his family. His brothers, Clarence and Gloucester, had their own claims and ambitions and both died violently. The Woodville relatives of his wife were notoriously unpopular, while great aristocrats, such as the Earl of Warwick, pursued their own interests and those of their families. In contrast, Henry VII had little close family. His uncle Jasper was childless and his strongest supporter. Of his male children only Henry VIII survived until adulthood and other claimants to the throne were harshly treated.

His own personality remains elusive. He has traditionally been portrayed as a cold and grasping man with a miserly attitude towards money. His actions certainly prove him to have been resourceful in his determination to maintain his grip on power. On the other hand, he appreciated that a king must maintain a lavish and impressive Court and he spent money freely where it suited him. His essential achievement is easy to grasp; he eliminated opposition and established his dynasty.

The continued debate amongst historians as to the significance of the accession of the Tudor dynasty in 1485 has already been referred to (*see page 2*). Recently historians have re-asserted the importance of 1485 as a turning point. Professor Charles Ross has undermined the reputation of Edward IV and A J Pollard has examined the severe weaknesses of the English monarchy in the fifteenth century. Of Henry VII's predecessors, Henry VI was deposed twice and then murdered; Edward IV took the throne by force and was himself deposed once; Edward V was murdered and Richard III, having seized the throne, was killed in battle.

In contrast, Henry VII founded a dynasty, which was to last for over a century, and all his heirs died natural deaths in possession of the throne. There were many conspiracies, but none of them succeeded. It was not until the reign of Charles I that another crowned monarch was overthrown.

This re-establishment of monarchical power and authority is now rightly seen as highly significant. What needs to be established is Henry VII's own responsibility for these developments. Undoubtedly, Henry enjoyed good luck. The lack of convincing rival claimants to the throne has already been mentioned. The rulers of France and the Low Countries had made significant interventions in English affairs throughout the fifteenth century, but during the 1490s the French became preoccupied with war in Italy and the attention of the European powers turned south. Nonetheless, Henry's techniques of government have intrigued historians and must be seen as a major factor in the restoration of stability. Historians, such as Penry Williams and S B Chrimes, have revealed his ruthless and manipulative attitude towards the great landowners in his drive to subordinate them to his will. This chapter will focus on Henry's establishment of a stable dynasty.

2 CONSPIRACIES AND RIVALS

After the Battle of Bosworth it was essential for Henry to move rapidly to establish his authority. He was crowned on 30 October 1485 and united the houses of Lancaster and York with his marriage to Elizabeth of York on 18 January 1486. He rewarded his supporters generously. His uncle Jasper was created Duke of Bedford and John de Vere, who was to prove an able military campaigner, was restored to the Earldom of Oxford. Henry's mother was now married to Thomas Stanley, whose support had been crucial to Tudor success at Bosworth. Stanley was created Earl of Derby and consolidated his position as the most powerful aristocrat in Cheshire and Lancashire.

Other men who had helped Henry, such as John Morton, Thomas Lovell, Reginald Bray, and Richard Fox were given the highest offices of state and most kept them for the rest of their days.

However important it was to reward these supporters, this did not in itself solve the problems of security which were to exist almost to the end of Henry's reign. Parliament declared Henry to be king and he formed a bodyguard of 200 men, the 'yeoman of the guard', but he would not keep his throne without the respect, consent, and co-operation of the landowning classes. There were many who had done well out of Yorkist rule; Richard III, for example, had enjoyed a great personal following in the North.

Henry VII acted with energy, and decisiveness in his dealings with all rivals of royal blood. Edward IV had attempted to buy off potential rivals with grants of land and office. Henry, in contrast, tried to neutralise any rivals before they could be used as figureheads by conspirators.

After the Battle of Bosworth, he confined Edward, Earl of Warwick, who was the son of the Duke of Clarence and the Yorkist heir, to the Tower of London. Edward IV's sister, Elizabeth, had married John de la Pole and was the mother of seven sons. Her surviving sons were inevitably drawn into conspiracies and Henry pursued them with great persistence and vigour. William de la Pole was imprisoned for thirty-eight years in the Tower. Archduke Philip, the ruler of the Low Countries, surrendered Edmund de la Pole in 1506 and he was executed in 1513, while Richard de la Pole remained in exile until his death in 1525.

Henry also seems to have been served by a far more effective intelligence service than either Edward or Richard, both of whom were surprised by conspiracies. Despite all of this, some untouchable opponents remained. In particular, Margaret of Burgundy, Edward IV's sister, was the effective ruler of the Low Countries for the early part of Henry's reign and consistently intrigued against him. It was also tempting for the rulers of France and Scotland and the semi-independent Irish aristocracy to attempt to capitalise on the various conspiracies against Henry, which will now be examined in detail.

Viscount Lovell had been a loyal supporter of Richard III and had served as Chamberlain of the Household, while Humphrey and Thomas Stafford were important landowners in Worcestershire. Their uprising in 1486 was shortlived and a comprehensive failure. One obvious problem was that they lacked a figurehead to be used as the claimant to the throne; the Earl of Warwick was in the Tower and Edward IV's sons were presumably dead.

The lack of serious claimants to the throne produced the strange phenomenon of the pretenders – Lambert Simnel and Perkin Warbeck. For the first fifteen years of Henry's reign, Simnel and Warbeck acted as the figureheads of a series of plots and conspiracies. Simnel claimed to be the Earl of Warwick, while Warbeck claimed to be Edward IV's son, Richard of York, and to have miraculously escaped from the Tower. The persistence of the intrigues of these bizarre figures illustrates the weakness of Henry's position.

Lambert Simnel was in fact the son of a joiner from Oxford and Henry could easily produce the Earl of Warwick, whom Simnel claimed to be. Despite this, he quickly attracted widespread support.

The main centre was Ireland. Edward IV's father, Richard of York, had been the Royal Lieutenant in Ireland during the reign of Henry VI. He had owned great estates and Ireland had become a Yorkist stronghold. The great Irish lords, such as Gerald, Earl of Kildare, were anxious to maintain their virtual independence from English control. One obvious way was to produce their own monarch and Simnel was crowned Edward VI in Dublin in May 1487.

The other major supporter of Simnel was Margaret of Burgundy. Lovell and John de la Pole, Earl of Lincoln, both fled to the Low Countries and were given 2000 German mercenaries under the leadership of Martin Schwartz, who was an able and experienced soldier.

A combined army of Irish and Germans landed in England in June 1487. At Stoke, on 14 June the rebels were defeated and Lincoln and Schwartz were slain. Simnel became the royal falconer.

Various conclusions can be drawn from the events leading to the Battle of Stoke. On the one hand the conspirators had picked up virtually no support in England and Henry acted decisively to meet the military threat; on the other hand a barely credible claimant had attracted a strong following from disaffected elements on the fringes of Henry's kingdom.

Warbeck first appeared in Cork in 1491. He was the son of a customs officer from Tournai in northern France. Like Simnel, he was essentially a useful pawn for the Irish and European opponents of Henry.

His first sponsor was Charles VIII of France who wanted to ensure that Henry VII did not obstruct his plans to take over Brittany. But after the Treaty of Étaples (3 November 1492), Charles agreed to abandon Warbeck.

Warbeck then went to the Court of Margaret of Burgundy who trained him for his role. Again Henry reacted forcefully. A trade war began with the Low Countries, while in Ireland the Earl of Kildare was dismissed from office. In England, Sir William Stanley, the brother-in-law of Henry's mother, was suspected of intrigue and executed in February 1495. All this ensured that Warbeck's landing at Deal in Kent on 3 July 1495 proved to be a complete fiasco.

After a brief stay in Ireland, Warbeck turned to King James IV of Scotland. The willingness of the Scots to participate in plots and conspiracies against the English Crown was a cause of concern and weakness throughout this period. In 1486, Henry had concluded a three-year truce with King James III. James was murdered in 1488 and his son, James IV, succeeded to the throne. Although the Anglo-Scottish truce was renewed for seven years in 1493, the traditional Scottish links with France and Burgundy were maintained and there was constant intrigue against Henry VII.

James IV welcomed Warbeck to Scotland in 1495 and gave him an aristocratic Scottish wife; he then invaded England in September 1496. Henry's response was to negotiate with James through Richard Fox, the Bishop of Durham; his aim was a marriage alliance with Scotland. At Ayton, in September 1497, a seven-year truce was agreed and James abandoned his support for Perkin Warbeck.

Far more significant was the development of this truce into a full alliance – the Treaty of Ayton – in September 1502. For the first time since 1328 an English king had agreed a full peace treaty with the Scots. The importance of this treaty was confirmed by the marriage of James to Henry's daughter Margaret in August 1503.

Warbeck returned to Ireland and then moved to Cornwall, but was captured and hanged in November 1499. Henry's success in dealing with conspiracies owed much to the conspirators, but also reflected his energy, persistence and ruthlessness. The best means of further strengthening his dynasty would be to neutralise potential foreign supporters of pretenders and conclude favourable marriage alliances for his family. For these reasons, a realistic and successful foreign policy was essential for the security of his dynasty.

3 THE FOREIGN POLICY OF HENRY VII

During the fifteenth century, England's international position had consistently declined. After 1453, only the toe-hold of Calais was retained on the continent, but Edward IV had still harboured the unrealistic and expensive dream of re-establishing Henry V's empire in France. France had grown enormously in power and by 1485 possessed far greater military and economic resources than England. France controlled much of the Channel coast and threatened to gobble up the Duchy of Brittany, which had traditionally been a useful counterweight to French power and influence.

England's other traditional ally had been the Duchy of Burgundy. The Dukes of Burgundy also ruled the Low Countries, which were of immense economic value and strategic importance to the English. The English economy depended on the export of woollen cloth to the port of Antwerp and this trading link was of vital importance to the two states.

It was not possible for Henry to pursue the traditional pro-Burgundian and anti-French policy. As has already been seen, Margaret of Burgundy was a bitter opponent of Henry VII and she and her son-in-law, Maximilian, the Holy Roman Emperor, consistently supported the conspiracies of Warbeck in the early 1490s. On the other hand Henry could exploit the close economic relationship between the two states as a means of pursuing his diplomatic aims.

The third major power of importance to England was Spain. The marriage between Ferdinand of Aragon and Isabella of Castile had created a dynastic union between the two states and their military success against the Moors confirmed the emergence of a major new power.

Henry's international position was not strong, but England was of sufficient importance and interest to the continental powers that it could not be ignored. His success lay in his realism.

He showed this realism in his relation to Brittany. It was clear that if the French succeeded in annexing it, they would gain complete control of the Channel coast and eliminate a potential ally of England. However, Henry was not in a strong position to stop the French. It was true that he had spent much of his youth under the protection of Duke

Francis of Brittany, but it was French support that had secured him the throne and he did not want France to support any other pretenders. Englishmen were notoriously anti French, but even more hostile to the high taxation that a lengthy war would require. Failure in war would almost certainly destroy Henry's insecure grip on the throne.

All these considerations justified Henry's one-year truce with France in 1485, which was later extended until 1489. But the death of Duke Francis in September 1488 provoked the inevitable crisis. His daughter Anne was still a child and feudal law entitled the French King to claim her as his ward. Henry's attempts to mediate failed and so he promised Anne assistance in September 1489 in the Treaty of Redon. He then sought international assistance and made a further treaty with Spain at Medina del Campo in March 1489.

None of these manoeuvres could prevent marriage between Anne and Charles VIII of France in December 1491. No other European country was prepared to fight France and the activities of Perkin Warbeck further weakened Henry's position.

There was little that Henry could do. To admit defeat in Brittany would be a national humiliation, but to invade France would be to invite disaster against a substantially stronger military power. Henry showed realism and made the most of a weak position. He could always use the traditional English claim to the throne of France to justify invasion and he landed at Calais in October 1492 and began to besiege Boulogne. This was undoubtedly no more than a ploy to improve his bargaining position in the inevitable negotiations with the French. A serious invasion would never be mounted as late in the year as October.

The result of the invasion was the Treaty of Étaples in October 1492. Charles VIII was eager to invade Italy and anxious to make peace. He agreed to pay Henry 745 000 gold crowns at a rate of 50 000 crowns per year; he also agreed not to support any rebels against Henry. Henry's policy was realistic. There was little that he could do to prevent the French takeover of Brittany and he had at least obtained significant financial compensation. War with France would have been ruinously expensive and almost certainly unsuccessful and the policy of good relations with France, which continued for the rest of his reign, was the wisest available. It was also the approach most likely to preserve Henry's grip on the throne.

Polydore Vergil was an Italian, who settled in England in the early sixteenth century and wrote a history of the country (*see page 417*). Here is his view of Henry's policies in 1492:

> There were many who believed Henry to have come to an
> understanding with Charles before he crossed the sea, partly
> through fear and partly through a desire to acquire money, and
> a lasting report of this charge so penetrated into the minds of

the public that even today many hold this opinion.   5
Nevertheless, as some argue, it was neither greed nor fear.
Henry, a man in general of the most prudent disposition, did
not fear the enemy, to whose forces his own were not unequal;
nor did he aim to secure cash, but was rather actuated by a
desire for honour and for his own safety. For it was at this time   10
that he learnt that Margaret, widow of Charles Duke of
Burgundy, had raised from the dead one of the sons of King
Edward her brother, a youth by the name of Richard; and that
this youth was with Charles to persuade the French king to
supply him with arms against Henry.   15

1 *Who was 'the youth by the name of Richard' (line 13)?*
2 *What events are referred to in the first two lines?*
3 *This document gives a variety of interpretations of Henry's foreign policy. Which do you find most convincing and why?*

Relations with the Low Countries were complex and fraught with difficulty. Close trading links bound the Dukes of Burgundy, who ruled the Low Countries, and the English together, while early in Henry's reign the support of Margaret of Burgundy for Perkin Warbeck threatened to drive them apart. Late in Henry's reign, the marriage alliance between Burgundy and Spain further complicated issues.

Henry's attitude towards the Low Countries was quite clear; he always gave priority to the interests of his dynasty over those of maintaining trade. By 1492, Henry could guarantee that neither Spain nor France would attempt to overthrow him, but Margaret of Burgundy would not abandon Warbeck and Maximilian, her son-in-law, resented Henry's peace treaty with France which had been concluded without consulting him.

Henry's reaction to these Burgundian intrigues was to place an embargo in 1493 on all trade with the Low Countries demonstrating the primacy of dynastic interests in foreign policy. The Burgundians responded with their own embargo in 1494 and further support for Warbeck.

Henry's position was strengthened by the involvement of the other European powers in war in Italy. Charles VIII's victories in Italy greatly concerned Maximilian and his son, Philip, and they were also concerned about the harmful effects of economic warfare. This led to negotiations, which were completed in 1496. Margaret of Burgundy agreed to abandon all support for Warbeck and faced the loss of her lands if she did not do so. More important was the trade treaty, known as the *Magnus Intercursus*, agreed in February 1496. This treaty allowed the English to sell goods in all Archduke Philip's Burgundian lands, with the exception of Flanders. Duties and tolls were to be no higher than the prevailing rate of the past fifty years; Flanders was included in the treaty in 1502.

The price for this treaty was that Henry joined the anti-French Holy League, but this was no more than a gesture and did not seriously interfere with the policy of peace with France, which continued to be the basis of Henry's foreign policy.

In contrast with closer neighbours, there was a natural affinity between Spain and England. Both could use the other as a counterweight to France and the Spanish involvement in the Mediterranean and Italian affairs ensured that there was no real clash of interests. The natural cement for such a relationship would be a marriage alliance. The Treaty of Medina del Campo (1489) illustrates the priority given to relations with Spain early in Henry's reign. Henry's young son Arthur was to marry Catherine of Aragon, the equally young daughter of Ferdinand and Isabella, the rulers of Spain. The value of this alliance was increased by the marriage of Catherine's elder sister, Joanna, to Archduke Philip, heir to the Burgundian lands.

In October 1501, Arthur and Catherine were married. Arthur's death in April 1502 was both a personal and diplomatic disaster for Henry VII, but the ensuing treaty of 1503, which arranged for Catherine to marry Prince Henry, who was Arthur's younger brother, maintained the marriage alliance with Spain although later problems postponed the marriage.

Henry's foreign policy until 1503 was both shrewd and realistic. He managed to keep out of the conflicts in Italy and maintained good relations with both sides. The dynastic union with Spain and indirectly Burgundy was clearly in the national interest and, more important to Henry, helped to secure his dynasty.

The Tudor dynasty became more insecure after 1500. Arthur's death in 1502 had followed the death of another son, Edmund, in 1500 and in 1503, Henry's wife, Elizabeth died. Prince Henry was now the only surviving son; in an age of frequent mortality, this provided no real security at all. Matters were not improved by Henry's failure to find another wife.

Events in Spain further weakened Henry's position. The marriage of Ferdinand and Isabella was a dynastic union between the separate states of Aragon and Castile. Isabella's death in 1504 threatened the break up of this state, which Henry had cultivated so assiduously. Catherine of Aragon no longer seemed such a diplomatic catch. In the immensely complex diplomacy of the years, Henry abandoned Ferdinand and looked to establish good relations with his son-in-law, Archduke Philip, who was prepared to challenge Ferdinand on behalf of his wife, Joanna, whom he believed should now rule Castile.

After Philip and Joanna were shipwrecked in England in 1506, Philip agreed a trade treaty – the so called *Malus Intercursus*, which never in fact came into effect, and handed over Edmund de la Pole, the Earl of Suffolk. But Philip's death enabled Ferdinand to regain control of Castile and seemed to wreck Henry's policy. Ferdinand allied himself to France in the League of Cambrai in 1508 and left England isolated.

It would be easy to dub Henry's foreign policy a failure. The French acquisition of Brittany and the ultimate failure of the Spanish alliance were certainly two blows. On the other hand, Henry's priorities must be understood. His main aim was to secure his dynasty and his own experience showed how vital foreign support could be for any usurper. His policies ensured that the major powers in Europe had abandoned support for any rival claimants to the throne by the mid 1490s. Moreover, he never faced an active alliance of hostile powers. This was partly a matter of good luck and the preoccupation with Italy, but it also reflected his diplomatic skill and the respect for him overseas.

A valuable contrast can be drawn with Edward IV. Edward still harboured fantasies that the English empire could be re-established in France. Henry's own invasion of France was a mere negotiating ploy and he never forgot that the need to maintain good relations with France was the basis of his policies. He can also be commended for his policy towards Scotland. The Treaty of Ayton and the marriage of his daughter to the King of Scotland benefited both the nation and the dynasty.

Above all Henry's avoidance of war must be commended. England was not powerful enough to wage war and could afford to be a bystander in the conflicts in Italy. This ensured that even exclusion from the League of Cambrai did not prove disastrous, since all its members were preoccupied in Italy. R B Wernham has summarised Henry's policies neatly: 'Peace with France and Scotland, reinforced by the reinsurance policy of alliances with Spain and the Netherlands, provided a pattern of relationships behind which England and the Tudor dynasty could prosper unmolested by Yorkist conspiracies or foreign interference.'

4 HENRY'S DOMESTIC POLICIES

Although an effective foreign policy was a crucial element in the establishment of a stable and secure dynasty, Henry's major priority was to be strong and effective in government at home. Much controversy has surrounded his aims and methods.

It was necessary for Henry to fulfil certain requirements if he was to maintain the throne. He needed to surround himself with able and effective councillors, upon whose loyalty he could rely. He also needed to establish a secure financial base, which would both enhance his prestige and enable him to enjoy greater independence and freedom of action. Most difficult of all, he had to secure the acceptance of royal authority throughout the country at a time when the machinery of law enforcement was weak and reliance on the co-operation of the nobility inevitable.

The survival of the dynasty would seem to suggest that he was successful in these basic aims. Historians, however, are as interested in his methods as his aims. There is, for example, much controversy over the degree of continuity between Edward IV and Henry VII. In contrast with Edward IV some see an authoritarian ruthlessness developing in his treatment of his most powerful subjects. Like all English kings, Henry needed the co-operation of the aristocracy, but he clearly determined to establish his supremacy.

Like all successful rulers, Henry also enjoyed good fortune. Henry VI and Edward IV had both suffered from the ambition and power of great aristocrats. Henry, on the other hand, was faced with a numerically declining nobility. In 1485, there were 50 peers, but in 1509 only 35. None of the remaining peers could match the power of men like the Earl of Warwick and Henry kept the lands of Warwick, Richard III and his brother Clarence, who were all now dead, in his own hands.

No marriages united two great aristocratic families during his reign. The Duke of Buckingham was only seven in 1485, the Earl of Northumberland was killed in 1489 and his heir was only 10 years old, leaving two of the greatest families without an effective head. Henry himself only created three new peerages. His policy was not anti-aristocratic, but he established a more dominant position than his predecessors.

Central administration – the Royal Council

The personal nature of government at this time must be stressed. In the words of John Guy, 'Henry VII governed England as his personal estate through his Council and his household.' It was, indeed, Henry's Council, which was the focal point of the government of the country.

At first sight Henry's Council seems an absurdly unwieldy body. During his reign, he appointed 227 councillors, but only about two dozen were regular attenders. Many of these had gained experience under the Yorkist kings and there is no evidence that Henry turned to men untainted by service to his predecessors.

The Council lacked a formal structure in the modern sense. There were no committees, or sub-committees. The Council of the North, which had emerged in Richard's reign, was not immediately re-created by Henry. There has been much controversy over the Act of 1487 which, some have maintained, established a separate 'Star Chamber' court, but this view has been discredited. The room known as the Star Chamber was simply a convenient location in which some members of the Council conducted legal business.

Henry's own inexperience was not shared by many of his most trusted advisors. John Morton attended virtually all the meetings of the Council of which records survive. He served as Lord Chancellor (a leading administrator and overseer of the courts of law) between 1486 and 1500 and later became both Archbishop of Canterbury and a Cardinal. Morton's career started under Henry VI and, after initial disfavour, he then served Edward IV and was a member of his Council. It was his dismissal by Richard III that seems to have turned him into a central figure in the conspiracy that brought Henry to the throne.

Henry's first Treasurer, Lord Dinham, had served Richard III in the vitally important position of Lieutenant of Calais. After his death in 1501, he was succeeded by Thomas Howard, Earl of Surrey. Howard's family had been Yorkist supporters and he had fought for Richard III at Bosworth. Despite this, Henry used him as his commander on the Scottish border after the murder of the Earl of Northumberland in 1489. In the words of J R Lander: 'Loyalty and ability were the only criteria of service – mighty lord, bishop, doctor of canon or civil law, or official, all were there, but only at the King's will.'

Henry clearly inspired and expected loyalty. The men, who most frequently attended Council meetings, such as Reginald Bray, Thomas Lovell, Richard Fox, and Peter Courtenay, tended to keep their positions for life. The Council's job was to give advice and put policy into practice, but it was Henry who made the decisions.

In the regions, for example, he subtly modified the approach of his predecessors. The Earl of Surrey, who was sent to the North in 1489 to succeed the Earl of Northumberland, had neither land nor influence in that region and was inevitably closely dependent on the King. When he was replaced in 1501, it was not by the fifth Earl of Northumberland, who was the greatest local landowner, but by a council under the Archbishop of York.

In Wales a council was created under Prince Arthur; on his death the Bishop of Lincoln became its president and he was not a great local landowner. Henry clearly wished to avoid Edward IV's creation of landowners with strong regional influence.

Although the 1487 statute did not establish the 'Star Chamber', it did create an important law court, which could deal with any disorder more swiftly and effectively than any existing court. Other new courts were created. The 'Court of Audit' dealt with many royal accounts; the 'Court of Requests' handled cases brought by the poor, while the 'Council Learned in the Law' eventually supervised all the King's royal and landed rights over his subjects.

Henry made far greater use of men with legal training than his predecessors and his tendency to keep his servants in the same posts encouraged a greater departmental specialization. This approach was markedly different from that of Edward IV and provided a more coherent structure in administration along with a speedier and more effective legal system.

Financial administration

If Henry has left any clear image for posterity, it is of a man obsessed with money. There is an underlying basis of truth in this view. It would not be fanciful to suggest that Henry's early poverty may have ensured that he had a firm grasp of the importance of money. It is also obviously true that the political strength of the Crown was, to a great degree, determined by its financial strength.

The lavishness of Henry's Court proves that he was no miser, but he was a cold political realist and this ensured that he took a close personal interest in finance for the whole of his reign. He had no experience to help him. In the words of S B Chrimes, 'no man has ascended the throne with such a lack of financial experience and resources as did Henry VII'.

Henry's most important source of revenue was the royal estates, which had significantly increased in size as a result of the death of many great landowners in previous years and the confiscation of other estates. Unlike Edward IV, Henry made few grants of land to political supporters and by 1509 the royal estates were probably larger than ever before. They now provided revenue of £42 000 p.a., which was four times as much as in 1433.

Henry could also raise revenue from his position as feudal overlord of the great aristocrats, who in theory still held their land from the King in return for military or financial services. The most important element in this so called feudal or prerogative revenue was wardship. If a great landowner died and his heir was still a child, the child became a ward of the king and the estates passed under royal control. Wardship was the most important source of prerogative revenue.

Remaining revenue came largely from Parliament. As was traditional, Henry was granted customs duties for life by Parliament and this completed his normal peacetime, or ordinary revenues. Extraordinary revenues in times of war and national crisis had to be voted by Parliament or raised by borrowing and Henry did his best to avoid both.

The fifteenth century had seen significant changes in the methods of financial administration. Traditionally revenues had been channelled to the Exchequer, but its methods were unwieldy and archaic. Gradually new techniques had been developed in the royal estates and under Edward IV and Richard III, revenues were increasingly directed to the Royal Household, or Chamber. This system was speedier and placed revenues directly at the King's disposal.

It does seem that Henry initially failed to grasp the importance of the development of Chamber finance under his two predecessors.

Chamber finance depended on the direct supervision of the monarch and his servants and the collapse of Richard III's government brought a collapse in royal revenue. Receipts from the royal estates declined from £25 000 in the last year of Richard's reign to £11 700 in the first year of Henry's. The methods of the Exchequer, which had regained its importance, were too cumbersome and rigid for effective supervision.

During the 1490s it gradually became clear that there were more efficient methods of running the royal estates. The Exchequer was too centralised and it was clearly more sensible to appoint agents with direct responsibility for raising revenue and running the estates. Sir Reginald Bray was one of Henry's most trusted servants and he managed the huge estates of the Duchy of Lancaster.

Thomas Lovell served as Treasurer of the Chamber until 1492, when he was succeeded by Sir Thomas Heron. By the end of Henry's reign 80 per cent of revenue went directly to the Chamber. Money was then immediately available for royal use and the Jewel House in the Tower of London became, in effect, a kind of crude royal bank where financial reserves were stored.

The Chamber was closely monitored by the King. Heron was called 'the general receiver of our lord the King' and the auditors employed by the Chamber were titled 'the general surveyors'. Henry involved himself directly in the affairs of the Chamber. Until 1503 every entry of a receipt was initialled by him and after 1503 every page. The receivers who collected royal revenue made frequent appearances before the King and his Council and Henry must take personal credit for the growing efficiency of financial administration.

Henry was also anxious to maximise his feudal prerogative. In 1503 Sir John Hussey was appointed the first surveyor of the King's Wards. The exploitation of the King's other feudal rights was a complex process. At first a series of commissions investigated means of increasing revenue; eventually in 1508 Edward Belknap was appointed the first surveyor of the King's prerogative.

Henry must be considered outstandingly successful in his management of royal finances in an age when all European monarchs constantly suffered from shortage of revenue. After some initial confusion he built on the experience of his Yorkist predecessors in his administration of the royal estates and raised revenue from about £10 000 p.a. in the last years of Edward IV to £42 000 p.a.

Taxation and customs revenue also increased and the French subsidy which Edward had enjoyed for seven years was paid to Henry from 1492 until his death in 1509. Indeed one major cause of Henry's solvency was his cautious and realistic foreign policy. By the end of his reign his annual revenue amounted to £100 000 compared with £65 000 in the last years of Edward IV.

The sophistication of Henry's financial system must not be exaggerated. The Chamber accounting system was crude – with all expenditure recorded in one lump sum – and there was no means of enforcing payment. The kings of France enjoyed far greater revenues. But in the words of John Guy, 'Henry VII perfected Yorkist techniques once he had appreciated their significance.' He also came close to fulfilling the fifteenth-century maxim that 'the King must live of his own'. But there were no innovations, and no new sources of revenue were discovered. He merely continued Edward's policy of more effective exploitation of the royal estates.

Where Henry showed a greater sophistication than Edward was in his understanding of the connection between economic and political strength. Henry never followed Edward's policy of granting large estates to his family and supporters. He appreciated that his financial strength would weaken political rivals and enable him to keep a firmer grip on the aristocracy.

Nevertheless, even if Henry's motives were not purely economic and his methods more dependent on diligent supervision than clever administrative techniques, any monarch who could lend £300 000 to the mighty house of Habsburg and leave one year's unspent income to his son must be considered an effective financier. Nor was he a miser, who accumulated wealth to no purpose. The lavishness of his Court has already been mentioned and a King whose accounts include £5 to pay card debts and £30 for a damsel who danced may have been more human than is sometimes believed.

5 THE PROBLEMS OF ORDER AND SECURITY

Any monarch preoccupied with establishing and securing the future of his dynasty was bound to be obsessed with the need to preserve order and retain the loyalty of his subjects. Indeed, it was in this area that Henry was seen at his most ruthless and his methods were certainly controversial and unpopular. In his defence the instability of the English monarchy over the previous forty years must be remembered.

The chief problem for all kings in this period was their relationship with the nobility. No king could rule without the co-operation of the nobility, which was largely responsible for conducting the king's business in the provinces, but loyalty and subservience had to be maintained. It has already been seen that Henry prevented the re-emergence of 'super nobles', like the Earl of Warwick, by his refusal to distribute royal estates in return for support. Under Henry, no aristocrat enjoyed a regional power-base similar to that of Richard III before he became King. Henry also lacked the difficult and ambitious male relatives, who had so troubled his predecessors. His refusal to distribute peerages showed that he believed in the importance of service to the Crown rather than hereditary titles. A good example was his treatment of the Earl of Surrey, who was not restored to his father's title of Duke of

Norfolk until after Henry's death. His Yorkist past may have been for-given, but it was not forgotten.

Retaining

The system of retaining was at the centre of aristocratic life in the fif-teenth century. Its significance and the problems associated with it have been much debated and much misunderstood. Retaining simply means the recruitment of followers by great aristocrats. The relation-ship was reciprocal; in return for their service, the retainers received the patronage and support of a powerful man.

There was nothing inherently wrong with the system of retaining. Indeed for Penry Williams, 'the existence of a body of retainers was essential to the whole mode of noble life' at a time when 'the principal centres of social influence and strength were the castles and house-holds of great nobleman'. It must also not be assumed that all retaining had a military purpose. Retainers could be household servants or bound by an indenture (contract) to do service for their lord. There were, however, numbers of men recruited for short periods, who did perform military duties. These men would wear the noblemen's 'liv-ery', which was some form of badge or uniform.

Henry relied on these noble retinues as the basis of his armed forces. He was also concerned, like all his predecessors, with the problem of 'maintenance' – the intimidation of juries on behalf of a retainer. But retaining was a far too useful and integral part of national life to be abolished. Henry simply followed Edward IV in aiming to control retaining by distinguishing between legal and illegal activity.

Four statutes dealt with the problems of livery and retaining. The earlier ones, such as that of 1487, essentially re-stated Edward IV's measures of 1468. In 1504, the most significant statute was introduced. At one time, it was believed that '*De Retentionibus Illicitis*' ended retain-ing. In fact retaining continued for at least another century and aboli-tion was never Henry's ambition. The first purpose of the statute was to reiterate the prohibition of illegal retaining; a system of 'placards' or licences was introduced. If the King himself had signed or sealed one of these 'placards', retaining could take place. This measure was to apply for the remainder of Henry's reign.

There is no evidence that this statute was enforced with great fre-quency. The only peer known to have been prosecuted was George Neville, Lord Burgavenny; Sir James Stanley, who was an uncle of the second Earl of Derby, was also fined heavily. Both fines were, however, suspended and it seems that the statute was mainly used as a means of intimidation. No written evidence of illegal retaining, which is com-monly found before 1485, has come to light for the reign of Henry VII.

He must, therefore, be regarded as more successful than his prede-cessors in controlling the system. The later career of Lord Burgavenny illustrates the distinction between legal and illegal retaining. He may have been a target for Henry because of his earlier involvement in the Cornish Uprising of 1497, but by 1510 he was sufficiently restored to favour to be made Constable of Dover and Warden of the Cinque Ports. In this position, he was licensed to retain as many men as he needed to meet the threat of the French.

Attainders, and Bonds and Recognizances

Throughout his reign, Henry's actions reflected a determination to preserve his throne and establish his dynasty. His methods became very unpopular and have been closely and critically scrutinised by historians. Most controversial was his use of Bonds and Recognizances (*see below*) to secure and maintain the loyalty of his subjects. As with many of Henry's policies, his basic techniques were not original, but they were applied in a distinctive and unprecedented fashion.

Henry's concern was to maintain his dominance over his most powerful subjects while retaining their co-operation. Certain weapons were available to him at the beginning of his reign, the most well known being the process of attainder. An Act of Attainder prevented a disloyal subject and his descendants from possessing or inheriting land. During Henry's reign, there were 138 attainders and only one Parliament (1497) failed to pass any. Forty-six attainders were eventually reversed. This was a relatively small number; the terms of reversal were often very harsh and did not include the complete restoration of lands. Henry's use of attainder was far more ruthless and severe than had been Edward IV's. It also enabled him to add to the royal estates.

In their most basic form, bonds are simply written obligations to pay some kind of penalty if certain conditions are not met. Recognizances were a form of bond, which referred to some previous action or misconduct and would impose penalties if good behaviour were not maintained in the future. It was a system not dissimilar to the modern procedure of being bound over to keep the peace.

Bonds and Recognizances were not a new practice. Edward IV had placed six peers and one peeress under political bonds, but under Henry there was a massive extension of the system. The English peerage consisted of 62 families; of these 36 were placed under bond to Henry at some point during his reign.

All of these agreements were negotiated with the King and his agents. Some dealt with legal obligations to the King, but many recognizances were far more dubious and were used, for example, after the Cornish Uprising of 1497, to secure the release of prisoners on trial for treason.

After 1502 the system became widespread. Henry effectively placed the aristocracy on probation in return for loyalty and good behaviour. The case of Lord Burgavenny has already been mentioned. He was fined the vast sum of £70 000 for illegal retaining. This was an impossible sum for him to meet, but the King used this offence and fine to force him to enter a recognizance of £13 000 that he would pay the King £500 p.a. over ten years. The Earl of Kent owed Henry money when he succeeded to the earldom. He was made to agree to a bond whereby he undertook to sell no land and give office to no man without royal consent or forfeit £10 000 should he break this bond.

Bonds were rarely actually used to raise cash and were often cancelled, or suspended; their value was a threat hanging over the nobility. Henry inherited a system sporadically used by his predecessors and converted it into an organised system of coercion. In doing so he certainly behaved in a crude and unscrupulous fashion. Whether he acted illegally is a far more complex question, but he certainly used all his powers to the absolute limit.

There is much debate as to how far this system was justified. Roger Lockyer argues that Henry VII did the dirty work and this allowed Henry VIII to dispense with the need to use such measures. J R Lander has argued in similar fashion: 'How else could Henry VII have controlled such a mob of aloof, self-interested magnates?'

The Council Learned in the Law

This was one of the few truly specialised bodies to emerge in the reign of Henry VII and became closely associated with the harsher side of government. Its most notorious members were Sir Richard Empson, who became Chancellor of the Duchy of Lancaster in 1504 and Edmund Dudley.

The Council's job was to collect debts owed to the King, which could, for example, stem from unpaid taxes or wardships. It was also involved in drawing up and supervising Bonds and Recognizances.

The Council and its members were widely hated. It acted without a jury and virtually had a free hand in fixing penalties. Empson and Dudley were believed to be corrupt and participants in a system of royal blackmail.

Henry VIII marked his accession to the throne by cancelling nearly 200 recognizances, imprisoning and eventually executing Empson and Dudley. A contrite Dudley wrote in the Tower:

> I have perused by books touching all such matters as I was
> privy unto and have written hereafter such persons as I think
> were hardly treated and much sorer than the causes required
> . . . and it is to be done in the honour of Christ his passion, most
> heartily and lowly. I record you all and also the pleasure and   5
> mind of the King's grace whose soul God pardon was much set
> to have many persons in his danger at his pleasure, and yet as
> well spiritual men as temporal men, wherefore many people
> were bound to his grace or to others to his use in great sums of

money, some by Recognizance, and some by obligation without   10
any condition, but as a simple and absolute bond payable at a
certain day, for his grace would have them so made. It were
against reason and good conscience that these bonds should be
reputed as perfect debts for I think his inward mind was never
to use them.   15

1   *Explain the meaning of 'Recognizance' (line 10).*
2   *According to Dudley what advantages did his methods bring to Henry?*
3   *What criticisms does Dudley have of Henry?*
4   *Dudley wrote this imprisoned in the Tower just after Henry's death. In
    what ways does this increase or diminish the value of the document?*

The Council Learned in the Law did not survive Henry's death. In a
sense, its abolition was a tribute to the effectiveness of its methods as
well as a testament to its deep unpopularity.

6 GOVERNING THE PROVINCES

Despite his harsh treatment of the aristocracy, Henry relied on them to
enforce his will in the provinces. Although there were occasional royal
progressions through the country, inevitably Henry spent most of his
time at Westminster. He had few paid servants; a small number
worked in the Exchequer, the Duchy of Lancaster and the customs service, but it has been estimated that there was only one paid official for
every 4000 inhabitants, while in France the figure was one for every
400 inhabitants.

To a great degree, therefore, Henry relied on the co-operation of
aristocratic families with strong local roots. The most famous of these
families was the Percy family in Yorkshire and Northumberland, but
the Stanleys in Lancashire and Cheshire, the Howards in East Anglia,
and the Berkeleys in Gloucestershire were equally important.

Henry preferred to win the support of these families by granting
them office rather than lands. It was still difficult, however, to assert
royal authority in the North. The murder of the Earl of
Northumberland, while trying to collect taxes in 1489, gave Henry an
opportunity to modify his approach. His principal officers became
Lord Dacre, who came from a great local family, and Thomas Howard,
Earl of Surrey, who was an outsider.

Henry's other important agents in the provinces were the Justices of
the Peace. They were unpaid and their main function was law enforcement. The King was obviously keenly interested in their work and concerned that they should do their job properly. Every Parliament of his
reign passed at least one statute concerned with the work of JPs. These
included measures to deal with rioting and the intimidation of juries.

The success of these measures is impossible to quantify. The murder of the Earl of Northumberland and the Cornish Rising of 1497, which was essentially another protest against taxation, are obvious examples of widespread disorder. Nonetheless, Henry's grip on his subjects was certainly firmer than his predecessors'. The fact that he did not need to travel the country continuously in order to assert his authority provides some evidence of the relative effectiveness of his government in the localities.

7 PARLIAMENT

Nothing is easier to misinterpret in English history than the role of Parliament. The main point to remember is that Parliament was important, but in a very different way from today. Parliament's role was one of partnership with, not opposition to the monarch.

Parliament played no role in the day to day government of the country. Whether or not a Parliament should be summoned was entirely the king's decision. Henry VII summoned seven Parliaments, five of which met in the first ten years of his reign. In the twenty-four years of his reign Parliament was actually in session for a little over a year and a half.

Parliament's structure was now fairly firmly fixed, although Henry did summon a small number of Great Councils, which consisted of the Lords without the Commons. Those peers entitled to attend the House of Lords were now a clearly defined caste and the towns and shires entitled to representation in the Commons were also firmly established. By 1489, it was accepted that an Act of Parliament was only valid if both the Commons and Lords had agreed to it. Measures of taxation now had to be initiated by the House of Commons, but the Lords enjoyed far greater prestige and power. Above all the King held the whip hand; it was he who summoned and dissolved Parliaments.

Parliaments were summoned for three reasons: for taxation, to make laws, and for general consultation. Over taxation Parliament's authority was undisputed. Henry's first Parliament granted the customs dues of tunnage and poundage for life as was now traditional. The other major Parliamentary taxes were Fifteenths and Tenths; these were taxes on movable goods in shires and boroughs respectively. Contributions from each parish were fixed and a maximum of only about £30 000 could be raised. Henry attempted to replace these unsatisfactory taxes by an open ended, directly assessed subsidy (a direct tax), which would bring in increasing amounts as national income grew. His first attempt in 1489 caused the murder of the Earl of Northumberland at Thirsk in Yorkshire, while the second led to the Cornish Uprising (*see page 481*). A major reason for Henry's declining use of Parliament in his last years was his growing financial independence and reliance on income from his own lands and the ruthless exploitation of all other sources of revenue.

The legislative role of Parliament was becoming more effective thanks to the development of printing. After the reign of Richard III, Parliamentary statutes were regularly printed, which allowed for a far stricter interpretation of statute law. Parliamentary statutes were the most significant example of co-operation between King and Parliament and required the participation of both.

Parliament's work in lawmaking and taxation assisted the King in his task of government. It also provided a forum for the statement of royal intentions and their discussion by the governing class, who in return could state their own views and pursue their personal ambitions with Henry. Essentially his Parliaments were co-operative ventures between the monarch and the governing élite; when their work was concluded, they were dismissed.

8 CONCLUSION

The year 1485 must be seen as a turning point in English history. Henry VII was not Edward IV mark two, but a far more realistic ruler determined to establish his dynasty.

Henry's foreign policy illustrates his realism and lack of illusion. Where Edward IV had still harboured delusions of re-conquering France, Henry VII pursued a limited policy based on peace with France and alliance with Spain; this enabled him gradually to eliminate the risk of conspiracies against his throne launched from overseas.

Edward had relied upon and rewarded the great aristocrats, while Henry was suspicious and parsimonious. Good fortune and his own lack of a close family had eroded the numbers of 'super aristocrats', but Henry did much to ensure that such a class did not re-emerge.

There is, however, no doubt that the massive expansion in the use of Bonds and Recognizances was both highly unpopular and of doubtful legality. Henry was harsh and unscrupulous in the use of these weapons to control his subjects.

The other basis of Henry's strength was his success as a financier. After initial confusion, he reverted to the methods of Edward IV and established a crude, but effective system, based on personal control and the support of loyal and long serving officers of the Crown.

Henry was a successful monarch. His reign saw the triumph of stability and realism, but at the cost of a growing number of harsh policies. His techniques were not 'modern'; he ran the country on a personal basis as a personal estate.

9 BIBLIOGRAPHY

S B Chrimes *Henry VII* (Methuen, 1977).
A Grant *Henry VII: the Impact of his Reign in English History* (Methuen Lancaster Pamphlet, 1985).
J Guy *Tudor England* (OUP, 1988).
R Lockyer *Henry VII* (Longman Seminar Studies, 2nd edition 1983).
C Rogers *Henry VII* (Hodder & Stoughton, Access to History, 1991).
P Williams *The Tudor Regime* (Clarendon, 1979).

10 DISCUSSION POINTS AND EXERCISES

A *This section consists of questions or points that might be used for discussion (or written answers) as a way of expanding on the chapter and testing understanding of it:*

1 What were Henry VII's disadvantages in 1485 and how was he able to overcome them?

2 How was Henry VII able to ensure the prevention or defeat of conspiracies against him?

3 Did the crisis over Brittany result in success or failure for Henry VII?

4 How was Henry VII able to neutralise the threat from Burgundy?

5 How well managed were England's relations with Spain under Henry VII?

6 In what ways was Henry VII's foreign policy particularly 'realistic'?

7 'The threat to Henry VII from "over-mighty subjects" was negligible.' Do you agree?

8 Was there anything new in the way the Royal Council worked under Henry VII?

9 Why were the royal finances so important and how did Henry VII improve them?

10 By what means, and how effectively, did Henry VII keep the nobility under control?

11 How did Henry VII maintain control over the provinces?

12 How did Parliament support the work of the King? Did it restrict his authority in any way?

13 What was the key to Henry VII's success as a ruler?

B *Essay questions*

1 How far were Henry VII's methods of government and administration based on those of Edward IV?

2   In what sense, if any, did Henry VII found a 'New Monarchy' in England?

3   By what means, and how successfully, did Henry VII improve royal finances?

4   Why was Henry VII able to establish his dynasty in England?

5   How did Henry VII prevent civil conflict from breaking out afresh?

6   'Ruthlessness and attention to detail brought him success.' How adequately does this characterise the reign of Henry VII?

11 EXERCISE – A COMPARISON OF EDWARD IV AND HENRY VII

Edward IV and Henry VII came to the throne in similar circumstances, after the violent overthrow of their predecessors. Both had lengthy reigns and were regarded as men of ability. Yet it was Henry VII, despite his remote claim to the throne, who went on to found a dynasty, while Edward IV's sons were murdered.

Historians are naturally fascinated by comparisons between the two men and their contrasting personalities and methods as a means of explaining why the Yorkists failed and the Tudors survived.

Compare the two men by looking at the following areas:

a   The advantages and disadvantages that each enjoyed when they took the throne.

b   The similarities and differences between their backgrounds and families.

c   Their aims, successes, and failures in foreign policy.

d   Their treatment of rival claimants to the throne.

e   Their choice of ministers.

f   Their attitude towards the nobility – in particular their use of patronage and legal restraints.

g   Their contrasting techniques in finance and administration.

1   How far do your conclusions explain Henry's greater success?

2   What comparisons and contrasts have you found?

III

HENRY VIII 1509–29

—

Henry VIII, anon.

1 INTRODUCTION

THE contrasting images of Henry VIII and his father are striking. Henry VII is remembered, if at all, as a cold and calculating financier with a cautious outlook in foreign policy. Henry VIII, in contrast, is unquestionably the English monarch whose name and deeds are most familiar to the average person.

Both his personality and the events of his reign have contributed to his fame. He came to the throne in his eighteenth year full of youthful vigour. He was in many ways a genuinely talented man. He was tall and strong, gifted musically, and more than competent academically.

The astonishing dramas of his reign have attracted the close scrutiny of many distinguished English historians. The saga of his divorce and six wives help to bring colour to this period. Even more fascinating to professional historians are the events of the 1530s, which saw the start of the English Reformation and much debated administrative and constitutional developments.

In contrast, his early years have attracted less interest. The reason is quite easy to understand. Much of the King's energy and the resources of the kingdom were concentrated in an apparently futile attempt to reproduce the victories of Henry V in France. The convoluted diplomacy and tortuous military campaigns of this period seem to have brought no lasting benefit to the country.

The other striking feature of this period is the dominant position of Cardinal Wolsey. By 1515, Wolsey had established himself as the King's chief minister and he maintained this position for the next fifteen years.

Wolsey has not enjoyed a good press. He was an Archbishop and a Cardinal, but also a very worldly man of affairs. It is easy to take him as a symbol of all that was corrupt and decadent in the Catholic Church in the years before the Reformation. It is also easy to paint his foreign policy as anachronistic and vainglorious.

In recent years, a more balanced view of Wolsey has begun to emerge. Peter Gwyn's 1990 biography was the first to be written since 1929 and gives a generally sympathetic view. He is prepared to justify much of Wolsey's work on Henry's behalf and show that this period has an importance of its own and not just as a precursor to the 1530s.

2 HENRY'S ACCESSION

The royal marriage

Henry VIII was born on 28 June 1491. It was not until the death of his elder brother, Prince Arthur, in April 1502 that he became heir apparent. There is no evidence that he was given any responsibility in government while his father was still alive, but as the only surviving male prince he was a very valuable commodity.

The question of his marriage was of critical importance. Royal marriage was not simply vital as a means of preserving the dynasty and national stability, it was also a valuable diplomatic tool. The choice of a wife from another royal family would help to maintain an alliance and cement diplomatic links. In the case of Henry VIII, his choice of wife was to determine the course of his whole reign.

Henry's elder brother, Prince Arthur, had been married to Catherine of Aragon, the daughter of Ferdinand of Aragon and Isabella of Castile, the rulers of Spain. It is not certain that the marriage had been consummated before Arthur's death.

In June 1503, Henry VII made a treaty for the marriage of Henry to

Catherine following Arthur's death; at this time, Henry was 12 years old and Catherine was 17. Canon law (the law of the Church) did not allow marriage to the wife of a dead brother and permission from the Pope was required before any marriage could take place.

Henry VII did not wholeheartedly commit himself to this marriage (*see page 40*) and continued to seek alternative brides for his son until his death. As soon as Henry succeeded to the throne, he married Catherine on 11 June 1509.

There were good reasons for haste. The previous fifty years had seen the crown of England constantly changing hands. Henry VII's ruthless and patient management of the country had more or less eliminated serious rivals for the throne, but the sooner Henry VIII could produce children the more stable the Tudor dynasty would be. Nonetheless, the marriage remained something of a legal oddity. The Pope had given a dispensation for the marriage to take place, but this was already six years old and a minority of Church lawyers had their doubts about its validity.

The fall of Empson and Dudley

The effectiveness of Henry VII's government cannot be denied, but by 1509 his methods had become deeply unpopular. Edmund Dudley and Sir Richard Empson were the two men most closely associated with Henry VII's ruthless financial demands and legal controls over the aristocracy and gentry. Henry had Empson and Dudley arrested in April 1509 and they were executed a year later. This freed him from association with the most unpopular aspects of his father's government. The Council Learned in Law, through which most of the work of Empson and Dudley had been conducted, was abolished and some of the bonds imposed by Henry were cancelled.

This was astute public relations rather than a dramatic shift in policy. Henry VIII could afford some moderation in his rule because his father had been so effective. It must not be assumed that he was in any sense a tolerant man. He was young, ambitious and in the words of John Guy 'egoistical, self-righteous and broody'. Any threat to his position as king was countered ruthlessly. In 1513, he ordered the execution of Edmund de la Pole, whom Henry VII had kept in the Tower because he had a claim to the throne.

3 HENRY'S AIMS AND PRIORITIES 1509–12

On his accession Henry swore in public that he would attack France. There is no doubt that this was no idle threat; war was his central aim. Henry's aggressive posture contrasted dramatically with his father's caution in foreign policy. Henry VII had been satisfied with an annual pension of £5000 from the French King, which had helped to stabilise the national finances.

There seems little to commend Henry VIII's desire to renew the Hundred Years War and revive the English claim to the throne of France. France was a far more powerful country than England and war was bound to wreck the national finances. On the other hand, it is important to understand the contemporary admiration for chivalry and military glory. The aristocracy was still essentially a military caste created for war. Henry VII's passivity had not been popular, partly because it denied the ruling class the chance to win success and booty in battle. It was seen as the King's duty to win honour for himself and his country, and the young Henry was bound to be drawn to this role.

Opportunities would also be available for the dispensation of patronage. Henry VII had been notoriously mean in granting aristocratic titles; in 1509, the Duke of Buckingham was the only hereditary duke in the kingdom. By 1514, Thomas Howard had been restored to the Duchy of Norfolk, taken from the family for their support of Richard III in 1485, and Charles Brandon had been created Duke of Suffolk. Both men had played important parts in the military campaigns of these years. The popularity of Henry VIII was undeniably increased by his aggressive posture of national leadership and lavish distribution of patronage.

Whether an aggressive foreign policy served the national interest is more debatable. European affairs were in a state of some confusion in 1509. The struggle for advantage between Ferdinand of Spain, Louis XII of France, and Maximilian, the Holy Roman Emperor, focused on Italy. It might seem reasonable to assume that Henry could benefit from his availability as an ally to any one of these contesting powers. There was always tension between the French, the English and Emperor Maximilian in north-western Europe. Maximilian ruled the Low Countries, while the English retained the valuable toe-hold of Calais. It could be argued that too passive a policy would encourage the French to try to seize Calais. At the same time Ferdinand of Aragon had his own claims against the French in southern France close to areas held by the English Crown until the 1450s.

Maximilian and Ferdinand were both, therefore, potential allies for Henry. Unfortunately, they were both veterans in European diplomacy and totally unscrupulous and untrustworthy. They were quite capable of manipulating the naive and hot-blooded Henry for their own purposes.

Henry inherited most of his father's counsellors. He was a young man notoriously addicted to games and amusements and unenthusiastic about day to day administrative tasks. It might be assumed that major decisions were initially made by men such as Richard Fox, Bishop of Winchester, and William Warham, Archbishop of Canterbury, both of whom were men of vast experience closely associated with the very different approach of Henry VII. This assumption should be rejected. Henry did require some time to acclimatise himself to his new position, but his ministers' duty was to implement Henry's policies and not create them. If the King was determined to fight a war, war would be fought.

4 WAR WITH FRANCE

Pope Julius II was increasingly unhappy with the League of Cambrai, which had temporarily united the other major powers against Venice, and was concerned that the true threat to Italy came from France. Henry sent a diplomatic mission to Rome in 1511 and England joined the Holy League against France, which Ferdinand, the Pope, the Swiss, and the Venetians had just formed.

Some kind of strategy now had to be developed. Henry agreed with Ferdinand on a joint expedition to the historically English territories in Aquitaine in south-west France close to the Spanish border. An English expedition was then despatched to San Sebastian in northern Spain in April 1512.

There seems little doubt that this expedition was organised for the benefit of Ferdinand rather than Henry. Ferdinand had his own claim to Navarre on the border between France and Spain and conveniently close to where the expedition had been sent.

The campaign proved to be a complete fiasco. Ferdinand captured Navarre, while the English troops under the Marquis of Dorset drank too much, mutinied, or died of dysentery. Despite promises of a renewed alliance in April 1513, once Ferdinand had achieved his objectives, he made peace and abandoned Henry.

The obvious base for any offensive against France was Calais. It had been in English hands for over 150 years and made an ideal base for transporting troops. Any campaign in northern France would require an alliance with Maximilian, the Holy Roman Emperor and ruler of the wealthy cities of the Low Countries. If anything, Maximilian was even less reliable than Ferdinand, but he did agree to join the English attack on France in April 1513.

The French were well aware of Henry's planned invasion. There were weaknesses in Louis XII's position; many French troops were in Italy and by the standards of the day the English army of 30 000 was huge and impressively equipped. It was the most threatening force sent to France since the battle of Agincourt. This organisational triumph was largely the work of a rising servant of the King, Thomas Wolsey, whose forceful and energetic personality came to be widely appreciated for the first time.

Despite the impressive quality of Henry's army, the French had some predictable but dangerous weapons with which to neutralise the

English. Chief amongst these was the 'Auld Alliance' with James IV of Scotland. Scotland was a poor and backward country and its kings were under constant threat from the powerful nobility, but a Scottish invasion of England still posed a very serious threat. The French would also be aware of the unreliability of Maximilian, who intended to exploit Henry for his own ends.

Henry also needed to clarify his own war aims. He maintained the traditional English claim to the throne of France and many French provinces. In practice, his main aim was to prove himself as a fine soldier and true man of chivalry, but any conquered territory would be valuable as a bargaining counter in peace negotiations.

The lack of a more specific purpose to the campaign is suggested by Henry's failure to move his army from Calais until 21 July 1513. As a result a considerable part of the summer campaigning season had passed before the army set out. It initially seemed that Boulogne was Henry's target. Its capture would be of great value, both expanding the Calais Pale and providing another friendly port across the Channel. Instead, on 1 August Henry marched on the fortress of Thérouanne. Thérouanne's fortifications did not seriously threaten the English, but they did threaten Maximilian's territories. Again it seems that Henry was serving his ally's interests rather than his own.

Nonetheless, success and glory was achieved. A French force sent to relieve the town was forced to flee in undignified fashion in the so-called 'Battle of the Spurs' giving Henry the genuine, if insignificant, victory that he craved. On 22 August Thérouanne surrendered and its fortifications were destroyed. This brought little benefit to the English, but pleased Maximilian.

The next English target was the city of Tournai. Tournai was a French city entirely surrounded by Maximilian's lands and a hundred miles from Calais. It was undoubtedly a wealthy city, but again it seems that its capture would be of benefit to Maximilian rather than Henry. If the English did capture Tournai, it was so far from the sea that maintenance of control would pose great problems and require vast expense.

On 20 September, the bombardment of Tournai began and three days later the city surrendered, passing unenthusiastically under English rule for the next five years. The English were forced to maintain a garrison and entirely re-build the defences of the city at great cost.

There is a case for regarding the campaign of 1513 as an absurd charade, in which Henry was the dupe of Ferdinand and Maximilian and was effectively fighting France in the interest of countries other than his own. On the other hand, Henry had flexed his muscles and proved that England could organise a large and well equipped army. Over the next years this military success brought Henry a leading role in Europe. He had proved himself a true king in the traditional manner and Tournai was at least a valuable possession for diplomatic bargaining. It was England's first military victory in France for seventy-five years and Thomas Wolsey had provided the organisational dynamism that Henry needed.

Ironically, Henry had nothing to do with England's greatest military triumph in 1513. On 9 September at Flodden Field the Earl of Surrey annihilated the army of James IV and was restored to the Duchy of Norfolk as a result. James himself was killed along with much of the Scottish aristocracy. Although Henry did not capitalise on this victory as effectively as he might, the military threat from Scotland dramatically diminished.

5 THOMAS WOLSEY

Thomas Wolsey was the son of a butcher and born in Ipswich in 1472 or 1473. He was educated at Magdalen College, Oxford, and became Bursar of the College and Master of the school attached to the College. In order to progress in the world it was essential that someone from Wolsey's modest background should attract the patronage of some great man. In Wolsey's case, it was initially through the Marquis of Dorset that he gained advancement. He then became chaplain to Henry VII and chaplain and almoner (distributor of alms) to Henry VIII

Cardinal Thomas Wolsey, anon.

before showing his outstanding qualities in the campaign of 1513.

Wolsey's indispensability to Henry was shown by the vast number of major offices that he accumulated over the next years. In 1514, he became Bishop of Tournai and of Lincoln; and in the same year Archbishop of York. In September 1515, he became a cardinal and later that year was appointed Lord Chancellor. Even more remarkable was his appointment as Papal Legate (i.e. representative of the Pope) on a temporary basis in 1518 and for life in 1524. This position effectively gave him control over the English Church and primacy over the Archbishop of Canterbury.

His accumulation of clerical offices, or pluralism, offers one explanation for the generally hostile attitude towards Wolsey from many historians. He held all these positions in the Church for the revenues that they would bring him. For example, he did not visit his diocese of York until his fall from power in 1528. He can easily be portrayed as the worst kind of cynical and worldly churchman.

Wolsey has also suffered because of his unpopularity with his contemporaries. Polydore Vergil, who wrote the most influential account of this period, had a personal grievance against Wolsey, who had caused him to be imprisoned in the Tower for a short period. Another contemporary historian, Edward Hall came from London, where anti-clerical attitudes were common, and was also suspicious of Wolsey's supposedly pro-French policies.

Henry's Poet Laureate, John Skelton, pointedly criticised Wolsey in his verse.

Why come ye not to Court?
To which court?
To the King's Court?
Or to Hampton Court?

Wolsey's palace at Hampton Court was indeed splendid and his greed for wealth and property cannot be denied.

Wolsey's bad press has continued in the twentieth century. The conscious or unconscious Protestant sympathies of English historians have been repelled by what is seen as decadence. There is a vigorous debate as to what his aims and motivation really were. For A F Pollard writing in 1929 (not to be confused with A J Pollard [see page 3]), Wolsey subordinated English foreign policy to the interests of the Papacy because of his own ambition to become Pope. In his biography of Henry VIII, Professor Scarisbrick argues that Wolsey's central aim was to be the peacemaker of Europe. Peter Gwyn's recent biography rejects both these arguments. He believes that Henry was always the master and Wolsey his loyal servant, whose aim was to promote the honour and glory of the King.

What no-one can deny is the power of Wolsey's personality and his extraordinary vigour and energy. Foreign policy absorbed the bulk of his time, but in recent years there has also been a growing interest in his work as Lord Chancellor and his involvement in the social questions of the day. Wolsey may only have been Henry's servant, but he was a remarkable man in his own right.

6 FOREIGN POLICY 1514–25

In these years Henry and Wolsey pursued a vigorous foreign policy involving a constantly shifting pattern of alliances. International affairs were much altered by the accession of new monarchs. In 1515 Francis I succeeded Louis XII as King of France. Francis was as youthful and energetic as Henry and yearned for success abroad. There was bound to be rivalry between two such similar characters. The changes in Spain and the Holy Roman Empire were in some ways even more significant. The deaths of Ferdinand of Aragon in 1516 and the Emperor Maximilian in 1519 completed the concentration of a vast empire in the hands of Charles, Duke of Burgundy, who eventually became Holy Roman Emperor and is usually known as Charles V.

Charles eventually ruled Spain, the Low Countries, Austria, and much of Italy where he contested control of the Duchy of Milan with Francis I. France was surrounded by territory ruled by Charles V, whose tenacity compensated for his lack of glamour in comparison with Francis and Henry.

The rivalry between Francis and Charles was greatly to the benefit of Henry. He was a potential and valuable ally for them both. England also occupied a crucial geographical position. The natural route for Charles from Spain to the Low Countries was by sea through the English Channel. It would be easy for Henry to assist or disrupt his communications.

Wolsey's first diplomatic achievement was peace with France in 1514. Ferdinand and Maximilian had proved to be unreliable allies and the peace settlement with France did not include them. The treaty was not unfavourable: England kept Tournai and the French pension originally paid to Henry VII after the Treaty of Etaples was renewed. In addition, Henry's unfortunate younger sister Mary was to marry the ageing Louis XII. The treaty was to last until one year after the death of whichever king died first. The war had cost vast amounts of money and Henry had failed to find reliable allies. On the other hand the French could no longer afford to ignore Henry and the formidable forces that he had managed to raise.

The death of Louis on 1 January 1515 and the accession of Francis ended any chance of lasting peace in Europe. Henry's sister Mary was the chief beneficiary as she was now free to marry Charles Brandon, Duke of Suffolk. But in every other way the accession of Francis weakened England's international position.

Events in Italy further strengthened the French position. A great victory at Marignano in September 1515 consolidated French power in Italy. Wolsey made funds available to both Maximilian and the Swiss in an attempt to build an anti-French coalition, but Francis made peace with the Swiss at Fribourg and Charles at Noyon (1516) and with Maximilian at Cambrai (1517). Once again potential allies had proved unreliable and England was left looking dangerously exposed and isolated internationally.

From this vulnerable position, through patient and opportunistic diplomacy, Henry and Wolsey engineered their greatest diplomatic triumph. In 1517 Wolsey sensibly opened negotiations with the French and achieved an initial success with the return of Henry's sister, Margaret, to Scotland, from where she had been forced to flee by intrigues sponsored by Francis.

The real impetus for peace, however, came from Pope Leo X. He was increasingly concerned about the threat of an invasion of Italy by the Ottoman Turks and proposed a universal peace in Europe followed by a crusade. Crusades were much discussed in Europe, but never with serious intent. Nonetheless, in 1518, Thomas Campeggio, a Papal Legate, was sent to England. This gave Henry the opportunity to obtain legatine powers for Wolsey.

The atmosphere created by the Papacy gave added impetus to the negotiations with France. Every other policy had gained small success, or failed altogether, so there was much to be said for alliance and friendship with France. Wolsey's triumph lay in combining peace with France with a general European peace.

On 2 October 1518, in London, English and French representatives agreed to a treaty binding the great powers to perpetual peace. Twenty other powers were eventually included in this agreement, which became known as the Treaty of London. On 4 October it was further agreed that Tournai should return to France in return for 600 000 crowns and that Mary, Henry's daughter, should marry the son of the French King.

The Treaty of London did not last and may be seen as nothing more than a series of high sounding and meaningless clichés. But Wolsey's intentions appear to have been genuine and earned much praise and honour for him and his master. It was also a brilliant recovery after three years of diplomatic disaster. The war of 1512–13 had cost £600 000 at a time when Henry's annual revenue was on average £100 000. As Peter Gwyn has written: 'Peace was a much cheaper way of securing England's dominant position in Europe than subsidising anti-French alliances.' England was the pivot of the Treaty of London as each state made their agreement individually with England and not with each other. Therefore, at no cost Henry and Wolsey were established as the peacemakers of Europe and England had secured an influence in Europe out of all proportion to its real power and wealth.

Wolsey had satisfied his own desire for peace and gratified Henry's desire for honour and glory.

Within three years of the Treaty of London war had again broken out between Francis I and Charles V. This might seem to point to the essential unreality of the agreement. In fact, the assumption of the imperial throne by Charles in 1519 was bound to lead to conflict with Francis since they directly clashed over control of the Duchy of Milan. Also, in strictly practical terms it was alliance with France that brought most benefit to Wolsey. It gave England the chance to exert some leverage over France, or desert and ally with Charles in an anti-French coalition. Both Charles and Francis, therefore, had reason to maintain good relations with England.

The events of 1520–1 provide evidence of the central position in diplomacy that Wolsey had engineered for Henry and himself. On 26 May 1520 Charles met briefly with Henry on his way from Spain to the Low Countries. The meeting had to be brief because Henry was about to embark for the most glamorous and spectacular of his meetings with Francis at the Field of the Cloth of Gold (*see page 424*), which was located in the no-man's land between Calais and French territory. A retinue of 5000 accompanied Henry and nearly two weeks of wrestling, dancing, and jousting was exactly the kind of lavish celebration, in which Henry most delighted, despite the embarrassment of losing to Francis in a wrestling match. The two kings parted on 23 June and exchanged vows of peace, after which Henry again conferred with Charles V at Gravelines and Calais. This shows how Henry and Wolsey were able to take advantage of their position as the third of three major powers, knowing that England's alliance with either of the other two would tip the balance decisively.

It was Francis who re-opened hostilities with the capture of Navarre from Spain in the spring of 1521. Charles V argued that Francis was in breach of the Treaty of London and tried to win Henry over into an anti-French alliance.

The English reaction gave rise to an extraordinary sequence of events. On 2 August Wolsey sailed for Calais for a conference whose ostensible purpose was to obtain a peace settlement between France and the Emperor. Yet on 14 August Wolsey made the short journey to Bruges and negotiated a treaty with Charles. This committed England to war with France if fighting continued. Henry and Charles would mount a joint campaign and Mary Tudor was to marry Charles instead of the son of the French King. After this meeting Wolsey returned to Calais and the peace conference.

His behaviour has been much discussed. Scarisbrick has argued that Wolsey always wanted peace and that there was an underlying conflict with Henry. Wolsey's consolation was to delay the commitment to war until May 1522. The most recent interpretation has come from Peter Gwyn. He argues that Wolsey was not looking for peace, but was a tough and uncompromising negotiator, who hoodwinked the French while conducting serious negotiations with Charles. Neutrality would seriously diminish Henry's role as a major international figure so assiduously nurtured by Wolsey since 1518, whereas an alliance with Charles might bring material gains and would be popular with the Pope, who was keen to expel the French from Italy.

In Wolsey's behaviour in 1521, Gwyn finds further justification for his view of the relationship and motivation of the two men: 'the most important thing was to dominate affairs, and by this means bring honour to his master – and, of course, to himself'.

War was actually declared on 29 May 1522 and lasted for three years. The only options available were to fight or opt out of European affairs altogether. The aim of the alliance with Charles was not to conquer France, but to use military success to enhance the influence of Henry and Wolsey in Europe.

Although England's population of two and a half million was barely one-sixth that of France and Henry's tax revenue was far less than Francis', he lacked the extensive commitments that Francis had to maintain elsewhere in Europe. There were signs of scepticism about war in the Parliament of 1523, but by August finance was available for another 'Great Enterprise' against France.

Problems in Scotland and fears that Charles V might prove an unreliable ally had caused some caution and delay, but in August 1523 the Duke of Suffolk crossed to Calais with a substantial army. The initial plan was to attack Boulogne, but Charles V persuaded the English to march on Paris. Initially no opposition was met and the army advanced to within 70 miles of the city before the campaign disintegrated.

The expense of the campaign and the failure of Charles V and the French traitor Charles of Bourbon to offer effective support brought growing disenchantment with the war. In 1524 negotiations were re-opened with the French. As before Wolsey used the alliance with Charles as a means of bringing pressure to bear on the French.

His classic balance of power diplomacy was dramatically disrupted by news of the Battle of Pavia in northern Italy in February 1525. The imperial armies destroyed the armies of France, and Francis and his two sons were captured. Henry's initial reaction was understandable. There really did now seem a chance that he could recover the lost territories in France and even claim the French throne. Another invasion was planned and a forced loan or 'Amicable Grant' was demanded from the English people. The English people, however, had lost interest in financing war and it proved impossible to raise the money. Moreover, Charles V clearly had no enthusiasm for Henry's plans and in August, Wolsey negotiated the Treaty of The More with the French. England abandoned territorial claims in France and the French resumed an annual pension of 100 000 gold crowns.

The war may have failed, but the peace treaty gave Henry the chance to continue to play a decisive and independent role in European affairs. There were those who argued that the imperial alliance should be maintained, but Charles was unreliable, and too close an alliance with one of the great powers would have made Henry appear a subordinate.

English diplomacy between 1515–25 failed to bring great gains to the country, but it did thrust the country into a major role that its wealth and population scarcely justified. Wolsey's aim was to serve his master and maintain his honour and influence. In hindsight this may seem vainglorious, but that is a rather anachronistic view. The conflict between Francis and Charles may have been inevitable and Henry and Wolsey did well to preserve an independent and active role and win glory, honour and prestige, which meant so much to Henry.

7 DOMESTIC AFFAIRS UNDER WOLSEY

Wolsey's main concern was always foreign policy, but his energy and vitality ensured that he played an active role in all aspects of government. After his appointment as Lord Chancellor in December 1515, he presided over the Court of Chancery and it was at this time that the Court of Star Chamber emerged as a distinct court separate from the King's Council.

Both courts saw a dramatic expansion in their work at this time. In Wolsey's fourteen years as Lord Chancellor, it is estimated that over nine thousand cases were brought before the two courts. In particular the Court of Star Chamber became far busier dealing with about 120 cases each year compared with only about a dozen in the reign of Henry VII. It is with this court that Wolsey was most closely associated.

Despite all his other responsibilities, he sat as a judge in the Court of Star Chamber several times each week. The value of Wolsey's work in Star Chamber has sometimes been questioned. It is true that he attracted so much business to the court that it could not cope and overflow courts had to be established, and that he failed to organise the court in an effective manner leaving this task to his successors. On the other hand recent historians, such as John Guy, have given Wolsey credit for his genuine support for 'impartial justice'. This simply means that anyone should feel that they could take their case to the Star Chamber regardless of their wealth or status. This was a radical idea in an age where rank and wealth expected deference from the poor and where the slogan 'Justice is a fat fee' realistically reflected the open bribery and corruption.

Like Henry VII, Wolsey was prepared to attack abuse of power by the aristocracy and such traditional problems as illegal retaining and bribery of JPs and sheriffs. Great aristocrats were brought before the Star Chamber and punished; in 1515 the Earl of Northumberland was sent to the Fleet Prison and in 1516 Lord Burgavenny was accused of illegal retaining. This harsh treatment was perhaps unusual, but reflected the energy of a man described by Peter Gwyn as 'an extremely active Lord Chancellor, who used that office's existing machinery to the full'.

It is nonetheless true that Wolsey's more ambitious schemes to reorganise the administration of the law never really bore fruit. A scheme of 1526 to send commissioners to every shire to hear cases was never implemented, but a permanent committee was established at White Hall in Westminster in 1519 specifically to hear cases brought by the poor, and Wolsey clearly did try to make himself accessible to all his King's subjects. According to the Venetian ambassador Guistinian he had 'the reputation of being extremely just: he favours the people exceedingly, and especially the poor: hearing their suits and seeking to despatch them instantly . . .' As a lawyer, Wolsey may not have been an innovator or a reformer, but he was diligent and fair in the administration of justice.

Enclosure

Professor Scarisbrick has encouraged a more sympathetic view of Wolsey in his discussion of Wolsey's attitude towards enclosure. The issue of enclosure is highly complex and much debated by economic historians. Essentially enclosure involves the conversion of land from crop growing to sheep rearing and is associated with the practice of clearing people off the land for this purpose (*see page 459*). In the late fifteenth and early sixteenth centuries, there was anxiety about the depopulation of the countryside. This is illustrated by three statutes (1489, 1514, 1515), which were concerned with rural depopulation. Enclosure was concentrated in parts of the south Midlands and was, in the words of Professor Scarisbrick, 'slow, erratic, and piecemeal, and as much the work of peasants as of big men'.

Wolsey showed typical drive and industry in investigating this problem. In 1517/8, he encouraged an enquiry into enclosure, whose returns provided material for the Court of Chancery to take legal action against those who had ignored the three statutes.

Between 1518–29, legal action was taken against 264 persons, many of whom were forced to rebuild houses and return land to arable farming. It may justly be argued that the overall effect of these prosecutions was small, but the nature of Wolsey's actions was unprecedented. Proceedings were taken against 9 peers, 3 bishops, 32 knights, 51 heads of religious houses, and several Oxford colleges. Wolsey was quite prepared to challenge the wealthiest and most powerful elements of society in court.

More important perhaps was his willingness to question the right of landowners to do exactly as they pleased in their own counties, where they would expect to be unchallenged. Wolsey's motives are interesting. His actions brought him no financial advantage and concessions over enclosure in the Parliament of 1523, where Wolsey was effectively forced to accept all existing enclosures, provide evidence of the unpopularity of his actions with the ruling classes. It seems that he was aware of the dangers of social and economic discontent and as a result directly questioned the right of great lords to do as they wished with their own lands.

It is neither fanciful nor anachronistic to see Wolsey as a man with a social conscience and a sense of duty towards all his royal master's subjects. It is equally clear that his actions in the Court of Star Chamber and over enclosure did nothing for his popularity with the great men of the realm.

Parliament

The enormous difference in the role and importance of Parliament in the sixteenth century compared with today must never be forgotten. The main purpose of Parliament was to make laws and not to participate in the day to day government of the country, which was the work of the King and his Council. Consent from Parliament was also required for certain forms of taxation. But it is essential to remember that the King, Lords and Commons were partners – the 'King-in-Parliament' made the laws.

Henry VII had summoned Parliament infrequently in the last years of his reign. His avoidance of war and clever financial management made him virtually self-sufficient and he had no need for additional revenue from Parliament. It must not be assumed that a lack of Parliaments was unpopular; attendance could be expensive and irksome, although private individuals did sometimes need Parliament to pass specific pieces of legislation.

There were six parliamentary sessions between 1510–15. The main reason for this was that Henry needed money to finance his extravagant foreign policy. Parliament made the customary grants of tunnage and poundage in 1510.

The most significant benefit to the Crown came with the modernization of parliamentary taxation. The traditional 'Tenths' and 'Fifteenths' were based on a fixed sum that had to be raised by each community. Since there was no form of tax assessment, the amount of wealth actually available to be taxed was unknown. Any attempts to change the system and introduce a more flexible and realistic form of assessment had met with violent resistance.

During the early years of Henry's reign the 'subsidy' was developed. This was based on an assessment of personal wealth and banded according to the ability to pay and proved a far more effective tax than its predecessors.

It is possible that the subsidy was Wolsey's idea. He used the new tax four times and raised far more revenue than had been possible with sole reliance on Fifteenths and Tenths. Between 1513–16, the subsidy raised £170 000, three Fifteenths and Tenths raised £90 000, while the clergy contributed £40 000.

Parliament met only twice (1515 and 1523) during the ascendancy of Wolsey. There was nothing unusual in this. Parliaments were generally summoned to provide cash for fighting wars and between 1518–22 the country was at peace. These Parliaments did provide substantial revenue, which was supplemented in the early 1520s by 'loans' from the people, many of which were never repaid.

Nevertheless, it does seem that Wolsey was never really at ease with Parliament. The Parliament of 1515 was dominated by concern over Church matters. A London merchant named Richard Hunne, who had been charged with heresy, was found dead in custody. Even though there was less widespread anti-clericalism at the time than used to be thought (*see pages 83/4*), the City of London was sensitive to any attack on one of its number by the Church and Hunne's death caused great controversy. At the same time a friar, Henry Standish, attacked 'benefit of clergy', which allowed men in holy orders the right of trial in Church courts, which were regarded as excessively lenient. 'Benefit of clergy' was notoriously abused.

Potentially these issues were very embarrassing for Wolsey, who was both a man of the Church and a royal servant. An Act of 1512 had restricted benefit of clergy and was due for renewal in 1515. The question of its renewal divided Church and State and on one occasion Wolsey was forced to kneel before Henry and assure him that he had no desire to limit the powers of the Crown.

Wolsey's role in this appears to be that of mediator. The Act of 1512 was not renewed, but the royal will had been asserted and the complaints of Parliament had found an audience. It would be pressing the evidence too far to suggest that the anti-clerical mood of Parliament in 1515 explains the lack of Parliaments over the next eight years, but Wolsey had undoubtedly been placed in a very delicate position.

The Parliament of 1523 was the only Parliament to be summoned while Wolsey was Chancellor; the 1515 Parliament had actually been summoned before he was appointed. The primary source material is very sketchy, but does suggest that Wolsey was ill at ease in his dealings with this Parliament.

Inevitably the main argument was over money. War had been renewed with France and Wolsey initially demanded over £800 000 on top of 'loans' of £260 000. It appears that Wolsey tried to bully Parliament by maintaining the session well into the summer. He did obtain some extra money, but at the cost of abandoning his campaign against enclosure and creating much ill feeling. It would be going too far to suggest on the available evidence that there was outright antagonism between Wolsey and the leading figures in the country, who sat in Parliament, but there was probably some insensitivity on his part.

The Amicable Grant

The conflicts of 1523 were swiftly followed by one of the most complex and controversial disputes of this period. The 'Amicable Grant' was to be a non-refundable contribution by the English people to finance the war in France after Henry's ambitions were rekindled by the destruction of the French army at Pavia in Italy in February 1525.

This new demand followed the forced loans and high parliamentary taxation of the previous three years. Popular reaction was swift and hostile. There were disturbances concentrated around the important cloth-making centre of Lavenham in Suffolk and extending to London and Kent.

There is no evidence that this activity was fomented by aristocrats, although many probably disliked Wolsey. Indeed the Dukes of Norfolk and Suffolk did their best to enforce the royal will. Opposition seems to have been spontaneous and based on poverty and inability to pay rather than on innate hostility to Henry's policies. No money at all was collected and peace was made with France. The Amicable Grant can be viewed as a humiliation for Henry and Wolsey, but it also suggests flexibility and realism in the face of united opposition. It is also possible that the campaign in France had been more or less abandoned before the unpopularity of the Amicable Grant became clear.

Too much should not be concluded from the lack of Parliaments while Wolsey was Chancellor, but he clearly did not always get his own way and his behaviour in 1523 was certainly clumsy. Nonetheless, vast sums were raised by the standards of the day and there is no evidence of any organised opposition to Wolsey. The fact that the Amicable Grant was not referred to Parliament is of no great significance; it may simply reflect the need for swift action after Pavia.

The discontent of 1525 was concentrated in East Anglia, at this time this was a prosperous region and under the influence of two of Henry's greatest courtiers the Dukes of Norfolk and Suffolk. Their concern is shown in this letter to Wolsey written in May 1525:

> Please it Your Grace to be advertised that continually more and
> more knowledge doth come to us, that the confederacy with the
> evil disposed persons of this town extended to many places, not
> only in this shire and in Essex, but in Cambridgeshire, the town
> and university of Cambridge, and divers other countries . . .   5
> And assured Your Grace may be that we will not depart hence
> unless that we see no manner of likelihood of no new business
> to arise after our departure; and yet we shall put such order in
> both shires that if any such should chance, all the power of the
> King's servants and ours shall be ready to withstand the same,   10

and chieftains appointed to lead therein; and we with all
possible diligence to return. And assuredly, all things well
considered that we hear and see, we think we never saw the
time so needful for the king's highness to call his council unto
him, to debate and determine what is best to be done . . .   15
Written at Lavenham, the 12th day of May at noon.

1   *What does this extract suggest about the role in government of these two
    men?*

2   *Why do you think that the two Dukes were prepared to act so vigorously
    to suppress these protests?*

3   *What do you think is the significance of their request that the King should
    summon his Council (line 14)?*

4   *What might be concealed in a document written by these men to
    Wolsey?*

8 THE KING, WOLSEY AND THE ARISTOCRACY

Historians are fascinated with the question of where power really lay
in Tudor England. In one sense the question is easily answered; power
lay with the monarch, who chose his servants and ultimately determined policy. But the monarch was always surrounded by ruthless
and ambitious individuals determined to gain for themselves position
and influence.

Some historians see Tudor government and politics as essentially
dominated by 'faction'. This term is best understood to mean the existence of competing groups ambitious for office and personal power
and anxious to deny these to their rivals. Faction was closely linked to
patronage – the use of personal influence to advance in society.
Ambitious men needed a wealthy and powerful patron, whom they
would support in return for office or other privileges, but of course the
ultimate source of all these things was the king.

No-one denies the importance of patronage in Tudor England, but
the significance of faction in the time of Wolsey is fiercely debated.
Wolsey was a man from a humble background, who came to control
vast patronage and massive wealth. It is argued by some that this
aroused antagonism from the great nobles on the King's Council, who
saw Wolsey as a barrier to their own advancement. Peter Gwyn,
Wolsey's most recent biographer argues that too much stress has been
put on faction. He sees Henry VIII as his own master, who made all the
important decisions and was not susceptible to manipulation.

The execution of the Duke of Buckingham in May 1521 is sometimes
seen as evidence of Wolsey's manipulation. Buckingham was the country's leading aristocrat; he had royal blood and at least as good a claim
to the throne as the Tudors. Polydore Vergil was the first to suggest

that Wolsey engineered his fall to prevent Buckingham exploiting anti-French feeling.

Modern historians have largely rejected this interpretation. Buckingham seems to have been an intelligent but arrogant man. He had resented both Henry's failure to appoint him to the prestigious office of Constable of England and Star Chamber action against Sir William Bulmer for wearing Buckingham's livery in the presence of the King. There is also evidence that Buckingham was raising troops and that accusations of treason were not wholly groundless.

David Starkey has made a close examination of Henry VIII's Court and drawn attention to the significance of the Privy Chamber, which was the heart of the Royal Household (*see page 119*). The King was based at Westminster, but used many other palaces, such as Greenwich and Eltham. In the summer he would tour the country usually remaining in the South and Midlands. The Royal Court was the largest single institution in the country. Its organisation was split between the Lower Household, which was the public face of royal life, and the Chamber, in which the King conducted his private life. Those servants who had access to the Chamber were the King's closest companions.

During the fifteenth century, the working of the Chamber became more specialised. The Privy Chamber was created in the 1490s. The gentlemen of the Privy Chamber were the King's most intimate private servants. The most important of these, the Groom of the Stool, looked after the royal commode (lavatory).

Henry VIII was a very different character to his father. His love of pleasure and lack of application to the day to day tasks of government inevitably attracted similarly youthful and extrovert courtiers. Starkey argues that as a result 'there were two main foci of power: the administrative, centring on the council, and the royal household or Court'. He argues that Wolsey continually sought control over the Privy Chamber which was obviously a rival influence over the King. The situation was complicated in 1518/9 by the creation of the office of Gentleman of the Privy Chamber. This gave an official title to the closest royal favourites.

Wolsey's ability and the vast amount of patronage that he controlled had diminished the importance of faction. His household of 500 matched Henry's and his palaces, such as York Place and Hampton Court, were another magnet for ambitious young men. But the Gentlemen of the Privy Chamber or 'minions' had daily contact with Henry and influence over the distribution of patronage. Wolsey's reaction to this development was to secure the expulsion of most of the 'minions' from Court in May 1519.

However, their return was inevitable. Henry needed the company of these vigorous young men and it was only the wars of 1522–5 that kept them from an active life at Court. When the wars finished, Wolsey's next ploy was to secure the so called Eltham Ordinances of January 1526. Ostensibly these were economy measures reducing the number of Gentleman of the Bedchamber from twelve to six, but the most polit-ically active were removed and the survivors were of no importance.

David Starkey's analysis of the politics of the early years of Henry's reign does carry much conviction. It is accepted that Henry was easily distracted from day to day politics. Wolsey held a dominant position in government and the distribution of patronage, but lacked the intimate daily contact with the King enjoyed by the 'minions', many of whom would naturally seek to influence the distribution of patronage or the direction of policy. For Starkey the battle between the Council, which was dominated by Wolsey, and the Court, which was dominated by Henry's favourites, explains the politics of this period and 'the struggle for control between the two was continuous and often bitter'.

Peter Gwyn argues that too much stress has been given to faction by modern historians. He suggests that Henry was always in charge and that the use of courtiers on military or diplomatic missions was inevitable, since they were best suited for this purpose, and did not reflect some conspiracy by Wolsey. By the same token the Eltham Ordinances were simply an economy measure and many of the Gentlemen of the Bedchamber were in fact promoted. For example, Sir William Compton, the Groom of the Stool for ten years, became under-treasurer of the Exchequer.

Gwyn's insistence on the dominance of the royal will is an interest-ing argument, but in his own words 'the factional view is now almost an orthodoxy'. The debate on faction has particular importance because it resurfaces in the late 1520s at the time of the royal divorce and the fall of Wolsey.

9 THE DIVORCE

Catherine's marriage to Henry had taken place under circumstances which aroused doubt in the minds of some prominent churchman. She was five years older than Henry and it does seem that she was a pious and loyal wife, to whom her husband was initially genuinely devoted. Catherine's problem was simply that she did not produce a son and heir. A daughter, Mary, was born, but five other children died in infan-cy and after 1518 there were no more pregnancies. Henry was not in fact a notable womaniser, but by 1524 Catherine and he were no longer living as man and wife and amongst his mistresses was a woman named Mary Boleyn, sister of Anne Boleyn.

Henry's arrogance and egocentricity were such that he was bound to seek a scapegoat for his misfortunes. During the 1520s he gradually convinced himself that the marriage was illegal and that no papal dispensation could overcome the biblical ban on marriage to a dead brother's wife. He saw the failure of the marriage to produce a son as divine punishment. According to Professor Scarisbrick Henry believed 'that it was not only his right to throw away his wife, but it was also his duty – to himself, to Catherine, to his people, to God'. Henry did have a case in canon law, but it was not a strong one and informed legal opinion largely opposed him. It would require exceptional good fortune and a very favourable international climate for any divorce to be granted by the Pope.

Henry did not suddenly decide to abandon Catherine. The exceptional personality of Anne Boleyn played a vital role in shaping events. Anne Boleyn was a woman of great character and intelligence. Her background was aristocratic. The Boleyns were originally London merchants, but Anne's mother was the daughter of Thomas Howard, the Duke of Norfolk, and Anne was also related to the Butlers – leading members of the Irish aristocracy. She was born in 1501 and a mature woman at the time of the divorce. In 1513, she became a maid of honour at the court of the Duke of Burgundy at Mechelen (Malines) in the Low Countries. This was the most glittering court in northern Europe, whose practices were aped by the admiring English. She learned French and then spent seven years in the household of Queen Claude of France only returning to England in 1521.

Her biographer, Eric Ives, stresses her 'elegance and independence' and 'continental polish'. She was probably not conventionally attractive (there are rumours of six fingers and a wart), but she had been a stylish member of two stylish courts and was also strong-minded and intellectually gifted. These qualities were enough to attract Henry at a Court pageant in 1522 where Anne played Perseverance. Henry's infatuation with Anne and dissatisfaction with Catherine were not initially connected. It is even possible that his relationship with Anne did not seriously develop before the decision to seek a divorce was taken in May 1527. Anne's main contribution to the developing crisis was her proud refusal to follow her sister Mary and become Henry's mistress. She was only prepared to accept marriage.

There is no concrete evidence of great initial hostility between Anne and Wolsey, despite some contemporary claims. Indeed, the delicate negotiations with the Pope that now seemed inevitable if a divorce was to be secured seemed entirely suited to Wolsey's talents. He was a skilled and experienced negotiator and renowned for his closeness to Rome, which had secured for him the coveted title of Papal Legate.

Wolsey's failure to secure the divorce destroyed him. Undoubtedly, he was exceptionally unlucky in the international situation. By 1526 the English were disillusioned with Charles V, who was of course Catherine's nephew. Pope Clement VII also feared Charles V's power in Italy after the destruction of the French at Pavia. The result of this was the formation of the Holy League of Cognac in May 1526. Its members were the Papacy, France, Venice, and Florence with the backing of England and it was directed against Charles V.

However, any realistic chance of co-operation from the Pope was shattered when the armies of Charles sacked Rome and captured the Pope. Although Clement was soon released he was obviously anxious not to offend Charles, who opposed the divorce. Two years of delicate negotiations by Wolsey failed to gain support from the Pope by 1529.

Wolsey also sought to enlist French military support. Francis I made an agreement with Wolsey at Amiens in August 1527 and by January 1528 France and England were both at war with Charles V. The French defeat at Landriano in June 1529 confirmed that Clement VII would remain in the power of Charles V. The Treaty of Cambrai in August 1529 allied Francis, Charles and the Pope and destroyed any remaining illusion that the Pope might view the divorce with sympathy. Through no fault of his own Wolsey had failed Henry and fatally weakened his own position.

10 THE FALL OF WOLSEY

In October 1529 Wolsey was stripped of his authority and departed for his diocese of York for the first time. His death on 29 November 1530 came five weeks after he was charged with treason.

Various explanations are advanced for the fall of Wolsey. The simplest comes from Peter Gwyn. He argues that Wolsey was Henry's servant, whose duty it was to fulfill his master's wishes. Through no fault of his own, his diplomacy failed as did all his other schemes, such as the Legatine Courts, which met in England in 1527 and 1529. His failure to get the divorce inevitably brought about his dismissal. In addition he was particularly vulnerable because of his close association with the Papacy.

Gwyn's explanation is simple and coherent, but not generally accepted. David Starkey and Eric Ives both argue that Wolsey was a victim of factional intrigues organised by leading aristocrats, such as the Duke of Norfolk, around the person of Anne Boleyn.

Anne, it is argued, had to enter politics to challenge the popularity of Catherine of Aragon. She weakened Wolsey's control of patronage by securing the rejection of Wolsey's candidate for the valuable position of Abbess of Wilton in 1528. Control of patronage was essential if a man like Wolsey was to maintain his hold on power.

During 1528 there was no serious split between Anne and Wolsey as he was her best hope of securing the divorce. It was only in the summer of 1529 that it became clear that Wolsey had failed. This enabled Anne and her faction to bring Wolsey down at a time when Wolsey had little close contact with the King. Ives argues that the fall of Wolsey was 'first and foremost Anne's success'.

On such matters differences between scholars are inevitable. It is clear that Wolsey failed the King on a major issue that involved personalities and politics. This was bound to weaken his position. It is equally clear that there was a constant battle for prestige and position in Henry's Court and that Anne Boleyn was a formidable figure in this struggle.

George Cavendish was an intimate servant and admirer of Wolsey. His biography provides one of the few sympathetic contemporary portraits and interesting insights into Court intrigues:

> As I heard it reported by them that waited upon the King at dinner, that Mistress Anne Boleyn was much offended with the King, as far as she durst, that he so gently entertained my lord [Wolsey], saying as she sat with the King at dinner in communication [conversation] of him, 'Sir,' quod she, 'Is it not a 5 marvellous thing to consider what debt and danger the Cardinal has brought you in with all your subjects . . . there is not a man within all your realm worth five pounds but he hath indebted you unto him by his means' [meaning by a loan that the King had but late of his subjects] . . . 'there is never a 10 nobleman within this realm that if he had done but half so much as he hath done but he were well worthy to lose his head. If my Lord of Norfolk, my Lord of Suffolk, my lord my father, or any other noble person within your realm had done much less than he, but they should have lost their heads or this.' 'Why 15 then I perceive,' quod the King 'ye are not the Cardinal's friend.' 'Forsooth sir,' then quod she, 'I have no cause nor any other man that loveth your grace. No more have your grace if ye consider well his doings.'

1 *To which loan is Anne probably referring (line 9)?*

2 *What impression is given of her personality?*

3 *How does this conversation illustrate the weakness of Wolsey's position?*

4 *Which modern interpretation of Wolsey's fall seems most justified by this extract?*

It is easy to deride the first twenty years of Henry's reign. His foreign policy seems anachronistic and unrealistic. Wolsey was undoubtedly greedy and vainglorious and an exceptionally worldly churchman. His achievement was to enhance the prestige of the country to a far greater level than its actual power merited. It might also have been very dangerous to stand on the sidelines when France and the Empire were struggling so fiercely for supremacy.

Wolsey may have achieved little at home, but he showed an energy and social conscience that must be respected. He was not an intolerant man and although he took action against the first stirrings of heresy, he was not a persecutor by temperament. He should be seen as the dynamic and imaginative servant of a capricious master.

11 Bibliography

G R Elton *Reform and Reformation* (Edward Arnold, 1977).
J Guy *Tudor England* (OUP, 1988).
P Gwyn *The King's Cardinal* (Barrie & Jenkins, 1990).
E Ives *Anne Boleyn* (Blackwell, 1986).
J J Scarisbrick *Henry VIII* (Methuen, 1968).
D Starkey *The Reign of Henry VIII: Personalities and Politics* (George Philip, 1985).

12 Discussion points and exercises

A *This section consists of questions or points that might be used for discussion (or written answers) as a way of expanding on the chapter and testing understanding of it:*

1 Why have Henry VIII's early years been given little attention by historians until recently?

2 Why did Henry VIII marry Catherine of Aragon so quickly after his accession?

3 What does the execution of Empson and Dudley reveal about Henry VIII's political methods?

4 Why did Henry VIII want war and in whose interests was it?

5 What did Henry VIII gain from the wars against France and Scotland in 1513?

6 Why has Wolsey's reputation been so controversial?

7 What influence did England have in European affairs 1514–22, and how was it achieved?

8 What motives lay behind Wolsey's foreign policy?

9 Why was the 1522–5 war against France a failure?

10 Did Wolsey achieve anything as a judge?

11 How did Wolsey tackle the problem of enclosure and why was he concerned about it?

12 How effective was Wolsey in his dealings with Parliaments?

13 Was the Amicable Grant simply an error?

14 'Wolsey could never finally master the factions which opposed him.' Why not?

15 Why did Henry VIII want a divorce?

16 Why did Wolsey fail to secure the divorce?

17 How far was Wolsey's downfall brought about by Anne Boleyn?

1 What were Wolsey's aims in foreign policy and how far were they fulfilled?

2 Did Wolsey's conduct of foreign policy subordinate England's interests to those of the Papacy?

3 Who achieved more in foreign affairs: Henry VII or Wolsey?

4 'Only distraction by foreign policy denied him full success in domestic affairs.' Discuss this view of Wolsey.

5 What constructive achievements can Wolsey claim?

6 Why did Wolsey fall from power?

13 ESSAY WRITING – ASSESSMENT

Wolsey continues to attract controversy. The size of his personality, the power that he obtained and the policies that he pursued intrigue historians.

A common type of essay asks the student to consider the successes and failures of a particular person. Wolsey is especially suited to this approach.

An initial difficulty with Wolsey lies in establishing what he was actually trying to do. Should he be seen as his master's loyal servant, or as pursuing his own ambitions? If you consider that Wolsey's aim was to serve Henry VIII, he can be judged by his success in doing so. It must also be borne in mind, for example, that the sixteenth-century conception of a successful foreign policy was very different to our own.

Consider Wolsey's successes and failures in the following areas:

a Diplomacy and foreign policy. In doing this you must carefully consider the differing views of historians and especially the interpretations of Peter Gwyn.

b His work as Lord Chancellor. Were there any achievements in administrative reform or policy towards enclosure?

c His relationship with Parliament, especially in financial matters.

d His relationship with the King and aristocracy. How important were faction and patronage and how effectively and by what means did Wolsey maintain his position with Henry VIII?

e The divorce. Was Wolsey's task impossible?

f Why did he fall from power? Was it a matter of personalities, policies or a combination of the two?

IV

Henry VIII: The Reformation

—

1 Introduction

RELIGIOUS practice has for many become a token gesture kept for the ceremonial occasions of life and it is difficult to grasp the immense importance of their religion to the people of the sixteenth century. And Henry VIII's reign was, of course, of immense importance in the history of the English Church. When he came to the throne England was an integral part of the Catholic Church, owing spiritual allegiance to the Pope (though what that meant exactly could be a matter for dispute) and participating to the full in the traditional practices of that Church. Henry himself had made a show of his piety and had taken up the pen in defence of Catholic doctrine and the Papacy against Luther when he wrote his *Assertio Septem Sacramentorum* (Defence of the Seven Sacraments), for which he received, and his successors still bear, the title of Defender of the Faith. By the time of his death the English Church had renounced any link with or allegiance to Rome, the King had declared himself Supreme Head of the Church, a variety of traditional practices had been banned, the religious orders dissolved, and a number of reformers looked, with some anticipation, for further, more blatantly Protestant, developments in the country. What brought about these changes? Was there a genuine need and demand for reform or was Henry motivated by personal and political considerations? What exactly were these changes, how did they affect the country, and were the Protestant reformers realistic in their hopes?

2 The Pre-Reformation Church

What was the condition of the English Church before the Henrician Reformation and how did contemporaries view the Church? These questions are important since one of the debates on that reformation is concerned with the extent to which it was imposed from above on an unwilling, or at best indifferent, country or whether it would be more accurate to see the initiative for reform coming from below and that all Henry needed to do was to channel this dissatisfaction towards his own ends.

A number of historians have put forward the idea that even without Henry's wish to divorce his first Queen and the policies he had to adopt to gain that end, England may have experienced some form of reformation. Supporters of this theory see in the pre-Reformation Church a variety of abuses and lack of spirituality that provoked unfavourable reactions from many contemporaries and so provided the necessary support for the King in his attack on the English Church. This criticism is often put under the heading of 'anti-clericalism', a term that can be used to cover hostility to the clergy in general or to certain abuses of their position or just to particular individuals. A leading exponent of this interpretation has been Professor A G Dickens whose book *The English Reformation* explicitly sets out to describe 'those basic conditions which made possible the dramatic and familiar changes of the years 1529–59' which, he maintains, 'had created before the meeting of the Reformation Parliament an atmosphere little short of explosive'.

This view certainly seems well supported by some of the contemporary evidence. In 1512, John Colet, Dean of St Paul's, preached the opening sermon to a meeting of the Convocation of Canterbury, an assembly of the leading clergy and representatives of the parish clergy, of the south of England. Having emphasised the need for reform in the Church, he then laid the blame for its current state on the shoulders of the clergy, from the most ill-paid of priests to the bishops. Many of his accusations were echoed by others. Shortly before the opening of the Parliament of 1529, a pamphlet entitled *A Supplication for the Beggars* was circulating in London. This was the work of Simon Fish, a lawyer and Lutheran activist, and is an example of anti-clericalism in its most extreme form. Unlike Colet, he did not suggest the clergy reform themselves but asked the King to take action – 'To tie these holy idle thieves to the carts to be whipped naked about every market town.'

Many historians are now taking a kinder view of the pre-Reformation Church. Contemporary complaints cannot be ignored but research beyond these into administrative records – for example, bishops' visitations or court proceedings – has helped to redress the balance in favour of the Church. Professor J J Scarisbrick and Dr Christopher Harper-Bill have presented a picture of a Church which, though far from perfect, was acceptable to the majority of its members and continued to enjoy considerable support at all levels of society.

To modern eyes the Church of the early sixteenth century would certainly seem very generously staffed. Some complaints seem to have been aimed at these large numbers but it should be remembered that many of these clerics were not involved in what we would consider to be priestly duties. Since entry to the clerical order was for some simply the only way to enter any form of professional or educated life any modern comparison would have to include large numbers of teachers and civil servants. However, even with this caveat there was undoubtedly no shortage of clerical manpower and inevitably such a large body of men provided material for criticism.

Both Colet and Fish agreed on the faults of the clergy. At all levels they were too ambitious, continually chasing after more and better offices. This led to the associated abuses of pluralism and non-residence. Pluralism was the holding of more than one office at a time, and with it of course went non-residence, failing to live in the parish from which one got one's income. When this happened, it was argued, the parishioners were all too often left without any spiritual leadership or had to make do with a substitute poorly paid and often inadequate. To make matters worse, men often gained their offices through nepotism or simony. The former meant appointment on the grounds of a family relationship rather than for any appropriate qualification and the latter was the outright buying of an office. Neither of these, it should be stressed, was officially sanctioned but both of them led to the appointment of people of inappropriate character whether as ordinary priests or bishops.

However, where studies have been made of different areas, using in particular records of bishops' visitations (or tours of inspection) of their dioceses, a rather different picture emerges. It now appears that most of the parish clergy carried out their duties conscientiously and to the satisfaction of their parishioners. In the diocese of Lincoln, for example, a study of episcopal records shows that in the years between 1514 and 1521 only 4 per cent of parishes complained about inadequate performance of spiritual duty by their clergymen, and in some cases this could be explained by old age. Investigations elsewhere have shown similar results. Non-resident clergy were properly licensed and seem to have found adequate deputies to take their place. Indeed the parish clergy as a whole were not as ill-educated as they have often been portrayed. Although rarely familiar with the latest ideas in learning such evidence as can be gained from the books they owned and the few references to those individuals who were inadequate, show a body of men generally well enough versed in the conventional and traditional learning and certainly able to cater for the needs of most of their parishioners. Bishops too have fared better in the light of further research. On the whole, the bishops of the early sixteenth century, even when involved with other secular tasks, devoted time to the administration and spiritual welfare of their dioceses. Archbishop Warham, for example, conducted a personal visitation of the Canterbury diocese in 1511–12, while still acting as Lord Chancellor of England. Other bishops showed a similar willingness to work in their dioceses whenever possible, even while serving the King in some way. Even when absence was necessary, the diocese could be adequately administered by his deputies and specifically episcopal functions carried out by suffragan (assistant) bishops.

But it was not just the clergy's alleged failures that provoked criticism. In some areas they were seen as being too efficient. The main source of income for the holder of a parish was what he gained from tithes – the offering to the Church of a tenth of each man's income, whether in the form of crops, animal products, commercial profits or wages. In addition there were the fees that a priest could demand in return for services over and above the usual routine, such as marriages and funerals. Not to be confused with this last was the priest's right to claim mortuary from the estate of a deceased parishioner; that is, a payment that, in theory, was meant to make up for any tithes that may not have been paid during a person's lifetime. Here, according to their critics, the clergy were too concerned with financial gain and pressed for payments beyond their due. The same complaint was made about the fees payable for probate of testaments – the proving and registering of a will which made it a legal document. But although some contemporaries targetted such clerical greed and modern historians have found some instances that seem to support this view, only a few cases involving tithe payments appear in the courts and rarely disputes over mortuaries or probate. A few extreme cases have been built up to provide a general picture that is very misleading.

The case of Richard Hunne, the London merchant, is an obvious example of this. In 1511, he refused his rector's demand for his recently deceased son's burial cover as a mortuary payment for the child. The rector took him to the ecclesiastical courts and in return Hunne attacked the rector in the King's courts, charging him with a breach of the Statute of Praemunire. Hunne himself was arrested and, on the basis of some books found in his house, was charged with heresy and imprisoned. Before his case had come to trial he was found strangled in his cell. A coroner's court declared that he had been murdered and accused the Bishop of London's chancellor and two others of the crime. The bishop managed to avoid having these men brought to trial but the whole affair apparently caused considerable resentment in the City of London, especially when the dead man was found guilty of heresy, his property confiscated and his widow and children reduced to poverty. But though this incident caused a stir, it was obviously unusual and should not be taken as typical.

It is the 'typical' attitude to the Church that Professor Scarisbrick has tried to unearth. Using a variety of sources, he has shown that the vast majority of people in England were more than content with their Church. Evidence from wills shows money and goods still being used for religious purposes. There are bequests to orders of friars and nuns, money is earmarked for traditional practices – the saying of Masses, burning of lights before statues and altars – and the parish church especially benefits with endowments for the fabric and furnishings and for the maintenance of 'services' provided at a parish level. Buildings themselves testify to this concern with large numbers of churches being improved or rebuilt at this period and mostly at the expense of the parishioners themselves. That this piety was essentially of a traditional nature is shown also by the kind of books that were being produced, bought and, presumably, read. All this indicates a people co-operating with the clergy in maintaining a Church that satisfied their needs. Far from the laity and clergy being at odds, they are seen acting in partnership.

Were there then no real voices of dissent? Obviously there were and Colet and Fish are examples of two in particular. Colet found much to complain about but he believed in the Church reforming itself. It did not require a new system, merely the conscientious implementation of existing rules. Colet represented a group of scholars who had come to prominence in northern Europe in the previous generation – the Christian humanists. (They were called humanists because, like the humanists of the Italian Renaissance, they believed in the central importance of the humanities, meaning then the study of classical Latin and Greek literature, alongside the Bible and religious works.) Inspired by the work of Erasmus, the great Dutch scholar and campaigner for reforms in the Church, these humanists wanted a simpler religion based on a more accurate version of the Bible. They wanted religion to be a matter of inner faith rather than just outward and mechanical ceremonial display. But this was the inspiration of moderate reform, and Erasmians, such as Colet, Sir Thomas More and John Fisher, Bishop of Rochester, stopped short of challenging Church doctrine or the religious authority of the Pope.

Fish on the other hand voiced the discontent of the heretic. The Church was beyond reforming itself and it was the task of the prince to take it in hand. His was not a lone voice. England had its native heretic tradition in the Lollards who anticipated a number of the beliefs of the new German heresy of Martin Luther – for instance, their attack on the role of the priest as an intermediary between laymen and God – and it is generally accepted that Lollard groups survived in the early sixteenth century, although their strength of organisation and importance are much debated. In the Midlands and Home Counties, for example, groups of Lollards were in correspondence with each other and the authorities were certainly convinced of the danger they posed.

To the Lollards could now be added the followers of Martin Luther. The German reformer's books were already arriving in England by 1519. The movement, though, was not widespread and was restricted mainly to areas in the east of the country which had relatively frequent contact with Germany through commercial activity. Some interest was also shown in academic circles, especially at Cambridge, where a group met regularly at the White Horse Inn to discuss the new ideas. It was only natural that there should also be contact between these new reformers and some of the Lollard groups, whose organisation could be used to circulate books and ideas and whose writings were now given a new lease of life. At times the Lutheran scholars could be rather dismissive of the Lollards and their inaccurate translations of the Bible. In 1525 William Tyndale produced an English translation of the New Testament which was printed in Cologne, smuggled into England, and proved so successful that it ran to several editions. However, despite some panic amongst the authorities, Lutheranism had few adherents in England and it would take more than just their efforts to effect any change in the English Church.

3 THE DIVORCE CASE

In 1509 Henry VIII had married his elder brother's widow, Catherine of Aragon. Although against the law of the Church a papal dispensation (special permission) had been granted by Pope Julius II. On 17 May 1527 Cardinal Wolsey, in his capacity as Papal Legate, summoned Henry VIII to a secret court to answer the charge that he had been living in adultery with his brother's widow for eighteen years. The King had prompted this to pave the way for a divorce from Queen Catherine.

For the politics surrounding the case see pages 74–7 – the issues included Henry's overriding desire for a male heir; his increasing and frustrated passion for Anne Boleyn; the Pope's reluctance to grant a divorce, being under the sway of Catherine of Aragon's nephew, the Emperor Charles V; and Wolsey's downfall owing to his failure to secure the divorce and his vulnerability to the faction which opposed him. Henry was fully determined on his divorce but he did, however, want to persuade his subjects, many of whom held Catherine in high regard, of the validity of his case.

In November 1528, Henry summoned 'his nobility, judges and counsellors with divers other persons' to his presence and explained his actions. The lawyer Edward Hall recorded Henry's speech.

> . . . But when we remember our mortality and that we must die, then we think that all our doings in our lifetime are clearly defaced and worthy of no memory if we leave you in trouble at the time of our death. For if our true heir be not known at the time of our death, see what mischief and trouble shall succeed to you and your children. . . And although it has pleased almighty God to send us a fair daughter of a noble woman and me begotten to our great comfort and joy, yet it hath been told us by divers great clerks that neither she is our lawful daughter

nor her mother our lawful wife, but that we live together abominably and detestably in open adultery... Think you, my lords, that these words touch not my body and soul, think you that these doings do not daily and hourly trouble my conscience and vex my spirits, yes, we doubt not but and if it were your own cause every man would seek remedy when the peril of your soul and the loss of your inheritance is openly laid to you. .. And as touching the Queen, if it be adjudged by the law of God that she is my lawful wife, there was never thing more pleasant nor more acceptable to me in my life both for the discharge and clearing of my conscience and also for the good qualities and conditions the which I know to be in her.

1   *What reasons does Henry give for questioning his marriage to Catherine and what fear might have persuaded his listeners to accept his reasoning?*
2   *What reason does Henry implicitly deny in this extract?*
3   'And if a man shall take his brother's wife, it is an unclean thing: he hath uncovered his brother's nakedness; they shall be childless'

(Leviticus 20:21)

Why might Henry maintain that the fate threatened in Leviticus 20:21 had befallen him?

It would not do to be too cynical about Henry's words. Which of his reasons for divorcing Catherine was dominant we cannot certainly say, and he may not have been able to do so himself; but by 1528 he had committed himself to removing Catherine and marrying Anne. He had also committed himself to the way he would present his case.

Henry's argument was a direct challenge to papal power. As he saw it, Leviticus expressly condemned the very kind of marriage into which he had entered. This was not just a law of the Church that could be set aside by the authorities in the Church but a scriptural prohibition that no-one, not even the Pope, could set aside. What he was asking Pope Clement VII to do in 1528 was to admit that his predecessor had gone beyond the limits of his authority. Unfortunately for Henry, this case was not a particularly strong one – most contemporary opinion and most precedents tended to support the idea that Popes could indeed dispense in such a case. A further problem was that Henry's case depended on the first marriage, between Arthur and Catherine, having been consummated, since without any such sexual relationship there was no impediment of affinity (being related) in the first place and the prohibition in Leviticus did not apply. Catherine always maintained, privately and publicly, that the marriage had not been consummated.

Although denying the Pope's power to dispense with Leviticus, Henry did recognise that his marriage problem was a spiritual matter that came within the sphere of the Pope's authority. His first efforts therefore were aimed at obtaining a hearing of his case in England, presided over by a compliant Cardinal Wolsey. Clement VII played for time as much as possible. The political situation in Italy was such that he could not afford to offend Catherine's nephew, the Emperor Charles V, by sanctioning his aunt's divorce; but neither did he want to offend Henry. In all fairness, he may also have felt that Henry's case was not strong enough. In September 1528, Cardinal Campeggio finally arrived in England with the ostensible purpose of presiding with Wolsey over a Legatine Court that would decide on Henry's case. This was just further playing for time and on 31 July 1529, despite Henry's demands that sentence be passed, Campeggio ordered that the court should adjourn until October. It never sat again. Shortly after the adjournment, it was learned that Clement had already called the case to Rome. It seemed that Henry would not, after all, have his case settled in England.

4 THE PARLIAMENT OF 1529

Shortly after the adjournment of the Legatine Court, writs were issued for the Parliament that was to meet in November. This was the first of seven sessions of what has become known as the Reformation Parliament. It was not finally dissolved until April 1536 and was remarkable for its length and the amount and nature of its legislation.

We do not know precisely why Henry decided to summon a Parliament at this point. When the new Lord Chancellor, Sir Thomas More, spoke at the opening ceremony at Blackfriars he made a vague reference to the need for new laws to remedy 'divers new enormities' but did not specify what he meant. Both the French and Imperial ambassadors reported in October that the coming Parliament was to be used against Wolsey but by the time it opened the Cardinal had been dealt with. In November, a committee of peers, with two Commons members, was to draw up a list of forty-four articles attacking Wolsey and his policies, but beyond presenting it to Henry and sending a copy to the Commons nothing was done.

The timing of the writs indicates that the summons to Parliament was somehow linked to the failure to settle the divorce question and that Henry hoped to make a new beginning with the help of his subjects. According to the Imperial ambassador, Chapuys, Catherine certainly thought the Parliament would be used against her. But if this was the case then it must be admitted that Parliament did remarkably little in the matter for more than two years.

The 1529 session of Parliament has been seen as demonstrating the anti-clericalism of the time, an anti-clericalism that Henry now wished to appropriate to his own use. The main source for this is Edward Hall, a London lawyer and Member of Parliament. Hall was also an early historian of the Tudor period, a great supporter of the Tudor dynasty, especially in the person of Henry VIII, a man of strong reforming sympathies, and an 'anti-clerical'. In his account of the proceedings in the Commons he laid great stress on their 'griefs wherewith the spirituality had before time grievously oppressed them' and their determination to have these dealt with. This determination bore fruit in three acts. Two dealt with mortuaries and probate of wills and imposed a scale of fees that could be charged for each of these and a third tried to curb the practices of pluralism and non-residence and clerical involvement in commercial agriculture and trade. But the picture of an anti-clerical Commons in action may be too simple. To begin with, these acts constitute only three out of twenty-six passed in this first session. They seem also to have been introduced by particular groups. The Mercers Company of London, for example, had pushed for action on probate and mortuaries, though only as the fifth of a five point programme otherwise concerned with trade. And for some members the target of this legislation may not have been the clergy but the memory and character of a particular cleric, Cardinal Wolsey. Finally the acts were greatly moderated by the time they passed the Commons as a whole and the sections on pluralism and non-residence so loaded with possible exemptions that it could have had little practical effect.

However, although the significance of these acts should not be over-emphasised, and their real effect may have been minimal, they did cause some stir among the clergy of the Upper House. They objected, perhaps naturally, to gratuitous lay interference in their domain, especially when they claimed to be taking action themselves. 'Or is there any of these abuses that the clergy seek not to extirp and destroy?' asked John Fisher. 'Be there not laws already provided against such and many more disorders?' This may be the true significance of the episode – not that a rampant anti-clericalism was being directed against the Church, but rather that the Church leaders could feel that they were under attack and were being put on the defensive. By the end of 1530 the attack was to come not from specific interests in the Commons but from the King.

5 HENRY VIII AND THE SUPREMACY

Despite the failure of the Legatine Court in London to grant him his annulment, Henry continued to pursue his case, hoping to gather enough support to persuade the Pope of the justice of his cause. He already had a team of scholars at work collecting material to present to the court on his behalf and he now wanted them to continue their efforts. His agents were sent to universities across Europe to win support for the King's cause to back up the pronouncements that were made on his behalf by Oxford and Cambridge early in 1530. Eight of these universities came out in his favour though this may have been in response to bribes or political influence. The European reformers were also canvassed for their views and provided differing answers. On the whole, the Swiss reformers were favourable but the majority of Lutheran divines maintained the validity of his marriage. Protestant leanings certainly did not guarantee support for this aspect of Henry's policy. William Tyndale, the English reformer who advocated royal control of the Church, wrote a treatise condemning the attempts to gain a divorce, which he blamed on Wolsey. Henry, however, had not given up hope. He had not abandoned the idea that the Pope might yet come round to his side, though whether this would be achieved by threat or persuasion was uncertain.

So far Henry had not attacked the Pope's authority in this matter. He was asking Pope Clement to judge the validity of his predecessor's dispensation. However, in 1530 he also developed further ideas. Undoubtedly Henry could be more confident of a favourable verdict if the case was heard in England and not in Rome, and by one of his own clergy; but instead of trying to gain this as a favour in this particular case, Henry now began to demand it as of right. Precedent, he claimed, showed that no case could be taken out of any court in England to the courts in Rome, without royal permission. This *privilegium Angliae*, it was maintained, had been recognised, indeed granted, by the Popes themselves and had been enshrined in, among other things, the Constitutions of Clarendon of Henry II's reign. The Statute of Praemunire (1353) had been an expression of this principle which, though neglected, could yet be applied more consistently. The argument was developed further – it became more than a national privilege claimed by the King of England alone. The Council of Nicaea (in 325) and subsequent councils of the Church had affirmed the principle that no case should be taken out of the ecclesiastical province of its origin. According to this, Henry's divorce had to be settled in England by his own archbishop. Henry's agents were now set to finding academic support in Europe for this new claim but were less successful than in their earlier attempts.

More radical however were the ideas that now claimed Henry's attention, that he need acknowledge no superior on earth, Pope or Emperor, and that within his realm it was his duty to exercise supreme headship over the Church – that is, Royal Supremacy. This was a long way from simply wanting the Pope to give a favourable verdict in a particular marriage case, but the two were nevertheless linked. In October 1528, William Tyndale had published his book *The Obedience of the Christian Man and How Christian Rulers Ought to Govern*. In it he set out the view that the ruler is supreme on earth, answerable only to God, in full charge of his subjects' temporal and spiritual welfare and commanding their total allegiance. Because of the heresies it contained, the book was banned in England but Anne Boleyn possessed a copy and through her it came to Henry's notice. At her instigation he read through it and was suitably impressed – 'This book is for me and for all kings to read.' These ideas were further developed by those scholars who had already been researching Henry's divorce case. By September 1530, they had prepared for Henry a manuscript known as the *Collectanea Satis Copiosa*. This was a collection of proofs and precedents, drawn from Scripture, the early Church, and British history, that claimed to show that Henry, like his predecessors, could indeed claim **imperial** authority, that is, that he was subject to no other earthly power, that within his kingdom he had complete authority, that this had always been the case in theory although in recent centuries the Papacy had usurped some of this authority. Marginal notes in Henry's own handwriting testify to his interest in this document. It provided the justification he needed to put his case for Supremacy.

Henry's actions in the years following 1529, therefore, should be seen in the light of these different, yet closely linked, themes and it is not always easy to see which is dominant at any one time. To what extent do his actions during these years represent attempts to put pressure on the Pope, directly or through the clergy in England, and to what extent do they represent Henry testing the water of Royal Supremacy? The possible double nature of royal policy is most apparent in his treatment of the English clergy.

6 THE ENGLISH CLERGY UNDER PRESSURE

In October 1530, fifteen members of the upper clergy, including several defenders of Catherine of Aragon, were charged with contravening the Statute of Praemunire on the grounds that they had accepted Wolsey as Papal Legate. Charges against these specific individuals were soon dropped but in January 1531, Henry threatened the whole of the clergy of Southern England, assembled in the Convocation of Canterbury, with this same Statute of Praemunire. The threat was only lifted when, in seeking a general pardon for any possible offence of this kind, they promised to pay Henry a fine of £100 000, the amount of a clerical subsidy. No doubt there was a financial motive in all this. Henry had no reserves of money and the possibility of an expensive international policy arising from the divorce case was present. But he also seems to have been using the occasion to show that he was fully prepared to come down heavily on the clergy and that it would be in their best interests to co-operate fully in his policies.

But there were other implications as well. When asking for pardon the clergy had also asked for a clearer statement of their liberties. Henry's response was to demand that he be recognised as 'sole protector and also Supreme Head of the English Church', and that this should include a 'cure of souls', that is, some direct responsibility for the spiritual welfare of his subjects. He had gone too far. Despite considerable pressure, Convocation refused to accept such a claim and it was only with reluctance that they were willing to concede to him the role of 'singular protector, only and supreme lord and, so far as the law of Christ allows, even Supreme Head'. Both sides could claim a minor victory. Henry had asserted himself and not been totally rebuffed, but the qualifying clause on the law of Christ meant that the clergy could justly maintain that there was in fact no change in the situation. Later, in May 1531, the Convocation of York received the same pardon on payment of £18 000.

Substantial pressure on the Pope was attempted early in 1532. In January a Bill in Restraint of Annates was introduced into Parliament. These annates were payments made to the Pope from their first year's income by the higher clergy, mostly bishops and abbots, whose appointment, in theory at least, lay with the Pope. On the grounds that the payments were a financial drain on the country, the bill set out to put an end to the practice. It also stated that if the Pope refused to ratify any appointments made by the King, then consecration of a new bishop should still take place with any papal action ignored. Although this would have made little practical difference, it was nevertheless an attack on papal authority. The bill faced considerable resistance, both in the Lords where all the bishops voted against it, and in the Commons, where the King thought his presence necessary to ensure a favourable vote. But the resulting act was not to come into operation for a year and then only if Henry chose to give it his official assent. It remained, therefore, as a threat to the Pope and was used as such. A copy was sent to Henry's agents in Rome who were instructed to show it to the Pope and let him know that, if he wished to avoid its possible consequences, then the answer lay in co-operation with the King of England. Henry, then, had still not given up the idea that it was the Pope who would provide him with his divorce.

At the same time, the English clergy were coming under pressure and again Parliament was to have a role to play. The starting point was the Commons' Supplication Against the Ordinaries (i.e. petition against those in ecclesiastical authority). This was a complaint about the extent and nature of the Church courts, and requested the King to take some action in the matter. Whether this was a genuine grievance is doubtful. It appears rather that the Supplication was introduced into the House by Thomas Cromwell and that by working through Parliament more weight could be given to the claim that Henry had the support of his country in his policy. It is likely that the King himself was unaware of this move, though he proved willing to take advantage of it. He was presented with the Supplication on 18 March and then passed it on to Convocation for consideration, only to be dissatisfied with their response which upheld the Church's legislative powers and their practices in the Church courts. He passed this on to a deputation from the Commons, remarking that 'their answer will smally please you'. Having aligned himself with Parliament in the matter, Henry now demanded that Convocation agree to acknowledge the King's right to supervise the process of ecclesiastical legislation.

With the possibility of parliamentary action against them and under pressure from some of the King's noble councillors who attended their meeting, Convocation gave way to the King's demands. Several bishops were absent, others expressed serious reservations, and there was strong resistance from the lower clergy. Nevertheless, on 15 May the Submission of the Clergy was passed in Convocation. According to the terms of the Submission, Convocation could only meet at the King's command and could enact no ecclesiastical legislation without royal consent. Provision was also made for the appointment of a commission of clergy and laity to review existing legislation in order to remove any that was prejudicial to the King's authority and secure the royal assent to the remainder. This commission was in fact never appointed but nonetheless the forced Submission of the Clergy was a definite denial of papal authority by the King. That this was a turning point was recognised by the leading Christian humanist, Sir Thomas More, who resigned as Lord Chancellor on 16 May. He was in favour of moderate humanist reform but he could not accept the King's policy when it threatened the universal Church with schism.

7 THE SETTLEMENT OF THE DIVORCE

In mid-1532 events began to move more swiftly. In August, the Archbishop of Canterbury, William Warham, died, thus removing a man who had on occasion proved staunch in his opposition to some of Henry's more radical moves and who, though willing to allow Henry's case for annulment, wanted the decision to come from Rome. Henry had the opportunity to appoint an archbishop of his own choosing, one whom he could expect to back him in all his policies. The man he chose was Thomas Cranmer. Cranmer had first come to Henry's notice in 1539. He was a fellow of Jesus College, Cambridge, who, according to one story, had first suggested to Henry the tactic of enlisting the support of the European universities. By 1530 he was certainly one of the group of researchers actively pursuing Henry's cause and was sent on a mission to Europe to canvass further support. He was also very much a reformer who not only supported the divorce but was committed to the idea of royal control of the Church. His doctrinal position at this date is debatable – he was most probably 'finding his way' – but his sympathy with the European reformers was shown when in 1531 he married, despite being a priest, the niece of a prominent Lutheran pastor in Germany. With Cranmer as his archbishop, Henry could expect more co-operation at least from the head of the English clergy.

By January 1533, Anne Boleyn knew she was pregnant. Just when she gave in to Henry is not certain, but it may have been on a trip to France and where their relationship was open enough for her to be given apartments connecting with those of the King. By the end of January, she and Henry were married in a secret ceremony.

The pregnancy and marriage indicate that by now Henry was prepared to seek a radical solution to his problem. Cranmer was consecrated archbishop in March. Despite papal approval having been sought and obtained for his appointment, he took pains to show, when taking his consecration oath, that he felt his first loyalty was to the King. He now set about his immediate task. A court was convened at Dunstable to hear the case between Henry and Catherine and in May Cranmer declared Henry's union with his first wife to have been no true marriage and that consequently his sole and legal wife was Anne Boleyn. It may have been something of an anti-climax in September when the longed-for child proved to be a girl, Elizabeth, and not the male heir for which Henry was waiting.

8 THE BREAK WITH ROME

Cranmer's action was a direct challenge to the Pope. The case was still under consideration in Rome and Clement had explicitly forbidden Henry to re-marry until it had been decided. But Henry had gone beyond simple disobedience and the years 1533–6 were to see the severance of all links between England and Rome. Though the process was to take place largely within the next three years, the overture had taken at least as long. Why did Henry hesitate for so long before committing himself to action? First, one should remember the radical nature of what he was doing, mentally as well as politically. Though he might criticise the Pope, though he might even try to bully him, it took Henry a long time to believe that he could really do without him. A peaceful succession might depend on his marriage and he had to have adequate authority to back him up – hence his refusal to countenance any hints from Pope Clement, who simply wanted to avoid publicly antagonising Charles V, that he should simply go ahead with marrying Anne and hope Catherine would retire gracefully. On at least two occasions in 1530 Henry consulted a gathering of nobility, bishops and judges as to whether he could ignore the Pope and simply have the divorce case settled in England and on both occasions he was told that it could not be done. It took time therefore to win over some of the faint hearts and also to convince Henry that his cause was strong enough to withstand opposition. But that time did come and the planning and implementation of the new policy was to a large extent the work of one man, Thomas Cromwell.

About Cromwell's early life we know very little. By his own account he had been something of a 'ruffian', travelling extensively abroad before returning to England where he joined Wolsey's household, at the same time acquiring enough legal expertise to be admitted to one of the Inns of Court in 1524. On Wolsey's fall he continued to defend the Cardinal, speaking up for him in the Parliament of 1529. But his career had already taken a new direction. By 1531 he was a member of the King's Council and in 1533 he was made Master of the King's Jewels. In fact his importance lay not so much in any particular office as in his personal influence on the King. He was obviously a man of high ability, skilled in the law, something of a linguist and with a genuine interest in scholarship for its own sake as well as for the use to which it could be put in practical affairs. In religion there is no doubt that, though he might profess to believe as the King believed, he was by inclination a reformer. Although Cromwell's may not have been the mind that originated the ideas behind Henry's policy, it was he who took the ideas and made them practicable.

This process can be seen in the Act in Restraint of Appeals, passed by April 1533. By this act no appeals were to be made from England to Rome in any matters concerning wills, marriages, tithes or payments to the Church; instead cases were to go from archdeacon to bishop, and then to archbishop. Beyond that, there was no appeal. It was with the backing of this act that Cranmer was able to decide the King's case at Dunstable. The relevance of the act to Henry's personal situation was even more apparent in earlier drafts where specific reference was made to the King's divorce and the problems of the succession and it may have been the active preparation of the act that partly decided the timing of the consummation of Henry's relationship with Anne. Early drafts also reveal something of the sources and justification for the assertion of such independence of Rome.

Preamble from the Act in Restraint of Appeals:

Where by divers sundry old authentic histories and chronicles it is manifestly declared and expressed that this realm of England is an empire and so hath been accepted in the world, governed by one supreme head and king having the dignity and royal estate of the imperial crown of the same, unto whom a body politic, compact of all sorts and degrees of people divided in terms and by names of spiritualty and temporalty, be bounden and owe next to God a natural and humble obedience; he being also institute and furnished by the goodness and sufferance of Almighty God with plenary, whole and entire power, pre-eminence, authority, prerogative and jurisdiction to render and yield justice and final determination to all manner of folk resiants [residents] or subjects within this realm, in all causes, matters, debates and contentions happening to occur, insurge or begin within the limits whereof, without restraint or provocation to any foreign princes or potentates of the world.

1 *What does this source tell us about the nature and justification of 'imperial authority'?*

The Act in Restraint of Appeals was a major piece of legislation and the following year saw a number of acts which gave its assertions more definition and substance.

A bill devised by Cromwell to transfer ecclesiastical annates to the King was dropped, probably because of opposition in the Lords and instead the Act in Restraint of Annates was passed in March 1534. It repeated the act of the previous year and gave statutory confirmation to Henry's ratification of that earlier act. In addition, it provided more details on the process whereby bishops were to be appointed by the King. Financial contributions to Rome were the subject of another act passed at the same time. This ordered an end to the laity's annual contribution to the Pope of 'Peter's Pence' and forbade payment of any other kind to Rome. Any dispensations that might formerly have come from the Pope were now to be sought from the Archbishop of Canterbury and would be issued under royal licence. The Act for the Submission of the Clergy repeated the details of the submission of 1532 but also extended the arrangements of the Act in Restraint of Appeals to all kinds of cases, not just those mentioned in the 1533 act. The First Succession Act declared that the succession to the throne was to lie first with the male heirs of Anne Boleyn, and then with the heirs male of any subsequent wife. After them, the Crown would go to the Princess Elizabeth and her children, and finally to any other daughters that might yet be born. This was not specifically a religious issue but the act required subjects to be prepared to take an oath accepting the rules for succession and stated that any deeds or writing that threatened the King or his title, or slandered his marriage, would be accounted high treason. This meant, of course, accepting the legitimacy of Cranmer's decision and the rejection of Rome that had made it possible.

Parliament returned to its work in November, when the Act of Supremacy declared that the 'King's Majesty justly and rightfully is and oweth to be the Supreme Head of the Church of England.' It did not make him Supreme Head but recognised his right to be such and, with this, his authority to administer the Church, oversee its legislation, institute reform, and ensure the soundness of its doctrine. Henry's title was given effective protection by a new and contentious Treason Act, which, after some opposition, was passed in November. This made it high treason to threaten Henry, Anne or his heirs, in words as well as in writing or by deeds, or to deny him his titles, or to accuse

Henry of being a heretic, tyrant or usurper. Finally in this session of Parliament, the Act of First Fruits and Tenths took up where the Annates Act left off. A year's income from all newly filled ecclesiastical offices and benefices (first fruits) and a tenth of all clerical income were now to be paid to the King. There is no record of there being any opposition on this occasion although the clergy must have been well aware of its effect on their finances. After only a year without such payments they now found themselves paying the King much more than they had ever sent to the Pope. Two years later, the whole process was rounded off with the Act Against Papal Authority. This blanket condemnation of the Pope left no room for allowing him any form of authority or influence in England, even in matters of heresy.

The need for such laws as the Treason Act of 1534 or that against papal authority – with its reference to the seditious 'imps of the said bishop of Rome' – show that these changes did not take place without argument or opposition. The Treason Act was passed shortly after the affair of Elizabeth Barton, the 'Nun of Kent'. She had spoken out against Henry's marriage to Anne Boleyn, declaring that it would lead to his being deposed. The judges maintained that there was no case against her in law and her execution was only secured by an Act of Attainder, whereby Parliament declared her a traitor and, therefore, subject to the death penalty. Once it was passed the Treason Act could be used against some of Henry's more eminent opponents. Three Carthusian priors and a member of the convent at Syon suffered death for denying Henry's Supremacy and in June 1535, they were followed by John Fisher, Bishop of Rochester. A staunch supporter of Queen Catherine and for a long time a prominent opponent of Henry's policies, he had also been implicated in the Elizabeth Barton affair. More circumspect in his approach, but still well-known for his opposition to Henry, was the ex-Lord Chancellor Sir Thomas More. Like Fisher, he had refused the oath accepting the Succession Act because it included a denial of papal authority but he had refused also to answer any questions on the subject. However, he was condemned on the evidence of Sir Richard Rich, the solicitor-general, who alleged that, in conversation with him, More had denied the King's title. More was executed on 6 July 1535.

There were other expressions of discontent. We have seen that the clergy did not give in without a struggle in both 1531 and 1532, and Parliament too was the scene of some contention, in the debates over the Act in Restraint of Annates, for example. There was an organised opposition group in the Commons that had links with More and the Imperial ambassador. Support for Queen Catherine was strong. In April 1532, Thomas Temys, member for Westbury, Wiltshire, wanted the Commons to ask the King to take Catherine back as his rightful Queen and Edward Hall, a supporter of Henry's policies, nevertheless testifies to the existence of much sympathy for Catherine. Throughout the reign examples occur of individuals speaking out against the changes that had taken place and criticising Henry and his advisers.

But at no point was this opposition strong enough to force Henry to call a complete halt. To begin with, the method used, consciously or not, in putting the changes through made opposition difficult. If, in 1532 or 1533, the final achievement of 1536 had been put forward in one programme more people may have understood what was happening and objected. But the changes came in stages and it was difficult to say at just what stage one should try to halt the process. Bearing in mind the circumstances of this reformation, many people may have had real doubts about the permanence of the changes. It was not unknown for kings and popes to quarrel, or for kings to bring pressure to bear on popes by asserting their own authority. Was there not a chance that when the divorce problem had been resolved or forgotten, then the old relations would be resumed?

If this was the case, opposition to royal policy would be difficult to justify, especially since this opposition might cause more harm than it prevented. People wanted good government, with as little disturbance as possible. It would have to be a pressing need that allowed any strong resistance to the source of that government. And Henry was that source, the anointed King. People expected to follow where their superiors led them. To obey was their first duty and if they were led astray then the fault was not theirs but their leaders'. There were of course those who did dissent but they could be dealt with. Intimidation, of whole groups or individuals, the threat of the treason legislation – these could be, and were, effective checks and they were applied with considerable success during this period.

9 THE DISSOLUTION OF THE MONASTERIES

So far we have looked at matters of 'high politics'. Important though the divorce and Henry's Supremacy were, the effect they had on the lives of the majority of people was limited. King or Pope? – Catherine or Anne? – these were questions of little direct concern to most people in the country. But the Henrician Reformation did not stop there and one of the most dramatic consequences, as regards numbers of people involved, was the process known as the Dissolution of the Monasteries.

It has been estimated that in the early sixteenth century there were 700–800 religious houses ranging from those with only a handful of inmates to the great foundations such as St Mary's in York or Westminster in London. Their importance can be judged in a number of ways. Some twenty-seven abbots and priors had the right to attend meetings of Parliament and the office of abbot could bring influence and prestige; Wolsey himself did not scorn the title and income of Abbot of St Albans (though he had never been a monk). In economic terms the religious communities in England and Wales are reckoned to have controlled approximately 10 per cent of the country's wealth and individual houses could still provide the economic centre for their area, employing a large number of estate workers. In addition they were religious and social centres, that in many regions were to be sorely missed. The very age of some of the foundations – they could have histories going back 500 years or more – and their physical presence – in some cases with a church as great as a cathedral – made them a dominant and apparently permanent feature of English society and the English landscape.

The process of dissolution

In spite of all this, the years 1536–40 saw the end of the monasteries. The details were masterminded by Thomas Cromwell. In January of 1535 he was created Henry's Vicegerent in Spirituals, an appointment which enabled him to act on the King's behalf and exercise the royal authority in the English Church. Almost immediately he sent out commissions to make a full survey of all property held by the Church and by the summer these findings had been brought together in the *Valor Ecclesiasticus* (the Ecclesiastical Valuation). And in September of that year Cromwell sent out another set of commissioners to conduct a visitation of all the religious houses in the kingdom.

Visitations in themselves were nothing new, but previously they had normally been the responsibility of the local bishop, had not been so hastily conducted and had been mainly concerned with reform. It is obvious from the speed with which Cromwell's visitors acted and the tone of some of their letters that they knew what they were looking for and were determined to find it. Cromwell soon built up a dossier illustrating the corrupt morals and spiritual laxity of the regular clergy and these findings were presented to Parliament early in 1536. These reports, combined perhaps with the King's own intervention, were enough to secure the passing of an act for suppressing the smaller religious houses – those worth less than £200 a year. These houses, with their estates and other forms of income, were now the property of the Crown. The dispossessed inmates could either transfer to other houses or join the secular clergy. (Parish priests and their superiors were the secular clergy; monks were known as the regular clergy.)

Now there appeared some popular reaction against the process of the Henrician Reformation. In October 1536, the people of Louth, in Lincolnshire, rose up in protest at the changes that were being imposed and they were joined by other communities. Although the Lincolnshire rising was soon suppressed, it was not before the movement had spread to Yorkshire, where the lawyer, Robert Aske, soon assumed leadership of the rebellion which now took the title of the Pilgrimage of Grace. The pilgrims entered York and Hull, took the castle of Pontefract, and moved to Doncaster. At the River Don they were met by the Duke of Norfolk, who had come north to deal with the trouble. He listened to their complaints and in return for their dispersal, promised that their demands would be investigated and that they would receive a pardon. However, a further outbreak of trouble in the north-west gave him the opportunity to break the promise (which neither he nor Henry seem to have had any intention of keeping) and the main leaders of the Pilgrimage were captured and eventually executed.

Even those who would see the Pilgrimage as essentially a political movement or the result of economic distress cannot deny the strong religious element. The title of 'Pilgrimage', its banner of the Five Wounds of Christ, the songs the pilgrims sang and the demands they made all point to support for the old order in religion as an ideal that many, if not all, had in common. There were fears for the future of the parish churches and their possessions, condemnation of the reformers and support for the Pope's spiritual supremacy, and, occurring in all the demands, the request that the dissolved abbeys be restored. The arguments were based on more than the spiritual role of the abbeys; they were also seen as centres contributing to the social and economic welfare of their areas. Some of the suppressed houses were restored during the Pilgrimage and a number of monasteries were closely associated with the movement. After it had been put down, the heads of five abbeys and one priory were attainted of treason and executed because of the support they had given to the Pilgrimage. Their houses were declared forfeit to the King – as if they had been their private estates – and immediately suppressed.

Henry's treatment of these monasteries had perhaps demonstrated to others which way the wind was blowing. Commissioners were sent round the remaining, larger monasteries to 'invite' their surrender to the Crown. Failure to accede to such a surrender could have unhappy consequences – the Abbot of Glastonbury, for example, was hanged; co-operation led to the provision of pensions and the possibility of preferment in the Church outside the monasteries. In 1539 a second Act of Dissolution was passed. This legalised the Crown's possession of all those monasteries that had already surrendered to Henry and those few that had yet to do so, which followed in 1540.

Reasons for the dissolution

Such was the process of dissolution, but why did Henry close the monasteries at all? To begin with, it should be recognised that the dissolution of the monasteries was not a necessary consequence of the split from Rome. However, both Henry and Cromwell may have resented the continued existence of the representatives of international orders in the now autonomous English Church, a situation which had already been addressed in one of the clauses of the Dispensation Act, but it is unlikely that either Henry or Cromwell saw the monasteries in general as centres of resistance to the King's new style. Most of them seem to have given way with as little fuss as the rest of the Church in England, and some monasteries took pains to stress their new allegiance in letters of loyalty to the King.

Nor was the split from Rome necessary in order to close the monasteries, or at least some of them. The selective closure of individual monasteries, or groups of them, was not unprecedented. Monasteries and nunneries had been closed in the past with papal approval and their resources directed to other, normally educational, uses. For instance, in 1518 and 1525 Cardinal Wolsey had secured permission to close a number of establishments in order to found his new college at Oxford and a grammar school in his home town of Ipswich.

The mere act of closing some monasteries, therefore, did not obviously mean a move away from Catholicism. It could in fact be seen in a much more positive light – a genuine attempt at removing the abuses that could arise in monasticism and so highlighting the good work and continued value of those houses that remained. And this was the official line that was expressed in 1536 in the first Dissolution Act. The reason given for the suppression of the smaller monasteries is the 'manifest sin, vicious, carnal and abominable living' to be found there and the need is stressed for the reformation of this situation and encouragement of the good work of the greater monasteries. Precedent and perhaps a sense of need following Cromwell's visitation meant that Henry was able to get his Parliament to agree to this first – and, as they then thought, only – stage in the dissolution process.

For some people there was a more fundamental objection to monasticism as simply being a misguided form of spiritual life as well as a waste of human and financial resources. Cromwell himself can almost certainly be included among these more radical reformers who wished simply to do away with monasticism altogether. Some indication of this mentality can be found in the association of the dissolution with the eradication of traditional practices, through the Injunctions of 1536 and 1538, which attacked the abuse of images and relics and discouraged pilgrimages. Reports of Cromwell's commissioners contain many references to these practices and the exposure of fraudulent relics and dismantling of shrines went hand in hand with the dissolution process. Monasteries were also too closely associated with the practice of praying for the dead to appeal to radical reformers who were now moving towards a denial of the doctrine of Purgatory, according to which souls had to be purified (a process speeded up by prayers for the dead) before admission to Heaven. In 1538 the Abbess of Godstow attempted to avoid the dissolution of her house by assuring Cromwell 'that there is neither Pope nor Purgatory, Image nor Pilgrimage, nor praying to dead saints, used or regarded amongst us'.

There was a body of thought, expressed particularly in Cromwell's circle, that the spirit if not the letter of the founders' intentions would be better served by re-directing the resources vested in the monasteries. In 1539 an act was passed in Parliament enabling the King to create new bishoprics:

> Forasmuch as it is not unknown the slothful and ungodly life which hath been used amongst all those sort which have borne the name of religious folk, and to the intent that from henceforth many of them might be turned to better use as hereafter shall follow, whereby God's word might the better be set forth, children brought up in learning, clerks nourished in the universities, old servants decayed to have livings, almshouses for poor folk to be sustained in, readers of Greek, Hebrew, and Latin to have good stipend, daily alms to be ministered, mending of highways, exhibition for ministers of the Church; It is thought therefore unto the King's Highness most expedient and necessary that more bishoprics collegiate and cathedral churches shall be established instead of these aforesaid religious houses . . .

1 *What judgement does this extract make on the religious orders and how does it differ from the official statements in 1536?*
2 *In what ways does this preamble suggest that the money from the monasteries should be used?*

Little was done that would fulfil this aspect of the reformers' ambitions and it is generally accepted that, for Henry at least, money was the main motive. In 1534 a plan had been suggested that would have enabled the Crown to profit from Church wealth. If this had been put into effect it would have meant all the income of the Church going to the Crown. Archbishops and bishops would have been paid salaries and monasteries granted money according to the number of inmates and the considerable surplus would have remained at the King's disposal. The plan was too radical but it shows that by the early 1530s the Church was being seen as a potential source of money to the Crown.

Closely linked to the financial motive is a second question – did Henry plan total dissolution from the start? The words of the 1536 act would seem to deny this. The act refers to 'great and honourable monasteries of this realm' and those monasteries where 'religion is right well kept and observed' – no room here for suppression, at least on the grounds of the 1536 act. And Henry seemed prepared to back his declaration with action when he exempted a number of the smaller monasteries on appeal and refounded two others.

In contrast to this, however, one could paint a much more cynical picture. Professor Scarisbrick has drawn attention to some advice that Henry was later to present to the rulers of Scotland on dissolving monasteries. Any plan should be kept secret and the first move should give the impression of being simply for reform. Leading clergy should be won over by promises of the worthy use of monastic resources and this, combined with an attack on the morals of the monks, should make for a quiet and easy suppression. Certainly in England the eventual use of monastic resources and Henry's failure to live up to his promises made or implied seem to show that he had practised what he now preached.

Some consequences of the dissolution

The dissolution resulted in about 9000 religious (monks and nuns) being forced to find some alternative way of life. The problem varied in nature and difficulty. Many of the male religious could be absorbed into the rest of the Church. Abbots, priors and the like sometimes found themselves becoming bishops or members of the diocesan hierarchy; others joined the ranks of the parish clergy. Those who were unwilling, or unable, to make such a change had to rely on pensions provided by the government from the proceeds of the dissolution. These pensions were calculated according to the wealth of the house to which they had belonged. Again, the senior members of the system did fairly well, with pensions that certainly put them on a par with the lay gentry, but the average allowance seems to have been about £5 p.a. which did not compare well with wages elsewhere. Nuns got even less, certainly not enough to live on, and at the same time the King's insistence that vows of chastity were inviolable meant that they could not turn to marriage as a way of finding support. In a society where the independent single woman was unknown their plight was serious. Lay employees of the religious houses were not so badly affected. Most of these would have been estate workers and they would be required under any new owners.

The immediate area around the monastery may well have suffered from the loss of monastic charity. In 1538, Thomas, Lord Audley, who wished the Benedictine monastery at Colchester to remain as a college for secular clergy, cited the importance of their charitable work. A letter to Cromwell, describing how the religious changes were being accepted in Nottinghamshire and Lincolnshire, maintains that the people saw the economic benefits of the dissolution and criticised the monks for their evil living but nevertheless 'they think there is . . . great loss of their prayers'.

As far as the government was concerned, the dissolution was undoubtedly a financial success. In 1536 a Court of Augmentations was set up to deal with the new income that it had generated and in the ten years between the first closures and Henry's death, the monasteries provided the Crown with over a million pounds. Some of the money came from the gold, silver and jewels that many of the monasteries had possessed. But the bulk of the income came from the monastic estates.

Whether either Henry or Cromwell wished to keep all the estates as a permanent addition to the Crown's resources is debatable; in fact this was not to be the case. By 1547 almost two-thirds of the land had passed out of Crown hands, realising a total income of about £800 000. There was still income to be had from the retained estates but this varied greatly from year to year.

With this income came liabilities – as well as pensions to the ex-religious, the Crown took on any outstanding debts – and a limited amount of money went on the kind of educational enterprises of which many of the reformers had had such high hopes. Wolsey's Oxford college was re-endowed as Christ Church, two college halls at Cambridge were refounded as Trinity College, and five Regius Professorships instituted at each of the universities. Six new bishoprics were also founded. These were Gloucester, Peterborough, Oxford, Chester, Bristol and Westminster, though the last did not survive beyond 1550. Thirteen had been projected but here, as with education, achievement failed to live up to expectation. Henry found other needs for the money, particularly defence, in the late 1530s and early 1540s, and his renewed intervention in European politics in the 1540s.

While the Church suffered a loss of land and revenue, the lay estate profited. Whether or not they had sought the dissolution, laymen were ready to take advantage of the opportunity to acquire more land and it was the nobility and gentry who gained most from this great change-over. Not only did it give them a chance to increase their landed wealth, it also gave them, through their new estates, a greater control of Church patronage. In the past a monastery had often been the 'rector' of a parish, receiving the tithes and, in return, appointing a salaried vicar. When the estates were transferred to laymen this role was seen as part of the property, so the new landlord continued to receive the tithes and continued to appoint the vicar, this was to persist over the following centuries.

Physically, the dissolution resulted in the loss of a great many buildings, of which large numbers were undoubtedly architecturally outstanding. Some survived to act as cathedrals or parish churches; others were adapted to secular uses, but most fell into decay. The disposal of the contents led to the loss of numberless examples of medieval art either by dispersal and disappearance or by being melted down or otherwise destroyed for the value of the materials. The loss to scholarship of the monastic libraries caused some concern even at the time. The antiquary John Leland, with Henry's encouragement, tried to salvage something from the destruction but we can only guess at the artistic and literary masterpieces which must have ended up on the rubbish heap.

10 THE RELIGIOUS REFORMATION

The situation in the 1530s

It would be inaccurate to see the legislation of 1533–6 as simply bringing in institutional or political change. Henry's assumption of the title of Supreme Head, with its accompanying functions, was a major religious change in itself. Although Henry did not claim to exercise the *potestas ordinis*, that is the powers proper to the ordained clergy such as the administration of the sacraments, he did lay claim to the *potestas jurisdictionis*, that allowed him to control ecclesiastical legislation and administration, to ensure that the Church remained doctrinally orthodox and to implement any necessary reforms.

The various pronouncements concerning this spiritual welfare were subject to a variety of influences. In breaking away from the Roman Catholic Church, Henry had enlisted the help of a number of men who saw Royal Supremacy not as an end in itself but as the means to a wider programme of reform. This group included the Archbishop of Canterbury, Thomas Cranmer, and others who were promoted to the bench of bishops during this period – Edward Foxe (Hereford, 1538), Hugh Latimer (Worcester, 1535) and Nicholas Shaxton (Salisbury, 1535). These had enjoyed the patronage of Anne Boleyn and her circle, but their cause did not suffer with the fall of the Boleyns in 1536 (*see pages 137–40*). This was due to some extent to Thomas Cromwell. Although it would be wrong to describe all of them at this stage as Protestant or Lutheran in their ideas, their reformist stance certainly seemed to be taking them in that direction. At the same time, the diplomatic situation seemed to favour the reformers.

In 1533 serious negotiations had been opened with the German Lutheran princes in the hope of gaining their help in distracting the Emperor from any possible action against England. They had demanded adherence to Lutheran teaching as expressed in the Wittenberg Articles as a condition of any alliance. But Henry, although he might seek a Lutheran alliance and even turn to Luther for support in his divorce case, was not yet prepared to go as far as the German reformer in some of his doctrines.

The Ten Articles

It was against this background that the Ten Articles were produced in July 1536. They were drawn up at Henry's request by Convocation and issued on his authority as Supreme Head. The introduction to the Articles stated that they were considered necessary to settle any 'outward unquietness which by occasion of the said diversity of opinions (if remedy were not provided) might perchance have ensued'. This concern over unity is understandable following the unsettling changes of the early 1530s. Certainly, in January 1536, Cromwell had felt it necessary to instruct all the bishops to prevent any form of religious extremism.

The fact that much of the wording of the Articles is directly based on that of the Wittenberg Articles has been taken as demonstrating some concessions in the direction of the Lutherans. If this is the case then the concessions were limited and were no more than the taking advantage of areas where there was some common ground and statements vague enough to satisfy both sides could be made. The article on the Eucharist was a particular example of this which requires some explanation of the doctrines concerned.

The Catholic doctrine of transubstantiation was based on the belief that anything can be divided into its **substance**, that is the real essence of its being which cannot be seen or experienced in any material way, and its **accidents**, that is its external properties such as what it looks like, feels like etc. According to this doctrine, at the words of the consecration during the Eucharist, the substance of the bread and wine is transformed into the substance of the body and the blood of Christ, while the accidents, the outward appearance, remain the same.

Although Lutherans did not deny the real presence of Christ's body and blood in the bread and wine, they did reject the doctrine of transubstantiation which attempted to give it some philosophical justification. The Lutheran view is sometimes dubbed 'consubstantiation' implying that Christ's body and blood are really present but so too is the whole and real nature of the bread and wine. In fact Luther preferred to abandon all such philosophical definitions and simply accept on faith that Christ's body and blood are really present.

The statement in the Ten Articles on the Eucharist could be interpreted in a Lutheran way but could just as well be seen as supporting Catholic teaching since the most that it says is that the body and blood of Christ is 'verily, substantially and really contained and comprehended' in the bread and wine. There is no reference to a complete change of substance (Catholic) nor to the continued existence of the substance of bread and wine with the body and blood (Lutheran).

The practice of praying for the dead, with its implicit acceptance of the doctrine of Purgatory, was on the other hand clearly commended. This would be rejected by Lutherans, who denied the existence of Purgatory and the efficacy of such prayers. However the compilers of the Articles refused to be explicit on the nature or even the name of Purgatory. The Ten Articles then did not signify any true doctrinal change but their ambiguity in certain areas did mean that they could be credited with some reforming character.

The following year a committee of bishops produced *The Institution of a Christian Man* (also known as the Bishops' Book). Henry allowed its publication and recommended it to the clergy though he had, on his own admission, only flicked through it and was later to make extensive criticisms of it. All seven of the sacraments (Luther accepted only baptism, the Eucharist and penance) are mentioned in this book, a concession to the conservatives that was qualified by the statement that the reinstated four were of lesser status, with no foundation in Scripture. But on the whole the book can be seen to follow the general tone of the Ten Articles and cannot be judged as having either furthered or hindered the reformers' cause.

The Royal Injunctions

The impact of the Bishops' Book was probably limited. Although Henry recommended it to his clergy, it was not compulsory reading and nobody was required to take any action as a result of it. Of more effect was the activity of Thomas Cromwell in these years. In 1536, acting as the King's Vicegerent in Spirituals, he issued the First Royal Injunctions to all the clergy of the realm. These started by stating clearly the clergy's duty to preach regularly in support of the Royal Supremacy. As well as this, in an attack on 'all superstition and hypocrisy', clergy were told not to encourage devotion to particular images or saints, and to dissuade people from the practice of making pilgrimages. This, together with the order that everyone should learn the Lord's Prayer, Creed and Ten Commandments in English, was certainly the influence of the reforming party. The remaining Injunctions were less contentious, being concerned with clerical behaviour, attention to duty, providing money for charitable and educational purposes and maintenance of church fabric.

Two years later, a second set of Injunctions was issued which went further. Priests had now, in at least four sermons a year, positively to discourage people from venerating images or relics, and if they had previously supported such practices, were now to recant. Perhaps most important for the reforming party was the order that an English translation of the Bible was to be placed in every church and everyone was to encouraged to read it.

The provision of a vernacular Bible was an important step for the reformers, and particularly in England which had a tradition of official hostility and suspicion towards such translations, mainly because of their associations with the Lollard heresy. Not all religious conservatives were against such a move. Sir Thomas More, while lamenting the misuse of Scripture by heretics, still believed that properly authorised translations should be made available for the laity to read. Nevertheless, the demand for an English Bible was a particular hallmark of the progressives in religion. Cromwell licensed the use of two separate translations, the first one by Miles Coverdale in 1535, and the second by John Rogers in 1537. Cromwell's interest did not stop here. He commissioned a revised translation, the production of which he helped to finance, and it was this Great Bible, which appeared in 1539, that he

Frontispiece to the Great Bible of 1539

probably had in mind in his Injunctions of 1538. At this stage Henry gave the policy his full support. It was his duty to see that his subjects received the word of God as expressed in the Scriptures and this was the image that was portrayed on the title-page of the 1535 and 1539 Bibles. On both of these Henry was shown giving the Bible to his bishops and nobility and through them to his people. Within a few years, however, he seems to have become somewhat disillusioned with the results. In 1543 an Act for the Advancement of True Religion attempted to limit Bible-reading to the nobility, gentry and merchant classes, and in his last speech to Parliament on Christmas Eve 1545, Henry complained at 'how unreverently that most precious jewel the word of God is disputed, rhymed, sung and jangled in every alehouse and tavern, contrary to the true meaning of the same'.

A conservative reaction

It is perhaps indicative of a degree of expectation that further changes were bound to follow that some individuals were prepared to state publicly beliefs that were either heretical or contrary to the discipline of the English Church. It seems likely that the King was disturbed by such demonstrations and that in this climate more conservative counsels would prevail in religious matters.

In 1538, for example, John Lambert was accused of denying the 'real presence', the physical presence of Christ, in the Eucharist. Henry himself, dressed all in white, presided at his trial and after displaying his own skills in theology, ordered Cromwell to read Lambert's sentence of death by burning. This episode was followed by a royal proclamation against sacramentaries (those who denied the real presence), unlicensed books and married priests. Clerical celibacy had already proved a block to any agreement with the Lutheran princes when Henry had informed their embassy that that was one of the points on which he would make no concessions. In the same letter he had asserted his belief in private Masses and that the laity should receive Communion only under one kind (receiving the bread only) and not, as most Protestants demanded, under both kinds (receiving both bread and wine).

The negotiations with the Lutheran princes were brought on by England's continuing need to find potential allies to use against the Emperor Charles, a need which seemed particularly acute by the beginning of 1539. The Pope was preparing to publish his Bill of excommunication against Henry, and Charles and Francis I of France, enjoying one of their brief interludes of mutual peace, seemed set to take joint action against England. But while Cromwell pursued the Lutheran alliance, Henry seems to have put more trust in demonstrating the orthodoxy of his Church and showing any would-be invaders that they would have no justification, in religion at least, in attacking him. Certainly Henry made little attempt to be conciliatory to the Lutherans, while he did ensure the passage through Parliament of the conservative Act of Six Articles.

First moves towards the Act were made in May 1539, when a committee of bishops was set up to discuss a possible statement that would ensure religious unity. Since this consisted of four conservatives and four radicals, little progress was made and in June, the Duke of Norfolk introduced into the House of Lords six questions which discussion and Henry's intervention, transformed into the Six Articles that formed the basis of the Act.

> First, that in the most blessed sacrament of the altar, . . . is
> present really, under the form of bread and wine, the natural
> body and blood of our Saviour Jesus Christ, conceived of the
> Virgin Mary; and that after the consecration there remaineth no
> substance of bread or wine, nor any other substance but the
> substance of Christ, God and man.
> Secondly, that Communion in both kinds is not necessary *ad*

salutem [for salvation] by the law of God, to all persons; . . .

Thirdly, that priests after the order of priesthood received, as afore, may not marry by the law of God.

Fourthly, that vows of chastity or widowhood, by man or woman made to God advisedly, ought to be observed by the law of God, . . .

Fifthly, that is meet and necessary that private Masses be continued and admitted in this the King's English Church and Congregation, as whereby good Christian people, ordering themselves accordingly, do receive both godly and goodly consolations and benefits, and it is agreeable also to God's law.

Sixthly, that auricular confession [i.e. heard by the priest rather than just made in prayer] is expedient and necessary to be retained and continued, used and frequented in the Church of God.

1   *What view of the Eucharist is described in articles 1 and 2?*
2   *Using information from earlier in the chapter, comment on the acceptability or otherwise of these articles to the reforming party.*

The penalties in the Act were severe. To dispute the first article in any way would be considered heresy and punishable by burning. Any solemn denial of the other five (for example, in sermons or teaching) was punishable by death. Anyone who broke a vow of chastity was also to be sentenced to death. Any other denial or transgressions of the Articles was to result in imprisonment and loss of property for the first offence, with the death penalty reserved for the second offence.

This was a victory for the conservatives, and reformers in England and Europe saw it as a setback. It was known as 'the whip with six strings'. Bishops Latimer and Shaxton resigned their Sees in protest. Cranmer, however, remained in office, although he felt it expedient to send his wife back to Germany. His belief in the Royal Supremacy overrode any doubts he must have had about some of the Articles.

Four years later, the conservative orthodoxy was reinforced by the publication of *The Necessary Doctrine and Erudition of a Christian Man*. This was subjected to Henry's personal scrutiny before publication and hence is known as the King's Book. In this book all seven sacraments are said to be of equal weight, the doctrine of transubstantiation is upheld and demands for Communion under both kinds dismissed. The Lutheran teaching of 'justification by faith alone'[1] (*see page 115*) is rejected. Prayers and Masses for the dead are acceptable but any financial abuses arising from a belief in Purgatory are firmly condemned.

But the 1540s did not see a total reversal in policy despite the triumph of a conservative faction following Cromwell's fall from favour and execution in 1540 (*see pages 141–2*). Although the doctrinal position did not change, further inroads were made or planned on some of the ceremonies and practices of the Church. Late in 1541, for example, Henry repeated his order that all shrines should be dismantled and declared that there should be lighted candles only before the Blessed Sacrament. He also encouraged Cranmer in his plans for an English liturgy (the 'script' for services) and allowed the publication in May 1544, of an English translation of the litany, a sequence of supplications to God and the saints. There is even some slight evidence to suggest that towards the end of his life, Henry considered the abolition of the Mass. Cranmer later reported that he had heard him make the suggestion in the presence of the French admiral, and that the idea had already been discussed by Henry and the French King. However, there is little evidence to support the sincerity of Henry's remark, and it is normally taken as an inexplicable element in his diplomatic arsenal. What was planned by the end of the reign was the dissolution of the chantries. These were foundations devoted to the saying of Masses for the dead and though the expressed intention of the dissolution was to gain the wealth invested in them, such a move could easily be associated with an attack on that practice and the doctrine of Purgatory.

11 THE KING'S RELIGION

In a situation where Henry, as Supreme Head, actively intervened in the formulation of doctrine and the imposition of order in the Church, his personal religious convictions were important. It is not easy to pin Henry down on this question. At different times during his reign he could be seen as the champion of the Papacy, or of humanist reform, or the hope of English Protestantism. External pressures such as the diplomatic situation or the influence of particular groups, could have an effect on the progress and timing of the religious changes; but Henry was no puppet and enough survives of his own writings and reported comments to show that he had and implemented his own ideas.

Henry himself was ready to acknowledge that his ideas changed. In 1521 he published his *Assertio Septem Sacramentorum* (Defence of the Seven Sacraments) against the teaching of Martin Luther. He was helped by others in writing this book but the final version was his own and he was prepared to put his name to it. In it he included a strong defence of papal authority, despite the advice of Sir Thomas More who warned him that it might be quoted against him in the future, and when More's warning came true in the 1530s, Henry admitted that as a result of further reading he had now changed his opinion. Whether one attributes such change to study and mature reflection, the influence of others, or the demands of dynastic politics is a matter of debate, but it had taken place; and there is no need to assume that it stopped there and did not continue to the end of his life.

It is relatively easy to see what Henry had moved from – a conventional Catholicism, publicly practised and backed by a knowledge of theology that was unusual in a King; but it is not so easy to see what he moved to. Having dispensed with Papal Supremacy, did he assume a position of conservative orthodoxy, or a policy of further reform?

During the 1530s he was certainly willing to fall in with the reforming notions of people like Cromwell and Cranmer, at least in some of the practices of the Church, discouraging veneration of the saints and relics, dismantling shrines and rejecting pilgrimages. This continued to the end of his reign. In 1546, it was Henry himself who added creeping to the Cross to the list of practices to be forbidden although he himself had been devoted to such practices only a few years before.

Much more difficult to unravel is Henry's doctrinal position. In broad outline, the official pronouncements seem to shift from the Lutheran-tinged ambiguity of the Ten Articles in 1536 to the straitened orthodoxy of the Six Articles in 1539, reinforced four years later by the King's Book. Professor Scarisbrick has shown that Henry's personal doctrine was rather more complicated. In some areas he represented religious conservatism itself. He was, for example, particularly strict in the enforcement of clerical celibacy and of vows of chastity in general. For him this was not just a question of discipline, but, as he insisted in inserting in the Six Articles, a 'law of God'. In the same act, he took care also to have the doctrine of transubstantiation set out with no possibility of misinterpretation and emphasised also that Communion under both kinds was unnecessary for the laity. He continued too to believe in the efficacy of prayers and Masses for the dead. In 1537, when the cause of reform seemed at its strongest, he still arranged for several thousand Masses to be said for the soul of Queen Jane and he made similar provision for his own soul in his will.

In other areas Henry was more radical. In his comments on the sacrament of holy orders, he went so far as to imply that the priesthood was not of divine institution and to play down the importance of the role of the priest. On the question of auricular confession, although he insisted on it as part of his Church, when it was debated in 1539 he refused to accept the idea that it was required by the law of God – a phrase which he deleted from the draft of the Six Articles – but only that it was 'expedient' and he grew very impatient with conservatives such as Gardiner and Tunstall when they insisted on arguing the point.

If consistency on the lines of an identifiable Catholic or Protestant stance is looked for in Henry's personal religion, then the result will be disappointment. To the end he remained susceptible to change and persuasion. He never abandoned his affection for his Archbishop of Canterbury, Thomas Cranmer, though he must have known of his marriage and on a number of occasions differed from him on doctrinal questions. Cranmer, for example, insisted on rejecting or correcting most of Henry's criticisms of the Bishop's Book of 1537. And throughout the 1540s, Cranmer continued to pursue reformist ideas within his diocese and in his clerical appointments. In 1543, when Cranmer was accused of heresy by his own clergy, Henry's response was to order the Archbishop himself to investigate the charges. Similarly, when accusations were made against his last wife, Catherine Parr (well-known for her reforming sympathies) she personally sought Henry's pardon and his anger was redirected against the accusers.

It was easy to see in Henry someone whose religious views were unpredictable and inconsistent. Partly this can be explained by the fact that he did not feel constrained to declare himself totally for or against any one set of prescribed beliefs. Partly too this was the result of his being, in theology, an amateur, and a lazy amateur at that. Turning to theology only in fits and starts, he had neither the time nor perhaps the inclination to develop what others would have considered a coherent body of doctrine. We know that it could be difficult getting him to begin work in the first place and even more difficult to prevent him from being distracted. He admitted to having only 'taken as it were a taste' of the Bishop's Book when asked to give his approval and in 1531 when, on his own initiative, he decided to study and amend the reforming ordinances of Convocation, his enthusiasm did not get him beyond the third page. He disliked writing intensely and where possible seems to have avoided reading. Cranmer, in a letter to the reformer Wolfgang Capito, gives some idea of how Henry worked.

Do you still want to know whether your offering was acceptable? Well, I will state, not what I myself know to be the truth, but what I have heard from others who have been at court more recently than myself. The King, (who is most acute and vigilant in everything) is in the habit of handing over books of this kind, which have been presented to him, and especially those which he has not the patience to read himself, to one of his courtiers for perusal, from whom he may afterwards learn their contents. He then takes them back, and presently gives them to be examined by someone else, of an entirely opposite way of thinking from the former party. And when he has thus found out everything from them, and has ascertained both what they praise and what they condemn, then at length he openly gives his own opinion on the same points. And this, I understand, he has done with respect to your book. And while he was much pleased with many things in it, there were also some things which he could by no means stomach and approve. I suspect they were the statements you made about the Mass.

1   *What does the letter tell us about how Henry arrived at his opinions?*
2   *To what extent might this letter explain the apparent inconsistencies in Henry's religious beliefs?*

12 BIBLIOGRAPHY

C S L Davies *Peace, Print and Protestantism* (Paladin, 1977).
A G Dickens *The English Reformation* (Fontana, 1964).
C Haigh (ed.) *The English Reformation Revised* (CUP 1987), especially Haigh's own contributions.
C Harper-Bill *The Pre-Reformation Church in England 1400–1530* (Longman Seminar Studies, 1989).
K Randell *Henry VIII and the Reformation in England* (Hodder & Stoughton, Access to History 1993).
J J Scarisbrick *The Reformation and the English People* (Blackwell, 1984).
W J Shiels *The English Reformation 1530–1570* (Longman Seminar Studies, 1989).

13 DISCUSSION POINTS AND EXERCISES

A *This section consists of questions or points that might be used for discussion (or written answers) as a way of expanding on the chapter and testing understanding of it:*

1 What did anti-clericalism consist of before the break with Rome?

2 How general was the demand for a reformation of the Church?

3 How important was Henry's annulment in bringing about the English Reformation?

4 How determined on reform was the 1529 Parliament?

5 What was the basis of Henry's claim to Supremacy?

6 How did Henry maneouvre the English clergy into submission?

7 Account for Henry's success in his attack on papal authority.

8 Why were the smaller monasteries dissolved three years before the larger ones?

9 'The monasteries were dissolved purely as a result of Henry VIII's greed.' Do you agree?

10 Apart from the King, who gained and who lost from the dissolution of the monasteries?

11 How radical were the Ten Articles and the Royal Injunctions issued by Cromwell?

12 'The whip with six strings' – how accurate is this as a judgement of the Act of Six Articles?

13 What was consistent and what was changeable in the King's religious outlook

14 Does 'Catholicism without the Pope' best summarise the religion of England at the end of Henry's reign?

B *Essay questions*

1   Comment on the proposition that 'the sole cause of the Reformation was Henry VIII's determination to secure a divorce'.

2   Why was there so little resistance to the Henrician Reformation?

3   'There was no blueprint for the Henrician Reformation; it just evolved stage by stage.' How accurate is this view?

4   How important was the role of Parliament in the Henrician Reformation?

5   'The dissolution of the monasteries was a disaster for the many but a golden opportunity for a few.' Discuss.

6   How extensive were the religious changes brought about by the English Reformation before the death of Henry VIII?

14 ESSAY WRITING – NARRATIVE AND ANALYSIS

A rule of thumb for A-Level essays is the less narrative the better. Re-telling the story can bring in much redundant material and obscure the argument when what is needed is clear, balanced analysis. However, some questions seem to demand narrative. Take, for instance, question 3 above: 'There was no blueprint for the Henrician Reformation; it just evolved stage by stage.' How accurate is this view?

At first sight it might appear to be a statement which is generally accurate, and its truth could be demonstrated by telling the story of the Henrician Reformation showing how one development led to another. However, it would be much better to organise the essay thematically. And a more balanced argument will result if any principles or strategies behind the Henrician Reformation are clarified and placed against the view of it as just one development leading to another.

To assist in this, plan to write each paragraph of the essay as if in answer to an appropriate question. The following are questions to illustrate this approach. Complete the list, decide which order the questions should come in and then write the essay.

a   Was there a consistent aim or principle which lay behind the legislation of 1533–6 or were the various acts just bargaining counters with the Pope?

b   How important was the financial motive in the Henrician Reformation?

c   Was a reformation necessary for the Crown to exploit the Church?

d   Why were reforms, such as the dissolution of the monasteries, made piecemeal rather than all at once? Because the government's plans were unformed or because there was a need to acclimatise the nation to change?

e   Did Cromwell have a clear view of where the Reformation was going or did he just adapt to circumstances and his master's whims?

---

[1] *A soul is 'justified' when it is made fit to enter Heaven. Roman Catholics believed in 'justification by faith and works', the works being good works such as pilgrimages or alms-giving. Protestants believed that human 'works' were as nothing compared with God-given faith – so they taught 'justification by faith alone'.*

V

HENRY VIII: GOVERNMENT AND POLITICS 1529–47

–

1 INTRODUCTION

THAT Henry should be the King most likely to be recognised of all England's monarchs is no accident. It results from the combination of Hans Holbein, one of the sixteenth century's great portrait artists, with a King who wished to impress upon the world an effective public image; and draws our attention to the importance, not just for Henry but for all the Tudors, of this kind of display (*see pages 424–5*). The main area where such display could be seen was the King's Court. This was the visible sign of the King's majesty. The magnificence of the Court was not simply personal extravagance but served to impress subjects and ambassadors alike, and had an important role in maintaining royal authority and prestige.

But the Court was more than a colourful facade. It was also a centre of government. However, the extent to which this was the case is debated. In 1953 G R Elton published a book entitled *The Tudor Revolution in Government*. In it he maintained that the 1530s saw a crucial change in the way in which England was governed and he attributed that change not to accident but to the conscious design of one man, Thomas Cromwell. And one aspect of that design was to take administration away from the Royal Household and vest it in a number of specialised, independent departments. The impact of this book is still with us. The thesis has always been controversial but criticism has recently become especially strong and Cromwell's role as an innovator and statesman has been challenged and the importance of the Household re-affirmed. And more attention has been paid in recent years to the faction-fighting which dominated politics.

Politics was also played out in other areas – in Parliament and in the provinces, and Henry needed to command general support in both these areas if he was to make his rule effective. But the emphasis nowadays, particularly with regard to Parliament, has shifted from seeing it as a potential source of opposition to regarding it as essentially a body that supported and co-operated with the King's majesty. Henry certainly made significant use of Parliament and so contributed to its development.

But parliamentary history and administrative reform were not what Henry would have thought important. He would build his reputation on the role he played in Europe and thought not in terms of a developing nation state but of personal triumphs in the dynastic and political struggles of his age.

2 THE COURT OF HENRY VIII

Courtiers

The Court was wherever the King was and though that might well be in Whitehall it might also be in a manor-house in the Home Counties or in a field in France. It is worth keeping this fact in mind because the importance of the Court depended not on a place but on a person, the King at its centre, and it was this that dictated first of all its function and secondly the way in which people regarded it.

In its broadest sense the Court could include a wide variety of people; numbers in attendance varied and it is virtually impossible to draw up a standard list of 'members of the Court'. It depended very much on what was happening and great events required great numbers. At the Field of the Cloth of Gold, for example, the King was accompanied by a total retinue of about 5000 individuals which included twenty-three peers, two archbishops and five bishops. This was admittedly the high point of Courtly spectacle but when the Court settled down for the winter season then the chosen palaces would be expected to accommodate about eight hundred people and the skeleton touring Court of the summer would be unlikely to consist of less than four hundred. This does not always take into account the extra retainers and servants which the higher-ranking members of Court might bring along. As a result privacy was a luxury that none but the most eminent could hope to enjoy and lower down the scale the servants endured the discomfort vividly described by Alexander Barclay early in the century:

> And sometimes these courtiers them more to incumber
> Sleep all in one chamber near twenty in number.
> Then it is great sorrow for to abide their shout,
> Some fart, some flingeth, and other snort and rout,
> Some boke and some bable, some cometh drunk to bed,
> Some brawl and some jangle when they be beastly fed,
> Some laugh and some cry, each man will have his will,
> Some spew and some piss, not one of them is still.

This was the more sordid side of Court life. Its public or official aspect was designed to present quite a different picture. One function of the Court was to act as a setting for the King for it was in the context of the Court that he made his public appearances. It was of the utmost importance for any monarch in the sixteenth century to make a great display since the appearance of power contributed to a large extent to the reality of power. Images were widely and effectively used to bolster social, political and religious ideas, and the royal Court was the supreme moving image. Here Henry could be seen enthroned in the midst of his nobility on state occasions or riding in procession accompanied by a host of courtiers and liveried attendants. The nobility of the realm were all expected at one time or another to attend the Court. It was of benefit to both parties. The King was enhanced by his nobles' presence and the nobleman could assert his own authority by his close association with the monarch. And attendance was vital if a man had a particular favour to ask since access to the King was only to be gained at or through the Court. To absent oneself from Court for a prolonged period was to risk oblivion and political suicide.

Household and Chamber

When it comes to looking at the political importance of the Court, then we must turn to the King's Household, which formed the centre of the Court. Its origins lay in the King's basic need for a staff of servants to feed and clothe him and by the beginning of Henry VIII's reign this could mean an establishment of up to 500 people.

Closest to the King was the 'Upper Household' or Chamber, headed by the Lord Chamberlain. At one time the Chamber had been just one room but by Henry's reign it had become a series of apartments, one leading into the other, and designed to serve the King's public and private needs. The diagram on page 119 shows the arrangement of the King's rooms at Hampton Court in the mid 1530s and, though details varied from palace to palace and at different times, will serve as a good example of the Chamber's physical organisation. The hall was the place where the Lower met the Upper Household and here the lesser members of the Court were entitled to eat. Behind the dais a door led through to the King's own rooms. However, at Hampton Court visitors would normally have proceeded to the first of the royal apartments, the Watching Chamber (or Guard Chamber). Almost any respectable-looking person who seemed to have a reason for being there was allowed this far and, under the eyes of the Yeomen of the King's Guard, could await access to the other rooms or the King's emergence from them, or mingle with other members of the Court. Access to the Presence Chamber was rather more restricted. The throne and canopy were in this room and it was the scene of the King's public audiences, with foreign ambassadors or deputations of his own subjects, and of

The King's Rooms at Hampton Court 1535

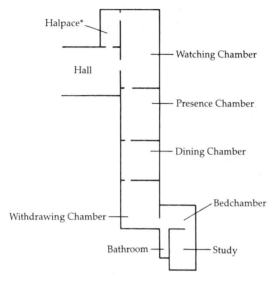

On the floor above were the king's library and jewel-house.

*a stair or ramp connecting two rooms on a different level

meetings with his Council. Finally in this public sequence there was the Dining Chamber, where the King would dine in state, attended and watched by those favoured or important enough. The personnel who were responsible for these rooms, as guards, servers, ushers and so on, formed the Chamber.

However, as the diagram indicates, this is not the whole story. The work of Dr David Starkey has shown that there was a third and very important sub-division of the Household to take into account and that was the **Privy Chamber**. (*See page 73 for a discussion of this in relation to Wolsey.*) He has argued convincingly that this first emerges as a distinct department in the 1490s and he sets it in the context of Henry VII consciously distancing himself from the rest of the Court in a set of totally private rooms where he could work unhampered by public ceremony and attended by personal servants with no expectations of political power or influence. (*See pages 44/5 to set this in the context of Henry VII's close personal control over finances.*) So, while the Chamber remained a public or semi-public area where the King was almost constantly on show, the suite of rooms known as the Privy Chamber became the King's private area to which access was severely restricted. Here the King was served by a small staff, separate from the rest of the Chamber in fact if not in theory, and headed by the King's most intimate personal servant, the Groom of the Stool.

This was the situation that Henry VIII inherited on becoming King, but while he maintained the private nature of the Privy Chamber, in another aspect he changed its character entirely. 'Company me thinks then best', he sang (or at least set to music) and here he broke with his father's practice. Henry VIII built up a circle of close companions with whom he spent his time both publicly and in the intimacy of the Privy Chamber, and these were not obscure bodyservants but younger members of the peerage or established members of the Court. And a second influx of younger favourites in the course of the 1510s brought further change. Because they were younger it was more natural for them to take over some of the functions of the official Privy Chamber staff in serving the King, and formal recognition of this new situation came in 1518 when, in direct imitation of the French practice, the office of Gentleman of the Chamber was created. At first this may have been seen as a temporary expedient. The King of France was on a visit accompanied by six of his own Gentlemen and six English equivalents were needed quickly to pair off with them. However, within a few years the office of Gentleman of the Privy Chamber had emerged and the new status of the King's bodyservant was recognised. In just over ten years a Privy Chamber staff of menial servants waiting on an isolated King had been transformed into an official circle of intimate and high-ranking companions.

The Gentlemen of the Privy Chamber possessed both access and status. We have already seen that attendance at the Court was necessary for political success and it is easy to see why. This was the age of personal monarchy when the King chose his own ministers and distributed the rewards of public life, and since the King was only to be found in the Court, then to the Court one must go and once there it was with the skills of the courtier that one made one's way. George Cavendish, who, as Wolsey's gentleman usher, could appreciate the politics of a Court, refers both to access and courtliness in explaining the rise of Thomas Cromwell. After the Cardinal's disgrace Cromwell was responsible for winding up some of his affairs and so 'had a great occasion of access to the King for the disposition of divers lands whereof he had the order and governance, by means whereof and by his witty demeanour he grew continually into the King's favour'. The staff of the Privy Chamber had the greatest occasion of access of all. They were with the King from the moment he awoke until he went to bed, and, being constantly in attendance, could judge what it was possible to get from the King and when it was possible to get it.

This access had been enjoyed by Henry VII's personal servants, but his son's Privy Chamber were drawn from a different class. These were men who were the King's companions as well as his servants and their new status can be seen from the ways in which they were employed.

They did not act simply as bodyservants to the King but were also sent abroad on diplomatic missions, given active military offices or had administrative posts in the regions. In all of this they wielded an added authority because of their intimacy with the King. Going from the Privy Chamber, they took with them in some way a sense of the royal presence, they became extensions of the King. This symbolism, strange to us, was understood well enough in the sixteenth century; but more than symbolism was involved. In diplomacy, for example, they had a very real advantage in going from one court environment to another, where their skill in a shared culture could help in establishing good relations. An early example is Charles Brandon who had risen to favour by his skill as a jouster. On a mission to France in 1514 his skill also drew the admiration of the French King, Louis XII, who thereupon showed much greater confidence in Brandon when it came to the negotiating table.

With men who had access to the King and the stature to use that access to further their own and other people's careers, the new-style Privy Chamber had become a potential centre for political activity and its importance as such was recognised from the moment it was given its new status. As was seen on page 73 in 1518/9 and again in 1526 Cardinal Wolsey had attempted to clear the Privy Chamber of individuals he saw as a threat to his hold on the King's confidence. After his failure and the success of the Boleyn party, the Court, and the Privy Chamber in particular, continued to provide a setting for the political struggles of Henry's reign.

3 THE TUDOR REVOLUTION IN GOVERNMENT

The Household was not just a political forum. It also had a part to play in the government and administration of the realm and the nature of this role and the extent to which it might have changed during this period have recently been much debated. Professor Elton argued that during the 1530s a system of government centred on the King in his Household gave way to a system of departments, freed from the vagaries of immediate royal control and run according to a formal routine.

During the 1530s the dominant figure in the King's affairs was Thomas Cromwell. (*See pages 93/4 for a discussion of his role in religious affairs.*) According to Professor Elton, he was also responsible for the changes in Tudor government and administration and deliberately so – 'working in effect to a master plan: confronted by the needs for administrative efficiency and effectiveness he promoted measures which incorporated the principle of national against Household government and relied on a bureaucratic organisation relatively independent of personal relationships'. In other words, this means that the government

Thomas Cromwell, 1st Earl of Essex, after Hans Holbein

and administration of the kingdom would be carried out by departments that had a formal organisation and set procedure. As a result it would not need a King (or a Wolsey or even a Cromwell) to keep the system going. Instead, each department would continue to function, following the rules laid down for it, without requiring the intervention of monarch or minister. This was the Tudor Revolution and there are three main areas in which it said to have taken effect: the Council, financial administration, and the role of the King's principal secretary.

The Privy Council

The early Tudor Council had varied in size and exercised a range of advisory, administrative and judicial functions. So, under Henry VII, although up to forty or more members might meet at any one time, it appears there were about twenty-five members who were summoned regularly and frequently, and that a normal meeting consisted of less than ten members. The kind of people summoned included the great officers of state, such as the Lord Chancellor or the Treasurer, judges, members of the nobility and bishops, and royal officials of lower rank; anyone in fact could be summoned that the King chose.

From 1529, the problem of Henry's marriage dominated royal policy and, not surprisingly, the King was showing unusual energy and personal commitment in the efforts to find a solution. And so he now drew about himself a small group of councillors who became once again a 'Council Attendant' upon the King. This had existed before Wolsey dominated the Council as a *de facto* inner ring, but one which did not as yet have any official status other than that of being part of the Council as a whole. By 1540, however, this inner ring has indeed become a new institution. The informal group around the King had become the Privy Council. This consisted of about nineteen members, most of them qualifying for membership by virtue of holding a particular office, whose separate and permanent status has been marked by the appointment of a clerk to record their decisions and whose activities were predominantly those of advising on and executing policy rather than the administration of justice. At the same time, the judicial aspects of the Council's work were continued by Star Chamber and the Court of Requests. Although the former consisted of the same personnel as the Privy Council, with the addition of the two chief justices, both it and the Court of Requests were now to be considered as separate institutions, with their own clerks and set times of meeting.

So much is generally agreed. Where historians differ is in the process and motives behind this change. For Professor Elton this is an obvious and characteristic part of Thomas Cromwell's master-plan. The old Council could be too large to be effective and this Privy Council, with its set pattern of membership, was more efficient and less dependent on the King's active involvement. He certainly seems to have been thinking along such lines because in June 1534 he made a note for himself: 'To remember the King for the establishment of the Council.' This implies that he was intending some formal recognition of the inner ring's status.

We know that Cromwell had an important role to play on the Council. By 1533 he appears to have been responsible for drawing up the agenda for Council meetings, possibly conducting the meetings and afterwards implementing the decisions. He kept his own record of Council decisions and it is probable that all the clerical work for the Council, including minuting, was carried out by Cromwell's staff. The 1530s then were the important years in the transition from inner ring to Privy Council and bearing in mind Cromwell's apparent plans for the Council and his domination of its affairs in those years, it would seem credible that he was responsible for this change. A few weeks after his death, the Privy Council consolidated its new status with the following decision.

That there should be a clerk attendant upon the said Council to write, enter and register all such decrees, determinations, letters and other such things as he should be appointed to enter in a book, to remain always as a ledger, as well for the discharge of the said councillors touching such things as they should pass from time to time, as also for a memorial unto them of their own proceedings.

1   *Why is the appointment important in the history of the Privy Council?.*
2   *How well does this appointment fit Elton's theory of a Tudor Revolution?*

It certainly seems to fit the Tudor Revolution. An informal and uncertain number of individuals, chosen by the King, gives way to a small and efficient body. At the same time and as part of the same process, Cromwell also gave the Court of Star Chamber and Court of Requests their final institutional independence.

But this view does not necessarily tell the whole story, and the emphasis placed on Cromwell's role in particular has come in for much criticism. To start with the conciliar courts – Star Chamber and Requests – these had their beginnings under Cardinal Wolsey. In both cases we find Cromwell not creating anything new but making a contribution to a development that had originated earlier in the reign. Nor should this separation of the judicial from the executive functions be seen as a necessary consequence of the establishment of the Privy Council, since they had gained their distinct identities before that had fully emerged.

Turning to the Privy Council itself, two main criticisms of seeing it as Cromwell's achievement are, first, that it represents an ideal that was sought after by others, especially among the nobility, and, secondly, that it could represent such a threat to Cromwell's own position that he would be unlikely to encourage it. The ideal in question was that government should not be in the hands of a single great minister, but conducted by a small and primarily noble council. According to George Cavendish, Wolsey's fall had been partly engineered by 'the great lords of the Council, bearing a secret grudge against the Cardinal because that they could not rule the commonweal [for him] as they would' and, in October of 1529, one of those lords, the Duke of Norfolk, told the Imperial ambassador Chapuys that government would in future be managed by the Council and not an individual. That Council, moreover, would consist of 'those who from birth and circumstances were more competent'. And this, to some extent, we see happening on Wolsey's fall, when Henry gathered a small group of councillors about him to help find a way out of his marriage problem.

As yet, however, there had been no formal change – the 'Council Attendant' was still an *ad hoc* group with no prescribed membership. The important date, when a change did take place, would appear to be 1536 and rather than it being planned, it happened as a reaction to the Pilgrimage of Grace. It was a time of danger to the King and also a time when Cromwell, under attack from the rebels, had to take a back seat while the Council assumed a more prominent role. Lists of Council members at this time indicate that membership was now greatly restricted in numbers. It is possible, therefore, that the 1536 crisis had heightened the importance of a small, select Council which could react swiftly and effectively in need. But as well as being smaller, there are indications that membership of this Council depended on holding certain qualifying offices (e.g. the Lord Chamberlain). This seems to have been the case by the spring of 1537 when a Council list shows that of fourteen members all but one were important office-holders.

The new importance of offices as a sign of status is demonstrated by the Act of Precedence of 1539. This laid down the order in which people would sit in Parliament and in sessions of the Privy Council and shows clearly that seniority was now based upon the holding of particular offices. Office-holding, then, was a criterion for membership of the Privy Council but ten of the eleven offices mentioned in the act were almost always held by noblemen and so this ensured a good proportion of noblemen on the Privy Council. So the Privy Council that emerged by 1540 seems to qualify, by reason of its size and membership, as a manifestation of the noble council sought after by the Duke of Norfolk and his like.

But where was Cromwell in all of this? Rather than the Privy Council being his creation, it looks as if it was a long-standing ideal that was helped into being by the events of 1536. However, it was then checked by Cromwell's return to prominence for what remained of the 1530s and any further institutional development was in fact halted because the Privy Council remained dependent on Cromwell's own staff for all its secretarial work. In this way he kept control, and it was important for him to do so since the kind of people who were on the Privy Council proved to be his political enemies. This is the second reason suggested for doubting a key role for Cromwell in creating the Privy Council. He was a skilled politician and was not likely to establish an important government body that virtually guaranteed membership to people who were his political rivals. It was to be his enemies on the Council who brought about his downfall in 1540 and only then was the Privy Council, freed from Cromwell's domination, able to complete its emergence as an institution with the appointment of a secretary.

In this argument, the view of the Privy Council as part of the assertion of an aristocratic ideal, expressed most notably by Dr Starkey, has been used, but it is worth expressing some reservations about this. Although the nobility might dominate the Privy Council, they did not by right form a majority of the members. And a good proportion of the peers were ennobled by Henry rather than being representatives of ancient, aristocratic families – Cromwell himself was created a baron and later Earl of Essex. So there must be qualifications to any view of an aristocratic reaction. Certainly the nobility were essential to good government and those who aspired or were born to titles expected a degree of power and responsibility. However, it was not given as an automatic right but was linked to the King's service.

Finance

The financial system based on the Household that was so effectively employed by Henry VII continued into the reign of his son. Royal revenue, particularly from the Crown lands, was paid in to the Treasurer of the Chamber in cash and stored away in one of the King's strongrooms, such as the Jewel House at Westminster. Regular audits were held by members of the Royal Household or specially-commissioned councillors. The advantages of the system were that close supervision by the King was possible, a realistic assessment could be made of the money at his disposal, and that money was readily available in cash. On the other hand, the efficient working of the system did rely on the close supervision of the monarch or his deputy. This system continued up to the 1530s with very little modification.

Meanwhile the Exchequer continued to function, dealing particularly with income from customs and from the administration of justice. However, although it was acknowledged as being effective in its accounting and collecting, it could also be very slow.

As the Treasurer of the Chamber turned more and more to dealing with income and expenditure at a national level, there was a growing need for someone to replace him in his original role of attending to the King's personal financial needs. This role was filled from the Privy Chamber by the Groom of the Stool, who, among his other duties, controlled the Privy Purse. The Privy Purse was at its most active during the years 1529–32, and it is no coincidence that these were the years when Henry VIII resumed personal control of political affairs. So it is that Privy Purse accounts for this short period show almost a third of its expenditure going on matters of state. At the same time, although the Treasurer of the Chamber still dealt with more money than the Groom, his business was of a routine nature such as the payment of wages and does not match the importance of the Privy Purse.

The importance was temporary. As Thomas Cromwell's influence increased, he started to take over control of the financing of policy, while the Privy Purse was once more restricted to the King's personal expenditure.

The creation of organised financial departments starts in 1536. The Office of General Surveyors, first seen in 1515 handling Household income, now became a permanent department and in the same year the Court of Augmentations was set up to handle the income from the lands of the monasteries. Augmentations, whose modern collecting and accounting procedures compared favourably with the Exchequer, became the model for further departments (or courts). In 1540 the Court of Wards was set up to handle royal revenue from wardship, and after Cromwell's death, the Court of First Fruits and Tenths, which collected the King's ecclesiastical dues, and the Court of General Surveyors, were organised on similar lines in 1541 and 1542 respectively. By the end of Henry's reign, therefore, there were six financial departments functioning independently of the Household and of each other, and, in contrast to the earlier Household arrangements, working within specific areas.

What brought about this change? It may owe something to Thomas Cromwell and a belief in bureaucratic institutions being better than the informality and uncertainty of the Household style of government. But if this was the case he was not willing to put it fully to the test in his own lifetime. He had, for example, kept the Court of First Fruits and Tenths very much under his own control, treating it almost like a Household department and using its resources to finance his policies. It only became a 'free-standing' institution after his death. As well as this, the creation of these departments can be seen as a response to particular needs. The 1530s saw an increase in royal income in a number of areas, the old system could not cope and so the new departments were set up. Nor, in daily practice, should the contrast between old and new be over-emphasised. Personnel could move with ease from one department to another or between departments and Household, or even work in two areas at once. This broke down any tendency to clear-cut differences between them.

There was still one area where the Privy Chamber played an important role. The new departments collected royal revenue and paid out the routine expenses for which they were responsible, but they did not keep the surplus. What happened to this is indicated in a government memorandum of 1537 which notes that all revenue-collecting departments should make a yearly account of income, expenditure 'and what the whole remainder to the King's use will yearly amount to'. This remainder, it concludes, is every year to 'be laid up for all necessities' and the places where it was laid up, or stored, were the King's Privy Coffers. These Privy Coffers were Henry's stores of cash, kept in his main palaces, but particularly in Whitehall, and which were administered by members of his Privy Chamber under the King's direct supervision. One might want to claim a bureaucratic revolution in the collecting and accounting of the royal income, but hoarding and spending was still very much a Household affair.

The Secretary

By the beginning of the Tudor period the role of the King's secretary was already regarded as a public office rather than simply that of a personal assistant to the King. His work can be divided into three main parts. First there was his secretarial work proper, that is the reading of the King's letters, providing his master with summaries of these and helping to draft and write the royal replies. Second, arising from this, he was in charge of the signet, the King's private seal which was used to authorise royal orders to government departments. This work was mostly routine but it did provide access to much government business and gave considerable scope to a man of ability.

When Thomas Cromwell took office the secretary was essentially a member of the Household, whose importance lay in access to the King combined with an intimate knowledge of royal affairs, but whose status was not of the first rank. Because the secretary's role was not restricted to any particular area, Cromwell managed to exploit it to the utmost. He was able to extend his influence to virtually every area of public life and in so doing set a precedent that could be followed by later secretaries. As far as Professor Elton is concerned, he took the secretaryship out of the Household and made it one of the offices of state. Its new status was recognised in the 1539 Act of Precedence where it was listed as one, though in precedence the least, of the 'great offices of the realm'. Although this was not aimed at improving Cromwell's personal position – he was already pre-eminent as the King's vicegerent in religious affairs – it certainly reflects the new importance given to the office by Cromwell's use of it.

But although Cromwell set a precedent and undoubtedly influenced the status in the short term, the new status did not persist. In 1540 Cromwell resigned the office which was then divided between two holders, Thomas Wriothesley and Ralph Sadler, and the secretaryship was officially restored to its pre-Cromwellian point in the order of precedence. Nor did Cromwell's successors come anywhere near to emulating his comprehensive control of affairs. Apart from the clerks of the signet office, Cromwell's staff as secretary had been those of his own household and he had not instituted any formal department to carry on his own work. It seems very much as if he had seen in the secretaryship the potential for personal advance and political control but had not envisaged any permanent change in the secretary's role. The importance of the secretary later in the sixteenth century may have owed something to his example but the ascendancy of Cromwell's secretaryship was primarily a personal one.

Was there a Tudor revolution in government?

Although Professor Elton still maintains that Cromwell supervised a change in governmental methods from Household practices to bureaucratic institutions, there are many objections to this view. Evolution seems as valid a concept as revolution. It can also be maintained that some changes were more pragmatic – the result of reacting to events. A vast increase in sources of wealth led necessarily to the creation of departments to handle that wealth, and, like the Privy Council, these departments were not fully institutionalised until Cromwell had left the scene. In fact, to some extent Cromwell acted as a brake on any bureaucratic development, and it is almost as though he dominated these different areas through his own household system. His own staff provided the Privy Council secretariat and John Gostwick, treasurer of First Fruits and Tenths, was effectively Cromwell's personal servant, and it was through him that Cromwell financed his policies. At the same time the Household retained an important role, if not in the accounting and collecting, certainly in the storing and spending of revenue. The distinction between Household and bureaucratic may not have been so clear in the 1530s and 1540s when the two areas could share the same personnel – the Privy Council met in the room opposite the King's bedroom, and councillors and secretaries shared the Household privilege of eating at the King's expense. Cromwell himself had been able to exploit the Household offices of Master of the Jewels and the King's secretary in his rise to power and later in his career he became Lord Great Chamberlain as part of his plan of keeping control of that important area of political life.

Professor Elton acknowledges many of these objections and he has shown himself willing to modify his original theory. He accepts that in some areas Cromwell was able to build on earlier work and he recognises the limitations to Cromwell's actions. Circumstances dictated that he could not make sweeping reforms, but he acted as the occasion demanded and the opportunity presented itself. Neither could he implement fully the changes that he wanted but had to retain a large measure of personal control in the 'unreformed' manner simply to guarantee at least some limited success. All of which presumes that Cromwell did at least set out to bring about change, and in the end the real difference between the supporters and critics of the Tudor Revolution idea seems to lie as much in their views on the character and motives of Thomas Cromwell as in any argument over what actually happened. What has remained constant for Professor Elton is that minister's commitment to introducing a new style of government in England; and he has continued to defend this central idea even while qualifying other aspects of his original thesis.

4 ROYAL AUTHORITY AND THE LOCAL COMMUNITY

Like so much else during this period, control of the provinces, away from the centre, was a mixture of the institutional and the informal. This control was important, especially at a time of change when it was necessary to have royal policy first of all communicated to the provinces and then put into effect. The religious changes of Henry's reign, for example, required action of this kind if they were to be at all effective. The raising of troops and the administration of the King's justice both needed adequate representation of the royal will in the local community. But although it was important, there was very little change in this area during Henry VIII's reign. What we do see is the exploitation and development of existing institutions and methods.

Cromwell saw such control as a necessary feature in his view of the 'unitary' state. Part of the country's imperial nature was that the King should have total control over all people and all areas within his realm, and he worked hard at putting this ideal into practice. Such changes as he did make are discussed elsewhere (*see pages 347–54*). These included the establishment of the Council of the North to administer royal policy in that area and the inclusion of Wales in the shire system. But these moves were aimed at making sure the whole country shared the same system – to the system itself Cromwell made no change.

The officers who were most regularly involved in administering the localities for the King were the Justices of the Peace, the JPs. Their duties covered a wide variety of responsibilities and increased steadily as they were called upon to enforce new statutes. As a result there was a short-lived attempt in 1542 to get the JPs to hold extra plenary sessions, presumably to make sure that all their duties were carried out. In the same year the Justices of Assize were given the authority to hear any charges against the JPs and a year later it was ordered that the Court of King's Bench should in future receive a transcript of the quarter-session proceedings in each shire. The nature of the Justices of the Peace had changed little but the amount of work they did was increasing and was seen to require greater supervision.

The gentry and nobility of the area, often joined by the leading churchmen were the JPs and other local officers of the King. They were chosen because they were the natural leaders of their locality. They expected to be given such responsibilities and readily accepted them, though they were largely unpaid and could be onerous. However, to be associated with the royal authority in this way enhanced their own position and was seen as an essential part of their role in society. The King was well aware of the need to cultivate these men. Since he could not afford to set up a system of fully-paid royal officials, he needed the co-operation of the leaders of the counties to secure his ends. Special efforts were made to build up a network of personal relationships between the King and individuals in the provinces, relationships that would ensure their particular loyalty and provide the King with instruments of his policy in those parts of the country where he was seldom seen. These 'King's men' could be linked to their monarch by a variety of means – patronage, the granting of lands and titles, or positions at Court that brought prestige but no duties requiring residence.

People who were important figures at the centre – in Court and Council – were also important in different parts of the country. Most members of the Privy Chamber were also Justices of the Peace and courtiers were sent to act on commissions or to raise troops for the King, often from their own followers. The Privy Chamber members provided a substantial proportion of the army when the King went to war.

5 PARLIAMENT

Another very important link between the centre and the provinces was Parliament. In a Parliament the King's subjects were able to express their opinions on aspects of royal policy and demonstrate their willingness, or otherwise, to pay for it, while the King used the meetings to present his policies to his people, win their consent to them and then send them away to enforce these policies in their own communities. For the ups and downs in this relationship in Wolsey's time see pages 69–71. In 1529 there were 51 lay peers and the number had been increased to 55 by 1534. The Lords Spiritual consisted of the two archbishops (of Canterbury and York) and normally 19 bishops, and about 29 abbots from the more important monastic houses. The House of Commons in 1529 consisted of 310 members. Seventy-four of them were knights of the shire, returned from thirty-seven counties, and 236 represented the parliamentary boroughs. County members generally combined a prominent role in their shire with some Court connection. A number of men of this type had also taken over the borough seats but there was still a sizeable proportion of genuine borough representatives.

Although the Upper House enjoyed a greater status and prestige than the Commons, when it came to parliamentary business the two houses were equal. There were two main reasons for summoning Parliament. One was financial and it had long been a principle that the King could not tax his people without their consent expressed in Parliament and the vote of the Commons was essential for this. The other reason was legislation and the assent of the Commons was as necessary as that of the Lords and King in the making of statutes. To help them in their conduct of business the Commons had already claimed with some success a number of privileges. In 1523 the then Speaker, Sir Thomas More, made the first recorded request that members should be allowed to speak freely on any matters put before them and generally speaking the spirit of the request was observed through Henry's reign. Such freedom was not without its limits and members still needed to watch their words. Later in the reign, one Thomas Broke found himself up before a panel of bishops to answer for his criticism of the Act of Six Articles.

By 1529 Parliament was seen as an important but irregular part of government, with specific functions in the areas of finance and legislation, and enough continuity to have secured certain privileges, such as a qualified freedom of speech in parliamentary debate. By the end of the reign, further significant developments had been brought about in the nature of the English Parliament.

To begin with there was an increased frequency of sessions during this period. From 1529 to 1536, the sessions of the Reformation Parliament took place almost annually; and in the eleven years left of

Henry's reign only four years did not witness a Parliament in session. By contrast, Parliaments had been held in only five of the first twenty years of the reign. The real change came not in 1529 but in 1532 and was due to the arrival of Thomas Cromwell. It has often been argued that Cromwell showed particular skill in turning to statute as the means of securing the breach with Rome – he took many of the ideas being discussed at the time and 'showed how they could be turned into reality by means of acts of Parliament' (*Elton*). But this can be exaggerated. After all, in matters of such high importance the King wanted to be assured of the (at least outward) consent of his important subjects and that any policy could be effectively enforced. For both of these Parliament was the obvious instrument. It contained the leaders of the political nation and its statutes were generally regarded as the highest form of positive, or man-made, law in the realm, which could be enforced with the fullest sanctions. The King could declare himself to be Supreme Head of the Church but he needed a statute to allow him to chop someone's head off for denying it. Nevertheless Cromwell did take great pains in the drafting of bills and showed a tendency to use statute even when it was not necessary.

As a result, Cromwell's rise to power witnessed a great increase in parliamentary activity especially in the sessions of the 1530s when an unprecedented amount of legislation was passed. And it was legislation of particular significance; after being involved with such major changes, many historians have argued that Parliament was not to be the same again. It had ventured into areas, such as religion, that it had not previously dealt with, and consequently there was a feeling that Parliament's scope had been widened and there were now no areas from which it could be excluded. According to Professor Graves: 'By 1540 King-in-Parliament had emerged as the sovereign legislator . . . Its laws were not only supreme but omnicompetent.' If one looks at the practicalities of the situation there is much to be said for this view, but in the 1520s and 1530s such a bald statement would not have been so readily acceptable. Limitations were still acknowledged:

> Every man's law must be consonant to the law of God. And
> therefore the laws of princes, nor the commandments of
> prelates, the statutes of communities, ne yet the ordinance of the
> Church is not righteous nor obligatory but it be consonant to
> the law of God.

(*Cristopher St Germain* Doctor and Student, 1529)

1 *What is meant by a law being consonant with the law of God?*
2 *How might the legislators of the break with Rome have turned this 'limitation' to their own advantage?*

Since Parliament's role was recognised as important, care was taken to ensure its efficient co-operation during sessions. After Parliament had been summoned in 1539, Cromwell wrote to Henry that he 'and other your dedicate councillors be about to bring all things so to pass that your Majesty had a never more tractable Parliament'. The methods were not exceptional – the use of direct royal influence in a few areas and the promise of co-operation from influential landowners in others would ensure the return of a sufficient number of councillors and royal 'men of business' to the House of Commons and, on the whole, this seems to have been seen as no more than the accepted use of patronage.

Despite any attempts to prevent it, the Crown could still face opposition in Parliament. In the early years of the Reformation Parliament in particular there seem to have been organised attempts to block Henry's policy in both the Upper and Lower Houses, led by supporters of Catherine of Aragon. Once sessions had begun, therefore, the royal men of business were needed to introduce, support and guide government legislation through the House. Individuals who were known to oppose the royal policy could be persuaded to absent themselves from the House, as happened to Sir George Throckmorton in 1534. This happened also to members of the Upper House who might cause trouble for government legislation. Henry also used his personal authority to bring pressure to bear. Groups of MPs might be summoned to his presence to be made aware of his feelings, as he did in 1532 when the Commons rejected his attempts to pass a bill that would have reasserted his right to feudal dues on all lands held by knight service. Occasionally he even went down into the House itself. In 1532, for example, criticism of the Annates bill led to Henry forcing the House to vote on the bill in his presence and in 1536 he may personally have delivered the bill for the dissolution of the monasteries. Opposition in the Commons was also encountered during the passing of the Treason Act, although there is no certainty as to what prompted this or if it had any affect on the final wording of the act. Opposition was not always in vain. In 1532 and again in 1539 the Commons successfully resisted royal demands for a parliamentary tax.

Nonetheless for the most part the relationship between King and Parliament was one of co-operation. Both stood to gain from its meeting. Henry gained the support of the realm, as represented in Parliament, for his policies in the practical form of legislation and money, and the members themselves could take advantage of the sessions to put forward their own bills and make their own feelings heard. By its role in a period of particularly important and wide-ranging legislation, Parliament as an institution gained a new prestige and a foothold in areas of competence that would later be expanded. This enhancement of Parliament's status was of particular importance to the Lower House and it became more common than before to introduce bills in the Commons, partly prompted perhaps by Cromwell's presence there at a crucial stage. The new significance of the Commons was reflected in the greater number of government men that could now be found there and also perhaps in the fact that by the end of Henry's reign it had acquired its own Journal. It had increased in size as well, with the addition of members from the shires of Wales and the Marcher territories and the creation of fourteen new parliamentary boroughs. The Lords had also seen a major change in the removal of all the abbots from its benches, with the result that the temporal peers began to enjoy a substantial majority.

6 POLITICS AND PATRONAGE

Privy Council and Court, Parliament and Privy Chamber – despite history students' efforts to simplify their own task by separating and analysing them, they could not be so neatly kept apart in the reality of sixteenth-century politics. An individual's life is too untidy to compartmentalise in this way, and the same person could be active in more than one of these areas, indeed almost inevitably, he was. A career that starts with a position in the Household could include sitting in the Commons before membership of the Privy Council and then perhaps a peerage. And the polished courtier of the Privy Chamber was also likely to be an active JP and in wartime the leader of an armed retinue drawn from his estates.

One element was essential to success in all the different areas that made up a man's career, and that was **patronage**, the system in which the patron bestowed gifts and rewards on his client. Or, in this context, the monarch granted titles, offices, or lands to the favoured subject. Patronage permeated the whole of Tudor society. There were no formal routes for advancement, relying on examinations or recognised qualifications; you did not gain office by filling out an application form listing personal achievements and certificates gained. Not even a bureaucratic Cromwell has been accused of favouring such a formalised system. But what Cromwell and his contemporaries would have appreciated in modern recruitment and selection is the personal reference. Because in the sixteenth century it was this personal recommendation that mattered. If a man had an office at his disposal, he gave it to someone he knew or to someone who had been recommended to him. And this worked at all levels of society – whether it was the King appointing a Chancellor or the local parish priest choosing an assistant clerk. At the summit of this pyramid of patronage was the King himself, the ultimate source of all honours and the immediate source of many of those plum jobs that gave a man power, prestige and wealth. Without his patronage there was no way to the top; but with it a politician could achieve eminence for himself and also the ability to reward his own clients in turn, because the person who found favour with the King could then become a channel of that favour for others. Attached to every successful careerist was a band of clients who relied on him for their current positions and future prospects. In return they gave him service and support.

Much of Tudor politics, therefore, was bound up with search for patronage. People sought access to the King, they tried to influence the King, they used persuasion, flattery and guile, but in doing all this they rarely tried to act alone. Individuals came together in alliances that are known as factions; and the consequent struggles between these groups have been given the name faction politics. Professor Ives has provided a good working definition of a faction. He sees it as a group of people who have come together to seek 'objectives that are seen primarily in personal terms'. This does not mean however, that they are entirely self-seeking and concerned only for personal power at the expense of their opponents. It is also possible to see other motives contributing to these groupings. In the 1530s there were those who stressed their loyalty to the old Queen, Catherine of Aragon, and then to her daughter Mary. Others found a community of interest in their sympathy for religious reform in contrast to those conservatives who wished to stem the tide of change. But none of these factions had a political agenda; alliances and membership could shift and change in response to events. Professor Ives would like to see faction recognised as a continual phenomenon in the sixteenth century, but he admits that there were times when the struggles between the different groups became more violent and intense. Under Henry VII such activity was negligible. The King was so obviously in control and by his isolation had so freed himself from any effective influence that there was no place for faction. His son's accession heralded the change although its extent is debated. (*See page 158 for Gwyn's view.*) Surrounded by people of potential political status even in his most intimate moments, Henry VIII provided the context in which faction politics could and did flourish.

7 THE FACTIONS AFTER WOLSEY

Wolsey's fall created a gap that no one person was able or called upon to fill. Henry was left with a continuing problem – how to set aside Catherine of Aragon and marry Anne Boleyn – but with no effective way yet suggested by which he could arrive at a solution. Groups that had previously had a common cause in bringing about the end of the Cardinal found that this unity did not extend to the question of how Henry should get his annulment, or indeed whether he should attempt to get an annulment at all. Those individuals who had been ranged against Wolsey now realigned themselves according to their different interests and loyalties and in the years that led up to the divorce and break with Rome these factions competed for the attention of the King as he cast about for a realistic policy.

At first it seemed that the aristocratic faction, together with Anne, had been totally successful. The French ambassador, Du Bellay, wrote to his master: 'The Duke of Norfolk is now made chief of the Council and in his absence the Duke of Suffolk, and above everyone Mademoiselle Anne.' As well as the Dukes of Norfolk, Anne Boleyn's uncle and Suffolk, others who can be identified with this group include the Earl of Wiltshire, Anne Boleyn's father, and Stephen Gardiner, the King's secretary from October 1531, and Bishop of Winchester. At first this was the most powerful group, and especially strong on the Council, but it lacked both initiative and coherence. Norfolk and Suffolk had little to offer Henry other than their loyalty and service. Both Dukes would go along with Henry's attempts at divorce and accept with equanimity the prospect of rejecting papal authority. Gardiner was more active in the cause of the King's marriage but, like Norfolk and Suffolk, he was essentially conservative in his attitude. As one of Henry's agents in Rome, he showed himself willing to put pressure on the Pope and was later to accept and defend Royal Supremacy in the church but he remained a traditionalist in his religious beliefs and his defence of clerical privilege in Convocation in 1532 cast him under a temporary cloud and he had to buy his way back into favour by giving one of his manors to Anne Boleyn.

Much more radical in its approach to the problem was the faction that grew up around Anne herself. Her main supporter was her brother George Boleyn, who, following expulsion in one of Wolsey's reforms, was re-admitted to the Privy Chamber in 1528 and who, as Viscount Rochford, from late 1529 was one of the two noblemen in the Privy Chamber, as well as being a member of the Council. Other members of the Privy Chamber committed to her cause were Sir Francis Bryan and Sir William Brereton. Sir Thomas Audley, the Speaker of the House of Commons in 1529, and later More's successor as Lord Chancellor, was to use his legal skills in supporting the divorce, helping the man who was possibly the single most important newcomer to the Boleyn camp, Thomas Cromwell. Thomas Cranmer, soon to become Archbishop of Canterbury, and Edward Foxe, one of the men behind the theory of the Henrician Supremacy, were also of this faction. This was the radical faction in more ways than one. First, it was prepared to use extreme measures in securing Henry's annulment, abandoning any reference to the Pope and establishing an autonomous Church that would make its own decision in the affair. Second, this was to be accompanied by reform in the English Church that went beyond Royal Supremacy to include some of the latest reforming ideas current at the time.

Fear for the safety of the universal Church as well as loyalty to Catherine of Aragon explains the existence of the third, Aragonese, faction that emerged at this time. It had its origins in the early years of Henry's reign and included a number of the nobility who felt aggrieved at the power wielded by Cardinal Wolsey. Henry Courtenay, Marquis of Exeter, a member of the Privy Chamber and the Council, was an old opponent and so too was Lord Darcy, who was responsible for drawing up a set of articles against the Cardinal that might be used in any legal proceedings against him. Both these men supported Queen Catherine and objected to the religious implications that attended the divorce policy put forward by Anne and her faction. Sir Thomas More, who succeeded Wolsey as Lord Chancellor, made no secret of his disagreement with Henry over the divorce which he seems to have made clear at Council meetings and Bishop John Fisher was even more outspoken in his defence of Queen Catherine. This faction had supporters in the Household, including some of those who felt they had suffered at Wolsey's hands such as Sir Nicholas Carew, a gentleman of the Privy Chamber, and Sir Henry Guildford, the Controller of the Household, who spoke out on Catherine's behalf at the Council table. It also had close connections, through More and others, with Members of Parliament who were expressing their support for the Queen in the House. Sir George Throckmorton, a member of the King's Household, and a number of other MPs seem to have met regularly at the Queen's Head tavern, and to have been identified as an 'opposition' group who spoke out against royal policy on the Church and the divorce.

In Council, Court and Parliament these three factions fought for the King's favour and it was the radical faction that won the day. In the face of the Pope's adamant refusal to decide in the King's favour, they provided him with the only effective way out of his impasse. They provided the justification for the break with Rome and the Boleyn marriage. Opponents were silenced, either by execution – More and Fisher were both beheaded – on royal disfavour – Lord Darcy was advised to absent himself from Parliament. It was, for the time being at least, a triumph for the radicals.

8 THE FALL OF ANNE BOLEYN

On 7 January 1536, Catherine of Aragon died. Henry rejoiced and so did Anne, who, pregnant with what she hoped was the longed-for son, must finally have felt secure as the rightful Queen of England. But far from marking the end of the Aragonese faction, which still survived in Court and Council, Catherine's death actually provided a spur for further action against Anne and her supporters.

In 1534 the first Succession Act had stated that Henry had never truly been married to Catherine and that consequently the line of succession lay with the children of his marriage to Anne Boleyn. Although no specific mention was made of Catherine's daughter, Mary was effectively excluded from the succession by reason of her illegitimacy and it was one of the aims of the Aragonese faction to have her place in the succession restored to her. Now that Catherine was dead, Henry would be spared the embarrassing consequences of any implied restoration of his first Queen that might have accompanied such a move. According to some canon lawyers there was a good case for arguing that since Henry and Catherine had genuinely believed in the validity of their marriage when their daughter was born, then Mary could be considered legitimate although the marriage itself could still be rightly judged as void. The enemies of Anne Boleyn had religious motives as well. Mary and her mother had remained loyal to Rome, but Anne and her party were closely identified with the reforming movement in the English Church. This was not just because Anne's marriage had depended on the rejection of the Papacy. She also showed signs of her strong commitment to some of the new trends in religion, encouraging the reading of the Bible in the vernacular and actively supporting the appointment of reforming churchmen such as Cranmer and Latimer. For many of Mary's supporters the removal of the Boleyns from power was also seen as part of the struggle for religious orthodoxy.

One other event in January of that year gave the Aragonese some hopes of success. The restoration of Mary and the ending of religious innovation required the removal of Anne Boleyn and Anne's position with the King was weakened on 29 January when she miscarried of a son. Later stories of the baby having been deformed are likely to have been exaggerated but there is no doubt that Henry's reaction put Anne's future in question. He saw it as a judgement of God on a marriage that had never been lawful and went so far as to mutter about having been bewitched into marriage. Anne's situation was made more vulnerable by the existence of a rival for Henry's affections. Jane Seymour had been a member of the Court since the early 1530s, first as one of Catherine's ladies-in-waiting and then as part of Anne's household, but she did not seriously attract the King's attention until 1535 or 1536. The affair was first noted by Chapuys by February and in the following month she was given rooms near the King. Mary's supporters were quick to cast her in the key role of seducing the King from his wife and she was carefully coached in how to win and retain his favour. It also brought into the affair her brother, Edward Seymour, already an established figure at Court who in March was appointed to the Privy Chamber.

Not only the Boleyns were threatened by these developments. Thomas Cromwell had already built up a strong following of his own, including dependents in the Privy Chamber, men like Sir John Russell and Sir Thomas Heneage who had once served Wolsey and had since transferred their allegiance; but his rise had been based on the success of the Boleyn marriage and the changes accompanying it and this association meant that he was an obvious target for any conservative reaction. However, he had already had his differences with Anne, largely over issues of patronage and also of foreign policy where his support for a pro-Imperial stance was at odds with the Boleyns' French sympathies. He decided therefore to throw in his lot with the Aragonese.

We do not know exactly when Cromwell decided to move against Anne, but he was later to tell Chapuys that he had made the decision on 18 April. On 24 April a commission was set up to investigate and punish treasons and lesser crimes in Kent and Middlesex and three days later writs were issued for the summoning of a new Parliament. This was less than a fortnight after the previous Parliament had been dissolved and the reason that was given for this unexpected summons at the opening of its first session on 8 June was that it was to settle the problems caused by Anne's fall. But at the end of April none of this had yet been mentioned. Henry was still acknowledging Anne as his wife and the possibility of having children by her, although there was some indication of a change in the political climate on 23 April when Carew was chosen as a Knight of the Garter in preference to Anne's brother, Rochford. Then, on 30 April, Cromwell had Mark Smeaton, a musician in the Privy Chamber, arrested and interrogated. Under torture he confessed to adultery with the Queen. On the following day Henry Norris, Henry's Groom of the Stool, was arrested and sent to the Tower, to be followed within the next few days by Anne herself, her brother, Lord Rochford, and two other members of the Privy Chamber, Sir Francis Weston and Sir William Brereton. They were accused of adultery, and in Rochford's case incest, with the Queen. In prison, Anne's injudicious conjectures on which of her words and deeds could have prompted the accusations were immediately reported to Cromwell and themselves became evidence. The flirtatious but innocent exchanges of courtly love were twisted into material for a conspiracy to bring about the King's death so that she could marry one of her so-called lovers. Smeaton's was the only confession to be obtained but they were all found guilty and sentenced to death. The men were executed on 17 May. On the same day Cranmer declared the King's marriage to Anne to be invalid, so barring their daughter Elizabeth from the succession. Two days later Anne herself was put to death, beheaded as a last favour, in the French fashion, with a sword. On the following day Henry was betrothed to Jane Seymour and the marriage took place on 30 May.

We cannot be certain of the extent to which Henry might have taken the initiative in what happened. As we have seen there were good grounds for believing that he had had enough of Anne Boleyn and was looking for the opportunity to cast her aside, having convinced himself that his second marriage, like his first, was condemned by God. In this case Cromwell's intervention could be seen just as much as a response to a royal command, explicit or not, as a reaction to a new development in the political situation at Court. Nevertheless, it was played out very much as a faction struggle and resulted in a re-ordering of alliances and swift attempts at making the most of the new opportunities available.

9 CROMWELL'S TRIUMPH AND HIS FALL

Having dealt with one faction, Cromwell now turned on his allies. He had not fought hard only to find his own influence and reforming ideals brought to nothing by a conservative backlash. They were accused – with justification – of attempting to get Mary restored to the succession. The succession was indeed changed but not to Mary's advantage. At the end of June 1536 Parliament passed the second Act of Succession. Unlike the act of 1534, this one specifically banned Catherine's descendants from the succession and also did the same to any descendants of Queen Anne. Instead the succession was to lie with the children of his marriage to Jane Seymour, his 'most dear and entirely beloved lawful wife'. In addition, in the event of Henry at no time begetting a legitimate heir, he was given the power to declare, by letters patent or in his will who the heir should be.

Cromwell had emerged the winner in all this. At the end of June he replaced Anne's father as Lord Privy Seal and on 8 July was ennobled as Baron Cromwell of Wimbledon. He took the opportunity of insinuating more of his followers into the Privy Chamber. Ralph Sadler and Peter Mewtas were two Cromwellians who gained Privy Chamber places in 1536, and the former was also awarded the estates of the executed Brereton.

Later in 1536, disgruntled members of the Aragonese faction, having failed in the struggles at Court, attempted to topple Cromwell, restore Princess Mary and reverse the religious changes, by resorting to armed uprising when they took part in the Pilgrimage of Grace. Lord Darcy's loyalty to the Aragonese cause has already been noted and Lord Hussey had been Mary's chamberlain. Their involvement in the Pilgrimage resulted in their execution in June 1537. Others, previously their allies, like the Marquis of Exeter, had remained loyal although undoubtedly in sympathy with the rebels' demands. Cromwell was to get them later, when in 1538, probably at Henry's instigation, he rounded up a number of potential opponents to the regime, many of whom were related to or associated with the exiled Reginald Pole. Pole was Henry's second cousin, a well-known figure in Rome who, when he wrote condemning Henry's religious policy and then followed that by an ill-fated attempt to raise continental support for the Pilgrimage, provoked the King's wrath which descended on his family. A series of arrests and executions followed, including the Marquis of Exeter, Pole's brother Lord Montague and two members of the Privy

Chamber, Sir Nicholas Carew and Sir Edward Neville. The last of the Aragonese had been flushed out and further appointments seemed to confirm Cromwell's hold on the Privy Chamber. His clients Thomas Heneage and Anthony Denny became Groom of the Stool and Chief Gentleman respectively, and Cromwell himself, in January 1539, was made Chief Noble of the Privy Chamber.

Cromwell was dominant but not unchallenged, and though he seemed to have tied up the Privy Chamber, he was to face a formidable threat from his opponents on the Privy Council. Foremost among these was the Duke of Norfolk, who had no sympathy with the changes he saw taking place around him and disliked Cromwell as a low-born upstart. Temporarily excluded from the Privy Council but still actively criticising Cromwell, and his religious policies in particular, was the Bishop of Winchester, Stephen Gardiner, in 1538 he returned from a stint as ambassador at the French court and was keen to build up relations with that country rather than follow Cromwell's plan for a German alliance. This conservative faction saw their chance of toppling Cromwell in 1540 when a combination of circumstances led to a weakening of his influence.

Jane Seymour had died in October 1537, shortly after giving birth to Henry's son, Edward. The King was sincere in his mourning but very soon turned his attention to finding a new wife and this time decided to use his marriage to serve his international rather than dynastic interests. Encouraged by Cromwell, he chose Anne, the sister of the Duke of Cleves, and a marriage treaty was signed in October 1539. A painting by Holbein and some reassuring reports from his agents convinced Henry that Anne would be personally as well as politically acceptable to him, but when he met her on 1 January 1540, he disliked her on sight, informing Cromwell that she was 'nothing as well as she was spoken of.' Since the political situation demanded it, he went through with the marriage, but it was never consummated – Henry did not have the inclination and Anne apparently had no idea of what was involved. Meanwhile the international situation had improved, Henry was left with a wife he did not want and Cromwell, whether justifiably or not, had to bear most of the blame. Henry wanted another divorce and Cromwell had to arrange it.

On the face of it nothing could be simpler than annulling an unconsummated marriage, but for Cromwell there was a distinct complication, because an alternative candidate for the King's hand had already been brought forward. Catherine Howard was the niece of the Duke of Norfolk and had apparently been introduced to Henry at the house of Stephen Gardiner. She was young, lively and co-operative and had so captivated the King that it was obvious to Cromwell that if he got Henry his divorce, then his enemy's niece would be the next Queen with a consequent strengthening of the conservatives at Cromwell's expense.

Even so, Cromwell might yet have survived, even with Catherine as Queen, for he was still high in the royal favour. In April 1540 he was created Earl of Essex and Lord Great Chamberlain, a post which he hoped to use to extend his control of both Chamber and Privy Chamber; and he demonstrated his value as a minister by managing to get a large subsidy from Parliament at a time when it was much needed. However, his opponents had another area in which they could attack, playing on what seemed to be Henry's desire to assert the orthodoxy of his Church in the face of religious disunity in the country. An investigation into the existence of a heretic 'cell' in Calais reported back in early April and amongst its findings implied that Cromwell had countenanced their continued presence despite the attempts of the Deputy, Lord Lisle, to deal with them. The details of what happened are not clear. Cromwell attempted to head off trouble by accusing Lisle of being involved in dealings with Cardinal Pole but the attempt was in vain. Cromwell's known sympathies in religion were enough to give credence to the charges of heresy that formed part of the attack made on him by his enemies and the King's impatience with the slow progress in getting his divorce tipped the balance. On 10 June Cromwell was arrested in the Council Chamber and taken to the Tower. His written appeals to the King, refuting the charges of treason and heresy, were ignored and on 28 July, having been condemned by act of attainder, he was executed, acknowledging no guilt and claiming that he died 'in the catholic faith of the Holy Church'.

10 FACTION IN THE 1540s

The events of 1540 proved a victory for the conservatives. Cromwell's fall was very soon followed by Henry's marriage to Catherine Howard. However, there was no clean sweep of either Chamber or Council, and most of Cromwell's clients remained in their places with relatively little disturbance. Nor were the late minister's religious ideals totally overthrown while Cranmer remained a favourite with the King.

Such ascendancy as the conservatives possessed was soon brought to an end and through the same woman who had first brought them into favour. Being the King's wife had not been enough to get Catherine to change habits that had apparently started before her marriage, and in November 1541, information was laid before the Council concerning her persistent adultery. Unlike the accusations made against Anne Boleyn, there is little doubt that these were substantially true and that the Council had a duty to inform the King. It appears no-one had the courage to tell the King until Cranmer, trusting to his special relationship, gave Henry a paper with details of the affair while he was at Mass. A more cynical view might stress Cranmer's opposition to the Howards, especially in matters of religion, and his satisfaction at being able to remove one of the main channels of their influence. When Henry had recovered from the shock of the revelation, he included Cranmer with other previous associates of Cromwell on the commission to investigate the accusations. Catherine's two lovers, one of whom was one of the King's favourites in the Privy Chamber, were executed in December, while Catherine and her accomplice, Lady Rochford, were beheaded in the following February. It was a severe blow to the Howard interest, especially in the Privy Chamber, from which Catherine's relatives were expelled, but the Duke of Norfolk speedily joined in the condemnation of his niece and, once again, the after-effects were limited.

The conservatives remained strong enough to make another attack on the reformers in 1543, this time taking Thomas Cranmer as their target. Using evidence provided by some of the clergy from Cranmer's own cathedral, Gardiner, in the Privy Council, accused him of heresy. But Gardiner had misjudged Cranmer's relationship with the King. When Henry was informed of what had happened, he sent for the archbishop and, instead of taking him to task for his heretical views, put him in charge of the investigation into his own activities. The harsh words he kept for those who had attempted to destroy Cranmer.

But no party had it all their own way and in 1544 Gardiner himself came under suspicion, following the execution of his nephew and secretary, Germayne Gardiner, for denying the Royal Supremacy. Cranmer, together with the Earl of Hertford and Viscount Lisle, two others who had adopted the reforming mantle, and the Duke of Suffolk, probably acting for personal rather than religious reasons, argued that Gardiner himself must have known and approved of his nephew's beliefs. Henry agreed that the bishop should be committed to the Tower for questioning, but Gardiner was informed by an ally in the Privy Chamber of what was happening and immediately sought a personal audience with the King when his abject submission to the royal mercy earned him a full pardon for any views he may have held in the past. Suffolk remonstrated with the King but to no avail; quick access to the King and a personal appeal had won the day. 'If I had suspected this, I would have had him in the Tower overnight and have stopped his journey to the Court,' complained Suffolk.

Although on this occasion Gardiner had won, the cause of the reformers remained strong at this time and especially in the Privy Chamber where ex-Cromwellians such as Sir Anthony Denny and Sir Ralph Sadler were still in office. The reformers were given further encouragement following the King's sixth and final marriage, in July 1543, to Catherine Parr. Though no scholar, the new Queen was openly committed to the new ideas in religion, to the extent that a work she wrote – *The Lamentations of a Sinner* – had to wait until after Henry's death before it could be published. Her influence on Henry's religious policy was limited but her household became a centre for the discussion and practice of new ideas in religion at Court. Nor did this take place in isolation, for a number of her ladies had husbands of a similar religious temperament in the King's Privy Chamber,

Catherine's role as an active supporter of the new religion is confirmed by the efforts made by the conservatives to associate her and her attendants with out and out heresy. In the summer of 1546, the Lincolnshire woman, Anne Askew, was arrested and interrogated on a charge of heresy. Her own heresy was soon established but her interrogators then tried to force her into including members of the Court in her confession, citing the Countess of Hertford and the wife of Sir Anthony Denny. Despite their personal – and illegal – efforts in operating the rack, Wriothesley and his fellow councillor Sir Richard Rich failed to extract the necessary information. Nevertheless, the conservatives decided to try a direct attack on the Queen and received the King's permission to investigate her activities. Catherine, hearing of this, judiciously threw herself on the King's mercy, admitting that she might have spoken out of turn on religious affairs but that she had discussed theology with Henry because she knew he had such an interest in the subject. In future, like a dutiful wife, she would accept her husband's judgement in such matters. The ploy worked and when Wriothesley arrived to arrest the Queen, he was given very short shrift.

By 1546, while official pronouncements on religion remained relatively orthodox and within the spirit of the Six Articles, a party committed to reform had grown up at the centre of affairs and had gained a strong position at Court in the households of both Henry and his consort, and faction politics had increasingly taken on an air of religious dispute. At the heart of the Court, in the King's Privy Chamber, the dominant figure was Sir Anthony Denny, Chief Gentleman and Groom of the Stool, with his own circle of relations and clients and an inclination for reform. From October 1546, the second Chief Gentleman was Sir William Herbert, brother-in-law to Queen Catherine Parr and one of a number of links between the two households. The man who was to lead the reforming alliance was Edward Seymour Earl of Hertford, who combined liberal doses of ambition and greed with his religious commitment, and whose sister's marriage to Henry had boosted an already successful career at Court which was then consolidated by his military activities in the 1540s. Closely allied to Hertford at this stage was John Dudley, Viscount Lisle, who had seen a rapid rise in 1542–3 when he gained his peerage, a place in the Privy Chamber and, with his appointment as Lord Admiral, on the Privy Council. By December 1546, the Imperial ambassador had this to say about them:

> Four or five months ago was a great persecution of heretics . . . which has ceased since Hertford and the Lord Admiral have resided at court.

1   *What does this tell us of Hertford's and Lisle's reputation and influence in December 1546?*

2   *In the context of faction politics, what heresy case in particular might be brought to mind by the ambassador's words and why?*

Influence in the Privy Chamber was not enough to guarantee success. Hertford's alliance had also to increase its power on the Privy Council where the conservatives could normally command a majority. The people who needed to be removed or made ineffective were Gardiner and the Duke of Norfolk. Gardiner had already weakened his own position by his part in the ill-fated attempt to expose heresy in the Queen's household back in July 1546, but his opponents further turned the King against him, apparently by telling Henry that the bishop had refused to agree to an exchange of lands. As a consequence Gardiner was excluded from the Council by the middle of November. And this time he was kept away from the King.

The removal of the Howards was a more dramatic affair and involved not only the Duke of Norfolk but also his son, Henry, the Earl of Surrey. On 2 December Surrey was accused of disloyalty to the King, and the Council ordered that he be taken into custody for interrogation and that his associates should also be questioned. The accused was already in some disfavour with the King because of his poor showing at the defence of Boulogne earlier in the year and, if the evidence against him is to be believed, had on a number of occasions spoken rashly of what should happen on the King's death and of his own family's right to act as regents for the young Edward. On 12 December 1546 Surrey and his father were both sent to the Tower. Surrey's trial took place in the following January and he was tried on only one of the many charges brought against him, that of quartering the arms of King Edward the Confessor with his own. To us it may seem the slightest of offences, but its consequences for the Earl of Surrey should be a reminder of the importance attached to such heraldic messages in the sixteenth century and the real significance of visual displays: the accused was found guilty and executed on 19 January 1547. Norfolk had already confessed to knowing of his son's treason and was condemned to die on 28 January, but he was saved by the King's death on the preceding night. But Hertford's purpose had been served. His two main enemies on the Privy Council had been removed from the political scene and at a time crucial to his plans.

Control of the Privy Chamber was vital for the success of these plans. It meant controlling all access to the King, a valuable asset when, as we have seen, a personal interview with the King might tip the balance in a politician's favour. It also meant control of the Dry Stamp. The Dry Stamp, when applied to a document, produced an impression of the King's signature that could then be inked in by the appropriate officer, and from the autumn of 1545 this had been the usual process for getting the royal signature. Custody of the Dry Stamp was entrusted to John Gates, a Gentleman of the Privy Chamber and brother-in-law to Sir Anthony Denny; and his servant William Clerk was responsible for its actual use. So Denny not only controlled access to the King, as Chief Gentleman of the Privy Chamber, but also had effective control of the royal signature. Both of these were to be crucial to the Hertford alliance in the last months of 1546.

The centre of interest late in 1546 was Henry's will in which the King, in accordance with the Act of Succession, could set out his final decision on the order of succession as well as naming the regency Council that would advise his son. At this stage it appears that the order of succession had been determined, with the Crown going first to Edward and his heirs, then Mary and her heirs, and then to Elizabeth and her heirs. The will also named the members of the regency Council of sixteen who, after the removal of Gardiner and Norfolk, appear to have had a majority of reforming sympathisers rather than conservatives. But this was not the last form of the will although it may have been the last version of which Henry was fully aware.

The date on the will is 30 December, but other evidence points to the will not having been 'signed' (i.e. dry-stamped and inked) until late January when Henry was actually dying or even already dead. The Clerk's register of documents places the will just before another document dated 27 January; and included in the will as a Councillor is Sir Thomas Seymour, who was not appointed to the Privy Council until 23 January. At some time during the intervening month, and presumably near the end, when it could be assumed that Henry would not recover enough to see the document, further changes were made to the will. To start with, contrary to the principle expressed earlier that the regency Council should always act in concert, it was made possible for the Council to invest authority in a single individual. Secondly, a clause was included which enabled the Council to put into effect grants of offices and titles which, it was claimed, Henry wanted to be made but had not lived to implement. This gave the members of the Hertford faction the opportunity to 'reward' themselves and to 'buy' the support of other significant figures where necessary.

So, control of the Privy Chamber had enabled Hertford and his allies to achieve two things. Their denial of access to the King for any but their supporters meant they would be the only ones to influence him as he drew up the final terms of his will. Their control of the Dry Stamp enabled them to produce a validly signed last will and testament even when Henry may no longer have been aware of what was happening. When Henry died on 27 January 1547, control of the Privy Chamber gave them one more advantage. News of his death was withheld for three days, an interval that gave Hertford time to gain possession of the person of the new King before the country at large had learned of the death of the old. The faction struggles of one reign had set the scene for the next.

11 FOREIGN POLICY: THE 1530s

England was not a first rate power at this period. That description can really only be applied to France and Spain (under the rule of the Emperor), both of which had at their disposal much greater resources for pursuing an active and aggressive foreign policy than England could normally hope to command, but, because for much of the time those resources were directed towards war against each other, it did give England a significant role as a potential ally for either side. England was important for two reasons. First, it was a strong enough power to effect a major change in the international situation if the King chose to enter into an alliance. Second, its geographical position was significant. At this stage of the Habsburg-Valois conflict, the King of Spain, Charles, was also the Holy Roman Emperor and the ruler of the Netherlands. If allied with Charles, then England could help to encircle France; if allied with France, then England could help to cut Charles' links with the Netherlands by way of the Channel.

The Netherlands were important to England since in Antwerp they had the main market for England's most important export, woollen cloth, and for this reason the rulers of both countries normally had to maintain good enough relations to allow that trade to carry on unhindered. In 1528, for example, when England was at war with the Emperor Charles, a truce was arranged that allowed the trade between England and Antwerp to continue.

If co-operation with the Netherlands was considered a natural state of affairs, then so too was hostility to France. The English King still maintained a claim to the throne of France, expressed by his bearing the royal arms of France with those of England; and the town of Calais remained a part of the English King's territories. All things being equal, hostility to France seemed the normal state of affairs. One factor that could influence the relationship was new and that was Henry's break from the Roman Church which at first led him to seek alliance with the French.

Finally, there is the question of the King's own prestige. Although we have spoken (and will continue to do so) of the countries by name – England, France and so on – there was a greater tendency in the sixteenth century to see foreign policy as relations between different rulers rather than between different countries, so one should think not so much of England allying with France as of Henry VIII allying with Francis I. In this kind of context, the prestige and ambitions of the individual ruler are obviously of great importance.

In the years after 1529, there were two main strands to English diplomatic activity, directed at Rome and France. Embassies continued to be sent to Rome to put the King's case for a divorce, seeking the Pope's agreement to the claim that the case had to be heard in England or, with veiled threats, attempting to get some more co-operative attitude in the matter. While his agents tried their best in Rome, others were sent to the French King, who, dissatisfied with the terms of the Treaty of Cambrai (1529), by which he had made peace with Charles V, was only too happy to find an ally against the Emperor. In June of 1532 Henry signed a defensive alliance with Francis I and then in October a meeting at Boulogne and Calais was arranged for the two Kings. But the relationship lacked firm foundations since their ultimate aims were too different. Francis' main concern was to recruit a new ally in readiness for when he once again took up arms against the Emperor, and at the same time he was working to win over the Pope to the same end. In October 1533, he met the Pope at Marseilles where the marriage was arranged between Francis' son, Henry, the Duke of Orleans, and the Pope's niece, Catherine de'Medici. None of this, however, seemed to help Henry Tudor. Admittedly he gained the services of two French cardinals in presenting his case in Rome and Francis had managed to get the papal sentence of excommunication delayed, but Henry had no interest in French ambitions in Europe nor in the formation of alliances with the Pope. Rather he seems to have hoped that if combined pressure on the Pope did not produce the desired results then he would gain French support for his split from Rome. The year 1533 saw a growing division between Henry and Francis. The former felt betrayed by Francis' Marseilles treaty with the Pope, and Francis was angered by Henry's marriage to Anne Boleyn and his envoys' aggressive attitude towards the Pope: 'As fast as I study to win the Pope, ye study to lose him.'

But Henry still felt the need for some support in Europe, especially in the event of the Emperor taking action in support of his aunt Catherine. Contact had already been made with the Lutheran princes in Germany and, in 1533, Henry's growing isolation from France led him to forget their theologians' condemnation of his annulment but rather to consider that they too had repudiated papal authority and that the Lutheran Schmalkaldic League was now defying the Emperor. Negotiations were set in motion for some form of alliance between England and the League and these continued in varying degrees of intensity for the next three years. However, the religious nature of the League was such that there could be no political agreement without some form of religious agreement as well, and the Protestantism of Luther was simply too strong for Henry to stomach.

By 1536 the international situation seemed to have improved for Henry. The death of the Duke of Milan in the previous year had immediately set off an argument between Francis and Charles over who should succeed him and this soon led to war between the two powers.

Neither of them was in a position to take any action against Henry and indeed would be more likely to seek his assurance of neutrality if not support. The death of Catherine of Aragon in January removed a major cause of tension between Henry and Charles, and Cromwell was able to inform the English envoys in France that they could now afford to be less conciliatory towards Francis. There were signs of a better understanding between England and Charles, which even the Francophile Boleyns felt it worth advocating, and after the execution of Anne, whose marriage Charles could never be brought to recognise, there seemed a real chance of some reconciliation.

In October 1537 Jane Seymour died and Henry almost immediately set about finding himself a new wife. With the birth of Edward, the continuation of the dynasty was no longer the main consideration and he saw in his fourth marriage the opportunity of establishing a firm relationship with another European power that would help deter any concerted action by Charles and Francis against England. For a year Henry put in bids for a wife to both the French and Habsburg camps, coming up with complicated plans for multiple marriage alliances that received little encouragement from any of the parties involved. His first choice in France was the widowed daughter of the Duke of Guise, but he was both disappointed and outmanoeuvred when she married James V of Scotland. His wish to see personally a selection of other French candidates merely resulted in a rebuke from the French ambassador for his unchivalrous attitude towards the ladies of France. On the Habsburg side he seriously considered Charles' niece, Christina, the 16-year-old widow of the Duke of Milan, but not only were there difficulties in the conditions he demanded, the girl herself had doubts about his marital record: 'Her Council suspecteth that her great aunt was poisoned, that the second was put to death and the third lost for lack of keeping her child bed.'

Not only did these negotiations fail to produce any marriage, they also failed to keep Charles and Francis apart. In June 1538, the Pope brought the two of them together at Nice where they signed a ten-year truce and this was followed shortly afterwards by a joint declaration of co-operation against the enemies of Christendom, which included the King of England. By the end of the year Pope Paul III was preparing to publish the Bull of excommunication against Henry and sent Cardinal Reginald Pole on a mission to encourage Charles and Francis to take up arms against England. Cardinal David Beaton was sent to Scotland on the same errand, and this, combined with the Scottish King's recent marriage, must have aroused fears of a closer relationship between Scotland and France that might result in concerted action against England.

The threat of invasion seemed very real in 1539 and Henry and Cromwell responded accordingly. In early February a survey of the kingdom's defences was ordered and work started on an extensive campaign of building and refurbishment of fortifications, largely financed from the proceeds of the dissolution and often using building materials from the plundered monasteries. Henry himself made a long tour of the new defences and most of the work, on the south and east coasts at least had been completed within two years. The navy, in which Henry had often shown an interest and had built up from his father's seven ships to a fleet of more than forty, was put on a war footing and a muster of the county militias held. In May, 16 500 soldiers marched through London and paraded before the King at a review at his palace of St James.

While these military preparations were set in motion, diplomatic efforts were also made to cope with the situation. In January 1539 Henry had again sent ambassadors to the Schmalkaldic League, hoping to dissuade them from coming to any agreement with the Emperor and asking for a delegation to come to England for further talks. The delegation duly arrived but the talks came to nothing and the passage of the Act of Six Articles in June showed that any religious settlement was impossible. That Act in itself has been seen as an attempt to show Europe that a campaign against England on religious grounds was unjustified.

Progress had been made on finding the King a wife. In January negotiations were opened with the Duke of Cleves on the possibility of a marriage with one of his daughters. In some ways it seemed the ideal alliance. The Duke, who was in dispute with the Emperor, had, like Henry, broken away from the Roman Catholic Church, but he had not adopted Lutheranism, although he was connected by marriage with some of the German Protestants. An agreement was signed in October and the marriage between Henry and Anne of Cleves took place in the following January 1540. Despite his personal aversion, Henry went through with the marriage since at the time Francis and Charles seemed particularly close. Francis had just given permission to Charles to cross France on his way to deal with a revolt in the Netherlands and the two rulers were meeting in Paris on the same day that Henry met Anne for the first time.

But the prospect of a European crusade against Henry proved to be an illusion and when in February of 1540 the Duke of Norfolk went on an embassy to France, Henry could be reassured that Francis and Charles were once more drawing apart and assuming their more usual hostile attitude to each other. The Cleves marriage was unnecessary and Henry could safely set aside his new Queen without jeopardising his security.

12 FOREIGN POLICY: FRANCE AND SCOTLAND 1541–47

As the hostility mounted between Francis and Charles, Henry, was once more seen as a desirable ally in any approaching conflict. During the early months of 1542 Francis tried to win Henry over by the prospect of a marriage between Princess Mary and one of the French princes, but while Henry allowed the negotiations to drag on, he had already taken the initiative himself in seeking an alliance with the Emperor. In June Henry and Charles agreed on a joint invasion of France, to take place in the following year. Then, in July 1542, Francis and Charles went to war.

Before Henry could commit his forces he had to make sure of his own safety at home and in particular this meant the security of his northern border. He had already made a number of conciliatory approaches to James V which were meant to have culminated in a meeting between the two Kings at York in the autumn of 1541. But James had rejected all Henry's advances and then humiliated him by simply not turning up for the York meeting. This slight, combined with the strongly Catholic and Francophile regime in the country, convinced Henry that some show of strength was needed if Scotland was to be kept in its place. A meeting of English and Scottish ambassadors took place in York in August 1542, but Henry professed himself dissatisfied with its outcome and as a result the Duke of Norfolk led an army on a raid across the Scottish border. In response, a Scottish army invaded England only to have its 10 000 men routed by an English force of 3000 at Solway Moss, with the capture of a number of Scottish notables. Shortly afterwards, in December, James V died, leaving as his heir his daughter, Mary, all of six days old.

Henry was now presented with the opportunity to do more than just overawe his northern neighbour. His long-term plan was the marriage of the new Scottish Queen to his son Edward when the two of them were old enough and in July the Treaties of Greenwich called for peace between the two kingdoms and arranged for the future marriage of Mary and Edward. However, these terms were unacceptable to most Scots, and by the end of the year the treaties had been rejected by the Scottish Parliament and the French party was once more in control. In May 1544, the Earl of Hertford led an expedition into Scotland which resulted in the burning of Edinburgh, the devastation of much of the Lowlands and the strengthening of anti-English feeling in the country. If the aim had been to further the English cause in Scotland, it had failed; but in the more limited terms of keeping the Scots too occupied to intervene in the English invasion of France, either by attacking England or sending an expedition to France, it could claim to have had some success. Hertford led another raid of the same kind late in 1545

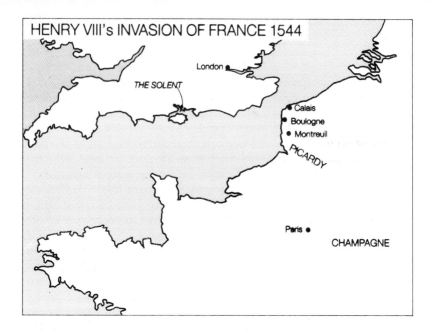

HENRY VIII's INVASION OF FRANCE 1544

London

THE SOLENT

Calais
Boulogne
Montreuil

PICARDY

Paris

CHAMPAGNE

and in the following year Cardinal Beaton, one of the leading members of the French party in Scotland, was murdered. But Henry's reign ended with the country still dominated by a pro-French, Catholic alliance.

While all this had been happening Henry's main interest was elsewhere. An official treaty had been made with the Emperor Charles in February of 1543 and in June 1544, an army of 40 000 went over to Calais where they were joined by Henry himself, marking by his presence the area of policy which he considered most important. The original plan had been for an advance on Paris, Henry marching through Picardy from Calais while Charles led his army through Champagne. But Henry now had second thoughts and decided that he could not be expected to march inland until he had strengthened his position in the area of Calais. Accordingly, he sent a part of his army under the Duke of Norfolk to lay siege to the town of Montreuil, while Suffolk was sent to capture Boulogne. Norfolk failed in his task, but on 14 September Boulogne surrendered and four days later Henry made a triumphant entry into the city and immediately began ordering the strengthening of its fortifications.

Charles had advanced through Champagne according to plan but, disappointed by what he saw as Henry's lack of co-operation, and with problems with the German Protestants requiring his attention, he readily made peace with Francis on the same day that Boulogne fell to the English. Henry was now alone in his war against France and negotiations started almost immediately for a peace settlement, but foundered on Henry's insistence that he should keep Boulogne and also that France would sever her ties with Scotland. Without allies, England now faced the prospect of a continued war with France while Scotland, reinforced by French arms, still presented a problem to the north.

In July of 1545 the war was carried into English waters when a French fleet sailed into the Solent but caused little damage beyond the affront to English honour and the sinking of the Mary Rose, due not to gunfire but the disorganised reaction to the appearance of the French. A landing on the Isle of Wight was easily repulsed, the French attempt to recapture Boulogne failed and a show of force by Scotland led to the Earl of Hertford's raid. Both sides were ready for peace and the Treaty of Campe was signed in June 1546. Henry was to keep Boulogne for the next eight years but it was then to be given back to the French in return for the payment of £600 000, and the French promised to resume the payment of an annual pension to Henry worth £35 000 p.a. They were a sop to Henry's honour rather than advantageous terms and when the new fortifications built by Henry were taken into account, Francis got Boulogne back at a bargain price.

In terms of material costs, during these last years of Henry's foreign policy England had paid a high price for very little gain. War was getting to be increasingly expensive both because of inflation and the greater numbers and more up-to-date weapons that were required. Apart from taxation Henry had access to the money he had made from the Church, but this was not inexhaustible. The expenses of these years also led to the debasement of the coinage which transformed a sound currency into one widely regarded with suspicion.

However, we should not look at the issue purely in account book terms and much of what Henry was hoping to achieve could not be measured in income or even land. In some ways the events of the 1540s have much in common with the early years of Henry's reign and not least in the motives which inspired his actions. Henry was fulfilling his role as the warrior king, leading his troops in war, though now he had to be carried in a litter rather than riding on horseback; and to be a partaker in great events, matching himself with the other rulers of Europe, was an end in itself. The prestige that it brought was sufficient reward. The point is made by a set of four paintings that still exist in the Royal Collection. Two of the paintings deal with his first campaign against France in 1513 and illustrate his meeting with Maximilian and his victory at the Battle of the Spurs; the other two record his departure for and arrival at the Field of Cloth of Gold. But although the subjects come from the early part of the reign, the pictures were actually painted in the mid-1540s. What we have in these pictures is an affirmation by Henry, at the very end of his life, of those aspects of his reign that he still considered to be important – the ambitious European venture to which he returned in the 1540s. The pictures celebrate the King's prominent participation on the international stage and demonstrate that its value was as great to Henry in the 1540s as it was in the 1510s and 1520s.

13 BIBLIOGRAPHY

C Coleman (ed.) and D Starkey *Revolution Reassessed* (OUP, 1986).
S Doran *England and Europe 1485–1603* (Longman Seminar Studies, 1986).
G R Elton *Reform and Reformation* (Edward Arnold, 1977).
G R Elton (ed.) *The Tudor Constitution* (2nd edition, CUP, 1982).
M A R Graves *Early Tudor Parliaments 1485–1558* (Longman Seminar Studies, 1990).
E W Ives *Faction in Tudor England* (Historical Association, revised 1986).
K Randell *Henry VIII and the Government of England* (Hodder & Stoughton, Access to History 1991).
D Starkey *The Reign of Henry VIII: Personalities and Politics* (George Philip, 1985).
D Starkey (ed.) *The English Court from the Wars of the Roses to the Civil War* (Longman, 1987), especially his chapter on 'Intimacy and Innovation: the Rise of the Privy Chamber, 1484–1547.'

14 DISCUSSION POINTS AND EXERCISES

A *This section consists of questions or points that might be used for discussion (or written answers) as a way of expanding on the chapter and testing understanding of it:*

1   What was the Court and why was it important?
2   Why was Henry VIII's Privy Chamber of **political** importance?
3   What, according to Professor Elton, constituted the Tudor Revolution in Government?
4   How did a Privy Chamber emerge and did it suit or obstruct Cromwell's ambitions?
5   How far did control of the royal finances become bureaucratic under Cromwell?
6   How important did Cromwell make the role of the King's secretary?
7   'There was no Tudor Revolution in Government.' Is that a fair comment on Elton's thesis?
8   How did the Tudor monarchy control the provinces?
9   What effect did Henry VIII's reign have on Parliament?
10 Why was patronage so important?

11 Which were the major factions after the fall of Wolsey and what held them together?

12 What brought about the fall of Anne Boleyn?

13 'Cromwell could generally master his conservative opponents but the King's personal affections defeated him.' How far were Henry's fourth and fifth marriages responsible for Cromwell's ruin?

14 To what extent was religion of importance in the faction politics of the 1540s?

15 Why was control of the Privy Chamber of ever greater importance towards the end of the reign?

16 Under what conditions did Henry's foreign policy become important in Europe?

17 Did Henry VIII achieve anything in his foreign policy in the 1530s?

18 What was gained and what was lost in the wars against France and Scotland in the 1540s?

19 How far was Henry VIII's foreign policy in 'the national interest'?

B *Essay questions*

1 How far was Thomas Cromwell an innovator in government?

2 Can the government of England under Henry VIII and Cromwell in the 1530s fairly be described as tyrannical?

3 'Cromwell was no policy maker – he merely carried out his master's wishes with ruthless efficiency.' Discuss.

4 How do you explain the downfall of so successful a minister as Thomas Cromwell?

5 Why were the last years of Henry VIII's reign after the fall of Cromwell so confused and difficult?

6 What were the aims and achievements of Henry VIII's foreign policy from 1529 to 1547?

15 DOCUMENTARY EXERCISE – WAS HENRY VIII MANIPULATED?

From George Cavendish The Life and Death of Cardinal Wolsey. (*Cavendish was Wolsey's gentleman-usher who remained with his master until the latter's death and then returned to his home county of Suffolk. He wrote this life during the reign of Queen Mary. This extract comes from Wolsey's death-bed speech. He is speaking of King Henry.*)

A.   He is sure a prince of royal courage, and hath a princely heart; and rather than he will either miss or want any part of his will or appetite, he will put the loss of one half of his realm in danger. For I assure you I have often kneeled before him in his privy chamber on my knees the space of an hour or two to persuade him therefro. Therefore, Master Kingston, if it chance hereafter you to be one of his privy council (as for your wisdom and other qualities ye be meet so to be) I warn you to be well advised and assured what matter ye put in his head; for ye shall never pull it out again.

From William Roper The Life of Sir Thomas More. (*Roper was a member of More's household from 1518 and married his daughter Margaret in 1521. His 'Life' was written in the 1550s. In this extract More, who has just resigned his office of Chancellor, is giving some advice to Cromwell on how to handle the King.*)

B.   'Master Cromwell,' quoth he, 'you are now entered into the service of a most noble, wise and liberal prince. If you will follow my poor advice, you shall, in your counsel-giving unto his grace, ever tell him what he ought to do but never what he is able to do. So shall you show yourself a true, faithful servant and a right worthy counsellor. For if a lion know his own strength, hard were it for any man to rule him.'

1   *In what ways do these two sources agree or disagree in their picture of Henry VIII?*

The French ambassador Marillac wrote this character sketch of Henry in 1540. He lists what he considers to be Henry's three main vices, or 'plagues'. The first is greed.

C.   Thence proceeds the second plague, distrust and fear. The King, knowing how many changes he has made, and what tragedies and scandals he has created, would fain keep in favour with everybody, but does not trust a single man, expecting to see them all offended, and he will not cease to dip his hand in blood as long as he doubts his people. Hence every day edicts are published so sanguinary [bloody] that with a thousand guards one would scarce be safe. Hence too it is that now with us, as affairs incline, he makes alliances which last as long as it makes for him to keep them.

The third plague, lightness and inconsistency proceeds partly from the other two and partly from the nature of the nation, and has perverted the rights of religion, marriage, faith and promise, as softened wax can be altered to any form.

John Foxe had supported religious reform in the reign of Henry VIII and on the accession of the Catholic Mary in 1553 had to flee the country. While in exile he collected and published accounts of the Protestant martyrs in England which he later published with additional material on earlier martyrs and the European reformers see page 421.

D.   So long as Queen Anne, Thomas Cromwell, Archbishop Cranmer, Master Denny, Doctor Butts, with such like were about him, and could prevail with him, what organ of Christ's glory did more good in the Church than he? . . . Thus, while good counsel was about him, and could be heard, the King did much good. So again, when sinister and wicked counsel, under subtle and crafty pretences, had gotten once the foot in, thrusting truth and verity out of the prince's ears, how much religion and all good things went prosperously forward before, so much, on the contrary side, all revolted backward again.

2   *What reservations might one have about each of sources C and D, bearing in mind the author and context of each of them?*

From D Starkey The Reign of Henry VIII . . . *(1985):*

E.   Henry was not the archetypal strong King. He was not weak either, but he was manipulable – and through his strongest defences, his suspiciousness and his refusal ever to give his confidence completely . . .

From D Starkey The English Court . . . *(1987):*

F.   The England of Henry VIII, in fact, experienced the politics of manipulation in an acute form. This was due, on the one hand, to the King's character, and, on the other, to the reconstructed Privy Chamber of 1518. For Henry VIII, behind Holbein's image of the archetypal strong king, was profoundly open to influence.

3   *Explain Starkey's reference to the Privy Chamber.*

4   *What similarities are there between Starkey's view and the opinion expressed by Marillac in source C?*

From J J Scarisbrick Henry VIII *(1968):*

G.   [In 1540] . . . the failure of the Cleves marriage exposed Henry once more at his most vulnerable point. Catherine Howard, Norfolk's niece, had been placed before a ready King, and the bait worked quickly. Cromwell was about to be trapped . . .
     His fall was very like Wolsey's. He was hustled out from below, the victim of a conspiracy waged by the same

Norfolk, aided by Gardiner and his fellows, who used Catherine Howard, as Anne Boleyn had been used before, as their pawn.

From J J Scarisbrick Henry VIII (1968):

H.   About eight months after Cromwell's death, Marillac reported that Henry was very gloomy and malevolent; that he suspected that his very ministers had brought about Cromwell's destruction by false accusations 'and on light pretexts'; that he had said so to their faces; that he now knew that Cromwell had been the most faithful servant that he had ever had. At the time, probably, Henry had never fully understood how and why Cromwell was suddenly swept away. The King had been stampeded by a faction bent on a *coup d'état* and swept along by it like the suggestible man that he was. It is no contradiction to say this so soon after asserting his complete absorption in, and command of, the policies which some have said Cromwell was furtively trying to foist upon him. For Henry was often this: a vulnerable and volatile thing, just at the moment when he seemed most assured and thrustful.

From P Gwyn The King's Cardinal: The Rise and Fall of Thomas Wolsey:

I.   But one thing Henry was not was someone who could be easily manipulated, whether by an individual or a faction, and even those he fell head over heels in love with, such as Anne Boleyn and, to a lesser extent, Catherine Howard, though they obviously affected what he did, were never able to manage him to any significant extent.

J.   Despite the efforts of his most outstanding modern biographer the [reference is to J J Scarisbrick], the prevalent view is that Henry was a King who was easily manipulated; indeed, so weak was he that he needed to be manipulated for anything to happen. This view has been attacked here. It was Henry who made Wolsey, and it was Henry who destroyed him, just as he was to make and destroy Thomas Cromwell. He made all the important decisions and appointments. In every sense he ruled.

5   *What is Gwyn's view on Henry VIII's character?*

6   *How well does Gwyn's view fit in with the view expressed by Scarisbrick?*

From E W Ives 'Faction at the Court of Henry VIII: the Fall of Anne Boleyn' History, *no. 190 (June 1972):*

K.   In fact there is no necessary incongruence between the mastery which Henry impressed on his subjects and vulnerability to pressure. One resolution lies in Henry's known inconsistency. At one time he would set a course which horrified his ministers, at another he would not interfere when a course was set which he disliked. The King was master, but never in a steady autocratic fashion. He would lead, follow, manipulate, assist, observe or ignore as it suited him. This very fact invited pressure; everything depended upon attracting or distracting the King's attention.

L.   In truth no one succeeded Cromwell, and Henry determined from now on to avoid reliance on single over-powerful ministers. From mid-1540 to mid-1546, he took sole responsibility for all that was attempted and done: those were the years of his truly personal rule. But if he supposed that he might thus free himself from the troubles of faction he was mistaken; behind the deceptive facade of a dominant kingship, the battles of ambition and policy continued as vigorous as ever.

7   *Summarise the different interpretations of Henry VIII given by sources E–L.*

Obviously there have been many views expressed on whether or not Henry was manipulated. The next exercise will ask you to make up your own mind on the problem (or at least to suggest a possible answer) and in doing so there are a number of points that you should bear in mind. What is meant by 'manipulation'? Are there areas where you would prefer to use the words 'influence' or 'persuade' – and what are the differences between them? Remember that you are dealing with almost forty years of a man's life – do you expect consistency of out-look and behaviour over this length of time? Would the ailing over-weight king of the 1540s react in the same way as the confident young athlete of the 1520s or can experience/cynicism/self-deception be taken into account? Look at the **ways** in which Henry could be manip-ulated and the **occasions** when it might have happened. Was Henry more vulnerable in some areas than in others? Consider why people might want to act in this way and how the structure of the political scene might have made it more or less likely.

8   *Use the information from Chapters III, IV and V to provide your own answer to the question 'Was Henry VIII manipulated?', providing evidence to back up your conclusions and comparing those conclusions to sources E–L given above.*

VI

EDWARD VI 1547–53

—

Edward VI, anon.

1 INTRODUCTION

THE whole period from 1540 to 1560 has sometimes been described by
historians as one of 'crisis'. A cursory knowledge of these years reveals
a number of obvious problems: difficulties of succession leading to a
boy King followed by two Queens; unsettling changes from Catholic to
Protestant, Protestant to Catholic and back again; frequent foreign
wars leading to government financial crises and wider economic difficulties for the English people; and a striking reduction in cloth exports.
All of this was aggravated by a dramatic price rise (*see pages 442-4*)
which was to have major economic and social consequences and which
was made worse by debasement of the coinage, a short term financial
maneouvre whereby the government reduced the content of gold or

silver in coins in order to make its money go further.

Most of these problems seemed to loom in 1547 when the 10-year-old Edward VI succeeded to the throne. While the young King already showed signs of piety and intellect, it would be some years before he could rule in person and the spectres of faction struggle and even of civil war arose in the minds of contemporaries. The two immediate precedents for a minority, those of Henry VI in 1422 and Edward V in 1483, did not inspire confidence. Moreover England's religious destiny was to say the least vague in 1547. It seemed likely that some form of Protestantism was to become the official doctrine, but powerful conservative forces remained among both clergy and laity. In foreign policy relations with Scotland and France were confused, and serious financial problems threatened the state in the likely event of war. If a war did break out the government would be tempted to debase the coinage, a move that was likely to further fuel inflation and hence to increase poverty and the possibility of domestic unrest.

Two factors might bring some comfort to this troubled legacy: even if one hesitates to accept Elton's theory of a 'Revolution in Government' it is clear that the Tudor state was more powerful than it had been earlier in the century before Cromwell's reforms. However, this advantage was weakened by a minority and hence by the uncertainty of who would wield this power and by the previous government's sales and gifts of former monastic lands. The second factor was the financial potential of Church wealth, but – as already just indicated – much of this had been disposed of and the scope for further spoilation of the Church was rather limited.

2 PROTECTOR SOMERSET

Henry VIII's will provided for a Council, but named no individual regent, although it did leave open the possibility of a Protector. On 12 March 1547, Edward Seymour, Earl of Hertford and Edward VI's uncle, obtained letters patent giving him near-sovereign powers as Lord Protector of the Realm and Governor of the King's Person. This gave him the right to appoint whom he wished to the Council. He also quickly secured advancement for himself to become Duke of Somerset. There were two fifteenth-century precedents for a protectorate during a minority: 1422 and 1483, and both these occasions involved the King's uncle. Finally Somerset, advised by his mentor Sir William Paget, forced Thomas Wriothesley, the Earl of Southampton to leave the Council.

Historians are divided in their view of Somerset. An older generation that included A F Pollard saw him as a high-minded idealist, a friend of the poor and an opponent of religious persecution. While only a handful of heretics perished during his period of government, the image of the 'good duke' has been seriously dented by more modern writers. He is seen as self-seeking, ambitious and arrogant by those who have researched his origins.

Edward Seymour was the son of a Wiltshire knight, whose family had risen through Jane Seymour's marriage to Henry VIII. He had amassed extensive estates in Somerset and Wiltshire, some of it extorted from William Barlow, Bishop of Bath and Wells. Thus his inherited landed income amounted to £2400 a year by 1540 and his gains since then had brought him a further £5000 a year. With this fortune he was able to build his own palace, Somerset House, knocking down part of a densely populated part of London including a cloister of St Paul's Cathedral in the process.

Once in government Somerset neglected the Council, except to use it from time to time as little more than a rubber stamp. He preferred to work through his own household, sometimes referred to as his 'new' council. Of its leading members – Smith, Stanhope, Cecil, Wolf, Thynne and Gray – only one (Smith) was a member of the King's Council.

Two of Somerset's early measures can be used to put this unfavourable impression to the test. The first concerns his treatment of his brother Thomas, who was executed for treason on 20 March 1549. Thomas had sought for himself a higher position in the state, being disappointed at not being named to the Regency Council formed in 1547. He had unwisely sought Wriothesley's support, but the latter denounced him and gained re-admission to the Council as a reward. His marriage to the former Queen, Catherine Parr, in April 1547 raised some eyebrows, although he had been betrothed to her before as early as 1543. When Catherine died shortly afterwards Thomas was accused of trying to seduce the 15-year-old Princess Elizabeth, and there were even rumours by December 1548 that she was pregnant by him. Clearly Thomas had sailed fairly close to the wind, but Somerset's treatment of his brother shows a streak of ruthlessness which would earn him few allies.

The second such measure is the act to repeal Henry VIII's treason laws and the more conservative religious legislation. The new act resembled Edward III's statute of 1352 which defined treason as plotting the King's death (or that of his consort or heir), waging war against the King or serving his enemies. To deny the Royal Supremacy in writing – or three times in speech – would also constitute treason, but no offence could be proved without two witnesses. In some ways then, this new act could be seen as a bid for personal popularity like Henry VIII in 1509 or Mary in 1553. However, a closer examination of the act shows that it was still fairly repressive for the dice were heavily loaded against the accused who had no right to confront hostile witnesses, no counsel of his own and little chance to prepare his case. Moreover Thomas Seymour, and indeed Somerset himself, were to discover that an Act of Attainder could be used in the last resort if the

1547 act did not apply. The Catholic bishops who opposed Somerset's religious policies all ended up in prison for refusing to carry out the new religious programme, while to control religious subversion a separate act of 1547 ordered prison for those who disturbed the peace by speaking irreverently of the Eucharist.

However, before a full picture can be arrived at it will be necessary to look closely at Somerset's better known policies – on religion, social reform and his reaction to the 1549 rebellions and on foreign policy.

3 SOMERSET'S FOREIGN POLICY

For the Protector, as he surveyed his responsibilities in 1547, the most important task was to face the twin challenge in foreign affairs of a hostile France and an unpredictable Scotland. Henry VIII's legacy in foreign policy was not just commitments against these two traditional enemies, but also the consequences of a growth of conscious national feeling, especially since the break with Rome. Englishmen's insularity – their sense of being in a world apart – had markedly increased. There was also the expense of embarking on modern warfare, which tended paradoxically to bind England more closely to the continent in a military sense, for the best firearms were to be had from Antwerp, and foreign mercenaries, needed to supplement the tiny standing forces, could only come from the continent too. Hence the need to borrow heavily in order to sustain a military campaign: in 1549 alone £250 000 was borrowed – half of it from abroad.

Somerset was determined to bring about a union of the royal houses of England and Scotland, asserting a claim to the Scottish throne that went back to the time of Edward I. He hoped, rather idealistically, to marry the 10-year-old Edward VI to the 5-year-old Mary, Queen of Scots, who had succeeded on her father's death in 1542. By March 1547, the pro-English Protestant party had collapsed to all intents and purposes, and on 31 July their last stronghold, the castle of St Andrews fell to a French force sent over by the new King Henry II, keen to cut a dash on the European stage by extending French influence in Scotland. Moreover he was keen to recover Boulogne from England immediately, although Henry VIII had agreed to return it to France by 1554. For the French there was also the prize of a marriage between the Dauphin Francis and the Queen of Scots.

Somerset's invading army in 1547 enjoyed early success at the Battle of Pinkie Clough, a mere 9 miles from Edinburgh, but Somerset had neither the military strength nor the funds to remain in Scotland in force. Thus he decided to leave a string of garrisons to guard strongpoints along the border and up the east coast as far as Dundee. These were designed to prevent concentrations of Scottish troops, to intercept French reinforcements and, more obliquely, to encourage the fledgling

Scottish Reformation. Unfortunately the English fleet could not seal off Scotland completely and several of the forts were difficult to resupply. The Protector's worst fears were confirmed in June 1548 when a French force landed at Leith with 6000 troops and spirited the child Queen away to Brest where she arrived in August. Somerset responded by sending up an army to relieve the garrisons, but almost all of them had had to be withdrawn by the autumn of 1549. The long effort to control Scotland seemed to have been counter-productive. Scotland had a pro-French government and a French army was poised on England's northern border. Meanwhile Henry II declared war on England on 8 August 1549 and proceeded to attack Boulogne.

It hardly needs to be said that the costs of the Scottish campaign were prodigious: out of £1 386 000 spent on military affairs during Edward VI's reign £580 000 was spent by Somerset on this one campaign. He spent £351 000 on troops alone – 50 per cent more than Henry VIII had spent in five years. Somerset paid for the wars by the usual expedients: he debased the coinage (£537 000 was raised in this way between 1547 and 1551), he tapped some of the resources released by the dissolution of chantries and colleges in 1547 (£110 000 had come from this source by Michaelmas 1548), he obtained a grant of parliamentary taxation (£335 000 was raised in this way during Edward VI's reign, of which £189 000 went for war and defence) and he resorted to the usual steps of Crown land sales and borrowing. The Protector's legacy in foreign affairs to his successor was failure in Scotland, a continuing struggle against France and extremely straitened finances.

4 SOMERSET AND RELIGION

Ever since 1546 the Catholic faction in English politics had lacked effective leadership. Norfolk was in prison, Gardiner, Bishop of Winchester, had been excluded from Henry VIII's Regency Council and Tunstall, the Bishop of Durham was too old to influence events. Wriothesley alone was the most effective member of the conservative group.

Meanwhile Protestant expectations from the new government grew apace as exiled preachers like Becon, Turner and Hooper returned. Foreign reformers also sought refuge in England, especially after the Battle of Mühlberg when the Emperor Charles V destroyed the forces of the Protestant Schmalkaldic League and ensured that Strasbourg was no longer a Protestant haven. Thus England became a major centre of Protestant theology as the continental reformers arrived: Bucer who became Regius Professor of Divinity at Cambridge, John a Lasco from Poland who settled at a London church, Peter Martyr Vermigli who secured the Regius Professorship at Oxford, Bernardo Ochino and John Knox recently released from a French galley.

In their wake fresh signs of religious radicalism appeared in

England: subversive preaching, the suppression here and there of the Mass (in 1548 alone thirty-one tracts appeared against the Catholic Mass), iconoclasm – the destruction of church sculptures and paintings which were condemned as being idolatrous. Services were said in the vernacular, while ballads, sermons and plays all seemed to herald a new Protestant dawn. Indeed the Council was so worried by this ferment that they re-imposed censorship in August 1549. It must be borne in mind, however, that total numbers of Protestants remained small – perhaps one-fifth of Londoners and smaller numbers concentrated overwhelmingly in the South, where Kent, Essex, Sussex and Bristol were particular centres. The printing presses were busy too – out of 394 books printed during the Protectorate no less than 159 were written by Protestant reformers.

The government's response seemed, by contrast, rather cautious. Edward VI himself had, of course, already been brought up to be a Protestant and many of Somerset's supporters were men of advanced religious views. Yet Mary Tudor's evident public Catholicism was tolerated and Somerset seems to have been keen to avoid antagonising Charles V, who could have caused difficulty by intervening in Somerset's Scottish campaign (*see pages 163–4*). The initial religious steps taken by Somerset's government were, therefore, rather hesitant. Thomas Cromwell's 1538 'Injunctions' (*see page 106*) were re-introduced with additions – these encouraged iconoclasm and the Bible in English, but they went little further than that. The reading of Cranmer's *Homilies* was also encouraged; these were sets of prepared sermons with a strong Protestant slant, for example the homily 'On Justification' which taught the Lutheran doctrine of justification by faith alone (*see page 115*). Finally some of the emphatically Catholic legislation from Henry VIII's reign was repealed along with the treason laws already discussed. Parliament met on 4 November 1547 to revoke the Act of Six Articles of 1539 which had affirmed the doctrine of transubstantiation, the King's Book of 1543 which reinforced it and the Act for the Advancement of True Religion also of 1543, which had effectively made Bible reading an upper class male preserve.

The remaining Catholics in the political nation were not slow to oppose these measures. Gardiner took the lead by pointing out that the re-issued 'Injunctions', the *Paraphrases* and the *Homilies* all contravened Henry VIII's religious laws from his last years. His case was of course much weakened by the repeal of Catholic legislation mentioned above. His protests led to a spell in the Fleet Prison from September 1547 to January 1548, followed by confinement to London. In June 1548 he was sent to the Tower and eventually deprived of his bishopric in 1551. Gardiner probably avoided a worse fate through his scrupulous regard for the law, but he was not the only one to suffer persecution. Edmund Bonner, the Bishop of London was deprived of his See in October 1549, while 1551 brought the resignations of Bishops Vesey of Exeter, Day of

Chichester and Heath of Worcester. Naturally these vacancies enabled ardent Protestants to take their places – the likes of Ridley, Ponet, Coverdale, Scory and Hooper.

The first real measure against the Catholic Church came in the Chantries Act of 1547, which completed the attack on the Church's corporate property begun by Henry VIII. A total of 2374 chantries and chapels, 90 colleges and 110 hospitals were dissolved. The reasons were partly doctrinal, as chantries were a clear expression of the Catholic doctrine of Purgatory, which encouraged good works like the founding of chantry chapels where prayers were said to keep the soul of the benefactor out of Purgatory. They were also material and political, for money was sorely needed for the Protector's wars against both Scotland and France. The cash yield from the chantries was in fact around £160 000, a sum about 20 per cent of that yielded by the dissolution of the monasteries. There were 2500 priests made redundant, of whom 2000 were found benefices. While the total number of schools seems to have been reduced slightly (*see page 415*). Most were refounded, e.g. as 'Edward VI' schools and by 1553 probably there were somewhat more schools than there had been in 1547. The act itself put of course its own gloss on the motives for the new law:

> . . . considering that a great part of superstition and errors in
> Christian religion hath been brought into the minds and
> estimation of men . . . by devising and phantasing vain opinions
> of Purgatory and Masses satisfactory to be done for them which
> be departed, the which doctrine and vain opinion by nothing
> more is maintained and upholden than by the abuse of trentals,
> chantries and other provisions made for the continuance of the
> said blindness and ignorance; and further considering and
> understanding that the alteration, change, and amendment of
> the same, and converting to goodly and godly uses, as in
> erecting of grammar schools to the education of youth in virtue
> and godliness, the further augmenting of the universities, and
> better provision for the poor and needy, cannot in this present
> Parliament be provided and conveniently done, nor cannot nor
> ought to any other manner person be committed than to the
> King's Highness, whose Majesty with and by the advice of his
> Highness' most prudent Council can and will most wisely and
> beneficially, both for the honour of God and the weal of this His
> Majesty's realm, order, alter, convert and dispose the same. . . .

1 *According to this document, what seems to have been the main religious motive for dissolving the chantries?*

2 *What does the extract claim to be the main practical reason for the attack on the chantries?*

3 *Does this document just obscure an underlying financial motive for the dissolution of the chantries or does it clarify other motives?*

Various other more minor religious measures followed: an act allowing priests to marry was eventually passed in February 1549, and around 20 per cent of priests did so – giving them of course a vested interest in the Reformation. Earlier in 1547 another act authorised the giving out of Communion in both kinds, but the major piece of religious legislation of the Somerset years was the Prayer Book of 1549 and its attendant Act of Uniformity. In some ways the new Prayer Book leant towards Protestantism: e.g. the idea of a 'Common' prayer book representing a dialogue between priest and people and suggesting the Lutheran idea of the 'priesthood of all believers', as opposed to the Catholic view of the priest as an intermediary between God and laymen. Yet on the central issue of the Eucharist the more moderate Catholics and Protestants could derive some comfort from the ambiguity of the Prayer Book's phrasing.

Radical Protestants like Bucer, Ridley and Hooper called for further changes, but Gardiner (from the Tower of course) could detect no actual harm in the new book. For him it was in no way ideal, but it was acceptable and he seized eagerly on the Book's ambiguities. Somerset had in fact, despite his own radical religious views, deliberately sought an unclear settlement in order to avoid upsetting Charles V.

Indeed he even assured Charles V that the Prayer Book was a conservative reform, and there was in reality a good deal about the new book that was conservative: priests still wore traditional vestments and there was still a railed-off altar at the east end instead of a more Protestant Communion table in the centre of the Church. Worshippers would also find other familiar features of Catholic ritual largely intact: candles, the chrism of consecrated oil, prayers for the dead, commemoration of the Virgin Mary and other saints, auricular confession, anointing at baptism and extreme unction. Conservatives could feel reassured that the line would now be held after so much had been lost: clerical celibacy, Communion in one kind only, images and wall paintings and the four ceremonies of Candlemas, Ash Wednesday, Palm Sunday palms and creeping to the Cross on Good Friday. Yet few Englishmen could have supposed in 1549 that the pace of religious reform would quicken following a series of events that led to Somerset's fall in the autumn of that year and his replacement by Northumberland.

5 SOMERSET, SOCIAL REFORM AND THE 1549 REBELLIONS

The popular disturbances of 1549 engulfed much of the country. In May there was unrest in Somerset, Wiltshire, Hampshire, Kent, Sussex and Essex. June saw the so-called Prayer Book Rebellion in Devon and Cornwall, while in July Norfolk, Suffolk, Cambridgeshire, Hertfordshire, Northamptonshire, Bedfordshire, Buckinghamshire, Oxfordshire and Yorkshire joined the list. In August, Leicestershire and Rutland followed. In most of these counties the restoration of order was carried out by the local nobility and gentry, but troops were called in from the Scottish campaign to deal with Oxfordshire, Buckinghamshire and Suffolk and there were set piece battles in the South-West (2500 deaths) and in Norfolk (3000 deaths).

Devon and Cornwall were among the remotest communities in Tudor England, and their isolation was accentuated by poor communications and by the retention by ordinary people – at least in Cornwall – of the Cornish language. Cornwall especially had a low standard of living and severe problems of law enforcement with no resident nobles. When the Prayer Book (Western) Rebellion broke out in Devon in June 1549 it was marked by religious conservatism. The parishioners of Sampford Courtenay found the new 1549 Prayer Book incomprehensible and helped to swell a force of rebels including Cornishmen, who gathered at Crediton by 20 June. Sir Peter Carew, a Devon gentleman lately living in Lincolnshire, saw the size of the rebel host at first hand and reported back in person to London. Somerset's reaction was cautious: he did not see the unrest as serious and he ordered pardons for those involved in the original commotion at Sampford Courtenay. It is easy to see the sense in the Protector's stance: he was already faced with enclosure riots in a good many other areas and the French might invade at any time. Therefore, instead of intervening himself, he sent Lord Russell to the West Country to enforce order on 24 June. By August the rebels still besieged Exeter and Somerset's diary entry of 27 July betrays a certain harshness – the rebels, he wrote, 'speak traiterous words against the King and in favour of the traiterous rebels, ye shall hang two or three of them . . . And that will be the only and best stay of all those talks'. Ten days later Russell had breached Exeter's walls and raised the siege, while at the same time war broke out against France, thus realising Somerset's growing fear that the French might help to keep the rebellion alive. The final struggle came in mid-August when thousands of rebels died in a pitched battle at Okehampton.

A study of the Prayer Book Rebels' demands shows an overwhelming call for a return to traditional Catholicism. It is clear that they misunderstood the new Prayer Book to some extent, believing that children could only be baptised on Sundays. They disliked particularly the new English language service, preferring Latin or Cornish and provoked Cranmer's comment that more Cornishmen must surely understand English than Latin. Nicholas Udall, a leading Protestant convert, maintained that the western commons had been deceived by the priests and he and other reformers seized on the propaganda opportunity to conclude that popery led inevitably to rebellion and anarchy.

While most of the Devon Articles are religious, anti-gentry feeling creeps in here and there: Article 13, for example, demands a reduction in the size of gentry households, probably because some retainers abused the social power of the landowning class. Article 14 urged the restoration of abbey and chantry lands acquired by the local gentry and giving them a vested interest in the progress of the Reformation. Indeed Somerset himself said of the rebels that they, 'hath conceived a wonderful hate against the gentlemen and taketh them all as their enemies'. His own attitude to social reform had helped to inspire this elsewhere as well.

Kett's Rebellion, which presented the authorities with an even more serious problem than the Prayer Book Rebellion, erupted also in June 1549. An anti-enclosure riot was followed by more disturbances in Norfolk led by Robert Kett, a well-to-do tanner turned country landowner who brought leadership to an incoherent series of anti-enclosure riots. By 10 July Kett was in Norwich and two days later he was on Mousehold Heath overlooking the city with no less than 16 000 rebels, equivalent to one-third of all men of military age in Norfolk.

The authorities' reaction to this outrage was low key: the local gentry made little effort to disperse them, preferring either to parley with them or to ignore them. In Norwich the city fathers took a similarly conciliatory view, remembering perhaps that unlike Exeter their city walls were not intact. Meanwhile Somerset ordered a herald to offer them a pardon if they went home – his proposal was insultingly refused and by 23 July the entire city of Norwich, the second city in the country, was in rebel hands. On 30 July William Parr, Marquis of Northampton and Catherine Parr's brother arrived with 14 000 men, including a contingent of Italian mercenaries. After a skirmish Northampton was driven off humiliatingly and the government had to put their faith in John Dudley, Earl of Warwick, who entered Norwich on 24 August. On 27 August he brought the Kett host to battle at Dussindale when as many as 3000 rebels were killed. Kett's execution for treason on 7 December completed the repression in which 48 others are also known to have died.

It is to some extent reasonable to blame Somerset for the outbreak of the movement. His genuine concern to help the commons encouraged rumours in East Anglia that he would redress the peasants' grievances and that he would condone direct action on their part. There is, however, no evidence for this latter belief and the Kett Rebels' demands ranged much more widely than Somerset's current concerns. These did mention enclosures, but they also complained about inflation, the erosion of commons' rights over common land and the rapaciousness of lawyers. In short the agrarian points in their manifesto seemed to hark back to some golden age of prosperity and justice at the end of the fifteenth century, before the onset of the 'Price Revolution', and to earlier disturbances in the county (1381 perhaps and the upheavals of 1525). As far as religion was concerned the Norfolk peasants seem to have been devout and loyal Protestants, for the new 1549 Prayer Book was used daily – on several occasions by Robert Watson, Canon of Norwich and Matthew Parker. Seven of the articles of complaint can be described as religious, all of them echoing sentiments from earlier Parliaments or Injunctions.

Yet how far is Somerset to blame for failing to stamp out the rising earlier? In East Anglia he could no more rely on the local gentry than he could in the South-West. The leading local magnate, the Duke of Norfolk, had languished in the Tower since 1547 and most of the fourteen upper gentry and the 424 gentlemen who remained in the county either lacked the resources to act or deemed it prudent to bide their time and see how things would develop. It is also possible, of course, that some of them may have wanted the rebellion to run its course in order to show Somerset the danger of his social policies. Somerset's reaction to the news from Norfolk resembled his response to the Prayer Book Rebellion. He still had important military commitments in Scotland and in France, where the new King, Henry II, declared war on England on 8 August and proceeded to attack Boulogne, and he was aware of threats to law and order elsewhere in England. Hence the Protector's initial response was a conciliatory one: he offered a pardon which was rejected by Kett on 21 July. Then Somerset authorised the sending of the forces commanded by Northampton, who was the highest-ranking Privy Councillor after Somerset himself, a relation of Henry VIII's by marriage and a veteran of the 1544 campaign in Scotland. Moreover he was accompanied by Lords Wentworth and Sheffield, who also had military experience. Following the ignominious dispersal of Northampton's forces and Sheffield's death at the hands of the mob Somerset was stunned. He blamed Northampton for ineptitude and realised that the Kett Rebellion was a much more serious affair than he had thought; thus he decided to send Warwick to put it down. Somerset could have supervised the repression himself, but Russell had coped in Devon and Warwick seemed up to the task in East Anglia.

An older generation of historians interpreted Somerset's apparent indecisiveness as a twinge of conscience, and for A F Pollard Somerset was choosing the path of principle over expediency. Yet Somerset's letters make clear his opposition to all rebellions – they were, he wrote, 'lewd, seditious and evil disposed persons'. His actions look more and more to modern eyes the only realistic military strategy, and one which seems to have enjoyed the confidence of the Council for a long while during the summer of 1549. After all Kett was not physically threatening the government unlike the rebels in 1381, 1450 and 1497; nowhere in the rebels' demands was there talk of releasing the King from the grip of evil ministers. Unfortunately the Kett rising was the occasion for the fall of Somerset by October 1549, and criticism of him built up in the Council and elsewhere as this letter shows, written to him by William Paget, one of his closest advisers, on 7 July 1549:

I told your Grace the truth, and was not believed: well, now your Grace sees it, what says your Grace? Marry, the King's subjects out of all discipline, out of obedience, caring neither for Protector or King, and much less for any other mean officer. And what is the cause? Your own levity, your softness, your opinion to be good to the poor. I know, I say, your good meaning and honest nature. But I say, sir, it is great pity (as the common proverb goes) in a warm summer that ever fair weather should do harm. It is a pity that your so much gentleness should be an occasion of so great an evil as is now chanced in England by these rebels . . . Consider, I beseech you most humbly, with all my heart, that society in a realm does consist and is maintained by mean of religion and law . . . Look well whether you have either law or religion at home, and I fear you shall find neither. The use of the old religion is forbidden by a law, and the use of the new is not yet printed in the stomachs of the eleven or twelve parts in the realm, what countenance soever men make outwardly to please them in whom they see the power rests. Now, sir, for the law: where is it used in England at liberty? Almost nowhere. The foot taketh upon him the part of the head, and commons is become a king, appointing conditions and laws to the governors, saying, 'Grant this, and that, and we will go home' . . . I know in this matter of the commons every man of the Council hath misliked your proceedings, and wished it otherwise.

1   *What qualities of character is Paget criticising in Somerset?*
2   *How fair are Paget's criticisms of Somerset's policy?*

Somerset's fall came soon after Warwick's suppression of the Kett rebellion, which represented at the very least a blow to his prestige as Protector. By the end of September 1549, a majority on the Council wanted to remove him, and the only way to achieve this was through some form of conspiracy. On 5 October, the Protector issued a proclamation calling all loyal subjects to rally to King and Protector at Hampton Court. Eighteen councillors including Russell and Herbert issued counter-proclamations, and by 14 October, Somerset was in the Tower. The reason for his fall was – as much as any other factor – his political isolation which sprang from his autocratic methods, his abrasive arrogance and his high-minded pride. The Kett fiasco came as an opportunity for his many enemies in the political community to combine to oust him – dismayed more by his authoritarianism than by any alleged weakness.

6 GOVERNMENT, POLITICS AND FOREIGN POLICY UNDER NORTHUMBERLAND

John Dudley, Earl of Warwick, was the eldest son of Edmund Dudley, one of Henry VII's tax-collectors who had been executed by Henry VIII in 1510. Warwick is normally referred to as Northumberland as he was raised to that Dukedom in October 1551. Having enjoyed a successful military career under Henry VIII he emerged as Lord President of the Council and Great Master of the King's Household on Somerset's fall after a series of skilful manoeuvres among the tangled factions of the Council. When Somerset was disgraced Warwick led a faction of seven councillors, including Cranmer, who favoured a further radical religious reform against fourteen councillors who favoured a more conservative position and a deal with the Emperor Charles V. Wriothesley, accused of plotting a second *coup*, was dismissed from the Council together with his leading supporter the Earl of Arundel. Following the fiercest struggle for power since the fifteenth century Warwick soon to be Northumberland now had a majority of the Council behind him including the Marquis of Dorset and the Bishop of Ely.

Northumberland's adverse reputation as the supplanter of the 'Good Duke' of Somerset and as the cynical schemer trying to deny the throne to Mary in 1553 has recently been challenged by historians. Certainly in financial affairs he could be seen as modestly successful after the insolvency that had marked Somerset's period of office. While he raised government revenue in many traditional ways: selling Crown lands, confiscating lead, coining bullion from Church plate and seizing episcopal lands, he was also more vigorous than his predecessor in collecting Crown debts, pruning government expenses and instituting regular audits. Above all perhaps, in March 1552 he appointed a Royal Commission to investigate the work of the revenue courts. Thus Smith, Cecil, Mildmay, Petre and Gresham cut their administrative teeth on what Elton has called 'a genuine reform administration'. Gresham was exceptionally useful as an exchange manipulator and agent in Antwerp where many of the government's loans were raised. He was able to ensure that the government's foreign loans were punctually renewed or paid out of new loans. While he could do little to reduce the total owing at Antwerp (£132 000 was still outstanding at the end of 1552, with a further £109 000 owing at home), he could derive some satisfaction from negotiating an interest rate of 14 per cent when Charles V was having to pay 16 per cent.

The link between financial and foreign policy is an obvious one – clearly Northumberland's retrenchment would only succeed if he also ended Somerset's wars. On 24 March 1550 England and France signed the Treaty of Boulogne, whereby France was to keep the town in return for £133 333, English troops were to leave Scotland and no marriage was to take place between Mary, Queen of Scots and Edward VI. A further treaty at Angers arranged for Edward to marry Henry II's daughter, Elisabeth of Valois for a dowry of 200 000 crowns. The peace settlement was no doubt inglorious (Pollard called it 'the most ignominious signed by England during the century') but it showed realism in cutting England's losses. If the wars had gone on, it might have led to an intolerable strain on England's social fabric. The 1549 upheavals were a very recent memory.

A strong case could also be made out for the success of Northumberland's administrative policy. While Somerset had neglected the Council, Northumberland revived it, giving it an influx of new blood – twelve councillors were appointed in 1550, all of course pro-Northumberland. Even Somerset was brought back on to the Council in that year, but he lost his place there in September 1551 and indeed his life in January 1552 when he began to challenge Northumberland's authority and to plot against him. In the provinces, meanwhile, the Lord-Lieutenants appointed in 1549 following a precedent of Henry VIII to control the levies of troops in the shires, were kept in being and the network was extended with new appointments. Thus the Earls of Huntingdon and Westmorland enhanced their local standing through their lieutenancies, but were rarely able to attend the Council. In these ways the administrative machine first expanded by Thomas Cromwell in the 1530s was revitalised and prepared for its role in keeping government going during the ups and downs of the next ten years.

Even Northumberland's social policy has come in for praise. The background of the 1549 disturbances, three poor harvests aggravated by bad weather, soaring wheat prices (from 9 shillings a quarter in 1548–9 to 15 shillings a quarter in 1549–50 and 19 shillings a quarter in 1551–2) and the 1551 crisis in the cloth trade struck fear into Northumberland's government. The Lord President realised that if disorder were to be avoided, the authorities would have to show some concern for social justice and try to alleviate the effects of economic trends. While Hales' sheep tax was abandoned and the Enclosure Commissions wound up, the number of prosecutions for depopulation increased markedly. In 1552 two acts were passed on social issues: one to protect arable farming and to stop usury (money lending often at extortionate rates of interest), the other a new poor law to collect funds for the relief of the 'deserving' or 'impotent' poor. It seems, therefore, that Northumberland's concern for social justice was more effective than Somerset's better known measures.

7 NORTHUMBERLAND AND RELIGION

Northumberland's personal religious views are an enigma. In some ways he had seemed to be a conservative, although he had tried to bring members of all factions together to oppose Somerset. Yet this was the same man who had tried to persuade both Wriothesley and Arundel that he wanted to stop further religious change, and perhaps even to go back on some of the Protector's reforms. Certainly he was no scholar and it may be that he was swayed by the arguments of Protestant zealots, or that he came increasingly to see the best chance to preserve his own power in a further reformation.

The first barometer of the religious climate came in May 1550 with the issue of a new Ordinal, the service book used at the ordination of new priests. It showed its radical tone by ending the minor orders of sub-deacon, acolyte etc. and by urging new ministers to preach the gospel. It was first used at St Paul's in June 1550 when John Foxe was ordained priest by the new Bishop of London, Nicholas Ridley.

Ridley was one of a number of unashamed Protestants who were appointed to bishoprics under Northumberland. Bonner, the former Bishop of London had to be replaced following his deprivation, and Ridley set about at once to impose a more radically Protestant stamp on the diocese. Altars were replaced by Communion tables in the centre of the church rather than at the east end in almost every London church by the end of the year. Such a change of location may seem unimportant, but to sixteenth-century Protestants it was vital to make clear that the congregation was participating much more closely in religious ritual than in a Catholic church.

Other episcopal appointments included Hooper, who was nominated as Bishop of Gloucester in July 1550. Hooper, who had recently returned from exile in Strasbourg and Zurich, was a far more extreme Protestant than Ridley and indeed he at first refused consecration at Gloucester as he would have to wear what he described as 'popish' vestments. Cranmer and Ridley refused to consecrate him if he continued to insist on scriptural justification for any ceremonial, and Hooper spent a short term in jail before he agreed to go through with the original ceremony. Once installed as bishop Hooper was extremely active, administering the Church courts and conducting exhaustive tours of the diocese. The worst problem that he faced was the ignorance of the clergy: in 1551 he found that 168 out of 311 of his clergy could not repeat the ten commandments – clearly he would need wider support if his ministers were to be effective missionaries for the Reformation.

These ardent reformers often received their opportunity through the deprivation or resignation of their conservative predecessors: Heath of Worcester went to prison in May 1550 and was deprived in October 1551, while in May 1552 his See was amalgamated with Hooper's. Gardiner of Winchester lost his post in February 1551, Day of Chichester suffered deprivation in October 1551, Tunstall of Durham a year later and Rugge of Norwich and Vesey of Exeter both resigned. By late 1551 their Protestant replacements ensured that most bishops now favoured further religious reform.

Such reform was not long in coming, for in 1552 the Second Edwardian Prayer Book was published. In every way the new book marked a radical revision of the 1549 Book, as it manifestly broke the earlier compromise between Protestant doctrine and Catholic form by insisting that only forms of worship derived from Scripture were valid. Even the terms 'matins' and 'evensong' disappeared to be replaced by 'morning prayer' and 'evening prayer'. Yet the real touchstone of the new book's religious tone was bound to be its treatment of the Mass. In fact the word 'Mass' was dropped in favour of 'the Lord's Supper' or 'Holy Eucharist' and the priest's familiar medieval vestments were abolished in favour of a plain white surplice. The crucial change, however, came in the words of administration: where the 1549 Book had 'The Body of our Lord Jesus Christ which was given for thee preserve thye body and soul unto everlasting life', the 1552 Book substituted 'take and eat this in remembrance that Christ died for thee and feed on him in thy heart by faith with thanksgiving'. The Catholic doctrine of transubstantiation, which held that a physical change took place in the bread and the wine once they had been blessed by the priest, now deferred to a purely spiritual presence of Christ. Meanwhile altars became Communion tables and to satisfy some Protestants' anxieties the so-called 'Black Rubric' was inserted by order of the Council to affirm that kneeling at Communion in no way implied adoration or any sort of real, i.e. physical, presence.

Like its predecessor the 1552 Book was accompanied by an Act of Uniformity to enforce its use:

> ... that from and after the feast of All Saints next coming, all
> and every person and persons inhabiting within this realm or
> any other the King's Majesty's dominions, shall diligently and
> faithfully, having no lawful or reasonable excuse to be absent,
> endeavour themselves to resort to their parish church or chapel
> accustomed, ... and then and there to abide orderly and soberly
> during the time of the common prayer, preachings, or other
> service of God there to be used and ministered; upon pain of
> punishment by the censures of the Church. ...
>
> And by the authority aforesaid it is now further enacted that
> if any manner of person or persons inhabiting and being within
> this realm or any other the King's Majesty's dominions shall
> after the said feast of All Saints willingly and wittingly hear and
> be present at any other manner or form of common prayer, of
> administration of the sacraments, of making of ministers in the
> churches, or of any other rites contained in the book annexed to
> this act than is mentioned and set forth in the said book or that
> is contrary to the form of sundry provisions and exceptions
> contained in the foresaid former statute, and shall be thereof
> convicted according to the laws of this realm before the justices

... by the verdict of twelve men or by his or their own confession or otherwise, shall for the first offence suffer imprisonment for six months without bail . . ., and for the second offence being likewise convicted as is above said imprisonment for one whole year, and for the third offence in like manner imprisonment during his or their lives.

1 *How does the first paragraph suggest opposition to the 1552 Prayer Book, or simply religious indifference, might be expressed?*

2 *Account for the level of severity of the penalties fixed in the second paragraph.*

Northumberland's religious reforms were completed by Cranmer's Forty-two Articles which represented a decisively Protestant interpretation of the Christian faith. Clerical marriage was allowed in a bill passed in 1549, and the deprivations of priests in Mary Tudor's reign give some idea of the extent of clerical matrimony: 88 out of 319 in Essex, 1 in 3 in London, a quarter in Norwich, at least 70 out of 616 in the Lincoln diocese and 1 in 10 in the York diocese. Not all were necessarily keen Protestants for clerical marriage had its practical aspects: sons to till the glebe, a wife to order the household, tend the poultry and organise relations with female parishioners, but they would nonetheless have a vested interest in the preservation of this aspect at least of the Edwardian Reformation.

Much had therefore been enacted in Northumberland's period of office in the area of religion, but even the most resolute Protestants wondered sometimes whether they had the time or the manpower to carry out the root and branch reformation for which so many of them yearned. Some changes indeed had to be shelved like the projected alterations to canon law through constraints of time and opposition.

8 THE FALL OF NORTHUMBERLAND

Edward VI had enjoyed a fairly healthy childhood contrary to the myth of a boy sickly since birth, but early in 1553 he showed signs of incurable pulmonary tuberculosis, a disease which often displays numerous rallies and relapses. Now Northumberland realised that he would have to work fast in order to prevent the accession of Mary Tudor, which was likely to reverse his religious changes and to spell the end of his personal ascendancy. Edward VI himself seems to have been a party to this 'Devise for the Succession' as it was termed, whereby the provisions both of Henry VIII's 1543 Act of Succession and of his will were set aside in favour of Lady Jane Grey, the grand-daughter of Henry's younger sister Mary. Such an arrangement ignored not only Mary Tudor's claim; it also neglected the Stuart line of succession descended through the line of Henry VIII's elder sister Margaret. In addition Northumberland had ensured that Lady Jane Grey should marry his own son Lord Guildford Dudley – thus the 'Devise' came more and more to look like a crude plot to secure Northumberland's continued control in the likely event of Edward's early death.

Events unfolded rapidly as the King's health worsened during the summer of 1553. On 21 June 1553 letters patent bastardised the Princesses Mary and Elizabeth in defiance of the claims not only of Mary Queen of Scots, but also of Lady Jane Grey's mother Frances who was still alive and who should enjoy a stronger claim than a daughter of hers. On 6 July Edward died and three days later Queen Jane was proclaimed.

Mary Tudor reacted quickly to the threat, leaving London where she would have been in danger of arrest and going to Kenninghall in East Anglia from where she mustered her forces at Framlingham in Suffolk having been proclaimed Queen Mary I at Bury St Edmunds. Over the next few days the conservative East Anglian gentry who had rallied to her initially were joined by national figures like Bath, Sussex and Derby and many gentlemen like the Protestant Sir Peter Carew in Devon and Sir Thomas Wyatt in Kent. Some nobles' rivalry with the Grey faction led them to take Mary's side – the Hastings family of Leicestershire would be an example of this category. On 14 July Northumberland left London for Cambridge and on the 19 July Mary was proclaimed Queen in the capital in what Bindoff described as 'the greatest mass demonstration of loyalty ever accorded to a Tudor'. One by one the Privy Councillors had begun to swing her way and the Earl of Arundel, a scion of England's most prestigious family, the Howards, was pardoned and re-admitted to the Council. On 24 July Northumberland was arrested. The Tudors had survived their greatest crisis.

Why then did Northumberland fail to hold on to power? One reason was certainly a practical one; he had paid off the Italian and German mercenaries whom he had hired to put down the 1549 risings, but probably more important was the respect for Mary's legitimacy. The 'Devise' looked like blatant interference with the legal succession, a fact recognised even by many confirmed Protestants like those listeners to a sermon of Bishop Ridley's on 9 July 1553 in which he tried to justify Northumberland's scheme. There may well have also been a popular element, hatred of Northumberland for his role in the Kett Rebellion and a desire for revenge on those gentry who had been involved in the subsequent repression. Yet at the same time it is striking how many nobility and gentry rallied to the new Queen, while what allies Northumberland had were too recently established and lacked status. Two other factors are worth mentioning: while there was an awareness that Mary Tudor was a Catholic in doctrine, it was not clear that she was a 'papist', i.e. that she intended to re-establish papal power in England or to act intolerantly or repressively towards

Protestants and much of England in any case was still conservative on religion. Finally there is no doubt that Northumberland had laid his plans too late; there is no evidence of a long-term plot on his part. Thus came to an end the rule of the man whom many historians now regard as a genuine and able reformer.

9 THE SIGNIFICANCE OF EDWARD VI's REIGN

It would be easy to agree with C S L Davies that Edward VI's reign represented 'an extraordinary tale of misfortune', for the picture can be painted so as to appear bleak: in foreign policy England was cheated by Scotland and defeated by France, in domestic affairs the government was dogged by corruption and financial embarrassment, forced to manipulate the currency and thwarted by uncertain foreign markets and a series of bad harvests. Moreover the reign saw the most serious law and order challenge in the form of the 1549 disturbances since Cade's Rebellion in 1450. The one positive achievement among so much apparent failure might seem to lie in religious policy.

Such a view would of course overlook much useful work in administration, especially under Northumberland, which enabled the government machine to survive – largely unscathed – into the reigns of Mary and Elizabeth I. Furthermore, while the 1549 risings were a close call for the regime, they were put down and steps were taken under Northumberland to attempt to deal with some of the social problems which were believed to have given rise to them. There remains, however, the religious problem. Clearly as Northumberland's succession plan failed, the accession of Mary put all the religious developments of the past six years in jeopardy. How far then had England gone along the road to Protestantism under Edward VI?

An immediate problem in answering this question is the lack of evidence, particularly of the views and beliefs of the common people – the vast majority of the population. Having said that there are some straws in the wind which may enable one to reach a tentative view. Certainly a number of vigorous reforming bishops worked assiduously to preach the reformed faith, and one thinks here of Ridley in London, Hooper in Gloucester and in Worcester too, when his diocese was enlarged, and Holgate in York. Their efforts must have been hampered, however, by the lack of time to train sufficient clergy for the job in hand, and this deficiency was not made up until well into Elizabeth's reign. Then there was the influence of those who clearly had a vested interest in the new order: married priests including Cranmer and Holgate themselves and those who had benefited from the confiscation and sale of monastic and chantry lands – by no means all radical Protestants. Magnates also played their part; while some were conspicuously conservative like Derby, Arundel and Shrewsbury others were clear radicals like

Pembroke, Northumberland, Dorset and the Dowager Duchess of Suffolk at Grimsthorpe in Lincolnshire. Their influence and that of sections of the clergy produced by 1553 a dedicated minority that was prepared to suffer for Protestantism, including a good many non-intellectuals – craftsmen, housewives, apprentices, some of whom were prepared to die for their faith in the Marian reaction. Such martyrs were few, however, for a mere 800 fled England in 1553 out of a population of around 3 million. More numerous proportionately were the 80 MPs out of 350 who voted not to repeal Reformation legislation at the beginning of Mary's reign.

Much recent research on this topic has centred on analyses of wills to determine the religion of the testator. It is true that wills in the sixteenth century were only made by a minority, but the preamble to a will should show the religious leanings of the writer: traditional Catholic usage mentions the Blessed Virgin and the saints, while Protestants tend to omit this. A comparative study can reveal some trends: thus in 1547 60 per cent of wills in Nottinghamshire and Yorkshire were traditional, by 1553 this figure had gone down to 40 per cent, while in Kent the equivalent figures were 40 per cent and 10 per cent.

A further point, however, explains why the pace of change in religious outlook was so slow is one made by many of the reformers themselves, namely that anti-papalism was not enough in itself to fuel a real reformation. Genuine missionary work was needed and many rural areas and small towns had little contact with reformed preaching, which was most prevalent in London, the two university cities of Oxford and Cambridge and in the South-East generally. Access to literature and to schooling of any kind in the provinces remained limited.

A reasonable and cautious conclusion would run something along these lines: by 1553 probably the great majority of people were not irrevocably committed either to Protestantism or to Catholicism; indeed it is unlikely that they would have thought in such hard and fast terms. The Reformation had made some impact in the south-eastern corner of the country, but it would require much more time and greater trained manpower for it to spread further afield. Neither resource was available in Edward VI's brief reign. In 1553 it remained an open question whether some of the same difficulties would prevent or delay the efforts of Mary Tudor to turn the religious clock back.

10 BIBLIOGRAPHY

C Cross *Church and People 1450–1660* (Fontana, 1976).
C S L Davies *Peace, Print and Protestantism 1450–1558* (Paladin, 1977).
G R Elton *Reform and Reformation* (Edward Arnold, 1977).
N Heard *Edward VI and Mary: A Mid-Tudor Crisis?* (Hodder & Stoughton, Access to History 1990).

J Pound *Poverty and Vagrancy in Tudor England* (Longman, 1971).
W J Shiels *The English Reformation 1530–1570* (Longman, 1989).
A G R Smith *The Emergence of a Nation State: the Commonwealth of England 1529–1660* (Longman, 1984).

11 DISCUSSION POINTS AND EXERCISES

A *This section consists of questions or points that might be used for discussion (or written answers) as a way of expanding on the chapter and testing understanding of it:*

1 Did Henry VIII bequeath a 'crisis' to Edward VI?
2 Was Somerset fitted for high political office?
3 How far could Somerset's measures be described as Protestant?
4 Was Somerset really a radical reformer in social and economic policy?
5 Did the rebellions of 1549 represent a real threat to the government?
6 Was Somerset's foreign policy a total failure?
7 How effectively did Northumberland as Lord President govern in respect of finances, foreign policy and administration?
8 'Northumberland's social policy was far more practical than Somerset's.' Is this true and, if so, in what ways?
9 By what means was England made more Protestant under Northumberland?
10 Was Northumberland's religious policy a case of a fanatical minority imposing its will on the majority?
11 Why did Northumberland fail to hold onto power in 1553?

B *Essay questions*

1 Compare Somerset and Northumberland as effective rulers of England during the reign of Edward VI.
2 How far did the problems of his reign stem from Edward VI's minority?
3 Was England in the reign of Edward VI governed well or badly?
4 Why was there so much upheaval in the short reign of Edward VI?
5 What basic weaknesses in Tudor government were exposed under Edward VI?
6 What progress had Protestantism made in England by 1553?

12 EXERCISE – RELIGIOUS GEOGRAPHY

Draw a map of Tudor England and on it mark London, Oxford, Cambridge, York, Winchester, Norwich, Lincoln, Gloucester, Canterbury, Rochester, Worcester, Durham, Essex and Nottingham. From sections 4 and 8 in the chapter mark on the map any area identified at any point in the text either with Protestantism or Catholicism under the following headings:

a Earnest Protestant bishops like Cranmer, Ridley, Hooper and Holgate.

b Catholic bishops deprived of their Sees like Bonner, Gardiner, Heath, Day and Tunstall.

c The universities and the reformed London churches under continental figures like Bucer, John a Lasco, Peter Martyr Vermigli and Bernardo Ochino.

d The areas with high and low proportions of married priests.

e Areas for which there is information about the religious complexion of wills, e.g. Kent, Nottinghamshire, Yorkshire.

f Magnates and their areas of influence and religious views: e.g. Derby in Lancashire and Cheshire, Arundel in Sussex and Shrewsbury in the northern Welsh Marches, Pembroke in Wiltshire and the Duchess of Suffolk in Lincolnshire.

How far was reforming activity of all kinds concentrated in one region of the country? How do you explain any such concentration?

VII

MARY TUDOR 1553–8

—

Mary I, Hans Eworth

1 INTRODUCTION

UNTIL relatively recently Mary was seen as an almost complete failure.
The two best known features of her reign have always been the burnings of several hundred Protestant heretics and the loss of Calais at the
end of a disastrous war fought against France in alliance with her husband's kingdom of Spain. The early twentieth-century historian
Pollard summed up the period as one of sterility and stagnation, only
rescued by the accession of Elizabeth on her death in 1558.

This picture of failure has been challenged by a later generation of
writers who have sought to find some positive achievements. They
have pointed to Mary's initial success in taking the throne under difficult circumstances in July 1553, and to the setting up, immediately after

her accession, of a strong Council, less divided by faction than that of the two previous reigns. It is of course true that councillors offered conflicting advice on the marriage question: some favouring the Spanish match and others an English suitor, but Mary reached agreement with her Council on the marriage terms with Philip of Spain and survived a serious rebellion in 1554 which whipped up anti-Spanish and anti-Catholic feeling.

No doubt Mary's determined efforts to restore full papal Catholicism ultimately failed – if only because her early death in 1558 left the way open for the accession of a declared Protestant, her half-sister Elizabeth. However, there is little doubt that the religious temper of England was more conservative than anything else in 1553, and most of the political nation was prepared to accept some kind of religious counter-reformation, provided that nothing was done to restore former monastic lands. The burnings did arouse opposition, but they were by no means the most unpopular of all Mary's actions.

A case can be made out to suggest that Mary was a capable administrator, helped perhaps by the reforms of Thomas Cromwell in the 1530s and the continuity of an efficient bureaucracy ever since. Her reforms of customs rates, coinage and revenue courts may be unglamorous, but they did provide Elizabeth with a good start on which she could build.

It is hard, nevertheless, to say much that is positive about Mary's foreign policy. The marriage agreement of 1554 specifically stated that England's foreign affairs would not lead to war on Spain's side. However, Philip's second visit to England in 1557 succeeded in persuading Mary and her advisors of the need to embark on war against Henry II of France. The war was not – at least initially – unpopular in England, for it enabled a large number of formerly dissident nobles to prove their loyalty. Yet the loss of Calais, England's only remaining possession on the continental mainland, remains the legacy of her pro-Habsburg foreign posture.

Clearly Mary's reign is never likely to be seen as a great period of history. There were undoubted failures and even those policies that seemed to be showing some success were cut short by the Queen's untimely death at the age of 42. This should not overshadow, however, her relative popularity on her accession and her painstaking care over dull administrative detail.

2 GAINING THE THRONE

On the day of Edward VI's death – 6 July 1553 – Mary was on her way to visit her half-brother at Greenwich. Hearing the news at Hoddesdon in Hertfordshire, she at once decided to return to Kenninghall in Norfolk, one of her own manors surrounded by sympathetic gentry.

She immediately began to act as a Queen: for example on 9 July she addressed a message to the Privy Council in London setting out her right and title to the throne. The success of her bid for the throne is analysed on pages 177/8.

On 19 July, Mary was officially proclaimed in London, which she entered on 3 August, becoming the first woman to occupy the throne in her own right since Matilda in the twelfth century. On 7 August, Cranmer and Scory conducted the late King's funeral according to the reformed rites.

Meanwhile Northumberland went to the block with several of his henchmen, but Lady Jane Grey's life was spared. What C S L Davies has called 'the only successful rebellion in Tudor England' had succeeded, but Englishmen were as yet unclear about what Mary would now do with her power.

3 FACTION AND POLITICS

Mary was understandably determined to fill the Council with loyal appointees but she could not prevent the rivalry between Gardiner, the Chancellor until his death in November 1555 and Paget, the Keeper of the Privy Seal from March 1555. This emerged, for example, in the discussions over the royal marriage in 1554, when Gardiner proposed Mary's English relative, Edward Courtenay, as the bridegroom, while his rival argued for Philip of Spain, the only working councillor to do so. It is easy, however, to exaggerate the importance of this rift. After all on many matters the Council maintained a united front, e.g. at the time of Wyatt's Rebellion in 1554, although there seems to have been some disagreement over punishment of the rebels. Some councillors, including perhaps Gardiner, may have had doubts over the effectiveness of the burnings of heretics, but they seem to have kept such doubts largely to themselves.

Despite the reservations felt by some councillors at some of Mary's policies, she did emerge successful in obtaining agreement for three key controversial steps: the full return to Rome in religion, her marriage to the heir to the Spanish throne and the declaration of war against France in alliance with Habsburg Spain. No doubt Mary was also influenced in these, and perhaps other policies, by the advice that she received from two further, unofficial advisers: Simon Renard, the Imperial ambassador who represented Philip's father, the Emperor Charles V at the English Court and Philip himself, who for all his inability to read and understand English and his infrequent visits to England must have made his views plain to his wife.

Thus we are struck by a relative lack of division in the highest ranks of government, and even by a continuity from previous reigns. Not only are there a number of familiar faces from the 1540s and early

1550s, there is also some continuity into the future. The most remarkable example of this is perhaps Winchester, who served as Lord Treasurer from 1550 to 1572. This prompts Professor Elton, the leading constitutional historian of the period, to see the Cromwellian reforms of the 1530s bearing fruit in the 1550s and beyond.

The same continuity can be detected in Mary's relations with her Parliaments. No less than five Parliaments were held during the reign: in 1553, twice in 1554, in 1555 and in 1558. Opposition was expressed from time to time to certain of Mary's policies: to the proposed Church lands settlement, to the plan to crown Philip and to the idea of removing Princess Elizabeth from the succession. There was, however, no sense of mounting opposition. Professor Tittler, one of Mary's most recent biographers, writes of 'a genuine spirit of compromise and co-operation which has not generally been observed either in the history of Tudor parliaments or of Mary's reign'. MPs often saw Parliament as a forum for the representation of local interests including patronage and they did not welcome long sessions that kept them away from their responsibilities in their localities.

4 THE SUCCESSION PROBLEM AND THE SPANISH MARRIAGE

Mary was crowned and anointed by Gardiner on 1 October 1553 according to the old Catholic rite. Thus the problem of the succession and her marriage loomed to haunt the new Queen. She was determined on two things: to marry and to bear children and to debar her half-sister Elizabeth from the throne on religious grounds. The question was: whom should she marry?

Two candidates presented themselves: an English suitor in Edward Courtenay and a foreign one in Philip of Spain. At first sight Courtenay's credentials looked impressive, for he was the great-grandson of Edward IV on his paternal grandmother's side. His father Henry, second Earl of Devon and Marquis of Exeter, had been a devout Catholic and a confidant of Mary herself. He had paid for his indiscretion with his life in 1538. Edward was 27 years old (compared to Mary's 37) and his claims were advanced on the Council by Gardiner who was keen to avoid a foreign match.

However, the Courtenay candidature presented significant difficulties, not least because it opened up the danger of reviving factional quarrels. Moreover his personal qualities suggested further disadvantages: he was intellectually astute but socially awkward, unreliable in religion, debauched, weak and lacking in common sense.

Mary herself much preferred a Spanish marriage – she was after all half-Spanish herself and Philip of Spain, the heir to the Emperor

Charles V, seemed to offer so much more than Courtenay. He was 26 years old, a widower with one son by his former marriage and experience as Regent in the Netherlands in 1549–50 and as Regent of Spain itself since 1551. He was also a Catholic, and supported in his claim by Paget and by his father, the Emperor. Charles who was to divide his huge territorial responsibilities between his two sons Philip and Ferdinand, was keen to strengthen Philip's inheritance by the addition of England. Philip, with Spain itself and the Low Countries to his name, would be in a better position to counter-balance the power of France if he was King of England too.

The official Spanish proposal of marriage was presented to Mary by Simon Renard, the Imperial ambassador, on 10 October 1553. At the end of the month Mary formally accepted the proposal and gazed longingly at a Titian portrait of her husband-to-be pending Philip's arrival in England.

Mary had, unfortunately, failed to anticipate the furore that the Spanish marriage proposal stirred up in England, seeing Spanish power as a threat to English liberties and commercial interests. There is little doubt that a majority of councillors opposed the match, and in November a parliamentary delegation tried to dissuade her. Eventually both the Council (on 7 December 1553) and Parliament (in April 1554) accepted the marriage treaty. Philip's title was to be that of King, and therefore to some extent joint sovereign with Mary, but he was not to enjoy the full prerogative. No aliens were to hold office in England, and England would not be expected to join Spain in a war against France. As for the succession, the eldest surviving child of the marriage would succeed to both England and the Netherlands. If Mary were to die before Philip, then he would have no further claim to the English throne. Finally, if Don Carlos, Philip's existing son died childless before Philip himself, any child of Mary's would inherit the whole Spanish Empire – including the Americas and much of Italy. Philip himself was a good deal less enthusiastic about the idea than either his father or his future bride. He seems to have been determined not to be bound by the terms, and he was somewhat slow to arrive in England to claim his bride. He was never crowned King of England and he never seems to have taken to England, regarding it perhaps in Professor Loades' words as 'a chilly land of barbarous heretics'.

The Spanish marriage was largely responsible for the one major disturbance of the reign, Wyatt's Rebellion from January to February 1554. There had in fact been plots and rumours of plots since the autumn of 1553 to engineer a Protestant succession and to secure a marriage between Courtenay and the 20-year-old Princess Elizabeth. The former seems to have been thrown into the plot by his petulance at being passed over by Mary in favour of Philip, but – unstable as ever – he divulged the details of the conspiracy to Gardiner. It is true that by December 1553 plans had been laid for simultaneous risings to erupt on 18 March 1554 in Kent, Hertfordshire, Devon and Leicestershire, and the Welsh borders – the first area to be led by Sir Thomas Wyatt, the third by Sir Peter Carew, the fourth by the Duke of Suffolk and his brothers and the last by Sir James Croft. The French ambassador Antoine de Noailles was also involved, promising naval support in the Channel and help in securing ports in the South-West. Unfortunately the scheme went awry as the government got wind of the plan in mid-January 1554 and Devon and Hertfordshire failed to rise. In Leicestershire only 140 joined Suffolk, who was quickly arrested by his neighbouring loyal rival, the Earl of Huntingdon. That left Kent where Wyatt was forced into premature action.

Wyatt had first come to prominence in 1549 as the author of a plan presented to Protector Somerset for a standing cadre of trained men in each county under a paid professional. Like Croft and Carew he had served Henry VIII in his French campaigns of the 1540s and all three now seemed worried about further advancement. However Kent was especially sensitive with a turbulent history and ready access to London propaganda. It was also strategically placed with many small interests and few great families. Wyatt himself, a large landowner in the county, had originally declared for Mary, but in January 1554 he managed to assemble a force of between 2500 and 3000. Wyatt whipped up anti-Spanish feeling by playing on fears of being dragged into war on Spain's behalf and of imminent arrivals of Spaniards in Kent. He posed as the rescuer of the Queen from foolish advice, but beyond this he appears to have left his aims deliberately vague.

Wyatt's plan might have had some chance of success if he had moved quickly on London either to compel Mary to abandon her plans or to replace her by Elizabeth, who was still legally the heir until Mary had children or Parliament decided otherwise. The slow government response also gave him opportunities, for Arundel and Shrewsbury (both known opponents of the marriage) failed to move, and the elderly Duke of Norfolk returned to Court having failed to block Wyatt's advance to the capital. Meanwhile the London militia confronted Wyatt on the left bank of the Medway but then moved over to his side. Wyatt who had by now acquired ships and cannon had a good chance of success. Why then did he fail?

Part of the answer lies in Mary's own response. She refrained from appealing to Charles V, realising perhaps that the presence of foreign troops would have played into Wyatt's hands. She also remained in London and ordered the fortification of the city. If she had left the capital, she would have left it vulnerable to attacks from other directions. On 1 February Mary issued a personal appeal from the Guildhall, despite Gardiner's advice to take refuge in Winchester. She played on Londoners' fears of an incursion into the city by armed men, as had happened in 1450 at the time of Jack Cade's Rebellion and received support from the more neutral councillors like Pembroke and Bedford, still at this time the Keeper of the Privy Seal. Above all she benefited from Wyatt's error in diverting his forces on 30 January to take Cooling Castle, held by Lord Cobham. The castle surrendered, but Wyatt had lost a whole day. He was therefore late in reaching the Thames at Southwark where London Bridge held out against the rebels. Wyatt did not cross the Thames until 6 February – at Kingston much further to the west – only to be defeated both in Kensington and in Fleet Street by Pembroke. Meanwhile on 9 February Princess Elizabeth was arrested for alleged complicity in the rebellion.

Paget urged leniency for the captured rebels, while Renard by contrast wanted the deaths of both Courtenay and Elizabeth. The latter two were spared in the absence of hard evidence to implicate them, but 100 perished including Lady Jane Grey, her husband Guildford Dudley, Carew, Suffolk and Wyatt himself. The bulk of the captured rebels numbering around 600 were freed and Elizabeth served a brief prison term before being sent to the royal manor of Woodstock. While the repression was harsh it was not vindictive.

Several questions still need to be asked about the rebellion. Firstly were the motives more complex than mere anti-Spanish xenophobia, sowing distrust of Philip and raising fears of increased taxes for foreign adventures? Professors Tittler and Dickens see religion as an important ingredient, especially as Kent was known as a Protestant stronghold. Professor Thorp has examined the religious leanings of several leading rebels, and out of 14 lay leaders he has found no Catholics, 8 definite Protestants, 3 probable Protestants and 3 whose religious sympathies are unknown. Of 9 clergy all seem to have been Protestants. It is also worth remembering that Kent produced no less than one-sixth of the Marian martyrs later in the reign. Professor Fletcher finds evidence for some other rebel leaders' Protestant sympathies: Carew seems to have been regarded as a Protestant, Croft had been instrumental in trying to introduce the Protestant liturgy into Ireland in 1551 and Suffolk had entertained the Protestant theologian Bullinger. It seems therefore that a distinct Protestant strand ran through these upheavals, although it is not possible to list Wyatt himself as Protestant.

Secondly was the Wyatt Rebellion obviously so much more serious to the government as Kett's Rebellion had been? Certainly its proximity to London is an important factor, but Kett had been seen by the political nation as a threat to itself rather than a quarrel within its own ranks as the 1554 events seemed to be. In 1554 the political community rallied out of loyalty to the Tudor dynasty and abhorrence of all rebellion. Kett's Rebellion had involved far greater numbers, but his host remained in Norfolk, 100 miles from the centre of power. Maybe Professor Wernham has a point when he sees the 1554 events as 'a protest designed to prevent the adoption of a particular policy, a protest made in advance. It was an attempt to join in the debate about what foreign policy should be. This was something new in English affairs.'

Finally did the Wyatt movement suffer from serious initial weaknesses? Certainly Wyatt found out the hard way that hostility to the Spanish marriage was strong, but not that strong when other factors were brought into play. The association of the Duke of Northumberland connection was an unfortunate stigma for Wyatt to overcome, and the only real magnate involved in the plots, the Duke of Suffolk, could only raise a paltry force. It is also the case that the orthodox Protestant leadership refused to get involved, and some even refused to be released by the rebels. Thus a conventional domestic revolt had little chance of success against a monarch sustained by enough magnates.

5 MARIAN GOVERNMENT

Recent writing on Mary's reign has commented favourably on Mary's success in the rather unglamorous area of financial administration. The most famous such measure is the amalgamation of the revenue courts which occurred in 1554 when the responsibility for First Fruits and Tenths and for Augmentations passed to the Exchequer, making this body responsible for most royal revenues for the first time since the fifteenth century. This may well have been the brainchild of Thomas Cromwell, but it was put into effect during Mary's reign by Winchester and Mildmay who also introduced advanced methods of auditing and accounting. The net yield of the former Court of Augmentations doubled, while a new survey of royal lands increased their revenue by more than £40 000. Meanwhile Sir Thomas Gresham's services were retained manipulating foreign exchange rates and negotiating favourable foreign loans.

Mary is also given credit for the issuing of a new book of customs rates in 1558. The background to this is a serious rise in the general costs of government at a time of pronounced inflation, warfare, greater government activity in other areas and the expense of Renaissance kingly style. The sale of Crown lands, offices and monopolies went some way towards solving the problem as did parliamentary subsidies which brought in ready cash for a short time but also entailed a political risk. Thus the government's attention turned to the customs which were still being levied according to the 1507 book with minor increases from 1536 and 1545. Indeed many goods remained wholly untaxed, and inflation quickly made the rates on those that were taxed obsolete. The average increase in valuation over the 1545 revision was nearly 120 per cent, and the modest yield of £29 000 for 1558 rose to £83 000 in 1559. Indeed the Marian book survived until 1604 giving Mary greater success in this area even than Henry VII or Edward IV. Two important new principles had been established: that rates could be determined by the Crown alone, and that the Crown could impose new export duties without Parliament's consent. Efficiency of collection also improved with the appointment of Sir Francis Englefield to the new post of Surveyor General of the Customs.

At the same time the government became more involved in domestic commerce and industry encouraging statutes like the Retail Trades Act of 1554 and the Woollen Cloth Act of 1557. Charters of incorporation of boroughs doubled and local authorities were encouraged to survey grain stocks and to enforce measures against hoarders.

At the same time the government actively fostered trade, seeking alternative ports to Calais such as Bergen, Bruges and Middleburg in the Low Countries. English attempts to break into the lucrative Spanish New World market were however thwarted, and commercial attention turned elsewhere. Following Willoughby and Chancellor's voyage to Russia in 1553 the Muscovy Company received its charter in 1555 and contacts developed with Morocco and Guinea in West Africa. The fact that traders did not protest at the higher duties in the new Book of Rates may well suggest a new alliance between the monarchy and commercial interests.

All of this would seem to challenge the view of an older generation of historians led by Pollard who wrote of the 'sterility' of Mary's reign. Despite some severe social and economic problems, including perhaps up to 200 000 deaths from the 1558 epidemic of sweating sickness, there were no violent uprisings based on such issues and no air of continuing crisis like that which hung over the reign of the incompetent Henry VI. It would nonetheless be wrong to see Mary as a great innovator in government. There was no sharp break with the past: rather Mary operated within a traditional framework of ideas. Hence the historian is entitled to wonder how far Mary herself can take the credit for administrative success and how far it may be due to an earlier generation of ministers headed by Thomas Cromwell himself and continued by their disciples well into Elizabeth's reign.

6 RELIGION

The prospects for religion in 1553

The present day historian knows with hindsight that the Marian attempt to restore Catholicism was doomed to failure after a mere five years, and that it was followed by a renewed English Reformation under Elizabeth. However few contemporary Englishmen could have anticipated this in 1553.

There was a widespread religious conservatism, which had hardly been touched by the Edwardian experiment in Protestantism. Most people shared an unintellectual and instinctive feeling for the familiar i.e. Catholic ritual and belief. Most people expected, and indeed hoped for, some sort of restoration of Catholicism, most likely that kind which prevailed in Henry VIII's latter years. Few people can have expected the full rigours of pre-1529 Catholicism, the papal allegiance, the violent persecution of heretics and the restoration of monasteries.

Protestantism had its problems too. In England it was identified with faction, corruption and economic crisis, while on the continent it seemed to have shot its bolt. All over Europe the reformed faith appeared to be in retreat: the Reformation was only now entrenched in northern and central Germany, Scandinavia and the Swiss Confederation. The first wave of reform was over.

Catholicism was meanwhile preparing itself, as the Counter or Catholic Reformation proceeded. The newly created Jesuit Order, the Council of Trent and the reformed Papacy all seemed in the ascendant. C S L Davies concludes, 'Far from Marian Catholicism being a symptom of hopeless, anachronistic reaction, as it may seem to us, to contemporaries it represented the flow of the current.'

Early moves towards Catholicism

Mary's first proclamation on religion issued on 18 August 1553 was remarkably tolerant. She deplored the diversity of religious opinions, but she promised that there would be no compulsion for the time being as she was convinced that no coercion would be necessary. The Queen believed that most apparent Protestants were really Catholics who had been led astray during her half-brother's reign and that true Protestants were only a tiny minority of fanatics. Hence she was sure that the restoration of the old faith would be easy to carry out. She also realised that little could be done to persecute Protestants even if she wished to do so without Parliament's approval to restore the fifteenth-century heresy laws. For a full return to Rome a special Papal Legate would also be required to absolve England and return it to the fold.

Some measures could, however, be taken at once. Seven bishops were deprived of their Sees, four of whom were imprisoned including Cranmer, Hooper, Latimer and Ridley. Three of the latter had to face debates against Catholic theologians in Oxford in April 1554 when it was expected that they would be humiliated and ridiculed. In this the government's hopes were dashed because, while Cranmer performed poorly in the debate and Latimer refused to dispute at all, Ridley managed to confound no less than thirty-three opposing divines. Clearly the intellectual battle against Protestantism and its champions would be harder than the authorities had envisaged.

Around a quarter of the clergy were deprived of their livings mostly for marriage. Of these 2000 clergy most were, not surprisingly, in the South and East, e.g. 243 deprivations in the Norwich diocese and 150 in London, while only 10 per cent of clergy lost their livings in the North. There was also a significant emigration of foreign Protestants like John a Lasco, Peter Martyr Vermigli and Bernardo Ochino that aggravated the Church's serious manpower shortage.

Mary's first Parliament (October 1553) repealed most of the reforming legislation from the previous reign including the two Prayer Books and their Acts of Uniformity, clerical marriage, Communion in both kinds and the Forty-two Articles Act, and the 1547 service was re-established. None of this happened without opposition, however, as between a quarter and a third of the Commons voted against these proposals and in Mary's second Parliament (April-May 1554), while the Spanish marriage was approved, members refused to re-enact the Act of Six Articles or to punish those who refused to attend church. The Royal Supremacy had also yet to be annulled, and to her embarrassment Mary remained 'Supreme Head of the Church of England', which she abbreviated to 'etc.' after her secular titles.

The Imperial ambassador Simon Renard wrote to the Emperor on 3 September 1554 as Cardinal Pole waited for the official invitation to visit England, to outline some of the difficulties which he foresaw in implementing the full rigours of pre-1529 Papal Catholicism which Mary seemed determined to re-introduce:

> Cardinal Pole presses for an answer whether or no he is to be received here as Legate, and writes that he wants a definite reply so that he may either go back to Rome or proceed on his journey. Of course one must take it for granted that zeal for religion alone moves him, but still doubts assail me. Affairs are not settled here yet, and the King has only been a few days in the realm. The Spaniards are hated, as I have seen in the past and expect to see in the future. There was trouble at the last session of Parliament, and disagreeable incidents are of daily occurrence. Only ten days ago the heretics tried to burn a church in Suffolk with the entire congregation that was hearing Mass inside . . .
>
> On examining the brief sent hither by the Cardinal and intended to dispense those who hold Church property, I have noticed that it is not drawn up in a suitable manner . . . It is my duty to inform your Majesty that the Catholics hold more Church property than do the heretics, and unless they obtain a general dispensation to satisfy them that their titles will never be contested they will not allow the Cardinal to execute his commission; and he certainly will not be able to do so until the question has been submitted to Parliament, former Acts of which have vested the title of Supreme Head of the Church in the Crown, the right of which to deal with all religious questions consequently stands firm.

1 *How reliable do you think Renard was as an observer of English affairs?*

2 *Summarise briefly the reasons, drawn from Renard's observations, for Pole to be cautious.*

Cardinal Pole

Reginald Pole was born in Worcestershire in 1500 the son of Sir Geoffrey Pole and Margaret, Countess of Salisbury. His mother was the daughter of George, Duke of Clarence making him a great-nephew of Edward IV. After higher education at Oxford and Padua in Italy he returned to Italy as an exile having quarrelled with Henry VIII over the King's 'Great Matter' in 1532. In the 1530s his reputation was that of a humanist and advocate of Church reform. Indeed in 1536 he collaborated on the famous *'Consilium Delectorum Cardinalium De Emendanda Ecclesia'*, whose report recommended far-reaching changes in the Catholic Church. He was rewarded with a Cardinal's hat in 1536 although he had not yet been ordained as a priest, and in 1545 he was chosen as one of three Cardinals to preside over the Council of Trent. In 1549 he failed by only one vote in the College of Cardinals to become Pope. Thus on the eve of his return to England in 1554 he was a respected senior churchman, an authority on pastoral care and clerical education and a respected diplomat.

Pole's arrival in the country of his birth was delayed until November 1554 partly because Charles V wanted his son to establish himself first and because Mary herself wanted to be strong enough to dissuade him from restoring all former Church lands. Pole arrived at Westminster to find Mary's third Parliament convened and prepared to abandon Royal Supremacy over the Church and to repeal the Act of Attainder hanging over him. On 28 November 1554, Pole addressed both Houses of Parliament and was reported as saying:

> . . . his principal business was to restore the nation to its ancient nobility. To this purpose he had an authority from His Holiness to make them part of the Catholic Church. That the Apostolic See had a particular regard for this island, and that to this, the Pope seemed to be led by the directions of Providence, which has given a preference to this country by making it one of the first provinces that received the Christian faith . . .
>
> If we require into the English revolt we shall find . . . avarice and sensuality the principal motives, and that was first started and carried on by the unbridled appetite and licentiousness of a single person. And though it was given out that there would be a vast accession of wealth to the public, yet this expectation dwindled to nothing. The Crown was left in debt, and the subjects generally speaking more impoverished than ever. And as to religion, people were tied up to forms and hampered with penalties and, to speak plainly, there was more liberty of conscience in Turkey than in England.

... The Church of Rome might have recovered her jurisdiction by force, and had an offer of the greatest princes in Europe to assist her pretensions. However, she was willing to waive this advantage, and apply to none but friendly expedients.

1   *How does Pole account for the 'English revolt'?*
2   *Comment on Pole's assertion that 'the Church of Rome might have recovered her jurisdiction by force, and had an offer of the greatest princes in Europe to assist her pretensions'.*

Two days later on 30 November 1554 Pole formally granted absolution to the whole realm and restored it to papal obedience. Parliament went on to revive the anti-Lollard heresy laws of 1382, 1401 and 1414 and to repeal all acts passed against the Papacy since 1529. Now Pole could work fully as Papal Legate, although he was forced reluctantly to agree to concede lay ownership of Church lands given out after the dissolution of the monasteries. The lay peers, supported by Paget, who himself owned former monastic land, opposed Pole's initial idea to restore monastic lands for obvious material reasons and also because they feared a revival of abbots' seats in the House of Lords which might well lead in turn to a renewed clerical majority in the Upper House.

Pole's strategy for the re-Catholicization of England emerges from the London Synod of 1555 when he tried to grapple with the Church's organisational and financial problems. He urged bishops to undertake regular visitations to detect non-residence, pluralism and tithes impropriated (taken over) by laymen, but even with the best episcopate this would take time – especially as some of the most senior prelates like Gardiner and Heath were often preoccupied with state affairs.

Pole's bishops were youthful, determined and well-qualified but few were outstanding. Gardiner, Tunstall and Bonner all former Henrician bishops returned to their Sees, while Pate of Worcester, Goldwell of St Asaph, Watson of Lincoln and Heath of Worcester and then of York were new vigorous incumbents, but they lacked of course the time needed for their labours to bear fruit.

Fourteen seminaries were set up to train priests, but Pole turned down the Jesuits' offer to preach and evangelise for Catholicization. He set greater store by visitations of the two universities, both of which he was to become Chancellor. He encouraged the founding of two new Oxford colleges, Trinity and St John's but he was to find few scholars to replace the likes of Bucer, Martyr or Fagius. While the MA degree course was shortened, the colleges would need much more time to become effective centres of Catholic renewal.

The same difficulties afflicted the attempts to bring in new books to counteract the effects of the Protestant Bible. A Catholic New Testament, a Book of Homilies and a new Catechism were prepared but there was little time to implement them.

There was probably more success in restoring features of Catholic worship in churches: altars, rood-lofts and images reappeared, together with vestments and the paraphernalia of the Mass but few shrines or relics were to be seen. However, the Injunctions of Archdeacon Nicholas Harpsfield of Canterbury on the condition of parish churches in his area in 1557 underscore the sorry state of the parish churches and the decay of church furniture necessary for Catholic worship.

The effectiveness of Pole's efforts was weakened partly by failure to motivate or inspire his subordinates or to understand the hostility to the Catholic Church that had erupted during his exile. It also suffered from the changes in his status in England. After Cranmer's death he became Archbishop of Canterbury in 1556, but the deaths of Popes Julius III and Marcellus II in 1555 brought his arch-enemy Caraffa to the Holy See in 1556 as Paul IV. In April 1557 he withdrew Pole's legatine authority, summoned him to Rome to face charges of heresy and refused to confirm his episcopal appointments. Thus the Cardinal's effective period as legate was to last little over two years.

Censorship and writing

Mary's government was prepared to use censorship on the lines of the Roman Counter-Reformation itself. In 1553 she issued decrees against seditious rumours, in 1555 an Index of proscribed writers was drawn up and in 1558 the death penalty was prescribed for those involved with prohibited books.

These measures were hampered partly by the pre-existence of around 19 000 copies of the outlawed 1552 Prayer Book and the continued output by Protestant writers at the height of the Marian persecution – even Latimer and Ridley somehow managed to write from their Oxford prison.

Some Protestant writers hurled invective against Mary to undermine her credibility and to sustain the faith and hopes of Protestants by urging purely passive disobedience. Some like Becon and Scory enjoined obedience to the Queen, interpreting her reign as punishment on the faithful for their sins. Others encouraged non-attendance at Mass and the continuation of Protestant rites to keep up the spirits of the faithful, and the works of continental reformers like Luther, Melanchthon and Calvin also enjoyed a vogue. There were, however, a few writers who developed theories of active disobedience. John Knox's chief theme was the illegitimacy of women rulers by natural law, and in *The First Blast of the Trumpet Against the Monstrous Regiment of Women* (1558) he ascribed the calamities that had befallen England to God's displeasure at the unnatural choice of Mary Tudor as queen. In 1558 he also published in Geneva *The Appellation of John Knox* urging the overthrow of women rulers.

Christopher Goodman, minister of the English exiles in Geneva published in 1556 *How Superior Powers ought to be Obeyed*, described by Professor Tittler as 'one of the most politically practical of such statements in the literature of sixteenth-century political thought'. Goodman put forward a limited concept of monarchy in which the sovereign held his or her authority from God, but only through a covenant whereby the people 'elected' the monarch. It followed, according to Goodman, that the king must fear God, respect his word and refrain from ruling by coercion. Equally the people must obey a godly monarch, but enforce God's will against an ungodly ruler. Goodman held that the magistrates – meaning nobles, councillors and judges – must get rid of an unsatisfactory sovereign. If they failed to do so, then the people should take matters into their own hands.

Finally Ponet in his *Short Treatise of Political Power* published in 1556 also argued against the absolutist nature of royal authority and stressed the ruler's obligation to protect the common weal. He did not, however, describe the specific means whereby a ruler like Mary might be brought to justice.

Catholic publications by contrast seem much more lightweight. The government could have made much more use of the opportunity to sponsor Sunday sermons at St Paul's Cross: Nicholas Harpsfield, the Archdeacon of Canterbury preached there only twice – once to praise the royal marriage and once to give thanks for the Battle of St Quentin, while Gardiner only spoke there in 1554 – to praise Philip and to announce the reconciliation with Rome. The authorities could have made greater use of an important platform to propagate their views.

Of the Catholic writers only Miles Huggard, John Christopherson and Thomas Watson are at all well known. Clearly Mary failed to inspire the intellectuals, few of her advisers had studied abroad and most of the really bright sparks were Protestants anyway. The Erasmian vitality of the early sixteenth century had died out. The intellectual void which they left was filled by the reactionary tide that flowed from the meetings of the Council of Trent. In any event about half of all publishers had left England and those who remained were kept busy by Pole printing missals, hymnals, homilies, breviaries, primers, psalters, etc., for which there was a ready and profitable market. Thus they were less willing to produce and sell polemical works with a more limited readership.

The persecution of Protestants

Only two religious extremists had been burned in Edward VI's reign: George van Parris, a Flemish surgeon who denied Christ's divinity, and Joan Bocher, an ex-Lollard turned Anabaptist, but once Mary's third Parliament had restored the treason legislation in January 1555 the way was open for the burnings of Protestants which is such a notorious feature of the reign.

The zeal for the executions seems to have come partly from Mary herself urged on by Spanish confessors like Carranza a Castro and Pole himself. Gardiner apparently became more sceptical just before his death in November 1555 and Simon Renard's dispatches to Philip suggest that he was also doubtful of the wisdom of the burnings. For example on 5 February 1555 Renard wrote to Philip to describe the death of John Rogers, the biblical translator, at Smithfield the previous day. Renard records a strongly emotional reaction from the crowd with weeping, prayers, the gathering of ashes and bones and threats directed against the bishops. Indeed the authorities seem to have become aware that the burning policy might be counter-productive and in London efforts were made to ensure that apprentices and servants stayed away from executions.

There were approximately three hundred victims including 50 women with most occurring in the South-East – there were for example 67 martyrs in London, 58 in Kent, 39 in Essex, 23 in Sussex and 18 in Suffolk. Only two took place north of the Trent and very few in the West or in Wales. Certainly the zeal and effectiveness of the regime was greatest in the South-East and there had been more Protestants there anyway.

The execution of Latimer and Ridley

The best known deaths were of course those of Ridley and Latimer in Oxford on 16 October 1555, of Cranmer also in Oxford on 21 March 1556 and of Hooper in Gloucester in 1555. In all twenty-one clergy died, but later victims tended to be humbler: artisans, labourers, yeomen and husbandmen. Their courage too impressed onlookers and Protestants became convinced that these must be God's chosen.

How far can the Marian burnings be compared with persecution before or since either in England or abroad? It may be that mid-Tudor England was less used to violence – after all Henry VIII had put only twelve Protestants to death. Yet in France Henry II's *'Chambre Ardente'* of 1547–50 killed more than the Marian campaign, and of course it was ultimately the Protestants who wrote the received version of the events of the Marian years. John Foxe's best-seller *Acts and Monuments* (better known as *Foxe's Book of Martyrs*) was published in 1563 and added significantly to an emerging English self-identity and to the 'Black Legend' of Spanish wickedness.

Protestants themselves did not disagree with the burning of heretics; they quarrelled only with the definition of heresy. Indeed among the Marian martyrs Philpot and Rogers had both accepted the need to burn Anabaptists. It also needs to be stressed that capital punishment was a frequent occurrence in sixteenth-century England, where no less than seven hundred were sentenced to hang after the 1569 Northern Rebellion and where between seventeen and fifty-four death sentences were handed down annually in Essex in Elizabeth's reign – often for small-scale theft.

About eight hundred Protestant men and women went into exile abroad to escape the persecution. Most settled in Switzerland or Germany to sit out what they expected would be a temporary inconvenience. The largest group were gentlefolk of which 166 have been identified, including Sir Francis Knollys and Sir Anthony Cooke. There were even two nobles: Francis, Earl of Bedford and Katherine, Duchess of Suffolk who made a stately journey from her Lincolnshire seat to Gravesend accompanied by six servants. Of the rest 67 were Protestant clerics, 119 theology students, 40 merchants, 32 artisans, 7 painters and 6 'professional men'. Among the women 100 were wives accompanying their husbands, and 25 were women on their own; there were also 146 children and 45 servants. Few of the exiles were labourers or husbandmen, no doubt because of the substantial resources needed to go into foreign exile.

In the long run the exiles' prolonged and direct contact with the second generation of continental reformers, who were running their churches without bishops, contributed to religious debates in Elizabeth's reign. They also had plenty of time to ponder Protestant theories of political opposition applicable to English conditions.

Finally, despite the persecution, quite a large Protestant underground remained in England. In London inns and private houses, congregations of up to two hundred listened to preachers of the calibre of Scambler, Fowle, Rough, Bernher and Bentham, many of whom appeared on Elizabeth's first bench of bishops. There were also similar congregations as far afield as Sussex, Kent, Hertfordshire, Essex, Suffolk, Lincolnshire, Leicestershire and Lancashire. There were even a few open preachers, of whom the best known is George Eagles (alias 'Trudgeover') who roamed over East Anglia until his capture and execution in 1557 at Colchester. When Paget suggested to William Cecil that Mary's prospects were good, he replied, 'My Lord, you are therein so far deceived, that I fear rather an inundation of the contrary part, so universal a boiling and a bubbling I see.'

Conclusion

Why was the attempt to re-implant Catholicism unsuccessful? Clearly in a reign that only lasted, in the event, for five years there was a limit to what Mary and her advisers could achieve to bring back the Roman Catholic faith. Of course delays at the beginning of the reign meant that the effective period available was more like three years. Mary died childless and the throne passed to her half-sister Elizabeth.

It is however still doubtful whether, given more time, Mary could in fact have achieved more in religion, for few of those directing religious policy really understood contemporary English religious sentiment. Neither Mary herself nor her husband were ever really in touch and Pole tended to think of the England that he had left in 1532. The tone of policy remained negative, lacking positive missionary zeal and failing to make use of native English spiritual or intellectual traditions. Moreover there was little compelling literary expression on the Catholic side and there was little money available in the straitened circumstances of the 1550s. Thus Mary's attempt to refound the monasteries produced only 100 religious in six houses by 1557. Finally Mary was left with most of the same clergy who had served under Edward VI, as even former married priests could officiate after putting their wives away and doing penance. There must have been many contemporary Vicars of Bray who were prepared to conform with every shift of religious flavour like Robert Parkyn in Aldwick-le-Street, south Yorkshire or Thomas Dobson in Cambridgeshire. If England was far from being a Protestant state in 1553, it was also far from being universally Catholic in 1558.

7 FOREIGN POLICY

The first half of Mary's reign saw England neutral in the great Habsburg-Valois conflict that had pitted France against Spain ever since Charles VIII's invasion of Northern Italy in 1494. These so-called

'Italian Wars' flared up into actual fighting from time to time relieved by periodic truces like that for five years solemnly agreed at Vaucelles in February 1556. In that year Philip II succeeded his father as King of Spain, Duke of Burgundy, ruler of much of Italy and a good deal else besides. In September 1556 Philip's armies under the Duke of Alva invaded the Papal States, provoking the furiously anti-Spanish Pope Paul IV to promise Naples to Henry II of France if he would help to drive Spanish forces out of Italy. By February 1557 war had resumed between France and Spain, and Philip looked to England for support, especially for naval supplies, funds and the presence of an English fleet in the Channel. Opinion in the English political community was, however, anxious to avoid antagonising the French who were useful trading partners and who could stir up trouble for the English on the Scottish border, in Ireland or in the Pale of Calais.

Luckily for Philip, Henry II's tolerance of English Protestant exiles and his willingness to allow them to use France as a base from which to attack England, forced her into the war. The Dudley Conspiracy of 1556 when de Noailles, the French ambassador encouraged Sir Henry Dudley to attack Yarmouth Castle in the Isle of Wight was followed in 1557 by Thomas Stafford's voyage from France to Scarborough with arms provided by Henry. He declared himself 'Protector of England' before his defeat by the Earl of Westmorland. Stafford's escapade revived traditional English fears of French expansion northwards and made English participation in the war inevitable.

The omens for the war seemed good at first, especially as the 1557 harvest promised to be good after disastrous ones in 1555 and 1556. War also provided a chance to unite a divided realm, not least giving Protestants an opportunity to show their loyalty in service. Francis Russell, the second Earl of Bedford and a Wyatt conspirator, fought valiantly at the Battle of St Quentin in 1557, while other Wyatt rebels like Cuthbert Vaughan, Sir James Croft and Sir Peter Carew also joined up. The most conspicuous example of loyalty was by the three surviving sons of the late Duke of Northumberland, Harry, Ambrose and Robert, who, pardoned in January 1555, all purged themselves further by fighting for Mary in France. Catholic and more neutral nobles were no less keen to serve and Pembroke, Rutland, Montague, Shrewsbury, Westmorland, Clinton and Grey of Wilton all joined up for honour and profit.

In October 1555 Mary's navy was in a parlous state: she could deploy effectively only three warships, when Henry VIII could dispose of twenty-one in 1547. By 1557 there were once again twenty-one men-of-war and five further ships, and during 1558–9 as much tonnage of shipping was built as during 1583–8, the height of the struggle against Spain. At the same time the administration of naval finances was entrusted to Lord Treasurer Winchester, who with Benjamin Gonson, the Naval Treasurer, had from 1557 a regular peacetime allocation for the fleet's upkeep that varied between £14 000 and £20 000 per year. Elizabeth I was to be glad of the fleet that Mary left her in her Scottish campaign of 1560.

Prior to 1558 the recruitment of land forces was to be achieved by two methods: a feudal knights' levy and a national militia system which had fallen into decay. Mary's Militia Act of 1558 required the ten newly appointed Lord-Lieutenants, JPs and Commissioners of Muster to raise a militia. Thus Mary laid the foundations of the Elizabethan military system.

War was declared on 7 June 1557, and on the same day Mary issued the following fulsome proclamation of war aims:

> Although we, the Queen, when we first came to the throne, understood that the Duke of Northumberland's abominable treason had been abetted by Henry, the French King . . . we attributed these doings to the French King's ministers rather than to his own will, hoping thus patiently to induce him to adopt a truly friendly attitude towards us. More, we undertook heavy expenditures to send our ambassadors to assist in peace negotiations between him and the Emperor; but our labours met with no return from the King . . . He has also favoured pirates, enemies of Christendom who have despoiled our subjects.
>
> We realise that nothing we can do will induce the King to change his methods. The other day he sent Stafford with ships and supplies to seize our castle of Scarborough, not content with having intrigued so long with a view to getting possession of Calais and other places belonging to us across the seas and having financed counterfeiters and encouraged them to put false coin into circulation in this country.
>
> For the above reasons, and because he has sent an army to invade Flanders, which we are under obligation to defend, we have seen fit to proclaim to our subjects that they are to consider the King of France as a public enemy to ourselves and to our nation, rather than suffer him to continue to deceive us under colour of friendship.
>
> We therefore command all Englishmen to regard Henry, the French King, and his vassals as public enemies of this kingdom and to harm them wherever possible, abstaining from trading or any other business with them. Although the French King has molested our merchants and subjects, without declaring war, we have seen fit to allow his subjects and merchants forty days to leave this kingdom with such property as the law permits them to export.

1 *Comment on the tone adopted in this document towards the French King.*

2 *Are there any other war aims not mentioned here?*

Historians have usually seen the Anglo-French war of 1557–9 in a harsh light: for Elton it is 'the most disastrous of the century', while Tittler writes, 'it is hard to think of any subsequent English campaign which has resulted in less material gain and more loss of face'. However, there was success in a number of theatres, the navy performing particularly well. All French shipping was cleared out of the Channel thus guarding Philip's supply lines to the Low Countries. Naval units also carried Pembroke and his army of 7000 across the Channel, and escorted the Atlantic fishing fleet, the Spanish bullion fleet and Sussex's expedition to Ireland. The Battle of St Quentin fought on 10 August 1557 was another success when Pembroke's detachment of 5000 English played their part in Philip's victory over the French. Finally the southwards march of the Scots was halted by bad weather and dissension.

By the autumn of 1557 Philip seemed to have all northern France at his feet. It came as a shock therefore to hear the news of the successful French attack on and seizure of Calais and its hinterland on 1 January 1558 by the Duke of Guise. Thus France gained the last English enclave on the French coast, and not only the port of Calais itself but also an area of land measuring 20 miles by 6 miles including the strategic forts of Guisnes and Hammes. Where then does the blame lie for such an unmitigated defeat? Certainly Wentworth, the English commander at Calais, and the Council must bear some of the responsibility for failing to reinforce the English garrison and for laying up the English fleet for the winter. However, there was a wider lack of enthusiasm for the war, shared even by Philip himself leading to low morale. It may well be that sheer bad luck played a part too, and – possibly – treason.

How serious then was the loss of Calais? The economic loss can be exaggerated as the Staple was already in decline, numbering only 150 merchants as long ago as 1540. Yet the loss to morale was considerable, and for Protestants the defeat symbolised the dire penalty imposed by God for Mary's rule and the hated Spanish link. When Mary died the conflict was not yet resolved, the war had provided no real rallying point to unify the nation – despite the military commands of a few former opponents – and the recruitment system proved sadly deficient.

8 MARY'S LEGACY

Mary died at St James's Palace on 17 November 1558; Cardinal Pole died later the same day at Lambeth. Shortly before her death Mary acknowledged Princess Elizabeth, thus confirming both the 1544 Succession Act and Henry VIII's will. Since her death Mary has had a bad press: Elizabethans were keen to justify her successor's Protestant uniformity and Victorians stressed the importance of the reign of Elizabeth as the historical basis for English liberty. Hence both groups tended to see Mary's reign as an aberration in the even flow of English history, an object lesson in the perils of Catholic and authoritarian rule.

There remain further difficulties in arriving at a balanced interpretation. Mary spent much time at the start of her brief reign establishing her regime, and her task was all the harder as she was attempting a sharp break in both religious and foreign policy. In short she had to reward supporters, deal with opponents and reweave the nation's whole political fabric at the same time. In a sense, therefore, it is hardly fair to ask even whether there was a distinctive Marian regime, as it was still being formed in 1558. Elizabeth after all took ten years to create an identifiable Elizabethan regime.

For all that, it may be possible to see Mary as a strong monarch with a relatively successful Council and a fair grip on the administration of justice, even though many of her policies were unfinished or unfulfilled by 1558. Many of her measures were brought to fruition under Elizabeth: the search for new trade routes, coinage reform and the revival of the navy. Sometimes these have been held up as unique accomplishments of Elizabeth I's rule! At the same time Mary survived early vicissitudes and carried out several significant policies like her marriage, the return to Rome and the declaration of war. In fact she was defeated on only one main plank of her platform, namely her husband's coronation.

Despite all this it is impossible to avoid criticising Mary if one is to be fair to the evidence. Pre-existing religious divisions deteriorated under Mary and intolerance and xenophobia increased. Yet, in a curious way, Protestantism benefited from her reign. Under persecution the reformed faith could prove its religious credentials. Furthermore, as the victim of an apparently alien tyranny, it could establish itself as peculiarly English. Mary's reign stopped just in time for a moderate Anglicanism to be possible, and her main legacy in religion may indeed be that she weakened and divided religious conservatism.

Yet it remains probable that the main causes of her unpopularity lay outside religious policy. The Spanish marriage and the French war cast a longer shadow than her religious persecution.

9 BIBLIOGRAPHY

C S L Davies *Peace, Print and Protestantism 1450–1558* (Paladin 1977).
G R Elton *Reform and Reformation* (Edward Arnold, 1977).
C Haigh (ed.) *The English Reformation Revised* (CUP, 1987).
N Heard *Edward VI and Mary: A Mid-Tudor Crisis?* (Hodder & Stoughton, Access to History, 1990).
J Loach (ed.) and R Tittler *The Mid-Tudor Polity* (Macmillan, 1980).
D M Loades *The Reign of Mary Tudor* (Benn, 1980).
R Tittler *The Reign of Mary I* (Longman 1983).

10 DISCUSSION POINTS AND EXERCISE

A *This section consists of questions or points that might be used for discussion (or written answers) as a way of expanding on the chapter and testing understanding of it:*

1 Which are the most debatable issues affecting the reputation of Mary Tudor?

2 Account for Mary's success in taking the throne in 1553.

3 How far did Mary's accession lead to an upheaval in government personnel?

4 Why was it Mary's preference to marry Philip of Spain?

5 Why were such close restraints on Philip's authority in England insisted upon in the marriage treaty?

6 What caused Wyatt's Rebellion and why did it fail?

7 Was Mary's religious policy doomed from the start?

8 Why could Mary only attempt to re-Catholicize England in stages? What were those stages?

9 What were Pole's methods in the re-Catholicization of England and what limited their effectiveness?

10 What was the effect of the burnings?

11 Is it correct to describe Mary's foreign policy as 'a complete disaster'?

12 'Mary Tudor was a failure, although there are many mitigating reasons for her being so.' Is this a fair judgement?

B *Essay questions*

1 'Her marriage to Philip of Spain was Mary's worst mistake.' Discuss.

2 Account for Mary's popularity in 1553 and her unpopularity in 1558.

3 How firmly was Protestantism established in 1553 and to what extent was it weakened by the policies of Mary Tudor?

4 'An interlude of sterility and stagnation.' Is this a fair judgement on the reign of Mary I?

5 How far can Mary Tudor's government be described as 'efficient but reactionary'?

6 What was Mary I's legacy to her successor?

11 EXERCISE – WAS THERE A MID-TUDOR CRISIS?

The idea that there was a 'crisis' in mid-sixteenth-century England, rather on the lines of the alleged crisis in early and mid-seventeenth-century England and the 'General Crisis' theory in the whole of seventeenth-century Europe, does have some obvious appeal. Among historians who have suggested this perhaps the best known is W R D Jones who entitled his book published in 1973 *The Mid-Tudor Crisis, 1539 to 1563*. Jones detects a serious threat to the continuity, security and power of the Tudor monarchy in the combination during the period of severe difficulties in four main areas: the royal succession, religion, foreign policy and the economy.

There is no doubt that the period saw considerable dynastic problems for the Tudors. Edward VI succeeded as a minor of 10 years old and died before reaching his majority or producing an heir. His half-sister Mary seized the throne in 1553 in what many historians regard as the only successful rebellion during the period, but she died after only five years failing to leave an heir. Finally Elizabeth acceded in 1558 as a young unmarried woman challenged by her cousin Mary Queen of Scots.

A study of religious developments reveals a similar whirlwind of changes. Henry VIII's 'Catholicism without the Pope' was rapidly altered under his son, as a more and more Protestant policy emerged under both Somerset and Northumberland. Mary reversed this trend dramatically and attempted a root and branch return to the old faith. Elizabeth tried to impose a moderately Protestant settlement in 1559. Religious fanaticism was a strong feature of the entire period and religious issues informed several of the revolts during the period. The Western Rebellion of 1549 was caused almost solely by religious changes, Kett's Rebellion had strong Protestant overtones as did Wyatt's Rebellion in 1554 – the only one of the three to mount a serious challenge to the government and dynasty.

In foreign policy Henry's military adventures against France and Scotland spilled over into Edward VI's reign. Much of the Crown's windfall profit from the dissolutions was squandered on warfare and debasement of the coinage stoked the fires of inflation. Northumberland's pragmatic policy of financial retrenchment and appeasement of England's traditional enemies was reversed by Mary who embroiled England in a futile campaign against France that lost Calais and further discredited the already unpopular Spanish alliance.

Finally, serious economic problems exacerbated general poverty and combined with natural hazards like poor harvests and disease to demoralise and even to reduce the mass of the population. Prices rose sharply, especially in foodstuff where costs doubled between 1540 and 1560. Rents also increased as landlords tried to escape from the inflationary spiral while manufacturing and exports declined, particularly in the vital cloth trade. Under these circumstances unemployment soared and Professor Bindoff's 'dangerous corner' was reached with a series of disastrous harvests, especially those of 1555 and 1556 – the worst of the century. Influenza epidemics hit a population weakened by malnutrition and at the most conservative estimate no less than 6 per cent of the population died of disease between 1556 and 1560. Kett's Rebellion of 1549 stands out among a widespread network of revolts across southern England and the Midlands caused by economic and social grievances.

The crisis only came to an end according to Jones in 1563 when Elizabeth was beginning to establish herself on the throne with a successful religious settlement in 1559, the expulsion of the French from Scotland in 1560 and the introduction of a firmer coinage in 1561. Meanwhile she embarked on a more cautious semi-isolationist foreign policy.

There are however substantial objections to this view and it has to be said that few recent historians have been convinced by it. The crisis theory overlooks the fact that the government never lost control, even in 1549. This may have been partly because the two rebellions in 1549 had limited aims and did not intend to topple the government. The Council functioned effectively from 1540 despite undoubted factional turmoil from time to time. At the centre ministers like Cecil, Paget, Gresham and Mildmay kept the show on the road, assisted in the provinces by the mass of JPs. The governing élites survived the most dangerous moment in 1553 when they decided to back Mary's legitimate descent rather than flirt with Northumberland's 'devise'.

If there was no real crisis for the authorities, what about the people? One wonders whether ordinary people were aware of a continuous crisis over the whole period, or even just between 1547 and 1558. Perhaps it is more reasonable to speak of a series of short-lived crises of the kind that may have been normal for any country at any time. It is even arguable that the English economy was undergoing a period of restructuring rather than a genuine crisis, with its accompanying symptoms of population pressure and inflation best seen as passing phenomena.

The foreign policy 'crisis' theory can also be challenged as there was never a real danger of foreign invasion, and even religious tensions can seem to look less threatening. There may well have been as much compromise as confrontation among the English élite in their approach to religion, and there can be little doubt that apathy and indifference to religious questions characterised the approach of many ordinary people to rival religious enthusiasms. The zealots on either side were a small minority.

Alan G R Smith is among contemporary historians who have been sceptical of the 'Mid-Tudor Crisis' idea. This is his conclusion:

The death of Mary can be seen as marking the end – or the beginning of the end – of the 'mid-century crisis' of Tudor England. But should we talk in such apocalyptic terms? It may be that the application of the word 'crisis' to a period of at least eleven and in the case of some historians (W. R. D. Jones covers the period 1539 to 1563) of over twenty years obscures as much as it illuminates. It seems essential at least to distinguish in discussion between the English people and the English state. There is obviously much to be said for the view that the middle decades of the century were a period of crisis (or perhaps better of crises) for the people of England. The years 1540–60 saw unprecedently rapid changes in the economy and in religion, arguably the two areas which affected most intimately the lives of ordinary Englishmen; historians are now emphasizing the profound psychological as well as material shocks which these upheavals must have meant for hundreds of thousands of men and women who had been accustomed to much less volatile conditions. It is doubtful, on the other hand, if the Tudor state was ever in quite as serious difficulties as the word 'crisis' implies. Between 1540 and 1558 the throne was occupied successively by a sick and rapidly ageing bully, a boy who was too young to rule and a woman of limited political abilities. In these circumstances what is significant and remarkable is not the weakness of government, but its relative strength. At no time during the period, except perhaps at the end of Somerset's Protectorate, was there a serious threat of the breakdown of administration, surely the fundamental test of a 'crisis' in the life of a state. The middle decades of the century certainly produced severe difficulties for the governments of the time, but the English State which Elizabeth inherited in 1558 was a fully functioning polity.

1 *What do you understand by the word 'crisis'?*
2 *Summarise the case for the 'Mid-Tudor Crisis' in about one hundred words.*
3 *Similarly give a summary of the case against the theory in about one hundred words.*
4 *How far are the different aspects of the 'crisis' – dynastic, diplomatic and military, religious and social/economic separate themes and how far are they inter-related? Look back over the previous two chapters to get ideas for this.*

VIII

ELIZABETH I: THE GOVERNMENT OF ENGLAND

Elizabeth I, Nicholas Hilliard

1 INTRODUCTION

THE long reign of Elizabeth I was in several respects an age of change. In particular, religious life again took a new direction, and there was a radical re-orientation of the country's foreign policy. However, the system of government through which Elizabeth ruled changed remarkably little. Institutions and practices waxed and waned, but there was no striking departure from the paths trodden by previous Tudor monarchs. Elizabeth's cautious conservatism was as evident in this respect as in any other.

This is not to belittle Elizabeth's achievement. The latter lay in mastering the existing system, producing from it a stability and strength few if anyone anticipated in 1558. The monarchy was certainly not at its most formidable when Elizabeth assumed the throne. The first two Tudors were immensely strong figures. It is clear, however, that during the reigns of Edward and Mary the stature of the monarchy was considerably diminished. This followed partly from their individual shortcomings and partly from the fact that in an age of religious excitement and division the monarch inevitably failed to command undisputed loyalty. Many looked to conscience rather than to the monarch's will for guidance in both religion and public affairs. In addition, Elizabeth inherited an empty Exchequer and a war which had inflicted great damage to the reputation and popularity of her sister.

Initially, Elizabeth's qualifications to restore the monarchy did not seem impressive. In 1558 she was a 25-year-old princess who had never been taught the arts of kingship which male heirs traditionally learnt from their fathers and tutors. As a woman, such were the assumptions of the age, she was not expected in any case to possess the capacity to govern. Many would have agreed with the words in John Knox's *First Blast of the Trumpet against the Monstrous Regiment of Women*, published just before Elizabeth's accession: 'To promote a woman to bear rule, superiority, dominion or empire above any realm, nation or city is repugnant to nature; contumely to God, a thing most contrary to his revealed will and approved ordinance; and finally, it is the subversion of good order, of all equity and justice.' In particular, it was felt that she would be unable to control the men around her. Mary Tudor's reign possibly eroded the prejudice, but the popular impression of the influence of Philip and Pole meant that the myth was by no means dispelled. Finally, the dubious claim to legitimacy of the daughter of Anne Boleyn added to the likelihood of discontent if Elizabeth alienated Catholics and invited them and the monarchs of Europe to look to the rival claimant, Mary Queen of Scots.

Expectation of weak government was almost a self-fulfilling prophecy. An institution which lacked the revenue to create a strong army and bureaucracy depended upon the image rather than the reality of strength. If the great men of England regarded Elizabeth as a weak ruler, half the battle to impose her authority was already lost.

Of course, Elizabeth had numerous advantages too. She had many of the personal qualities of a good ruler. From Henry and Anne she inherited intelligence, cunning, the capacity to charm and a remarkable strength of will. She had a quick temper which intimidated all who ever experienced its unleashing. Anne's unfortunate fate and Elizabeth's need under Mary to dispel suspicion of her treason and heresy had made her a wily and defensive politician. In addition, the Tudor dynasty was by this stage firmly established, and Elizabeth's place within it and consequent right to rule were accepted by the vast majority – notwithstanding the dangers of a provocative religious policy. During Mary's long illness in 1558 there was no move made to prevent Elizabeth's accession. In fact, Mary's mistakes made Elizabeth's arrival on the throne a welcome relief to many.

Finally, for all the reservations about this young woman's ability to rule, the nation did want her to provide firm, strong government. The memory of how weak monarchy led to civil war in the previous century had become entrenched in the political culture. The factionalism and civil disturbance of more recent years underlined the point. Elizabeth could clearly draw not only upon her own talents but also on a reservoir of goodwill among her people. She ascended the throne in 1558 with no little confidence and relish for the task ahead.

2 THE MONARCH AS GOVERNOR

Elizabeth had a clear perception of the need to project the glory and splendour of the monarchy, and of the consequent need to maintain an impressive Court. Expenditure at Court and the size of its inner circle, the Household, were smaller than under Edward and Mary, out of financial necessity. But shrewd use of the money available meant that there was no decline in the opulence of the Tudor Court. The brilliance of the clothes, jewellery and tapestries and of the frequent tournaments, plays, pageants, banquets and other entertainments, the grace and charm of Elizabeth, the rigorous attention to etiquette, and the frequent attendance of the great aristocrats created an impression of royal magnificence among all who came into contact with the Queen and her Court. The fact that she went 'on progress' to most of central and southern England – although never to the north or west – exposed the glittering array to the gaze of a significant proportion of her people. And, of course, the courtiers carried to their localities news of the majesty which they saw and associated with the name of Elizabeth.

Poets praising the Queen as Gloriana or the goddess Astraea and a vast number of portraits of Elizabeth appearing in paintings, miniatures, medallions, woodcuts and engravings created 'the cult of Elizabeth' – and of a monarchy which came closer than any other in English history to divine status. (*This cultural development is discussed in fuller detail on pages 425–30.*) Perhaps English Protestants found in the glorification of Elizabeth an alternative to the Catholics' 'superstitious' adoration of saints and use of religious imagery. In particular, Frances Yates has suggested that Elizabethans may have found in the Virgin Queen a Protestant substitute for the Virgin Mary; as one poet advised, the cry of *Vivat Eliza!* should take the place of *Ave Maria!*.

Notwithstanding the efforts of propagandists, it was on her performance as the head of government that Elizabeth's success or failure ultimately depended. That performance was manifested in the directions taken in national policy, and subsequent chapters will assess the merits of her moderate religious policy and independent foreign policy. But one must, in addition, consider the extent to which Elizabeth displayed application, skill and character in her everyday conduct of affairs. She certainly had a large capacity for work and involved herself in the smallest details of government. This could annoy her ministers – 'I would to God, her Majesty could be content to refer these things to them that can best judge of them, as other princes do', complained Walsingham on one occasion – but it did keep them 'on their toes' and it developed in Elizabeth a considerable knowledge of every issue. She also possessed intelligence and sound political judgement. But her most notable quality was her strength of character, her unbending will, and it will be obvious from what follows that this was the basis of her domination of the political system.

She had vices, too, of course: she could be unreasonable and self-centred, and her wilfulness often resembled blind obstinacy; her excessive caution and indecision were probably major, damaging faults, as the succession question demonstrated. Nevertheless, it would be churlish indeed to deny that Elizabeth had the personal qualities of an effective ruler.

Elizabeth had a clear idea of her place within the English constitution. The Privy Council had an important and valued advisory role. But the ultimate decisions belonged to the Queen. This was the essence of the 'royal prerogative', and Elizabeth had such a forceful, intimidating personality that no minister ever dared to question it. Similarly, she did not permit Parliament to make decisions on national affairs, and, further, denied its right, with mixed success, even to discuss 'matters of state' without her consent (*see Chapter X*).

More than any other Tudor, except perhaps Henry VII, she was in charge of policy. William Cecil, despite the accusation of his rivals that he was *roy plus qu'elle*, acknowledged his duty to 'obey her Majesty's commandment and no wise contrary the same'. The Earl of Leicester, Cecil's principal rival for almost thirty years, allegedly learnt more painfully to know his place. In the early 1630s, Sir Robert Naunton recalled that:

> The principal note of . . . [Queen Elizabeth's] reign will be that she ruled much by faction and parties which herself both made, upheld, and weakened, as her own great judgment advised; for I dissent from the common received opinion that my lord of Leicester was absolute and above all in her grace . . . [When he presumed to threaten one of her officials with dismissal] she replied with her wonted oath (God's death!), my lord, I have wished you well but my favour is not so locked up for you that others shall not partake thereof; for I have many servants unto whom I have and will at my pleasure bequeath my favour and likewise resume the same. And if you think to rule here I will take a course to see you forthcoming. I will have here but one mistress and no master . . . which so quelled my lord of Leicester that his feigned humility was long after one of his best virtues . . .

1 *What light does Naunton throw upon the personality of Elizabeth?*

2 *Why was it important that Elizabeth's 'favour' should not be given to one man but to her 'many servants'?*

3 *Why must one question Naunton's reliability when he relates a story which promotes the idea of Elizabeth's greatness?*

On some points the Queen resisted clear majorities within the Council and Parliament, and on others she was so remarkably wilful that even unanimity among her ministers could not change her course. The demands of the more radical Protestants, the Puritans, many of them supported by her leading Councillors, foundered upon her obstinate refusal to alter the religious settlement of 1559. And it was her recalcitrance which, defying a clear majority in the Council, delayed for many years England's joining the Dutch rebels against Spain. Her role in determining religious and foreign policy is discussed more fully in Chapters IX and XI. The following examples of Elizabeth's strength are drawn from an area in which her jealous protection of the royal prerogative was probably most complete: the related questions of the succession, Mary Queen of Scots and her marriage – in her view, matters *par excellence* into which no subject had the right to enter unasked.

In October 1562, Elizabeth nearly died of smallpox, raising the spectre of civil war in the event of a disputed succession. She came under intense pressure to name her successor. But Elizabeth was aware that men would inevitably rally to the nominee, and might even plot treason to secure an early succession. As she told the Commons, 'I am well acquainted with the nature of this people; I know how easily they dislike the present state of affairs; I know what nimble eyes they bear to the next succession . . . When my sister Mary was Queen, what prayers were made by many to see me placed in her seat . . . Now then, if the affections of our people grow faint . . . In how great danger shall I be . . .? Assuredly, if my successor were known to the world, I would never esteem my state to be safe.'

Other conspiracies might form around disappointed claimants, perhaps Jane Grey's sister, Catherine, especially in view of the fact that the successor whom Elizabeth favoured on the basis of strict legitimacy, Mary Queen of Scots ('I know not who should be before her'), would be anathema to many English Protestants. So, in spite of strong pressure year after year from her Councillors, successive Parliaments, and the nation at large, Elizabeth never gave her decision on the issue, not even on her deathbed in 1603. It was a remarkable example of her obdurate strength.

In 1567 Mary Queen of Scots, generally thought to have connived at the murder of her husband, Lord Darnley, was deposed. Indignant at the liberties taken by the Scots with a fellow-monarch, Elizabeth protested vigorously against Mary's imprisonment and dethronement – this without reference to a Council which for the most part welcomed

Mary's fall. The Scottish Queen's arrival in England in 1568 to seek refuge raised new problems. From the beginning, she was suspected of plotting against Elizabeth. In 1571, she was at least acquainted with the Florentine banker Ridolfi's plan to overthrow Elizabeth by inviting armed Spanish intervention. Her principal English accomplice, the Duke of Norfolk, was executed for his part, but Elizabeth, defying the overwhelming majority in both the Council and the Parliament of 1572, refused even to agree to a bill to bar Mary from the English succession. In fact, only Elizabeth's determination to protect her cousin stood between Mary and the scaffold. Thereafter, Mary figured prominently, though for the most part passively, in the treasonous plans of English Catholics and their Spanish, French and papal allies. It took irrefutable proof of Mary's complicity in the Babington Plot of 1586 to destroy Elizabeth's resolve, after almost twenty years, and permit the Council to decide the issue which led to Mary's execution in 1587. Though ultimately defeated on this, the affair as a whole bears eloquent testimony to her dominant role in the decision-making process.

Marriage and child-bearing would have solved many of these problems. The inevitability of the Queen's marriage was generally taken for granted in the first decade of the reign. Elizabeth initially concurred. But Mary's experience with Philip showed that the English would not easily accept a foreign king, and the choice of an Englishman would provoke jealousy (*see page 216 on Dudley*). Also, Elizabeth clearly feared that a husband would detract from her power. ('I will have here but one mistress and no master.') As early as the mid-1560s, she may have decided to remain single; after this, she happily reaped the diplomatic benefits of courtships with foreign princes, but she frustrated the efforts of those who sought to complete the process. The candidature of Austria's Archduke Charles was favoured by Norfolk, Sussex and Cecil. But Leicester and his friends feared the coming of a husband indebted to their rivals. Elizabeth found it easy, in December 1567, to latch onto the Protestant scruples of the Leicester circle to reject the suit. There were subsequent discussions about marriage to two French princes, brothers to the King – the Duke of Anjou in 1570–2, and in 1578–82 the Duke of Alençon (also known, somewhat confusingly, as Anjou after his succession to his brother's title). These proposals similarly foundered upon the Queen's lack of serious intent, despite the efforts on the first occasion of a significant portion of her Council.

Of course, the Virgin Queen never did marry. Elizabeth was very much 'her own woman'; she was a strong monarch whose right to decide upon national affairs was beyond question.

The picture drawn so far is by no means complete. Elizabeth was no autocrat. Financial weakness was a major constraint on the monarchy; no ruler had the capacity to govern without the co-operation of the propertied classes and both the Privy Council and Parliament had indispensable roles. A comprehensive view of the Queen's role is possible only after the other parts of the body politic have been described. However, while the monarch did not govern alone the other institutions of government existed more to serve than to restrict her power.

3 THE PRIVY COUNCIL: COMPOSITION

After the fall of Thomas Cromwell in 1540, the Council was expanded to include both ministers and magnates (men chosen in acknowledgement of their status as great men in the localities). For this reason, the Council contained up to forty members under Edward and fifty under Mary. Though modern historians have argued the effectiveness of the Marian Council, Elizabeth was clearly unimpressed; she felt that 'a multitude doth make rather discord and confusion than good counsel'.

Elizabeth essentially returned to the Cromwellian idea of a smaller, working body. Her first Council had only nineteen members. That it contained several magnates, and that some of these were moderate Catholics, indicates that Elizabeth did not or could not entirely forsake the benefits of a Council which represented influence and opinion. Such men would give her government more stature and authority, they would help her to govern their counties, and in times of unrest or warfare their loyalty was indispensable. But her priority was a Council of professional administrators, men selected for their competence and for their reliance upon her continued favour.

Almost immediately an inner ring of fewer than ten such people emerged, the others seldom attending. Later, the magnates ceased to be members, death rather than dismissal claiming a majority. They were not replaced. In the 1590s, the membership sank at one point to as low as nine, and the regular attendance to four or five. The eleven-member Council of 1597 and the thirteen-member Council of 1601 each had only one member who did not hold office. The virtual exclusion of the magnates illustrates the self-confidence of the regime, but Christopher Haigh has suggested that the Council thereby became 'dangerously narrow and weak in its membership'.

The vast majority of Elizabeth's first Council had earlier experience of high office. Some had served Henry and Edward, and ten of the nineteen had been on Mary's last Council. However, this understates the extent of the change wrought in 1558–9. Mary's principal adviser at the end of her reign, Paget, was dismissed. William Cecil (sometimes known by his later title, Lord Burghley), the new secretary, was his effective replacement. The strongest Catholics were omitted, including Nicholas Heath, Lord Chancellor and Archbishop of York (Canterbury was vacant after Pole survived Mary by only twelve hours). The balance shifted in favour of pragmatic Protestants like Cecil. They were flanked by the more radical Francis Knollys and Bedford and moderate, non-papist conservatives in Winchester, Arundel, Shrewsbury and Derby. Few of the retained or conservative Councillors (Lord Treasurer Winchester being the main exception on both counts) entered the inner circle of active ministers. None of the retained conservatives survived beyond 1572, and only two new conservatives (Croft in 1566 and Worcester in 1601) were appointed. In sum, Elizabeth's Council, especially the active element, was very much her own creation, and its Protestantism indicates that the change from Mary's Council was more than a simple matter of personnel.

The revival of Cecil's career was especially important, for he went on to become one of the greatest administrator-politicians in English history. From 1550 he served as surveyor of Elizabeth's estates and in 1550–3 was Northumberland's Secretary of State. Under Mary, he was naturally out of favour, but he avoided persecution by conforming to Catholicism, despite his Protestant views. In 1558, he became Secretary of State again, and in 1572 (now as Lord Burghley, 1571) he was appointed Lord Treasurer, a post he held until his death in 1598.

Cecil's ability and loyalty were greatly valued by Elizabeth, and during his forty years in office he was the Queen's most influential and reliable adviser. But he was never able to monopolise Elizabeth's favour. His greatest rival was Robert Dudley, Earl of Leicester (1564). Dudley tried in the early years of the reign to win Elizabeth's hand in marriage, much to the annoyance of Cecil, and their rivalry was subsequently aggravated by the difference between Cecil's moderate Protestantism and Leicester's incautious radicalism. Leicester's lack of ministerial office – he had only minor Household posts, as Master of the Horse and Lieutenant of Windsor Castle – demonstrates the irrelevance of formal office, for he was a major political force until his death in 1588. Elizabeth's Councillors also included men of the calibre of the Marquis of Winchester, Lord Treasurer 1550–72, Sir Francis Walsingham, Secretary of State 1573–90, and William's son, Robert, Secretary of State 1596–1612.

Finally, Elizabeth's Councils included remarkably few clerics. Whitgift was the only one of Elizabeth's three Archbishops of Canterbury to enter the Council, and no Archbishop of York joined it after Heath's removal. No other practising clergyman was made a Councillor. Initially, this probably owed much to the steadfast Catholicism of the bishops inherited from Mary. But the pattern persisted. The remarkable expansion of lay education during the century had created a reservoir of talent. Elizabeth's preference for active ministers over representatives of specific interests was also a factor. But it may well be that the dearth of clerical influence at the summit of political life also reflected the diminished stature of the post-Reformation Church.

4 THE PRIVY COUNCIL: DECIDING NATIONAL POLICY

Its executive role demanded most of the Council's attention, and this will be discussed below. It also acted as an advisory body to the Queen, taking the initiative, generally, in proposing policy. She normally took no part in the Council's discussions; her role was to receive the Council's view or views and proceed to make a decision. Of course, Elizabeth sought and accepted advice from men who were not Councillors at all. Every courtier was a potential adviser. However, the Household tended to be a less important forum of political discussion after the formation of the Privy Council – all the more so because the Privy Chambers of Mary and Elizabeth were predominantly female (though the regular access which Household members had to the Queen probably did give them a significant role in the distribution of patronage). In fact, the leading officers of the Household tended themselves to be Councillors rather than to rival the Council. The Council was the Queen's only regular source of advice.

The members of Elizabeth's Privy Council found various means to influence the Queen's decisions. They could be skilful manipulators of public opinion. In 1560, there emerged the prospect of Elizabeth marrying Robert Dudley (Earl of Leicester from 1564). The young Queen was clearly infatuated with him. Many, however, were alarmed that, as her husband, Dudley would achieve a monopoly of influence and favour; indeed, it appeared that this ambitious son of the infamous Duke of Northumberland would appropriate the powers of the monarchy. An explicit opposition to the marriage would have infuriated Elizabeth – she imprisoned two courtiers for their criticism. So Cecil chose a more devious course. He encouraged a rumour that Dudley was plotting to poison his wife, Amy Dudley. Amy's death in September 1560 (she was found at the bottom of a staircase; the cause of death is not known) seemed to confirm the story and meant that a marriage would provoke popular outrage. Also, it may have been Cecil who made public in 1561 Dudley's plan to win Philip II's support for the marriage by pledging the restoration of Catholicism; this time the public outcry against the marriage was probably fatal.

Much later, in 1579, the Queen entertained seriously the prospect of marriage to the (second) Duke of Anjou. A vigorous anti-Catholic and anti-French campaign, seen in plays, broadsheets and sermons, convinced her that public opinion was set against the idea, and she felt compelled to give it up. But the campaign was almost certainly instigated by Leicester and Walsingham. Haigh has written that Elizabeth 'told Alençon [Anjou] that her people would not consent to the marriage. In fact, it had been dished by the Privy Council.'

The Councillors could sometimes rally influential support from more unexpected sources. As well as stirring popular opinion against the Dudley suit, Cecil also persuaded the Spanish ambassador to advise Elizabeth of its disadvantages. Indeed, both foreign ambassadors and English ambassadors abroad were often covertly recruited to support the views of Councillors. More rarely, the Queen's ladies were used; in 1581, when the Anjou project was revived, Leicester and Hatton induced the women of the Privy Chamber to 'weep and wail about the horrors of marriage'. As shown below, Councillors were often responsible for Parliament's more agitated endeavours, notably on marriage and the succession. In fact, the tendency of Councillors to manipulate information went even farther: most of the correspondence with the Queen was received by Cecil as secretary, so he was in a position to deny her knowledge entirely, prepare an appropriate interpretation, choose the moment of presentation (minding well the Queen's mood), or solicit a more convenient, contrary view.

The eventual fate of Mary Queen of Scots shows that the Council could make decisions in areas where Elizabeth's will was not clearly expressed despite the Queen's earlier determination not to proceed against her cousin. In July 1586, Mary (allegedly) dictated the infamous letter in which she endorsed Babington's plot to murder Elizabeth. Walsingham's agents, aware that Mary used empty beer casks to smuggle secret correspondence from her prison home at Chartley Manor, duly intercepted the letter. Mary was tried by a special commission, found guilty, and sentenced to death. But Elizabeth baulked at the idea of killing a fellow monarch. Walsingham was driven to fabricating the 'Stafford Plot' to murder Elizabeth, to show the Queen that her life remained in danger as long as Mary lived. In the end, the decision to despatch the warrant for her execution was taken by the Privy Council, and Elizabeth was informed after the deed was done on 7 February 1587. Her fury had no lasting effect, except on the ruined career of the scapegoat, the second secretary William Davison.

However, it is misleading to dwell so long on the more covert and devious stratagems to which Councillors had recourse. Quite simply, Elizabeth respected the views of the extremely able men she appointed. Such men were not mere ciphers. Cecil in particular won her trust as a man of considerable judgement, but she also had a high regard for the less wide-ranging talents of Leicester, Walsingham and other of her Councillors. Experience showed that their advice was often correct. And they were capable of presenting their views persuasively and diplomatically. In 1559, Cecil's arguments and persistence (possibly assisted by a resignation threat) induced a reluctant monarch to help the Scottish Protestants to drive out the French. When Mary first arrived in England, in 1568, Elizabeth's first instinct was to help her regain what was indisputably her right, the throne of Scotland. But Cecil's tentative expression of the danger posed by a restored Mary and constant emphasis on Mary's possible guilt in the murder of her husband (as well, more deviously, as his encouragement of Regent Moray and the Scottish Protestants to oppose restoration) were the influences which checked Elizabeth (even before Mary betrayed her trust by plotting secretly to marry the Duke of Norfolk and, later, to have Elizabeth deposed).

Clearly, then, the Council intervened constantly in the making of policy. However, the execution of Mary was unique; it was the only major decision made by the Council. The fact remains that it was Elizabeth who made the decisions on national policy. All the strivings of her advisers serve to underline the point. And, for all the exceptions noted above, it is necessary to recall the frequency with which the Queen's formidable will decided (or refused to decide) policy, even against the wishes of those who surrounded her. The Council had a significant role, but there is no disputing the primacy of the monarch.

5 FACTION

Elizabeth's Council was rarely a united body. Indeed conflict was endemic. It was mainly concerned with the struggle to win the Queen's favour, for this was the key to a successful political career. The honour and glory associated with a leading role in government was one incentive to competition. But control of patronage was the major prize in this political game.

Policy differences also arose. Unfortunately, it is not always possible to separate advocacy of policy from the quest for favour. Leicester's pressure for intervention in the cause of the Huguenots in 1562 probably owed more to his desire to match Cecil's earlier Scottish triumph than to any assessment of the merits of the policy; but one cannot be sure. In 1569–70, there was a concerted attempt by numerous Councillors to destroy Cecil; the impulse came in part from resentment against the secretary's hold on Elizabeth's favour, and partly from the conviction that his foreign policy was placing the country in great danger (this was in the aftermath of the seizure of the Spanish treasure [*see Chapter XI*]). The long dispute between Cecil and Leicester on the issue of intervention in the Dutch Revolt against Philip II probably marked a genuine difference on policy; but in the wider context the rivalry between the two began as, and remained primarily, a competition for favour. The last great dispute of the reign was between Robert Cecil, who in effect took over from his father as the Queen's chief minister when William Cecil died in 1598, and the Earl of Essex, who was successor in the Queen's affections to Leicester who had died in 1588. The dispute was mainly concerned with Elizabeth's favour, in particular with the consequent control of royal patronage, although the Earl's association with an aggressive, Protestant foreign policy deepened the rift.

Men naturally formed alliances in the course of these disputes. But it would be wrong to characterise them as 'parties' in the modern sense of political groups identifiable by common policies and organised support. In the first place the political alliances were so unstable. In 1568, Norfolk was Cecil's friend and the bitter rival of the over-ambitious Leicester; within a year he was Leicester's ally in the drive to depose Cecil. By retaining the Queen's confidence, Cecil moved from friendless isolation in 1569 to general approval in 1572. Secondly, even between rivals there was co-operation in the business of government; if it had been otherwise, Elizabeth would have frowned upon such 'discord and confusion'. The idea of parties uniting to press for particular measures would have been considered an unconstitutional infringement of the monarch's right to determine policy. One must reject, therefore, the concept of 'parties' in Elizabethan England.

The concept of 'faction', in other words a loose association of politicians with similar aims and interests, is favoured by many historians. These groupings too were unstable. Politics which placed more emphasis on the distribution of spoils than on principle were incapable of generating lasting alliances.

Elizabeth never gave exclusive power to any single individual or faction. Giving over a monopoly would deny the Queen control of policy, and both deprive her of the benefits of patronage and provoke discontent among those denied favour. Whether Elizabeth deliberately fomented difference, according to the principle of 'divide and rule', is much more debatable. On numerous occasions she sought to resolve differences – to achieve harmony, a working relationship, between rivals. However, for all the advantages of a united government, on balance the fact of so much conflict strengthened her hand, helping her to dominate. There is some evidence that she appointed men of opposing factions and varying views; for example, Norfolk and Dudley were admitted to the Council together in October 1562, and Archbishop Whitgift was one of several moderate Councillors nominated in 1586 to balance the aggressively Protestant Leicester and Walsingham. Such men competed for her favours. And the Queen was able to receive varying advice, often interviewing Councillors individually, and to make decisions which had the support of at least part of the Council. The prime example of Elizabeth's ability to exploit the divisions within her Council was the way in which the concurrence of Cecil, Sussex and a few others helped her to resist the pressure from a majority for intervention in the Dutch Revolt.

A Council united against her would have been a formidable prospect. But there existed no system of collective responsibility by which Councillors united behind one, majority view. The politicians were too ready to devour each other in order to achieve purely personal goals. And such a system would have been regarded as an unconstitutional threat to the royal prerogative to decide national policy –

regarded as such by most, and by a monarch whose intimidating personality did not encourage the expression of an alternative view.

6 THE PRIVY COUNCIL: ITS EXECUTIVE ROLE

Councillors were rather more free to make decisions in the administrative role which claimed most of their attention. It is quite startling to the modern mind the extent to which the Privy Council was involved in the minutiae of everyday life. Elton cites one, typical day on which 'the Council considered the Catholic Lady Stonor's house arrest, trade with Spain, a minor land dispute in Guernsey, a poor man's complaint against the Bishop of Hereford, various matters connected with recusants, the report that a man had spoken in favour of [the Jesuit] Edward Campion, a land dispute between the Earls of Northumberland and Bedford, a merchant's losses through Turkish pirates, Sir Peter Carew's debts, seven passports to foreign vessels released from embargo, and the provision of post hirses for a messenger'. On other occasions, the Council discussed such trivial matters as the cost of a pond in St James's Park and the alleged use of lewd words by a William Holland of Sussex.

It would appear, then, that no aspect of life was beyond the scope of the Council. Served by only a few clerks, it issued a constant and extraordinarily varied stream of orders to officials great and small in the provinces. And it was the Council which appointed those officials. It also supervised the Queen's accounts and authorised every act of expenditure by the Exchequer. In the 1580s, the campaign to suppress Catholicism saw the Council discussing the fate of hundreds of individuals. From 1585, the war against Spain was organised by the Council, a massive undertaking which included training of the militia, production of munitions, the building of ships and recruitment of privateers, and decisions about individual military operations.

The Council also had a quasi-judicial role. It investigated many crimes, especially those, like treason, sedition and popular disorder, which threatened the security or stability of the state. Torture was commonly used in the process. These crimes would ultimately be tried by the courts. In addition, disputes between private individuals were often brought before the Council. These private cases consumed much valuable time. Several attempts to order suitors to apply instead to the courts proved futile; suitors naturally sought the support of the great men of government, and the latter felt compelled to hear the grievances of friends and dependants.

Such a centralised system imposed an enormous burden of work on the Council. In the early years, the Councillors usually gathered three times a week, in either the morning or the afternoon. Towards the end of the reign, with the war in particular adding greatly to its duties, the Council met almost every day, including Sundays, often all day.

That this overloaded system yielded efficient government is eloquent testimony to the industry and ability of the Councillors. Cecil's role was pivotal. His office of Secretary of State (1558–72) formally meant he was the Queen's secretary. Essentially, however, he was also the secretary of the Council. He procured information, set the Council's agenda, and took responsibility for the dissemination and enforcement of its decisions – all this across the whole, extraordinary range of the Council's business. When he became Lord Treasurer in 1572, it would appear that his involvement in administrative detail became only marginally less close and pervasive – possibly at the expense of the attention which Crown finances sorely required (*see pages 230–5*).

The administrative work of the Council is not without relevance to the more political, advisory role discussed above. The Councillors were not men who merely considered and advised upon policy. Such figures, however wise, would have been relatively expendable. Instead, the Council was the indispensable hub of the entire machinery of government. The possible loss of such invaluable servants could not be treated lightly. Standing or falling together, they could have been replaced only with great difficulty and disruption. As shown above, however, Elizabeth was faced with no such united front – and consequently with a Council which did more to supplement than detract from her power.

7 GOVERNING THE PROVINCES

The system

The experience of most English people was largely confined to their locality. Many never left their county, and it was the latter they often meant when they referred to their 'cuntrie'. They were only vaguely and intermittently aware of the activities of the central government in London. The Crown's weak finances precluded the maintenance of an extensive bureaucracy; its paid agents in the provinces numbered only a few hundred revenue collectors, customs officials and wardship administrators (feodaries). So, the government of every county was principally the responsibility of voluntary, unpaid members of the local nobility and gentry.

Under the Tudors, and especially during the reign of Elizabeth, there was a substantial increase in the burdens imposed on this local governing class. This arose from the government's more active efforts to regulate the economy, deal with the poor, secure religious conformity, and promote the country's military preparedness. As the burden grew, so was the organisation of local government changed, again especially under Elizabeth, though the Crown's shortage of money meant there could be no departure from reliance on the local élites.

The role of the sheriff continued its long decline. Appointed for only one year, and responsible for a variety of onerous and expensive tasks, the office was accepted with increasing reluctance. The sheriff's place at the head of county society was taken, under Elizabeth, by a relatively new creation, the Lord-Lieutenant. Originally, during Henry VIII's reign, this figure was confined to responsibility for the local militia, and it was an occasional and short-lived appointment determined by military circumstances. The post developed under Henry's successors, with the Elizabethan war against Spain in particular bringing it to a new level of importance. In the 1580s, Lord-Lieutenants were appointed to almost every county and permitted to retain the office for life. Their duties were filled out to include the levying of forced loans, enforcement of economic regulations, supervision of the JPs, and a general responsibility for acquainting the Council with events in their county. To hold this position became a great honour; it was a mark of the Queen's favour or of one's pre-eminence in the county – in most cases of both. It was held usually by a peer, and in half the counties by a Councillor. Much of the work was done by the several Deputy Lieutenants; a post created in the 1560s, it bore its own considerable prestige and was filled by the larger, resident landowners.

The Justices of the Peace were both 'the mainstay of the Tudor system of law enforcement' and, increasingly, 'the general executive agents of local administration'. Their number rose fivefold under the Tudors, to an average of about fifty per county. To become a JP was to be acknowledged as a member of the leading gentry. The JP's workload grew with the great increase in statute (parliamentary) law under the Tudors. He had a major judicial role, as the magistrate responsible for deciding upon the vast majority of disputes and offences, from murder to the theft of swan's egg. In addition, especially under Elizabeth, the JP acquired numerous administrative duties, notably in relation to the Poor Law and economic regulation (*see Chapter XV*), maintenance of highways and bridges, licensing of alehouses, and the management of houses of correction.

Special commissions were sent out to perform those tasks which could not be left to the existing officials. Used by all the Tudors – one thinks of the men who investigated the monasteries in Cromwell's day – they appeared particularly often during Elizabeth's reign. For example, the oath to the Royal Supremacy, according to the religious settlement of 1559, was imposed by special commissions, and from 1583 staunchly Protestant commissions were deployed to enforce the persecution of Catholics. Initially, the use of these bodies was a significant departure from the principle of local men for local government, but it appears that under Elizabeth they were more often than not dominated by local men, albeit specially selected.

Below county level, in the hundred and the parish, constables, churchwardens, overseers of the poor (from 1597) and other officials carried out numerous functions, for example road maintenance, the control of vermin, policing, and poor relief, under the supervision of JPs and sheriffs. The emergence of the parish as a secular (non-religious) unit was another important development under Elizabeth. In the towns, borough councils – mostly narrow, propertied oligarchies whose members were co-opted rather than elected – appointed those who carried out a similar range of duties there.

An assessment

This system of government had many imperfections. Though the office-holders at county level were formally appointed by the central government, the degree of control exerted by the latter was far from complete. With the posts carrying little or no remuneration – the sheriffs received nominal fees, and the JPs were given small allowances for attending sessions – men did not depend on the government for their living in the way that members of a modern civil service do. The channels of communication, especially with the northern provinces, were far from adequate, so that one could not even be sure what was happening. The fact that the JPs met increasingly often meant that they developed an *esprit de corps* which led to emphasis on local interests to the exclusion of wider concerns.

Not surprisingly, then, office-holders did not always co-operate with the policy of the government. The majority of JPs were relatively inactive, regarding their appointment more as a badge of honour than an obligation to serve. Some abused their positions for personal profit. According to one complainant, 'A Justice of the Peace is a Living Creature that for half a dozen of Chickens will Dispense with a whole Dozen of Penal Statutes . . . unless you offer sacrifice unto these Idol-Justices, of Sheep and Oxen, they know you not.' In many parts of the country, recusancy fines (for non-attendance at church) were not enforced because JPs were sympathetic to the plight of their Catholic neighbours where they were not themselves of that persuasion. Often the militia was inadequately prepared; local opposition to both service in it and the expense was shared by the gentry and prevailed over any wider conception of the national interest. As shown on page 233, the subsidy commissioners appointed to collect parliamentary taxation permitted outrageously distorted assessments which greatly diminished Crown revenue.

The problem reached new proportions in the 1590s. The country was simultaneously exhausted by the demands of war and afflicted by high inflation and (in 1594–7) bad harvests. There was resentment against parliamentary taxes, the new poor rates, ship money (in place of ships), militia rates, militia service, and conscription to fight abroad or, even worse, in Ireland; and it is clear that in many places the local governors shared the popular disaffection and obstructed the enforcement of these measures. Given that the country's national defences were jeopardised by the Crown's lack of a dependable bureaucracy, it is apparent that much more than administrative efficiency was at stake.

The composition of local power structures could also be a serious problem. Some families were of such eminence, owning vast tracts of land and exerting a perhaps centuries-old sway over the minds of all in their proximity, that they had more effective say than distant London in the running of their counties. To try to circumvent their power would amount to open confrontation with county society, when the whole idea of the system was to win the latter's co-operation. Only in the far north, where the loyalty of the great Percy, Neville and Dacre families was particularly doubtful, did Elizabeth try to exclude magnates in advance of rebellion. Generally speaking, the great men and their friends – often their nominees – remained dominant.

This inability to install local governors who could check the power of the magnates – most directly by commanding the local armed forces, the militia – meant that there was a danger of rebellion. The Earl of Derby's sympathy with Catholics and dubious loyalty to Elizabeth were well known, but his dominance in Lancashire had left the government little choice but to place his friends in power and make him Lord-Lieutenant – and then hope for the best when the Northern Rising broke out in 1569. (The Northern Rising was a rebellion led by the Earls of Northumberland and Westmorland against the Protestantism and, even more, the centralisation of the Tudor regime which was reducing their local influence.) The Duke of Norfolk and the Earl of Cumberland were others who might have raised their dependents in that year. Fortunately, they remained loyal. But the tension of those weeks, when Elizabeth waited for the great men of England to show their hand, bears testimony to the regime's dangerous reliance on the provincial élites not only for everyday government but for its very survival.

On the other hand, one must not overstate the difficulties. Parliament, drawing representation from every part of the kingdom, acted as a focus of national unity. For most people, local sentiment though strong did not preclude a sense of nationhood and loyalty to the seemingly age-old Tudor dynasty. 'Allegiance was not single and undivided.' (*Penry Williams*) Tudor propaganda and Church teaching relentlessly expounded the subject's duty to obey. Above all, most people wanted the peace which quiet loyalty brought. The Pilgrimage of Grace had shown even the particularist North that rebellion was futile and disastrous.

The magnates, even if capable of raising their own, were more often bitter rivals than potential allies against the Crown. The Northern Rising of 1569, for all the alarm it initially provoked, quickly collapsed – failing even to rally all the dependents of its leaders, and more than meeting its match in the forces which other magnates put in the field for the Crown. The Essex revolt of 1601 (*see pages 498–9*) failed even more miserably, merely resulting in some commotion on the streets of London. The Crown had few men in the provinces on whom it could absolutely rely, but those who wished or dared to issue an open challenge were even thinner on the ground.

As for the problem of ensuring good government in the more general sense, the difficulties were not insuperable. England was a small country, in terms of both territory and population; with only about 2000 families of substantial influence, the Councillors could have an acquaintance with a large part of the political nation. These people constantly travelled to the unquestioned centre of national life, London, and were often present at Court (and, less continuously, in Parliament). The industry of the Privy Council ensured a remarkably close supervision of life in England, as suggested in the previous section. The office of Lord-Lieutenant was such a great prize its holders preferred to co-operate rather than risk deprivation. The Lieutenancy, collecting information and transmitting instructions, became the major link between the Council and the provinces. Where it proved inadequate, the Council had the use of the bishops, the circuit judges, and the special commissions.

Uncooperative officials could be and often were removed. Perhaps one-third of the JPs were replaced soon after Elizabeth's accession, and many more were struck off subsequently. The result for the purged official was something as dreadful as the collapse of a civil service career: a loss of prestige, of one's place in the all-important local hierarchy. There was usually, especially in the South, a substantial 'pool' of men who were conscientious, respected and well-disposed. The vast patronage at the disposal of the Crown exerted a strong pull, so that personal ambition often led to ready co-operation. Most perceived an interest in good government and felt a duty to serve their Queen. They were keen to lend their assistance where religious principle and material well-being were not directly at stake, and the Council was sufficiently wise and sensitive to avoid antagonising them. Obstructionism was especially great in the 1590s, but it did not prevent the Council both improving the national defences and completing the conquest of Ireland; and it did not breed a permanent reluctance to act as the local servants of the Crown.

Finally, it must be concluded that men of local standing were far more appropriate than anonymous bureaucrats to the government of a country so varied and of a people who spent their lives in awe of their gentry and peers. The system, as Elton put it, 'exploited local knowledge and loyalties in the interests of the state, a thing no centralised bureaucracy could hope to achieve'. In many places, government by the local squire was the best of all worlds.

However, Elton may go too far in describing the system of local government as a 'success'. There was so much variation between (and within) counties, generalisation is almost bound to mislead. Certainly, some areas were badly governed, from the perspective of both Crown and people. But for the most part central government succeeded in having its policy implemented – rather better than the French monarchy with its 40 000 bureaucrats. It succeeded, indeed, in considerably increasing the scope and activity of government. Though finances precluded radical reform, the modest changes made during Elizabeth's reign were clearly beneficial. Above all, the Council worked the system with a skilful mixture of conciliation and coercion – and, of course, with remarkable industry. The result was by no means unimpressive.

8 PATRONAGE

Royal patronage – the range of benefits distributed by the Crown – was the essential lubricant of Tudor government, as has already been seen (*see pages 72–4 and pages 134–5*). Elizabeth governed England through the voluntary efforts of the men of substance. But these men knew that loyal service might be well rewarded. The Crown had at its disposal a vast array of patronage: a large number of offices in the legal system, the Church, the armed forces, the central bureaucracy, local administration, and at Court; honours such as peerages and knighthoods; favourable treatment regarding the payment of taxes and debts; the capacity to sell or lease Crown lands cheaply (though Elizabeth gifted very little land); customs farms, licences and monopoly rights; pensions and annuities.

The Queen was happy to maintain such an array because her purpose was to satisfy the aspirations of as many substantial figures as possible. Pluralism was rife; it was not inconsistent with the Queen's objective. The 200 positions at Court, for the most part, had more to do with securing loyalty and gratitude than with administration, and Williams has argued that such institutions as the Duchy of Lancaster and the Council in the Marches of Wales were continued as sources of 'political rewards, through which the monarch could foster loyalty to his regime'.

At the lower levels, patronage might yield a modest income along with status and the ability to use one's position to assist friends and neighbours. For a few, it meant a great deal more. Most Crown appointments carried poor remuneration in terms of salaries. The Secretary of State received £100 a year, the Attorney-General £13 6s. 8d., and the Solicitor £10. But official positions also yielded set fees for business completed, and gifts and gratuities from those who depended upon one's decisions.

> For nothing there is done without a fee:
> The Courtier needs must recompensed be.

> (*Spenser*, Mother Hubberd's Tale)

Gratuities were essentially bribes, but it must be understood that such rewards were regarded by society as due payment for services rendered and were indispensable in view of the pitifully low official salaries. Only in the 1590s, when the expense of war meant that royal patronage flowed less freely, and inflation ate into other sources of income, did the demands become excessive and 'corruption' become the appropriate description.

Robert Cecil used his position as Master of the Court of Wards to extract £3000 a year, of which only £233 was made up of his official salary. (Men paid handsomely for the right to exploit the wealth of minors.) Additionally, the successful courtier might hope for other forms of patronage from which he could derive income – a monopoly (the sole right to sell a good or service), a customs farm (the right to collect customs duties on a particular good, and to retain any surplus over and above the fixed sum required by the Exchequer). Great wealth was attainable. Earlier in the century, Wolsey set an outstanding example. Under Elizabeth, the Dudleys re-emerged to claim a vast fortune, and the Cecils rose from the ranks of the gentry to become the great aristocratic dynasty which was soon (in the next reign) to build Hatfield House. Many others, too, made considerable if less spectacular fortunes.

However, more than mere wealth was at stake. The Queen personally made many of the decisions on Crown patronage. She settled the major appointments, of course, but she often interfered in minor matters too (one thinks of her reading the lists of JPs and indicating those who were to be omitted from the next commission). Such were the benefits she gained from patronage, she never allowed any other individual or faction to appropriate exclusive control of its distribution. But she could not make every decision. Much of the royal patronage was dispensed by politicians; for example, department heads appointed most of the less senior officials (in the Exchequer, this meant 65 of the 94 staff). And even when the Queen was formally responsible she often had little choice but to rely on them for advice. In other words, those closest to the Queen were in a position greatly to influence the distribution of that patronage from which so much wealth and status flowed.

The results were dramatic. The men who acquired such influence acquired also legions of expectant or grateful friends. As Neale wrote, 'Success not only meant money: it meant power. On it depended the quality and size of a statesman's faction – his entourage of household servants, followers and clients, thronging his chamber and constituting a minor court within the Court proper. The world saw his greatness reflected therein.' When Essex placed friends well, it was said that 'Those which are lukewarm will trust more in him; and such as be assured unto him will be glad to see he hath power to do his friends good.' When, much earlier, Dudley won the Queen's affection, 'Men of all ranks turned to him to obtain personal favours from the Queen. Even the fragments of his correspondence which are all that survive reveal half the English earls, cap in hand, at the favourite's door, asking his aid or pledging their hopeful friendship . . .' (*MacCaffrey*). On the other hand, he who could no longer influence the flow of patronage stood to lose much; as Essex complained when he failed to secure favour, 'Who will be desirous to come under a roof that threateneth ruin?' Thus it may be seen that men's 'greatness', and political alliances, rose and fell according to the Queen's decision as to whom she allowed a say in the distribution of patronage.

The Queen derived much advantage from the patronage system. Loyal and reliable men could be placed in sensitive positions, for the tentacles of royal patronage extended to every aspect of government and part of the country. Of course, the receipt of favour created loyalty, gratitude and dependence – among Councillors and magnates as well as the less exalted. Hopeful suitors were respectful, flattering (and Elizabeth quite pathetically craved outlandish praise), and generous with their New Year gifts. The fact that men became rivals for royal patronage meant that they competed to please her, and that they were incapable of political unity against her.

But there were problems too. For patronage reasons, men were given 'sinecures', positions which had no duties attached; in view of the Crown's shortage of money, this was not the most economical use of resources. Others (including pluralists, by necessity) having gained posts through gratuities or favour, either neglected their duties or delegated them to deputies who were not accountable officials. Of course, the prevalence of favour, gratuities and other inducements meant that many decisions appear unjust. There were many wardships, for instance, which were granted not to caring guardians but to those prepared to pay Robert Cecil's price for the privilege of extorting the wealth of the ward. Frequently, ability failed to secure appointments, a situation which not only blighted the careers of talented men but also acted to the detriment of royal administration.

Humiliating ingratiation and public ridicule were often the lot of the suitor:

> Full little knowest thou that hast not tried
> What Hell it is in suing long to bide;
> To lose good days that might be better spent;
> To waste long nights in pensive discontent;
> To speed today, to be put back tomorrow;
> To feed on hope, to pine with fear and sorrow;
> To have thy Prince's grace, yet want her Peer's;
> To have thy asking, yet wait many years;
> To fret thy soul with crosses and with cares;
> To eat thy heart through comfortless despairs;
> To fawn, to crouch, to wait, to ride, to run,
> To spend, to give, to want, to be undone.

(*Spenser*, Mother Hubberd's Tale)

1   *What does this poem suggest about the workings of the patronage system?*
2   *Given that Crown appointments rarely paid well, why were people*
    prepared to suffer such indignities to acquire them?

Above all, the patronage question provoked much bitterness and jealousy throughout society. It will suffice to mention some of the more notable examples. The Percy family's exclusion from important local positions during the 1560s created the anger and despair which, far more than their Catholicism, produced the Northern Rising in 1569. Very different was the problem created by monopolies during the later years of the reign. Elizabeth, pressed by the expense of war, greatly increased the number of monopolies, as forms of patronage which did not drain the Treasury. The monopolists were able to raise the prices for many goods and services, making large profits. But consumers were outraged, the Queen's popularity suffered, and the monopolies debate in 1601 led to a unique Commons victory over the Crown (*see Chapter X*). However justifiable, Elizabeth's excessive use of this form of patronage was seriously misjudged.

The same decades also saw bitter rivalry within the Council, and one wonders how many good men and measures fell victim to the ceaseless competition. The 1560s were the years when Leicester's star shone brightest, and he provoked much resentment by attempting to monopolise the royal patronage. The followers of Leicester and Norfolk bore arms and came near to violence in 1565–6. Fortunately, after 1570, the Queen's appreciation of Cecil's wise counsel and great industry grew as her devotion to Leicester cooled. Cecil, perhaps aware of Elizabeth's requirements, was not (until much later) overly aggressive on his own and his friends' behalf; he gave Elizabeth relatively disinterested advice on patronage, and the Council's divisions, therefore, had less of the virulence of the 1560s.

This situation changed again, dramatically, during Elizabeth's last decade. From the early 1590s, the Earl of Essex posed a strong challenge to the influence of the Cecils. His desire to monopolise the Queen's favour encountered stiff opposition first from William Cecil (by then Lord Burghley), till his death in 1598, and then from Robert Cecil, whose own greed for patronage was considerable. Elizabeth, arguably, was mistaken when she at first encouraged the Earl's excessive ambition with her generosity and later cut him off entirely from her favour. Essex was able to win support for the view that a narrow circle of Cecil associates dominated Elizabeth's government and were responsible for the many ills which then afflicted the country. The former accusation was certainly correct, though it arose largely in reaction to the Earl's own, monopolistic tendencies. His loss of the valuable customs farm for sweet wines and failure to gain the Mastership of the Court of Wards, which went to Robert Cecil, inflicted both humiliation and bankruptcy on Essex. In 1601, he made the desperate attempt at revolt which cost him his life. Though little more than a small riot in the streets of London, the revolt frightened Elizabeth and left her more dependent on one faction, Robert Cecil's, than she had ever been before.

In sum, for all the benefits patronage brought the Crown, the dangers were also considerable. Any system which distributed such great prizes according to criteria (often personal whims) so lacking in objectivity was almost bound to cause difficulty. In the hands of a young, inexperienced Queen, as in her excessive favour for Leicester, and finally in the hands of a monarch in decline, as the Essex crisis shows, much damage could be inflicted. However, in the intervening years of stability, Elizabeth's judicious and even-handed approach to the distribution of patronage was not the least of her virtues.

9 THE FINANCIAL PROBLEM

No consideration of Elizabethan government would be complete without discussion of the financial realities which constrained the workings of the system. Elizabeth and her government did not give Crown revenues the fundamental reform they badly needed. Both Mary and James, her maligned predecessor and successor, achieved more. This was probably the area in which Elizabeth's cautious and short-sighted approach to government proved most damaging.

The achievements

The Crown's finances were supervised and even administered by the Council as a whole and not merely by the finance ministers (namely the Lord Treasurer, his Chancellor of the Exchequer, and the Under-Treasurer). Elizabeth did not involve herself in the detailed supervision of the accounts, but she did make a major contribution by sharing Winchester's and Burghley's perception of the need for economy. (They were Lord Treasurers in 1550–72 and 1572–98, respectively.) Expenditure was kept on a tight rein. There was virtually no building, bureaucracy was not permitted to expand, official salaries were more or less frozen at their low levels, the Household was reduced and compelled to cut its spending, gifts and pensions were much less freely given than before or after, and courtiers were instead rewarded with wardships and monopoly rights – the latter being forms of patronage which involved no outlay by the Treasury. And, of course, for most of her reign Elizabeth avoided the crippling expense of war. Not surprisingly, then, critics of the Elizabethan record on finance have not faulted her on expenditure.

Under Elizabeth, ordinary revenue, whose principal components are discussed below, increased from about £200 000 a year to about

£300 000, keeping pace with inflation. With the tight control of expenditure, the Treasury was able to record a large annual surplus on the ordinary account, pay off the substantial debts (£227 000) left by Mary, and produce an accumulated cash reserve of £300 000 by 1585. Small wonder that, in 1576, Chancellor of the Exchequer Sir Walter Mildmay exultantly told the Commons that,

> Her Majesty hath most carefully delivered this Kingdom from a
> great and weighty Debt, wherewith it hath long been burdened.
> A Debt begun four years at the least before the death of King
> Henry the Eighth, and not cleared until within these two years,
> and all that while running upon Interest, a course able to eat up
> not only private men and their patrimonies, but also Princes,
> and their Estates; but such hath been the care of this time, as
> Her Majesty and the State is clearly freed from the eating
> corrosive . . . By means whereof the realm is not only acquitted
> of this great burden . . . but also her Majesty's credit thereby
> both at home and abroad [is] greater than any other Prince for
> money, if she need have, and so in reason it ought to be, for that
> she hath kept promise to all men, wherein other Princes have
> often failed to the hindrance of many.

1 *Why might the Commons in particular need to be persuaded of Elizabeth's financial prudence?*

2 *In what way was Mildmay's statement influenced by the fact that Philip II had gone bankrupt in 1575?*

Elizabeth's most impressive financial achievement was the funding of the great war against Spain, from 1585, and of the hard-fought struggle (1593–1603) to complete the conquest of Ireland. In 1600, the latter consumed £320 000 out of a total expenditure of £459 840. To cope, spending in all other areas was reduced. Notably, there was a more systematic exploitation of purveyance, the Crown's right to buy goods for the royal Household at below market price. And there was a great increase in the granting of monopoly rights, as a cheap form of patronage. Crown land worth over £600 000 was sold, including virtually all of the remaining monastic property. Parliamentary taxation (*see pages 282–3*) was requested more frequently and in multiples. Forced loans were imposed. Privateers who attacked Spanish shipping had to share the booty with the Crown. Local rates were imposed to build fortifications and prepare the militia, and ship money (a tax originally on coastal areas for their defence) was demanded ever more widely and farther inland. In the end, Elizabeth bequeathed a debt of only £350 000 – a highly creditable sum in the circumstances. And this was achieved without having recourse to an inflationary debasement of the coinage.

The shortcomings

Unfortunately, such a superficial account disguises some less palatable realities. The principal sources of ordinary revenue – land rentals and customs duties – produced disappointing yields. During the reign, the overall rate of inflation was roughly 75 per cent. But the revenue from land rose by only 25 per cent, to £100 000 a year, and customs revenue barely rose at all, holding at around £90 000. This was despite the fact that there was greater vigour in the collection of both rents and customs duties, and wide recourse to customs farming. Quite simply, the government failed to increase duties in line with inflation, the charges reflecting the quickly-outdated values established by Mary's Book of Rates of 1558. Rents, too, were not raised sufficiently, and, of course, the land sales meant a narrowing base for this source of revenue. In addition, another, potentially major source of ordinary revenue, wardships, yielded only a small part of the income achieved from them in the next century. There were various forms of Crown debt which favourites were allowed to leave unpaid. The most damaging was the permission to office-holders to use the revenues in their charge; thus Leicester and Winchester headed a long list with unpaid debts of £35 000 and £34 000 respectively.

The impressive rise in the ordinary revenue mentioned earlier is attributable to other factors. In the first place, the figures are not entirely reliable; at least in the first half of the reign, some of the receipts from extraordinary, parliamentary taxation found their way into the ordinary account. Also, ordinary revenue was boosted by such measures as diligent collection of debts (those of favourites excepted), fining recusants (Catholics who would not attend church), and exploiting the revenues of vacant dioceses (Oxford stood vacant for 32 of the 45 years of the reign). These were finite sources. They merely staved off the problems posed by inflation and the failure to act boldly on Crown rents and customs duties.

Parliamentary taxation – primarily the so-called subsidies, assessed on property and income – yielded about £2.5 million during the reign, a massive sum. According to custom, parliamentary taxation was to be requested only in times of war, revolt, or other extraordinary need, and only very rarely had previous Tudor monarchs asked for it when there was no such emergency: Henry VIII in 1534, Edward (Northumberland) in 1553, and Mary in 1555. In normal times, the Crown's ordinary revenue was expected to suffice. Increasingly, this was an outdated idea which ignored the difficulty faced in meeting the rising cost of everyday government. Elizabeth frequently secured subsidies during the years of peace, and used some of the receipts for ordinary, non-military expenditure. This might have been the fundamental reform of Crown revenue which was needed. Unfortunately, the traditional assumption was not boldly addressed and dispelled. Elizabeth's government maintained a pretence of extraordinary need when they justified their requests to Parliament; there was no acknowledgement of the use of parliamentary taxes for ordinary expenditure. No permanent solution was found, then, and Elizabeth's successors would find great difficulty in securing money from Parliament.

In addition, parliamentary taxation was not efficiently administered. The collectors (subsidy commissioners) were often negligent or corrupt. The records of ownership were allowed to fall hopelessly out of date, leaving many potential payers untaxed. Above all, the assessments of wealth and income upon which people were taxed were made on the basis of the payer's unsworn declaration, inviting undervaluation. Indeed, the latter was common practice. The Council complained of 'the notable and evident abasing and diminution of many men's values heretofore in their assessments under all reasonable proportions, specially of men of the better state of livelihood and countenance'. In 1593, Robert Cecil told the Commons that 'he knew one shire of this realm wherein there were many men of good living and countenance, but none of them in the said last subsidies assessed at above four score pounds land per annum. And that in the city of London also, where the greatest part of the riches of the realm are, there was no one assessed at above two hundred pounds goods a man . . .' Yet William Cecil, Lord Burghley, Robert's father and now the Lord Treasurer, was a prime offender, declaring an annual income of £133 6s. 8d. when his real income was about £4000. In 1534, 15 nobles were assessed at over £1000, in 1571 there were 9, and in 1601 there was 1, figures all the more incredible in view of the Tudor inflation. The result was not just that receipts failed to rise in line with prices; even in nominal terms, without adjusting for inflation, the value of each subsidy fell from £140 000 at the start of the reign to £80 000 at the end. This meant that subsidies had to be requested in multiples, and although Parliament accepted them (*see page 284*), they were psychologically much less acceptable than taxes which adjusted automatically to inflation.

In sum, Elizabeth and her ministers allowed the financial position of the Crown to weaken and did not even attempt the reforms necessary to avoid the problem. She was in a difficult situation. Any conceivable policy to increase government revenue would inevitably have alienated many. In particular, the tenants on Crown lands and the merchants would have resented increases in rents and customs duties in order to improve ordinary revenue. The propertied classes in general would have objected to an abandonment of the idea that parliamentary taxation was acceptable only in extraordinary circumstances, and they would not have welcomed revision of the assessments. The result of reform would probably have been conflict with Parliament and obstructionism in the provinces. The historian denouncing rulers who shirk those difficult decisions which cause unpopularity is often guilty of unsympathetic severity. Nevertheless, the courageous boldness of Henry VIII and Cromwell might have cured the ills rather better than the caution and conservatism of Elizabeth and William Cecil.

The effects

How harmful was the financial problem? Able to employ little more than a thousand professional bureaucrats, the Crown relied upon unpaid volunteers in the provinces and, within the departments of state, on the personal servants of the officials. Their lack of direct accountability hardly ensured good government. But it is important to remember that the system of rule by the local élites had more than financial advantages (*see above*), and Alsop has shown that the personal assistants of the formal administrators were sufficiently conscientious and ambitious to perform well. Of course, the remuneration of officials was poor; as a result, their decisions were excessively dependent on the gratuities offered, rather than on the merit of a case, especially in the closing years of the reign.

More serious, perhaps, were the implications for defence and foreign policy. The defences of the country were severely damaged by the financial weakness of the Crown. England was unable to create or maintain forces equal to those of continental rivals, leaving her perpetually vulnerable. And Elizabeth might have acted earlier, to good effect, to check the threat from Spain, had financial constraints not dictated a passive policy (*see Chapter XI*).

Not surprisingly, the internal politics of the country were put under strain as the government sought ways out of its difficulties. The need to employ such extraordinary measures as ship money created discontent. It was manifested in a widespread avoidance of ship money and culminated in the great dispute of 1601 over monopolies, exclusive rights sold or granted to courtiers, to market certain goods at inflated prices (*see page 283*).

Above all, the financial legacy of the reign was a poisoned chalice. The parsimony of Elizabeth's later years caused a pent-up thirst for more generous patronage, before which James I, a Scot who had to win friends in his new kingdom, had little choice but to give way. This had disastrous results for royal finances. The enforced reliance on monopolies and purveyance, the former especially, caused much dissatisfaction with the Stuarts. On the revenue side, James was quickly forced to the conclusion that he must raise customs duties, to catch up on decades of rapid inflation (and Elizabethan neglect); this led to the Impositions crisis of 1608 and a long history of protest against taxation not approved by Parliament. The land sales, as pointed out, had left a major source of ordinary revenue much diminished; Elizabeth reaped the benefit, the Stuarts faced the shortfall.

Even the fruits of peace were contaminated by the legacy. The frequent use of multiple subsidies had exhausted the patience of the payers. So, when peace was made in 1604, the outdated view that parliamentary taxation could cease was enthusiastically embraced; the Stuarts, accordingly, found Parliament unsympathetic to their plight. In general terms, Elizabeth's success in papering over the cracks without major innovation created the mistaken impression that the Stuarts sought new taxes for selfish or dangerous purposes.

Nevertheless, despite all of the above, there is reason to regard the Crown's financial weakness as a blessing. Given the inadequacy of its ordinary revenue (certainly as it was administered at that time), the monarchy was financially dependent on Parliament. The latter would never finance the creation of a strong, standing army and a bureaucracy. The lack of them brought problems for the state, but it was the nation's principal defence against an over-mighty ruler, against royal absolutism. This point was more fully appreciated in the seventeenth century than in Elizabeth's day, and the long struggle against Stuart tyranny (as it was perceived) was conducted largely in terms of the revenues of the Crown.

10 CONCLUSION

Elizabeth needed the co-operation of her Council, Parliament, and the propertied classes of England. She had not the power of a despot. Rather, she ruled by consent. And yet, she was unquestionably a strong monarch. She controlled the policy of her government, making almost all of the major decisions. Perhaps, as a woman, and therefore not expected to prevail in a man's world, this simple fact represented her greatest success. Her dominance rested upon the desire of the political nation to see (and assist) strong government, on the broad acceptability of her religious and foreign policies, on her diplomatic but firm handling of Parliament, and on the impact of her daunting personality. She owed a great debt to the Privy Council; but it was her wisdom which gave the Crown such able and hard-working ministers.

The reign was markedly less impressive in its closing years. The war, economic difficulties, the execution of the dashing Essex after his abortive revolt in 1601 and Elizabeth's declining personal charms combined to ruin the Queen's popularity; many lamented the fifty years of 'petticoat rule' and welcomed the news of Elizabeth's death. The problems were mainly caused by the special circumstances of the time, the war in particular contributing high taxes and rates, conscription, financial stringency, corruption in government, and the spread of monopolies. But it cannot be said that the system of government coped well. The inadequacy of Crown revenue, the competition for and abuse of patronage, and the lack of fully dependable servants in the provinces were exposed as serious shortcomings. The Stuarts quickly found the same; Elizabeth bequeathed a system of government which collapsed within four decades.

However, one must not deduce too much from a period of extraordinary difficulty. For most of the reign, the system provided stable and effective government. Dedicated and industrious ministers performed herculean tasks which left little time for the contemplation of possible, future problems. One cannot be surprised if the relative success of the earlier years undermined the prospects of substantial change. Also, any change would probably involve disruption and conflicts of interest. In contrast Henry VIII and Cromwell had proceeded undaunted and began a revolution which very few wanted. After three decades of government-led change the country probably needed a period of peace and stability; the relatively cautious and conservative Elizabeth and Cecil provided it. As Elton wrote, 'originality can be overvalued . . . the startling burst of originality associated with Thomas Cromwell gave his successors quite enough to do'. Finally, it is surely unfair to denounce Elizabeth for tolerating the continuation of problems which caused insurmountable difficulty not for her but for the less able rulers who followed.

11 BIBLIOGRAPHY

C Haigh (ed.) *The Reign of Elizabeth I* (Macmillan, 1984).
C Haigh *Elizabeth I* (Longman, 1988).
J Hurstfield and A G R Smith *Elizabethan History: State and Society* (St Martin's Press, 1972).
E W Ives *Faction in Tudor England* (Historical Association, 1979).
D M Loades *The Tudor Court* (Historical Association, 1989).
W T MacCaffrey *The Shaping of the Elizabethan Regime* (Cape, 1969).
W T MacCaffrey *Queen Elizabeth and the Making of Policy, 1572–1588* (Princeton, 1981).
J E Neale *Essays in Elizabethan History* (Cape, 1958).
A G R Smith *The Government of Elizabethan England* (Edward Arnold, 1967).

12 DISCUSSION POINTS AND EXERCISES

A *This section consists of questions or points that might be used for discussion (or written answers) as a way of expanding on the chapter and testing understanding of it:*

1 How difficult was Elizabeth's position on her accession?
2 Why did Elizabeth and the Council take so much trouble with her public image?
3 How well did her character fit Elizabeth to govern?
4 In which ways did the Privy Council help Elizabeth to govern?

5 How far could the Privy Council wield power independently of the Queen?

6 What was the importance of faction?

7 How well did the Privy Council cope with the burden of business?

8 What changes in local government were made in the reign of Elizabeth?

9 What were the principal weaknesses of local government?

10 Why was there such bitter competition for patronage?

11 What were the shortcomings of the patronage system?

12 What were the main strengths and weaknesses of the Elizabethan system of Crown finances?

13 Why did Elizabeth do so little to remedy the faults in Crown finances?

14 Why did Elizabeth's financial legacy prove so damaging?

15 'Elizabeth I was right not to have initiated reforms; in that she showed a striking sense of realism.' Do you agree?

B *Essay questions*

1 How well was Elizabeth served by those who helped her to govern England?

2 Should the Elizabethan system of government be considered a success?

3 What features of Elizabethan government were responsible for its success?

4 What were the principal constraints on the power of Elizabeth?

5 Why, and in what ways, did government operate less successfully in the last decade of Elizabeth's reign?

6 How far did the Elizabethan system of government differ from that of Henry VIII?

13 EXERCISE – AN ASSESSMENT OF WILLIAM CECIL, LORD BURGHLEY

Study the sections in the chapter relevant to Cecil, read the following documents and then answer the questions below.

Lord Burghley to Sir Robert Cecil, 23 March 1596:

. . . I do hold, and will always, this course in such matters as I differ in opinion from her Majesty; as long as I may be allowed to give advice I will not change my opinion by affirming the

contrary, for that were to offend God, to whom I am sworn first; 5
but as a servant I will obey her Majesty's commandment and no
wise contrary the same, presuming that she being God's chief
minister here, it shall be God's will to have her commandments
obeyed, after that I have performed my duty as a councillor,
and shall in my heart wish her commandments to have such 10
good successes as I am sure she intendeth . . .

J Clapham (one of Burghley's clerks), Elizabeth of England:

About the fourteenth year of the Queen's reign Cecil was made
Knight of the Garter, and, after the death of the Marquis of
Winchester, Treasurer of England, he succeeded him in the 15
treasureship, which office he enjoyed till his death; ordering the
affairs of the realm in such a manner as he was respected even
by his enemies, who reputed him the most famous councillor of
Christendom in his time; the English government being then
commonly termed by strangers Cecil's commonwealth . . . In 20
matters of counsel nothing for the most part was done without
him, for that nothing was thought well done whereof he was
not the contriver and director. His credit with the Queen was
such as his wisdom and integrity well deserved . . . the
necessity of his service would not any long time permit his 25
absence from the Court and the greatness of his place procured
him the envy of those who otherwise could not but
acknowledge his virtues . . .

1   *What does Burghley's letter suggest about (a) the minister's and (b) the
    Queen's role in decision-making?*

2   *Describe three major issues on which Burghley felt he had to 'differ in
    opinion from her Majesty' (line 3).*

3   *Which 'virtues' gave Burghley such great 'credit with the Queen'
    (line 23)?*

4   *Discuss the view that, in fact, Burghley's 'subtle and complex influence
    over the Queen was greater than he would ever acknowledge'. How
    accurate were those who called England's government 'Cecil's
    commonwealth'?*

5   *What, in retrospect, were Burghley's principal shortcomings?*

6   *How does Burghley compare with his illustrious Tudor predecessors,
    Wolsey and Cromwell?*

IX

Elizabeth I: Religion

—

1 Introduction

The Queen's religious persuasion

'Until now I have believed that the matters of religion would continue
in the accustomed manner, her Majesty having promised this with her
own mouth many times; but now I have lost faith, and I see that by little and little they are returning to the bad use.' This judgement by a
Venetian observer was made some six weeks after Elizabeth I acceded
to the throne on 17 November 1558, and highlights the changes in religion which were beginning to take place in the early critical months of
the reign. The new Queen herself had conformed to the Roman
Catholic practices, reintroduced by Mary after the return to Rome in
1554, whilst maintaining a low political profile. Almost 300 burnings of
heretics and her rumoured involvement in Wyatt's rebellion, illustrated how little room for manoeuvre she had. Furthermore, her half-sister
Mary had been the rightful ruler, and Elizabeth's conservatism in such
matters led her to accept the return of Catholicism as a matter for the
monarch's royal prerogative and not to be challenged.

Her religious beliefs can never be fully known but as the daughter
of Anne Boleyn and brought up under the protective wing of the
Seymour faction at Court, she was a convinced Protestant from her earlier days, a living symbol of the break with Rome. Her tutor had been
Sir Roger Ascham, the Cambridge humanist of the Henrician Court,
and it was the moderate religious position of these reforming men
which she adopted as her own. She was in favour of priestly celibacy,
supported such Erasmian aims as the reform of Church abuses and
repudiated transubstantiation and the authority of the Pope. She disliked religious dispute, long sermons and desired moderate ceremony
which included the use of copes and crucifixes and music in her own
private devotions but which prohibited the use of incense. Private
devotion was indeed the core of religion to the Queen, not wanting, in

Sir Nicholas Bacon's words, 'to make windows into men's hearts'. She preferred a Church which was flexible enough to accommodate the wide range of religious beliefs among the committed, and the large number of confused men and women, unsure of the correct form of worship after the changes.

To be as tolerant as possible under a very moderate Protestant umbrella, was Elizabeth's personal style or policy when it came to the doctrine of her Church, but she demanded obedience and outward observance of those things which were deemed necessary by her, and complete loyalty to her God-given authority. In this she reflected her father's Reformed Church of the 1530s, whilst in doctrine she represented those influences such as Cranmer and Ridley who had been among those responsible for the two Prayer Books of 1549 and 1552. Once her Church was established, she would be committed to the status quo, believing that innovation would lead to that instability she had been appointed by God to guard against.

The struggle for power

The creation of the Elizabethan Church Settlement has been the subject of historical debate in recent years. The old tradition from John Foxe to A F Pollard suggested that Elizabeth set out to create the Church of England according to her wishes, and that she succeeded despite Catholic opposition. This view was challenged in the 1950s when Professor J E Neale proposed that Elizabeth was enough of a conservative to be aiming merely at restoring Henrician Catholicism without the Pope, and that the Church of England was the creation of returning religious exiles who forced her to compromise with their demands, voiced through a Puritan 'choir' or party in the House of Commons. This interpretation has more recently been challenged by a number of historians, in particular Dr N Jones in 'Faith by Statute'. Here, the focus has been the struggle in the House of Lords between the Queen and her Council, and the Marian bishops, who nearly wrecked the new government's plans. The House of Commons has been shown to have been much more pliant towards the proposed legislation, and recent research has indicated that the exiles had not returned in sufficient numbers by 1559, nor were they yet sufficiently organised.

Surrounded by her new Council, many of whom were ex-Edwardians supportive of Protestantism, such as Cecil, who had stayed close to Elizabeth during the difficult years, Elizabeth sought to revive the Royal Supremacy over the Church and reintroduce the 1552 Book of Common Prayer as soon as possible. This required statutory reform by Parliament and a delay for the issuing of writs. Meanwhile there was a danger that the Protestants might be difficult to control, now Elizabeth was at the helm, and a series of proclamations sought to slow down reform. For instance, on 28 December she silenced all preachers until Parliament had met 'for better conciliation and accord of such causes as at this present are moved in matters and ceremonies of religion'. This action did not appease the Catholics. Bishop White of Winchester preached at Mary's funeral that the 'wolves are come out of Geneva' to prey on the English flock and rumours began of armed resistance to religious change and the release of heretics.

In addition to raising funds for war and the Crown, and to recognising her as rightful monarch, Elizabeth's first Parliament had to act quickly to establish the religious framework when it assembled on 25 January 1559. The problem lay less in the Lower House where Protestant patronage gave the new government a decisive advantage over ardent Marians, but rather in the Upper House where the bishops, along with conservative peers such as Viscount Montagu, sought to resist. They would not have been pleased to witness Elizabeth's dismissing the Westminster Abbey monks' procession with lighted tapers in the Catholic style saying 'Away with these torches, we see very well'. Faced by the Lords' opposition the Commons were forced to declare that 'no persons shall be punished for using the religion of King Edward's last year' and to accept an altered Supremacy and Uniformity Bill as the best deal they would get. By Easter 1559, Elizabeth and Cecil were faced with a serious impasse, the nation's religion still yet unsettled.

Fortified by the successful peace negotiations with the French concluded on 2 April at Câteau Cambrèsis, by which Elizabeth preserved national honour in maintaining technical possession of Calais and thereby boosted her reputation, the Queen decided to try again over the religious issue rather than to dissolve Parliament and accept the Mass. The key was to win control of the Lords where the Marian bishops denied Parliament's right 'as to be accounted judges in such matters' in the words of Bishop Scot of Chester in March 1559, and where the Protestant John Jewel despaired of 'having none there on our side to expose their artifices and refute their falsehoods'. However, two leading Catholic bishops were afterwards arrested and sent to the Tower, in a clear attempt to overawe the opposition by strong arm methods and sway the opinions of the conservative lay peers.

2 THE RELIGIOUS SETTLEMENT OF 1559

The Act of Supremacy

Reverting to the initial policy, separate Bills for Supremacy and Uniformity were introduced so that the Queen's Supremacy would be established even if the form of worship were not. And she was not to take her father's title of 'Supreme Head' of the Church, rather she was to be 'Supreme Governor', a tactical ploy to ease the consciences of the

Catholics, for whom the Pope was the Head of the Church on earth, and of those Protestants who found it difficult to accept a human, and a woman at that, as Head of God's Church. Importantly, the Bill also incorporated an oath of loyalty for clergy and officials, the penalty for refusal being loss of office, it repealed the Marian heresy laws, guaranteed freedom of worship for Protestants and allowed Communion in both kinds as enacted in 1547, and established the Commission for Ecclesiastical Causes (or High Commission) to impose order and stamp out error. The Queen and her Council successfully forced these measures through the 'back door', the Bill gaining wide approval in the Commons and Lords despite the united episcopal opposition.

The Act of Uniformity

Such ease of passage did not await the Uniformity Bill. Distinctly Edwardian in its Protestantism, it sought to blend the personal religious moderation of the Queen with the more advanced attitudes of some of her Council; hence it fused into one the 1549 Uniformity with the version of 1552. The 1552 Book of Common Prayer was re-imposed for use in all churches upon pain of imprisonment, and church attendance on Sundays and Holy Days was enforced, a fine of 12*d*. per absence, to be collected by the churchwardens for poor relief. Heavy fines and imprisonment awaited those who sought to slander or libel the Book, or tried to prevent its proper use. To persuade conservative peers, prepared to accept the Supremacy and reject the Pope, but for whom the rejection of transubstantiation contained in the 1552 Prayer Book was unacceptable, a compromise had to be forged with 'two sentences only added in the delivery of the Sacrament of the communicants, and none other or otherwise'. The two sentences were those embodied in the 1549 Prayer Book: 'The body/blood of our Lord Jesus Christ which was given for thee, preserve thy body and soul until everlasting life.' Thus a deliberate ambiguity was incorporated into the Communion, allowing for a broad spectrum of interpretation including the belief in transubstantiation. This wish to placate traditionalists, provided other changes such as the abandonment of the reference to 'the Bishop of Rome and all his detestable enormities'.

The ornaments of the Church and the dress or vestments of the clergy were to be used as in the second year of Edward VI's reign, 'until other order shall be therein taken [given] by the authority of the Queen's Majesty'. The latter was a particular blow to the Protestant reformers but was not expected to be permanent, nor was the wearing expected to be enforced, only that they could not be removed from the Church. But Elizabeth defined such matters as *adiaphora* (matters indifferent to salvation and therefore for her to decide) and she sought to impose by law a common code of practice for peace, due reverence and the advancement of God's glory. Passed by the Commons, the Lords passed the Bill of Uniformity only by 21 to 18 with 2 bishops and the Abbot of Westminster absent or imprisoned. The Queen and her Council had secured a narrow triumph over the conservative peers and bishops, through the use of propaganda, censorship, physical force, compromise and sharp political practice. By the end of June 1559 the Settlement began to be implemented with the requirement of the Oath of Supremacy by the new Court of High Commission. All but one of the Marian bishops (Andrew Kitchen of Llandaff) refused the Oath and were deprived of office, furnishing Elizabeth with the chance to pick a bench of Protestant bishops with old Edwardian, Matthew Parker, as the new Archbishop of Canterbury. Only perhaps as few as 4 per cent of the lower clergy (c.300 out of 8000) refused the Oath.

Royal Intervention in the Settlement

In addition to the two great Acts of the Settlement, royal prerogative power was also brought to bear on the country in a series of Injunctions issued by the Queen in 1559 to further establish a sound basis for the new Church. The clergy were ordered to wear the 'seemly habits, garments and such square caps', used in Edward's reign; clerical marriage was discouraged requiring the permission of the bishop and two Justices of the Peace; and commissions were issued for visitations to enforce order and deprive those who refused to comply. The content and timing of sermons against 'all usurped and foreign power' and 'idolatry and superstition' were laid down; the clergy were to preach at least four times a year; each parish was to have 'one book of the whole Bible of the largest volume in English'; each cleric was to buy his own copy of the New Testament in Latin and English, and was not to haunt alehouses, drink or play dice but conduct himself decently. The doctrine of the Church of England was left to Convocation (the Church's assembly) to sort out. Archbishop Parker looked to the Forty-two Articles of Religion of Edward's reign as a suitable basis and the revision and emergence of these as the Thirty-nine Articles of the Church of England in 1563 were fully approved by Convocation. In this forum, the establishment line was nearly wrecked by the radical Protestant group, largely made up of returned exiles and determined to reform further the English Church along continental lines. As a result of their pressure, the article on the Eucharist specifically denied any physical presence of Christ in the Eucharist thus being offensive to Catholic and Lutheran alike. The Queen ordered the article to be omitted when the other thirty-eight were published and later quashed an attempt in 1566 to allow the articles to be given statutory support.

Control of the new Church also gave Elizabeth the chance to exploit its wealth at a time when her regime was short of cash. The ecclesiastical taxes of First Fruits and Tenths, returned to Rome by Mary, were taken back by the Crown providing about £40 000 in annual revenue.

Mary's refounded monasteries and charities were again dissolved, the property reverting to the Crown. Yet it was on the question of the new Church's lands that the Religious Settlement caused such problems, and Elizabeth proved to be as voracious as her forebears in her appetite for economic exploitation at great cost to the welfare and estate of the Church. The 1559 Act of Exchange allowed Elizabeth to exchange the episcopal lands of a vacant See for royal property of the same value. In practice, she transferred to the Crown the better Church lands. And many Church revenues had fallen into other lay hands since the Dissolution of the Monasteries.

The implication for the new Church was clear – it was vulnerable to exploitation, it was poor and it was weak. In October 1559 Archbishop Parker and other newly nominated bishops petitioned the Queen to halt the exchanges but to no avail. Elizabeth delayed appointing some of her new men until 1560 solely to direct the revenues into the Exchequer, and her policy caused much hardship for her bishops.

Conclusion

By the end of 1559 Elizabeth had laid the foundations of the Religious Settlement, had achieved that very moderate blend of authority and form of worship which harkened back to the early days of Edward VI and which reflected her own personal inclinations. Hers was fundamentally an English style of settlement, owing little to the European centres of reform, from where the exiles were returning. It was a compromise dictated by the need to sell it to the conservatives in the Lords. Protestantism's relationship to the vast majority of the English population was that of a new-fangled, disruptive set of beliefs which undermined the traditional ways. It should not be forgotten that the 1552 Prayer Book was in use for less than a year in many places, and that there had been a general acceptance of the return of Catholicism in 1554. The success of Protestantism was, therefore, by no means inevitable in 1559, its return was greeted with little widespread enthusiasm. Yet, for the Queen, the new Church was legally established by statute, supplemented by royal prerogative, and it was fixed. Hers was a static view, of a true religion formally restored with Crown and Church relations clearly established by law. It was, for her, unchangeable, a '*via media*' (middle way) carved in stone, providing the politically vital flexibility to embrace the widest number of her countrymen in loyalty and good order and outward conformity. It was not a view shared by Catholics, radical Protestants, nor indeed did it satisfy those moderate Churchmen, theologically in advance of the Queen, who made up her first episcopal bench and clerical appointees.

ELIZABETH AND THE CATHOLICS

3 CONFORMITY AND SURVIVALISM

The intention of the Queen and her Council after the establishment of the 1559 Settlement was gradually to squeeze the life out of the 'Old Religion' of Catholicism until it withered away through lack of priests and lethargy, and conformity to the new Church replaced it. Cardinal Pole's decision to renew English Catholicism from the top via the London Synod of 1555, might have paid dividends if Mary had lived longer, but her death allowed the Catholic bishops to be isolated and deprived, and exposed her failure to reinvigorate Catholicism amongst the lower clergy. That only 300 priests were deprived for refusing the Oath was a testament to this failure, and the political acumen of the Crown. In 1559 English Catholics were faced with a difficult problem of whether to conform to the new Anglican Church or to try by persuasion or force to restore their Faith. The deliberate ambiguity of the Settlement enabled many Catholics to accept, if not agree with, the new State Church and to indulge in outward conformity to its requirements (known as 'Church Papistry') thus remaining loyal to the Queen.

Yet what was the nature of Catholicism in England at the time? John Bossy characterised it in *The Character of English Catholicism* as 'less concerned with doctrinal affirmation or dramas of conscience than with a set of ingrained observances which defined and gave meaning to the cycle of the week and the seasons of the year, to birth, marriage and death. This has been aptly termed survivalism.' It was found, for instance, in the more remote parts of Kent, Sussex or the peripheral lands of the North and West, although here and elsewhere, Catholicism was forced to retreat to the protection of relatively independent landowning households. The external shows of this religion such as festivals and processions were lost, but the personal and spiritual mainstream of its Faith e.g. fasting, marriage, christenings and burial remained intact and in private. In 1558 conservative religion was still powerful in many counties, adhered to by the vast majority of the population as the 'natural' religion and this survivalism and gentry protection formed the substance of early Elizabethan Catholicism.

The Acts of Supremacy and Uniformity imposed mild penalties for passive resistance by the Catholic laity involving a 12d. fine for failure to attend church and loss of office for refusal to take the Oath. Saying Mass or arranging for it to be said led to the death penalty, mere attendance at Mass resulting in a 100 mark fine. Whilst the fine was levied in some cases, Elizabeth ensured that the death penalty was not implemented before 1577, partly from a personal preference for a softly-softly approach, and partly from the fact that a wholehearted commitment to apply such punishments would have been more than the government had the ability to impose and would have seriously disrupted county and local government, setting Protestant against Catholic and dissolving the ties of kinship and good lordship on which the fabric of society was based. Imprisonment was the preferred alternative, as in 1568 when a number of prominent Catholics, including Lady Brown and Lady Cary, were arrested for celebrating Mass.

During the 1560s there was little threat from Catholicism. According to a 1564 Privy Council Survey many Justices of the Peace were Catholic, and at least sympathetic to the cause or putting local loyalties first; a minimum of conformity was almost universally observed by the heads of households, whilst maintaining their traditional practices behind their own doors. Several ministers provided the official Church practices in public and Catholic ones in private, some tried to incorporate Catholic practices such as elevating the Host, or the use of Communion wafers, into the Prayer Book Service. Thus clerical conformity to the rules of 1559 were implemented reluctantly in some areas and took up to twenty years as in Weaverham, Cheshire where little had changed at all by 1578.

With this process of slow erosion and gradual conformity in the 1560s, there was relatively little recusancy, though some evidence survives. The recusants were those Catholics who refused to attend the Anglican Services or those who refused the Oath of Supremacy and, if priests, were deprived or resigned in 1559. Lancashire had some forty recusant priests in the 1560s. However, the dominant trend of these early years was one of outward conformity to the Church of England among the Catholics, their own devotions unmolested owing to the problems of enforcement of penal legislation in the localities, especially in Catholic areas. This in turn meant there was little separation from parish church into recusancy.

A significant responsibility for this must be the government's successful policy, but there were external reasons. There was a lack of spiritual guidance on this matter from the Papacy. Under pressure from Philip II, who wanted to avoid making an enemy of Elizabeth, only in 1562 did the Vatican prohibit Catholic attendance at Anglican services. Although Spanish and papal policy appears to have hardened after 1565, Phillip II was too preoccupied with the Mediterranean and the Netherlands to take serious action. In the absence of strong leadership, it was left to individuals to continue the fight for their religion.

One exile in Louvain, Thomas Harding, translated devotional works for the English market and engaged in a vigorous published dispute with some of the Protestant bishops, especially John Jewel, in defence of his faith. Such literature smuggled into England helped to introduce ideas of reformed continental Catholicism and to boost morale. Perhaps most significant was William Allen who founded a seminary at Donai in the southern Netherlands in 1568, to educate Catholics abroad and to train priests to return to England.

4 REVOLT AND TREASON: THE NORTHERN EARLS

Circumstances were beginning to change, however, by 1568 and to disrupt the comfortable *modus vivendi* of Elizabeth's first decade. The crushing of the Calvinists by the Duke of Alva in the Netherlands, the flight of the Queen of Scots into England (May 1568), and the seizure of Phillip II's bullion ships (December 1568) as the culmination of growing antagonism between English and Spanish merchants, placed the English in a more threatening international and domestic position, and relations between the government and the Catholics became more strained with the Revolt of the Northern Earls of 1569 (*see pages 494–8*).

The arrival of the Queen of Scots on English soil in January 1568 provided an immediate focus for followers of the 'old' religion; if Elizabeth were to die, then a Catholic heir would lead them back into that fold. As Elizabeth had been the centre of the hopes and intrigues of the religious opposition in her sister's time, so Mary Queen of Scots became in her cousin's. For the Northern Earls of Westmorland and Northumberland religion appears to have been a genuine motive and, though by no means the only one, it was the glue which held a wide range of political and economic causes together. Enthusiasm for the Catholic cause certainly motivated the lesser players; Richard Norton, Sheriff of York, who had worn the badge of the Five Wounds of Christ in 1536; Thomas Markenfeld, his son-in-law, and Dr Morton, both of whom had been to the Continent in the 1560s and had returned fired with zeal to awake the North.

The rebellion in the autumn of 1569 failed. Mistimed to perfection was the Pope Pius V's response, the excommunication and deposition of Elizabeth by the Bull '*Regnans in Excelsis*' in 1570, which had been requested by the Earls and the exiles to coincide with the revolt. By its terms English Catholics were absolved from any oath of allegiance and commanded to disobey the Queen on pain of similar excommunication. In practice the vast majority ignored the Bull. However, this is to miss the point. It was a marked change in theory and that was not lost on Parliament, the Established Church nor Phillip II who criticised 'this sudden and unexpected step [which] will make matters worse and drive the Queen and her friends the more to oppress and persecute the few good Catholics remaining in England'. Obedience to Rome meant treason towards the Queen and it was taken, in Professor Elton's words as 'an unmistakable declaration of war' threatening to break the bonds between monarch and her people. Every Catholic was to be treated as a potential traitor.

The Catholic cause was not helped by the Ridolfi Plot of March 1571 involving Mary Queen of Scots and the Duke of Norfolk as a married alternative to Elizabeth, backed by Spanish arms and cash. As a result the Duke of Norfolk was executed for treason (June 1572) and the Spanish Ambassador was expelled. The massacre by Catholics of

French Huguenots on St Batholomew's Eve in 1572 in Paris led Archbishop Parker to claim that Catholics were 'rejoicing much at this unnatural and unprincely cruelty and murder'.

New legislation, such as the Treasons Act of 1571, was passed to deal with the Catholic threat. However survivalism continued, Church Papistry (lip-service to the State Church) rather than recusancy being the usual means whereby the majority of Catholic households steered clear of the new stiffer legislation, with local mutual interest and social sentiment proving stronger than adherence to the letter of the law. In practice, Catholic loyalty to the regime had been shown by the failure of the Northern Earls' Revolt and the Ridolfi Plot to generate conservative support. For her part, the Queen still sought to maintain her policy towards her Catholic subjects and tried to control the pressure building up in Parliament for more draconian legislation.

5 THE MISSION TO ENGLAND

Within the framework of the Church of England conservative opinion remained widespread but two factors destabilised it. The first was the inexorable drive of hard-edged Protestantism. Secondly, the conservatives always had the potential to return to the Catholic fold. The recusant Marian priests having largely died off, priests from seminaries on the continent and then the Jesuits sent trained young priests to England for the presentation and augmentation of the Catholic faith. It was this impetus which increased recusancy.

The seminary at Douai, founded by William Allen in 1568, was established firstly to educate Catholics abroad, and then to train a priesthood for England. Its priests were not prepared simply to maintain the Elizabethan compromise and lay supremacy but sought to introduce a purer style of Catholicism in the manner of the Council of Trent reforms. Seeing the Settlement as unlikely to collapse and an intolerable burden, they were prepared to accept the notion of foreign invasion to help their task of reconversion. They were thus perceived as spies and traitors by the Protestants, a threat to the security of the state. Yet this should not blind us to the mission's purpose of sustaining and strengthening existing Catholic practices and faith. In 1580, Edmund Campion, a Jesuit, outlined his task: 'to preach the gospel, to minister the sacraments, to instruct the simple, to reform sinners, to confute errors and, in brief, to cry alarm spiritual against foul vice and proved ignorance wherewith my countrymen are abused'.

From the mid-1570s onwards the Catholic threat increased as the influx of seminary priests began in earnest at the rate of about 20 per year 1576–9, rising to 29 in 1580. In June 1580 Campion and Robert Parsons were the first two Jesuit missionaries, bringing with them all the determination and dedication expected of Loyola's 'Soldiers of the

Faith'. These men provided the organisation and structure of the mission which the seminary priests had failed to do since their first arrival in 1574. They had tended to operate as isolated individuals after sheltering near the coast. By the 1580s London was the nerve-centre for the shelter and distribution of immigrant priests and by 1584 Allen and Parsons were working together on the supply of priests from the Continent into England. Once arrived, a network of Catholic gentry gave them shelter in their households, though they were unevenly distributed across the country. They were concentrated mainly in the South and East, despite the best efforts of Jesuits such as Robert Southwell, Henry Garnet and John Gerard to broaden the mission's range into Yorkshire, Durham and Worcestershire.

Against the background of the mission, the international situation seemed to suggest a turning of the tide against Protestantism. The election of Pope Gregory XIII (1572–85) strengthened the Papacy's resolve to overthrow Elizabeth 'as the cause of such great harm to the Catholic faith and of the loss of so many millions of souls'. The Throckmorton Plot of October 1583, whereby French Catholic forces were to invade, backed by Spanish and papal money, and liberate Mary Queen of Scots to start a Catholic rising, involved both the Jesuits and William Allen. Government fears were again intensified by the assassination of William of Orange and the Treaty of Joinville between Philip II and the Catholic League in France in the following year. Furthermore, the Duke of Parma was clearing the Netherlands for Catholicism at an alarming rate.

Not surprisingly, the effect of this international backdrop in which forces of good and evil, Christ and Anti-Christ, were waging a struggle to the death, further heightened English Protestant suspicion that Catholics were fundamentally traitorous and potential assassins like Anthony Tyrell (1581) and Dr Parry (1584). Edmund Campion claimed the Catholics were 'as true subjects as ever the Queen had' but religion could not be separated from politics and persecution intensified as fears increased.

An Act of 1581 redefined treason to include those who withdrew English subjects from allegiance to the Queen or her Church. Recusancy fines were increased to £20 and fines were introduced for saying or hearing Mass, thereby blocking the loop-hole for Church Papists who could attend the local Anglican Church and then hear Mass privately. It was still not an offence to be a Catholic – just to become one.

In 1585 Parliament ordered the expulsion of priests, and it now became treason to become a priest, with the death penalty for those who helped priests in any way. This harsh legislation aimed to undermine the organisation of the Mission and between 1586–1603, 123 out of 146 Catholics executed were charged under this Statute – 'Act Against Jesuits and Seminary Priests'. Treason was extended to cover those who were the cause for which others plotted treason, specifically Mary Queen of Scots. As part of the enforcement of this legislation a series of questions were devised in 1581 for use with captured priests. The sixth and last question became known as 'The Bloody Question':

> If the Pope also by his Bull pronounced her Majesty to be deprived and no lawful Queen, and her subjects to be discharged of their allegiance, and if the Pope or any other by his authority do invade the realm, which part would you take, or which part ought a good subject of England to take?

1 *What precisely was meant by 'a good subject of England'?*
2 *Why were the replies published by the Authorities?*

The impact of this welter of penal legislation was varied. It was clearly an attempt by the Protestant regime to destroy the missionary priesthood and to force the native Catholics into maintaining at least the conformity of Church Papistry as it had done since the Settlement. For the priests, the dangers involved did not put them off – for such trained and dedicated men, imprisonment, torture and the traitor's death by hanging, drawing and quartering were an accepted, even welcomed, risk. Between 1581 and 1586, 30 priests were executed and 50 were put in prison, yet a further 179 arrived in the same period. In 1588 21 priests were put to death and a further 53 between 1590 and 1603. Overall, A F Pollard argued that 187 priests died for the cause and certainly the government was not able to halt their arrival.

As far as the Catholic laity was concerned, the increase of the recusancy laws coupled with the impact of the mission led to a polarisation between those who conformed fully to the Anglican Church, and those who shifted from outward conformity to recusancy. The evidence does vary from region to region, with the greatest movement into recusancy in the North, but it was also evident in and around London and in Sussex. However, fines acted as a brake on recusancy. By 1592 Cardinal Allen had accepted there would remain Church Papists among English Catholics, albeit as a declining proportion amongst Catholics.

The success of the mission is an issue about which there has been much debate. Certainly Dr Haigh has suggested that the survival of English Catholicism owed little to the missionary priests as had been suggested by Professor J Bossy, but owed much more to the strength of native survivalism. He has argued that the mission did not focus its efforts on the stronger Catholic areas of the North but rather devoted its manpower disproportionately to the needs of the wealthier in the South and East. After 1580, 50 per cent of the missionary priests resorted to the South-East where only 20 per cent of detected recusants resided. Professor Bossy on the other hand argued that survivalism decayed as the Marian clergy died off, and that the evangelising role of the mission was crucial in maintaining the 'old faith' into the next century and beyond.

Professor McGrath has convincingly argued that the mission was important even if it failed to reconvert England or fully transferred conservatives into recusancy. For a Catholic, a priest to celebrate the Mass was essential and thus without the efforts of the seminary priests and Jesuits, Catholicism would have largely disappeared. The gentry were crucial in providing shelter, priest holes and funding for priests as domestic chaplains who cost around £30 p.a., and could not be afforded so easily in the North. The ports of entry were in the South and East, and hence London became, with its ease of communication, the focus of the organisation. The expansion of Catholicism under the greater tolerance of the Stuarts was a testament to the efforts of the mission and a measure of its achievement in creating a gentry form of Catholicism, though it did certainly fail to maximise the size and distribution of the potential Catholic community.

It should not be imagined, however, that even committed Catholics and recusants automatically supported the mission's aim of supplanting Elizabeth and many drew the line at this. Above all, they showed their loyalty to Elizabeth in not rising to meet the Armada of 1588, despite Allen's wishes. Many recusants wished to fight against the Spanish, once more illustrating as in 1553 that patriotism and the defence of a hereditary monarch were greater priorities than personal religious conviction. Indeed one group of Catholics appealed against the militancy of the mission, particularly in the form of George Blackwell, appointed 'Archpriest' in 1598. This group became known as the Appellants.

Not a large group, the Appellants did, however, reflect a strand of conservative English Catholicism which wished to see a return to some toleration of their faith. In a sense this marked a triumph for the Settlement of the Queen, by which loyalty was the greatest test, even though Catholicism had not been squeezed to death as the Queen and Council had wanted in 1559. Much of the old survivalism had been absorbed into the Church of England; what remained was the leaner, fitter Catholicism or recusancy which existed outside the religious consensus. The proportion within this group were expanding by the end of the reign whilst Church Papistry still existed for the wealthy heads of families, but in far fewer numbers than the 1560s. By 1603 the Church of England was established as a wholly Protestant national Church with the vast majority of the English population within its embrace and the Catholics on the outside.

ELIZABETH AND THE PURITANS

6 THE DEFINITION AND ORIGINS OF PURITANISM

The immediate problem the historian is faced with is one of definition. What does the term mean, 'Puritan'? It is certainly useful as a broad brush for the student of Elizabethan Protestant religion but it needs careful handling. Firstly, it was not a term in much use at the time. It first surfaced in 1565 among works of the Catholic exiles and is taken up by the Chronicler John Stow in 1566. In fact, it was used more as a term of abuse in the seventeenth century. The Puritans themselves used phrases such as 'True Gospellers' or 'the Godly' and were regarded in general as 'hotter' Protestants or 'precisians'. Secondly, they believed in Calvinist 'double predestination' of the 'elect' (destined for Heaven) and 'the reprobate' (those destined for Hell). They believed that the Bible was the only source of religious instruction in God's Word, and that a 'godly' life required total conformity to that Word. Preaching of the Word was the means whereby the country could be proselytised (converted) and cleansed of the last remnant of the Catholic Anti-Christ, the Pope and his Church, that 'rose-coloured whore seated upon the Beast'. The problem is that these criteria also apply elsewhere, to many of the bishops for instance. They, too, were concerned about extending the impact of Protestantism, about low standards of clergy, the large number of non-preaching clergy, about the need to purify the Church of the relics of popery, and stricter observance of the Sabbath.

Two other issues, however, did differentiate the Puritan of the 1560s from his fellow Protestants. Firstly, the speed at which the Church was to be fully reformed; for them it was to be done as quickly as possible, irrespective of the practical problems which this might entail. Meanwhile they would adapt the standards set down in 1559 to create a more 'Godly Church' closer to the purer Reformed Churches abroad. Secondly, there was the issue of obedience to the princely power and the relationship between Church and State embodied in the 1559 Settlement. This is what Professor Collinson has called 'the geological fault-line between Anglicanism and Nonconformity'. The Queen, and in varying degrees her bishops, insisted that in matters indifferent to salvation (*adiaphora*), the will of the prince must be obeyed, thus placing a restraint on true Christian liberty. For the radical Protestants or Puritans, if such things were not in the Bible, then a Christian, dictated to only by the Word of God, was free to ignore them. For them, loyalty to God came before loyalty to the Prince and a truly reformed Church had to be separated from the power of the monarch. Professor McGrath defined Puritans conveniently as those 'whose ideas and actions on matters concerning religious belief, religious practice, church government or church organisation brought them into conflict with the Church established by law and with the policy of the Supreme Governor'.

Many of these Elizabethan Puritans had been part of the struggle to establish Edwardian Protestantism. What brought a new dimension to the thoughts and actions of these men was their exile abroad under Mary. That exile was seen as a test of true faith before inheriting the Promised Land, a punishment by God for the ungodliness and worldliness of the English Church between 1547–53. Radicals amongst the exiles thought this necessitated a change of approach, as suggested by Thomas Becon's 'A Comfortable Epistle' in 1554. Importantly, these radicals had gathered in Geneva where they absorbed Calvinist ideology at first hand and witnessed churches run, not by bishops, but by their ministers and leaders of their congregations under a *classis* or Presbyterian model. This vision of an alternative style of Church was fundamental to the creation of that Elizabethan Puritanism of the 'hotter' sort: the moderates, however, were also affected by living face to face with Continental Calvinism and this body of men, some of whom became the first generation of Elizabethan bishops, were certainly reinvigorated by their ordeal.

7 THE PURITANS AND THE 1559 SETTLEMENT

The return of both groups throughout 1559 and into 1560 marked a pleasing end to the test of exile and gave an opportunity to reconstruct the Protestant Church and begin converting the mass of survivalist Catholics. What the 'Puritans' found was a Religious Settlement which had compromised the 1552 Prayer Book. Furthermore, the 'ornaments' rubric of the Act of Uniformity, requiring the use of Catholic vestments, had incorporated the 'rags of Popery' into the Church service; stone altars had not been removed and a royal injunction allowed the use of unleavened wafers reminiscent of the Mass rather than the bread as prescribed in the Prayer Book. The Queen's own conservative brand of Protestantism and her desire to attract the conformity of the majority of Catholics and conservatives had created a '*via media*' which was unacceptable to the newly-returned Puritans. For them the 1559 Settlement could represent only the starting line, for the Queen it marked the finishing tape. The appointment of the old Henrician, Matthew Parker, never a Marian exile, as Archbishop of Canterbury further underlined the mediocrity of the Settlement to radical eyes.

The first decade saw the Puritans focus their attention on achieving further official reformation of the Church as established in 1559, in the meantime adapting unofficially the Settlement to create a more 'godly' Church at the local parish level. They took strong exception to Clause 12 of the Act of Uniformity requiring the use of eucharistic vestments which were reminiscent of those worn by Catholic priests and even found the white surplice prescribed in the Prayer Book as 'the preaching signs of popish priesthood' and 'the garments of the Idol'. In the 'Vestiarian' Controversy the godly ministers rejected such vestments as lacking Scriptural basis, despite Archbishop Parker's assertion at the instigation of an irate Queen, that they were '*adiaphora*'. These ministers, supported even by some bishops, began to develop a general pattern of godly churchmanship rejecting also the sign of the cross on the forehead at baptism, shortening the service to allow for extended sermons or metric psalms, giving Communion with bread to seated, rather than kneeling, congregations, and objecting to plays and merrymaking on holy days especially on the Sabbath.

It was this style of godly churchmanship which led the Puritans to launch a campaign in 1563, which would further purify the Church in practice beyond that established by statute in 1559. The Convocation of Canterbury met to define the beliefs of the Church of England, based largely on the forty-two earlier Edwardian articles. Convocation agreed that 'Holy Scripture containeth all things necessary to salvation' but did not accept the Calvinist doctrine of 'double predestination' – it was accepted that God fore-ordained some to Heaven but not that He deliberately fore-ordained others to Hell. Even worse, six articles of reform of a strongly Puritan flavour representing godly churchmanship were narrowly defeated by the moderates in authority by 59 votes to 58.

Three of the six articles put forward in 1563 were:

> 2. That in all parish churches the minister in common prayer turn his face towards the people; and there distinctly read the divine service appointed, where all the people assembled may hear and be edified...
>
> 4. That forasmuch as divers communicants are not able to kneel during the time of the Communion, for age, sickness and sundry other infirmities, and some also superstitiously both kneel and knock (beat their breasts), that order of kneeling may be left to the discretion of the Ordinary (the bishop or his representative) within his jurisdiction.
>
> 5. That it be sufficient for the minister, in time of saying divine service and ministering of the sacraments, to use a surplice; and that no minister say service or minister the sacraments but in a comely garment or habit.

1 *Why was it felt important that the minister should face the people?*

2 *What was thought superstitious about kneeling at Communion?*

3 *Why were these demands unacceptable to the Church authorities?*

The ecclesiastical authorities, by careful management of elections, never again gave the Puritans the chance to attack the Established

Church in Convocation. When in 1566 Archbishop Parker's 'Advertisements' in dealing with the issues of clerical dress and ceremonial, enforced the Queen's desire to keep to the letter of the Settlement, some forty London clerics were deprived of their livings for refusing to accept the orders, leaving congregations untaught or served by ignorant hirelings. As a result the Puritans had to look to other means of achieving their further reformation of the Church than through Convocation, dominated as it was by the bishops and the hierarchy of the Church establishment. Any change of the Religious Settlement of the Church had now to come through the support of influential laymen such as the Earl of Leicester or through Parliament.

8 THE PRESBYTERIAN MOVEMENT

Puritan radicals turned their attention upon the body of the bishops, recalling their Swiss exile experience to highlight the Episcopacy as a popish institution responsible for the delays in reforming the Church. A central figure in this pressure group was Thomas Cartwright, appointed Lady Margaret Professor of Divinity at Cambridge in 1569. In a series of lectures on the Acts of the Apostles in 1570 he advocated the abolition of Episcopacy on the grounds that bishops had no biblical basis for their existence, and suggested their replacement by a Presbyterian Church organisation based on the Calvinist 'classis' system. He was the first university theologian to support Presbyterianism and saw Church and State as necessarily separate. Although a monarch-led Reformation was a welcome beginning, it needed furthering by following the examples of Continental churches, so that obedience to God, and to the Queen, were both possible but separate.

Against a backdrop of the Northern Earls' Revolt and the Bull 'Regnans in Excelsis', Parliament became the focus for the Presbyterian attack; because of its role in creating the Settlement, it might be prevailed upon to alter it. In 1571 William Strickland, a radical Puritan MP, introduced a Bill to Reform the Book of Common Prayer and abolish the surplice. It was defeated in Parliament, but John Field, an influential Presbyterian radical, emerged as the link between the 'godly' congregations and Puritan MPs in the Commons, under the patronage, amongst others, of the Earl of Leicester. The Queen was, however, forced to allow the Thirty-nine Articles to be given statutory recognition, a move she had quashed earlier, but which now gave Parliament a new central interest in religious affairs, a fact not lost on the Presbyterian radicals.

The following year, 1572, against a background of continuing anti-Catholic sentiment, two 'Admonitions [or warnings] to the Parliament' were presented, the first by Field and a fellow radical Puritan minister, Thomas Wilcox, the second by Thomas Cartwright. Though addressed to MPs, the first warning was a bold appeal to public opinion which landed Field and Wilcox in Newgate Prison. They argued that instead of the popish hierarchy of the Church of England as established, an equality of ministers was needed who, along with godly elders, would form a consistory (governing body) for each congregation as in the Genevan model and thereby improve discipline and order. Field's own church at Wandsworth was run on these lines and one effect of the 'Admonitions' debate was to spawn a revival of 'godly' Puritan churches separated from the Established Church, which was seen as dangerously slow in reforming itself further.

Defeated in Parliament and faced by the hostility of the Queen and her bishops, the radical Puritans kept a lower profile for the rest of the decade, Thomas Cartwright seeing fit to flee abroad into exile in 1574. The appointment in December 1575 of Edmund Grindal as the new Archbishop of Canterbury was an encouragement to Puritans of all shades. As a Marian exile with some Swiss experience, he had proved to be more sympathetic to Puritan grievances than Archbishop Parker. Many looked forward, on the basis of Grindal's record as Bishop of London and then Archbishop of York, to a closing of Protestant ranks and the establishment of a common ground against popery and ignorance. Indeed, Grindal had ordained Field as a minister in 1566 and had supported the Puritan stance over vestments. Field, for his part, abandoned his attacks on the Church hierarchy and turned to denouncing the Catholic common enemy.

Between the radical Puritans and those more willing to accept the Church establishment there was a broad consensus over 'prophesyings'. These were meetings for prayer, preaching, discussion and instruction from the Bible. They had sprung up in various parts of the country during the 1560s and 1570s as part of the Puritan impulse to further reform by improving the standard of conservative clergy, many of whom were ordained under Mary and ignorant of the new ways. Most of the bishops turned a blind eye to these 'prophesyings' out of sympathy and a sense of common Protestant purpose. However, the Queen did not approve.

9 CLIMAX OF THE RADICAL PURITAN CAMPAIGN

Consensus was destroyed by the suspension of Archbishop Grindal by the Queen over his refusal to suppress prophesyings in the southern province of Canterbury (*see pages 263–4 below*). The Presbyterian response was to utilize the limbo period of the Primate's suspension (1576–83) to further develop the *'classis* movement', which aimed to continue reform at grass-roots level in spite of the Church of England's hostility. Owing much to Calvin's model in Geneva, extended to France, the Netherlands and Scotland, the *classis* or Presbyterian meetings were organised by Field and others, using Walter Travers' *Full & Plain Declaration of Ecclesiastical Discipline* (1574) as the book of worship, rather than the Book of Common Prayer. The Book required ministers and congregational leaders (lay elders) from a number of parishes to form themselves into a *classis* to maintain discipline and uniformity of belief. Each *classis* would elect representatives to a provincial synod and they in turn would elect men to a national synod. In 1582 the first national synod met in Cambridge, and another in 1587 in London, to co-ordinate plans for a forthcoming parliamentary session. It was hoped that this Presbyterian hierarchy would ultimately replace the traditional system of bishops and archdeacons but do so from within the Church of England in an unofficial and subversive way.

One way in which the movement sought to do this was to have a 'godly' minister selected by the *classis* for a vacancy who would then recommend him for ordination by a sympathetic bishop, or more likely, exploit lay patronage. Puritan gentry who held the advowson (right of appointment) could be approached by the *classis* to support the candidate, who would be prepared to conform in the use of the Prayer Book, but adapt it to more Puritan consciences. The incidence of the '*classis*' movement is difficult to gauge but appears to have been strongest in London, the south Midlands and the South-East, interestingly coinciding with areas where the major thrust of the Catholic mission was directed. However, by the time of Field's death in March 1588, the attempt to establish a clandestine national Presbyterian organisation had failed due to an aggressive campaign by the Church authorities and because it was supported only by a small minority of Protestant, lay and clerical.

The appointment of John Whitgift, as Archbishop of Canterbury on the death of Grindal in 1583, saw a return of anti-Puritan pressure. Supported by a bench of bishops who were less sympathetic than their predecessors to Puritan ministers, Whitgift tried to force conformity upon them, no longer prepared to turn a blind eye to their loose interpretation of the Prayer Book. His attempts to restore discipline led to uproar and the Puritans sought redress of grievance against the Church establishment once again through the agency of Parliament.

Throughout 1584 the Puritans organised petitions to Parliament on the condition of the Church, the silencing of so many ministers and on the new Archbishop's methods. Through the Puritan laity these complaints were transferred to the Parliament of 1584–5 which met against the backdrop of reviving Catholic fortunes abroad. Ignoring the Queen's order that religion was not a subject for discussion, they listened sympathetically to the Puritan demands. A bill by Dr Turner to establish a Presbyterian system was refused introduction, however. Nevertheless, 1586 saw a concerted attempt by the Puritans to persuade Parliament to remodel the church A 'General Supplication' of evidence from 2537 parishes, summarised by Field, was presented to

Parliament in 1586, along with petitions complaining about the suspension of godly ministers.

On 27 February 1587, the Puritan MP, Anthony Cope, introduced his 'Bill and Book' proposing the abolition of all existing laws and customs of the Church and replacement with a Presbyterian system of government and worship based on a revised Genevan Prayer Book. It was a carefully prepared assault on the status quo by Travers and Field centred on the simultaneous meeting of the National Synod in London. When the Speaker, as the Queen's agent in the Commons, warned the House 'not to meddle with this matter', four Puritan MPs still pressed for the Bill to be read. Its subsequent confiscation by the Queen caused Peter Wentworth to launch his famous attack on royal interference in Commons' business. He and his four Puritan colleagues were sent to the Tower charged with holding private meetings to plan parliamentary business – an offence not protected by parliamentary privilege.

This represented the high water mark of radical Elizabethan Puritanism. Denied again their opportunity through Parliament, the zealots were forced back upon the unofficial implementation of their programme by godly ministers at local level, since 'seeing we cannot compass these things by suit, nor dispute, it is the multitude and people that must bring the discipline to pass which we desire'. Unfortunately for them, circumstances prevailed against them. Foreign affairs and the Armada of 1588 concentrated moderate minds on the need to pull together behind the Queen, whilst the removal of the Queen of Scots in 1587 as the internal focus of Catholic hopes, denied the radicals a vital weapon with which to beat the established authorities. Even worse, the deaths of John Field and his patron, the Earl of Leicester, in 1588 were matched by the demise of other powerful Court patrons of the Puritan cause such as the Earl of Bedford (1585) and Sir Walter Mildmay (1589).

The 'Martin Marprelate Tracts', violent and abusive attacks on the bishops and Anglican Church (1587), possibly the work of the separatist John Penry, further scandalised religious opinion and alienated political support from the radicals. William Cecil, Lord Burghley, viewed them as subversive and in need of curbing. The way was open, therefore, for Whitgift to launch another campaign against the Puritans, one which he was to maintain until his death in 1604.

Not that the Presbyterians were the most radical of the Puritan strand of Protestantism. The 1570s had seen the development of a body of Protestants, who had as little time for a Presbyterian national Church structure, as they did for the Anglican one. These extremist sects first developed around London after the Admonitions controversy of 1571–2 and wanted each congregation to run its own affairs in the manner of the separated congregations of the Marian exile. Frustration at Presbyterian inertia led to a declaration by one Robert Browne called a 'Treatise for Reformation without Tarrying for Any' which denied the Royal Supremacy, and sought a covenant or agreement among his supporters to create a truly reformed Church within their congregations in a loose confederation. Another separatist group emerged in London later under the leadership of Henry Barrow. These early congregationalist sects saw themselves as the 'saints' of a true but invisible church and sought immediate reformation of the Church in England by separating away from the evil Church of England as established in 1559. To the authorities they were guilty of the same crime as the missionary priests and active recusants – denying loyalty to the Queen and, worse, their separatism threatened the whole social order. In 1583 two Brownists, Tasker and Copping, were hanged for treason under the recusancy laws, in 1593 John Greenwood and Henry Bacon were hanged for sedition and in the same year Parliament passed 'An Act against Sectaries'.

10 RADICAL CONFORMITY

In the aftermath of political defeat, the Puritans directed their energies towards preaching, pastoral work and the development of piety whilst conforming within Anglicanism. Puritan social and moral values, and particularly the preservation of the Sabbath as the Lord's Day against the temptations of alehouse, theatre or sports, developed as the characteristics of a radical wing within the established Church. This practical Puritan piety, so characteristic of seventeenth-century Puritanism, had its roots in the withdrawal of radical Puritanism from the national political arena in the 1590s.

Presbyterianism had never been a widespread and well supported body of opinion. It was a minority group which made an impact far in excess of its numbers through astute propaganda, shrewd tactics and sympathetic patronage on the Council e.g. Warwick and Walsingham. Although its political organisation was crushed nevertheless, according to Professor Collinson a reconstructed form of radical Puritanism spread its social and moral influence within the body politic in the form of Puritanism's 'reform of manners' under James I and Charles I. Elizabethan radical Puritanism went underground in the 1590s, if not into exile, to create a pressure group within the Church of England dedicated to the furtherance of the 'godly' reformation through practical personal piety. In this they formed a consensus with their more moderate brethren.

THE CHURCH OF ENGLAND

11 THE STATE OF THE CHURCH – 1559

It was one thing to establish the Church of England by statutory authority in 1559, but was quite another for the old Edwardian establishment to guarantee its survival. The new Protestant Church was intrinsically linked to the health of the Queen – Mary's short reign proof enough that change could be soon overturned. Elizabeth's longevity was certainly a crucial factor in her Church's survival and had she died of smallpox in October 1562 the religious history of the late sixteenth century may have been very different. It was not the case. Elizabeth's Church was new and fragile, a compromise designed to squeeze Catholicism into acceptance, through being sufficiently attractive and traditional, yet not sufficiently reformed to please the returning exiles. As Professor Collinson has remarked 'The result must have seemed precarious and provisional, not a settlement to last for 400 years.'

The majority of the population probably did not want change. The exiles after all had numbered only 700 and Protestantism was largely the religion of the educated élite within the political nation and clergy. Most of the English population believed in a quasi-magical set of beliefs involving miracles, the limbo of the unbaptised, and witchcraft (*see pages 388–96*). The unreformed Catholic Church had not sought to challenge this but to acknowledge it, whilst providing the necessary rites of passage and the Mass. Replacing all this by ideas of faith, doctrine and God accessible to all via the Scriptures, needed time for assimilation. As Dr Haigh has shown in his study of Lancashire, there was still loyalty to the traditional ways and hostility to Protestant innovation as late as the 1590s and beyond. Nor was the political nation attracted to Protestantism for necessarily religious reasons. Elizabeth's first Parliament was dominated by private bills to recapture ex-Church land granted to them by Edward VI then returned to the Church by Mary. Some, therefore, supported the Elizabethan Act of Supremacy for the material gain of lay property rights and acquiring a clear land title but disliked the Act of Uniformity because of its attack on the Mass.

Within the body of adherents to the Church of England, there was not one universal religious view. The student of the Elizabethan Church of England must not look for the simple hues of black or white to denote its followers but must appreciate the sophisticated shades of grey which the Church embraced. The numbers of Presbyterians, Separatists and Recusants remained quite small and this suggests a growing broad conformity which developed during the reign but underneath the orthodoxy, imposed in 1559, there existed many tensions concerned with the direction and character of the new Church.

The economic condition of the Church in 1559 also gave cause for concern. The bishops lost many of their best properties in 'exchanges' with the Crown – see page 244. Appointed less for their administrative skill and more for their brand of Protestantism, a number struggled to cope with the economic position they had been presented with. Bentham died after twenty years in office owing £1000 to the Crown, and £200 to the See. The impoverishment of the Church meant that the livings were also poor and less attractive to men of the right education and religious persuasion. As a result, vacant livings, if filled at all, sometimes had to be filled by ex-Marian priests who conformed, or the ill-educated and the non-committed, thus enhancing the criticisms about the condition of the new Church under the unreformed episcopal structure.

The new Church, and the Royal Supremacy over it, did have its defenders against doubts expressed by Catholics and radical Protestants. The essence of the argument was Erastian – ecclesiastical as well as secular power must lie completely in the hands of the Christian magistrate or prince. (The doctrine was named after its originator, a Dr Erastus, physician to the Elector Palatine.) The most significant work to this effect in England was that of John Jewel, Bishop of Salisbury, who in 1562 sought to justify the Church and the Settlement. His *Apology or Answer in defence of the Church of England* (published 1564) was aimed at the Catholic critics, especially Thomas Harding, who argued that Parliament had usurped the spiritual power belonging solely to the Pope. Jewel's ideas formed the basis for later works in defence in the 1559 Settlement such as Thomas Bilson's *True Difference between Christian Subjection and Antichristian Rebellion* (1585) or Richard Hooker's *Laws of Ecclesiastical Polity* published in the 1590s.

12 DEMANDS FOR CHANGE UNDER ARCHBISHOP MATTHEW PARKER 1559–75

For the Queen the 1559 Settlement was to be enforced effectively by Archbishop Parker (installed December 1559) and his bench of bishops. But an end to clerical abuses, a preaching and pastoral role for the Church, an end to worldliness, were as much objectives of bishops such as Jewel and Aylmer as they were of the 'hotter' sort of Protestant. They supported moves for more diocesan visitations and the use of lay superintendants and rural deans to overcome the administrative problems in the size of some of the dioceses. That of Lincoln, for example, was spread over nine counties.

Presbyterian demands for a preacher in every parish highlighted the Church problem of getting men of quality into the field but ministers made weekly visits to the bishop to improve their standards and moderaters supervised prophesyings in local market towns. The Queen for her part felt one or two preachers per county was sufficient and sought to suppress prophesyings. This was the essential difficulty – the Queen refused to acknowledge formal change and disliked the circumvention of ceremonial requirement, so common outside the environs of London. With the die cast against officially sponsored change, informal modifications had to suffice, to the frustration of moderate reformers.

Elizabeth was to attack the marriage of clerics in 1561, despite official sanction in 1559, with the proviso of approval by the relevant bishop and neighbouring gentry. She refused to revive the Edwardian act for the marriage of priests and in 1561 issued another royal injunction forbidding any cleric to live with his wife and family in any college or cathedral close. Parker was forced to defend clerical marriage whilst Bishop Cox thought it would lead to non-residence. The Queen backed down over the cathedral closes but not colleges. Over ceremonial she was determined to impose discipline and curb the informal changes to the Settlement. Most bishops outside London refused to implement royal policy and allowed a certain amount of license over uniformity e.g. to clerics in Essex who refused to wear the surplice as required of them on the grounds that it was a visible vestige of popery. In January 1565 the Queen demanded conformity of the clergy on pain of loss of office, blaming Parker and his bishops for allowing 'these errors, tending to breed some schism or deformity in the Church' and requiring that 'uniformity of order may be kept in every church and without variety and contention'. The bishops were squeezed between their own ideas and the Queen's view of their role. Forced to choose between God and the Monarch, they backed Elizabeth's desire for order and disciplined the 'hotter' Protestants in accordance with her wishes. This process undermined the common ground between bishops, moderate Puritans and the more radical sort.

After a decade of existence, the Church of England found itself under threat of the Catholics on the one hand and the Presbyterianism of the radical Puritans on the other. The forms by which the Queen had been at pains to keep the Catholics loyal, had created tension inside English Protestantism which had proved impossible to control. However, the dangers posed by external Catholic threats persuaded many to defend the Anglican Church and Presbyterianism seemed too disruptive in its implications for the body politic. The mainstream of moderate Puritans wished to develop a learned ministry, spread the Word, and make inroads on general ignorance whilst remaining within the Church.

The Queen and her Church needed defending against a worsening international crisis not thrown over at the whim of a minority, jeopardising the conversion of rank and file to Protestantism and enabling Catholics to champion social conservatism. More cynically, Presbyterianism threatened gentry and aristocratic land rights gained by the Reformation. The First 'Admonition' stressed the need to remove advowson (the right to appoint a local minister) and impropriations (the taking over of tithes by a layman) which would have hit the landowning classes financially. It is not surprising that Parliament, the forum of the landed interest, should have refused to surrender their own privileges in support of Presbyterianism – they after all were part of that hierarchical structure the radicals seemed likely to demolish.

13 EDMUND GRINDAL 1575–83

The translation of Edmund Grindal from York to Canterbury on the death of Parker in May 1575 was a political move. Highly thought of by his contemporaries, he had been an exile in Strasbourg and as Bishop of London had helped establish London as a centre for Protestantism. In the Vestiarian Controversy (*see pages 253–4*) he had upheld royal authority despite his sympathies for the non-conformist cause and had been translated to York in 1569, in the wake of the Northern Earls' Rebellion, to maintain the pressure on Catholic survivalism. As President of the York Ecclesiastical Commission and in alliance with the Earl of Huntingdon as President of the Council in the North after 1572, Grindal tried to make an impact with Protestantism in the rural, backward North. He resisted translation to the southern province because he felt his job was not finished. However, influential courtiers supported him as the one most likely to contain within the Church those 'hotter' Protestants alienated by Parker's unswerving and sterile defence of the status quo. In this way it was hoped to take the steam out of Presbyterianism, by reforming from within, and closing Protestant ranks against revitalised popery. He quickly encouraged the publication of a translation of Scripture known as the Geneva Bible, which Parker had suppressed, and attacked non-attendance, pluralism and dispensations. These were practical reforms not attempted earlier and quickly caused the Queen irritation, though controversy between the Protestants began to recede.

It was the issue of prophesyings, with their preaching and prayer outside the normal framework of church services, which brought about the clash between Archbishop and Monarch. Elizabeth thought two or three preachers per county was sufficient, each armed with a Book of Homilies from which to read, safe, prepared sermons. She had not changed her mind about 'prophesyings' as the cause of Presbyterian unrest and disquiet, not conducive to maintaining the *via media* of her settlement. In late 1576 Elizabeth ordered Grindal to suppress them, upon which Grindal, who encouraged them, consulted his bishops. He found that 10 out of 15 were in favour of prophesyings and out of conscience he refused suppression, writing to the Queen (20 December 1576) to ask 'how this strange opinion should once enter into your mind that it should be good for the Church to have few preachers'. He continued with two petitions:

> The first is, that you would refer all these ecclesiastical matters which touch religion, or the doctrine and discipline of the Church, to the bishops of divines of your realm, according to the example of all godly Christian emperors and princes of all ages . . .
> The second petition I have to make to your Majesty is this: that when you deal in matters of faith and religion, or matters that touch the Church of Christ, which is His spouse, brought with so dear a price, you would not use to pronounce so resolutely and peremptorily, as from authority, as you may do in civil and extern[al] matters; but always remember that in God's causes the will of God, and not the will of any earthly creatures, is to take place . . .

1 *Why was this advice so unacceptable to the Queen?*
2 *What can we learn about Grindal's religious views from the extract?*

Unlike the Vestiarian Controversy in which he could, in conscience, uphold royal authority with regard to what he saw as *adiaphora*, the suppression of prophesyings was not 'indifferent'; it struck right at the heart of mainstream moderate evangelical Protestantism and Grindal was forced to choose between God and the Governor of the Church. He was suspended in the summer of 1577 until his death in July 1583 and narrowly escaped deprivation while constantly refusing requests from the Privy Council to compromise. His fall marked the last chance for that overtly moderate reform to create a consensus between the Establishment and radical Puritans based around Grindal's moderate Puritan instincts. It ended the hopes of official reformation of the Church from within and the commitment to an open-ended reform of the Church which had been such a central plank of Protestants since the exile had ended.

It was a sharp turning point for the Church of England under Elizabeth but perhaps should not be over-stated. Prophesyings were not suppressed in the northern province, deemed necessary for the fight against ingrained survivalism; monthly preaching exercises began in the diocese of Chester in 1584. In the southern province they re-appeared as 'lectures by combination'.

14 JOHN WHITGIFT 1583–1604

During the six years of Grindal's suspension, the radicals were able to re-establish themselves and develop the *classis* system, free from inter-ference from the Archbishop of Canterbury. And they continued to benefit from a certain amount of leniency towards their co-religionists shown by some bishops, which Parker had been largely unable to control and which Grindal had condoned. The crackdown on the radicals coincided with the translation of John Whitgift from Worcester to Canterbury in September 1583. Elizabeth had found an Archbishop who would defend her Church against Catholic and Puritan alike.

Whitgift was one of the second generation of Elizabethan bishops, a product of the Elizabethan Settlement who had come to the fore in 1570, when as Head of Trinity College, Cambridge he attacked in print Thomas Cartwright's lectures on the Acts of the Apostles. Whitgift had argued that there was no scriptural basis for Presbyterianism and that the structure of the Church was a matter indifferent. He was a vehement supporter of the Anglican hierarchy as established in 1559 and, although an opponent of Calvinist church structure, he was a committed Calvinist predestinarian in his belief.

According to Professor Neale, Whitgift's appointment marked 'one of the decisive events of the reign'. He and his allies replaced Grindal's style of moderate Puritanism with a push for uniformity and orthodoxy, according to statutory requirement. A sermon preached on 17 November 1583 was an uncompromising demand for obedience to the Church as fixed in 1559. In this policy he was supported by the Queen and by the changing character of his bench of bishops caused by the death of first generation bishops, such as Pilkington of Durham in 1576, Horne of Winchester in 1580 and Bentham of Coventry and Lichfield in 1579. Whitgift immediately demanded that all the clergy of the southern province subscribe to three articles recognising the Royal Supremacy, agreeing to all of the Thirty-nine Articles and accepting that the Prayer Book contained nothing contrary to the Word of God. In other words he endorsed conformity to established Church government, doctrine and liturgy. To help him he used the Court of High Commission to deprive non-conforming clergy.

In this court, Whitgift used the 'ex officio' oath, the most violently disliked of his procedures, which had been employed in the North against Catholic priests since 1562. However, its use against fellow Protestants caused anger. By it, the suspected minister swore to answer all questions truthfully before he knew what the questions were and before any charge had been made. For a Puritan to lie about his actions would mean prison for contempt of court and to admit to Presbyterianism meant deprivation. The court, therefore, gained vital information and could benefit from self-incrimination by the ministers. Between 300–400 ministers refused to swear an oath that the Prayer Book contained nothing contrary to the Word of God and, although only a handful were deprived, hundreds of preaching ministers were silenced. A wave of protest from the Council and the counties forced Whitgift to climb down and require full subscription only from new ministers. Even so, Whitgift was appointed to the Privy Council

(February 1586) as the only Elizabethan churchman to exercise significant political influence.

The defeat of Presbyterianism in Parliament of 1586–7, the common sense of national purpose occasioned by the Armada and the deaths of radicals and their supporters in the late 1580s, provided Whitgift with the opportunity to relaunch his attack on the Presbyterian ministers. However, unlike in 1583–4, this campaign was more selective in its target and moderate Puritans' support for the State Church afforded them some protection from rigorous enforcement of the 1559 Settlement.

Much of this controversy among Protestants, however, took place in the southern province and was a debate about the Church's direction where it had been securely established. In the North, as Grindal had found, the style of Protestantism was secondary in importance to the struggle to overcome Catholicism. The northern High Commission Court was never used as a weapon against radical Puritans and, apart from two deprivations in 1567 in Durham, no minister willing to work within the settlement was deprived. 'Prophesyings' were not suppressed in the North by Grindal or his successors. And limited conformity continued unabated in the North, where as Dr Haigh has shown, Catholicism still had a strong foothold in the 1590s.

Whatever these practical limitations, the Church of England was strengthened by intellectual developments in its support. There were a number of writers who were influential but between 1594–7 the pendulum swung most strongly towards the established Church with the publication of Richard Hooker's *Laws of Ecclesiastical Polity* which refuted Presbyterianism in a superbly effective intellectual defence of the national Church and laid the foundations for the later intellectual development of '*ius divino episcopacy*' (divine right of bishops) in the following century.

Such writers as Hooker and the bishops themselves, while supporting the the Royal Supremacy and maintaining an Erastian position, did not necessarily reject all the beliefs identified with Puritanism. Whitgift, for instance, was forced to intervene in the controversy in Cambridge in the 1590s concerning Calvinist teaching on predestination. The heads of houses appealed to Whitgift to intervene, which he did by producing the Lambeth Articles of 20 November 1595, supported by Richard Fletcher, Bishop of London. In the Articles he defined a clearly Calvinist view that 'God from eternity predestined certain men to life and condemned others to death' and that election was due to God's will alone. Elizabeth moved quickly to prevent publication of the Articles and to put an end to such potentially divisive debate. Whitgift, the most sympathetic of Elizabeth's archbishops, was forced to back down but the Articles mark a clear statement of the Church's Calvinist doctrine in the late years of the reign and reinforced the belief of the godly that further reform might be attained.

15 THE GODLY MAGISTRATE

Throughout the reign the alliance between convinced lay Protestants and godly ministers generated a Puritanism which was the cutting edge of Protestantism's campaign against tradition and inertia. Protestantism required the infusion of Scripture into the populace, yet the Church lacked a proper preaching ministry and adequate provision to fund one. It was this role which the 'godly' magistrate filled.

At the head of these agents of change stood those powerful landed magnates who operated at Court and Council and whose contribution to the cause of Protestantism would be hard to exaggerate. Through their patronage networks, men of acceptable religious stance gained either secular or spiritual promotion. The Earls of Bedford, Huntingdon, Leicester, Sir Francis Knollys and Sir Francis Walsingham provided a nucleus of such patrons and nor should William Cecil, Lord Burghley, be forgotten.

As Chancellors of Oxford and Cambridge universities, both Burghley and Leicester were prepared to appoint divines who were more radically Protestant than suited the Queen, or to secure men of godly Puritanism as Fellows or Heads of Colleges. Leicester's influence was brought to bear in defence of such radicals as John Field in 1572 or Thomas Cartwright in 1586 and to protect Puritan ministers from episcopal pressure. The Crown was the largest holder of advowsons (rights to appoint parish ministers) and the livings were distributed by the Lord Keeper or the Lord Chancellor. The committed Protestant, Sir Nicholas Bacon, was estimated to have presented to an average of 113 benefices per year as Lord Keeper. These godly magistrates were also able to use the forum of Parliament to advance their interests. The drive to advance Protestantism was by no means left to a group of opposition MPs.

The key to Protestantism's successful impact was the alliance between the godly local layman and the zealous cleric, seeking to build a fully reformed Church in their localities and more concerned with practical reforms than rival systems of ecclesiastical government. Such laity demanded high standards of their church officials and used their patronage (advowsons) to present the right nominee to their benefices, effectively echoing their own religious sentiments and supporting the patron's social position and policies in the locality. In 1602 Sir Francis Hastings revealed it was his duty 'to father a good people to a good minister, a longing people to hear and a labouring speaking minister to teach them'.

In the towns where livings were small and poor, most with a stipend of less than £10 p.a., corporations sought to improve the position by buying the advowson and paying more to attract zealots, such as Robert Cooke who was brought to Leeds in 1588, or by establishing town lectureships as permanently endowed posts, as in Coventry or

Ipswich or Colchester. Supplementation of the incumbent's stipend was one way the godly magistrate could attract a zealous minister or new posts, distinct from the official living, were created. The growing economic power of the godly laity by the end of the century certainly made such intervention affordable.

16 THE UNIVERSITIES

The increasing demand for a learned ministry stimulated supply. There was a rapid expansion of higher education, and between 1558–90 numbers at Oxford and Cambridge universities grew steadily. In the dioceses of London in 1560, 40 per cent of the clergy were graduates, whereas by 1595 this number had risen to over 70 per cent. Not every area reflected a similar pattern, especially in the peripheral areas, but growing education facilities seem also to have enhanced the godliness of the magistracy. Many such gentry did not take degrees but went for a general education, and to enjoy themselves, but were nevertheless exposed to Protestant ideas, some quite advanced.

In 1584, Sir Walter Mildmay, Chancellor of the Exchequer, founded Emmanuel College, Cambridge as a 'seed-plot', according to the Preface of the College Statutes, 'of the most noble plants of theology and learning which would be transplanted to all parts of the Church' to produce 'a faith of purest doctrine and a life of most holy discipline'. In 1596 Frances, Countess of Sussex, founded Sidney Sussex College as a similar 'nursery of Puritanism' as William Land was later to remark. The period also saw a growth in the connections between the colleges and the local grammar schools, often but not exclusively Edwardian foundations, via closed exhibitions and endowments, strengthening the bond between godly magistrate and minister and making the universities significant agents for religious change.

17 CONCLUSION

By the time of the Queen's death in 1603 the Church of England had been securely established and was to be governed by a committed Scottish Calvinist, prepared to uphold episcopacy as a vital bulwark to monarchy: 'No Bishop, No King' was James I's famous reply to attempts to reconstruct the Anglican Church upon his arrival. The Church was still suffering from the economic spoil imposed by the last of the Tudors and could still not maintain the level of active preaching ministers it might ideally have liked. But it had survived attacks from both religious wings and had in the first three decades held the middle ground, successfully broadening its scope to encompass all but the recusant and the separatist. In this, it was a triumph for Elizabeth's policy of creating a *'via media'*, of preventing division, of not wishing to make windows into men's souls. She had successfully upheld the 1559 Settlement in which loyalty to the Governor of the Church was of ultimate importance and in John Whitgift she finally found a churchman prepared to enforce the conformity she desired.

However, the Church itself in 1603 had developed from that of 1559. The Queen had viewed the Church as the product of an act of state, a Church which was to remain fixed. This static view had been challenged by moderate and radical Puritan alike, whose dynamic views emphasised a continuing process of reformation until the Anglican Church was a true, fully reformed Church. By the end of her reign, the Church of England had progressed along these lines. An acceptance of Calvinist 'double predestination', the development of a Puritan piety, the growth of a teaching and preaching ministry, were all achieved informally. The Church of 1603 was in this way also a triumph for that moderate Puritanism promoted by men such as Edmund Grindal and it represented the mainstream of Church of England Protestantism under Elizabeth's successor.

18 BIBLIOGRAPHY

R J Acheson *Radical Puritanism* (Longman Seminar Studies).
P Collinson *English Puritanism* (Historical Association, 1983).
P Collinson *The Religion of Protestants* (OUP, 1982).
C Cross *Church and People 1450–1660* (Fontana, 1976).
A Dures *English Catholicism 1558–1642* (Longman Seminar Studies, 1983).
C Haigh (ed.) *The Reign of Elizabeth I* (Macmillan, 1984). (Especially the articles by Haigh, Jones and Collinson.)
P V McGrath *Papists and Puritans* (Batsford, 1967).
G Regan *Elizabeth I* (CUP, 1988).
J Warren *Elizabeth I: Religion and Foreign Affairs* (Hodder & Stoughton, Access to History, 1993).

19 DISCUSSION POINTS AND EXERCISES

A *This section consists of questions or points that might be used for discussion (or written answers) as a way of expanding on the chapter and testing understanding of it:*

1   What problems did Protestants face on the new Queen's accession in 1558?
2   How do the historiographical interpretations of the first year differ?
3   'Protestantism returned only through the use of force.' Do you agree?

4 Did Elizabeth get the Settlement she wanted?

5 How did Catholicism adapt in the first ten years of the Settlement?

6 Was religion the real issue for the Northern Earls?

7 Assess the achievements and failures of 'The Catholic Mission'.

8 'The conflict between Catholic and Puritan in the 1580s can only be fully understood when set against events abroad.' How fair is this assessment?

9 What had happened to English Catholicism by 1603?

10 On what issues did the various shades of English Puritan agree and how did they differ in their doctrine and in their reaction to the Settlement?

11 How effectively did the Crown curb the more extreme Puritans in the first two decades of the Settlement?

12 Why did Puritans turn to Parliament as the forum to achieve their aims in the 1570s and 1580s?

13 How did Puritans react to political failure at the end of the reign?

14 Assess the achievement of Matthew Parker as Archbishop of Canterbury?

15 Why was Grindal suspended and why did he refuse to back down?

16 'In John Whitgift, the Queen finally got her churchman.' Discuss this verdict.

17 By what means was Protestantism established throughout the country at local level?

18 How secure was the position of the Church of England by 1603?

B *Essay questions*

1 How real was the danger from the English Catholics?

2 Which constituted the greater threat to Royal power under Elizabeth I – the Catholics or the Puritans?

3 What part did Archbishops Parker and Whitgift play in upholding the Elizabethan Settlement of Religion?

4 How well did Elizabeth's Archbishops of Canterbury support her in the maintenance of her 'Religious Settlement'?

5 Why, and with what success, did Elizabeth resist Puritan attempts to modify her Religious Settlement?

6 How and when was the Religious Settlement of Elizabeth's reign achieved?

20 DOCUMENTARY EXERCISE – ELIZABETH AND HER CHURCH

Read these extracts and then answer the following questions:

Jewel to Martyr, 14 April 1559:

A. It has happened that the Mass in many places has of itself fallen to the ground, without any laws for its discontinuance. If the Queen herself would but banish it from her private chapel, the whole thing might be easily got rid of . . . She has, however, so regulated this Mass of hers (which she has hitherto retained only for the circumstances of the times) that although many things are done therein, which are scarcely to be endured, it may yet be heard without any great danger. But this woman, excellent as she is, and earnest in the cause of true religion, notwithstanding she desires a thorough change as early as possible, cannot however be induced to effect such change without the effect of law . . .

Queen Elizabeth to Matthew Parker, 25 January 1565:

B. We thought, until this present, that by the regard which you, being the primate and metropolitan would have had hereto according to your office . . . these errors, tending to breed some schism or deformity in the Church, should have been stayed and appeased. But perceiving very lately . . . that the same doth rather begin to increase . . . we . . . have certainly determined to have all such diversities . . . as breed nothing but contention . . . and are also against the laws, good usages and ordinances of our realm, to be reformed and repressed . . . And, therefore, we do by these our present letters . . . straitly charge you . . . to confer with the bishops your brethren . . . and cause to be truly understood what varieties, novelties and diversities there are in our clergy . . . either in doctrine or in ceremonies and rites of the Church, or in the manners, usages and behaviours of the clergy themselves . . . and thereupon . . . to proceed by order . . . of such laws and ordinances as are provided by act of Parliament . . .

Edward Dering – Sermon before the Queen 1570:

C. Look upon your ministry, and there are some of one occupation, some of another: some shakebucklers [swashbucklers], some ruffians, some hawkers and hunters, some dicers and carders, some blind guides and cannot see; some dumb dogs and will not bark: and yet a thousand and more iniquities have now covered the priesthood. And yet you in the meanwhile that all these whoredoms are committed, you at whose hands God will require it, you sit still, and are careless, and let men do as they list. It toucheth not belike your commonwealth and therefore you are so well contented to let all alone. The Lord increase the gifts of his Holy Spirit in you, that from faith to faith you may grow continually till that you be zealous as good King David to work his will.

The Queen's letter suppressing prophesyings, 1577:

D. Right reverent father in God, we greet you well. We hear to our great grief that in sundry parts of our realm there are no small number of persons, presuming to be teachers and preachers of the Church though neither lawfully thereunto called nor yet fit for the same, which, contrary to our laws established for the public divine service of Almighty God and the administration of His holy sacraments within this Church of England, do daily devise, imagine, propound and put in execution sundry new rites and forms in the Church, as well by their preaching, reading and ministering the sacraments, as well by procuring unlawful assemblies of a great number of our people out of their ordinary parishes and from place far distant, which manner of invasions they in some places call prophesying and in some other places exercises; by which manner of assemblies great numbers of our people, specially the vulgar sort, are brought to idleness and seduced and in a manner schismatically divided amongst themselves into variety of dangerous opinions, and manifestly thereby encouraged to the violation of our laws and to the breach of common order, and finally to the offence of all our quiet subjects that desire to serve God according to the uniform orders established in the Church, whereof the sequel cannot be but over dangerous to be suffered.

The Queen's Speech to both Houses of Parliament, 29 March 1585:

E. Yet one matter toucheth me so near, as I may not overskip; religion, the ground on which all other matters ought to take root, and being corrupted, may mar all the tree. And that there be some fault finders with the order of the clergy, which so may make a slander to myself and the Church, whose over-ruler God hath made me; whose negligence cannot be excused if any schisms or errors heretical were suffered . . .

I see many over-bold with god Almighty, making too many subtle scannings of his blessed will, as lawyers do with human testaments. The presumption is so great as I may not suffer it (yet I mind not here to animate Romanists, which what adversaries they be to mine estate is sufficiently known) nor tolerate new-fangledness. I mean to guide them both by God's holy true rule . . .

Sir Robert Cecil to Archbishop Whitgift, 5 December 1595:

F. Her majesty . . . hath commanded me to send unto your grace that she mislikes much that any allowance hath been given by your grace and the rest of any points to be disputed of predestination, being a matter tender to and dangerous to weak, ignorant minds, and thereupon requireth your grace to suspend them. I could not tell what to answer, but do this as her majesty's commandment, and leave the matter for your grace who I know can best satisfy her in these things.

1 *Cite specific instances from the sources to show Elizabeth's concern for upholding the law in Church matters.*

2 *What evidence is there to show that Elizabeth was prepared to interfere as Supreme Governor above the heads of the bishops?*

3 *Who are likely to have supported Edward Dering's harsh judgment (document C) and why?*

4 *What criticisms does the Queen level at the reformers? Why?*

5 *'The Queen's view of her religious settlement was essentially static.' How far do these extracts support this conclusion?*

X

ELIZABETH I: PARLIAMENT

—

1 INTRODUCTION

THE rise of Parliament is one of the epic stories of English history. Subordinate to the Crown in its medieval youth, it grew to become the dominant institution in English politics. Eventually, in the nineteenth century, the will of Parliament outweighed that of the monarch, becoming the principal factor in deciding the policy and constitution of the government. The course of this great change is a subject which has provoked much disagreement. In particular, the significance of any single period in Parliament's development has been a recurrent theme of historical debate.

For several centuries, Elizabeth's reign was seen as part of the 'Tudor despotism' which halted or even reversed the rise of Parliament. Great power was wielded by exceptionally strong ('new') monarchs who dominated their Parliaments. In 1920, A F Pollard ventured a different interpretation, and this was established as the dominant view by the work of Sir John Neale (notably in his *Elizabeth I and her Parliaments*, published in two volumes in 1953 and 1957). Neale argued that Parliament, or, rather, the House of Commons, made significant progress during the reign of Elizabeth. An effective opposition arose in the Commons, inspired mainly by Puritanism. This opposition was strengthened by development of the privileges and procedures of the Commons. It was upon this achievement that the Stuart reigns were to see the power of Parliament built up against that of the Crown. Neale's argument held sway for several decades, but it has been vigorously assailed in the 1970s and 1980s. It was Neale's former pupil, Geoffrey Elton, who led the way, and the research done by Michael Graves in particular has done much to convince historians that Neale misinterpreted the evidence. These critics ('revisionists') have not gone so far as to revive the idea of Tudor despotism. But they have contended that the Commons did not even attempt to act as an opposition to

Elizabeth and did not rise at the monarch's expense; there is some evidence, indeed, that it entered a period of decline.

2 Elizabeth's Parliaments – an Outline

Parliament	Dates of sessions
1559	25 January – 8 May
1563–67	12 January – 10 April 1563(I) 30 September 1566 – 2 January 1567 (II)
1571	2 April – 29 May
1572–81	8 May – 30 June 1572 (I) 8 February – 15 March 1576 (II) 16 January – 18 March 1581 (III)
1584–85	23 November 1584 – 29 March 1585
1586–87	29 October 1586 – 23 March 1587
1589	4 February – 29 March
1593	19 February – 10 April
1597–98	24 October 1597 – 9 February 1598
1601	27 October – 19 December

Elizabeth summoned a total of ten Parliaments during her long reign. The first she called immediately after her accession to the throne, and it duly met in January 1559. According to a long-established principle of Tudor government, it voted the customs revenues for the life of the new monarch. It granted additional taxation to cover the expense of the current war against France. Finally, the main point of controversy, a new Religious Settlement was authorised; England was again made a Protestant country.

As is well known, a large number of people found fault with the new Church (*see Chapter IX*). Its hybrid character meant that it satisfied neither brand of purist, Protestant or Catholic. Protestant discontent was frequently voiced in Parliament (Catholics were excluded from the Commons from 1563). In the 1560s and 1570s, most notably in 1566 and 1571, the Church reform proposals tended to be limited, and while some were rejected by a Queen who was determined to maintain the settlement of 1559, others passed into law. The Parliaments of 1584–5 and 1586–7 saw a more extreme, Presbyterian Puritanism urged in the Commons. In whatever form, the religious debate was an ongoing feature of Elizabethan Parliaments.

Elizabeth's second Parliament, which met in 1563 and again in 1566–7, was called primarily to deal with a financial shortfall created by the military interventions in Scotland in 1560 and France in 1562–3. However, it earned its fame from the way in which members agitated the question of Elizabeth's marriage and the succession. The crisis of 1568–71: the arrival of Mary Queen of Scots in England, the Northern Rising of 1569, the Papal Bull calling on Catholics to withhold their loyalty from Protestant Elizabeth, and the Ridolfi Plot to force the restoration of Catholicism, caused Parliaments to be summoned in 1571 and 1572. Again, taxes were voted (in 1571), but activity centred on the need for laws to curb the threat from 'raging Romanist rebels'. A new Treasons Act made it treason to deny the Royal Supremacy or call Elizabeth a heretic, promulgation of a Papal Bull was made treasonable in another law, and measures to disinherit or execute Mary Queen of Scots were urged (unsuccessfully) upon Elizabeth.

The sense of crisis recurred frequently thereafter, as the conflict with Spain developed. The Parliament elected in 1572 met again in 1576 and 1581, and six new Parliaments were summoned between 1584 and 1601. All imposed taxes, initially to pay for expensive military preparations and eventually to fight the Spanish war that began in 1585. In addition, the enemy within, the potential allies of Philip II, were repressed by the vicious anti-Catholic legislation of 1581 and 1584–5, and the Parliament of 1586–7 lent its weight to the pressure which finally induced Elizabeth to sanction the execution of Mary Queen of Scots. The strains of war were also largely responsible for the monopolies row of 1601, the last and possibly greatest crisis in the history of Elizabeth's Parliaments. (Many MPs deeply resented the use of monopolies as royal patronage – a courtier would be granted the exclusive right to sell a particular commodity, at a huge profit.)

These issues provided the major points of controversy in Elizabeth's reign. Parliament also addressed many other questions. Some, like the Statute of Artificers of 1563 and the Poor Law of 1598 (*sees page 468–9*), were of national importance. Hundreds more were of private and local interest. It is clear that most of the subjects before Parliament did not cause conflict between MPs and the Queen. However, the significance of the differences that did exist has divided historians, and it will be necessary to consider the argument that Parliament was a centre of opposition before going on to describe the view currently dominant that co-operation was the norm.

3 THE LEGACY

There was every likelihood that Elizabeth's reign would see Parliament assertive and confident. Since 1529, Parliament had met in the great majority of years. It had passed an unprecedented mass of legislation, on such a wide variety of topics that there was no longer any area that seemed beyond the competence of Parliament. Its central role in the system of government seemed assured. Parliament had much to offer the monarch. Its meeting provided an invaluable opportunity to sound out the governing class. Every regime requires a flow of information between the centre and the outlying provinces, and Tudor governments were particularly anxious to learn the views of those, the peers, gentry and burgesses, who enforced law and order, collected taxes and generally conducted the business of government. Parliament was, as Elton said, a 'point of contact'. Above all, the government's measures acquired additional authority (legitimacy) when they were agreed by the nation's representatives. Sir Thomas Smith described the effect:

> The most high and absolute power of the realm of England consisteth in the Parliament. For as in war, where the King himself in person, the nobility, the rest of the gentility and the yeomanry are, is the force and power of England: so in peace and consultation where the prince is to give life and the last and highest commandment, the barony for the nobility and higher, the knights, esquires, gentlemen and commons for the lower part of the commonwealth, consult and show what is good and necessary for the commonwealth . . . That is the prince's and whole realm's deed; whereupon justly no man can complain but must accommodate himself to find it good and obey it. That which is done by this consent . . . is taken for law . . . For every Englishman is intended to be there present, either in person or by procuration and attorneys, of what pre-eminence, state, dignity or quality soever he be, from the prince (be he king or queen) to the lowest person in England. And the consent of the Parliament is taken to be every man's consent.
>
> (*Sir Thomas Smith*, De Republica Anglorum, 1565)

1 *What institutions was Smith referring to when he mentioned respectively 'the barony for the nobility and higher' and 'the knights esquires, gentlemen and commons for the lower part of the commonwealth'?*

2 *Why did Tudor monarchs value the role of Parliament and how had some of the major events of the English Reformation demonstrated this?*

The particular circumstances of the new reign made Parliament's role all the more indispensable. Certainly, Elizabeth would have to secure Parliament's approval for a new Church. She could hardly have dismantled the Marian religious settlement without the consent of that body, Parliament, which had established it. Parliament's co-operation would also be necessary in financial matters. Given that Elizabeth inherited an empty Treasury (and an expensive war) and an inadequate ordinary revenue (despite recent improvements), she had to turn to parliamentary taxation. Such dependence on the consent of Parliament threatened the power of the monarchy. That Elizabeth was a young and inexperienced woman can only have encouraged the expectation that Parliament would achieve greater power and stature.

Of course, Elizabeth rapidly emerged as a formidable politician who would not preside over a decline in monarchical power. She was fully aware that Parliament had an important role to play, but it was to assist rather than gain ascendancy over the Crown. Parliament would not have an independent power to make decisions on national policy, and, as shown below, even their freedom to discuss such affairs was restricted. Unfortunately for Elizabeth, Parliament had strong views on the very issues on which she wished to retain the initiative.

4 CONFLICT

On numerous occasions there was significant disagreement between MPs and the Crown. Protestant zeal, as Neale argued, was a major motivating factor for many members. They felt passionately not only about the nature of the Church but also about the need to secure it against the Catholic threat that persisted throughout Elizabeth's reign and seemed likely to prevail upon the accession of another Catholic queen. The other disruptive force identified by Neale was the growing tendency (begun under Henry VIII) of the country gentry to acquire the representation of boroughs, displacing the townsmen who traditionally held these seats. This meant that more and more MPs (eventually four-fifths of the House, in the later Parliaments) belonged to that independent and increasingly well educated class. Furthermore, a growing proportion (rising from 26 per cent in 1563 to 44 per cent in 1593) had some legal training, which made them more confident (and competent) law-makers. It is easy to imagine how the assertiveness of such members posed problems for a monarch determined to control the reins of power.

Religion

The religious question proved particularly difficult. The new Queen had considerable trouble in securing the original settlement, for the Parliament of 1559 contained men who were either more conservative or more radically Protestant than Elizabeth. Historians have differed on the course of events in 1559 (*sees page 240–4*), but that Elizabeth encountered problems in Parliament is not in dispute. Thereafter,

Puritan MPs frequently tried to secure legislation to make the Church more thoroughly Protestant. They naturally sought to promote their views through the institution whose decisions bound every subject, and they argued that Parliament's role in establishing the Church gave it a right to initiate reform. Faced with Elizabeth's unsympathetic response to their concerns, and aware that their ultimate accountability was to a higher authority, God, the Puritans felt compelled to put religious duty before their desire to be obedient servants of the Crown. In Neale's view, the Puritans formed an organised opposition which devised parliamentary strategies and co-ordinated their activities in the Commons; and, far from involving a purely negative attempt to defeat government policy, this was 'an opposition in a significantly new sense: one with a positive programme which . . . professed to aim at the fulfilment of its Protestant destiny'. A contemporary writer identified forty-three members of the Parliament of 1563–7 – 'our choir', as he described them – whom Neale cast as the leaders of the Puritan agitation. Equally zealous Protestants took up the struggle in the subsequent Parliaments. But all such efforts encountered resistance from a monarch who wished not only to preserve the Religious Settlement unchanged but also to deny Parliament's right to raise the question.

In 1566, 1571, 1572, 1586–7 and 1593, Elizabeth objected to Puritan bills on the grounds that Parliament had no right to raise the questions without her permission. They infringed 'the prerogative of the Queen', an argument to which this account will return later. Her displays of 'indignation' generally caused the measures to be abandoned – but not always immediately. When William Strickland proposed a bill, in 1571, to reform the Prayer Book, Elizabeth's order to exclude him from the Commons roused members to such angry protest that she quickly re-admitted the offender. Though she explicitly 'commanded the House not to meddle' in religious matters, Puritan measures continued to be advanced and to upset relations between Elizabeth and the Commons. In 1586, she sent Cope and his Presbyterian supporters to the Tower. In 1593 Morice's bills in defence of recalcitrant Puritans elicited a particularly strong rebuke:

> Mr Speaker stood up and said, That he had a message to deliver from her Majesty to the said House . . . it is in me and my power (I speak now in her Majesty's person) to call Parliaments; it is in my power to end and determine the same; it is in my power to assent or dissent to anything done in Parliaments. . . . it was not meant we should meddle with matters of state or causes ecclesiastical . . . She wondered that any could be of so high commandment to attempt (I use her own words) a thing so expressly contrary to that which she had forbidden; wherefore with this she was highly offended . . . her Majesty's present charge and express commandment is that no bill touching the

said matters of state of reformation in causes ecclesiastical be exhibited. And upon my allegiance I am commanded, if any such bill be exhibited, not to read it . . .

Marriage and succession

Elizabeth was equally loath to allow Parliament to discuss her marriage and the succession. These formed the second priority of the Puritans, but MPs in general, desperate to avoid a disputed or Catholic succession, were unwilling to leave them unsettled. The result was continual acrimony. Elizabeth rebuked the Commons in 1559 for presuming to urge her to marry. Then, in 1566, the issue came to a head. The Commons, supported by the Lords, apparently resolved to hold up the Subsidy Bill until Elizabeth settled the succession. According to Neale, 'There can be little doubt that making supplies depend on redress of grievances was the deliberate and concerted policy of the group organizing this agitation: of our "choir".' An angry Queen duly promised she would 'marry as soon as I can conveniently' in order to have children ('otherwise I would never marry'). But the House was neither satisfied with this vague declaration nor intimidated by her defiant manner (it was, she said, 'a strange thing that the foot should direct the head in so weighty a matter . . . Though I be a woman, yet I have as a good a courage, answerable to my place, as ever my father had. I am your anointed queen. I will never be constrained to do anything'). When she issued an 'express commandment' that the Commons should stop discussion of the matter, Paul Wentworth led the members in a famous protest in defence of 'the liberty of the free speech of the House'. Elizabeth withdrew her order and remitted one-third of the subsidy. But she refused to be bound further on the marriage and succession, saying that 'all things have their time' and warning the two Houses to 'beware . . . you prove [test] your prince's patience as you have now done mine'.

These attempts to press the succession issue, coming on top of the proposals for Church reform, finally persuaded Elizabeth to dissolve prematurely the Parliament of 1563–7, giving up much of her government's legislative programme 'to be rid of an intolerable House of Commons'. 'The choir' wrote Neale, 'returned to their homes, having conceived and employed such arts of opposition and displayed so resolute a spirit that no House of Commons before their time could furnish the like. The men of 1566 deserve place pre-eminent in our country's parliamentary history.'

The succession problem was aggravated in 1568 by the arrival in England of the legitimate but Catholic heir to the throne, Mary Queen of Scots and consequently by her own connections with those who organised the Northern Rising of 1569 and the Ridolfi Plot of 1570–1. In 1571, 1572 and 1584, Parliament urged exclusion or execution of Mary, or both. Elizabeth refused to accept Parliament's right to initiate measures against a fellow monarch. The successful demand for execution that was made by the Parliament of 1586–7 was the only one that did not involve conflict, for Parliament discussed the matter at the Queen's request. Then, in 1593, a bill to settle the succession so upset Elizabeth, 'as a matter contrary to her former strait commandment', that the Council imprisoned the MPs responsible, and their leader, Peter Wentworth, Paul Wentworth's brother, remained in the Tower until his death in 1597.

Clearly, then, the succession was an issue which agitated members throughout the reign.

Free speech

Closely involved in all of these matters was the issue of free speech. The members who raised such issues as Church reform, the Queen's marriage, and the succession encountered objections based not on the merits of their proposals but on their right to initiate discussion of them. Thomas More, when Speaker in 1523, had described Parliament's traditional right to discuss freely those matters legitimately before it; this meant that in most areas of national policy it had to await the initiative of the Crown. Elizabeth essentially shared More's conception, and she enforced it more rigidly than her predecessors, Henry VIII, Edward and Mary, all of whom in practice permitted more freedom of debate.

Elizabeth elaborated upon More's view, distinguishing between matters of 'commonweal' and matters of 'state'. The former were mostly private and local matters, and also national social and economic questions (like the Poor Law). These Parliament was free to discuss (though its final decisions did, of course, require the Royal Assent). The matters of state were those in which the monarch had a direct interest and acknowledged primacy, matters which, to use the contemporary terminology, belonged to the royal prerogative: religion, foreign policy, the Queen's marriage, the succession, and such Crown rights as purveyance (the Crown buying goods below market value) and the granting of monopolies. Members were not even permitted to discuss these issues except 'such as should be proponed unto them' (*Lord Keeper Bacon, 1571*). The Crown's claim to the sole right of initiative in these areas meant that Parliament was expected to await the legislative proposals of the government. Only twice, in 1572 and 1586, was Parliament invited to discuss a matter of state (the fate of Mary Queen of Scots, on both occasions) when a specific government proposal was not involved.

Many MPs, impelled chiefly by their zealous Protestantism, went beyond this to take the initiative in matters of state. As Neale wrote, 'Elizabeth was justified constitutionally and historically in her definition . . . But constitutional niceties make little appeal in passionate revolutionary times.' On several occasions, MPs, the Wentworth brothers in particular, explicitly took issue with the Queen's restrictive view and advanced the idea of Parliament's right to complete free speech. For example, Peter Wentworth asserted the claim in his famous speech to Parliament in 1576:

> . . . in this House, which is termed a place of free speech, there is nothing so necessary for the preservation of the prince and state as free speech, and without, it is a scorn and mockery to call it a Parliament House, for in truth it is none, but a very school of flattery and dissimulation, and so a fit place to serve the devil and his angels in, and not to glorify God and benefit the commonwealth . . .

Finances and economic issues

Given the inadequacy of the Crown's ordinary revenues, Elizabeth had to ask Parliament to vote subsidies in peacetime as well as during the war that broke out in 1585 and lasted until the end of her reign. MPs were loath to impose new burdens on their constituents and required the Councillors to justify every demand. The holding up of the Money Bill of 1566 has been regarded as an attempt to force the Queen's hand on another issue, the succession. Neale has argued that further examples of supply (of taxes) being made conditional on redress of grievances occurred in 1571, 1585 and 1601. In other words, the reign of Elizabeth witnessed the development of a major instrument of parliamentary opposition, one that was to be wielded to great effect under the Stuarts. In 1587, a Commons committee offered a benevolence (additional vote of money) on condition that Elizabeth accepted sovereignty over the Low Countries. She declined, having no wish to acquire the latter, but it was another notable attempt to use Parliament's control of the purse strings to influence policy.

At other times, the differences on money were more purely financial. In 1589 and 1593, MPs expressed their dissatisfaction with the heavy tax burden. On the latter occasion, when the Commons prepared to vote an insufficient two subsidies, Burghley (Cecil) used the Lords to propose an additional subsidy. This provoked a row in which some members objected to the greater burden itself ('The gentlemen must sell their plate and farmers their brass pots ere this will be paid . . . in histories it is to be observed that of all nations the English are not to be subject, base, or taxable', said Bacon) and the Commons, in addition, insisted on its sole right to initiate votes of money.

As matters of 'commonweal', social and economic questions could be raised, even in Elizabeth's restrictive view, on the initiative of members. This narrowed the scope for conflict. For example, the Crown accepted the Poor Law initiated by private members in 1597 as well as major additions to the government bill which was to become the

Statute of Artificers of 1563 (*see pages 454–6*). However, the Queen's prerogative might be at stake here, too, given that such royal rights as purveyance and monopolies were major economic grievances. So, differences occasionally arose. For example, in 1563 the Commons introduced two bills to limit the abuse of purveyance (the Crown's right to purchase goods at low, outdated prices). One bill passed through both Houses, but it was vetoed by a Queen determined to protect her prerogative powers against statutory encroachment. Far more important, however, was the issue of monopolies (*see page 234*). These raised prices to the consumer. Discontent grew intense during the economic crisis of the 1590s, but a financially straitened Monarch felt impelled to have increasing recourse to this costless form of patronage. The Commons protested in 1597, to no avail. In 1601, the House furiously assailed the practice – in a debate of such turbulence that Robert Cecil rebuked the members for conduct 'more fit for a grammar school than a court of parliament' – and the Queen, desperate to secure additional taxes, felt compelled to withdraw the most hated monopolies and submit the rest to challenge in the courts.

5 CO-OPERATION

This is a substantial catalogue of conflict. It was, however, spread across a long reign of almost forty-five years. Neale's emphasis on such 'dramatic aspects' – a function of his interest in the long term rise of the Commons at the expense of the monarch – has obscured the fact that there was usually co-operation between monarch and Parliament. As Michael Graves has written, 'the revisionists' study of parliamentary business places conflict in its right perspective. It was not the norm nor even a common occurrence, but an occasional isolated episode in a general climate of co-operation.'

The principal difficulty encountered by the Council was the way that the profusion of members' bills ate up the time available. Hundreds of private and local bills were proposed, dealing with matters as diverse as the settlement of individual wills and the export of horses. The problem was compounded by the garrulousness of many speakers and their ignorance of parliamentary procedure. It was the inefficiency of Parliament, the relatively inexperienced and disorganised Commons in particular, that caused ministers more problems than any deliberate intention to oppose. In the event, Elizabeth's Parliaments considered and passed a much greater number of laws than their predecessors, averaging 33 acts per session (out of 126 proposed), of which about two-fifths (166 of 432) dealt with private matters. This was a considerable feat of management, given that the average session lasted fewer than ten weeks.

Of course, many measures were in no way controversial. But the government's success in securing the passage of its own bills was significant. There was no substantial opposition to the great majority of its proposals. Parliament proved compliant even in areas where one might have expected members to hold strong views. For example, the money difficulties discussed above must be placed in perspective. Almost invariably, the Subsidy Bill went through easily and speedily. Indeed it has been suggested that Parliament's consideration of supply was a routine formality; the justificatory speeches of the Councillors were ritual signs of respect rather than necessary attempts to persuade; the supply bills usually passed through both Houses without hostile comment or amendment. Alsop has concluded that 'the Commons's role in initiating and deliberating on supply came very close to being a constitutional fiction under Elizabeth. Privy Councillors . . . expected no opposition, and were generally proved correct.'

Elizabeth was never denied funds, and 1566 was the only occasion on which she felt it wise to accept a reduced sum. Note that Parliament voted taxes in years of peace as well as those (from 1585) when taxation was clearly justified by the war. As far back as 1534, Parliament had passed a subsidy when the country was at peace. Under Elizabeth, a military pretext was still considered necessary, but it is striking how flimsy this could be; 'the orthodox doctrine of extraordinary need was stretched to the very limit without known complaint' (*Alsop*). During the war years, members offered only minimal opposition to the requests for **multiple** subsidies (two in 1589, three in 1593 and 1597, and four in 1601). For example, in 1589 only one member objected to the double subsidy, and he lamented the lack of opposition from any other. Such votes were unprecedented; no Parliament had ever before passed multiple subsidies, Mary's attempt to secure a double subsidy in 1558 having foundered (apparently) on Commons opposition. The tax burden was lightened by the inefficiency of the collection, but, nevertheless, the multiple subsidies were a striking innovation and Parliament's ready acquiescence speaks volumes about its co-operative mentality.

The alleged examples of supply made conditional on redress of grievances (in 1566, 1571, 1585 and 1601) have recently been reappraised. Elton in particular has contended that, while the supply debates of those years witnessed discussion of grievances, there was no attempt to hold up supply until they were remedied. Certainly, there is no conclusive evidence that this tactic was adopted. This applies even in the famous case of 1566; 'the connection between supply and succession was not as substantial as Sir John Neale believed' (*Alsop*). The idea of 'no supply before redress of grievances' was not an established strategy or principle, and the events of 1566 did not make it one. The later attempt to bribe Elizabeth to take the Dutch throne involved an **additional** vote and did not affect the proposed subsidy. The Commons did protest about the money Burghley proposed in the Lords in 1593; but the Commons initiative in money matters was preserved by the decision of the Lower House itself to propose the extra subsidy – hardly the recourse of a body disposed to confrontation. It would appear, in sum, that Elizabeth had less trouble securing supply than either her predecessors or the Stuarts. This owed much to the political nation's acceptance that her needs were legitimate (compared, for example, with those of her war-mongering father and the distrusted Stuarts). But the fact remains that on the vital question of money there was harmony between Elizabeth and her Parliaments.

Parliament hardly ever intruded into the royal prerogative to conduct foreign policy, despite the high level of Protestant discontent with Elizabeth's unwillingness to support the Dutch Revolt. Domestic religious issues caused more problems, but it is important to keep these too in perspective. The most important legislation enacted in the whole reign was that which created the Religious Settlement of 1559. Neale argued that the Settlement was imposed on Elizabeth by the Commons. The Queen proposed initially to go little further than the Supremacy Bill of February 1559 'to restore the supremacy of the Church of England &c. to the Crown of the realm'. The bizarre tacking onto this bill of Communion in both kinds was for Neale 'the vital clue', for it showed that a separate bill on the doctrine of the Church was not intended in this first Parliament. Elizabeth changed her mind as a result of the Protestant demand for a renewed doctrinal Reformation, a demand advanced in the House of Commons by men who adopted the 'superb, even astounding' tactics of 'an organized movement'.

However, another scholar, Norman Jones, has led recent historians back to the view first expressed by John Foxe. Jones identified numerous indications of Elizabeth's commitment to doctrinal Protestantism. He questioned the numerical and organisational strength ascribed by Neale to zealous Protestant MPs; there were only 20–25 religious radicals, of varying opinions, in a House of 400 members. And he rejected Neale's attribution of the doctrinal bills to those members ('the best guess is that they were part of the government's plan to restore English worship to the standard of 1552'). It was the House of Lords, led by the Marian bishops, that rejected the combined Supremacy-and-Uniformity Bill proposed by the government and carried in the Commons. Though she faltered briefly, Elizabeth decided to persevere. After Easter 1559, the Supremacy and Uniformity (with minor amendments) were separated into two bills and again passed the Commons easily. By using all of her influence with the lay peers, and arresting two of the bishops, the Queen overcame the opposition of the Lords (by only three votes in the case of the Uniformity Bill) and England was given a Protestant Church. The precise nature of the Religious Settlement has already been discussed (*see page 244*). The point here is that, according to the Jones view, the new Church was established by an alliance of Crown and Commons (against the Lords). One cannot be completely sure which of the views is correct. The dispute has arisen because of the inadequacy of the evidence ('meagre and baffling', as Neale described it) and for the same reason it is possibly beyond resolution. For the moment, however, this episode can no longer be seen as typifying conflict between Crown and Commons.

As for the Puritan agitation of later years, Graves has shown that the 'choir', Neale's heroes of the first campaign to reform the Church and settle the succession, was not at all an organised opposition. Neale's misinterpretation of the events of 1559 made him expect to see such an opposition in the next Parliament. He read the 'choir' document of 1566 as evidence of an organised body of men when it was merely a list of members appointed to consider the Succession Bill of 1563 (Elton's view) or may have been no more than a list of prominent personalities. Elton has concluded that 'the members of that "choir" formed no party and few of them were Puritans'. The Puritans, and discontented members in general, either acted individually or formed shifting alliances which varied from issue to issue. They pressed grievances without any thought of forming an opposition to the government or seeking to assert the power of Parliament against that of the Crown. The Puritan members did become better organised in 1571, but this was under Council leadership (*see below pages 287–9*). Above all, the Presbyterians in the Commons co-operated closely in 1584 and 1587, but they were a small minority in the House and their radical proposals foundered upon their colleagues' as well as the Queen's animosity. There is, in sum, no evidence of a significant Puritan opposition which was willing or able to lead the Commons against the Crown.

The great monopolies row of 1601 was not the work of an organised opposition movement; there is no evidence that members met in advance to plan their assault. Similarly, the disputes over parliamentary privilege involved either spontaneous reactions to official acts or the initiatives of isolated individuals. Elizabeth quickly and sensibly defused the incidents of 1566 and 1571 (*see above pages 278–81 on the succession and religion*). Peter Wentworth's call for the liberty of free speech in Parliament had a greater impact on succeeding generations than on his fellow MPs. In fact, it was the Commons that imprisoned him for four weeks for his crude and outrageous criticism of Elizabeth in the famous speech of 1576 ('her Majesty hath committed great fault, yea, dangerous faults to herself . . . It is a dangerous thing in a Prince unkindly to intreat and abuse his or her nobility and people, as her Majesty did the last Parliament'). In 1587 and 1593, when Peter Wentworth and a few allies were sent to the Tower, having pressed grievances outside as well as in the House, there was no general outcry. Most MPs who raised forbidden topics had no wish to confront Elizabeth on the principle involved and rarely persisted when the Queen indicated her hostility. As A G R Smith has written, Peter

Wentworth was 'essentially a maverick, a man whose views on free speech, which were of great significance for the future, were too far ahead of their time in the Elizabethan period'. Michael Graves is even more damning: 'the Wentworths were standard-bearers without an army', Peter was 'little more than a parliamentary nuisance'.

Finally, Parliament did not attempt to claim a role in the everyday administration of the country. The Queen was the head of the executive. Parliament did not even seek to supervise or audit the spending of the taxes it voted or to monitor the execution of its laws. Above all, it claimed no right to control the appointment of the Queen's servants. Some ministers were disliked; one thinks, for example, of the resentment felt against Robert Cecil's tactless and scolding manner. But criticism was muted, and on no occasion was the dismissal of Elizabeth's 'evil counsellors' demanded. Indeed, no Tudor Parliament encroached on the royal prerogative of choosing ministers. Parliament had demanded the removal of ministers during the previous two centuries, and it was to do so again under the Stuarts. So the Tudors offer a striking exception. Whatever the degree of opposition to Elizabethan and Tudor measures (or the lack of measures), there was no attempt to secure parliamentary government.

6 THE COUNCIL IN OPPOSITION

Much of the activity traditionally regarded as examples of Commons opposition involved the use of Parliament by Councillors to influence the monarch. Far from representing a growth in the assertiveness of Parliament, these episodes merely underlined the extent to which it failed to emerge as an independent power. When Councillors wished to change the mind of their obstinate Monarch, they frequently tried to convince her that the political nation demanded the measures they favoured. In particular, most of the activity associated with the so-called Puritan opposition was inspired by Councillors who shared the values and concerns of the less extreme (non-Presbyterian) Puritans.

The Queen's marriage and the succession were raised in 1563 and 1566 on the initiative of leading Councillors. The Commons petition of 1563 was drafted by a committee which was chaired by a Councillor (Sir Edward Rogers, Controller of the Household) and included all eight of the Councillors who sat in the Lower House, and the subsequent bill was guided through the House by one of the Council's unofficial helpers, Thomas Norton. In 1566, Lord Keeper Bacon in the Lords and Cecil in the Commons organised the joint delegation of the Houses to Elizabeth on the succession, Cecil helped to write into the preamble of the subsidy bill the Queen's promise to marry and name a successor, and it was the Councillors and their friends who took the major part in pressing the issue in Parliament.

Similarly, the Council supported the 1571 bill to punish all who failed to take Communion within the Church, an anti-Catholic measure to which the Queen refused to give the Royal Assent. In addition, it was the Council which launched the legislative assault on Catholicism in the 1580s; for example, the tough law of 1581 against recusancy (non-attendance at Church) was initiated by the Chancellor of the Exchequer's request for measures against 'evil affected Subjects', and it was Norton who responded by proposing and then leading a committee on the subject and drafting the bill. This is not to say that all Puritan measures emanated from the Council. The more radical bills – like Strickland's proposed reform of the Prayer Book in 1571 and the Presbyterian programme of the 1580s – they could not countenance, and these quickly failed.

In 1572, the Council possibly tricked Elizabeth into agreeing to a Parliament, arguing the need for money when their real purpose was to seek measures against Norfolk and Mary Queen of Scots. Certainly, Cecil (now Burghley) and his colleagues took the lead in demanding Norfolk's execution. They also led the joint committee of the Commons and Lords which drafted two bills against Mary, one finding her guilty of treason and the other excluding her from the succession. Despite Norton's speeches and the Council's success in rallying support in Parliament ('there can be found no more soundness than in the Common House, and no lack of appearing in the Higher House', Burghley wrote), Elizabeth's hostility forced the abandonment of the Attainder (treason) Bill. The Council secured the passage of the Exclusion Bill, only to be defeated again by Elizabeth. As Burghley later wrote to Francis Walsingham.

> Now for our Parliament, I cannot write patiently. All that we laboured for and had with full consent brought to fashion – I mean a law to make the Scottish queen unable and unworthy of succession of the Crown – was by her Majesty neither assented to nor rejected, but deferred until the Feast of All Saints; but what all other wise and good men may think thereof, you may guess.

In fact, Parliament was not recalled in 1572 on All Saints' Day (1 November); it remained prorogued until 1576. In 1586–7, again, it was the Council which initiated Parliament's attacks on Mary. In the wake of the Babington Plot, the Council pressed for a Parliament in 1586 ('We stick upon Parliament, which her Majesty misliketh', wrote Burghley), and then led the two Houses in demanding Mary's execution – this time successfully.

These were by no means the only occasions on which the Council tried to use Parliament to force the hand of a Queen who liked to think that she ruled with the love of her people. Neale was clearly aware of the views of the Councillors on many of the above questions. But he did not perceive the extent to which they actually led the Commons. He saw the above episodes as examples of the Commons in opposition, when in reality the House was a powerful weapon in the hands of the ministers. Expecting to find the beginnings of the opposition that the Commons raised against the Stuarts, Neale misread the evidence.

One important error in Neale's interpretation was his allocation to the ranks of the Commons opposition men who were in reality the allies and servants ('men of business') of the Council. Thomas Norton was one such man. One of Neale's heroes of opposition and 'princes of debate', Norton, as Michael Graves has shown, was actually 'Cecil's client' (*Graves*) and 'the Crown's most energetic assistant' (*Elton*). He proudly declared, referring to bills carried in 1581, that 'all that I have done I did by commandment of . . . the Queen's council there, and my chiefest care was in all things to be directed by the Council'. Graves has also found that William Fleetwood, Thomas Digges and others of Neale's opposition were really agents of the Privy Council. They actively promoted the Council's wishes in the Commons and were especially useful when it came to expressing views which Councillors could not openly support without losing the Queen's favour. These discoveries dramatically alter the way in which one must interpret the proceedings of the Commons. Bills and speeches considered by Neale to have been acts of Commons opposition were, in fact, the work of the Council.

7 CONTROL AND CONSENSUS

There were many reasons for Parliament's failure to mount a strong opposition to the monarchy. The Queen had means by which to 'manage' Parliament. The power of patronage was an especially useful weapon. Few MPs held paid office. But a majority prized their positions in local government and aspired to greater things in that and to the acquisition of pensions, monopolies and other benefits. So, the possible withdrawal of favour was a major sanction available to the monarch. The Crown did not have the ability directly to control the election of more than an insignificant number of MPs – most of them from Duchy of Lancaster land. But rather more were dependants of Councillors and loyal courtiers.

Thanks to the co-operation of such friends as the Duke of Bedford, Burghley nominated 26 MPs in 1584, and his son Robert may have chosen 30 in 1597 and 31 in 1601. The 'great men', who generally supported the Queen's government, controlled perhaps 40 per cent of the seats. The boroughs, in particular, were often so small that their voters could be subjected to irresistible pressure from the individual who owned much of the area and held the reins of local patronage – and some voters acquiesced on the understanding that the patron would relieve the borough of the need to pay a member's expenses. Although patronage was not sufficient to enable Elizabeth to 'pack' the Commons with nominees and other dependants, it did provide a useful nucleus of such people.

The Councillors worked assiduously and efficiently to expedite the business of the Crown (generally but not always, as shown above, with the Monarch's agreement). They carefully prepared their measures before Parliament met. In every new Parliament, the Speaker of the House of Commons was officially elected by that House. But the candidate proposed by the government was invariably elected, unopposed, so he was effectively a royal nominee. (The Crown's choice was disputed only once, in 1566, on purely technical grounds.) The Speaker controlled the proceedings of the Commons, and the Council ensured that his powers were used in the Crown's interest. In 1601, Robert Cecil 'spake something in Mr Speaker's ear' and the Speaker duly ended the session before a proposed Monopolies Bill could be read. Government measures were favoured in the order of business, and ministers did not find difficulty in being called in debate.

Behind the scenes, members were approached individually to court their support. The Councillors did not do all of this work. As shown above, they had unofficial helpers, and these men gave invaluable service. In particular, after his own elevation to the Lords in 1571 removed the government's most effective manager from the Lower House, Burghley relied heavily on the likes of Norton and Fleetwood to handle affairs in the Commons. In the later Parliaments, the number of Councillors in the Commons fell, to as low as three in 1597. Graves has argued that this decline would have been less harmful had the ability and experience of the Councillors not deteriorated as well. And the 'men of business', ambitious lawyers increasingly, compromised their reputation for independence by accepting government office, thereby weakening their leverage in Parliament. These deficiencies possibly contributed to the monopolies crisis of 1601. However, in the reign as a whole, the picture is of efficient and successful management.

Members were aware that the Queen could dissolve a troublesome Parliament, as she did in 1567. Also, she could withhold the Royal Assent. She did so more than sixty times in all. In almost every case (the major exception was the Communion Bill of 1571, and in 1572, though disclaiming any such intention, she effectively refused the assent to the bill to exclude Mary), this power of veto was used to block bills of little political importance. It meant merely that Elizabeth had responded to lobbying in a private interest or that she felt the measure was rushed through too quickly at the end of a session. But the awareness that the power existed meant that bills to which she objected were often abandoned at an early stage or appropriately amended. To persist with doomed measures would be futile, and Elizabethan politicians, belonging to a small political nation from which the masses were excluded, were less concerned than their modern equivalents to make vain gestures in order to attract popular attention.

The Crown also used the more compliant Lords to good effect. Few of its lay members owed their place to Elizabeth, for she made only eighteen peers in the whole reign. But the purge of the Marian bishops meant that all but one of Elizabeth's bishops (there were twenty-six at any time) owed their appointment to her. Other peers were Councillors, members of the Household, or in receipt of some royal favour. So, dependants of the Crown constituted more than half of the eighty-odd members of the Lords and of the substantially smaller number who regularly attended. The majority were personally close to the Monarch, seeing themselves (and regarded by Elizabeth) as principals in the service of the Crown. Of course, in a relatively small House of quite stable composition, any act of opposition was easily noticed by the Queen and her Councillors. Occasionally, the Upper House obliged the government by defeating unwanted Commons bills. More often, the government introduced into the Lords those measures which were likely to meet with stiff opposition in the Commons. A bill passed by the Upper House had at the very least to be given serious consideration by the Commons. The peers also served the Crown by means of the influence they could exert over their clients in the Commons (*see pages 226–30 on patronage*), and many were junior members of noble families.

The Crown could exercise more directly coercive powers. For as long as Parliament was in session, parliamentary privilege forbade imprisonment of a member on a private suit. But this did not affect the Crown's right to proceed against a member. His exemption from prosecution for words spoken in Parliament was not yet conclusively established. Elizabeth wisely avoided putting the question to the test, and she was aware that a too repressive attitude would deprive her of honest advice. But it was not difficult to find in a critical member's words or deeds outside Parliament some breach of the many and extremely vague laws against rumour-mongering and sedition, and there was a specific law forbidding the discussion of parliamentary business outside. It was under the latter that Peter Wentworth and several others were imprisoned in 1587 (for conferring about Puritan measures) and again in 1593 (when the issue was the succession). The possibility of such a fate may well have curbed opposition.

However, the main responsibility for the cordial relations which usually existed between Parliament and Crown lay not so much in members' resignation before the latter's power as in the view they had of their own function. The image of MPs striving to increase Parliament's power at the expense of the monarch is one that sixteenth-century men would not have recognised. Most were enthusiastic defenders of local interests, and put their energies into securing the appropriate legislation. In the area of national policy, MPs did not hold an exalted conception of their role. They were there to assist the government by passing legislation. The idea that they were called to advise the monarch was generally understood in the narrow sense that their job was to help the government to tailor its measures to the views and interests of the nation. MPs did not claim a right to give unsolicited advice or have it accepted. In other words, they shared Elizabeth's own view of the matter. As for the notion that they should organise themselves in order to promote particular policies, any such approximation to the concept of 'party' was regarded as a conspiracy against the Crown. Of course, Parliament did have the potential to oppose more vigorously; in particular, it might have used its power of the purse to force measures on Elizabeth. But any attempt to starve the Crown of funds would have undermined that good government to which Parliamentarians wished to contribute.

An awareness of the MPs' limited view of their role is crucial to an understanding of Elizabeth's Parliaments. Numerous circumstances fore-stalled grander ambitions. Most members came up to London from the small communities of provincial England, and Neale has probably overstated the extent to which such country gentry moved confidently in the rarefied atmosphere of national politics. They were easily intimidated by the splendours of the Court and the daunting presence of the Queen and her great Councillors. About half of the MPs in each House of Commons were novices who began with little knowledge of either the procedures or the rights of Parliament. Many came without any determination to pursue even local interests. There were numerous self-seeking men who wished to attract the favour of the Monarch or another patron. Non-attendance was a serious problem, despite a system of fines. Those who did attend were often keen to settle affairs quickly and terminate the expense of residence in London. An opposition could not be fashioned out of such material.

Finally, it is necessary to underline the personal contribution of Elizabeth. The world of high politics was a narrow, intimate one in which the character and personality of the leading players counted for more than the historian, so distant from the events, can easily imagine. The Queen was so much the focus of attention and activity that her demeanour counted at times for everything. She produced displays of fury and obstinacy that indicated the hopelessness and even danger of persisting with an unwelcome measure. But she was also tactful. Her concessions to pressure – for example, in 1566, 1587 and 1601 – were well judged to curtail rather than encourage opposition. She was aware of the benefits (especially financial) of a co-operative Parliament and had the diplomatic skills to promote good relations. The first drafts of her speeches were often indignant and aggressive, but she then toned them down; when pressed on the succession issue in 1566, she at first wished to accuse the members of treason, but she thought better of it. The contrast between Elizabeth's respectful attitude to Parliament and the offensive declamations of James I was certainly much noticed during the latter's reign. Above all, she was charming, especially when addressing the 'wise and discreet men' of the Commons. One suspects that she was willing and able to take advantage of men's desire to deal graciously with a woman. The language of many of her addresses smacks more of flirtation than politics. For example, in 1601, she addressed a Commons deputation with words which were clearly intended to restore harmony after the acrimonious monopolies debate:

> Though God hath raised me high, yet this I count the glory of my Crown, that I have reigned with your loves . . . I was never so much enticed with the glorious name of a king or royal authority of a queen, as delighted that God hath made me his instrument to maintain his truth and glory and to defend his kingdom from peril, dishonour, tyranny and oppression . . . Though you have had and may have many mightier and wiser princes sitting on this seat, yet you never had nor shall have any that will love you better . . . And I pray . . . that before the gentlemen depart into their counties you bring them all to kiss my hand.

For all these reasons, co-operation was the dominant theme in relations between Elizabeth and her Parliaments. Rarely did differences lead to agitation of constitutional issues which might have created deeper and more lasting rifts. In this respect, Elizabeth was a great deal more successful than her successors, the Stuarts, whose lack of political acumen often permitted narrow differences to develop into major questions of constitutional principle.

On the other hand, the revisionist view must not be carried too far. The 'romance' was not an untroubled one. Elizabeth, a woman, could never be as formidable as Henry VIII. The means to 'manage' came nowhere near to giving Elizabeth control of the Commons. Neale was probably correct when he argued that the infusion of gentry into the Commons made it harder to manage. Regular members grew in experience and confidence with the passing years. Local interests caused members to speak assertively on national issues; the latter, in the form of taxation, militia service, religious policy, poor relief, and so on, intruded on local concerns which even the most deferential member was bound to advance. Issues like the succession and religion aroused such passion and alarms that discontent was inevitably voiced, and not all of it was controlled by the Council. Finally, the general disillusionment of the 1590s made Elizabeth's last years a period of particular difficulty and suggest that the bitter monopolies row of 1601 should not be regarded as an isolated event.

It is hard to say whether Elizabeth encountered opposition more or less frequently than her predecessors. Certainly, it is relatively easy to find examples of conflict under Elizabeth. But the evidence on the Commons, in the form of diaries especially, is much more abundant for her period than for the other Tudors. The apparent calm of earlier

Parliaments probably owes much to the scarcity of evidence. It is not possible to compare the reigns with any certainty.

8 PRIVILEGES, RECORDS AND PROCEDURES

With regard to the suggestion that Parliament successfully established a right of free speech, the evidence discussed above (*see page 286*) shows one must be sceptical. To assert a claim is not to establish it. Elizabeth never acknowledged Parliament's right to unrequested discussion of questions of State. Her summary treatment of the Wentworths and their allies made this clear. Lord Keeper Puckering's famous statement of 1593 is the clearest evidence we have of her unchanging determination to hold the line in this matter:

> . . . her Majesty granteth you liberal but not licentious speech, liberty therefore but with due limitation. For even as there can be no good consultation where all freedom of advice is barred, so will there be no good conclusion where every man may speak what he listeth, without fit observation of persons,   5 matters, times, places and other needful circumstances . . . For liberty of speech her Majesty commandeth me to tell you that to say yea or no to bills, God forbid that any man should be restrained or afraid to answer according to his best liking, with some short declaration of his reason therein, and therein to have 10 a free voice, which is the very true liberty of the House; not, as some suppose, to speak there of all causes as him listeth, and to frame a form of religion or a state of government as to their idle brains shall seem meetest. She saith no king fit for his state will suffer such absurdities, and . . . she hopeth no man here longeth 15 so much for his ruin as that he mindeth to make such a peril to his own safety.

1   *What did Elizabeth mean by 'liberal but not licentious speech' (line 1)?*

2   *What examples did Elizabeth possibly have in mind when she denounced the presumptuous efforts of 'idle brains' (line 13)?*

3   *Why did Elizabeth find no great difficulty in limiting Parliament's discussions?*

The other main issue of privilege during the reign was the Norfolk election case of 1586, when the Commons claimed the right to decide upon disputed elections to the House. The Queen insisted that this should remain the task of the Lord Chancellor in the Court of Chancery, and the Commons did not press the matter. Elton has concluded firmly that, 'The history of the Commons' privileges in Elizabeth's reign testifies neither to any growth in power nor to the forging of weapons for a fight.' One feels that the intrusions into for-

bidden areas probably did amount to the setting of informal precedents which paved the way for later Parliamentarians to feel that they
could express their views. But it is certainly true that most members
did not deliberately seek to extend their rights and that Elizabeth did
not concede an inch of ground in this respect.

The Journal of the House of Commons survives from 1547. But there
were probably earlier records which have now been lost, and Neale
was wrong to conclude that this accidental date signified a stage in the
development of the House. Similarly, the improved Commons Journal
from 1571 is not attributable to the growing maturity of the House (as
Neale claimed). The new clerk, Fulk Onslow, brought his own preferred habits, and it is a mistake to contrast the scribbled notes that survive from his predecessor with the fair copy left by Onslow. Onslow
was apparently the first clerk who noted the speeches made in the
Commons. But they were not inserted into the Journal, and it is possible that they merely reflected Burghley's need to have a fuller account
of Commons proceedings after his elevation to the Lords. The Stuart
clerks did not invariably maintain the progress to better records, varying according to individual approach and political circumstances. In
sum, one must agree with Elton that it is 'inadvisable to read institutional, let alone constitutional significance into what happened'.

Even where procedural change certainly did occur, its interpretation
has been problematical. The House of Commons established during
the sixteenth century a more precise set of procedures and regulations,
dealing with the handling of bills, joint conferences with the Lords, and
much more. Neale argued that these developments were meant to
make the Commons stronger. However, Elton has shown that the
major changes predated Elizabeth; 'the parliaments of 1559 and 1601
are the same sort of institution and do not testify to institutional development'. In addition, the changes did not make Parliament more politically powerful and were not meant to do so. They were intended,
rather, to make it a more efficient place of business.

For example, Committees of the Whole House were much used in
Elizabeth's last three Parliaments; this procedure replaced the Speaker,
a royal nominee, with an elected chairman, and Wallace Notestein concluded that it served to strengthen the independence of the Commons.
In fact, it was merely a device to suspend the normal rules of debate
and thereby to speed up legislation. Elizabeth, anxious to make the
Commons a more efficient legislative machine, did not resent or
oppose such changes; the idea of the Committee of the Whole House
actually came from her Council, and the latter's members were the
main beneficiaries of the resultant freedom to speak more than once
during a debate. The Commons experienced more such development
than the Lords not because it was 'rising' faster but because the Lords,
the more mature House, had already developed the procedures it
required. Elton has clearly shown, by investigating the origins of such

changes, that 'as a temperature chart for political or constitutional developments the history of procedure is suspect'.

9 FREQUENCY

The fact that Parliament met so rarely under Elizabeth hardly suggests that it rose in power or importance. In the thirty years preceding Elizabeth's accession, there were twenty-six sessions of Parliament. In Elizabeth's reign of forty-five years, Parliament met only thirteen times, each session lasted for an average of fewer than ten weeks, and an average of more than three years lapsed between each session. In twenty-six calendar years Parliament did not meet at all. Parliament's legislative role was important and not questioned by Elizabeth. But, as a cautious, conservative monarch, she made only a limited number of those changes which would require Parliament's approval. As a result, Parliament largely lost the central role it acquired during the years of revolution after 1529.

Administration, as ever, was carried out by the Monarch, the Council, and the servants (some paid, most voluntary) they employed. Similarly, the national politics of the reign were played out at Court and in the Council, permanent institutions. Parliament's role was occasional and, in respect of the great issues, much taken up with continuing, in another forum, the ongoing politics of the Court. Called so infrequently, Parliament could play only a peripheral part. The extraordinary decline in the frequency of Parliament lends considerable weight to the idea that the institution actually declined under Elizabeth. It certainly does not suggest that the reign witnessed another chapter in the long rise of Parliament.

10 CONCLUSION

Parliament did rise under the early Tudors. It became a more regular feature of the system of government and extended its competence to embrace almost every conceivable type of subject. Statute was confirmed as the supreme form of law, and the monarch (and the judges) lost the power unilaterally to change it. Furthermore, the Commons gained institutional equality with the Lords (each had the same power to initiate and defeat measures). However, these changes were effected before 1540, mostly by Thomas Cromwell in the 1530s. Also, for the most part, they served to strengthen rather than challenge the power of the monarch. During the reigns of Edward and Mary, Parliament retained its new standing and in some respects added to it (for instance, there is its authorisation of the Religious Settlement in 1549). Historians were tempted by the idea that Parliament continued to rise under Elizabeth and entered the Stuart age poised to engage in a great struggle against the Crown. It seemed logical that Elizabeth's Parliaments constituted one of the links between the two Cromwells. More recent studies of Elizabethan Parliaments in their own right have shown what little basis this view has in the evidence.

There were many instances of conflict between Crown and Parliament. But they were not typical. Above all, they were not as meaningful as Neale imagined. With each Parliament containing about 500 individuals, there was bound to be a variety of views on many subjects. But when they emerged as acts of defiance, they not infrequently revealed the reluctance of most members to oppose the Crown. Rarely, and then only in the most rudimentary form and embracing a small minority of members, was there any attempt at organised activity against the policy of the Crown. Much of the pressure on Elizabeth was inspired from within her own government, by leading Councillors, and cannot be regarded as evidence of Parliament's assertiveness. Opposition generally failed to achieve anything. Certainly, the Commons acting alone rarely changed Elizabeth's policy. It was strong only when in harness with the Council and the Lords. Nor did the Commons overtake the power of the Lords; the latter probably remained its political superior.

Of course, the dominant institution in the Tudor system of government remained the Crown. For most of the time, it ruled without a Parliament. The latter was called when its assistance was required, usually to pass laws and taxes. Members took advantage of the meeting of Parliament to secure all manner of private and local benefits and to express their views on national issues. However, the rise of the Commons at the expense of the Crown was not an objective. Co-operation with the Crown in the pursuit of good government was the purpose of most Parliamentarians. Many of the causes of the conflict that took place in the next century may be traced back to Elizabeth's time. But the rise of Parliament was not one of them.

11 BIBLIOGRAPHY

D M Dean and N L Jones (eds) *The Parliaments of Elizabethan England* (Blackwell, 1990).
G R Elton *The Parliament of England, 1559–1581* (CUP, 1986).
M A R Graves *Elizabethan Parliaments, 1559–1601* (Longman, 1987).
M A R Graves *The Tudor Parliaments: Crown, Lords and Commons, 1485–1603* (Longman, 1985).
C Haigh (ed.) *The Reign of Elizabeth* (Macmillan, 1984).
C Haigh *Elizabeth I* (Longman, 1988).
J Loach *Parliament under the Tudors* (Clarendon, 1991).
J E Neale *Elizabeth I and her Parliaments*, 2 vols (Cape, 1953, 1957).

A G R Smith *The Government of Elizabethan England* (Edward Arnold, 1967).

12 DISCUSSION POINTS AND EXERCISES

A *This section consists of questions or points that might be used for discussion (or written answers) as a way of expanding on the chapter and testing understanding of it:*

1   Summarise the view of Elizabethan Parliaments first put forward by Neale. Does the narrative outline of Elizabeth's Parliaments tend to support or contradict this view?

2   For what reasons might one have expected Elizabeth's Parliaments to be vigorous and assertive?

3   On which issues did Elizabeth find Parliament especially troublesome and why?

4   What evidence is there that Elizabeth found Parliament a willing source of finance?

5   How powerful an opposition was there in Parliament to Elizabeth's Religious Settlement? Was there a 'Puritan choir'?

6   What evidence is there of Council leadership of Parliament's 'opposition' to Elizabeth?

7   What role did patronage play in relations between Elizabeth and her Parliaments?

8   What evidence is there that parliamentary opposition to Elizabeth was unusual, limited and unsuccessful?

9   What can one conclude from a study of the frequency of Elizabeth's Parliaments?

B *Essay questions*

1   How successful was Elizabeth in handling her Parliaments?

2   What part did religion play in causing conflict between Elizabeth and her Parliaments?

3   To what extent did Parliament act as a check on royal power during the reign of Elizabeth?

4   'The history of the Elizabethan Parliaments is not one of conflict, but of co-operation and consent.' Do you agree?

5   'Elizabeth's parliamentary critics were mainly concerned with national security and the succession.' Discuss.

6   Why did Elizabeth find it so easy to 'manage' her Parliaments?

13 HISTORIOGRAPHICAL EXERCISE –
THE CHARACTER OF ELIZABETHAN PARLIAMENTS

Study these excerpts from the writings of Neale and Elton, and then answer the questions which follow.

From Elizabeth I and her Parliaments *by J E Neale*:

A.   At the opening of the sixteenth century Parliament was
     essentially a legislative and taxing body, its meetings
     intermittent. Even at the end of the century the same
     description might be formally applied to it; but in the
     meanwhile it had become a political force with which the   5
     Crown and government had to reckon. The change was
     brought about by developments in the power, position,
     and prestige of the House of Commons . . .
     Puritan Members of the House of Commons became what
     Protestants had been in Mary Tudor's reign: an opposition.   10
     But it was an opposition in a significantly new sense: one
     with a positive programme which was not hostile to the
     regime, but professed to aim at the fulfilment of its
     Protestant destiny. Sir Thomas More's definition of
     freedom of speech, adequate for simple obstruction, was   15
     not capacious enough for their need. They wanted to
     initiate: to introduce bills and motions of their own, to
     frame the agenda of Parliament. Having little historical
     sense and a convenient memory for precedents, they read
     into the vague phrase, 'freedom of speech', a meaning that   20
     was bound, if it prevailed, to lead to the destruction of
     personal monarchy as the Tudors knew it, and to the
     evolution of parliamentary government as the world has
     known it.

From The Parliament of England, 1559–1581 *by G R Elton*:

B.   In the reign of Henry VIII, politics in Parliament achieved
     their aim because the monarch, proprietor of Parliaments,
     took the lead. In the reign of Elizabeth, political debates in
     Parliament and especially in the Commons never achieved
     anything because the monarch was entirely free to ignore
     them and usually did so . . . The old-established search,
     beloved by historians, for some growth or development in
     the political power and authority of Parliament and
     especially of the Commons is chimerical because in fact
     that power never changed in its fundamental
     characteristics . . .
        . . . Ultimately the existence of Parliament, and especially

of the Commons, made it possible to bring the raw contest for power out of the closet and make it look like orderly government – not an inconsiderable achievement but a very different one from that which traditional historiography ascribed to Parliament in the familiar story of the 'rise' of constitutional rule and a limited monarchy. And of that achievement no genuine trace can yet be found in the reign of Elizabeth. In that age of a strong monarchy wisely using the inherited institutions of government, the Lords and Commons, with the agreement and toleration of the Crown, formed a convenient and really rather ingeniously devised instrument for raising supply by consent and for making laws binding upon the agencies of enforcement. Its law-making power further offered a useful service to private and local interests . . . As a gathering of men of standing and influence it could be useful to its manipulators – usually the monarch but sometimes others. The rest was pretence, even if that pretence could at times deceive the pretenders.

1 *According to Neale what was the difference between 'Sir Thomas More's definition of freedom of speech' (line 14) and the interpretation of 'opposition' members in Elizabeth's time?*

2 *What do you understand by 'personal monarchy' and 'parliamentary government'? (lines 22–3)*

3 *What name did Neale use elsewhere to describe the parliamentary opposition, and how have the revisionists responded to his adoption of the term?*

4 *What evidence supports the conclusion that Parliament was indeed a 'rather ingeniously devised instrument' for certain governmental purposes?*

5 *Specify the points on which Elton would challenge Neale.*

XI

ELIZABETH I: FOREIGN POLICY

—

1 INTRODUCTION

It is ironic that Elizabeth shared none of the aggressive ambitions of
her father and yet led England into a war that not only dwarfed those
fought by Henry VIII but was one of the great wars of English history.
Its most famous episode, the victory over the Spanish Armada, is a
celebrated event in the country's folklore, and it has contributed much
to the making of Elizabeth's formidable reputation. One must question, however, the success of a foreign policy that led ultimately to
war against the world's strongest power. The reign saw massive
change in the country's foreign relations, substantial and commendable achievements, and, in the final analysis, a sorry failure to isolate
the country from the dreadful religious warfare that afflicted continental Europe.

Elizabeth did not seek either the Spanish or any other war. She did
not share the traditional ruler's estimation of the glories to be won in
war. In addition, Elizabeth was aware of England's limited capacity to
wage war. England's population was only one-quarter that of France
(and half of Spain's), and the Crown lacked the financial resources to
create an army that could match those maintained by other countries.
Even Scotland, in the 1540s, had proved beyond England's ability to
conquer, and Mary could not even attempt the recovery of Calais. With
an extensive militia and considerable naval power, despite their
neglect in the years before 1558, the English had a formidable defensive capability; as the Venetian ambassador wrote in 1557, the country
could 'resist any invasion from abroad, provided there be union within
the kingdom'. But the militia existed to defend their own counties and
were not a professional army with the capacity to fight abroad.
England did not rank with the continent's two great powers, France
and Spain, even if it was more than a 'bone between two dogs'.

In view of England's relative weakness and her personal inclination,

301

Elizabeth's foreign policy was primarily defensive. She did not seek to conquer new territory and, in particular, did not assert the centuries-old claim to the throne of France. The only exception was Calais, whose loss to France in 1558 was a hard pill to swallow. Henry VIII had tried to conquer France with the help of Spain. But his wars proved that such assistance could not be relied upon, for the Spanish showed on several occasions that they did not wish to raise England to the stature of a strong potential rival. One must conclude that Elizabeth's lack of grand, expansionist ambition was wise; her defensive foreign policy was imbued with a highly beneficial dose of realism.

An important part of Elizabeth's inheritance that she fully intended to continue was the close relationship between England and Spain, even if its purpose was no longer so exciting and ambitious. The war that erupted in 1585 was barely imaginable when Elizabeth came to power. Spain was England's principal ally. France posed a significant threat to England at the beginning of Elizabeth's reign, and it was clear that Spain therefore continued to be an invaluable friend; the Spanish alliance, which had culminated with Mary Tudor's marriage to Philip II, was the country's first line of defence, ensuring as it did that the French were never free to deploy all their power against England.

Discussion of Elizabeth's foreign policy begs the question of how much control the Queen herself exerted over the policy. She valued the advice of numerous individuals, both in and outside her Council, and was fortunate that in William Cecil and Francis Walsingham, between them Secretaries of State for thirty years, she was assisted by two of the most able men ever to serve the Tudors. However, there can be no doubt that Elizabeth made the final decisions. Foreign policy was not just another responsibility of government. To sixteenth-century monarchs it involved not so much business between countries as personal relations between the rulers themselves. It was family business, involving the family of princes. As such, it belonged within the royal prerogative, so much so that it was hardly possible to conceive of a monarch who did not decide his country's foreign policy. The fact that the question of Elizabeth's marriage, another prerogative matter, would inevitably feature prominently in English foreign policy made Elizabeth even more determined to maintain control. Elizabeth often followed advice, but as shown below, her will was the ultimate deciding factor in every issue.

2 EARLY DIFFICULTIES

In February 1559, Philip II acknowledged the mutual benefits of the Anglo-Spanish relationship by asking for Elizabeth's hand in marriage. In her first major foreign policy decision, she refused. She was well aware that her half-sister's marriage to Philip had been deeply unpopular among a people who considered it equivalent to Spanish conquest, and it was clear that Mary had brought England into the current war against France in order to serve her husband. The decision highlights an important element in Elizabeth's foreign policy: a determination that England would avoid both the reality and appearance of falling under the control of a foreign power. This might appear an obvious goal. But it was one that many Englishmen feared was beyond a woman ruler and that Mary had not even attempted to achieve. Many years later, it would cause the great war against Spain. However, the refusal to marry Philip did not, and was not intended to, cause a rift between the two countries. Far from feeling rebuffed, Philip was relieved that the difficulties caused by his previous marriage were not to be repeated. The underlying reasons for an alliance of Spain and England remained compelling on both sides. Its most immediate benefit was felt in Philip's success in persuading the Pope, despite French pressure, not to declare the new Queen illegitimate and a heretic; the Pope's silence was to be a major factor in limiting Catholic opposition to the Elizabethan Religious Settlement.

In August 1558, several months before Elizabeth's accession, the representatives of Spain, England, France and Scotland began to negotiate an end to a war that had been fought to the point of exhaustion on all sides. When the Peace of Câteau Cambrèsis was signed in April 1559, Calais was effectively given up; the French promise to restore it after eight years or forfeit 500 000 crowns was a thinly veiled English surrender, for all knew that the French intended to keep Calais. Its cession was a realistic and necessary step, for Philip was unwilling to continue the war and England could not have continued alone against France, certainly not with any prospect of regaining Calais. The port had been a financial drain, and, given Elizabeth's limited ambitions, it would no longer have been useful as a launching pad for aggression against France. Nevertheless, the loss of Calais was damaging. England no longer had the same domination of the narrow Straits of Dover, the principal route between Spain and the Netherlands as well as France and Scotland; one of England's levers of power against the might of Spain and France was forfeited. Above all, the loss of Calais after over 200 years was a major blow to English prestige and in particular to the pride of a Queen who was opening her reign in the most ignominious manner. Elizabeth was determined to retrieve what she and her people considered a part of England's national territory.

Of course, French power was still to be feared. With Calais in French hands and with Mary of Guise Regent of Scotland on behalf of her daughter, Mary Queen of Scots, Henry II was 'bestriding the realm, having one foot in Calais and the other in Scotland' (*Cecil*). As Jane Dawson has written, 'An English bridgehead in France had been replaced by a French bridgehead in Britain.' It seemed likely that the

French would challenge the legitimate succession of Anne Boleyn's daughter and support instead the claim of Mary Queen of Scots, the wife of their own King's son and heir. The threat from France grew appreciably when, in May 1559, the Scottish Protestants rebelled against the government of Mary of Guise. Mary had appointed Frenchmen to numerous positions of power in Scotland and in March 1559 launched a campaign to suppress Protestantism. The speedy success of the rebels, promising the institution of an anti-French and Protestant regime, was naturally welcomed in England, Elizabeth secretly sent money and arms, and some Scots even proposed a 'joyful conjunction' of the two kingdoms.

However, a very different outcome seemed likely when the French prepared to send a large army to suppress the revolt. French control would be reasserted and, even worse, this new army would be in a position to threaten England from the north. 'The old postern gate where the Scots could create a diversion had become the front door through which a French army might march' (*Dawson*).

In July 1559, fate dealt England a further blow. Henry II died after being struck in the eye at a joust held to celebrate the peace with Spain. He was succeeded by Mary's husband, Francis II, but the royal couple were no more than 'flexible instruments' in the hands of the Guises, Mary's uncles. These ambitious men were determined to help their sister assert French control of Scotland and to advance Mary's claim as the legitimate Queen of England. The wider context made the position even more dire. Philip was weary of war, short of money, and preoccupied with the aggression of the Ottomans; he would not have welcomed another struggle against France. Indeed, he was soon to marry Elisabeth of Valois, sister of the new King of France, in order to build better relations. Also, Philip was disappointed that Elizabeth had returned England to Protestantism, and he disapproved of assistance to Protestant rebels even when the enemy was France. England faced a dilemma: its traditional ally was not disposed to fill the role of protector, and any action the English might themselves take to forestall the danger would merely confirm their isolation and leave them to face alone the superior might of France.

It was Cecil who persuaded first the Council and then Elizabeth of the necessity of intervention, at one point threatening to resign if his advice was not accepted. He was driven by an ingrained fear of France that never left him. But there was a positive vision too. Dawson has argued convincingly that Cecil formulated a coherent, long-term 'British strategy' that aimed at ensuring England could face Europe without fear of the enmity of Scotland or Ireland. The chance to secure a Protestant, Anglophile Scotland should not be missed. 'Any wise kindle the fire, for if quenched, the opportunity will not come in our lives.' His handling of Elizabeth was masterly. She abhorred the thought of helping rebels ('It is against God's law to aid any subjects against their natural princes or their ministers'), and, far from feeling sympathy with fellow-Protestants, she shrank from the subversive Calvinism of John Knox and the Scots. So, in petitions that Cecil framed on behalf of the Scots, he had them declare emphatically their loyalty to their Queen ('in no wise withdrawing their hearts from their sovereign lady', Mary) and omit any reference to religion. Elizabeth was won over, rather, by emphasising the French threat to England, and Cecil's genius was evident in his method of communicating this to her: he played upon the instances of French questioning of her right to be Queen, knowing well that her extreme sensitivity on this point made it the key to exciting her to action.

Finally, in February 1560, under pressure from the Council, Elizabeth sent Norfolk to conclude the Treaty of Berwick with the Scots, and English soldiers were duly marched into Scotland. Their attempt to storm the French garrison at Leith was defeated by their own military ineptitude, the stout French resistance, and the effectiveness of the horde of Scottish prostitutes who threw stones, burning coals and wood in defence of their customers. But gales had destroyed the task force sent from France and financial crisis ruled out another attempt at relief. The Guise faction was preoccupied at home with the opposition of other noble families and the emerging Protestant threat, and their will to continue the struggle was finally shattered by the death of Mary of Guise in June 1560. By the Treaty of Edinburgh of July 1560, both England and France agreed to withdraw their forces from Scotland and Mary gave up her claim to the English throne; soon afterwards, the French effectively conceded self-government to the Scots, and Protestantism was established by the Scottish Parliament.

Scotland's new rulers were grateful, fellow Protestant allies of England. The 'Auld Alliance' between France and Scotland no longer existed, and a centuries-old threat to English security was, in large part, removed. 'England's postern gate was closed and the continental powers could invade her only by sea, where her naval strength must make them think twice before risking the attempt' (*Wernham*). The English wisely resisted any temptation to occupy or conquer Scotland, a task that Henry VIII's and the French experience showed was fraught with difficulty. In the following years, events north of the border often caused concern, but the work of 1560 was never to be undone. Wernham has argued that Elizabeth's reluctance to send an army to Scotland was justified. January and February were not good months in which to march an army into Scotland, time allowed political circumstances within France to work in England's favour, and she was surely right to fear Spain's reaction to her assisting Protestant rebels. Nevertheless, Elizabeth 'trembled indecisively' (*MacCaffrey*) throughout, and it is hard to believe, given her natural caution and hostility to rebellion, that she would have made the necessary commitment without Cecil's and the Council's pressure. To Cecil must go the principal credit for what was one of the outstanding achievements of Elizabeth's reign.

3 OPPORTUNITIES AND MISTAKES

From the early 1560s, France was weakened by internal religious division. The struggle between the Protestants, known as the Huguenots, and the Catholic majority greatly reduced the threat posed by France and instead made that country vulnerable to the intervention of other powers. The first of the French Wars of Religion began in June 1562, following the Duke of Guise's massacre of a Huguenot congregation, and the Catholics quickly gained the upper hand. Lord Robert Dudley (later the Earl of Leicester) and Sir Nicholas Throckmorton, anxious to match Cecil's recent Scottish success, strongly urged intervention on the side of the Huguenots. Without help, the latter seemed likely to collapse and a reunited France would again become a formidable enemy of England; in particular, the Duke of Guise would seek to revive French influence in Scotland through his niece, the now returned Mary Queen of Scots (*see page 307 below*). There was even the possibility that intervention could repeat the achievement secured in Scotland, for military success might give the 3Huguenots at least a share in the government of France. Elizabeth readily agreed, encouraged as she was by the Scottish success, eager to please her favourite, Dudley, and led by Huguenot representatives to believe that Calais could be regained. Again, there is no evidence of religious motivation in Elizabeth's policy; Cecil wrote that there were two principal goals, 'one to stay the Duke of Guise, as our sworn enemy, from his singular superiority, the other to procure us the restitution of Calais, or something to countervail it'.

In October 1562, an English army sailed to France and occupied Le Havre. Philip of Spain complained that Elizabeth was again supporting heretical rebels. As a result, she did not allow her troops to leave Le Havre to join the Huguenots. The latter were beaten at Dreux in December 1562. Many patriotic Huguenots were already alienated by England's stated desire to secure Calais, and they were now persuaded to make a peace that involved the promise of religious toleration of the Huguenots in return for their joining the government forces in defence of France against the invader. The newly united French duly defeated the English, forcing the surrender of Le Havre in July 1563.

By the resultant Treaty of Troyes (April 1564), Elizabeth formally renounced the English claim to Calais. It could be argued that Elizabeth had been right to seek an advantage when the opportunity arose. Also, the enterprise usefully reminded the French that their internal divisions made England a dangerous enemy, giving rise in particular to an unwillingness to intervene in Scotland or to support

Mary's claim to the English succession. But clearly the intervention was mismanaged, displaying little regard for the needs of the Huguenots, and the final result was a military debacle. Elizabeth certainly considered it a failure, and, for better or worse, she became more than ever reluctant to commit English forces in support of Protestant rebellion. As MacCaffrey wrote, Le Havre 'ended the spurt of adventurousness which had characterized the regime up to this point; the years after 1563 were ones of cautious isolationism in foreign affairs'.

The remarkably favourable position in Scotland was threatened by the return of Mary Queen of Scots, to her native land in August 1561 after the death of her French husband. Half-French by birth, she had lived at the French Court from 1548, having gone there when only 5 years old to escape English invaders, and she came back hoping to revive her country's traditional alliance with France. Her return, understandably, was not welcomed by Elizabeth and her government. In addition, Mary considered her claim to the English throne to be superior to Elizabeth's, Mary's deriving from Henry VIII's sister Margaret (her grandmother) while Elizabeth was the daughter of a woman, Anne Boleyn, whose marriage to Henry no Catholic thought legitimate. Mary was sufficiently realistic to accept Elizabeth's title, but she immediately asserted her claim to be the next in line, Elizabeth's successor. Elizabeth privately recognised Mary's right.

The likelihood of a Catholic successor was bound to upset England's Protestants and encourage the survival of Catholicism, and might even tempt some of the latter's adherents into assassination or rebellion. So, both in foreign policy terms, and in relation to England's domestic affairs, Mary's return to Scotland was a potential disaster for Elizabeth.

Of course, Scotland was then ruled by Protestant Anglophiles and Mary's return was accepted by them on condition that she did not try to alter the country's new political and religious orientation. Even with Mary on the throne, Scotland did not support France during the English intervention there in 1562–3. Indeed, her great desire to receive Elizabeth's nomination to the succession meant that Mary could not support the French cause or do anything else openly to oppose English interests. Elizabeth's refusal to pronounce on the nomination, though it owed much to her natural indecision, neatly served to ensure Mary's good behaviour for several years. Perhaps, however, Elizabeth overplayed this hand. Her attempts to make Mary change her religion, to forbid her marrying a European prince, and even in 1564 to try to arrange a marriage with her own rejected suitor, Robert Dudley – these were bound to alienate the proud Queen of Scots. In 1565, Mary married Lord Darnley. Darnley's own claim to the English title, as the child of the daughter of Margaret's second marriage, and, above all, his popularity with English Catholics, among whom he was raised, seemed to strengthen Mary's hand. English Protestants, the Council included, were accordingly alarmed. But Wernham has doubted if Elizabeth concurred; better by far the Darnley match than marriage to a prince from France or another European country. Certainly it suited Elizabeth to have Scotland's ties with the continental powers remain weak. She facilitated the marriage by allowing Darnley to go to Scotland, and may even have encouraged the whole business.

If Elizabeth did help to effect the Darnley marriage, she must bear some responsibility for an event which brought disaster to Mary and eventually grave danger to Elizabeth herself. Mary's apparent complicity in the assassination of Darnley – almost trumpeted in her marrying the murderer, Bothwell – led to a rebellion which forced her to abdicate in July 1567. The restoration of full Protestant control, which had been undermined in the mid-1560s by an increasingly assertive Mary, was beneficial to England in view of the Anglophile views of the Earl of Moray, who became the Regent of Scotland, and his supporters. But Elizabeth actually contemplated using force to restore Mary, so opposed was she to the idea that the Scots could depose their lawful monarch. Subsequently she urged the Scots to restore Mary to nominal sovereignty, a measure which past experience made unacceptable to them and to the wiser heads in her own Council.

In addition, Elizabeth's refusal to destroy Mary's reputation by publishing the evidence of her complicity in Darnley's murder – and the conferences held at York and Westminster in October-November 1568 did hear convincing evidence – sustained Mary's supporters in both Scotland and England. In 1570, Regent Moray was murdered and Elizabeth, pressed by her Council, had to send forces into Scotland to bring Mary's supporters to heel. In England Mary was to be a catalyst of rebellion and plotting that caused hundreds of deaths, especially in the Northern Rising of 1569, invited the repression of Catholics, and might have cost Elizabeth her throne and her life. One must conclude that Elizabeth's handling in the late 1560s of Scotland and its errant Queen did not well support the interests of her country. The turbulent nature of Scottish politics did ensure, to be fair, that no English ruler could have avoided difficulties there, and it is true that neither Mary's behaviour nor Elizabeth's response destroyed the essence of the achievement of 1560.

4 THE FIRST QUARRELS WITH SPAIN

Spain and England found it increasingly difficult to reconcile their interests. Elizabeth's adoption of Protestantism and, even more, her apparent willingness to support Protestant rebels (in Scotland and France) were injurious if by no means fatal blows to the relationship with Catholic Spain. The latter was so exhausted by decades of war that Philip desperately sought a lasting peace with France. Philip was fearful that Elizabeth's provocative actions in Scotland and France would drag him into another round of conflict. His attempts to urge restraint on the English could not be pressed too far, for England was too useful an ally. But Philip concluded that Elizabeth's regime posed a danger to Spanish interests as well as to true religion.

The first real crises between them centred upon the Netherlands. Crucially, Cardinal Granvelle, Philip's chief minister in the Netherlands until 1564, was prepared to meet Elizabeth's heretical policy with force. The efforts of English traders to spread Protestantism in the Netherlands caused him particular dismay, and Elizabeth's armed intervention in France convinced him that their actions were sponsored by her government. Also, problems arose with regard to the wool trade. The Netherlands' clothmakers resented the higher prices charged by the English merchants to cover the increased taxes of the Book of Rates of 1558, and they felt the pressure of competition from the growing number of English producers who made the finer cloths (the 'New Draperies') in which the Netherlands' workers had held a monopoly. In 1563, this tension was worsened by the way that English privateers exploited Elizabeth's encouragement of attacks on French Catholic shipping to go after the richer ships of Spain and the Netherlands.

Granvelle decided to teach Elizabeth a lesson by stopping the wool trade on which English prosperity depended. In the autumn of 1563, a severe outbreak of plague in England provided an excuse and he banned the import of English cloth. Elizabeth replied by banning all Netherlands imports; Granvelle reciprocated, and trade between England and the Netherlands ceased. The dispute was so damaging to both sides that trade was re-opened in 1564. But lasting harm was done. The English learnt the danger of exclusive dependence on Antwerp; they were never to regain entirely their confidence that the Netherlands' trade was both vital and secure. Events soon dealt it further blows. In 1566, Calvinists rioted in the Netherlands, and these disorders again made English merchants seek other ports into Europe; Hamburg was chosen by only a few merchants, but, significantly, its use continued permanently. Trading links with the Baltic and Russia were also developed considerably, providing more alternatives to Antwerp. These changes to trade had a major impact on foreign policy. They meant the erosion of one of the principal advantages of the alliance between England and Spain. Anglo-Spanish co-operation no longer seemed to be an economic necessity. One hesitates to accept that 'English foreign policy was to feel the benefit in a greater freedom of manoeuvre' (*Wernham*). These events constituted, after all, a step in the direction of war with an ancient ally.

The turning-point in Anglo-Spanish relations came in 1567. In August of that year, the Duke of Alva marched into the Netherlands at the head of a great Spanish army sent to prevent a recurrence of the unrest that first flared in the Netherlands in 1566. Philip had no intention of using it against England, whose alliance against France he continued to value, despite the recent difficulties. But things appeared very differently from England. For centuries, English leaders had concerned themselves with the state of the southern coast of the Channel, from Brittany to the Netherlands. From these shores would come any conceivable foreign invasion. The years of conflict with France underlined the importance of ensuring that other parts of the coastline were in friendly hands. This explains, for example, the important contributions of Calais and the former alliances with the Duchies of Brittany and Burgundy. Spanish possession of the Netherlands was beneficial in that it prevented a French takeover there; indeed, after the fall of Calais, the Spanish were the major obstacle to French occupation of the entire coastline.

However, the presence of Alva's army created an entirely new state of affairs. This great army possessed such overwhelming power that it seemed to present its own threat to England. The tensions of recent years had made the English apprehensive of Spanish power, but it was only when the strongest army in Christendom arrived on England's doorstep that Spain rather than France became the principal object of fear. The religious aspect was of major importance here. Many Protestants were convinced that their faith was locked in a life-and-death struggle with Catholicism. In particular, it was thought that the greatest Catholic power, Spain, would seek the destruction of Protestantism everywhere, not least in its strongest bastion, England. Once Alva's army had defeated the Netherlands' Protestants, there seemed every chance that it would be turned against England's so-called heretics. Elizabeth shared in the general anticipation of danger. For all that she did not allow religious prejudice to dictate her own foreign policy, she did not trust the piously Catholic Philip to respect England's independence if he acquired the power to enforce its return to the Church. Her sense of alarm was probably justified. Philip and Alva did not set out in 1567 to conquer England; but many of the King's advisers followed Granvelle in advocating a harder line against England

The outbreak of the second of France's Wars of Religion, when the Huguenots rebelled in September 1567, meant that Spanish power would not be checked by that of France. Indeed, it raised the possibility of victory for the pro-Spanish Guise faction and a united Catholic effort against heretical England. The army of William of Orange, leader of the Dutch rebels, was easily defeated by Alva in 1568 and the Netherlands was so completely pacified that the day seemed to be fast arriving when Alva's forces could be deployed elsewhere. In the spring of 1568, Philip expelled England's ambassador to Spain, Dr John Man, and replaced the Anglophile Guzman de Silva as ambassador to England with a man, Guerau de Spes, who quickly displayed his antipathy to the Protestant regime of Elizabeth by making contact with Mary and other Catholic malcontents. The changes may have had innocent reasons – Man was a Protestant zealot who informed his hosts that the Pope was 'a canting little monk', de Silva was the initiator of his own withdrawal, and Philip's instructions to de Spes clearly stated that he was to work for Elizabeth's continued friendship – but they nevertheless appeared to show that Philip was no longer an ally and added to the state of apprehension created by Alva's nearby presence.

Finally, another issue came increasingly to damage relations between England and Spain. The Spanish claimed all of northern and central America and attempted to prevent unauthorised trade between the settlements there and the seamen from other European countries. English sailors featured prominently among the latter, and one of the most famous, John Hawkins, had Elizabeth's support (and the investment of three of her ships) in his triangular slave trade between Africa, the West Indies, and Europe. Spain's efforts to stop this trade culminated in a Spanish squadron's attack on Hawkins's fleet in the Mexican port of San Juan de Ulua in September 1568. The treacherous nature of the attack (Hawkins received the Spaniards in peace, as servants of an allied power), as much as the losses inflicted, constituted yet another grievance between England and Spain.

Initially, however, this was a peripheral issue, affecting both countries' vital interests much less directly than European matters. The great Spanish army in the Netherlands was the principal source of tension in 1568 and for decades thereafter. Elizabeth was surely right to regard the army as a danger to England's security and to seek its removal. Her way of going about this gradually drove Philip to consider England an irreconcilable enemy, and the eventual result was to bring on the invasion that her policy was intended to avoid.

5 THE AFFAIR OF THE SPANISH BULLION

At the end of 1568, Anglo-Spanish relations were plunged into a state of crisis. The extraordinary story of this quarrel contains its fair share of mystery. In November 1568, five Spanish ships sailed towards the Netherlands carrying £85 000 to enable Alva to pay the costs of his massive army. Bad weather and privateers forced the ships to take shelter in Plymouth and Southampton. Elizabeth at first agreed to provide the ships with an armed escort, but she then decided instead to retain the money for her own use. The money had been borrowed from the bankers of Genoa, and legally it remained their property until it was delivered to Antwerp. Elizabeth contended that, far from stealing the money from the King of Spain, she was merely taking over the loan, a move to which the Genoese were apparently agreeable.

It is difficult to know if the Queen's reasoning was quite so straightforward. The action may have been a response to the massacre at San

Juan de Ulua, but it is unlikely that anything more than vague rumours of the incident had yet reached England (Hawkins and Drake did not arrive home until January 1569). Far more probably, she was using the opportunity to remind the Spanish that England's domination of their sea route to the Netherlands meant that the army could not be maintained indefinitely against Elizabeth's opposition. The seizure of the bullion was a lever designed to induce the army's withdrawal now that the Netherlands situation no longer necessitated its presence.

Instead, the measure did rather more to provoke Spanish hostility than achieve any goal Elizabeth might have desired. Alva's position in the Netherlands – presiding over an army owed months of back-pay – was so dire that he could only regard the seizure as the act of an enemy. Also, de Spes insisted, writing from London, that only the most vigorous response would bring Elizabeth to heel; following the ambassador's counsel, on 29 December Alva ordered the seizure of the English ships and goods in Netherlands ports and banned all trade with England. In fact, de Spes had advised this on 21 December, seven days before Elizabeth officially confirmed her intention regarding the money, and Wernham has argued that his precipitate action helped to bring on the crisis. Elizabeth immediately retaliated, the conflict escalated, and trade with Spain, as well as the Netherlands, came to a halt. The English government cannot have foreseen such an outcome. In fact, a majority of Councillors attacked Cecil, the man who had urged the seizure and thereby brought England into conflict with the formidable power of Spain. Genuinely alarmed as well as hopeful of destroying Cecil's influence, they launched a major campaign for his removal. For several months, a factional struggle raged as Cecil's enemies sought to turn the Queen against him. That he survived is a measure of the respect she had for his abilities.

The affair was never likely to provoke a Spanish invasion. The French would have opposed any attempt to extend Spanish power, Philip had his hands full with the revolt of the Moors of Granada that broke out in December 1568, and the Turks continued to threaten in the Mediterranean. Elizabeth must have been aware of the weaknesses of Philip's position. This is not to say, however, that she had anticipated the furious response to her seizure of the bullion and calculated that it would not prove fatal. Almost certainly, Elizabeth and Cecil had underestimated the extent to which it would alienate the Spanish. The measure was a mistake. Its outcome was not as disastrous as many feared in the early months of 1569. But a traditional ally and great power was alienated and virtually nothing was gained.

During the succeeding, crisis-ridden years, Elizabeth paid a price for her impetuosity. In November 1569, the Northern Rising broke out in the far north of England. It cost almost a thousand lives, mostly those of the rebels. De Spes, Spain's ambassador, had played a role in encouraging the northern Earls, and Elizabeth's discovery of their connection with de Spes possibly helped to drive them to rebellion. Three months later, in February 1570, the Pope, without reference to Philip, issued the Bull in which he called upon English Catholics to withhold their loyalty to Elizabeth. Together, the Rising and the Papal Bull produced widespread alarm and sparked off the first wave of repression of Catholics. Finally, in 1571, Ridolfi, a Florentine banker, plotted a Catholic rising to overthrow Elizabeth and replace her with Mary. De Spes was enthusiastic, and Philip and Alva (when visited by Ridolfi) agreed to despatch an army to England once 'the first steps' were taken by Norfolk and his English Catholic allies. In the event, the plot was uncovered, thanks largely to Ridolfi's inability to hold his tongue, Norfolk went to the block, and ambassador de Spes was expelled.

These events demonstrate the harmful effects of the breakdown in Anglo-Spanish relations. Many English Catholics regarded Spain as their natural protector. They were open to Spanish influence, and the latter was now used, albeit sporadically, to undermine the existing state. With the benefit of hindsight, one can conclude that the majority of English Catholics were fundamentally loyal to Elizabeth. Nevertheless, a plot like Ridolfi's certainly did pose a danger. In addition, the atmosphere of panic induced by the actions of some Catholics disturbed the religious peace of the country, producing repressive measures and encouraging Puritan demands that set Elizabeth at odds with much of the political nation (*see Chapter IX*). The rift with the premier Catholic power inevitably gave rise to dangers and tensions in a country that was divided in its religious affiliations.

The bullion dispute had much less damaging effects on England's economy. The country quickly overcame the loss of assets seized in the Netherlands and Spain; indeed, it was outweighed by the Spanish property taken over by England. The cloth trade, denied access to Antwerp, was switched to Hamburg. When the half-yearly cloth fleet reached the German port in May 1569, the English merchants sold their entire cargo, at good prices, and Hamburg's capacity to handle the trade was proven. Even when Antwerp was re-opened in 1573, Hamburg remained the major destination. Crucially, it was clear from 1569 that England was no longer dependent on Antwerp. The disruptive effect of the bullion issue was to outlast the fury it created, for it brought to an end a compelling reason for Anglo-Spanish friendship.

6 THE FRENCH ALLIANCE

The most striking departure engendered by the conflict with Spain was England's alliance with France, the traditional enemy. Catherine de Medici, the Queen Mother, was aware of France's vulnerability to English intervention in the religious strife that continued to plague her country. Elizabeth, on the other side, knew that friendship with France would force Philip to compete for her favour. Also, as Cecil especially was aware, it might help to restrain French ambition in the Netherlands. Finally, it would stave off the possibility that the two great Catholic powers would unite against heretical England – a generally remote possibility, but always dreaded and a particular concern during conflicts between England and Spain.

Late in 1570, Elizabeth began to encourage the idea of a marriage between herself and the Duke of Anjou, one of King Charles IX's younger brothers. The match won the support of Cecil and others, convinced as they were of the need to settle the succession (without admitting Mary), and keenly aware of the foreign policy advantages. They were hopeful that the Duke would at least play down his Catholicism to acquire the English throne. Perhaps their enthusiasm was less wise than Elizabeth's opportunism. Probably she never really intended to enter a marriage that would have diluted her power, endangered England's independence (particularly in the event of the younger Anjou's surviving her to rule alone as King of England), and provoked popular unrest (the thought of a French Catholic monarch being even more alarming than a Spaniard). She proceeded, then, to encourage the French suit, safe in the knowledge that 'the knotty point of religion' could always be used to prevent its reaching fruition.

After the expulsion of de Spes in December 1571, representing as it did a further stage in the collapse of Anglo-Spanish relations, Elizabeth proposed a formal alliance between England and France. The marriage question was shelved; the idea of a league against Spain was attractive to both sides even without a more lasting union through marriage. The Treaty of Blois of April 1572 constituted a diplomatic revolution, aligning England and France in opposition to Spain. It created a defensive alliance whereby they would help each other in the event of an attack on one by a third country. Elizabeth 'had gained a French shield' (*Wernham*) against the might of Alva's army. But she avoided committing herself to any offensive action. To join the French in the latter would create new dangers in the Netherlands and greatly damage the prospect of eventual reconciliation with Spain. The treaty met England's requirements precisely and was a commendable achievement. Another positive attribute was the treaty's failure to make any mention of Mary Queen of Scots in its reference to Scotland, an implicit abandonment of Mary by her former French patrons.

For all its advantages, however, the new alliance was plagued with difficulty. History bequeathed such a burden of animosity and mistrust that England and France could not suddenly live together as true and trusting friends. One source of difference was the Netherlands. Just as fear of Alva's army was the cement that held the alliance, so the question of what should follow Alva's departure served to alienate England from France. Earlier, in the summer of 1571, Charles IX's Council proposed a joint attack on Alva by France, England, and the German

Protestants. After expelling the Spanish, the victors should partition the Netherlands, with France acquiring Flanders and Artois, England the northern provinces of Holland and Zeeland, and the Germans the rest. Leicester and Francis Walsingham (then the English ambassador to France) welcomed the prospect, in particular the 'spiritual fruit [the spread of Protestantism] that may thereby ensue'. But Elizabeth and Cecil had no desire for continental territory whose retention might be militarily burdensome and inordinately expensive.

Above all, the thought of French expansion into the Netherlands was alarming in the extreme. Their hold on the southern coastline of the Channel would be extended to embrace the land east, as well as west, of the narrow Straits of Dover. Elizabeth preferred a restoration of the traditional balance between France and Spain in an area so crucial to English security. A substantial gain by England's traditional enemy was certainly not the best solution. An apprehensive Cecil had advised against an Anglo-French alliance that did not end the French threat permanently by including a marriage bond. Elizabeth, unwilling to marry, rejected his counsel, but she shared his wariness of French intentions. There was little prospect of agreement on positive action in the Netherlands – and as long as the latter was the major issue of the day relations between England and France would remain brittle.

Despite these misgivings the Treaty of Blois had been signed but the first crisis within the alliance arose only weeks later. In April 1572, the Dutch Sea Beggars (privateers) seized the port of Brill in south Holland and launched what became the Dutch Revolt. When, in addition, French Huguenots marched from the south, and William of Orange, leader of the Dutch rebels, threatened with a mercenary army from Germany, Alva was in the direst of straits. It required only an attack by the King of France to threaten the survival of Spanish power in the Netherlands. The reaction of Burghley (as Cecil had become) was revealing. He wrote on this subject in a Memorial for Matters in Flanders in June 1572:

> If . . . the French begin to possess any part of . . . the maritime parts, then it is like that the French . . . may be too potent neighbours for us and therefore [it] may be good for us to use all the means . . . to stay that course.
>
> If the French proceed to possess the maritime coasts and frontiers it seemeth to be good that . . . the Duke of Alva were informed secretly of the Queen's Majesty's disposition to assist the king his master by all honourable means she might in the defence of his inheritance, so as it may appear to her that he will discharge his subjects of their intolerable oppression, restore them to their ancient liberties, reconcile his nobility to him, deliver them from the fear of the Inquisition and continue with

her Majesty the ancient league for amity and traffic in as ample sort as any others, dukes of Burgundy, heretofore have done.

1 *In what respects could Burghley's attitude and policy be described as being very traditional and backward-looking?*

The possible resolution of England's principal foreign policy problem since 1567, the threat from Alva'a army, was not to be bought at any price. Spain must be sustained as a counterpoise to French power, so strong was the continuing English fear of the old enemy.

This premise had important implications for England's long-term policy in the Netherlands, as will be seen. In June–July 1572 Elizabeth permitted Sir Thomas Morgan and Sir Humphrey Gilbert to lead substantial forces of volunteers across to Flushing in Zeeland, and the correspondence between Burghley and these men reveals that their principal purpose in the minister's view was to hold the port against the French. Elizabeth had already suggested to Philip's unofficial ambassador, Antonio de Gueras, that she should hold Flushing for Spain, and she warmly welcomed Alva's proposal of talks on the bullion dispute. The old allies were converging again in order to check their old adversary. In the event, a renewal of the French Wars of Religion forced the Huguenots to withdraw from the Netherlands and prevented intervention by the King of France. The anticipated French threat evaporated. However, the events of 1572 served to remind the English government of the danger posed by France.

The division between England and France was deepened by the circumstance that caused the latter's collapse once more into religious warfare. On 24 August 1572, stung by the growth of Huguenot influence, the Guise faction initiated a massacre that claimed the lives of 13000 Huguenots within a month. The St Bartholomew's Eve Massacre had a profound effect on English opinion. It demonstrated the treachery of Catholics and their resolve to eradicate Protestantism. Walsingham in Paris thought it 'less peril to live with them as enemies than as friends'. Elizabeth was genuinely alarmed by the Massacre, and even when her fears subsided she had to take account of the hostility English Protestants felt towards the French monarchy. For both secular and religious reasons England and France were not easily reconciled.

7 THE GREAT DEBATE

The mainly Protestant rebels in the Netherlands continued after 1572 to resist the Catholic and repressive government that Philip sought to impose through Alva. For as long as it lasted, the rebellion in Holland and Zeeland relieved Elizabeth's fear of Alva's army. The latter was not free to be deployed against England. Equally, France posed no threat during its civil war, notwithstanding the alarm caused by the initial Catholic assault in 1572. With the two great powers of western Europe so embroiled in domestic difficulties, England's security could hardly have been better ensured. Even their capacity to incite rebellion within England (or Scotland) was limited by the certainty that Elizabeth could respond by intervening to aggravate their internal problems. However, it was always unlikely that both Spain and France would be weakened for good. As soon as one of them prevailed at home, England would again be faced with a powerful neighbour.

It is possible to damn Elizabeth's excessive caution, to accuse her of failing to exploit the temporary advantages of the 1570s to achieve permanent security. The latter, arguably, required bolder action to gain a favourable outcome in the Netherlands or France, or both. The perils her country encountered in the next decade may be attributable to the fact that she did not give enough assistance to the Dutch rebels and thereby allowed Spain to recover to a position of awesome, threatening power. In this view, Elizabeth must at least share responsibility for the great war that had then to be fought.

This line of criticism of Elizabeth's foreign policy has featured prominently in the work of historians, notably in Charles Wilson's *Queen Elizabeth and the Revolt of the Netherlands* (1970). In her own time, too, there was widespread support in England for the idea of military action on the side of the Dutch rebels and the Huguenots of France. The same motives had featured among Protestants from the beginning of the reign – for example, in Cecil's attitude to Scotland – but they acquired new vigour when the Dutch Revolt and the St Bartholomew's Eve Massacre initiated a period of sustained and ferocious religious conflict.

In addition to the strategic benefits of intervention, many Englishmen felt a strong obligation to help their fellow Protestants as they struggled against Catholic domination. For them, the conflicts in the Netherlands and France were the first stages of a general European war between Protestantism and Catholicism, Good and Evil. England had a duty to fight the cause of true religion. Moreover, failure to join the struggle would result in the victory of Catholicism on the continent and a massive assault on the one, remaining stronghold of Protestantism, England. Led by the Earl of Leicester and Sir Francis Walsingham (Secretary of State from December 1573), a majority of Elizabeth's Councillors favoured vigorous intervention for these reasons. Burghley shared their general outlook even if a naturally moderate and defensive mentality – and possibly a fear of alienating Elizabeth – made him more cautious in practice.

The problem was Elizabeth. Demonstrating great strength of will, she withstood all the pressure for a full and open intervention in the Protestant cause. She disliked the uncertainties of war and feared a lessening of her authority among those who would consider a female monarch unequal to the task of fighting one. Her sympathy with the plight of continental Protestants was undermined by dislike of their intolerant and uncompromising Calvinism. She did not feel the need to strike out in order to preclude a general Catholic onslaught, for she was more confident than her ministers that the traditional rivalry between France and Spain would keep them apart. Above all, she saw that England's national interest would be endangered by involving the country in a religious war; 'whatever the religious zealots, the pious men of blood, might say, she would not gamble England's future on so barbarous and unpredictable a holocaust' (*Wernham*). The idea of Elizabeth as a secular politician, though unacceptable in its fullest sense, is surely applicable here. She did not share the ideological imperatives of Puritans like Francis Walsingham.

Elizabeth's instinctive loathing of rebellion made her reluctant to give it support. Also, treacherous subjects were likely to be treacherous allies, as the Huguenots had proved when their fickleness led to the rout of the English army in 1563. Elizabeth never forgot that bitter lesson. She had to consider, too, the financial cost of a major campaign on the continent. To pay and equip an expeditionary army would entail massive expense. It would require the imposition of burdensome taxes that, for all their initial fervour, the people might come to resent and Parliament might prove reluctant to pass.

Elizabeth's limited objective in the Netherlands dictated a limited commitment. Her goal was the restoration of the semi-independent status that the Dutch enjoyed during the reign of Charles V. Alva's army must be removed and the country returned to a state of virtual demilitarization. Philip must also restore government through the elected States General and grant religious liberty (freedom from 'the fear of the Inquisition'). She did not want to end Spain's sovereignty over the Netherlands. Possibly a majority of her Councillors wanted to expel the Spanish. But for Elizabeth (and Burghley) the Spanish presence checked French ambitions there and prevented French acquisition of the entire southern coast of the Channel. '(It is) necessary for England', wrote Cecil, 'that the State of the Low Countries should continue in their ancient government, without either subduing it to the Spanish nation or joining it to the Crown of France.' The fact that the outright defeat of Spain was not sought inevitably made Elizabeth's intervention more limited and defensive than it might have been. She had only to intervene sufficiently to keep alive the resistance of the Dutch and convince Philip of the need to conclude a reasonable settlement.

8 A LIMITED SUCCESS

During the French wars of 1572–7, English Protestants sent money to help the Huguenots, some even crossed over to join the struggle, and Huguenot fighters used England as a base for several military operations. Elizabeth permitted these unofficial actions, formally authorised the sending of munitions, and once (in 1574) granted a loan of £15 000 for the hire of German soldiers. But the Huguenots made a remarkable recovery from their losses of August 1572 and, for all the anxiety of their English supporters, did not require more substantial assistance. France remained weak and divided. Elizabeth's forbearance meant that, although occasionally accused over individual actions, she did not fall out with the French monarchy. The latter remained her ally against Spain, and Blois was renewed in 1575. Moreover, aware of their vulnerability to intervention, the French avoided any action in Scotland or the Netherlands that might have threatened England's interests. Elizabeth's policy was perfectly adequate for the duration of the French civil war.

Elizabeth took a more positive role in relation to the Netherlands, as she sought to stave off both French expansion and a Spanish victory that would leave Spain's army unencumbered and dangerously close to England. She was suspected of involvement in the Sea Beggars' seizure of Brill in 1572. It was her earlier expulsion of the privateers from English ports that drove them across to Holland, but it is impossible to know if she had intended or even colluded in the attack that followed. Indisputably, however, she allowed both Dutch refugees and English volunteers to join the Sea Beggars in starting the Dutch Revolt in 1572. When the French threatened to take advantage, she sent Gilbert and his volunteers across to hold Flushing until the Dutch could take it over towards the end of 1572.

On several occasions in the following years, Elizabeth sent money and permitted volunteers to cross to the Netherlands to fight the Spanish army. She allowed privateers, many of them English, to close the Channel to Philip's ships, cutting off Spain's best means of communication with the Netherlands. She formally approved (and invested in) Drake's expedition of 1577–80 to the Pacific and probably hoped that he could seize sufficient gold and silver from the Spanish not only to fill her coffers but also to aggravate Philip's financial problems and make the Netherlands army even more difficult to sustain. All of these actions were sufficiently covert to avoid open conflict with Spain; Elizabeth later wrote of giving the Dutch 'such indirect assistance as shall not at once be a cause of war'. Her purpose was to ensure the continuation of the Dutch Revolt and convince Philip of the need to end it by granting the sort of settlement desired by Elizabeth.

The policy did not succeed. The Spanish, anxious to end England's troublesome interference, conceded much to England, re-opening trade in 1573, settling the bullion dispute in 1574 (by the Convention of Bristol), banishing English Catholic refugees from the Netherlands, and permitting English traders to practise their Protestant religion freely. They did not, however, settle with the Dutch, except briefly and under duress in 1577. English efforts at mediation, begun in 1573, were politely rejected.

Elizabeth at times contemplated more drastic action. In 1576, the 'Spanish Fury', a violent, anarchic mutiny of the Spanish soldiers, drove all seventeen Netherlands provinces to revolt and promised a Spanish collapse. French preparations to intervene in favour of the Dutch led Elizabeth to warn Henry III that any such action would cause her to send forces to fight on the side of Spain. However, in 1577 she agreed to send an expeditionary force to help the Dutch, and preparations were duly made. Spain's army, now regrouped under Don John of Austria, began the re-conquest of the Netherlands in earnest in the early months of 1578. Thousands of volunteers went over from England to help the Dutch and Elizabeth lent the States General £20 000 to hire mercenaries. Walsingham and most of the Council, Burghley probably included, pressed for the previously approved military intervention. Elizabeth vacillated, but her reluctance to risk war against Spain proved insuperable.

To compound the problem, the Dutch, frustrated with Elizabeth's half-heartedness, turned to France. The Duke of Alençon, Henry III's brother, was persuaded to accept the title of 'Defender of the Liberties of the Low Countries' and come to their aid with a sizeable army.

Though initially concerned, Elizabeth realised that Henry III of France was unwilling to risk war with Spain and would give minimal support to Alençon's 'private venture'. She decided that she could control Alençon ('her Frog') by encouraging his marriage suit; induced to hope for the kingship of England, he would not oppose Elizabeth's wishes in the Netherlands. Alençon was an erratic individual, however, and Elizabeth, ever reluctant to intervene decisively in the Netherlands, was dependent on his good behaviour and that left England at the mercy of forces over which she had little control.

The Dutch held off the Spanish in 1578, but the latter's victory was always a distinct possibility from this point. The impressive Duke of Parma took control of the army after Don John's death in October 1578. Alençon withdrew his exhausted forces by the end of 1578. Part of the southern Netherlands, alienated by the intolerant and aggressive behaviour of the Calvinists, made peace with Parma in January 1579. The goal of Elizabeth's policy, the restoration of the traditional status of the Netherlands, was certainly not achieved. Her Puritan critics were justified in their alarms and in their view that Elizabeth's excessively cautious approach was not sufficient to force a settlement on Spain. The policy of the 1570s was no more than a holding operation, in effect, and the failure to achieve any lasting solution in the Netherlands meant continuing and seemingly interminable danger.

9 SPAIN ASCENDANT

In the early 1580s a series of events enormously strengthened Spain. The male line of the royal house of Portugal died out in 1580. Through his mother, Isabella of Portugal, Philip could fairly claim a better title to the throne than his rival, the illegitimate Don Antonio. A Spanish army conquered the country in 1580 and Philip was proclaimed King of Portugal in April the following year. The two largest empires in the world became one, bringing to Spain the riches of Portugal's African and Oriental possessions. Ominously, the Portuguese navy had ten ocean-going ships. Most of Spain's navy consisted of smaller vessels capable only of sailing the quiet waters of the Mediterranean. But several larger ships had been built in order to protect the routes to America. Combined, the Spanish and Portuguese navies had an ocean-going capability that came close to matching England's.

In 1581, Elizabeth contemplated sending Drake to seize the Azores on behalf of Don Antonio and abandoned the idea only when Philip warned her that any support for his Portuguese rival would mean war. In the meantime, with the conquest of Portugal completed in September 1580, it seemed likely that the Spanish would turn their full attention back to the Dutch Revolt. Alarmed at the possibility of outright victory for Spain, Elizabeth had from 1579 sought an alliance with Henry III of France, in what MacCaffrey has called 'the boldest and by far the most ambitious initiative taken by her government since the Scottish enterprise of 1559–1560'. The Queen argued that they could not 'leave the King of Spain to increase to such greatness as hereafter neither the force of France nor England nor any that may confederate with them shall be able to withstand any thing that the King of Spain shall attempt'. She pressed Henry to intervene in the Netherlands and promised secret English assistance. It was Protestant opposition at home that made Elizabeth unable to deliver the Alençon marriage, as the French demanded. But it was really her own indecisiveness that scuppered the alliance, making her dither before the central problem;: she still wanted to minimise and keep secret English intervention in order to avoid war with Spain, while not facilitating French expansionism. Henry was unwilling to become Elizabeth's pawn and fight Spain alone, without even the benefit of his family's securing the English throne by marriage. So, he was not won over. Elizabeth and Henry failed to unite against the emerging Spanish threat, and it is probably fair to comment that bolder leadership at this stage would have saved them and their countries much future pain.

To check Parma, Elizabeth became Alençon's chief backer; she funded his private ventures in 1581 and 1582 to the tune of almost £100 000. This left him far short of the capacity to acquire mastery for himself or France but also incapable of preventing Parma's continued progress. Philip, aware of her role, was increasingly convinced of the enmity of the English Queen. In August 1583 his great admiral, the Marquis of Santa Cruz, proposed that he should lead an armada from Spain to overthrow 'the heretic woman', and Philip proceeded to order the building and hiring of some large ships suitable to this 'Enterprise of England'. However, with the Netherlands still unconquered and France unlikely to remain neutral in the event of a Spanish assault on England, Philip felt unable to proceed. He temporarily turned a deaf ear to those – for example, Mary Queen of Scots, the Duke of Guise, the English Jesuits, and his own ambassador to England, Bernardino de Mendoza – who manufactured a series of plots against Elizabeth. Most notably, in 1583 he refused to contribute the several thousand Netherlands-based soldiers requested by those behind what became known as the Throckmorton Plot to overthrow Elizabeth and install Mary. Throckmorton was arrested and his confession, drawn from him on the rack, revealed Mendoza's part in the conspiracy. Elizabeth expelled Mendoza in January 1584. The affair added considerably to the tension.

The possibility of a Spanish attack on England was increased further by the turn of events in the Netherlands and France. In 1582–4, Parma re-conquered most of Calvinist-held Flanders and Brabant. Alençon, cash-starved, ineffective, and reduced to war against Dutch allies who could not trust a papist Frenchman, withdrew in June 1583 and died a year later. Then, in July 1584, William of Orange, the military strong-man among the Calvinists, was assassinated. This heralded disaster for the Dutch cause. The Union of Utrecht became a 'headless common-wealth' that seemed likely to fall apart for want of an agreed leader. 'The final reduction of the whole Netherlands under Spanish rule looked to be only a matter of time.' (*Wernham*) The menace of a victorious Spanish army seemed closer than ever before.

Almost simultaneously, England's 'French shield' was removed. Alençon's death and Henry III's childlessness made Henry of Navarre the legal heir to the French throne. Henry, as leader of the Huguenots, was unacceptable to the French Catholics. They prepared to fight to force Henry III to disinherit Navarre and to destroy the Huguenots once and for all. To this end, the Catholic League (which commanded greater support than the king) called on aid from Philip and Spain. By the Treaty of Joinville of December 1584, they acknowledged Philip as their protector and received his promise of assistance. Philip now knew that he could deal with England without fear of the reaction of France.

England's position was one of great jeopardy. There was every like-lihood that Spain would soon be able to deploy both a large navy and an unbeatable army against England. France, in which a renewal of civil war appeared inevitable, could offer no protection. Indeed, if the Catholic League took over the government, France would be ruled by Philip's grateful and dependent ally. Spain threatened to become the dominant power in all of western Europe. England would be at its mercy. This was the great crisis of Elizabeth's reign.

10 THE OUTBREAK OF WAR

Because the Treaty of Joinville was initially a well kept secret, the full extent of the calamity was not immediately apparent in England. Nevertheless, the imminent collapse of the Dutch Revolt clearly required a decision on England's policy. Elizabeth's hopes that Henry III would assist the Dutch gradually faded in the early months of 1585. She had to come to terms with the fact that if England did not intervene forcefully the Dutch resistance would quickly collapse and the Spanish army would be free to attempt the Enterprise of England. Walsingham, Leicester and most of her Councillors were convinced both of their religious duty to save the Dutch Protestants and of the certainty that the great Catholic power would indeed try to destroy Protestantism in England. The past behaviour of Granvelle, de Spes and Mendoza, not to speak of the growing mythology surrounding the Spanish Inquisition and the supposed evils practised by Catholics throughout Europe, left them in no doubt of Philip's hostile intentions. They advocated a major military commitment by England to the Protestant cause in the Netherlands.

Still Elizabeth and Burghley hesitated. Elizabeth's antipathy to rebellion was undiminished. There was a chance, too, that Philip's hostility would lessen once the running sore of the Dutch Revolt was finally healed. France, they thought mistakenly, would continue to deter Spanish aggression. War would be enormously expensive and, given Spain's great power, potentially disastrous. Fortification of England would give as much security as intervention in the Netherlands, without provoking certain war. Even victory over Spain in the Netherlands would, in the long term, serve France more than England.

Elizabeth's caution was finally overcome in the spring and summer of 1585. On 20 March, the Catholic League took to arms and demanded that Henry III should root out heresy, and on the same day Walsingham received word of the Treaty of Joinville. Henry submitted to the League in June. Philip's hostile intent was indicated by his seizure of English shipping in Spanish ports at the end of May. And, all the while, Parma's army was closing on Antwerp and bringing the Dutch under control. These events, particularly Henry's capitulation to Philip's allies, brought Elizabeth and Burghley to an awareness of the awesome power Spain was acquiring and forced them to acknowledge the need for action. On 10 August 1585 Elizabeth and the Dutch signed the famous Treaty of Nonsuch, by which she became the protector of the Dutch and agreed to despatch an army of over 7000 soldiers. The vanguard arrived in August and Leicester, able at last not only to fight for Protestantism but also to seek the military glory he coveted, crossed over to take command in December. At the same time, Elizabeth sent Drake to attack Spain's ports to free the English ships. War, though it was never to be declared officially, had begun.

The merits of the policy that led to war will be discussed below. The final decision to fight was probably correct. True, the open support for rebellion within his empire made Philip decide to invade England; detailed preparations were ordered in January 1586. It is impossible to know for sure if Philip would have launched such an enterprise had Elizabeth continued to hold the Dutch at arms length. But there was clear evidence of Philip's growing hostility to the troublesome and heretical Queen of England, and to permit him to achieve total dominance in western Europe would surely have been a mistake. The intervention in the Netherlands was designed to deny Spain such a position, by reviving the Dutch resistance. Elizabeth had little choice but to conclude that it was a necessary measure, and, in this respect, historians have not found reason to question her judgement.

11 THE WAR

Elizabeth initially failed to appreciate that England and Spain were now engaged in a struggle that was entirely different from the angry encounters of the previous two decades. In her mind, the military initiative of 1585, though much more overt and substantial than earlier interventions, still did not make full-scale war inevitable. She hoped, rather, that Philip would see reason and conclude a settlement with the Dutch. In 1585 and again in 1587, Elizabeth turned down Dutch offers of the throne of an independent Netherlands, and she was enraged when Leicester implied her consent by assuming the post of Governor-General soon after his arrival. Her objective remained a self-governing Netherlands under Spanish sovereignty, and she knew that acceptance of the throne would be a hostile (and entirely illegitimate) act that would provoke a major war. Similarly, Elizabeth's attitude was revealed by her continuing readiness to seek a negotiated peace; secret talks on the future of the Netherlands went on intermittently from November 1585 until mid-1588, but Spanish success on the battlefield made them unwilling to concede a settlement that could satisfy England.

Despite his urgings, Elizabeth refused to expand Leicester's original army beyond the 7000 men promised at Nonsuch. Any great increase in size would produce the sort of escalation of the war that she wished to avoid. As one might expect, the Crown's perpetual shortage of money was another, compelling reason for the modest commitment, and Elizabeth failed to fund adequately even the small force that did exist. At the same time, for all her hopes of a limited conflict, Elizabeth was aware of the threat of invasion. She was determined that financial and military resources should not be expended in the Netherlands when they might be required in England itself. Indeed, the priority she gave to defending England was shown even in the way that the army was deployed in the Netherlands; it concentrated on denying Spain control of the major ports, leaving most of the fighting to the rather disgruntled Dutch. The whole enterprise bore the stamp of the cautious and prudent woman who was determined to restrain her impetuous, crusading favourite.

English soldiers were present in the Netherlands for the rest of Elizabeth's reign. Their first leader, Leicester, proved inept, squandering money and squabbling with his officers and the Dutch; twice he was re-called in near-disgrace. However, his army played a part in halting Parma's advance in 1586, and the great Spanish gains of 1587 did not go so far as to win them Flushing or any other deep-water port in which to receive the Armada in 1588 – a crucial failure. During the next five years, harvest failures combined with the Dutch naval blockade to cause starvation among Parma's army, the Dutch and English improved their performance in battle, and (from 1589) many of the Spanish troops were diverted to the civil war in France.

The Dutch Captain-General, Maurice of Nassau, arguably the only great General of the whole war, scored a string of successes. He required the assistance of relatively few men from England (only 8000 in 1589–95) and very large subsidies (£750 000 in the same period). By 1593–4, the northern part of the Netherlands was under Dutch control, while the south was retained by Spain. For most of the period until 1648, when Madrid finally recognised the independence of the northern Netherlands, the war continued. So, Spain was checked by the Dutch and yet remained in the southern Netherlands as an obstacle to French expansion. It was not the solution Elizabeth sought before (and during) the war, but it achieved the same end in limiting the power of her two great neighbours.

France provided the second principal arena of the war. Elizabeth's envoys initially failed to persuade beleaguered Henry III to back Henry of Navarre against the League. In 1589, however, the League's rebellion finally forced Henry into this alliance, he was assassinated, and Navarre claimed the succession as Henry IV (July 1589). The civil war then began in earnest. Philip gave the struggle for France priority over the Dutch war and sent thousands of Spanish soldiers to join the League. The English role, previously limited to a loan (£39 000) to Navarre in 1586, also became substantial. Elizabeth sent 20 000 troops and £300 000 in 1589–95. Though outweighed by the contributions of Protestants from France itself, the Netherlands and Germany, the English played a part in ensuring Henry's survival. His conversion to Catholicism in 1593 – with the comment, it is said, 'Paris is well worth a Mass' – was no defeat for England. By bringing peace with the League, it ensured that England's ally would retain the throne. By ending the civil war, it effected a revival of France as a check to Spanish power. The Franco-Spanish war of 1595–8 was a boon to England, notwithstanding Henry's ingratitude in making a separate peace with the common enemy in 1598. All in all, the position in France, too, was an immense improvement on the calamity that threatened in 1585.

At sea, Drake and Hawkins failed to intercept nearly as much of Spain's American silver as the Queen's fast-emptying coffers badly needed. Drake did achieve a magnificent success in 1587, entering Cadiz and destroying perhaps thirty Spanish vessels – hence his boast that he had 'singed the King of Spain's beard'. It severely disrupted the Armada preparations and led Drake and Hawkins to argue that an offensive approach, deploying ships to harry and blockade the Spanish coast and search out the silver fleets, was England's best defence. But here too Elizabeth was cautious and defensive. She insisted that her ships should concentrate on forming 'the wall of England' in the Channel. She was probably wise to rein in her naval forces, even if inherent caution was more the cause than any strategic awareness. The number of expeditions that yielded little or nothing demonstrated the uncertain benefits of a long-range strategy, while the Armada threat meant that priority had to be given to securing the home waters.

The 130 ships of the first Spanish Armada, carrying 17 000 troops and intended to bring the same number of Parma's men across from Flanders to England, reached the Channel in July 1588. It was met by the full strength of the navy – the Queen's own ships, privateers' vessels and merchantmen – a force that just outnumbered the Armada's warships. The English ships were also quicker and better armed with long-range guns than the Spanish. The Armada's strong defensive formation meant it lost only 2 ships as it passed up the Channel. Off Calais, however, the English scattered the fleet with fireships. They then ravaged the Armada at the Battle of Gravelines, sinking only 4 ships but forcing the northwards flight of the battered survivors. The fierce Atlantic gales encountered off Scotland and Ireland caused the vast majority of Spanish losses, with dozens of ships sinking or finishing on the rocky shores. Only half of the Armada made it back to Spain.

The defeat of the Armada fully merits its place among the great military exploits of English history. In the years after 1588, England's sailors took many Spanish prizes, and the destruction of Cadiz in 1596 was a striking success. But they frequently abandoned military advantage in order to seek booty ('there was no money to be made from sinking Spanish warships'), and they could not stop the New World silver reaching Philip in record quantities. Their raids on Spanish and Portuguese ports did not prevent the reconstruction of Philip's navy. Fortunately for the English, the armadas of 1596, 1597 and 1599 were all scattered by strong winds. The final verdict must be that the naval war was secondary to the land war in Europe. For all its remarkable feats, the navy could not win the war for England; it could only, as in 1588, prevent invasion and defeat.

The Earl of Tyrone's rebellion in Ireland in 1595–1603 made that country the fourth major, indeed the biggest, arena of warfare. The arrival of 3400 Spanish troops in 1601 marked Philip III's willingness to respond in kind to the English intervention in the Netherlands. As shown in Chapter XII, the Irish (and Spanish) were eventually defeated. But the struggle required the deployment of 25 000 English soldiers and a massive expenditure of £2 million, a diversion of resources that can only have damaged the war effort against Spain.

It was just as well that the other element in the 'British dimension' did not prove troublesome. Reaping the benefit of twenty-five years of sound diplomacy, the English did not have to worry about their northern border at a time when any show of hostility from Scotland might have brought disaster. The young James VI, strongly Protestant, hopeful of securing the English succession, and attracted by an annual pension of £4000, joined Elizabeth in signing the Treaty of Berwick in 1586, making the two countries firm allies. Even the execution of his mother, Mary Queen of Scots, in February 1587, did not break the alliance. Instead it made James the next in line after Elizabeth, and he knew that he had only to remain England's friend (and a Protestant) in order to succeed her on the English throne. This ambition was the principal basis of the alliance. But Burghley would have been justified in looking back to 1560 and musing on how different things would have been had he not driven out the Guises and created an entirely new relationship between England and Scotland.

12 CONCLUSION

Philip II having died in 1598 and Elizabeth in 1603, it was left to their heirs, Philip III and James I, to acknowledge that neither side could benefit from continued warfare. The Treaty of London of 1604 ended England's formal intervention in the Netherlands at a time when the Dutch were well capable of carrying on alone. England did not defeat Spain. In the first place, the military contributions of the Dutch and French surpassed those of England, even if the latter's was certainly substantial. Secondly, the war was fought to a stalemate, with neither side emerging as clear winners. On the other hand, the English and their allies succeeded in preventing Spanish hegemony in France and the Netherlands. Spain, for all its might, lacked the capacity to control all of western Europe. So, the purpose for which England went to war in 1585 was, by and large, achieved, as the spectre of overwhelming Spanish power was exorcised. At the end of Elizabeth's reign, the country was much more secure than it appeared in 1585. In this vital respect the war achieved much for England.

This is not to say that the foreign policy that led to war can be called a success. It was a war Elizabeth had long sought to avoid, and its occurrence must therefore be considered a policy failure. Indeed, any policy, whatever its objective, that led a middle-ranking country like England into war with the greatest power in the world must be considered a failure. Moreover, as shown in other chapters, it was a war that produced much disruption and unrest, causing as it did an oppressive level of taxation, dislocation of trade, enforced and bitterly resented military service, a profusion of detested monopolies, and widespread corruption in public life. The war was mainly responsible for the collapse of the Queen's popularity in the last years of her reign. It threatened her authority even more directly; so dominant at home, she found that commanders like Drake, Leicester and Essex constantly disobeyed her orders – usually to ill effect. They had little respect for a woman's knowledge of military matters and were ever-hopeful that success would bring glory and forestall retribution. In the end, Essex, heady with popular acclaim, sought her overthrow. Of course, the war's eventual outcome was indeed compatible with English interests but the war and the policy that failed to prevent it must not be confused.

One wonders, however, if any other strategy could have worked better. To identify failure is not necessarily to attribute blame. It is true that war in the 1570s, as desired by Puritan opinion, would have been preferable. By 1585 Spain was more powerful and dangerous, and England's French and Dutch allies were in disarray. But, as shown above, Elizabeth's forbearance in the 1570s had good reasons: the fear of France, the lack of financial resources, and so on. She had more sound argument on her side than could be found among those whose views were coloured by passionate fear of Catholicism. Even if one accepts that her cautious approach owed as much to her perpetual hesitancy and indecisiveness as to rational calculation – and a strong case can be made – it is difficult to see how a reasoned assessment of the circumstances of the 1570s dictated a policy of war with Spain.

More recent criticism of Elizabeth draws heavily on hindsight. She could not have foreseen the extraordinary series of events in the early 1580s, in Portugal, France and the Netherlands, the events that forced her to go to war. It might be added that the policy of every Tudor monarch would have been wrecked by the collapse of the great rivalry between France and Spain which had been for a century England's best protection. Elizabeth had to deal with a novel and highly dangerous situation. She did so by avoiding war as long as possible and then making war when it became a necessity. Many have done worse.

13 BIBLIOGRAPHY

J E A Dawson *William Cecil and the British Dimension of Early Elizabethan Foreign Policy, History*, 74, 241, (1989).
S Doran *England and Europe, 1485–1603* (Longman, 1986).
C Haigh (ed.) *The Reign of Elizabeth I* (Macmillan, 1984).

C Haigh *Elizabeth I* (Longman, 1988).

W T MacCaffrey *The Shaping of the Elizabethan Regime* (Cape, 1969).

W T MacCaffrey *Queen Elizabeth and the Making of Policy, 1572–1588* (Princeton, 1981).

R B Wernham *After the Armada: Elizabethan England and the Struggle for Western Europe, 1588–1595* (Clarendon, 1983).

R B Wernham *Before the Armada; The Growth of English Foreign Policy, 1485–1588* (Cape, 1966).

R B Wernham *The Making of Elizabethan Foreign Policy, 1558–1603* (University of California Press, 1980).

C Wilson *Queen Elizabeth and the Revolt of the Netherlands* (University of California Press, 1970).

14 DISCUSSION POINTS AND EXERCISES

A *This section consists of questions or points that might be used for discussion (or written answers) as a way of expanding on the chapter and testing understanding of it:*

1 Why was England in a vulnerable position in 1558–9?

2 Was England's intervention in Scotland in 1560 vindicated by its results?

3 In the early and mid-1560s how well did Elizabeth manage the relationship with: (*a*) France?
                                        (*b*) Scotland, after Mary, Queen of Scots' return?

4 Why did England's relations with Spain deteriorate so markedly during the first decade of Elizabeth's reign? Was the seizure of the Spanish bullion in 1568 as rash and foolish as Cecil's critics claimed?

5 Why was an alliance with France to restrict the power of Spain so problematic?

6 Were the 1570s a decade of lost opportunities in English foreign policy?

7 How did the balance of power change in favour of Spain in 1580–5?

8 How far should one regard the outbreak of war with Spain as a major failure in English foreign policy?

9 How was England able to hold its own against the superior might of Spain?

10 Did the results of the Spanish war vindicate Elizabeth's decision to fight?

B *Essay questions*

1 What were the main principles of Elizabeth's foreign policy?

2   To what extent did Elizabeth's foreign policy lack consistency and
    tend to lurch from one nervous expedient to the next?

3   How and why did Anglo-Spanish relations change between 1558
    and 1585?

4   To what extent did religion influence Elizabethan foreign policy?

5   How far and why did Elizabeth I abandon the foreign policy
    pursued by previous Tudors?

6   How did foreign affairs and domestic politics interact in the reign
    of Elizabeth?

15 DOCUMENTARY EXERCISES

Walsingham's analysis, October 1572

Walsingham to Sir Thomas Smith, 8 October 1572:

A.   ... If her Majesty stick now to spend or put in execution all
      those things that tend to her safety, she must not long look
      to live in repose, nay, she must not long look to keep the
      Crown upon her head. The cause of her former quietness
      proceeded of her neighbours' unquietness; which being   5
      removed, she must now make another account. The
      Admiral Coligny [the Huguenot leader] is now dead, and
      the Duke of Guise now liveth; the Prince of Orange is
      retired out of Flanders, but the Duke of Alva remaineth
      there still. I need not to conclude, for that to man's   10
      judgement it is apparent what will follow. Is it time now,
      think you, Sir, to stir, or is it not time to omit any remedy
      that may tend to her Majesty's safety? As far as I can learn,
      there is none yet sent to deal with the Princes of Germany,
      and yet there is here almost daily conference between the   15
      Pope's Nuncio, the Ambassador of Spain, and them here.
      They omit nothing that may tend to our peril. I would we
      were as careful not to omit any thing that may tend to our
      safety. It may be said that I fear too much. Surely,
      considering the state we stand in, I think it less danger to   20
      fear too much than too little. It may be said also that the
      jealousy that Spain has of the greatness of France, will not
      suffer him to endure to let France have any footing in
      England, and that like affection reigning in France, if Spain
      should attempt any thing. I confess it to be true, and yet I   25
      see no reason but that they both may consent to advance a
      third person, who pretendeth right to the Crown,
      especially being provoked thereto by the Pope, which is
      my chief fear.

It may also be alleged that the offer of the marriage 30
sheweth that they have no evil meaning towards her
Majesty. First, it may be doubted whether, considering
how nowadays their speech and meaning disagreeth, they
offer as they mean . . . I am now ready to think the same to
proceed of abuse, only to lull us asleep in security; for any 35
thing that I can perceive, the best way not to be deceived
by them is not to trust them . . .

Walsingham to the Regent of Scotland, 7 October 1572:

B. . . . Can we think that the fire kindled here in France will
extend itself no further? That which was concluded at the
late Council of Trent [a General Council of the Roman
Catholic Church which had finally condemned
Protestantism], as also that which was agreed on at Bayonne 5
[a meeting between the regent of France, Catherine de
Medici and the Duke of Alva], for the rooting out of the
professors of the Gospel, may in reason induce us to think
the contrary. Let us not deceive ourselves but assuredly
think that the two great monarchs of Europe together with 10
the rest of the Papists do mean shortly to put in execution
that which in the aforesaid assemblies was concluded. It is
seen that when two brothers are at discord, yet when a
stranger or a third person shall offer them any injury, nature
teacheth them to agree to withstand the stranger. 15

1 *Which 'third person' (line 27A) did many Protestants fear would be set on the English throne?*

2 *What did Walsingham mean by 'the offer of the marriage' (line 30A)?*

3 *Why did Walsingham fear that 'the two great monarchs of Europe' (line 10B) would forget their historic rivalry and unite against Elizabeth?*

4 *What did Walsingham mean by his discussion of the contrasting fortunes of leading men in France and the Netherlands, and what did he think 'will follow' (line 11A)?*

5 *Walsingham soon wanted to do more than 'deal with the Princes of Germany'. Briefly describe the foreign policy urged by English Puritans during the 1570s.*

6 *Why was Elizabeth so reluctant to intervene more vigorously to assist the Dutch Revolt?*

The debate on intervention in the Netherlands, October 1584

Extracts from the Calendar of State Papers, Foreign Series:

Sir Walter Mildmay's opinion:

Dangers if her Majesty do not aid the United Provinces.

The King of Spain will overrun those countries,
overthrowing their religion and ancient privileges and
subjecting them to his will.

Being settled there, he will be moved to pick quarrels with   5
this country by his nearness to it; the shipping which Holland
and Zeeland will yield him; his quietness in other parts; his
riches from the Indies, increased by the Low Countries.

Of all which will follow a dangerous war . . .

He will hope more easily to breed trouble here through the   10
ill-affected subjects when he is settled near them.

Her Majesty . . . may never have the like occasion to stop the
King's designs. Much better for her to keep him occupied
abroad than bear the war at home, when he shall be stirred up
by the Pope, Jesuits abroad, and Jesuits at home, and like   15
enough also by the Scots Queen and her son . . .
Dangers if her Majesty shall aid them.

. . . The enterprise. . . will draw on a war between him and
her Majesty, bringing with it great danger and inestimable
charges, the burden whereof she cannot bear herself, and   20
doubtful how her subjects will like to contribute to what most
will think an unnecessary war.

The offers he will make to the Scots Queen and her son to
trouble her Majesty, which is more perilous than any other war,
considering the readiness of their dispositions; and his stirring   25
up evil-disposed subjects to join with him.

His ability to maintain wars greater than the Queen's. Small
surety to find in the Low Countries a sufficient party, or
steadfastness in them . . . and if by the charge of the war she
should be driven to leave them, then is their danger greater, for   30
now they may make reasonable composition both for their
privileges and religion . . .

Burghley's Report on the Conference:

. . . The conclusion was:

That it was better for her Majesty to enter into a war now,   35
whilst she can do it outside her realm and have the help of the
people of Holland and their parties, and before the King of Spain
has consummated his conquests in those countries, whereby he
shall be so provoked with pride, and solicited by the Pope, and
tempted by the Queen's own subjects, and shall be so strong by   40
sea and so free from all other actions of quarrels, yea and shall
be so formidable to all the rest of Christendom, as that her
Majesty shall no wise be able with her own power nor with aid
of any other, neither by sea nor land, to withstand his attempts;
but shall be forced to give place to his unsatiable malice, which   45
is most terrible to be thought of, but most miserable to suffer.

1 *Why did Mildmay fear trouble from 'ill-affected subjects' (line 11)?*
2 *What made Elizabeth's ministers so suspicious of Philip's hostile 'designs' (line 13)?*
3 *In what ways do the above extracts suggest that intervention in the Netherlands was a very dangerous policy?*
4 *Which points in the source reveal why, nevertheless, the Council did opt for intervention?*

XII

THE FRONTIER REGIONS

—

1 INTRODUCTION – THE MEDIEVAL INHERITANCE

THE duties of a medieval king were essentially twofold: to preserve law and order within his realm, and to defend his subjects from external attack. By today's standards these may seem to be very modest requirements. But the English kings of the fifteenth century had no police force or standing army with which to fulfil these obligations. Their 'civil service' hardly exceeded 1500 men. The institutions of central government did little more than dispense justice inefficiently, and handle the Crown's finances. To make their rule effective in the country the kings had no choice but to work through those members of the aristocracy and gentry who volunteered their services as sheriffs and Justices of the Peace in the localities. This system worked reasonably well in lowland England, what G R Elton called the 'normal setting' of Tudor government. However, in the north of England, in the Principality and the Marches of Wales, and in the English colonies in Ireland and in France, there were special circumstances which created considerable difficulties for the kings of England.

The Calais Pale

After the loss of Normandy (1450) and Gascony (1453), the Calais Pale, a tract of land only 34 km long and 12 km wide, was the only territory on mainland Europe held by the English Crown. As such it was regarded as England's most important frontier. Since 1337 every English monarch claimed to be the true King of France. However audacious this pretension was, successive English kings were mesmerized by the possibility of winning glory and great fortune on a French battlefield. As long as they kept possession of Calais they continued to dream of using it as a base from which to conquer large tracts of French territory. It was not until 1803 that the English monarchy formally abandoned its claim to the sovereignty of France.

Despite the fact that it was a financial liability the kings of England were very much committed to their French colony. Edward IV (1461–83) spent much money in 1467 to strengthen the Pale's defences in preparation for a war in which he hoped to re-conquer Normandy and Gascony. Henry VII was less ambitious than Edward, yet in 1492 he attempted to extend the Calais bridgehead by capturing Boulogne. Henry VIII spent enormous sums on conquering and maintaining Tournai (1513–18) and Boulogne (1544–50). By comparison, little money was spent in extending English power in either Britain or Ireland. Indeed, it is apparent that, despite the predilections of particular ministers such as Cromwell, the kings and queens of England were much more anxious to acquire continental possessions than they were to consolidate their national territory.

Wales

The Welsh maintained their independence of the Anglo-Saxons throughout the early Middle Ages. However, by 1100 much of eastern and southern Wales was occupied by Norman barons. The English Crown granted these Marcher or Border lords a whole series of privileges so that they would defend England from the Welsh. The main concessions made to the Marcher lords were the right to build and garrison their own castles, to levy military service from their tenants and to create boroughs. Their lordships were made into liberties where the king's writ did not run. Indeed, they were completely free of the king's judicial system.

In 1403 a great Welsh lord named Owain Glyn Dŵr launched a tremendous revolt against English rule in Wales and succeeded in liberating most of the country. There can be no doubt but that his success owed much to a sense of grievance among the Welsh under foreign rule. The poets, especially, were conscious of their distinctive Welsh history and culture. However, the Welsh could not withstand the greater power of England for long and their revolt was eventually crushed. Nonetheless, throughout much of the fifteenth century the kings of England were wary of the Welsh in case they would rise again.

The Principality of Wales was regarded as the private estate of the Prince of Wales, who was normally the heir to the English throne. The prince managed this estate through his personal council. Throughout the later Middle Ages, the princes of Wales did not possess a residence in the Principality and few of them ever visited the area.

The Justices of the Principality were normally appointed from among the English Marcher lords, but their deputies were often Welshmen. Sheriffs in the Principality were almost invariably English, but the coroners and lesser officers were usually Welsh. While it is true the 'mere Welsh' (*meri Wallici*) suffered an inferior legal status in Wales compared with the English, it was possible to purchase letters of denizenship (naturalization) to acquire the same rights as an Englishman. Indeed, the Herberts and Tudors demonstrated that Welsh blood did not automatically disqualify one from promotion to a peerage – nor even from the Crown of England!

Despite the fears of Englishmen, the Principality of Wales remained subdued after Glyn Dŵr's defeat. The region was kept effectively under English control with the co-operation of some of the Welsh gentry. Several of the lordships in the neighbouring Welsh Marches, most notably Pembroke, were in the Crown's possession and were well ordered. However, Wales had an unenviable reputation for lawlessness. In part, at least, this was because there were few villages in the mountainous parts of Wales, and criminals could avoid capture by finding shelter in the wild and desolate terrain. On the other hand the multiplicity of legal jurisdictions among the independent Marcher lordships generated confusion and hindered the apprehension of felons who disturbed the peace of the Principality, and the bordering shires of western England. It seems that lawlessness, and not nationalist discontent, posed the greatest threat to English government in Wales in the age of the Tudors.

The north of England

Once Edward III's final attempt to subjugate Scotland ended in failure in 1341 he and his successors lost all interest in England's northern frontier. Instead they directed their ambitions against France and were content to delegate responsibility for defending the North to the local aristocracy. The Crown granted very extensive estates to the Earls of Northumberland and Westmorland to help them to keep the Scots at bay. By the fifteenth century these two magnates dominated England north of the Trent. Their personal councils and households were scarcely less elaborate than those of the king. Their extensive network of patronage, or 'affinity', bound the gentry throughout the North to their service.

To the landed power of these northern nobles the Crown added royal offices. Of these, the most important office was that of Warden of a March. There were three Marches: the West March encompassed much of Cumberland and Westmorland, the East and Middle Marches (which were always held by the same man) included almost all of Northumberland. The Warden was responsible for protecting his March from the Scots. He was, in effect, the military governor of a border zone. However, apart from the small garrisons in the royal castles in the March, he had no professional soldiers with which to repel an invasion. The defence of the realm was dependent on the Wardens drawing heavily on their private resources. Yet, while the powerful Percies and Nevilles ruled the North, England was safe from the Scots.

Like Wales there was much lawlessness in northern England. The region's many mountains and moors offered extensive areas of refuge for bandits and cattle-rustlers. The North was sparsely populated and local communities were unable to muster sufficient numbers to protect themselves from marauders. Furthermore, the men of the North, who constantly readied themselves to fight Scottish invaders, were easily provoked into violence. Blood feuds were common down to the seventeenth century. More mundane crimes seem to have been a fact of everyday life. In this environment of blood-letting and theft the people looked in vain to the Crown to curb the disorders, and to offer redress to the victims of crime.

The authority of the sheriffs and Justices of the Peace was greatly limited in the North by the existence of numerous liberties and franchises in which royal officials had little or no jurisdiction. The king's writ did not run at all in the County Palatine of Durham, nor in a number of smaller franchises held by the Archbishop of York and a number of northern monasteries. Apart from the notorious example of Tynedale and Redesdale, from which bands of thieves and thugs launched raids on unsuspecting people outside the honour, the secular liberties did not enjoy such complete freedom from the Crown's jurisdiction. Serious crimes committed in baronies and honours could be tried by the king's courts. However, the king's officials had no right to enter these liberties and they had to depend on the lord of the liberty to serve royal writs and execute the Crown's decrees. If, for any reason, the lord proved unhelpful there was nothing the king or his sheriff could do about it. Unfortunately, there were many lords who refused to hand over their relatives or retainers for trial and punishment.

The appointment of the northern earls as JPs for the North brought greater stability to the region, but certain problems persisted. The earls often broke the law themselves, and they were reluctant to prosecute their friends and supporters even for grievous crimes. More seriously, the fact that the Crown had virtually abandoned its responsibilities for governing the North to the local aristocracy meant that men there knew no prince other than a Percy or a Neville. The great magnates themselves were not always loyal and trustworthy subjects. They were extremely powerful and ambitious men. Throughout the Wars of the Roses the northern earls played key roles as king makers and king breakers. They were themselves part of the problem of the North.

Ireland

The claim of the kings of England to be lords of Ireland rested on the twin foundations of Pope Adrian IV's grant of the lordship in his bull *Laudabiliter* (1155), and the partial conquest of the country by Henry II and his successors. By 1300 the English Crown controlled two-thirds of Ireland, and most of the lowlands in the east and south of the country were effectively colonised. However, the English colony in Ireland was greatly weakened during the course of the fourteenth century by a massive Scots-Irish campaign in 1315–18, by the Black Death in 1348–9 and by persistent Irish attacks on the outlying colonial communities. As the Gaelic 're-conquest' progressed a great many English settlers abandoned the lands they occupied in Ireland, and returned to England. By 1460 two-thirds of Ireland was ruled by Irish lords.

The English lordship of Ireland was governed by a Lord-Lieutenant or Deputy. He was head of the civil administration, and a military commander with a garrison of 300–400 soldiers. He was supported in his tasks by an Irish council. The colonial administration at Dublin was a small-scale replica of its English counterpart. However, with a paltry annual income of £900 in the mid-fifteenth century the colonial administration governed effectively only in part of four counties around Dublin – the English Pale.

Beyond the Pale the English Crown delegated its responsibilities to a number of great Anglo-Irish magnates – the Fitzgeralds of Kildare and Desmond, and the Butlers of Ormond. These earls enjoyed almost complete autonomy from Dublin and they ruled their extensive territories with private armies. The earls, and the lesser gentry affiliated to them, continued to hold their estates by English feudal tenure. However, in the absence of a Crown legal system in their lordships, the magnates employed Irish judges. Beyond the Pale and the larger boroughs, Irish law had effectively displaced the English common law by the early fifteenth century.

One of the most insidious problems facing English government in late medieval Ireland was the process of 'Gaelicisation'. At first the peasantry, and later the gentry, in peripheral regions of the colony became culturally assimilated with their Irish neighbours. By 1460 English culture in Ireland was predominant only in the inner Pale, south Wexford and in the south of Ormond's country. Indeed, even in these areas the proportion of the population of Irish culture continued to increase into the sixteenth century. Worryingly for the Crown, cultural assimilation often preceded political alienation from England.

As early as 1297 the Crown attempted to legislate against cultural assimilation. The Statutes of Kilkenny (1366) are infamous as the most comprehensive code of laws designed to segregate the two communities in Ireland. The colonists were prohibited from marrying Irish people, and from adopting Irish customs, laws, language or dress. Even Irish sports were proscribed. Irish men were not to be advanced to positions of responsibility in government, nor could they be admitted to ecclesiastical benefices in the colony. Despite the fact that the great majority of the population of the colony were Irish, Irish men and women were denied any rights under English law. In the courts of the Pale, the Irish (*meri Hibernici*) had the legal status of serfs or bondmen. Those beyond the colony were officially designated 'the king's Irish enemies'.

The legal discrimination practised against the poorer Irish by the English courts was paralleled in the Principality of Wales by the inferior status accorded to the Welsh peasantry. However, the treatment of the native landowners in Ireland and Wales was very different. While the Welsh gentry were encouraged to participate in the government of the Principality, albeit in the lesser offices, Irish landholders were wholly excluded from the colonial administration. Indeed, the English rulers were committed to dispossessing the Irish nobility of their lands if they ever succeeded in subjugating the whole country. Under such circumstances there could be no question of the Irish gentry acquiescing in English rule as their Welsh counterparts had done.

Since the defeat of Rory O'Connor in 1171 Gaelic Ireland had no single ruler. Disputes between magnates were often resolved by battle. This source of division in Gaelic Ireland was compounded by the Irish system of succession – tanistry. This involved the succession to political power of the eldest and worthiest member of a ruling clan on the death of the lord. The succession could sometimes be contentious and lead to fratricidal war.

There was little political co-operation between the great Irish magnates. Consequently, they were no match for a large, well-equipped English army. When confronted by a sizeable English force the Irish lords sometimes found it expedient to submit for the time being – as Richard II discovered during his first, futile campaign in Ireland in 1394–5. More often the English armies searched in vain for an enemy to fight, but found themselves constantly ambushed by small, mobile bands making effective use of the local terrain. Once the English soldiers had gone the Irish lords were free to raid bordering settlements in the colony once more.

By 1460 the English colony in Ireland was in serious difficulty. Crown government was effective only in a small enclave around Dublin. With the recent English loss of Normandy and Gascony it seemed to many colonists in Ireland that English rule was about to collapse there also.

2 THE REVIVAL OF ROYAL GOVERNMENT

Although there is debate about his capabilities Edward IV (1461–83) was one of the more effective kings of late medieval England (*see pages 17–23*). In the regions he relied, at first, upon local noble families. In Wales Edward IV depended on William Herbert, whom he created Earl of Pembroke in 1469. The King entrusted the north of England to his then good friend Richard Neville, Earl of Warwick. However, after Warwick's rebellion caused Edward IV to briefly lose his crown, from September 1470 to March 1471, the King adopted a new approach to imposing royal control in peripheral regions. He established members of his immediate family in the North and Wales to act as foci of loyalty for the dynasty. From this expedient developed the provincial councils which proved to be of considerable importance for the revival of effective royal government in these regions under both the Yorkists and the Tudors, although at the cost of building up 'over-mighty' subjects in Edward's case.

The Council in the Principality and Marches of Wales.

In July 1471 Edward granted to his 9-month-old son the Principality of Wales, the Duchy of Cornwall and the County Palatine of Chester. A council was set up to manage these estates on behalf of the infant Prince. The Prince of Wales and his mother were sent to the Welsh border in the spring of 1473. Edward IV hoped that by their presence the Prince and his mother would generate greater loyalty towards the royal family in a troubled region.

The Council of the Prince of Wales was originally intended to do no more than administer the boy's possessions. However, when the House of Commons complained in 1473 that crimes were going unpunished in Herefordshire and Worcestershire, Edward IV directed the Prince's Council to address the situation and do anything that was required to improve the effectiveness of royal government in the two shires and later in adjoining counties.

Unfortunately, little evidence survives of the activities of the Council of the Prince of Wales during Edward IV's reign and there is debate about the King's intentions. On the other hand, the fact that Richard III intended to establish an identical body to help govern the north of England suggests that it had impressed him with its effectiveness. In any case it is probable that the Welsh Council ceased to exist when Edward, Prince of Wales, was lodged in the Tower by his uncle Richard III in 1483.

Though Henry VII's claim to the Crown was weak and he faced a number of challenges from the Yorkists, his position was reasonably secure in his native Wales. It was only after the council he established in the North had proved itself successful that he addressed the problems of his home region. As in the North, Henry VII adopted the practices of Edward IV. In 1493 Henry gave Arthur, Prince of Wales, possession of the Principality of Wales and a number of the Marcher lordships which had come into the Crown's hands. He established a Council for the Prince and made him responsible for overseeing the administration of justice in the Principality and Marches of Wales, and in the adjoining counties of Shropshire, Herefordshire, Worcestershire and Gloucestershire. Unfortunately, little is known of the work of the Welsh Council during Henry VII's reign.

Henry VIII was far more concerned with winning glory in France than he was in providing better government for his subjects. However, the King's demand for heavy taxation to finance his foreign adventures in 1523–5 exposed the weakness of royal government in the outlying regions. Wolsey attempted to address this problem by dispatching Princess Mary to Shropshire to head the Council in the Principality and Marches of Wales, and by sending the King's illegitimate son Henry Fitzroy to Yorkshire with a newly established Council of the North. Princess Mary's Council was presided over by John Veysey, Bishop of Exeter. It toured through Wales and the neighbouring English counties to oversee the administration of justice. However, under Veysey the Council was largely ineffective in tackling the disorders afflicting the Welsh borderlands.

The Council of the North

In 1471 Edward IV sent his brother Richard, Duke of Gloucester, to the North to take the place of the traitorous Earl of Warwick. Gloucester received half of Warwick's estates. Edward IV made Gloucester the greatest landowner, as well as the most important government official north of the Trent.

However, his authority did not extend over the county of Northumberland at this time. In 1470 Edward IV restored Henry Percy to the Earldom of Northumberland. Only when war broke out with Scotland, in 1482, did the Duke of Gloucester become Edward IV's sole Lieutenant in the North, with full authority over all royal officers north of the Trent.

Gloucester and Northumberland governed effectively in each of their separate spheres of influence. They successfully ended the disorders which had long been endemic in the North. As Justice of the Peace for the North (or High Commissioner as he became known) the Duke of Gloucester took an active interest in improving the quality of royal government in the North. He set himself against corrupt and feckless judges. He offered redress to all those who were denied justice in the royal courts. He agreed to arbitrate in legal disputes between local communities.

Having become Richard III, he made Henry Percy, Earl of Northumberland, the Warden-General in July 1484, giving him sole responsibility for the defence of the three Marches on the Scottish border. Richard III appointed his nephew John de la Pole, Earl of Lincoln, as the King's Lieutenant in the North and placed him at the head of the King's Council of the North which acted in effect as a court of justice.

Since its records have not survived it is not possible to assess the effectiveness of the Council of the North established by Richard III. With the usurpation of Henry Tudor to the throne of England in August 1485 the Council ceased to exist. Henry VII's first priority on becoming King was to secure his position in lowland England – the focus of the monarchy's strength. Only later did he consider the need for effective government in the outlying regions of his realm.

Henry VII appointed the Earl of Northumberland as Lieutenant in the North and Warden of the East and Middle Marches in January 1486. His was a military appointment. He was given no provincial council. He was directed simply to crush any sign of insurrection against the new regime. Henry VII was obviously wary of Yorkist dissension, but the risings which broke out in the North in 1487, 1489 and 1492 were motivated by economic rather than political grievances. The progress of enclosure impoverished a great many lesser folk and generated great resentment which broke out in armed rebellion. The Earl of Northumberland was killed by a revolting mob in 1489.

Northumberland's successor as Lieutenant was the Earl of Surrey. Surrey acted as Lieutenant-Warden of the East and Middle Marches for Henry's eldest son Prince Arthur, whom the King appointed as Warden-General. Lord Dacre of Gisland took charge of the West March. Henry VII established a council to assist the Earl of Surrey in governing Yorkshire. The council was clearly modelled on that devised by Richard III. Under Surrey and his successors the Council of the North became a Court of Requests, addressing the grievances of the poor folk being oppressed by the rich and powerful. As such the Council did much good work. However, the lords of the North were antagonised by its interference in their affairs. When Henry VII died in 1509 they successfully petitioned the new King for the dissolution of the Northern Council.

It was at Wolsey's instigation that the Council of the North was revived in 1525. The tax revolt of that year had exposed the weakness of royal control north of the Trent. Henry VIII, therefore, agreed to make his illegitimate son Henry Fitzroy, Duke of Richmond, the Lieutenant in the North and Warden-General of the Marches. Richmond was given a Council, whose members were chosen by Wolsey, and he was directed to supervise the government of all of the shires north of the Trent – save Durham. The Duke's Council made good progress in improving the government of Yorkshire, but its attempt to rule the border shires was an utter failure. By 1528 the East and Middle Marches were once more entrusted to the Earl of Northumberland, while Lord Dacre returned as Warden of the West March.

The Kildare ascendancy in Ireland

The reign of Edward IV marked the beginning of a revival of royal government in colonial Ireland, as in Wales and the north of England. Edward's accession in 1461 was widely welcomed in the colony. The Earls of Desmond and Kildare were enthusiastic Yorkists. The Earl of Ormond had been killed at Towton fighting for the Lancastrians.

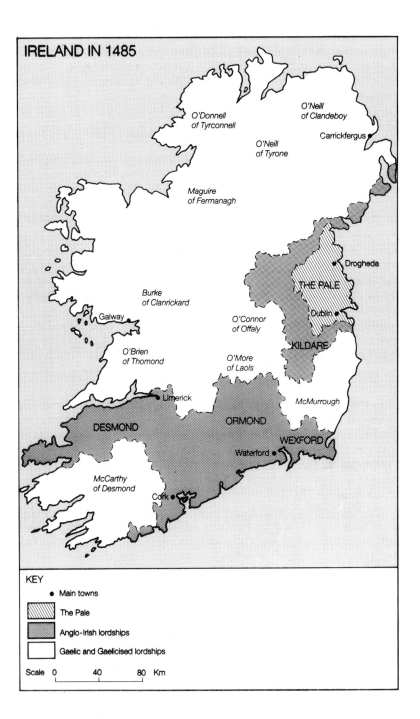

IRELAND IN 1485

O'Donnell
of Tyrconnell

O'Neill
of Clandeboy

Carrickfergus

O'Neill
of Tyrone

Maguire
of Fermanagh

Drogheda

THE PALE

Burke
of Clanrickard

Galway

O'Connor
of Offaly

Dublin

KILDARE

O'Brien
of Thomond

O'More
of Laois

McMurrough

Limerick

ORMOND

DESMOND

WEXFORD

Waterford

McCarthy
of Desmond

Cork

KEY

● Main towns

The Pale

Anglo-Irish lordships

Gaelic and Gaelicised lordships

Scale 0   40   80 Km

343

Edward IV appointed Thomas Fitzgerald, seventh Earl of Desmond, as Deputy in Ireland in the spring of 1463, in recognition of his success in crushing a Lancastrian uprising led by the Butlers of Ormond. The Earl of Desmond dominated much of south-western Ireland, but his appointment was remarkable in that he had previously taken little interest in the affairs of the colonial administration. Nonetheless, Desmond governed the colony effectively even if the expedients he resorted to finance the defence of the Pale were unpopular in some quarters.

In 1467, Edward IV felt secure enough in England to assert direct control over the colonial administration in Ireland. He sent one of his most trusted servants, John Tiptoft, Earl of Worcester, to the colony as his Deputy in place of Desmond. Tiptoft was appalled at the extent of Gaelicisation within the colony, and by the degree of independence enjoyed by the colony's 'over-mighty subjects'. In February 1468, Tiptoft had the Earls of Desmond and Kildare arrested on a charge of treason. The official reason given was that the two had breached the Statutes of Kilkenny (1366) by inter-marrying with the Irish, and by forming political alliances with them. Desmond, the most gaelicised magnate, was summarily beheaded. Kildare was fortunate enough to escape from custody. Kildare joined with Desmond's family and their Irish allies to attack the Pale in retaliation for the judicial murder. Tiptoft was unable to cope with the chaos he caused before he returned to England to support Edward IV against the Lancastrian uprising in 1470.

Tiptoft's appointment as Deputy clearly proved to be disastrous. He proved incapable of performing the primary duty of the King's governor in Ireland – that of protecting the Pale from Irish attacks – even with a garrison of 700 men. He had irrevocably alienated the Fitzgeralds of Desmond from the English Crown, and thereby lost almost all of south-western Ireland to English influence. For Edward IV the lesson of Tiptoft's deputyship was clear: he could either entrust colonial Ireland to a local magnate, or pay a very high price trying to govern the colony directly. With the Butlers of Ormond attainted, and the Fitzgeralds of Desmond alienated, Edward IV had little choice but to appoint the one remaining magnate Thomas Fitzgerald, seventh Earl of Kildare, as the Deputy-Lieutenant of Ireland from May 1471 and, after further attempts at direct control between 1475 and 1479, the King was forced to appoint Garret Mór Fitzgerald, the next Earl of Kildare, as Deputy-Lieutenant.

Garret Mór was a remarkable individual. He was clever, ambitious and forceful. He ably exploited his position as the greatest magnate in the Pale, and his near monopoly of the deputyship, to build up tremendous power and influence within the colony, and far beyond it. It was Garret Mór who gave his family an unrivalled ascendancy within Ireland. Kildare also set about conquering borderlands from the Irish.

By 1483 he had expelled Irish lords from the south and west of County Kildare and from the north of County Carlow.

Steven Ellis, in his book *Reform and Revival: English government in Ireland, 1470–1534*, observed that Irish historians have long failed to recognise that the territorial expansion of the Earls of Kildare also involved the expansion of English power in Ireland. The eighth Earl of Kildare has been portrayed as some kind of 'separatist' governing the colony in the best interests of Ireland, rather than England. Dr Ellis argues that such portrayals are grossly anachronistic. In fact, there was no necessary conflict between a magnate's aspirations and the Crown's interests while the magnate was loyal to the monarch. The seventh and eighth Earls of Kildare were both faithful to the House of York.

The accession of the Lancastrian, Henry Tudor, to the throne of England in August 1485 placed the Earl of Kildare in a new and unenviable situation. Fitzgerald, and the colonial administration at Dublin, remained Yorkist in sympathy. They were slow to recognise the change of dynasty. Fortunately, Henry VII was not in a position to intervene in Ireland while his hold on the English Crown was still unsure. He left Kildare in charge of the colony.

Early in 1487 a young boy, Lambert Simnel, set up to be Edward, Earl of Warwick, arrived in Ireland (*see page 35*). He was crowned in Dublin but despite this provocation Henry VII decided to be lenient with Kildare in the hope of avoiding a military commitment in Ireland. He chose to maintain the Deputy in office and issue a general pardon to the colonial élites – on condition that they entered into bonds whereby they would forfeit large sums of money if they ever again broke their oaths to the King. Yet Kildare and his allies refused to accept even this condition, and Henry VII's emissary was obliged to issue the pardons in return for nothing more than simple oaths of allegiance.

In November 1491 Perkin Warbeck arrived in Cork claiming to Edward IV's second son Richard (*see page 36*). The Earl of Kildare took care not to get involved, but he did not exert himself to deal with this latest attempt on Henry VII's crown. The King himself took no chances. He sent a small army to Ireland and, when Warbeck lost heart and left for France, Henry VII dismissed Kildare from office. The King chose two local notables to govern the colony but, without Kildare's co-operation, they encountered insurmountable difficulties. When news reached Henry VII that Warbeck was to return to Ireland, the King sent Sir Edward Poynings to the colony as Governor with a small army in September 1494.

Poynings proved to be an effective governor. He protected the Pale by making peace with the Irish. After an obscure incident in south Ulster, he arrested Kildare on a charge of treason and sent him to England. He crushed the ensuing rebellion by Kildare's brother James and he saw off Warbeck and his forces. Of even greater significance, perhaps, was the Parliament over which Poynings presided at Drogheda. The Parliament of 1494–5 passed an important statute, subsequently known as 'Poynings' Law', which precluded the holding of any Parliament in Ireland without the prior consent of the King, and which prevented the Parliament from considering any bill which had not received the King's sanction. Another statute abolished Ireland's legislative independence from England. An Act of Resumption was passed to recover some of the Crown lands which had been alienated during the turbulent course of the fifteenth century. Parliament also granted a new annual subsidy, and a new customs levy to help finance the colonial government.

By the time Poynings was re-called, in December 1495, he had greatly strengthened the Crown's control over the colony's administration and institutions. He had transformed the financial basis of the colonial government. Furthermore, the threat from Yorkist pretenders was effectively ended: when Warbeck returned to Ireland in 1499 he was universally spurned.

Henry VII re-appointed Kildare as Deputy in Ireland in August 1496. The King is reputed to have said that 'If all of Ireland cannot rule this man, then he is meet [suitable] to govern all of Ireland!' The Earl's son and heir was detained at Court as a guarantee of his good conduct. Kildare repaid the King's trust by working energetically to revive English government in Ireland. In fact, Kildare gave Henry VII what no one else could – an efficient administration in Ireland which was entirely self-financing. When Henry VII died in 1509 the English Crown no longer had an 'Irish problem'.

Garret Óg Fitzgerald became the ninth Earl of Kildare in 1513. He enjoyed enormous power and prestige as his father had done. After the crippling expense, and patent futility, of his adventures in France, Henry VIII looked to Ireland for some tangible success. He decided to cut Kildare down to size by stripping him of his office of state, and in his place appointed Thomas Howard, Earl of Surrey, as Lieutenant of Ireland in May 1520. Surrey was instructed to consider how all of Ireland might be brought under English rule. In a famous phrase, Henry VIII indicated that he believed that this could best be achieved 'by sober ways, politic drifts and amiable persuasions founded in law and reason': that is, by diplomacy. Surrey, however, disagreed. From his experience of the country he felt that Ireland could only be brought under English rule by conquest. This would take many years and prove enormously expensive. As it was, Surrey's garrison of 550 men cost the Crown £10 000 a year simply to defend the colony from attacks. The logic of the situation was unanswerable and Surrey was re-called.

Despite Surrey's failure Henry VIII and Wolsey were anxious to demonstrate that they could govern the colony without Kildare. Over the next ten years there were eight changes of Governor as the Crown vacillated between accepting the efficient and economical government of Kildare, and expensively demonstrating that the Earl was dispensable. The cumulative effect of the Crown's inconstancy was to weaken the colonial administration and destabilise relations with the Irish lords.

3 CROMWELL AND THE UNITARY STATE

G R Elton has argued that Thomas Cromwell achieved a 'revolution' in the administration of England, implementing many important reforms designed to transform the Tudor domains into a unitary commonwealth. Other historians dispute the extent to which Cromwell's changes may legitimately be termed revolutionary (*see pages 128–9*). Nonetheless, Cromwell certainly wished to ensure that the King's government functioned uniformly and effectively in every part of the realm. Through the Act for Resuming Certain Liberties to the Crown (1536) he destroyed the privileges of those areas where the King's writ had not run or was greatly circumscribed. The Lords of Liberties and Franchises were deprived of their jurisdiction in criminal causes. From 1536 only the Crown could appoint judges and justices in any part of England and Wales. It remained only to impose the King's laws to equal effect throughout his domains.

Cromwell's initial efforts to improve the effectiveness of the King's government in the outlying regions were strikingly conservative; in effect he did little more than change the personnel in charge. However, the schism from Rome created widespread disaffection and resistance, which was particularly open where the Crown's authority was at its weakest. In Ireland in 1534–5, and in the north of England in 1536–7, Catholic hostility to religious innovation was demonstrated in armed rebellion. Fear of rebellion was not Cromwell's sole motivation in strengthening royal authority in the periphery – but it highlighted the need for more radical approaches to these areas than the minister may previously have considered.

The Calais Pale

The Henrician schism exposed England to the possibility of attack by the Catholic rulers of France and the Holy Roman Empire. Calais became the country's first line of defence. It had to be well governed and well guarded. Unhappily, the Deputy of Calais, Arthur Plantagenet, Lord Lisle, was pathetically incompetent. In August 1535 Cromwell sent a royal commission to Calais to investigate its problems and to offer remedies.

The Calais Act (1536) entrusted the government of Calais and its Pale to an executive council comprised of eleven members, headed by

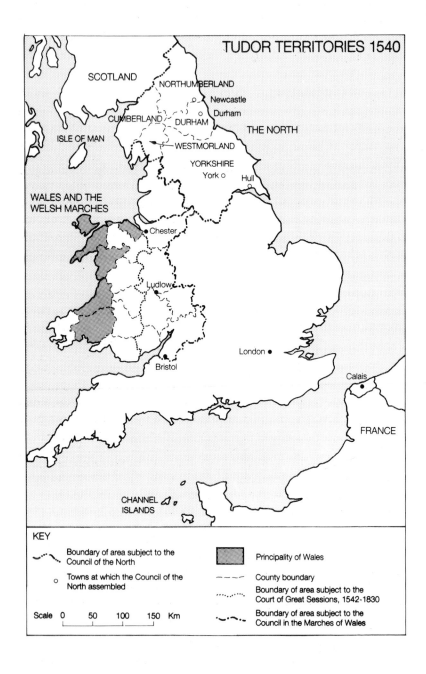

TUDOR TERRITORIES 1540

SCOTLAND

NORTHUMBERLAND

CUMBERLAND

Newcastle

Durham

DURHAM

ISLE OF MAN

THE NORTH

WESTMORLAND

YORKSHIRE

York ○

Hull

WALES AND THE
WELSH MARCHES

Chester ●

Ludlow ●

London ●

Bristol ●

Calais ●

FRANCE

CHANNEL
ISLANDS

KEY

- Boundary of area subject to the
  Council of the North

○ Towns at which the Council of the
  North assembled

Scale 0   50   100   150 Km

Principality of Wales

County boundary

Boundary of area subject to the
Court of Great Sessions, 1542-1830

Boundary of area subject to the
Council in the Marches of Wales

the Deputy. Most strikingly, Calais was granted the privilege of sending two MPs to the House of Commons to represent its interests. It is remarkable that Calais was represented in the English Parliament: in effect the territory was incorporated into the kingdom of England. This strongly suggests that Cromwell had no time for his master's delusions about winning possession of French provinces, if not the crown of France itself!

From 1532 the English Crown spent large sums of money on Calais' defence and Henry VIII extended the Pale by capturing Boulogne in 1544. But, when that town was liberated by the French in 1550, England was left with nothing to show for the £3.5 million she had spent on Henry's war with France. And when in 1557 England joined Spain in invading France, the French King, Henry II, decided to take his revenge by capturing Calais. On 1 January 1558 a large French army penetrated the outer defences of the Calais Pale. The French assault was audacious and caught the English garrison completely off-guard. Within eight days England lost Calais, her last possession on mainland Europe.

Wales

Under Bishop Veysey of Exeter, the Welsh borderlands continued to be disordered and relatively lawless. In 1534 Cromwell appointed Rowland Lee, Bishop of Coventry and Lichfield, to take Veysey's place as President of the Welsh Council. Lee was a very determined man of great physical energy but with limited intellectual powers. His ferocity in governing Wales was to be remembered for decades after his death.

The main problem besetting Wales and the adjoining English shires was the prevalence of homicide and theft. Lee's solution was simple and direct:; murderers and thieves were hanged whenever possible. Indeed, the bishop seemed obsessed with hunting down and hanging felons. He boasted of having hanged 5000 men in his first six years in Wales. In Lee's view one could only govern the Welsh through fear.

More importantly in 1536 Cromwell initiated a revolution in the government of Wales. It seems likely that Cromwell was influenced by Sir Thomas Englefield, a member of the Council in Wales, into establishing a uniform system of government in Wales as in England. In a statute of 1536 Justices of the Peace were established in the counties of the Principality of Wales, and in the Crown lordships of Pembroke and Glamorgan, with the same powers as their English counterparts. More importantly, the English Parliament in 1536 enacted the 'Act for Laws and Justice to be ministered in Wales in like form as it is in this realm':

> Albeit the dominion, principality and country of Wales justly
> and rightly is, and ever has been, incorporated, annexed, united
> and subject to and under the imperial crown of this realm [of

England], as a very member and joint [part] of the same, whereof the King's most royal majesty . . . is truly head, King, lord and ruler; yet notwithstanding, because in the same country, principality and dominion diverse rights, usages, laws and customs be far discrepant from the laws and customs of this realm, and also because the people of that same dominion have and daily use a speech nothing like, nor consonant to, the natural mother tongue used within this realm, some rude and ignorant people have made (a) distinction . . . between the King's subjects of this realm, and his subjects of the said dominion and principality of Wales, whereby great discord, variance, debate, division, murmur and sedition have grown between his said subjects. His highness, therefore, of a singular zeal, love and favour that he bears towards his subjects of his said dominion of Wales, minding and intending to reduce them to the perfect offer, notice and knowledge of his laws of this his realm (of England), and utterly to extirpate, all and singular, the sinister usages and customs differing from the same . . .

That his said country or dominion of Wales shall . . . continue forever from henceforth incorporated, united and annexed to and with this his realm of England; and that all and singular person or persons born, or to be born, in the said principality, country or dominion of Wales, shall have, enjoy and inherit all and singular freedoms, liberties, rights, privileges and laws within this his realm . . . as other the king's subjects, naturally born within the same, have, enjoy and inherit.

1   *What reasons does Cromwell give for passing this so-called Act of Union?*
2   *Judging from these extracts what advantages and what disadvantages would this Act bring to the people of Wales?*

By this Act the Welsh shires were each given the right to elect one MP to the English House of Commons, while the boroughs of each shire could vote collectively to elect a second MP.

A second statute in 1543 defined the union of Wales with England in much greater detail. The Welsh Marches were merged into hundreds and shires after the English fashion. The new shires of Denbigh, Montgomery, Radnor, Brecknock and Monmouth were created. Each of the new shires was entrusted to a sheriff and JPs as in England. However, the whole of Wales, excluding Monmouth which was transferred to England for administrative purposes, remained outside Westminster's system of court sessions. This separate system of justice in Wales lasted until 1830.

The Council in the Principality and Marches of Wales was re-organised as a permanent bureaucratic institution to direct and supervise the government of Wales and the adjacent English shires of

Cheshire, Shropshire, Herefordshire, Worcestershire, Gloucestershire and Monmouthshire. Through the Council all royal proclamations were made and orders transmitted to local government officers in the region – in Welsh translations whenever necessary. The Council continued to act as a judicial court, though the destruction of the privileges of the liberties and franchises made the task of law enforcement in the region much easier than in the past.

Certainly the reformed Council in Wales made a significant contribution towards the effective enforcement of English law in the region. No less important, one suspects, were the two so-called Acts of Union which allowed the Welsh landowners and burgesses to participate in local and national politics to a degree never previously possible. One indication of the success of these developments is the fact that despite the religious and economic upheavals which led to rebellions elsewhere in the Tudor domains, Wales remained peaceful into the seventeenth century.

The north of England

To tackle the disturbed and disordered state of the north of England Henry Percy, Earl of Northumberland, was appointed Lieutenant in place of Richmond in 1533. As with Kildare in Ireland, Henry VIII resented his dependence on the 'over-mighty' magnate, but he was not prepared to spend the money needed to govern the region directly from Westminster. However, Henry Percy was childless and heavily in debt. At Cromwell's suggestion Percy's debts were acquired by the Crown and used as a lever to force the Earl to bequeath his estates to the Crown in his will. An Act of Parliament confirmed this transaction in 1536. Cromwell planned to exploit the Percy estates to strengthen the Crown's position in the North.

However, the destruction of the Earldom of Northumberland alienated the wide-flung Percy affinity and caused many northerners to resort to rebellion to redress this major grievance. At the same time, the Crown's religious policies, most especially the suppression of the monasteries, were deeply unpopular in the North. Opposition to these two developments coalesced in the uprising known as the Pilgrimage of Grace. This uprising made it necessary to move more quickly than originally intended to reform the government of the North.

In autumn 1537, after the Pilgrimage was over, Cuthbert Tunstall, Bishop of Durham, was made Lord President of the Council of the North. This appointment was important because, henceforth, the North was no longer governed by a great magnate assisted by a council, but by a permanent bureaucratic council. The Council of the North was made the supreme executive authority for the shires north of the Trent – excepting the Duchy of Lancaster. With the Percy estates in the Crown's possession, and the suppression of the independent liberties and franchises (saving only the County Palatine of Durham which retained some minor privileges) there were no outstanding obstacles to the operation of royal government throughout the region. The Council of the North was the sole agent through which all royal proclamations were made, all royal orders were transmitted to sheriffs and justices, and all demands for collecting subsidies were issued. More important-ly, the Council was responsible for supervising the local government officers – in Church and State. After the Pilgrimage of Grace the Crown depended on the Council of the North to enforce its religious policies as much as its political policies.

The records of the Council of the North reveal that it was very active in chastising sheriffs and justices who failed to perform their duties as well as required. It ensured that the northern bishops implemented the Crown's religious policies within their dioceses. At its general sessions the Council sought to administer speedy and impartial justice to rich and poor folk alike. By addressing such issues as enclosures, food sup-plies, and the maintenance of private armies the Council was able to ameliorate many of the grievances of the common people. Dr Rachel Reid, in her definitive study *The King's Council in the North*, concluded that the re-constituted Council was singularly successful. The north of England was well and thoroughly governed by the Crown through the Council. The problem of the North, she declared, had been solved at last, although it was not to be without its disturbances (*see pages 494–8 on the rising of the Northern Earls*).

Ireland

As was the case in Wales and the north of England, Cromwell's initial strategy to strengthen the King's government in Ireland was conserva-tive. In effect he simply continued Cardinal Wolsey's policy in attempt-ing to avoid delegating the government to a local magnate, in favour of a bureaucratic regime controlled more firmly from Westminster.

As Wolsey had done before him, Cromwell decided to detain Garret Óg Fitzgerald, ninth Earl of Kildare, in England and appoint an Englishman as Deputy of Ireland in his place. When Kildare was sum-moned to England he insisted on some guarantee. He had already been detained in England from 1519 to 1523 and from 1526 to 1530, and was understandably reluctant to lose his freedom once again. In February 1534 Kildare was allowed to appoint his son Thomas, Lord Offaly, as his Deputy while he visited England. Nonetheless, once Kildare arrived at Court in May 1534 he was detained again.

Cromwell's choice of governor to replace Kildare was remarkable: Sir William Skeffington was a relative nonentity, a soldier who had tried to govern Ireland briefly in 1530–2 and failed. Skeffington was given command of a paltry army of 150 men, and supplied with copies of a pamphlet entitled 'Ordinances for the government of Ireland'. The

Ordinances comprised a modest programme of reform which advocated traditional remedies to longstanding problems. It is difficult to see how Cromwell's strategy could have achieved any progress.

On learning of his father's fate, Lord Offaly ostentatiously resigned as Vice-Deputy on 11 June 1534, and denounced the King's policies before the Council of Ireland. Perhaps the young man intended only to put pressure on the King to secure the Earl's freedom. Henry VIII, however, refused to be blackmailed. Kildare was lodged in the Tower. Offaly then launched a full-scale rebellion, claiming to lead a Catholic crusade against the heretical King.

The rebellion was spectacularly successful. The Kildare affinity was very extensive, and the appeal against English mis-government and religious innovation was very popular. The clergy were widely involved in mobilising support against the heretical King and his minions. However, contacts with Catholic dissidents in Wales and the north of England did not result in uprisings there. The Emperor and Pope gave the rebels their praise and prayers but failed to provide any military support.

In mid-October 1534, Skeffington landed near Dublin with 2300 soldiers, the largest army seen in Ireland since 1399. The Pale gentry abandoned the rebellion in the face of such an overwhelming force. Offaly (the Earl of Kildare since his father's death the previous autumn) surrendered on 24 August 1535 on being promised that his life would be spared. The young Earl was, in fact, executed along with his five uncles in the aftermath of the Pilgrimage of Grace. Kildare's son, Gerald, was most fortunate in that a league of Irish nobles spirited him to safety on the continent. The rebellion cost £23 000 to suppress and left the colonial administration in disarray. Cromwell was forced to recognise the need for more thorough-going changes than he had previously envisaged.

On 1 January 1536 Lord Leonard Grey was sent to Ireland to govern the colony. Subsequently four commissioners were sent to Ireland to investigate the problems facing the colonial administration. From the commissioners' recommendations Cromwell devised a new policy for the colony. The Dublin administration was to extend its government to the full extent of the colony. The Statutes of Kilkenny were to be revived within that area. However, the Irish lordships beyond the colony were not to be interfered with. The colony's frontier was to be fortified, but peace was to be negotiated with the bordering Irish lords wherever possible. The English army in Ireland was to stand at 340 men; 140 men on garrison duty, with another 200 ready for active service on the border. But also Henry VIII was determined that the Dublin administration be self-financing, which was simply impossible if it were to achieve the new goals Cromwell set for it.

In practice, there was little real change. Deputy Grey, in any case was a soldier, and not a caretaker. He tried to win glory for himself through an aggressive policy towards the Irish lords beyond the colony. He succeeded only in forcing the Irish lords to join a league, which was in effect a national alliance of Irish lords hostile to Dublin's militarist policies, and the promotion of Protestantism in Ireland. The league launched a large-scale assault on the Pale, but was repulsed. England sent large numbers of reinforcements to Ireland to deal with the threat. With no hope of mustering sufficient resources to defeat the English by themselves the league approached the King of Scotland in the spring of 1540 and offered him the sovereignty of Ireland. Nothing actually came of that venture, but it was clear that Grey's government was seriously endangering the English colony in Ireland. In April 1540, Grey was dismissed from office. He left behind him an impoverished administration in Dublin, a country in turmoil and a longing for the peaceful and prosperous days of the Kildare ascendancy.

4 THE IRISH CONSTITUTIONAL REVOLUTION

In June 1541 Ireland's constitutional status was changed from that of a feudal lordship, subject to the English Crown, into what seemed to be a sovereign kingdom. Historians had long assumed that Henry VIII was responsible for this initiative, and that it was no more than a cosmetic exercise. However, Brendan Bradshaw, in his book entitled *The Irish Constitutional Revolution in the Sixteenth Century* (1979), revealed that Henry received the title of King of Ireland with great misgivings. In fact, it was forced upon him by his Lord Deputy in Ireland as part of a wider, revolutionary strategy designed to peacefully unite the Irish people and the colonists in Ireland under English rule.

The constitutional 'revolution' was the brainchild of Sir Thomas Cusack, a minor official in the Dublin administration. Cusack had been deeply influenced by humanism during his legal studies at the Inner Temple in London, and returned to Ireland with a sense of mission. He wanted to see the government of Ireland reformed so that the native Irish and the colonists could live harmoniously together within a common political framework. Amazingly, he believed that this could best be achieved through peaceful means. Cusack's dream might never have had a chance of becoming a reality but for the support he won from Sir Anthony St Leger, whom Henry VIII appointed as his Lord Deputy in Ireland in July 1540.

The constitutional revolution got underway with the sitting of the Anglo-Irish Parliament on 13 June 1541. The Parliament declared that Ireland was, in fact, a kingdom, and Henry VIII was its King. The preamble to the Act for the kingly title (1541) stated that the 'lack of naming the King's majesty and his most noble progenitors as kings of Ireland . . . hath been great occasion [i.e. cause] that the Irishmen and inhabitants within this realm of Ireland have not been so obedient to the King's highness and his most noble progenitors, and to their laws, as they of right and according to their allegiance and bounden duties ought to have been'. St Leger and the Irish council hoped that by making Henry King, and not simply Lord of Ireland, the Irish might be encouraged to accept and obey him as their true sovereign. But the Act had far deeper implications. It abolished the constitutional and juridical division of Ireland between the English colony on the one hand, and the independent Gaelic lordships on the other. It made all of the Irish into subjects of Henry VIII, with the same rights and privileges as the King's English subjects. Henry was now honour bound to dispense justice and good government throughout his new kingdom.

The Irish Parliament of 1541–3 was historic in that an Irish nobleman attended the House of Lords for the first time ever. He was MacGilpatrick, who was made Baron of Upper Ossory only two days before the Parliament was convened. St Leger invited many other Irish lords to attend the Parliament as observers. The presence of these Irish nobles in the Parliament was a revolutionary innovation. It signified that in the future the Irish Parliament would become the representative assembly of all the people in Ireland – Gaelic Irish and colonists alike. By involving the two communities in the government in this way St Leger and Cusack hoped to break down the barriers between them.

With the constitutional framework in place, St Leger set about solving the most difficult issue dividing the Irish lords from the English Crown – the question of land tenure. It was clear that as long as the kings of England claimed ownership of the lands held by the Gaelic and Gaelicised lords there would never be peace in Ireland. To address this problem Cusack and St Leger devised the policy known to historians as 'surrender and regrant'. In essence, this involved the Irish lords surrendering their territories to the Crown, in return for letters patent by which the King regranted them their lands with a title valid under English law. This formula was designed to regularise the relationship between the Crown and the greatest Irish lords. It also began the process by which the independent Irish lordships were transformed, more or less as they stood, into feudal lordships held of the Crown of Ireland.

As part of the surrender and regrant process each Irish lord had to agree to abandon his Gaelic title and accept instead an English title of nobility, such as earl or baron. He agreed to assist and obey the King's officers, do military service for the Crown and pay taxes. Furthermore, the lord was obliged to learn to speak English and adopt English clothes and customs, and reject the Pope's authority.

St Leger realised that his revolution could not be achieved overnight. He worked to bring about change gradually and peacefully. The first breakthrough came in January 1541 when James Fitzgerald, eleventh Earl of Desmond, was formally reconciled to the English crown. Desmond was a great magnate whose family became estranged from the Crown since the murder of the sixth Earl by the government in 1468. Through St Leger's persuasion the eleventh Earl submitted to Henry VIII, and brought his many underlords with him. As Cusack observed, 'the winning of the Earl of Desmond was the winning of the rest of Munster at small charge'.

Progress with the Gaelic lords was necessarily more difficult and slow. The surrender and regrant process took time. Yet in September 1542 Conn O'Neill, Lord of Tyrone and descendent of the ancient Kings of Ireland, travelled to the English Court to become the first Earl of Tyrone. On 1 July 1543 Murrough O'Brien, Prince of Thomond, travelled to Court to become the first Earl of Thomond. With him went Ulick MacWilliam Burke, a magnate from south Connacht, who became the first Earl of Clanrickard.

The Cusack-St Leger initiative was making remarkable progress towards a peaceful settlement of the political divisions in Ireland when it was suddenly suspended. In July 1543 Henry embarked on a futile war with France and Scotland. The constitutional revolution never recovered from the suspension. Soon after the King's death, St Leger was replaced as Lord Deputy in Ireland by Sir Edward Bellingham, a soldier. Bellingham abandoned the experiment with gentle persuasion in favour of brute force.

Since the publication of Professor Bradshaw's book historians have debated about the extent to which the Cusack-St Leger initiative constituted a revolution. No one denies that the programme was very ambitious. If it had succeeded the independent Irish lords would have become the King's vassals and loyal peers. The political disorder in Ireland would have been brought to an end, and the new kingdom could have become an asset to the English Crown, rather than the financial liability it was destined to be. However, so little was achieved before it was suspended that the programme seems more revolutionary in its implications than in its implementation. The Dublin administration, for instance, was neither reformed nor expanded to deal with its greatly increased responsibilities. The Irish were not granted political and legal rights equal to those of the colonists. The King of Ireland was a legal fiction. The change in Ireland's constitutional status led to no recognisable improvement in the disposition of Henry VIII towards his Irish colony.

Nonetheless, the Cusack-St Leger initiative remains one of the most significant developments in sixteenth-century Irish history. Because of it, most of the Irish lords acknowledged the sovereignty of Henry VIII as King of Ireland and committed themselves to the 'surrender and regrant' process. In the case of those lords whose status had been regularised by July 1543, the extension of royal authority was very real. The Earls of Clanrickard and Thomond were especially noteworthy for their co-operation with the Crown during the remaining decades of the sixteenth century.

The remarkable progress achieved by St Leger in the first three years of his deputyship shows clearly that the subsequent resort to conquest and colonisation was unnecessary. The Tudor wars in Ireland were appallingly costly in terms of Irish lives, and English money. Bradshaw is certainly correct in seeing the aborting of the revolutionary initiative in July 1543 as a terrible tragedy whose consequences affect us still.

5 THE YEARS OF CONFUSION IN IRELAND 1547–64

St Leger's constitutional experiment reflected his sophisticated understanding of the social and political realities in Ireland. However, the English government did not apprehend these realities, and sought simple solutions to complex problems. From 1547 English policy towards Ireland became increasingly aggressive. Attempts were made to forcibly extend English power there by military action. Yet, for all the blood shed, Crown policy lacked purpose and direction. During Edward's short reign alone there were no less than six changes of governor in Ireland! The Irish lords were confronted by a colonial regime which behaved violently and erratically. The years of promise during St Leger's first term of office in Ireland were succeeded by years of turmoil and confusion.

Sir Thomas Radcliffe, Lord Fitzwalter, was an inexperienced young man who was not particularly intelligent. He became Deputy of Ireland in 1556 because he was related to the Queen and came from an important family, he succeeded his father as Earl of Sussex in 1557. He was a soldier at heart, not a politician, and his approach to governing Ireland was both ill-conceived and ham-fisted.

The new governor was directed to make English justice more widely available in Ireland, promote a plantation in Laois and Offaly, and expel the Scots from Antrim. Once in Ireland, however, he soon launched a number of military expeditions, destroying large quantities of grain and livestock in the hope of starving the Irish, as well as the Scots in Ireland, into submission. When a group of Anglo-Irish councillors remonstrated with Queen Mary, telling her that Sussex's manoeuvres were counter-productive as well as costly, he purged the Dublin administration of colonial office-holders and promoted Englishmen in their places.

In September 1560, Sussex presented a programme of reform to Queen Elizabeth. It is an incredible document from a man who had spent four years governing Ireland. It reveals a degree of ignorance about Irish politics which is simply staggering. In essence he believed that almost all of Ireland – Irish and colonial – was divided into two factions: the 'good guys' led by the Earl of Ormond, and the 'bad guys' led by the Earl of Kildare. He argued that if Kildare were taken to

England and given lands there in place of his estates in Ireland then the whole country would be content to enjoy English rule! Needless to say this proposal was not acted upon.

Sussex was discredited by his failure against Séan O'Neill, Lord of Tyrone, whom he was trying to bring to justice as a murderer and usurper. His enemies at Court questioned the Deputy's competence. In spite of massive subsidies from England, Sussex had achieved little during his long term in office. The Scots remained in east Ulster. The plantation of Laois and Offaly only got underway in 1563, and then proved to be an expensive failure. Sussex's sole success was the introduction of a system whereby English captains, with small bodies of troops, took the place of Irish lords in the administration of a number of minor lordships bordering on the Pale.

Sussex was almost universally hated in the Pale. He had alienated the Palesmen from the Dublin administration by excluding them from office and influence. He reduced the Irish Parliament into a cipher which failed to reflect the views of the colonial community. He seriously undermined the economic well-being of the colony by the constant wars he provoked. He debased the Irish coinage so much to help finance his large armies that it became practically worthless, and prices became grossly inflated. Finally, he imposed very high levels of cess on the Pale – a practice whereby the Crown requisitioned provisions from landowners, and subsequently paid for them at official prices. Since the debased coinage fueled massive inflation the 'official' price of produce usually bore no relationship to the market price.

Once Sussex was humiliated by Seán O'Neill, the political leaders of the Pale began an orchestrated campaign to have him dismissed from office. A royal commission was set up to investigate Sussex's administration. The Earl took 'sick leave' in May 1564 and never returned to Ireland.

6 PROGRAMMES OF CONQUEST 1565–78

On 13 October 1565 Sir Henry Sidney was made Deputy of Ireland. Sidney was well qualified to take command of the Dublin administration. He had gone to Ireland with Sussex, his brother-in-law in 1556 and served as Under-Treasurer. From 1560 he was President of the Council in Wales. He was a member of the Leicester faction and was thus guaranteed some influence at Court.

In an important book entitled *The Elizabethan Conquest of Ireland: a pattern established, 1565–1576*, Professor Nicholas Canny argued that Sidney's appointment marked 'a new departure' for Tudor policy towards Ireland. The new Deputy accepted office only when Elizabeth agreed to endorse his programme to extend English control throughout Ireland. Sidney promised to subdue the country in the space of only three years if the Queen provided him with an army of 1500 men, financed directly from England.

Sidney arrived in Ireland in January 1566. He immediately set about reforming the administration of justice in Leinster. By April he was ready to establish the Council in Munster with Warham St Leger, son of the popular Deputy, as President. St Leger was welcomed by the Earl of Desmond, but was opposed by the Earl of Ormond who feared having his independence curbed in the Palatine County of Tipperary. Ormond – known affectionately as 'Black Tom' by his cousin Elizabeth – persuaded the Queen that it was insufferable that he should be subject to the Council in Munster, as though he were no better than the unreliable Earl of Desmond. The Council was scuppered before it was even launched.

Meanwhile, Seán O'Neill, posing as the defender of the Catholic faith against English heresy, was negotiating with the governments of France and Scotland for military assistance to overthrow English rule in Ireland. He also built up a formidable army of his own in central Ulster. Elizabeth ordered Sidney to set his programme to one side, and overthrow O'Neill as quickly as possible. After losing ground to rivals as well as to Sidney, O'Neill he turned to the MacDonalds of Antrim for support; they murdered him and sent his head to Dublin. For Sidney this was a stroke of luck he determined to make the most of. He travelled to Court in October to negotiate new terms for his administration.

Sidney returned to Ireland as Deputy in April 1568 with a revised programme for conquest. The essential elements of the original scheme were retained but he now intended the provincial councils in Ireland, intended to draw the gentry into the service of the Crown, to become self-financing within a short period. He prepared a bill for the Irish Parliament to outlaw the private armies of Irish and colonial magnates, and to change the exactions through which the population had been forced to maintain them into a tax – called composition – to support the councils. This was an intelligent strategy to de-militarise the provinces and bolster the Queen's government at no expense.

An important element of Sidney's revised programme was the encouragement of private plantation ventures to help Anglicise Ireland. In September and October 1568 the Deputy reconnoitred the east coast of Ulster with a view to assessing the scope for colonising the area. He hoped to take advantage of Seán O'Neill's demise to subdue Ulster. Sidney planned to dispossess the Irish and Scottish landowners east of the River Bann, and then colonise the region with English settlers. He intended to impose a radical version of 'surrender and regrant' on the province west of the Bann by breaking up the great Irish lordships into small, harmless estates. The region would then be subject to a military council for an indefinite period.

However, Sidney discovered that Seán O'Neill's successor, Turlough

Luineach O'Neill, was employing hundreds of tough Scottish mercenaries to defend his territory from English aggression. In the circumstances Sidney could only play for time. He formally recognised O'Neill's position in Tyrone, while he secretly promoted the establishment of colonies in eastern Ulster.

Sidney promoted plantations in other regions of Ireland also. Warham St Leger acquired the Barony of Kerrycurrihy, which lay adjacent to Cork city, and settled it with an English population. More notoriously Sir Peter Carew, a descendant of one of the twelfth-century Anglo-Norman *conquistadores*, was encouraged by Sidney to establish claims on large areas throughout the colony. These ventures were remarkable in that they were directed against long-established members of the old colonial community. Unsurprisingly, they generated great anxiety and hostility among the colonial community. Fierce opposition to Carew and the other English adventurers was voiced in the Parliament of 1569–71, but to no avail. Also in 1569–71 serious disturbances were provoked in Connacht by insensitive religious policies and the imposition of English laws and customs. In Munster martial law was declared and there was ruthless suppression of suspected rebels. By April 1571 a kind of calm was imposed on Munster and Connacht, and Sidney was re-called from Ireland.

In the years 1568–71 Sidney's administration had cost IR £147 000. His programme was in disarray. His plantations and councils had sparked off widespread rebellions within the colony itself! His legislation in Parliament had encountered unprecedented opposition. Elizabeth came to the conclusion that programmes of conquest were simply too ambitious. The next Deputy, Sir William Fitzwilliam, set himself the modest goals of improving the quality of royal justice in Leinster, and delegated responsibility for the other provinces to the local nobility.

In Ulster, Sidney's plantation schemes came to fruition during Fitzwilliam's term of office, despite the new Deputy's hostility to such adventures. Sir Thomas Smith's attempt to colonise the Ards peninsula began in May 1572. Smith was influenced by classical Roman example, and by recent Spanish activity in the Americas. He planned to banish the Irish landowners and replace them with English settlers. The peasants were to be retained to perform manual labour for their new masters. A small colony was established at Newtownards. However, the local gentry, led by Sir Brian O'Neill of Clandeboy, offered very stiff resistance to Smith and his followers. When Smith was killed by one of his Irish labourers in autumn 1573, the entire venture came to an end.

Walter Devereux, Earl of Essex, launched a more ambitious scheme to colonise Antrim in August 1573. It soon faltered as Essex's followers deserted him when they discovered that Antrim was not quite the paradise they had been promised. Essex's entire fortune was tied up in the venture and he grew increasingly desperate as time passed. He was responsible for some appalling atrocities – most notoriously the indiscriminate murder of the entire population of Rathlin island! Fitzwilliam disapproved of the enterprise and did little to salvage it. By 1575 the writing was on the wall and Elizabeth ordered that the whole sordid affair be brought to an end.

Fitzwilliam's standing suffered through the failure of the Ulster projects, and the Leicester faction was able to exploit his embarrassment by having Sidney restored to office. Sidney was anxious to redeem his reputation by succeeding in Ireland. The Deputy arrived in Ireland in September 1575, determined to avoid the mistakes he made in 1568–71. He made a treaty with Turlough Luineach O'Neill, acknowledging him as Lord of Tyrone, in return for the latter ceding a portion of his lordship to Hugh O'Neill, Baron of Dungannon. Sidney travelled through Connacht and Munster to reassure the gentry that they had nothing to fear from his administration. There would be no new plantations. He persuaded them to agree to disband their private armies and to pay a modest composition rent to the provincial councils.

Encouraged by successes in Munster and Connacht, Sidney sought to impose composition on Leinster. In return he promised to end the feudal obligation of the Palesmen to fight in defence of the colony. The colonial community was unimpressed. In 1578 the Palesmen, backed by the Earls of Ormond and Kildare, sent a delegation of the Queen asking for a change in government policy. They insisted that Sidney's programme was likely to provoke a general revolt in Ireland. The Deputy's mass murder of the O'Mores and O'Connors who answered his summons to Mullaghmast, County Kildare, earned him infamy throughout Ireland, and especially among the Irish population. Sidney was ignominiously dismissed from office in late 1578. The programmatic approach to subduing Ireland was abandoned.

7 THE TUDOR REFORMATION AND IRELAND

The people of Ireland remained Catholic, despite the efforts of the English Crown to make them Protestant. Protestantism failed to win any significant following in the towns or in the countryside, among the Irish or among the old colonial community. The reasons for this overwhelming failure remain a matter for debate among historians.

Irish historians have long recognised that the Irish Church before the Reformation was in need of reform. John Watt, in *The Church in Medieval Ireland*, identified four chief causes for the decline of the Church in the later Middle Ages:

1. The use of the Statutes of Kilkenny to exclude Irish priests from benefices in the colony was divisive, and hence detrimental to Christianity in Ireland.

2. The Irish clergy had largely abandoned celibacy and transmitted Church offices to their sons.

3. The monastic orders were in grave disorder, a fact confirmed by Father Brendan Bradshaw's definitive study of the Irish religious orders before their dissolution by Henry VIII.

4. The papal *curia*, or bureaucracy, interfered with the Irish Church outside the Pale and colonial towns by providing all kinds of men to benefices, sometimes even laymen.

However, Watt's analysis is not entirely adequate. In the first comprehensive survey of the Irish Church on the eve of the Reformation Henry Jefferies identified the pervasive poverty of the Church as its most profound weakness. Most of the parish clergy in Ireland lived in poverty. While the benefices of the wealthy diocese of Dublin were worth IR £15 0s. 2d. on average, those in Cashel diocese were worth only IR £2 18s. 0d. The incumbents of the Ulster parishes in Armagh diocese received only IR £1 13s. 5d. on average. Such incomes were incredibly low by European standards.

A further handicap from which the Irish Church suffered was that half of the parishes were impropriated, that is, between 66 per cent and 100 per cent of the parochial tithe went to a monastery which then appointed the parish priest. Sometimes a vicar was appointed to serve the parish and he received about 33 per cent of the tithe, a Church tax on agricultural produce. The tithe had been much diminished owing to the unsettled political state of much of Ireland depressing Irish agriculture. However, it was common in Ireland for a curate to be appointed with no income but the altarages; the fees received for performing such services as baptisms, marriages and funerals. Such priests were very poor indeed.

Along the borderlands of the Pale, and between Irish and colonial lordships, many parishes were laid waste in times of war. The visitation of Tuam in 1565–7 revealed that 10 per cent of the archdiocese's parishes lay waste and depopulated. A visitation of the two northern deaneries of Armagh archdiocese in 1546 found that half of the churches visited were in ruins, lacking a roof and often a wall or two as well. In fact there are many contemporary references to widespread dereliction of Irish churches. Only to a limited extent, though, was this the result of war. In most instances the decay of the church buildings simply reflected the poverty of the parishes. Remarkably, the Armagh visitors found that the parish clergy continued to perform their pastoral duties despite the ruined state of their churches.

Evidence on the quality of the Irish clergy is scarce, yet Jefferies argues that the traditional image of ignorant and undisciplined priests may have been over-drawn. There was no university in Ireland until 1594, but Irish students could be found at Oxford and other foreign universities throughout the Middle Ages. Within Ireland there were a few grammar schools in the colony, while in the Irish lordships there were *studia particularia*, institutions where one could study canon and civil laws, the humanities, music or medicine to an advanced level. Certainly, at a time when graduate parsons were very rare throughout Europe, and most priests were trained through an 'apprenticeship', the Irish priesthood was probably as well trained as was its counterparts in other countries.

Clerical indiscipline was indeed a problem for the Irish Church, but its extent was curbed by bishops conducting visitations and citing delinquents before the Church courts. The chief sin that the Irish clergy were addicted to was concubinage, or the forming of illicit 'marriages'. If one does not take an overly critical view of this weakness it is apparent that the Irish clergy were hardly more indisciplined than were priests in similarly disturbed borderlands elsewhere in Christendom.

Ireland's Church leaders were long conscious of the need for reform. This is reflected in the decrees regularly endorsed by diocesan and provincial synods. Our records show many bishops endeavouring to improve the quality of the Church's pastoral mission, raise standards of clerical competence, and tackle clerical poverty by uniting benefices. Unfortunately, their efforts were undermined by the political turmoil and the poverty it caused.

The Irish laity, like other Europeans, wished the Church to be reformed. Nonetheless, there are many indications of voluntary lay support for the Church. The fifteenth and early-sixteenth centuries saw widespread rebuilding and embellishment of parish churches by the laity. Chantries were formed throughout the colony. Bequests to the Church in wills were often strikingly generous. Most remarkable was the founding of ninety friaries between 1400 and 1508, mostly in Connacht and Ulster, a development which was unparalleled in Christendom.

The Kildare rebellion dramatically demonstrated the extent of colonial hostility to Henry VIII's religious policies. Some of the colony's best educated and most senior clerics promoted the rebellion as a Catholic crusade against a heretic King. In the Irish Reformation Parliament of 1536–7 the proctors, or representatives of the parish clergy, who formed a third house in the colonial Parliament, vigorously opposed the bills for the Royal Supremacy and the breach with Rome. The King had to abolish the third house to have his religious legislation enacted. The position of the bishops in unclear. A document of 1559 suggests that 'special men' had been summoned to the Irish House of Lords in 1536–7 to outvote the spiritual peers.

Brendan Bradshaw, in his study of the Parliament, revealed that the Reformation statutes were supported in the Commons by a body of colonial reformers. These men had encountered 'commonwealth' ideas while studying in England and they hoped that Henry VIII and Cromwell would implement a thorough reform of the Church and society in Ireland. Bradshaw argued that as long as the Crown enjoyed the support of these local reformers it could hope to carry the colony along with its ecclesiastical and political changes. The English Crown gained IR £4070 p.a. from the dissolution of Irish monasteries, and won political credit by sharing some of the spoils with members of the colonial élite.

To spearhead the Henrician schism in Ireland, the King made George Browne, a former English friar, Archbishop of Dublin in March 1536. Browne was no zealot but he did his duty as expected. He promoted the Royal Supremacy and the Crown's religious programme throughout the ecclesiastical province of Dublin. The clergy generally offered passive resistance, refusing to preach or promote the Royal Supremacy. A handful openly condemned the innovations and suffered imprisonment. However, once the Act of Six Articles (1539) made clear the Catholic nature of the King's religion much of the bitterness began to fade.

St Leger applied his consensus approach to enforcing the Henrician schism in Ireland. In effect, he dissociated the Royal Supremacy from doctrinal novelty. He committed his administration to supporting the Church against magnate interference and exactions. He also employed political pressure to persuade the bishops to take the oath of Supremacy. This combination of practical support and coercion succeeded in getting twenty-four of Ireland's thirty bishops to take the oath by the end of Henry VIII's reign. When the first Jesuit mission was conducted in Ireland in 1542 it met with a frigid response from the Irish lords engaged in negotiations to secure the benefits of 'surrender and regrant'.

The Edwardian Reformation was imposed on the colony in Ireland with energy. The first Book of Common Prayer was introduced into churches throughout English speaking districts. The English Privy Council authorised the publication of an Irish language version of the Prayer Book in 1551, but nothing materialised. Opposition to the Edwardian Reformation was widespread in Ireland. With no Protestant-Irish clergy available the Crown appointed Englishmen to the Sees of Armagh, Kildare, Leighlin and Ossory. One of these new bishops, John Bale of Ossory, was a zealous preacher. Despite the opposition of the local clergy, Bale built up a following among the young people of Kilkenny. However, as soon as Mary ascended the throne the Reformation in Kilkenny came to an end. Elsewhere the Protestant prelates failed utterly to convert the priests or people.

Mary's reign was universally welcomed in Ireland. Catholic services were spontaneously restored in the English-speaking districts where the Prayer Book had been used. The small number of clergy who had married under Edward VI were soon weeded out and local Catholics were installed in all of the dioceses and parishes. The Parliament of 1557–8 formally completed the work of restoring the Roman Catholic Church in Ireland. Brendan Bradshaw has argued that the Counter-reformation became firmly established in Ireland during Mary's reign and gained a momentum which was never lost.

However, Jefferies' study of the Irish Parliament of 1560 revealed that the Parliament endorsed the Elizabethan Settlement in the remarkably short space of three weeks. Some bishops actually voted in favour of the ecclesiastical legislation in the House of Lords while only three are thought to have opposed it. It is clear from the actions of most of the Irish bishops and the Parliamentarians generally, that the Counterreformation had not taken hold in Mary's reign. On the other hand, there was no Protestant 'party' in the assembly. The ecclesiastical bills were endorsed because the colonial élite felt that they had little choice in the matter, and they had won concessions allowing the retention of Latin in Church services beyond the enclaves where English was widely spoken, and the continued use of the paraphenalia of Catholic worship in the 'reformed' Church of Ireland.

The enforcement of the Elizabethan Settlement in Ireland has yet to be studied systematically. In Bradshaw's view the Tudor Reformation made progress as long as the moderate Erasmian colonial reformers exercised some influence over government policies. However, as English political initiatives in Ireland grew increasingly militarist and oppressive, the local humanists were displaced by intolerant English Protestants. The Crown's aggressive political programmes and its coercive Church reform strategy alienated the colonial reformers, and their opposition was seen as critically important in the ultimate failure of the Tudor Reformation in Ireland. In Bradshaw's view, Sussex's appointment as Deputy in 1556 marked the turning point for progress of the Reformation in Ireland.

In contrast Professor Canny has pointed out that Bradshaw's colonial reformers continued to support the established Church in Elizabeth's reign. The colonial community generally conformed, attending Church services though they refused to receive the Anglican Communion. Even clergymen with conscientious objections generally conformed and adapted the Prayer Book services to make them as Catholic as possible. Some priests read 'little or nothing' from the Book of Common Prayer and regaled their congregations with stories of St Patrick or the Blessed Virgin. Nonetheless, Canny argued that as long as the colonial community conformed there was the possibility that it might be won to Protestantism in time – as happened in Wales and the conservative north of England.

Canny saw the collapse of colonial conformity to the established Church by the 1590s simply as a manifestation of the alienation of the colonial population from the harsh militarist regime governing Ireland. He declared that the Reformation failed to strike roots in Ireland during the years of conformity because of the lack of Protestant preaching.

A consensus has emerged which sees the towns as the key battlegrounds in the religious struggles in sixteenth-century Ireland. An article by Bradshaw on the south-western Irish cities showed that the pre-Reformation church was vibrant and popular, that there was no support in them for a Reformation 'from below', and that the Reformation made no headway in the cities before Elizabeth's reign. Until the 1570s and 1580s the city churches continued to be staffed by Catholic priests who may have conformed outwardly to the state religion, while subverting it as best they could.

A key failure of the reformed Church was its inability to provide schools good enough to compete with those run by recusant priests. The Catholic priest-teachers may have saved the Catholic faith in Ireland by inspiring the younger generations with a tremendous commitment to Rome. Many scholars from the recusant academies went on to study in Catholic colleges on mainland Europe, among whom a high proportion returned to Ireland as Jesuits or seminary trained priests.

Unable to recruit more than a handful of Irish Protestants into its ministry, the Protestant Church in Ireland began to employ English clerics. Some of these men preached zealously among the English-speaking towns-folk though, with the exception of Galway, apparently to little effect. However, the intrusion of English Protestant ministers into Irish benefices proved very unpopular. Englishmen were already gaining a virtual monopoly of high office in the civil administration in Ireland, and they showed themselves greedy for a share of Irish land and commercial opportunities. The colonial community came to regard the Anglicisation of their Church as part of a wider English Protestant assault on their heritage.

The crisis point was reached when the English administration in Ireland made extortionate demands for tax on the colony to finance the wars it was fighting against the Irish, and when Irish seminary priests returned from mainland Europe to propagate the Counter-reformation. These factors were conjoined in Waterford and the south-east of Ireland in 1577–9; in Dublin and the Pale in the early 1580s; and in Galway, Limerick and Cork in the 1590s.

The seminary priests were drawn mainly from the patrician class in the Irish towns. They were able to exploit their backgrounds to win the commitment of the urban élites in Ireland to the Catholic cause. The priest demonstrated such zeal and courage in their ministry that they commanded respect even from their adversaries.

The following extract is from Edmund Spenser's book, *A view of the present state of Ireland* (1596). The book is based on his first hand experiences as an English planter in Ireland. While reading the extract it is important to remember that Spenser was a Protestant, and was strongly opposed to the Catholic Church:

> ... it is [a] great wonder to see the difference which is between
> the zeal of the popish priests and the ministers of the gospel; for
> they [i.e. the priests] do not hesitate to come from Spain, from

Rome and from Rheims, by long toil and dangerous travel to
here, where they know peril of death awaits them, and no
reward nor riches is to be found, simply to draw the people to
the Church of Rome; whereas some of our idle ministers,
having a way of credit and esteem thereby opened onto them,
and having the livings of the country offered onto them,
without pain and without peril, will neither for the same nor
any love of God, nor zeal of religion, nor for all the good they
may do by winning souls to God, be drawn forth from their
warm nests to look out onto God's harvest, which is ready for
the sickle, and all the fields yellow long ago.

1 *What comparison does Spenser draw between the Catholic and the
   Protestant clergy in Ireland?*

2 *What might Spenser have hoped to achieve by making this comparison?*

The newly arrived Jesuits and seminary priests quickly set up a
Church structure parallel to that of the State Church. Recusancy on a
massive scale followed. The congregations which had attended the
Protestant services simply deserted *en masse*. In Cork city, for instance,
Bishop William Lyons complained that whereas previously hundreds
of people had attended the Protestant cathedral services, by 1596 there
were only a handful. The borough, with a population of 2000, had ten
Catholic priests who openly celebrated the Mass and the other religious ceremonies. The Protestant ministers were shunned; people
labelled them 'devils' and hurried past them in the street, making the
sign of the cross for protection against diabolical contagion. The scale
of the Protestant collapse in Cork, and everywhere else throughout the
colony where the Reformation had been imposed, was overwhelming.

One may conclude then, that the Catholic Church in Ireland, despite
its failings, enjoyed the support of the people in Ireland before the
Reformation. Their commitment to Catholicism seems to have made
the population resistant to Protestant preaching, even in the colonial
towns. The absence of any significant number of native Protestant clergy forced the Protestant Church in Ireland to resort to employing some
of the dregs of the Church of England. This, however, served only to
emphasis the alien nature of the State Church in Ireland.

Alan Ford, in *The Protestant reformation in Ireland, 1594–1641*, demonstrated that the Protestant Church of Ireland tried and failed to convert
the Irish to Protestantism in the early seventeenth century. Eventually,
the Protestant clergy, who were virtually all English or Scottish, abandoned hope of success and took refuge in the Calvinist doctrine of predestination: the Irish were simply not destined for Heaven!

8 THE BLOODY FINALE TO THE CONQUEST OF IRELAND

From the start of her reign Elizabeth faced two contradictions in Ireland. In theory she was sovereign of all of Ireland yet she had no control over much of the kingdom. Also in theory she was the 'supreme governor' of the Irish Church, but in reality the Pope was the spiritual leader of the great majority of Irish Christians.

By 1579, however, the English administration in Ireland included several individuals who were determined to resolve these contradictions. These 'New English' men were zealous Protestants who regarded Catholicism, and by extension Irish Catholics, as an abomination. These same men typically possessed an understanding of cultural evolution which predisposed them to regard the Irish people as barbarians who could be dispossessed or killed without any qualms of conscience. Professor Canny's comparative study of 'The Ideology of English colonization: from Ireland to America' has shown that many English colonisers regarded the Irish and the American Indians as inferior peoples who might be 'civilised' only through the use of terror and brute force. Edmund Spenser, the famous English poet, and planter in Ireland quoted earlier, went so far as to advocate the utility of genocide against the Irish! With such men in power in Ireland bloodshed was inevitable. This was especially true when more and more Irish and colonial noblemen saw the need to resort to arms to defend their Catholic faith from the Protestant Crown.

On 17 July 1579 James Fitzmaurice Fitzgerald arrived in Ireland with Dr Nicholas Sanders, a leading English Catholic, together with sixty soldiers from a larger force financed by Pope Gregory XIII. They called on the princes and people of Ireland to rally to the papal banner against the heretical Queen of England. The Earl of Desmond opposed the Catholic confederates at first, but the Earl's followers deserted him until he reluctantly got involved.

Thousands of soldiers were sent from England to reinforce the colonial regime. On 3 October 1579 Sir Nicholas Malby, recently appointed military governor of Munster, defeated the confederate army at Monasternenagh, County Tipperary. The confederates were forced into south-west Munster while the more vulnerable estates of the Earl of Desmond were systematically burned and all of their inhabitants, men, women and children were slaughtered.

Arthur, Lord Grey, was appointed Deputy of Ireland on 15 July 1580. Almost immediately there was further revolt, led by Viscount Baltinglass and in reaction Munster was systematically destroyed by the English army to create a famine in which the confederate soldiers would starve to death along with the civilian population. Grey's secretary, Edmund Spenser wrote that as a result the people of Munster 'looked [like] anatomies of death, they spoke like ghosts crying out of their graves, they did eat of dead carcasses . . . In short space there were none almost left, and a most populous and plentiful country [was] suddenly left empty of man or beast.'

Meanwhile, in the Pale, it was revealed that William Nugent, brother of Baron Delvin, was involved in the Baltinglass insurrection. Grey reacted hysterically. In December 1580 he arrested Delvin, the Earl of Kildare and many other Pale gentry and had twenty of them killed before the English Privy Council intervened. In fact, the gentry of the Pale had been very hostile to Baltinglass' rebellion, however much they sympathised with his motives. Grey's executions profoundly alienated the Palesmen from the Dublin administration. The 'New English' administrators, for their part, were convinced that the old colonial community were in fact treacherous papists who posed a greater threat to Protestant English power in Ireland than did the Irish.

By November 1582, the Earl of Desmond had been killed and the Catholic uprising was crushed. After a period of ominous calm Sir John Perrot was appointed Deputy in January 1584 with a new programme to impose English control throughout Ireland. Perrot summoned the Irish Parliament to meet on 26 April 1585 and he laid before it a number of bills prepared in England to endorse the Crown's confiscation of the estates of the Earl of Desmond and other Catholic confederates to ratify a new composition settlement ('nationalised' taxation) for the whole of Ireland; and to enact harsher legislation against Catholics.

The Parliament attainted Desmond and the other confederates. However, the opposition to the composition and anti-Catholic bills was overwhelming. Indeed, the government bills caused the old colonial community in Ireland to rally openly behind the twin causes of Catholicism and constitutional separatism. They became conscious of themselves as being 'Old English'. They were loyal to the English Crown, yet argued that Ireland was constitutionally autonomous from England i.e. they wanted a kind of 'dual monarchy'. They were zealously Catholic, and scornfully dismissive of the religious innovations of the 'New English' Protestants. The Old English argued that they could win the Irish population to accept English government and culture through education and persuasion. Few of the Old English were yet ready to join with the Irish in seeking an independent Ireland, despite their shared religion, and attachment to Ireland.

Once Desmond's estates were confiscated by the Crown, Perrot began a process of colonisation. A total of 574 645 acres were declared forfeit to the Crown. Detailed plans were drawn up in England to settle 8400 English people on the planted estates. The plans proved inadequate because too little care had been taken to ascertain exactly what land was confiscated, and what was not. Many innocent landowners were dispossessed along with confederates. Long standing tenants on the confiscated estates were evicted by alien settlers who took over their houses and farms. By 1590 the plantation of Munster was functioning with about 2000 settlers. The native population were forced to accept a servile status on their former lands. Few of the innocent victims of the plantation were compensated.

In Connacht a new composition scheme was implemented with the support of the Earls of Clanrickard and Thomond. The Earl's private demesnes were made exempt from the tax, and they received a share of the composition to reflect the incomes they had levied on their underlords under the Gaelic system of taxes. By this composition, Bingham, the English governor of Connacht, known as the President, was able to levy an annual income of IR £3645. With his revenues assured Bingham set about extending his control into north Connacht. When, as he expected, his ambitions were resisted he sent English troops to impose military control over Mayo in 1588–9, and Leitrim 1589–90.

By the beginning of 1590 the three southern provinces were effectively occupied by English troops. The colonial administration was determined to subdue Ulster as soon as possible. Hugh Rua MacMahon, lord of Monaghan, was callously provoked into rebellion, was then executed and his lordship was broken up into eight small units. Similar action was taken against other lords. Bingham took possession of Sligo Castle, which guarded the western gateway into Ulster. With other English garrisons in the east Ulster castles of Carrickfergus, Newry and Blackwater Fort, a ring of steel was steadily tightening around independent Ulster.

Hugh O'Neill, Earl of Tyrone, watched the English penetration of Ulster with some anxiety. He had been educated in the Pale, and afterwards he had been a soldier in the English army. Elizabeth expected Tyrone to strengthen English power in Ulster. However, Tyrone's education helped to make him a committed Catholic. His time in the English army gave him first hand experience of the disdain with which Irish people were held by English administrators and soldiers alike. As an Irishman Tyrone enjoyed less respect and trust than a nobleman of his standing might otherwise expect. To maintain his honour and freedom Tyrone offered to govern Ulster on behalf of the Queen, free of supervision from Dublin. Since the Queen did not accept Tyrone's services he was faced with a dilemma . . . how could he hope to resist an English army if his independence was threatened.

In June 1594 Hugh Maguire besieged the English garrison occupying Enniskillen, with support from Hugh Rua O'Donnell, lord of Tyrconnell. When an English battalion tried to break the siege it was repulsed by Tyrone's brother. Tyrone negotiated in vain with Dublin for responsibility for Ulster. Finally, in May 1595 the Irish Earl was at war with England.

Tyrone was ready for war. He had employed English and Spanish captains to train the men of his lordships to fight in modern warfare. He employed Scottish gunsmiths at Dungannon to produce armaments. He imported large quantities of guns and ammunition to equip his soldiers. He secured hundreds of Scottish mercenaries. Tyrone's ally, Tyrconnell, fielded a much less modern army, but he was able to secure large numbers of Scottish soldiers through his Scottish mother, Finula MacDonald. In 1595, the Ulster confederates had an army of 1000 cavalry, 4000 musketeers and 1000 pikemen. It was the most formidable and professional army ever fielded by Irish lords.

The Dublin administration calculated that the Ulster lords would be unable to maintain a large standing army for long. They reckoned that it was only a matter of time before Tyrone and Tyrconnell would be forced to capitulate. In fact, the Ulster lords had so developed the province's economy that they could maintain an army of 5000–6000 men almost indefinitely. However, they knew that they could not expel the English from Ireland without support from the gentry of the southern provinces, or without military assistance from Spain.

In July 1596, Tyrone and Tyrconnell appealed for support for their cause throughout Ireland. However, English military control was too firm for the Irish lords of the southern provinces to break free. The Old English lords simply refused to be drawn into rebellion. Philip II of Spain sent a great armada of one hundred ships to Ireland in October 1596, but the fleet was overwhelmed by a tremendous storm. Thirty-two ships were sunk, and the remainder struggled back to Spain. Late in October 1597 a second armada was sent to Ireland, but it too was forced back to Spain by dreadful storms.

The war in Ireland escalated gradually as the English Crown sent more and more troops there to crush the confederates. By 1599 the English garrison in Ireland numbered 17 300 soldiers – the largest English army of Elizabeth's reign. The Ulster lords stoutly defended their province and won a series of stunning victories against the English, most notably at the Battle of Clontibret in February 1595, and at the Battle of the Yellow Ford in August 1598.

The victory at the Yellow Ford was spectacular. An English army of 4200 men was smashed. The English garrisons elsewhere lost heart while the Irish everywhere were inspired. Tyrconnell gained mastery over Connacht. The midlands plantation was overthrown. Owen MacRory O'More brought 700 men to Limerick, and helped to overthrow the Munster plantation. The confederates established James Fitzgerald, a cousin of the last Earl, as lord of Desmond. English power in Ireland seemed to be on the verge of collapse.

Thousands of more English troops were sent to Ireland to retrieve the situation. In March 1599 Robert Devereux, Earl of Essex, was made Deputy of Ireland with a force of 17 300 men. Essex proved to be no match for the Irish lords though. An army he sent against Tyrconnell was smashed in the Curlew Mountains, County Sligo. Essex's men deserted him *en masse*. He only marched against Tyrone when the Queen threatened him. Even then he sued for a truce when the Irish lord confronted him. The truce proved to be his undoing. Essex fled to Court to justify his actions to the Queen. He later staged a foolish *coup* and was beheaded.

When the truce expired in January 1600, Tyrone asserted the confederate cause throughout the length of Ireland. In February 1600 Charles Blount, Lord Mountjoy, became Deputy of Ireland. He was a very able, if ruthless general, with 13 200 troops at his command. He deployed his superior forces skillfully. He set up a string of garrisons around Ulster, and established a fort behind Tyrone's lines at Derry. He made Sir George Carew president of Munster, and gave him a force of 3000 men. Without strong local leadership and effective soldiers against Carew's army the confederates soon lost control of Munster. When Mountjoy attempted to invade Ulster though, he was repulsed at the Moyry Pass.

On 21 September 1601, 3400 Spanish soldiers landed at Kinsale, County Cork. The Spanish force was smaller than expected, but it did represent a tangible contribution to the Catholic cause by Spain. The confederates desperately needed foreign assistance if they were to succeed. Therefore, though it was mid winter the Ulster earls marched their forces almost 500km southwards. Between the Irish armies and the Spanish force in Kinsale was the English Deputy Mountjoy with 7000 troops. On 21 December 1601, Tyrone was in the process of deploying his forces into their battle positions when the English struck. The Irish were caught off-guard and were routed. The Spanish force played no part in the fighting. They surrendered on 2 January 1602.

The battle of Kinsale was decisive. Tyrconnell went to Spain to secure more assistance, but it never came. Within Ireland the confederate cause crumbled. The English army penetrated Ulster's defences and systematically destroyed the province. There were mass killings of civilians by the sword and man-made famine. In June 1602 the O'Sullivan castle at Dunboy fell to the English after a valiant defence. Tyrone held out until 30 March 1603 when he was offered his life, and very generous terms. Though he did not know it at the time Elizabeth had died six days earlier.

9 EPILOGUE

On 24 March 1603 James VI of Scotland became King of England and Ireland. In England he inherited a kingdom which was internally peaceful and united. The King's writ was as effective in the north of England as it was in Middlesex. The Welsh élites had been successfully assimilated into the English polity. With few exceptions, the English and the Welsh were Protestant. In Ireland, however, the situation was very different. Large parts of the kingdom had been devastated. Buildings had been burned down, crops razed and livestock slaughtered. The population had been decimated by the mass starvation brought about deliberately in order to subjugate the Catholic confederate forces. The economy had been severely disrupted, the Irish coinage had been so debased that it was worthless, and the trading towns were in decay. As if to crown all of that, the Catholic faith was proscribed, and the church buildings and properties were transferred to the Protestant Church of Ireland which enjoyed virtually no support in the country. The people of Ireland, need it be said, were unimpressed by the Tudors' legacy.

Steven Ellis has remarked that by setting himself realistic goals Henry VII enjoyed greater success in his policies towards Ireland than did any other Tudor monarch. Admittedly, the Crown's authority beyond the Pale and the towns was tenuous. However, under the great Earl of Kildare the colony in Ireland financed itself, and showed definite signs of progress. Unfortunately, after the Kildare ascendancy the government of the colony fell to too many men who had unrealistic expectations about what could be achieved. Even Sidney, who was one of the more intelligent and experienced governors, persuaded Elizabeth that he could conquer Ireland with a small army within three years! More than anything else, it was the determination of the English Deputies to 'force the pace' of change in Ireland which resulted in such turmoil and bloodshed.

Undoubtedly, more might have been achieved had the English Deputies received sufficient funds from England. Instead, deeply unpopular exactions alienated the colonial community who ought to have been the bulwark of English power in Ireland. Ironically, the Deputies' efforts to relieve this source of tension involved them in further ill-conceived efforts to subjugate the Irish as quickly as possible.

The introduction of the Tudor Reformation into an already difficult political environment was most unfortunate. It was certain to be resisted, particularly by those whose loyalties to the Tudor Crown (assuming they had any) were far less strong than their commitment to Catholicism. That the Irish should have resisted Protestantism was almost inevitable. More importantly, in some ways, was the decision of the colonial community to identify their cause with Catholicism. The colonial élites would have been displaced from the Dublin administration by the English newcomers in any case. However, once the Dublin government was in the hands of 'New English' Protestants, the colonial élites were forced to develop a new understanding of themselves. They began to conceive of themselves as 'Old English'; Catholic, yet loyal to the English Crown and the rightful representatives of English interests in Ireland.

At the end of the Nine Years War Ireland had finally been conquered, at a cost of £2 million! However, the Old English, as well as the Irish population, were alienated from the English administration in Dublin. The enforcement of the penal laws against the Catholic religion in the seventeenth century, together with a range of policies to dispossess the Catholics of Ireland of their properties and political rights, eventually forced the Old English to make common cause with the Irish against the predatory Protestant establishment. The Irish were not to be assimilated into the English polity as the Welsh had been. English Protestantism and ideologies of colonisation predisposed Ireland's new rulers to perceive the Irish Catholics as being inferior to themselves. The sectarian and racialist elements in British thinking about Ireland would hinder Anglo-Irish relations for centuries to come.

10 BIBLIOGRAPHY

B Bradshaw *The Irish Constitutional Revolution in the Sixteenth Century* (CUP, 1979).
F W Brooks 'The Council in the North' in *The Tudors* J Hurstfield (ed.) (Historical Association, 1953).
C S L Davies 'England and the French War, 1557–59' in *The Mid Tudor Polity, 1540–1560* J Loach and R Tittler (eds) (Macmillan, 1980).
S G Ellis *Tudor Ireland: Crown, Community and the Conflict of Cultures, 1470–1603* (Longman, 1985).
T Herbert and G Elwys Jones *Tudor Wales* (Open University, 1988).
G Williams *Recovery, Reorientation and Reformation: Wales c.1415–1642* (Clarendon, 1987).

11 DISCUSSION POINTS AND EXERCISES

A *This section consists of questions or points that might be used for discussion (or written answers) as a way of expanding on the chapter and testing understanding of it:*

1 What particular difficulties did the English kings of the later Middle Ages face in the government of the outlying regions?

2 By what means did Edward IV and Henry VII overcome some of these problems?

3 In what ways, and why, did Cromwell become more radical in implementing royal policies in the frontier regions?

4 Why were Cromwell's efforts to reform the government of the English colony in Ireland so unsuccessful?

5 How close did Ireland come to a 'constitutional revolution' in the 1540s, and why did it fail?

6 Why was the record of the Deputies in Ireland between 1547–64 so dismal?

7 What were the consequences of Sidney's attempts to find a permanent solution to the problems of governing Ireland?

8 Why did the Reformation fail in Ireland?

9 Why did the English find it so difficult and so costly to subdue the Irish in the closing years of Elizabeth's reign?

10 Why had the problem of governing Ireland grown so greatly during the course of the Tudor century?

B *Essay questions*

1 How far did the north of England and Wales came under increasing central control in the first half of the sixteenth century?

2 Was Cromwell's approach to governing Wales and the North more creative than that of Henry VII?

3 What problems did Ireland present to English governments between 1496 and 1553, and how successfully were they dealt with?

4 To what extent was English power in Ireland extended during the reign of Elizabeth I?

5 How effective were the Tudor monarchs in coping with the problems posed by Ireland?

6 'Success in Wales and the North; abject failure in Ireland.' Is this a fair summary of Tudor government of the frontier regions?

12 DOCUMENTARY EXERCISE – THE CONQUEST OF IRELAND

A. Tudor Warfare in Ireland
i) Contemporary account of Deputy Mountjoy's tactics in Ulster (1600)

> . . . where other deputies used to assail the rebels only in summer time, this lord prosecuted [i.e. attacked] them most in winter, being commonly five days at least in the week on horseback all the winter long. This broke their hearts; for the air being sharp, and they naked, and they being driven from their homes into the woods [which were] bare of leaves, they had no shelter for themselves. Besides that, their cattle were also wasted by travelling [for safety] to and fro. Add to that they were . . . troubled in the seed time [and] could not sow their ground. And in the harvest time both the deputy's forces and the [English] garrisons cut down their corn before it was ripe, and then in winter time they [English troops] carried away or burnt all the stores of food in the secret places where the rebels had conveyed them.

[Munster] was a most rich and plentiful country, full of corn and cattle . . . yet before one year and a half they [the population of Munster] were brought to such wretchedness as that any stony heart would have rued the same. Out of every corner of the woods and glens they came creeping forth upon their hands, for their legs could not carry them; and they looked [like] anatomies of death; they spoke like ghosts crying out of their graves; they ate dead animals, [and were] happy where they could find them; yea, and one another soon after, insomuch as the very bodies they spared not to scrape out of their graves; and if they found a plot of watercresses or shamrocks, there they flocked as to a feast for the time, yet not able long to continue withal; that in (a) short space there were none almost left, and a most populous and plentiful country [was] suddenly left empty of man and beast; yet, sure, in all that war there perished not many by the sword, but all by the extremity of famine . . .

1 *With reference to the two documents above, describe exactly how the English armies sought to destroy their Irish opponents.*

2 *How reliable are these documents as evidence?*

3 *How was the reputation for such murderous tactics likely to affect Irish attitudes towards the English Crown, and its servants in Ireland?*

B. *The Earl of Tyrone's Terms for Peace (1599)*

1. That the catholic, apostolic and Roman religion be openly preached and taught throughout all Ireland, as well in cities as borough towns, by bishops, seminary priests, Jesuits and all other religious men.
2. That the Church of Ireland be wholly governed by the Pope.
3. That all cathedrals and parish churches, abbeys and all other religious houses, with all tithes and church lands, now in the hands of the English, be restored to the Catholic churchmen.
4. That all Irish priests and religious men, now prisoners in England or Ireland, be set at liberty, with all lay Irishmen that are troubled for their conscience, and to go where they will, without further trouble.
5. That all Irish priests and religious men may freely pass and repass, by sea and land, to and from foreign countries.
6. That no Englishman may be a churchman in Ireland . . .
8. That the governor of Ireland be at lest an earl, and of the privy council of England, bearing the name of viceroy.

9. That the lord chancellor, lord treasurer, lord admiral, the council of state, the justice of the laws, Queen's attorney, Queen's serjeant and all other officers appertaining to the council and law of Ireland, be Irishmen . . .

11. That the master of ordinance, and half the soldiers with their officers resident in Ireland, be Irishmen.

12. That no Irishman's heirs shall lose their lands for the faults of their ancestors . . .

14. That no children, nor any friends, be taken as hostages for the good behaviour of their parents and, if there be any such hostages now in the hands of the English they must be released.

15. That all statutes made against the promotion of Irishmen, as well in their own country as abroad, be repealed.

16. That the Queen nor her successors may in no sort force an Irishman to serve them against his will . . .

18. That all Irishmen, of what quality they be, may freely travel in foreign countries for their better experience, without making any of the Queen's officers acquainted withal . . .

21. That all Irishmen that will may learn, and use, all occupations and arts whatsoever.

Tyrone's articles of 1599 represented the conditions under which he, and the other Irish confederates, would accept Elizabeth's claim to sovereignty in Ireland.

1   *What changes did Tyrone wish to bring about in the English government's treatment of the Roman Catholic Church in Ireland?*

2   *What changes did Tyrone wish to bring about in the English government's treatment of Irish people generally?*

3   *Why do you think that Sir Robert Cecil, Elizabeth's chief minister, dismissed Tyrone's articles as 'utopian'?*

XIII

CULTURE AND SOCIETY
I: POPULAR CULTURE

———

1 INTRODUCTION

CULTURAL histories of England are sometimes merely descriptions of the glorious arts of the past, intended to inspire admiration rather than a critical understanding of our heritage. But many historians challenge this passive approach, recognising the need to decode the culture of the past and make its inner workings understandable. Rather than simply admiring Tudor culture, historians are using it to explore the inside of the Tudor mind.

This means that great art is not the only subject of cultural history. An increasing amount of work has been done on popular culture – the stories and customs through which most people entertained and expressed themselves; the festivities and processions which gave communities an identity; and the beliefs, such as in magic and witchcraft, which gave meaning to people's lives and conditioned their actions. To research into popular culture all sorts of evidence has been examined, evidence which used to be passed over or categorised as the remains of a quaint folklore – records of processions, or woodcuts (cheaply distributed cartoons) or popular ballads.

Such enquiry into popular beliefs and traditions takes on particular importance in Tudor history, given the impact on them of the religious upheavals of the period. This was a major concern of Keith Thomas in his *Religion and the Decline of Magic*, published in 1971. Influenced by the way anthropologists analyse primitive societies, he also mapped out new ways to approach the evidence of popular culture. Such work has given historians the will and the means to go beyond a history of the literate élite.

Popular culture and the high culture of the élite are to be considered in successive chapters, but a general question for historians is how far they can be separated. For instance, one of the debates about Shakespeare concerns the degree to which his plays appealed to the people at large when they were first written, or just to the more educated classes. However, there is no doubt that Shakespeare did draw on the common stock of popular culture. An illustration of this is in *As You Like It* – the duke was to be found living the simple life in the forest of Arden 'and a many merry men with him; and there they live like the old Robin Hood of England'.

The oral tradition of sixteenth-century popular culture, shared by the élite and the lower orders alike, was transmitted through diverse tales told in the tavern and the home (with many, fortunately for the historian, eventually printed). However, one tale stands out – the numerous contemporary references across a wide geographic and social range, suggest that Robin Hood is the ideal case study of values expressed in the oral tradition and of its development through the period.

2 ROBIN HOOD – A CASE STUDY IN POPULAR CULTURE

Robin Hood is, in his way, a living legend. Stories about him probably first started to circulate in the thirteenth century, and still Robin and his merry men can be seen defeating the Sheriff of Nottingham in books and films. Certain aspects of the stories make them everlastingly popular, whatever the historical circumstances. Above all they celebrate freedom. The greenwood is the opposite of the confinement of ordinary living, be it in medieval or Tudor manor or a modern town. Food is there for the taking in the form of the king's deer and there is no given authority, whether of family or magistrate; the merry men are an entirely free association under a natural leader, Robin. That association has many of the characteristics of a youth gang, idealising cool and successful combat, and disdaining those who try to impose order from above. The escapism has a universal appeal and the tales restore a sense of primitive justice, where a trickster triumphs by outwitting a tyrant or oppressor. But Robin is not just an eternal, mythical character, he also has a historical existence in the development of his story, and possibly in reality as a medieval outlaw.

In the last thirty years the search for the real Robin Hood has quickened. One thing is for certain – the oldest known tales, especially the *Gest* [tale] *of Robin Hood*, place him in a clearly described Barnesdale in south Yorkshire, with Sherwood Forest merely as an additional, shadowy area of operations, perhaps originating from a different cycle of tales. Research in the nineteenth century suggested that he had not been a contemporary of good King Richard and bad Prince John in the

1190s but that he had existed more than a century later in the early 1300s. However, recent work has turned up references to Robin Hood, or variants on his name, as early as 1225, so maybe he was alive and active at the time of Richard the Lionheart and the crusades.

In the end, the search for a real Robin, however enthralling some historians have found it, may be to miss the point. In his recent definitive study, J C Holt has suggested that Robin is likely to be a composite figure, made up of a number of outlaws in the late medieval period. Socially, Robin was at first a yeoman, either meaning one of the rising class of richer farmers in the late Middle Ages, as Dobson and Taylor argue, or a junior member of an aristocratic household as Holt claims is more likely. It was not until the sixteenth century that Robin acquired his aristocratic status and then became the wronged Earl of Huntingdon. It was clearly in the early modern period that Robin and his tales became more diversified to meet the needs of different occasions and different audiences.

The familiar characters only joined Robin gradually. A combative friar, for instance, first makes a full appearance in *Robin Hood and the Curtal Friar*, published in the seventeenth century but probably dating from the later Middle Ages. In the tale the friar fights with Robin, dumps him in the river, sets his dogs on him and finally submits and joins the band of outlaws. The name Friar Tuck, however, had definitely been associated with Robin Hood in the fragment of a play in 1475 and may have originated by 1417 when the name was used as an alias for a poaching, thieving chaplain from Lindfield in Sussex. But Friar Tuck's importance did not come from his origin or even his ebullience in Robin Hood narratives. Although sometimes anonymous, the fat friar, a symbol of joviality and indulgence, made his appearance every year on streets and commons up and down the land during the May Games.

The passing of time through the year was structured by festivals, and the May Games, celebrating the full seasonal return to warmth and fertility, were of particular importance. Morris dancers took their place in the Games, locked in cheerful, ritual combat with their staffs, much as Robin would appear in contemporary versions of his tales. Leading the revellers would be the queen of the May, identified with Maid Marion. She made her first appearance in a medieval French romance along with a lover who was named Robin, but who at that stage had nothing else in common with the outlaw of the greenwood. By the sixteenth century, however, he had become identified with Robin Hood, taking his place alongside Maid Marion in the May Games. So, in the Tudor period, the festivity of the May Games was combined with the freedom celebrated in the tales of the greenwood.

The popularity of the tales was not confined to the lower orders. Henry VIII liked to play at being a guest of Robin Hood. In 1515 he took his queen, Catherine of Aragon, and his Court to Shooters Hill as part of the May celebrations. Upon a whistle from the King, two hundred archers, clad in green and led by Robin Hood, appeared and, having exhibited their skills as archers, invited the royal party into the greenwood for an outlaws' breakfast of venison. But there were those who would have liked to have seen far less of Robin. Bishop Latimer complained of an occasion in 1549 when he was frustrated in his attempt to preach. A local parishioner told him, 'Syr thys is a busye daye wyth us, we can not heare you, it is Robyn hoodes day. The parish are gone a brode to gather for Robyn hoode.' This is one instance of why many evangelical clergy wished to repress popular culture and festivities which they thought prevented people from paying proper attention to the Word of God. But Robin Hood was not just a distraction from religion. He also represented crime.

Holt sees echoes of Robin Hood in the criminology of the sixteenth century. Thomas Harman in 1566 cited a 'ruffler' justifying his mugging of an old man: 'Good Lord, what a world is this! How many a man believe or trust in the same? See you not, this old knave told me that he had but seven shillings, and here is more by an angel. What an old knave and a false knave have we here.' That is akin to Robin's 'moral code' of only robbing those who lied to him. And rioters or criminals frequently brought Robin's name into disrepute as in the case of Roger Marshall of Wednesbury against whom a case was heard in Star Chamber in 1498. He had appeared at Willenhall fair, it was alleged, calling himself Robin Hood and threatening to strike down any man of Walsall who dared to show himself. That was intimidation rather than the traditional good humour and is one reason why Holt sternly reminds us that Robin Hood could be read as 'a glorification of violence to young and old alike'. Certainly there is darkness in the early tales such as 'Robin Hood and the Monk', where an innocent page is killed by one of the 'merry men' because he might be a witness against them. Robin's influence in popular culture was not necessarily benign.

Robin's excuse is usually his generosity with other people's money along with the generally objectionable character of those he steals from. What is not clear is how far these character traits of violence and generosity appealed to the poor and the oppressed. Eric Hobsbawm has shown how bandits could be transformed into heroes in the eyes of the peasantry; they were primitive social rebels. Holt will not accept that this applies to Robin Hood as, while Robin may be an enemy of an individual abbot or sheriff he makes no challenge to the system or to the landholding class. Nonetheless, while it is true that Robin was no social revolutionary, he did relish being outside the law and excelled in defeating officials of Church and State. The evidence to prove how peasants responded to Robin Hood is not available, but it is hard to believe that there was no joy taken in his symbolic destruction of oppressive authority.

Ultimately Robin remained successful in early modern popular culture because he was a master of disguise, just as in the tales. He would turn up at the royal Court or at an inn or market-place. He could appear with all the courtliness and chivalric valour of a wrongly dispossessed earl. But he could also appear, to the delight of a less socially exalted audience, fighting with tinkers and bakers and, in one tale, knocked out by a pedlar and throwing up all over Will Scarlett and Little John. He could be the leading character in a play performed at the Inns of Court or he could oversee the May Games. And he was given a new lease of life by the invention of printing. Wynkyn de Worde, Caxton's successor was the first to print the *Gest of Robin Hood* sometime after 1492 and it was reprinted many times in the 1500s. A century later the minstrel tales were frequently printed in broadsides as ballads to be sung. Whatever the message of Robin Hood, he adapted readily to the new medium of print just as in this century he has leapt, with consummate ease, onto the screen.

3 STREET CREDIBILITY – FESTIVALS AND PROCESSIONS

The May Games in which Robin Hood took part were just one of many festivals and processions which gave shape to the life of a community in sixteenth-century England. We know how important they were, given the efforts of religious reformers and secular authorities, particularly after the Reformation, to suppress or at least control them. But they were difficult to suppress, given that credibility as a member of a community came from participating in them, and custom going back to time immemorial often mattered more than the law. And sheer enjoyment of them must have been a factor as well.

It is a result of the authorities' panic that we know about these street customs in the first place. Aside from limited references in parish registers, it is anxious sermons and legal records which provide the most detailed evidence of dicing or other forms of gambling, of bear-baiting or cock-fighting and of festive occasions. In 1583 Philip Stubbes described a festive street procession in 'The Anatomy of Abuses' (akin to an extended sermon): 'Thus all things set in order, then have they their Hobby-horses, dragons and other Antiques together with their bawdy Pipers and thundering Drummers to strike up the devils dance withall. Then, march these heathen company towards the Church and Church-yard, their pipers piping, their drummers thundering, their stumps dancing, their bells jingling, their handkerchiefs swinging about their heads like madmen, their hobby-horses and other monsters skirmishing amongst the route . . .' The historian always has to be aware of the bias and partial knowledge in his evidence, and it is pretty obvious in the case of Stubbes. But there is a particular challenge in trying to correct the distortions of the hostile witnesses of popular culture when those who were actually out on the street participating in it all left very little trace of their own views behind them.

You can see, however, why Church ministers and magistrates were alarmed by Carnival. Lasting days or even weeks before the surrender to the austerity of Lent (the forty days of fasting before Easter), Carnival was a period of gross self-indulgence in food, drink and sex and a time when the usual order of things was subverted, when the world was turned upside down. Mikhail Bakhtin, whose work has inspired much of the study of Carnival, emphasised the 'uncrowning' that went on in the parody of hierarchy which was at the centre of the festival. A crown, the greatest symbol of authority, became a silly hat and all similar symbols were degraded.

Carnival was ruled over by its personification, described by one anonymous observer as 'sole-man of the Mouth, high Steward to the Stomach . . . Baron of Bacon flitch, Earle of Egg-baskets, and in the least and last place, lower Warden of the Stinke-ports'. Shrove Tuesday, the last day before Lent began, could be devoted not just to pancakes, but to flatulent foods ensuring a good number of powerful, laughter provoking farts. Contrary to the contemplation of higher things, of the spirit, this was the celebration of the body, in particular the lower body.

The whole thing was a travesty – literally, one of its most consistent features was cross-dressing. 'Bessies', men dressed as caricatures of outrageous, shrieking women, perhaps rather like pantomime dames, would parade through the streets. Historians can only speculate as to why they did it – for instance, it could be seen as the re-assertion of masculine authority over 'unruly women' who threatened the patriarchal system. The 'Bessies' themselves probably conceived of it differently – it was hilarious. It was an energetic, exciting liberation from the conventions of ordinary life. The way to celebrate that liberation was by parading the opposites of normality. A 'Bessy' was an opposite twice over – opposite to the man who was playing 'her' and opposite to the contemporary ideal stereotype of a subdued but attractive woman. Some cultural anthropologists argue that such double oppositions form patterns which are basic to all culture.

It is hard to tell what lasting social effect such 'travesty' might have. For, behind all this uninhibited behaviour, structured by opposites and speeded up by the rhythms of pipes and drums, there lay the understanding that it took place in privileged time, that there would have to be a return to normality, leaving ordinary social conventions undamaged. That was why, for all its parody of hierarchy, it was not a form of serious rebellion but a comic ritual.

Some historians would not accept this view that Carnival was a socially neutral comic ritual. A famous French example, the Carnival of

Romans of 1580, apparently demonstrates how subversive it could be, given that it was the occasion for great riots. An alternative view is that Carnival works like a social safety valve and, far from being a cause of rebellion, is therefore essentially conservative. With tensions released for a few days in a world turned upside down, so the argument goes, people would be more willing to accept the regular and often repressive hierarchy encountered in everyday life.

It was not just Carnival, however, that turned the world upside down. There were 'Lords of Misrule' at Christmas, as well as such inverted authorities at Carnival time. The difference between the solar and lunar year is twelve days, the equivalent to the twelve days of Christmas, a gap in regular time. Students would elect a 'lord' as part of the Christmas festivities, such as the 'King of the Cockneys' at Lincoln's Inn, one of the London communities of practising and student lawyers. Christmas was also the season of the year for plays which turned everything upside down, an obviously relevant example being the comic reversals of Shakespeare's *Twelfth Night*.

The whole year was structured by saints' eves – perhaps thirty of them, it varied from place to place – celebrated as 'wakes' which were, in effect, all night parties, and feast days, of which there could have been as many as ninety-five. (Much energy was devoted in the course of the Reformation to suppressing as many of these as possible.) A large number of these days were attached to specific community events. Just before the feast of the Ascension were the Rogation Days when the congregation would process around its parish boundaries – this 'beating of the bounds' affirmed the physical space occupied by the parish. Historians debate the balance between how Christian and how pagan such festivals were in the minds of people who had never received a theological education. At least two further festivals seemed to represent the breaking out of an older, terrifying pagan vision into a Christian ordered world – St John's Eve and Hallowe'en. We still celebrate the latter, of course, although it has been locked away in the safe, commercial world of modern entertainment.

Pagan practices and figures could also make an appearance on the streets of sixteenth-century towns and villages. To dance around a Maypole, a practice particularly loathed by Puritans, was clearly no Christianised ritual. The 'wodevose' or 'wodehouse' would appear in Midsummer pageants, a wild man dressed in skins and foliage brandishing a torch, personifying untamed nature. This was a variant of the 'Green Man' which was sometimes presented in effigy made out of foliage, encased in branches and then burnt. The Church, even before the Reformation, distrusted but could never quite eliminate these symbolic manifestations of pagan traditions and deep responses to the natural world. Modern culture has been more successful, relegating the dance around the maypole to being an asexual game for children, and reducing the image of the Green Man to pub signs.

In stressing the symbolic as against the social importance of popular festivities, one characteristic of them may too easily be overlooked – they provided reassurance, and a policing, of communal identity. Festivities expressed identity, whether for a community as a whole as in a carnival, or for groups such as youth fraternities whose rituals, in relation to Christmas, were described above. Sometimes cruelty would be mixed with the mirth, as in the 'charivari' where youths would band together to mock a young man marrying an older woman. He had betrayed his companions by abandoning them and threatened the fertility of the village, for an older woman might bear few children. If popular culture was the symbolic life of the community, it was also part of the enforcement of communal values on the individual.

Every individual and every group had a place within the larger community with little conception of any personal choice. (There was little individualism as we know it today, although it was beginning to develop by the end of the period [*see pages 394–5*].) In villages the community was defined mainly by family lineage. In towns, where there was greater social mobility, it would most clearly be seen in a religious procession which could be read like a social map. The best example of this is the procession of Corpus Christi, literally the Body of Christ. Taking place shortly after Whitsun, the whole of the town's corporation and gilds would process in order of importance, the most eminent coming last. The dominant image was that of the body, Christ's mystical Body, which united the faithful in the celebration of the Mass, and the social body, the community in procession. The mayor was the head, with the officers and the gilds being the limbs. All would be at one in 'good unity, concord and charity', according to the Tailors of Newcastle upon Tyne in 1536, when gild brothers 'amicably and lovingly . . . in their best apparel and array go in the procession'. This was, at any rate, the ideal. If things went wrong there could be riots instead of concord, one gild or 'limb' against another, battling over precedence.

In many towns Corpus Christi involved more than a procession. There were also pageants made up of mimes on wagons or fullscale mystery plays as at York. ('Mystery' in this context refers to a craft rather than to the modern idea of a mystery.) Not to present a play meant that the gild would be dishonoured, and it was obvious who should present what – the Bakers, for example, were usually the choice for the Last Supper and any Watermen performed Noah's Flood. This was the popular drama of the time where a community presented its stock characters and its values to itself.

It was not to last in that form. The Corpus Christi processions were abolished in 1547, condemned as papist superstition. And along with this abolition of religious images in drama went the destruction of visual images, paintings and sculptures which had adorned churches as visual aids, theological 'books for the unlearned' – Protestants feared they would inspire idolatry. (*See pages 422–3 for a more detailed discussion of the new religious élite's attack on visual images.*) The Reformation, and also social changes, were to affect much of the material of popular culture.

Even before Protestantism brought them to an end, however, the Corpus Christi processions were in decline. Gilds were growing poorer; population growth and economic change were disrupting the customary order of the towns. As this occurred the town élites, newly conditioned by humanist education (*see pages 413–17*) became more authoritarian and more remote from a popular culture starting to appear alien and dangerous. Religious figures, such as Noah, had been lampooned in the mystery plays and what had once seemed funny came to seem disrespectful and threatening. Many processions were reserved to the magistracy and its pomp alone, with the rest of the community excluded except as passive spectators. Drama did not disappear but there was less room for it on the increasingly controlled streets and it was gradually transferred into the private space of the theatres that were being newly built.

Although the Reformation united the authorities of Church and State in England, the country was fracturing in other ways. There had always been differences between life in towns and villages but, at the beginning of the sixteenth century, with only the largest cities approaching 10 000 people, towns had been very closely tied to the rural economy and culture. By 1600 urbanisation was quickening with the pace of commerce, and, for townspeople, the festivities of the agricultural year were becoming gradually more remote. The slow erosion of traditional popular culture had begun.

Traditional popular culture itself had not been unchanging – the Corpus Christi procession, for instance, dated from the thirteenth century rather than from time immemorial – but it did unite successive generations and, for all the authorities' distrust of riotous enjoyment, it brought together the various classes. In the sixteenth century not only did urbanisation speed up, but a new idea of what was vulgar and to be avoided took hold as the gentry and wealthier merchants separated themselves off more from common folk, at least in the less remote parts of the country. (See the next section on the transformation of the concept of hospitality and page 402 on the emerging culture of the gentleman.)

All this is not to say that we should be nostalgic for the happier, more harmonious Middle Ages, along with those who promote fictions of 'Merry England'. As noted above, scope for individual choice and cultural pluralism, which many in modern society value so highly, were hardly known in medieval and Tudor England.

4 HOSPITALITY

In 1595 the Lord Keeper of the Seal made a speech calling for house-hold charity to be renewed. This was, in part, an appeal to restore a golden age of social solidarity which had never fully existed, an appeal prompted by the harvest failures of the 1590s and fears that the hungry would rebel; but in part there was real cause for anxiety about the dying away during the Tudor age of an ideal of hospitality.

This ideal prescribed that when a stranger appeared at the gate, he must be fed and watered. This was a unifying popular concept, apply-ing to the cottage and the great house. It was symbolic of the code of hospitality that the gate was kept open during the day to all comers, except at meal times. The host's welcome to the guest was as important an exchange as money in other circumstances – the guest received sus-tenance and in return the host gained in honour. And, as Felicity Heal has put it, hospitality was 'a coded language, designed to articulate both power and magnanimity'. The more public hospitality a host was able to offer, the more influence he could wield in his community.

By 1600 the old inclusive ideal of hospitality was being much modi-fied, especially in the upper reaches of society. This could be seen in the layout of great houses. All meals had been taken in the Hall where the master presided over his household and guests, rich and poor. Having retreated first into a semi-private chamber, more and more of the nobility and gentry during Elizabeth's reign were cutting them-selves off in private dining rooms. There were still occasions for public hospitality, such as the Christmas gift-giving from tenants to lords in return for beer, bread and broth, but most hospitality was confined to social equals. It was not just a matter of being social equals by birth or economic status, however important these were; by the mid-Tudor period an increasing number of gentleman hosts expected guests to speak the same language learned in a humanist education.

The Reformation also, of course, played a role. Protestant doctrine took away any virtue from the giving of alms, and hospitality was, in part, displaced by organised charity. Instead of the reciprocal exchange of host and guest and the absorption of the poor into households, the Poor Laws of 1598 and 1601 (*see pages 468/9*) separated out the giving and receiving. And the stranger at the gate became the vagrant to be whipped back to his own parish. Organised charity was only for the really destitute; the able-bodied individual had to look after him or herself.

Increasing commercialisation and social mobility were fostering individualism at the expense of communal solidarity. It was therefore in areas in the North, in Wales and in Ireland, more remote from the centres of commercial development, that the old culture of hospitality survived more nearly intact, and still does in some areas where tourism has not dealt it a final death blow.

The decline of traditional hospitality meant the disappearance of a code giving clear guidance to people's behaviour. This cultural uncertainty led to many social stresses and strains, the needy nursing resentments as they were turned away from the door and the householder being confronted by guilt for having done so. (This may have prompted accusations of witchcraft [*see pages 394–5*].)

5 MAGIC AND POPULAR BELIEFS

There is nothing ridiculous in a belief in magic. Men and women always have wanted, and always will want, to control their environment; unable to do so themselves, they defer to experts apparently qualified by a special knowledge of how the world works. Today we have a blind faith in scientists; in Tudor England people turned to experts in magic, the 'cunning' men or women. Scientists, of course, are supposed to work on the basis of experimental fact and demonstrable cause and effect. However, our trust in them is another thing: a placebo, for instance, can apparently effect a cure whether it is prescribed by a modern doctor or a Tudor cunning man or woman. For most people (now as then) it is the authority which counts.

Magic was very often used for healing. A jumble of herbal recipes and incomprehensible incantations were available for the treatment of every problem. One Elizabethan wizard would cure the toothache by writing down on a piece of paper the names of the spirits he identified as causing the malady, whisper some spells (all the more powerful because secret) and then burn the paper. Many healers used touch as part of the cure. One particularly macabre example is the lifting up of sufferers from goitre (caused by iodine deficiency) to be touched by the dead hand of a freshly hanged man. But an example of great political importance was the touching for the King's evil, the power, supposedly granted to both the kings of France and England, to cure scrofula, a skin disease, by the laying on of hands. This apparently supernatural gift bolstered monarchical authority.

These healing spells and practices may seem absurd. However, as Keith Thomas argues, the drama and the symbolism of it all could work very well as a sort of primitive psychotherapy, and magical treatment could be more benign than the contemporary 'scientific' treatment by Tudor physicians with their purging and leeches. Herbal remedies were often very effective and, as forests and thousands of species of plants disappear in the modern world, it is increasingly and belatedly understood how much modern medicine can draw on them. Tudor herbalists did not understand in our terms how their remedies worked – they believed that every herb had a 'signature', an almost mystical characteristic which revealed its properties – but long practice and trial and error had enriched traditional lore and made much of it effective.

Divination, the revelation of hidden knowledge, was another task of cunning men or women. The location of a lost object might be pointed to by shears and sieve, or key and book. Criminals could be identified – the skill of the diviner was, of course, to give the name of someone already suspected. In a 1590 arson case, one Thomas Harding, accused a cunning man of fraud because he refused to identify those he, Thomas, had already said were guilty. Reassurance, the firming up of intuition, serving the preference to take some sort of action rather than do nothing in the face of adversity – these psychological and social needs were answered by the cunning folk.

The telling of fortunes was even more important in a period when natural or personal disaster was ever threatening. The fame of some seers spread far and wide beyond any single village. Elizabeth Barton, the Holy Maid of Kent, for instance, made herself very unpopular with Henry VIII by prophesying that he would die young if he married Anne Boleyn. A backhanded compliment was paid to the power of her prophecy (which was being exploited by those who opposed the Royal Supremacy) when she was executed in 1534. Similarly an inhabitant of County Kildare found that prophecy could bring retribution when his ears were cut off in 1593 for foretelling that an O'Donnell would one day be king of Ireland. Prophecy could enhance resolve or simply assuage natural curiosity but, where it applied to the great and, through them, the whole community, it could threaten the state.

Living prophets could be dealt with through the harsh rigour of the law but, unfortunately for the authorities, the popular imagination was host to a whole range of legendary prophets whose sayings were held to have contemporary force. Although there were those, including Caxton, who doubted that King Arthur ever existed, Merlin was still often quoted as an authority on present and future events. He was a danger to the state in that his name could be used to foster Welsh resistance to the Saxon – English – invader. There were numerous rhymes and riddles involving mythical or heraldic beasts such as the Red Dragon or the Boar of Cornwall. They could be interpreted to give legitimacy to more or less any political cause. In an age lacking any concept of progress, such a cause had to be wrapped up in some sense of the restoration of a lost age or the force of destiny. Indeed prophecies multiplied during times of disturbance. The Earl of Northampton in the late 1500s observed of a century earlier: 'When the Civil War was hottest between York and Lancaster the books of Beasts and Babies were exceeding rife and current in every quarter and corner of the realm, either side applying and interpreting as they were affected to the title.'

Less dramatic but perhaps more pervasive in its effects was astrology. It made sense that the stars were placed in the heavens for a purpose and the emotional effects of the moon seemed obvious. The learned cosmology of the time, placing the heavenly bodies in their various spheres (*see page 430*), was perfectly in harmony with the notion that they should influence natural and human events. And astrology had the great advantage of prestige in its being classified as a learned science at the same time as it could be easily, and profitably, popularised in the form of almanacs, pamphlets which made broad predictions and specified which days of the year would be best for sowing or reaping, wooing or marrying, or whatever activity might be of concern. The casting of individual horoscopes also made many astrologers both busy and rich.

Any threat to the status of astrologers did not come from being proved wrong: their general predictions and horoscopes were presented as only the likely outcomes of complex influences rather than as certainties which could be verified. And in any case reassuring advice was wanted from the astrologer as much as information, just as counsellors (or modern astrologers) might provide today. Many of the clergy saw astrologers as rivals in seeking the confidence of their parishioners. Calvinists in particular denounced the idea that control over human destinies came via the stars rather than directly from God; for them astrology smelt of diabolism. However, belief in astrology was too deep for the clergy to do anything to uproot it in the Tudor period. Indeed, many a clergyman himself found an almanac a handy book of reference.

According to the Whig interpretation of history (a school of thought powerful well into this century, which saw English history in terms of ever upward progress towards rationalism and liberty) there should be a clear chronology for the disappearance of magic and divination. They belong with, what were from the Whig point of view, all the other dark superstitions of late medieval Catholicism which should have been brought to an end by the Reformation and its triumphant preachers; this would then have paved the way for the emergence of modern, rational science. This chronology is, however, too simple. While the rituals of the pre-Reformation Church did lend themselves more to diversion into magical practices (such as the use of holy water for the magical purpose of making the land fertile), ecclesiastical leaders spoke out against them, albeit with limited effect. But then the triumph of the Reformation did not spell any quick end to magic either. The religious emphasis was shifted from ritual to belief, and the scope for a magic which made its own use of Church rituals was thereby reduced, but a congregation could just as well leave church after a long, hard sermon (which they might have regarded as penance in a new guise as much as a revelation of Scriptural truth) and return to the practical solutions offered by the cunning man or woman. Even those who listened to the preacher and believed what he said may not have had their own belief in magic reduced. It is one of the errors of some scholars to think that, because their belief system is entirely coherent, others are incapable of holding a number of contrary beliefs at one and the same time.

Astrology defies the simple chronology as well. If anything, it was resurgent by the middle of the sixteenth century, having been much more neglected in the early, pre-Reformation years of the century, and it has by no means disappeared in the modern world. Science too was not necessarily an enemy to magic; on the contrary it was allied to it in the sixteenth century. Magic depended on an animistic view of the material world – that is, the belief that all the matter around us is moved by spiritual forces which humans can harness through spells and rituals. Some significant science in the later sixteenth century, in line with neo-Platonism, a philosophy derived from Renaissance Italy, also worked on the principle that matter was imbued with spirits. Advances in mathematics grew from beliefs in the mystical qualities of numbers and not just from disinterested enquiry. The alchemist, with his repertoire of strange symbols and ritual incantations was not simply to be overthrown by the modern scientist, not even in the following century as the Scientific Revolution gathered momentum. Isaac Newton is famous as the father of modern physics – but he spent just as much of his time and intellectual energy on alchemy. So, just as the chronology is not simple, there is no simple division here between 'irrational' popular belief and 'rational' élite learning.

Magic, of course, was eventually to decline but not just because the clergy and (eventually) the scientists told the people to stop believing. Economic changes making existence less precarious, population movement into towns causing natural spirits to seem increasingly remote and, above all, the displacement of magical practices by modern technologies led to a gradual decline in magic and the animistic belief system which supported it. In the end it made more practical sense to drain and fertilise fields properly than to sprinkle them with holy water. Keith Thomas argues that magic declined before these material changes really got going and that it was therefore the belief system that changed first. But it is difficult to find evidence for his claim that there was a 'trickle down' effect in beliefs from newly enlightened scientists other than among the educated classes, and although the evidence for magical practices starts to dry up by 1700, that may be because the élite became dismissive of it rather than because magical practices ceased to exist. Magic can easily disappear simply by being recategorised as folklore or the superstition of the ignorant.

But alongside material needs, one thing that sustained a belief in magic throughout the early modern period, as much amongst the reformed clergy as their credulous parishioners, was fear of it in its malign form – witchcraft.

6 WITCHES

On 8 March 1579 the 4-year-old Susan Webbe died. Death in infancy or early childhood was all too common, but on this occasion the cause was reckoned to be witchcraft. And the guilty one seemed obvious. Ellen Smyth was the daughter of a condemned witch; her stepfather had become ill after a quarrel over an inheritance; she had a familiar, people said, a toad which, when burnt, caused Ellen pain; her son described her three spirits kept in bottles and in a wool-pack discovered in her house. She had another familiar, a black dog, which sent Susan Webbe's mother mad. Ellen Smyth was tried, found guilty of witching Susan to death, and hanged.

It was cases like this which characterise English witchcraft. There was no witch 'craze' or sudden epidemic of prosecutions – such cases as Ellen's were commonplace, although the bulk of them were in the later Tudor and early Stuart periods. In England there was none of the paraphernalia of continental witchcraft and the folklore which has come to represent it. There were no supposed flights by broomstick; witches like Ellen operated alone and not in covens enjoying a witches' sabbath. There were few reports of sexual excesses with an 'incubus' (i.e. the Devil playing the male part) or any bewitching of genitals, a fear of which, presumably for personal reasons, obsessed some continental commentators on the black arts. Instead in England there was generally just *maleficium*, the doing of harm to people or property. What the cunning folk could do for good, the witch could do for ill. The standard pattern was that a neighbours' quarrel would lead to cursing. If injury or damage then followed, then witchcraft would be talked of.

Ellen Smyth's case was typical of this pattern in most respects, except that Susan Webbe died almost immediately. Witchcraft was most often thought of when there was a lingering illness with plenty of opportunity to reflect on what had caused it and time to try to do something about it. But Ellen did have her familiars which are the most distinctively English feature of witchcraft. Familiars hardly figured in European witchcraft otherwise, except some instances in the Basque country. And the black cat was not necessarily the standard familiar. Ellen had her toad and black dog. One Joan Prentice was famous for her Bid the Ferret, which livened up the pamphlet account of Joan's witchcraft by being able to talk.

The first reaction of anyone fearful of malice from the like of Ellen or Joan had usually been to employ counter-magic. A cunning man or woman could help identify – or rather confirm suspicion – of the source of *maleficium* and perhaps provide a charm or advice on how to combat it. The pre-Reformation Church had also been a rich source of counter-magic with its exorcisms and holy water and other ritual devices. Only in the last resort did the supposed victim of witchcraft resort to the law.

There were a series of statutes relating to witchcraft. Henry VIII's 1542 statute connected it with heresy but this was repealed in 1547. Another was passed in 1563 at a time of concern at the false prophecies which sustained treason. Finally, the 1604 statute under James I, who thought himself to be an expert, was yet more severe, imposing the death penalty on a second offence for simply intending injury.

Recourse to the law became ever more common in the latter half of the sixteenth century and on into the seventeenth. It was not just because of these new statutes – where injury or damage could be proved, it had anyway been possible to bring cases against witches. According to Keith Thomas the law filled the gap when the Reformation stripped most of the devices used in counter-magic from the Church. That does much to explain the timing of witchcraft accusations – they increased in number as the Reformation became established. And certainly other explanations do not seem to tally with the statistics. Trevor-Roper argued that witch hunting was part of the hysteria generated by conflict between Catholics and Protestants, but there is little correlation, at least in England, between an increase in witchcraft cases and intense periods of religious conflict. Nor were witches used as scapegoats in bad times. In the late 1590s, despite disastrous harvests, there was no surge in prosecutions. In Essex, an example exhaustively studied by Alan MacFarlane, there were notable increases in the 1580s and 1640s, but he argues these resulted more from one or two determined prosecutors than from general conditions. Witchcraft accusations were not like an epidemic disease breaking out occasionally. They were a regular part of village life.

In Essex over half the villages had at least one witchcraft case in the Tudor and Stuart period. An Essex clergyman, George Gifford, who wrote two books on witchcraft in 1587 and 1593, quoted one character as saying:

> I was of a Jury not many years past, when there was an old
> woman arraigned for a witch. There came in eight or ten which
> gave evidence against her . . . One woman came in and testified
> upon her oath that her husband upon his death bed, took it
> upon his death, that he was bewitched, for he pined a long time. 5
> And he said further, he was sure that woman bewitched him.
> He took her to be naught, and thought she was angry with him,
> because she would have borrowed five shillings of him, and he
> denied to lend it to her. The woman took her oath also, that she
> thought in her conscience that the old woman was a witch, and 10
> that she killed her husband . . . Then followed a man, and he
> said he could not tell, but he thought she was once angry with
> him because she came to beg a few pot-herbs, and he denied
> her: and presently after he heard a thing as he thought to
> whisper in his ear, thou shalt be bewitched. The next day he 15

had such a pain in his back, that he could not sit upright: he said he sent to a cunning woman, she told he was bewitched, and by a woman that came for pot-herbs ... Then came in two or three grave honest men, which testified by common fame that she was a witch. We found her guilty, for what could we do 20 less, she was condemned and executed: and upon the ladder she made her prayer, and took it upon her death she was innocent and free from all such dealings.

1   *In both the specific accusations cited above (lines 4–5 and 15–16) what did each victim think started the chain of events leading to their being bewitched?*

2   *What is meant by the 'common fame' referred to in line 19 and what made it believable?*

3   *Analyse the reasons why the accused came to be thought a witch.*

Village communities were very tight knit and conformity to precise roles was demanded. Some would not, or could not, conform. The cackling old hag cursing the ordinary villagers is an over-drawn, fairy tale image but it has something in it. Witches did tend to be women past child-bearing age – that could make them marginal, of little further use to the future of the community and they might understandably have shown resentment at being pushed aside. Also some witch accusations may have been part of an attempt to reassert patriarchal authority over 'unruly women' (as satirised in Carnival). This does not mean that **all** witches were old and were women – neither do the court statistics nor the pamphlet literature of the time suggest that witchcraft was gender specific or that being old was an absolute prerequisite. However, it was older women who were often the most dependent on their neighbours; and where they were too demanding, tensions could grow and lead to quarrels and then to accusations of *maleficium* when something went wrong.

Surprisingly few supposed witches came from the poorest sections of the community, although they were usually poorer than their accusers. Possibly the poorest were too thoroughly under the heel of the rest of the community, whereas one almost universal characteristic of accused witches was a willingness to make a nuisance of themselves, to the point of cursing. And nothing, it seems, led to cursing more quickly than being turned down when requesting traditional, neighbourly charity.

Traditional hospitality seemed to contemporaries to be in decline in the Tudor period (*see pages 387–8*) and other forms of charity were being neglected. Alan MacFarlane sees in this the gradual rise of individualism at the expense of the old, closed, mutually supportive life of traditional communities. Village life was being disrupted by the economic and social changes of the early modern period – inflation, more trade, more movement up and down the social and financial scales, more migration from place to place, and particularly from villages to towns. With individualism developing as part of these changes, so neighbours were expected more to fend for themselves or rely on official sources of support, such as the parish. Also, since the Reformation the giving of alms had not been seen as a way of earning reward in Heaven. So there were ever more scenes where 'five shillings' or 'pot-herbs' would be denied to the old woman who asked for them, while the old moral imperative to give to neighbours still hung on in the background as a part of the inherited culture. The result was that the one who requested charity and was refused felt a right had been denied, and consequently she might well curse or try to frighten her way into getting what she asked for. (And the historian can never know how many 'witches' there were who were not prosecuted simply because they were successful in terrifying their neighbours into giving them what they wanted.) Equally, the neighbour who had denied a request might well feel guilty and seek to dispel that guilt by proclaiming the disappointed and angry old woman to be a witch.

Keith Thomas argues that witch beliefs 'reinforced accepted moral standards' because they made it clear that unneighbourly behaviour would have dreadful consequences. 'They were a check on the expression of vicious feelings by both the likely witch and her prospective victim.' In other words, witch beliefs were conservative in effect, keeping the old charitable ethos alive despite all the economic and social changes. MacFarlane places much more stress on what Thomas only passingly accepts – every time a witchcraft prosecution took place, however traditional it looked on the surface, the refusal of charity was being justified. In the longer run, witch prosecutions (rather than just witch beliefs) could help to destroy the old charitable obligations and, therefore, have a truly radical effect on village society. They helped to bring about 'a change from a "neighbourly", highly integrated and mutually interdependent village society, to a more individualistic one'. News of the hanging of a witch from a nearby village might just make an old woman think twice about pushing her demands for 'five shillings' or 'pot-herbs' too far, however much in an earlier period she might have been able to expect them as of right.

Apart from an upsurge in the chaotic 1640s, witch prosecutions gradually declined through the seventeenth century. Keith Thomas emphasises the cultural explanation – that the triumph of a mechanistic view of the universe did not allow for demons and black magic, or magic of any sort, and that gradually 'trickled down' to the lower orders (*see page 39*). Certainly eighteenth-century judges were to laugh witch prosecutions out of court even before the 1736 repeal of the relevant statute. That took away the legal ritual which had helped to sustain witch beliefs. MacFarlane, on the other hand, places greater emphasis on the social explanation – once individualism had triumphed and the old integrated communities had virtually dissolved, the tensions which had brought about witch accusations simply did not arise.

None of this happened quickly. Lynchings of supposed witches continued after the repeal of the law, the last known instance being that of Ruth Osborne at Tring in 1751. (The usual story – she had been refused buttermilk by a farmer who subsequently fell ill.) And witch beliefs survived even longer, continuing in some rural areas well into the nineteenth century and even into the twentieth. Although the intellectual, social and economic life of the larger society was transformed, popular culture in its local contexts, whether with regard to witch beliefs or any of its other forms previously discussed, showed a remarkable capacity to endure.

7 BIBLIOGRAPHY

F Heal *Hospitality in Early Modern England* (Clarendon, 1990).
J C Holt *Robin Hood* (Thames & Hudson, revised 1989).
M E James *Society, Politics and Culture: Studies in Early Modern England* (Cambridge, 1986).
F Laroque *Shakespeare's Festive World* (Cambridge, 1991).
A MacFarlane *Witchcraft in Tudor and Stuart England* (Routledge, 1970).
K Thomas *Religion and the Decline of Magic* (Weidenfeld and Nicolson, 1971, Penguin 1973).
J A Sharpe *Early Modern England: A Social History 1550–1760* (Edward Arnold, 1987).

8 DISCUSSION POINTS AND EXERCISES

A *This section consists of questions or points that might be used for discussion (or written answers) as a way of expanding on the chapter and testing understanding of it:*

1   Why has 'popular culture' been studied more in recent years?

2   Why were tales of Robin Hood popular in the Tudor period?

3   What do responses to Robin Hood reveal about attitudes to crime in the sixteenth century?

4   What was the significance of Carnival?

5   How did festivities and processions express the identity of a community and why was that changing by 1600?

6   Why was magic so universal a phenomenon in sixteenth-century rural life?

7 What shaped the attitudes to magic, prophecy and astrology of
  (*a*) the secular authorities?
  (*b*) the clergy?
  (*c*) scientists?

8 What eventually brought about the decline of magic?

9 What were the common causes of witchcraft accusations?

10 Why did such accusations increase in number towards the end of
   the sixteenth century?

11 What were the social characteristics of the witch?

12 What were the general social effects of witch trials and why did
   they decline?

B *Essay questions*

1 What constituted 'popular culture' in sixteenth-century England
  and how subject was it to change?

2 How far did the Reformation transform popular culture in Tudor
  England?

3 'Popular stories and festivities can reveal the fundamental
  characteristics of a society.' Is this true of the period 1450–1600 in
  England?

4 Who believed in, and practised, magic in sixteenth-century
  England, and why?

5 What caused the rise and then the decline of witch trials in early
  modern England?

9 ESSAY WRITING EXERCISE – CONTROLLING A BROAD TOPIC

Many essays, particularly in political history, refer to a well-defined
topic, a minister or a monarch, or a debate such as that surrounding
'the Tudor Revolution in Government'. They are often preferred by
students because the necessary information seems more manageable,
both in terms of its range and the way it divides easily into sub-sec-
tions or paragraphs. However, broader topics covering social or cultural issues across a whole period can allow for more creative thinking,
and they need not be peculiarly difficult to handle, given a methodical
approach.

The question to be used as an example is number 2 above: 'How far
did the Reformation transform popular culture in Tudor England?' Re-
read the chapter in the light of this question and then go through the
following stages:

1   List the aspects of popular culture to be considered – folk tales, Carnival, and so forth.

2   Number these aspects in order of the Reformation's impact on them.

3   In putting the various aspects of popular culture in order, certain problems of evidence may have come to light. For example, it is not immediately clear how far the Reformation affected Carnival and similar processions. That may require further research, but the readily available evidence can also be reviewed carefully. In this case look again at Philip Stubbes' hostile account of a street procession on page 382. What does the date of his account suggest about the immediacy of the Reformation's impact? There were repeated attempts to curtail carnivals and similar processions through preaching and lawsuits – what does **repetition** suggest about the success or otherwise of such attempts?

    Questioning the evidence in this way may not lead to certain conclusions but one of the techniques in dealing with a broad topic is to indicate, as you write, where you are on sure ground and where your analysis is necessarily more tentative.

4   Jot down any more general points which you need to take into account as you write. Such points are often concerned with:

    (*a*) the nature of the evidence; (*b*) comparison; (*c*) the long term view.

For instance:

a   Scrutiny of what Stubbes wrote should have reminded you that our view of popular culture may be distorted, given that the evidence often comes from hostile sources. We know most about what reformers were keen to control – there may be much popular culture which has gone unrecorded and on which the Reformation had no impact.

b   It would be useful to contrast the importance of the Reformation with other forces for change, such as urbanisation.

c   Some general reading would enable you to glance ahead from the Tudor period towards the seventeenth century. Popular Protestantism was by then far more widespread and had come to displace more aspects of traditional popular culture – even Christmas festivities disappeared for a time in the middle of the century.

5   Finally, frame your overall argument. It is often helpful to summarise it in a sentence or two so that you have a clear sense of direction. A starting point here would be: 'Reformers wished to control popular culture wherever they suspected it distracted from a godly life or smacked of popery or paganism. However, they

could only quickly transform what came under the direct control of the Church, such as religious processions and images; secular practices and beliefs, transmitted in the home, in the tavern and on the street, may have been condemned by reformers as immoral but were much more resistant to change.'

XIV

CULTURE AND SOCIETY
II: THE CULTURE OF THE ÉLITE

—

William Shakespeare, anon.

1 INTRODUCTION

Whatever the growing importance of 'history from below', the literate
élite in the age of Renaissance and Reformation has remained a vital
area of study. What enhanced the significance of Renaissance classical
studies in Tudor England was the introduction of printing to England
by William Caxton in the late fifteenth century and the expansion of
education beyond the clerical, academic élite to include a fair proportion of the nobility and gentry. Kings before the Tudors had had to win
credit with their subjects through displays of piety. Henry VIII was the
first king who saw the need to show the world how learned he was.

The culture of the élite took on particular importance under the Tudors, as did popular culture, because of the Reformation. This fundamental event of Tudor England was not just a religious and political watershed. It was also a cultural crisis. The leading writers of the age – men called humanists because of their training in the classics – had varying attitudes to the Reformation. The Tudor regime thought it vital that they should support the break from Rome, that their writings should legitimise the Royal Supremacy. The recent work of Alistair Fox and John Guy have shown the complexities and importance of this cultural struggle in Tudor England.

The Reformation was in one aspect the cause of destruction, with the looting of monasteries by Henry's commissioners or the wrecking of medieval shrines by Protestant enthusiasts. But the Reformation also stimulated much cultural creativity. The printing presses turned out huge quantities of what some might be tempted to dismiss as Protestant propaganda, but which had a profound effect on the way people wrote and thought. Religious works, such as the translations of the Bible, provided models of expressive English which have affected writers from generation to generation.

The image of a newly austere religion cutting away the cultural luxuriance of the old is also belied by the Protestant culture which grew up at the Tudor Court. This reached its height under Queen Elizabeth, with poetry and ceremonial produced by courtiers, surrounding her with a cult which made use of Renaissance symbols to bolster the Royal Supremacy and portray the justice and glory of the godly state of England. (*See pages 425–30 for a discussion of this cult in its political context.*) Frances Yates did more than any other historian to reveal this cultural programme of Elizabeth's courtiers. Its residual power is evident in the way that people today, who may know nothing of Elizabethan government, still have an impression of Elizabeth presiding over a golden age as 'The Virgin Queen', as 'Gloriana' or 'Astraea'.

Beside this enduring image of Queen Elizabeth, the other great icon of our cultural heritage originating in the late Tudor period is William Shakespeare. His genius is felt by many to transcend history, to articulate what is universal in human experience. But no man is free from history: Shakespeare's writings are embedded in the particular cultural context of late Tudor and early Jacobean England. E M W Tillyard sought to lay bear this context in his *The Elizabethan World Picture*, published in 1943. This offers the clearest insight into the structure of ideas which conditioned the educated mind of the period. Some more recent literary critics and historians, such as the so called 'New Historicists', prefer to investigate the competing, changing ideas of the time rather than to try to identify a static 'world picture'; they are looking for all the tensions and complexities in a period's thought, for the struggle rather than the structure. And there is much material, apart from

Shakespeare and his fellow dramatists, to fuel further debates about sixteenth-century culture, given the innovations then in printing and education which multiplied both texts and their readers.

2 REVOLUTIONS IN LEARNING – PRINTING AND EDUCATION

The popular culture examined in the last chapter was not just the preserve of the lower orders. From Robin Hood through mystery plays to belief in the powers of cunning folk and witches, the display, the pleasures and the values of popular culture were shared by a full cross-section of society, despite the clergy sometimes being suspicious of areas of communal life they could not control. However, although popular culture endured as a common stock of ideas and motifs, in the sixteenth century a more distinctive élite culture began to emerge which eventually led to the spurning of much popular culture as being vulgar. (The history of the word 'vulgar' itself charts this change in attitude. It originally just meant 'of the people'; by the seventeenth century it had taken on the current meaning of 'coarse, lacking in good taste'.) This élite culture was made possible by the printed book and by education. It was the culture of the gentleman.

It is difficult to assess how deep this cultural change went. The gentleman might be able to adorn his library with books but he did not necessarily read them; and while his son could attend Oxford or Cambridge or the Inns of Court he was as likely to dedicate himself there to riotous living as to the pursuit of learning. (In Elizabeth's reign William Harrison complained that when charged with disorder such roisterers 'think it sufficient to say they be gentlemen which grieveth many not a little'.) A distinction must be drawn between a show of culture which is made to win status, and culture which involves real participation.

It is also the case that ordinary people were not necessarily excluded from the printed word and education. Elementary education was widely available in 'petty' schools and there were charity schools such as Christ's Hospital in London open to the poor. Nonetheless, there is much debate about literacy rates. At the beginning of Elizabeth's reign about 20 per cent of men and 5 per cent of women were literate, on the evidence that they were able to sign their names. However, Thomas More estimated that about half of the population were literate. This could be a quite accurate impression, although it may apply only to London. The tradesmen and craftsmen of the capital were much more likely to be literate than the inhabitants of a remote rural community. And More can only have been referring to men. Literacy was subject to great regional and social variations and it would be hard to generalise even if the statistical evidence was clear.

Henry VIII and Henry VII, detail from the cartoon drawing for the *Tudor Succession*, Hans Holbein

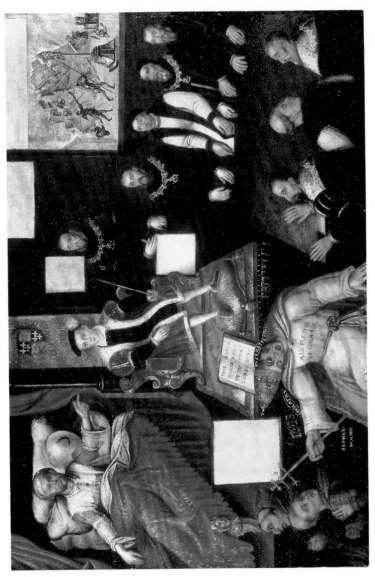

Allegory of the Reformation under Edward VI, anon.

Coronation Portrait of Elizabeth I, anon.

Allegory of *The Tudor Succession*, Lucas de Heere

Frontispiece to the *General and Rare Memorials* by John Dee

Elizabeth I, *The Sieve Portrait,* attribution either Cornelius Kitel or Federico Zuccari

Elizabeth I, *The Ditchley Portrait*, Marcus Gheeraerts the Younger

NON·SINE·SOLE·
IRIS·

Elizabeth I, *The Rainbow Portrait*, Marcus Gheeraerts the Younger

Despite the statistical uncertainties Lawrence Stone argued that the dynamic growth of literacy in the late Tudor period, coupled with the growth of schools and higher education, amounted to an 'educational revolution' lasting from 1560 to 1640. David Cressy's researches have supported this view, postulating that there was an upsurge in literacy to about 30 per cent of men and 10 per cent of women by the mid-seventeenth century. However, this still leaves the cultural impact of such a revolution unclear. Literacy, for instance, might have enabled an apprentice or a yeoman to read a 'gest of Robin Hood' or an almanac (*see page 390*) but these were extensions of popular, oral culture not displacements of it.

Printing

William Caxton set up the first printing press in England in 1476. This was some twenty years after printing with moveable type had been developed by Gutenberg in Mainz. Such a time lag suggests it was not so much a technological breakthrough as a businessman's judgment that there was sufficient demand for books which spurred on the development of printing. Caxton's press was certainly a wise investment and flourished under his careful assessment of the cultural market and that of his successor, Wynkyn de Worde. They published mainly religious works and chivalric romances such as Malory's *Morte d'Arthur*.

Caxton's printing press did not lead to immediate cultural change. Much of what he published was the same as the texts copied by scribes in a monastic scriptorium. However, although the contents of books might not have been immediately affected by the advent of printing, a new consumer came into existence. There had been private libraries before printing – the most famous is probably that of Duke Humphrey of Gloucester, a brother of Henry V, who donated his great collection to the University of Oxford – but most books were in abbeys and most scholars were monks. Literacy amongst the gentry had already started to improve in the fifteenth century but books had been scarcely affordable. Printing brought learning within their reach.

The debate on the effect of printing and education at the start of this section focused on the horizontal division in society between the gentleman and the lower orders. However, it should not obscure what happened to the vertical division between laity and clergy. Aside from some merchants and courtiers and religious enthusiasts such as the Lollards, the clerical monopoly on learning was so definite an assumption that it was sufficient to prove that you could read to claim 'benefit of clergy' and escape the full rigour of the secular law courts. Now, even before the Reformation weakened the division between the clergy and the rest of society, printing had done much to break their monopoly and open up the world of learning to the laity.

Printing brought a new freedom of ideas, and this could be a challenge to the state as well as to the clergy. It led to repeated attempts by the government to control the presses. The year 1529 saw the first list of prohibited books in reaction to the upsurge of Protestant literature and in 1538 censorship was extended to secular as well as religious works. Finally, in 1557 the Stationers were incorporated as a company to police printing in return for a monopoly of licensed presses in London, leaving the only competition in Oxford and Cambridge. Commercial incentive proved the most effective means of censorship.

Printing was not, of course, just a threat to the state. It furthered its development towards the modern state we know today. Administration was made easier – the latest statutes, for instance, became more accurately and quickly known when printed. Government propaganda could be spread much more efficiently, as when Cromwell assembled a team of writers to communicate his view of the Reformation. More subtly the national state could be supported by a stronger national identity as printing helped to ensure the supremacy of an increasingly standardised English, at least among the ruling classes, at the expense of provincial dialects.

Education

Both colleges at the universities and schools had been founded in the later Middle Ages by pious benefactors to promote a godly life and sound learning. In the Tudor period there were three new impulses which were to transform the character and the quantity of English education – humanism, the Reformation and the increasingly perceived need to maintain social order.

Humanism was the name nineteenth-century scholars gave to the movement which promoted the study of carefully edited Latin and Greek authors in place of the corrupt texts and arid, logic chopping disputes of the medieval scholastic philosophers. The humanists aimed not just to reflect on ideas but to use literature and rhetoric to motivate right action in the world. There is debate about whether humanism was ever a coherent movement in Italy, but English humanism did take on a definite character from the pervasive influence of one humanist – Erasmus of Rotterdam. He was the scholar of greatest international repute at the turn of the sixteenth century. He had a large following of correspondents and friends amongst England's leading scholars, such as More and Colet. Even Henry VIII felt it necessary to show off his Latin to him. Although he was to repudiate Protestantism, one of Erasmus' main aims was to break down the idea that only the clergy could be truly close to God. Hence he and his associates were known as Christian humanists. And he saw a liberal, classical education as the key to an improved religious life.

At the universities there were advances towards the humanist ideal of education. One of Erasmus' associates was John Fisher, Bishop of Rochester and chaplain to Henry VII's mother, Lady Margaret Beaufort. He co-operated with her in founding two new colleges to promote humanist learning at Cambridge, St John's and Christ's. There were also new foundations at Oxford, including in 1517 Corpus Christi College which established the first lectureship in Greek.

This change in the quality of learning was matched by quantity in terms of students. The records suggest the number of students matriculating, that is officially entering the two universities, more than doubled from 300 under Henry VIII to 700 under Elizabeth. (The conclusion has to be tentative as the evidence for Henry VIII's reign is incomplete.) Add to this the Inns of Court in London, which took 100 students per year in the first half of the Tudor period and 250 by the end of it, along with new institutions such as Gresham's College in London, founded in 1597, and it becomes clear that higher education was becoming an ever more important qualification for those with social aspirations.

The victory of humanism in the universities was, however, by no means complete. Erasmus' idyllic vision of the student like a bee sipping the nectar of humanist learning applied best to dedicated, independent scholars. Meanwhile, the curriculum remained much the same. It was divided between the *trivium* made up of grammar, rhetoric (how to express yourself clearly and forcefully) and logic, and the more advanced *quadrivium* consisting of arithmetic, geometry, music and astronomy. Students might thereafter move on to more specialised studies such as law or medicine while all had some acquaintance with the 'queen of the sciences', theology. The philosophical basis of most learning in the universities continued to be the medieval understanding of the ancient Greek philosopher, Aristotle, rather than Plato who was favoured by the humanists. And the humanists often had to struggle to maintain their foothold in the universities. For instance, conservative elements at Oxford sniped at the 'Grecians', the humanists of Corpus Christi. In response to their attacks Thomas More wrote his letter to the 'Trojans' in 1518, defending the new learning. More's eloquence made sure that that particular encounter was won, but humanists had to defend their position for some time to come.

The humanist programme was more clearly established in schools largely because of the model provided by the Dean of St Paul's, John Colet, in his foundation of St Paul's School in 1512. The school statutes drawn up in 1518 laid down very firm principles:

> A child at the first admission, once for ever, shall pay 4d. for writing of his name; this money of the admissions shall the poor scholar have that sweepeth the school and keepeth the seats clean.
>
> . . . And thrice in the day prostrate [the children] shall say the prayers with due tract and pausing, as they be contained in a

table in the school, that is to say, in the morning and at noon and at evening.

. . . If any child after he is received and admitted to the school go to any other school to learn there after the manner of that school then I will that such child for no man's suit shall be hereafter received into our school, but go where him list, where his friends shall think be better learning . . .

[Having recommended approved authors such as Erasmus, Colet continues]:

. . . All barbary, all corruption, all Latin adulterate which ignorant blind fools brought into this world and with the same hath distained and poisoned the old Latin speech and the very Roman tongue . . . I say that filthiness and all such abusion which the later world brought in, which may rather be called blotterature than literature, I utterly abanish and exclude out of this school and charge the masters that they teach always that is best, and instruct the children in Greek and Latin in reading unto them such authors that hath with wisdom joined the pure chaste eloquence.

1   *To what extent was St Paul's intended to be socially exclusive?*
2   *What do the tone and content of these statutes suggest concerning Colet's purpose in founding the school?*

Colet's work at St Paul's was copied in several respects. The Merchant Taylors founded a school in 1560 and copied the St Paul's statutes almost word for word. Of even more far reaching importance was the grammar of William Lily, the first master of St Paul's School. In 1540 Henry VIII proclaimed: 'We will and command . . . all you schoolmasters and teachers of grammar as ye intend to avoid our displeasure, and have our favour, to teach and learn your scholars this English introduction, here ensuing, and the Latin grammar annexed to the same, and none other.' This is an example of something like a National Curriculum, with a government feeling the need to intervene in a time of flux and uncertainty.

Cardinal Wolsey fully intended to complete the work Colet had begun. Alongside his foundation of Cardinal College at Oxford, he founded a new school at Ipswich. It was to be the first of a series of schools which would be established in every diocese in the country. This ambitious plan would have had a major effect on the education system and on culture in England, but it collapsed with Wolsey's political position in 1529. The humanist schemes for education, which Wolsey had shared, were to be reshaped by the Reformation.

The dissolution of the monasteries appeared to promote education with the founding of eighteen schools under the authority of Henry VIII between 1535 and 1547, and bishops were instructed to establish schools in their dioceses. But the bishops rarely carried out the instruction and the apparent gain of Henry VIII schools must be set against the losses of monastic schools. And other schools lost endowments which meant they could no longer offer free places. The dissolution of the chantries in Edward VI's reign (*see page 166*) at first had even more mixed effects with many schools supported by chantry funds being threatened by the confiscation of endowments. However, there was a pressing need to educate youth in Protestant thinking and avoid any relapse into popery owing to ignorance. That ensured the re-foundation of schools in nearly every part of the country, and they were often less haphazard in the way they were organised than when so much had depended on the very variable skills and commitment of the chantry priests. The Edwardian initiatives in education continued – in Elizabeth's reign there were 136 foundations of endowed grammar schools.

The keenly perceived moral and religious importance of education brought into question the character and status of the schoolmaster. The statutes of Shrewsbury School decreed that masters should not be 'common gamesters, not common haunters of taverns or alehouses, or other suspect houses'. Nicholas Udall, a humanist and Court poet, had a career which could excite such fears. Although described by Haddon as 'the best schoolmaster of his time, as well as the greatest beater', he did not just thrash his pupils – he was imprisoned in 1541 having been suspected of being involved in a robbery carried out by two of the boys, with one of whom he confessed to having an illicit relationship. In his great work 'The Schoolmaster' published in 1570, Roger Ascham concentrated on the general failings of the schoolmaster rather than the criminal exceptions. He argued that a teacher should encourage and teach by example rather than beat lessons into their unfortunate pupils, which could just stunt their understanding.

Little was done to inspire the schoolmaster or raise his status; he was paid as little as half what he could earn as a clergyman and, with one assistant, he might have a class of 140. Instead the state sought to control him. From 1559 on, bishops were instructed to examine schoolmasters, and controls became tighter as the reign wore on with growing fears of hidden Catholics.

The status of women and their education was not so pressing an issue at the time although the Tudor period produced a number of well known examples of highly educated lay women. Sir Thomas More was proud of the humanist achievements of his daughter, Margaret. However, this may have been the result more of his pride in his own ability as an educator than genuine belief in the capacity of women; his attitude towards his second wife suggests an entirely traditional view of the woman's role and he once remarked that 'if the soil of woman's brain be of its own nature bad . . . the defect of nature may be redressed by industry'. Other examples of highly educated women include Mary Tudor, whom Catherine of Aragon employed Juan Luis Vives to educate, and Elizabeth I, whose tutor was Roger Ascham. They did at least provide models to be copied amongst the higher nobility but the numbers of educated women remained small. In 1581 Richard Mulcaster argued strongly that women should be educated but he also stressed that he would not have them go to grammar schools or the universities. He said: 'If I should seem to enforce any novelty I might seem ridiculous and never see the thing which I tender so much . . .' He was sensitive to the strict limits imposed by the conventions of the time. Improving the status of women was not at all a major concern in Tudor education.

The third impulse in educational reform, alongside humanism and the Reformation, was the increasing concern for the common weal – that the state should be administered by those sufficiently educated, that schooling should help to alleviate the poverty and idleness which might breed disorder, and that the economy in general be well served by training and education. The keeping of official parish records, for instance, began under Cromwell and that required an educated clerk. The Royal Injunctions of 1536 declared that 'through sloth and idleness diverse valiant men fall some to begging some to theft and murder . . . where, if they had been well educated and brought up in some good literature, occupation or mystery, they should . . . have profited . . . to the great commodity and ornament of the common weal'. One educational theorist, Juan Luis Vives, suggested that students 'should not be ashamed to enter shops and factories, and ask questions from craftsmen, and to get to know the details of their work'. The idea of work experience is not entirely new. While it remained most important to ensure through education that the people were godly, for which read Protestant, the expanding administration of the realm and the increasing commercialisation of English society were certainly connected with the upsurge in education. The need for a well educated ruling class was apparent.

Having passed through a grammar school and a university or one of the Inns of Court, a gentleman could discourse with his peers in a refined vernacular, and confirm that he was truly a member of an international cultural élite if he also had an acquaintance with French, the Latin of the humanists and perhaps some Greek as well. He could demonstrate his judgment by '*exempla*', instances drawn from classical literature of good and evil men and the consequences of their actions. However, the gentleman's education was not just acquired at school or university. In 1531 Sir Thomas Elyot published *The Governour*, the leading handbook for a gentleman's education. It drew heavily on *The Courtier* by Castiglione, the great work of the Italian Renaissance which laid down not just the book learning but also the manners (at table, for instance) and the pastimes (such as hunting or dancing) necessary to life in an aristocratic society. This is a vital part of what Norbert Elias identified as a civilising process in Europe, which brought order to an otherwise unruly nobility. Certainly Elyot saw the dangers of a lack of order leading to 'perpetuall conflicte'. And Elyot's extremely thorough scheme of education had one central aim that noble children 'may be found worthy, and also able to be governors of the public weal'. The nobility and gentry were not just born to rule. It was education, and at least acknowledgement of the culture which arose out of it, which secured to them the position of a ruling class.

3 HUMANISTS AND POLITICS

Sir Thomas Elyot regularly dedicated his books to the King. He was seeking patronage and political advancement. Indeed he was rewarded with a brief period as ambassador to Emperor Charles V. In return for preferment he offered counsel to the King and, perhaps more importantly, added intellectual prestige to his Court. Lord Mountjoy, an eminent humanist wrote of Henry VIII: 'Our King is not after gold, or gems, or precious stones, but virtue, glory, immortality . . .' These words, certainly exaggerated and in most respects untrue, only make sense in the context of culture having become a part of political competition. Henry's real qualities were of little importance as long as he could compete with his fellow European monarchs. That was why he was very keen for the universally respected Erasmus to settle in England rather than in France or the Emperor's dominions.

Politically-motivated patronage often just produced standard eulogies, praising the subject's forebears and deeds, and making ludicrous comparisons with classical heroes, but sometimes it caused works of greater substance to be created. An outstanding example is the history of England finished by the Italian humanist Polydore Vergil in 1512. Although the use of the evidence is variable, there is a departure from medieval history writing in that the uncritical reporting of supernatural events was spurned and a clearer, more linear sense of progression through time was established. Along with its literary quality this ensured that Polydore Vergil's work remained one of the standard sources for English history for centuries. He aimed to show how the moral order of the country was restored by the advent of the Tudor dynasty. In carefully structured prose he showed, for instance, how the fatal flaws of Edward IV's character – his proneness to lust and his oath-breaking – undermined his otherwise benevolent traits and plunged the country into renewed moral chaos resulting in the tyranny of Richard III. The country could only then be rescued by the accession of Henry VII. This was, and is, great literature and enhanced the legitimacy of the Tudor claim to the throne.

The game of patronage was a difficult one for the aspiring humanist to play. However high the quality of his work, the political situation often led to disappointment for the ambitious writer. Paradoxically, this frustration could give rise to great creativity. An example is the satire of John Skelton, an inveterate enemy of Wolsey, fulminating against him from sanctuary in Westminster Abbey. Despite often very complex allegory his portrayal of character in *Speke Parrott, Collyn Clout* and *Why Come Ye Nat to Courte?* is unforgettably vivid and precise.

Frustration was also a source for the creativity of Sir Thomas Wyatt who was one of the two leading poets of Henry VIII's reign, along with the Earl of Surrey. He fell in love with Anne Boleyn, which posed political, as well as personal, difficulties. Wyatt had been responsible for introducing the sonnet, devised by the Italian Petrarch, into England and he sublimated his doomed love in poems lamenting the cruelties of fate and his mistress. He did, however, have extraordinary luck mixed in with his ill fortune. Implicated as a suitor of Anne Boleyn he escaped with his own life, despite having been forced to witness her execution. Rehabilitated by his friend Cromwell, he became ambassador to the Emperor (clearly a job where cultural prestige was a valued qualification), but when Cromwell fell from power it came out that Wyatt had been in contact with the 'traitor', Cardinal Pole. Having had to witness his friend Cromwell's execution, Wyatt then just escaped with his own life once more, this time owing to the intervention of Catherine Howard on condition that he returned to his wife – whom, sadly, he loathed. He wrote the Penitential Psalms and died (of natural causes) in 1542, having once again been restored to the King's favour. Wyatt's career may be exceptional but political disaster was common enough for writers.

The politics which writers had to cope with was not just that of the Court. They jockeyed for position intensely amongst themselves. Fierce debates sprang up which were by no means just scholarly. Even the pious Fisher became involved in a vitriolic dispute with the French humanist, LeFevre d'Etaples. Erasmus despaired of such behaviour: 'What ill spirit is it that troubles the tranquillity of studies by polemics of this kind? How much better it is to wander in the gardens of the Muses and to live in good understanding.' Again, Erasmus' idyllic vision did not fit the realities of his world.

Added to the politics of state and the political wrangles amongst scholars themselves, there could be conflicting political ideas which an individual writer had to struggle to make sense of. An example is *The History of King Richard III*, written by Sir Thomas More between 1513 and 1518. More was, albeit often unwillingly, a professional politician. At various stages he was Speaker of the House of Commons, Under-Sheriff of London, an ambassador, royal advisor and finally Lord Chancellor in succession to Wolsey. In *Richard III* he was trying to write a humanist history which followed the convention of contrasting good and evil. However, the contrast kept dissolving as his narrative charted the effects of power on politicians. Even Cardinal Morton, a great and respected influence on More, is shown to have been crafty and ruthless in luring the Duke of Buckingham to his destruction. More never finished his history and Alastair Fox argues that it is because of this conflict in his ideas. More wrote of the politics he was describing: 'And so they said that these matters be Kings' games, as it were stage plays, and for the more part played upon scaffolds. In which poor men . . . that sometime step up and play with them, when they cannot play their parts, they disorder the play and do themselves no good.' More was to be a regular actor in the political theatre and in 1535, having refused to declare acceptance of the Royal Supremacy, he was finally to play his part upon the scaffold. He knew that humanists could never write the political script, for all their intellectual prowess. He could, however, perhaps in compensation, create the perfect republic in his imagination – *Utopia*, which he wrote in 1516.

Alistair Fox has categorised works produced by the likes of Skelton, Wyatt and More as 'the literature of anxiety'. He argues that it constituted the last really imaginative writing before the emergence of Shakespeare and his contemporaries towards the end of the century. In between came the Reformation with its demand for propaganda and a disavowal of complex personal writing in favour of simple public messages.

There is a debate as to whether the influence of humanist scholarship languished as much as did imaginative literature owing to the Reformation. Certainly the executions of More and Fisher in 1535, and the decline, and then death, of Erasmus in 1536 seem to form a natural break in the development of humanism. Christian humanism, the emphasis these men placed on the reform of the Church through satire, moral example and Scriptural knowledge, was obviously displaced by the more radical programme of the Reformation. However, the intellectual struggle involved in the Reformation put a high premium on the literary and scholarly skills of humanists.

With regard to the Divorce some humanists lined up with Catherine of Aragon and some with Henry VIII. (On the Continent yet more lined up with Emperor Charles V as he was the highest bidder.) As the King moved towards the break with Rome, it was humanists such as Thomas Starkey and lawyers such as Christopher St German who supplied him with a theory of statute which under-pinned the Acts of the Reformation Parliament. A team of scholars, probably led by Edward Foxe, assembled historical sources called the *Collectanea Satis Copiosa* which made clear Henry's imperial sovereignty. This is not the continuation of a specifically Erasmian humanism as argued by James McConica, but it does show the flexibility and survival of the 'New Learning' in a more general way.

An example of one of the humanists who identified himself with the Reformation is Thomas Starkey. By 1535 he was chaplain to the King and one of Cromwell's most able propagandists. He was a thinker of considerable depth as was shown in the *Dialogue between Reginald Pole and Thomas Lupset.* This discussion of different forms of government was not just abstract theorising – his ideas concerning the need for education and support for the poor in order to preserve social order were very much in tune with Cromwell's thinking. However, in the end Starkey's influence came to little. In 1536 his old patron Pole came out decisively against the King and that helped to end Starkey's career. In any case the urgent political dictates of the 1530s ruled out any of the long term reforms which were envisaged in humanist thinking.

Humanism was of great use to politicians but it had little independent political force. Yet its very breadth and neutrality helped to preserve the achievements of the New Learning. There was no imperative to uproot it from the education system when political circumstances changed and one set of ideas fell out of favour. And even contacts with European humanists remained fairly open. For all the upheaval of the mid-century, humanism remained the basis for the great cultural flowering to come in Elizabeth's reign.

4 THE REFORMATION AND ENGLISH CULTURE

The crisis of the Church in the Reformation was also a crisis of culture. The words and images the Church sanctified were a vital part of everyday life. On the one hand, the Reformation was to enrich English as a literary language with the English Bible and other texts; on the other it stripped away much of the visual heritage of medieval Catholicism.

There had been translations of the Bible into English from the official Latin version (known as the Vulgate) before the sixteenth century, but they were associated with the heretic Lollards and were therefore condemned and very limited in circulation. None at all were printed until William Tyndale started to produce his translation of the New Testament in 1525. Copies were smuggled into England and eagerly bought despite attempts at suppression by the authorities. The start of the German Reformation made it all the more urgent to prevent the Bible from being too easily read by those who might challenge the authority of the Church.

The first complete translation of the Bible had to await publication until the English Reformation had begun. Miles Coverdale produced it in 1535. It was not an original translation, unlike that of Tyndale who had gone back to the Hebrew and Greek sources, but it had the King's approval. In 1539 Coverdale's Bible was superseded by an authorised translation known as the 'Great Bible', and all other versions were banned in the 1540s. It was also decreed that 'no woman (unless she be noble or gentle woman), no artificers, apprentices, journeymen . . . or labourers' should be permitted to read the Scriptures. The authorities were anxious to stop the Reformation from becoming too popular a movement and, therefore, uncontrollable. They could not, however, halt the new biblical scholarship. Exiles in Geneva during Mary's reign produced the 'Geneva Bible' (*see page 263*) which circulated widely in England in (the wealthier) private homes despite a further attempt to license just one official version in the form of the 'Bishops' Bible' of 1568. Finally, under James 1 the Authorised Version of 1611 was to be established as the standard until the twentieth century.

The language of these translations, honed and reworked through the sixteenth century, became the single greatest resource for English literature. Despite the restrictions under Henry VIII the Bible was the text everybody grew up with, even the illiterate as they heard it read out in church. Its vocabulary, its idioms and its rhythms were the basis, along with the classics, for the humanist trained élite, for everyday writing, such as letters and diaries, as well as the treatises and the poetry of 'high culture'. It became the core of English culture.

There were two other major texts associated with the Bible in fostering a common culture. One was the Prayer Book (*see page 167, page 175 and page 242 for its various versions*). As Cranmer put it in 1549: 'And whereas heretofore there hath been great diversity in saying and singing in Churches within this Realm . . . now from henceforth all the whole Realm shall have but one Use.' It was fortunate that Cranmer's English was amongst the most sensitive and elegant. The other major text was Foxe's *Book of Martyrs* which was less sensitive and less elegant but powerfully written and of enormous influence.

John Foxe first published his *Actes and Monuments of these latter and perilous Dayes*, commonly known as the *Book of Martyrs*, in 1563. In forthright prose it described the sufferings of Protestant martyrs at the hands of 'Bloody Mary'. It kept alive the revulsion felt towards the Marian persecution and the Spanish influence and was thereby of enormous importance in consolidating popular, emotional support for the Elizabethan Settlement. When a corrected edition was published in 1570 a copy was placed in every collegiate church in the country. It was the most widely known and influential work of the Tudor period.

Foxe is most famous for his tales of brave Protestant martyrs sustained by their faith as they faced the dreadful agonies of being burnt at the stake, but that was only one part of his work. His narrative covered centuries and told of the great medieval struggle between Emperors and Popes, which for him simply meant good against evil. Such history writing had little to do with the beginnings of critical scholarship in the Renaissance; the evidence was made to fit Foxe's schematic design, showing how the Popes gradually usurped the God given authority of secular rulers until the Reformation. Queen Elizabeth, acting as a new Constantine (the Emperor responsible for adopting Christianity as the religion of the Roman Empire), was then presented as restoring a golden age.

The ideology of an imperial monarchy (*see pages 94–5*) obviously predated Foxe but it was his work which gave it its greatest cultural impetus. And it was his imagery and language which did much to ensure that the ideology of Elizabethan Protestantism outlasted the conditions which had given rise to it in the sixteenth century. Foxe's influence could be felt right into our own era in literature and religious attitudes.

The images of Scriptural figures and saints which had covered the walls of churches and cathedrals had had such staying power through centuries of medieval Christianity. The Crucifix was the most striking image of suffering and the essential symbol of the Christian faith, representing the sacrifice which brings redemption. By the end of the sixteenth century it had generally been removed from the road screen (separating chancel and nave) and replaced in many cases by the royal coat of arms. On the other walls of the church the lives of saints and prophets had been whitewashed over and statues destroyed or decapitated. (This was not universal – some medieval images did survive until the Puritans in the English Civil War finished the job.) Instead of learning from images the congregation now had to concentrate on the words of the preacher. If there was anything to be seen on the walls it consisted of verses from the Bible or the Ten Commandments. A culture of images gave way to a culture of words.

The destruction of images was not simply vandalism. It was iconoclasm, the elimination of images which might be worshipped in themselves or treated as magical objects rather than as representations of higher spiritual truths. Suspicion of images pre-dated the Reformation. The Lollards had attacked them and some Christian humanists, such as Erasmus, thought they were external distractions from the inner spiritual life. The first major onslaught, however, came with the Henrician Reformation. The sixth of the Ten Articles still allowed for images which were genuinely 'laymen's books to remind us of heavenly things' but commissioners had been instructed to destroy 'abused' images associated with miracles, shrines and pilgrimages. So, for instance, the shrine of St Alban in St Albans Abbey was smashed at the time of the Dissolution – it was a centre for theologically unacceptable pilgrimages, it sustained the prestige of the Abbey, and there were also precious metals and jewels which could be carried away to fill the King's coffers.

The cultural change all this entailed was profound. The Reformation enriched the literary element of English culture as it reduced its visual tradition. Along with printing, according to Frances Yates, it transformed the structure of thinking. In the Middle Ages without regular access to books, huge quantities of information had to be memorised and one method used was 'memory places', visual images which were associated with data and ideas and which could be summoned up in the imagination far more easily than abstract words. It was common to have in the mind's eye a particularly spacious memory place in the form of a 'memory palace' with information recalled in the form of different objects placed in different rooms which could be toured in the imagination when it was necessary to recall them. (You might try it when revising.) With printing rendering 'memory places' less necessary and the Reformation breeding suspicion of images which might mislead in their associations, this way of organising ideas and data declined. Or at least it was displaced into the symbols to be found in the great poetic creativity of the later sixteenth century and beyond, or the burgeoning images of royalty. John Phillips commented that 'the cult of the royal image was created in order to buttress public order at a time when the religious image had proved disruptive of that same order'.

5 THE IMAGE OF ROYALTY

In England there was no standing army to shore up royal authority. A revolt such as the Pilgrimage of Grace (*see pages 485–90*) or that of the Northern Earls (*see pages 494–8*) showed just how easily the monarch's authority could be disrupted and that made the image of royalty all the more important. In the absence of coercive power the majesty of the Crown had to be self-evident to make obedience at least more likely.

A late medieval king such as Edward IV drew on a European tradition of chivalry, largely in the form of the pageants and tournaments developed by the Dukes of Burgundy. It was a culture of violence tempered by Christian virtues, the ideal of which was the heroic, selfless knight. Edward placed himself at the heart of this culture when he built St George's Chapel, Windsor as the church of the knights of the Garter. This was part of the revival of the Order of the Garter which had been founded in the previous century by Edward III. Each of the knights, the élite of the realm, were bound to the king by ties of loyalty and comradeship.

Henry VII appeared to be more remote and calculating than chivalric but he knew how to employ symbolic display for political purposes. In 1486 he conducted a royal progress receiving the ritual submission of the cities on his route. During this, the Tudor rose made its appearance – the red rose of Lancaster united with the white rose of York to represent dynastic peace. Another device which Henry employed was the Red Dragon. This was the emblem of the Welsh prince of the Dark Ages, Cadwalader, who had prophesied that a hero would return to restore the British race. Henry used this mythical connection to consolidate support – it was unlikely to have been coincidence that his route through Wales to England and Bosworth fitted closely to the bards' tales of Cadwalader and that he unfurled the standard of the Red Dragon on the battlefield.

Henry VIII brought a new dynamism and character to the royal image; it became co-terminous with his own ego. Henry both sponsored chivalric tournaments and fought real wars so that he could bask in glory. In contrast with his careful father, Court festivities under the young King were more elaborate, colourful and costly. He much enjoyed being a player in scenes of courtly love, the medieval tradition of lovelorn suitors using all the devices of poetry, song and dance to win fair but disdainful ladies. A variation on this theme was an entertainment put on for the Imperial ambassador in 1522 by William Cornish, the highly skilled Master of the Revels. It showed eight beautiful ladies, the personifications of virtues imprisoned in a castle, the 'Schatew Vert'. Henry appeared as 'Ardent Desire' (prophetically so – one of the imprisoned ladies was played by Anne Boleyn) and with his friends attacked the castle with oranges and dates. The ladies retaliated with rose water and the evening concluded with the triumph of the suitors and with dancing.

Such display can sound rather ludicrous now but the civilised quality of his Court had played its part in winning Henry VIII the reputation he desired. Francesco Chieregato wrote to Isabella d'Este: 'In short, the wealth and civilisation of the world are here: and those who call the English barbarians appear to me to render themselves such . . . [Pre-eminent amongst the English] is this most invincible King, whose acquirements and qualities are so many and excellent that I consider him to excell all who ever wore a crown.'

The diplomatic value placed upon extravagant, competitive display can be seen with the Field of the Cloth of Gold, Henry VIII's meeting with Francis I, which took place on neutral territory in northern France in June 1520 (*see page 65*). Henry attempted to outclass Francis' splendid pavilion by erecting a prefabricated palace, complete with fountains which ran with wine or beer whenever the French were near enough to be impressed. The theme of the meeting was peace and brotherhood, although the suspicions and quarrels over precedence showed how skin deep this was. In fact the whole event was an elaborate bluff as Henry moved closer to Charles V.

The palaces Henry built were like stage sets for his courtly display. Nonsuch, begun in 1538, was intended to compete with Francis I's Fontainebleau, and under the supervision of the Italian architect, Nicolò da Modena, it did achieve grandeur. The palace of Whitehall in contrast appeared to be little more than houses strung together; in response to an impatient King, it had been constructed far too fast.

The interior of Whitehall, however, was another matter. There were elaborate carvings, much covered in gold leaf and fine tapestries. Above all there was the fresco (a painting on fresh plaster) which dominated the Privy Chamber, the heart of Henry's private and his political world (*see pages 118–21*). It was the portrait by Hans Holbein, the great Flemish artist, of Henry VIII and his third wife, Jane Seymour, along with Henry VII and Elizabeth of York. Painted in 1537, it was destroyed in a fire which consumed the palace in 1698, but it is known through a complete copy and also a surviving cartoon by Holbein of the left half containing Henry VIII and his father (*see page 403*). The fresco as a whole propagates the stability and power of the Tudor dynasty but it is the portrait of Henry VIII which was the pattern for a multitude of copies and has endured in the popular imagination. As Roy Strong put it: 'No one ever thinks of Henry VIII in any other way than as this gouty, pig-eyed pile of flesh.' He also asserts that this is where royal portraits as 'propaganda in the modern sense of the word begins'. How such propaganda worked is explored further in the portraits exercise on pages 403–10 and 436–8.

The Holbein fresco in 1537 marked a highpoint for Henry VIII. The Pilgrimage of Grace had been crushed the year before, there was no foreign threat and Prince Edward was born in the October. But gone were the revels of the first half of the reign. Not only was the King ageing but the Reformation had made the royal image an ever more serious matter as a means of consolidating royal authority. This can be seen most graphically in the frontispiece of the Great Bible of 1539 with Henry ensuring that the Word of God reaches his people (*see page 107*). In this the royal and divine images almost become one. Stephen Gardiner wrote that God set princes on earth as 'representours of His Image unto men'. Such seriousness can also be seen in the antithetical religious projects of Edward VI's reign and of Mary Tudor, but in the mid-Tudor period there was nothing of the vigour of Henry VIII in the projection of the royal image. It was Elizabeth I whose carefully cultivated role as a symbol, even an icon, for her people, gave rise to a huge outpouring of cultural creativity.

6 THE CULT OF ELIZABETH I

In the first decade of Elizabeth's reign there was no sign of this cultural distinctiveness. For instance, portraits of her were standard, even second-rate and show an intelligent but unexceptional young woman. The cult of Elizabeth was first developed in the 1570s. There had been the revolt of the Northern Earls in 1569, the papal excommunication in 1570 and the plots surrounding Mary, Queen of Scots. To combat the insecurity these gave rise to, and the fear that the Elizabethan Settlement might have been only a temporary respite. Elizabeth's ministers and courtiers (she left it to them – it was cheaper) competitively commissioned and encouraged artists and poets to turn the Queen into a timeless symbol of peace, justice and stability.

In the process, two fundamental causes of social anxiety were transformed triumphantly into sources of confidence. Firstly, the destruction of the images, processions and ceremonies of the pre-Reformation Church left behind much disorientation and few physical expressions of communal identity. From the 1570s the gap was filled by images, processions and ceremonies associated with the Queen. Secondly there was the continual worry over Elizabeth's marriage – what was wanted was an heir to calm memories of the Wars of the Roses and the uncertainties of the mid-Tudor period. As the prospect of a marriage receded, however, there emerged the cult of the Virgin Queen – her purity and chastity would safeguard the realm whatever the insecurity of the dynasty. It is impossible to quantify its political effects but clearly virginity as a symbol had tremendous cultural power; it drew strength from the psychological roots left behind by the pre-Reformation cult of the Virgin Mary. And through this cult of the Virgin Queen, Elizabeth and her ministers, her painters and her poets, turned what must have been thought her worst handicap, her gender, into a significant source of her authority.

Before the Reformation the calendar had been structured by saints days. They were replaced by festivities associated with Elizabeth, in particular her Accession Day on 17 November. It rapidly became one of the great events of the year. In churches up and down the land sermons were preached stressing the importance of that day for the preservation of the realm and of true religion. They drew heavily on Foxe and his imperial theme – Elizabeth was identified with Constantine (*see page 421*), ushering in a golden age and renewing the Church; the idea was spread of history beginning again with the Accession. In stark contrast the Pope was pictured as the seven headed beast of the Apocalypse or the Whore of Babylon, with only the Queen to fend off the darkness. Such sermons played an invaluable role in consolidating the Elizabethan Settlement and provided the form in which the image of Elizabeth entered the popular imagination.

At Court a resurgence of chivalry characterised the Accession Day celebrations. From about 1572 Sir Henry Lee, the Queen's champion, began to stage the Accession Day Tilts. There was nothing new about tournaments, of course, but the Tilts took on a specific character and importance. They were not just contests of martial arts but an occasion when the Queen herself could be made the focus of all attention, as the fair lady to whom all the knights dedicated themselves. (Elizabeth, however, could show a refreshing indifference to eulogies – on one occasion, when she was bored by endless dedications, she said she would not have come had she known there would be so much talk of her, and went to bed.) The Accession Day Tilts incorporated new cultural elements. Onto the Burgundian traditions of the tournament were grafted Italian devices known as *imprese*. They were emblems made up for the occasion and could often carry a significant political message, such as the *impresa* Essex used in order to represent his feud with Robert Cecil, showing a pen on some scales outweighing a cannon. In devising the Tilts, Lee was also likely to have been influenced by Ramon Lull, a Spanish writer translated by Caxton, who pictured knights in pastoral settings being instructed by a hermit. In Lee's hands the hermit's instruction came to stand for the Protestant mission. How far that mission was progressing was shown by Lee at his retirement

Tilt in 1590 when he showed the Pillars of Hercules (which guard the straits dividing the Old World of the Mediterranean from the New World of the Atlantic), representing the potential for maritime expansion of Protestant England in the aftermath of the Armada. The new chivalry was backward looking in some of its forms but not necessarily in its themes.

The resurgence of chivalry went beyond the Accession Day Tilts. Edward VI had tried to do away with the tradition of St George as yet another popish superstition. Following Edward IV, Elizabeth very deliberately revived the cult of that saint and the ceremonials associated with the Order of the Garter. It was useful not only to consolidate the loyalty of the English élite, with the Queen very obviously the fount of honour, but also to cross the religious divide for diplomatic reasons, as when Charles IX and later Henry III of France were invested with membership of the Order.

Frances Yates has characterised all this as the 'imaginative re-feudalisation' of culture. It was not just true of England in the sixteenth century – a number of European regimes used 'the apparatus of chivalry and its religious traditions to focus fervent religious loyalty on the national monarchy'. The poets who dedicated themselves to Elizabeth ensured that the cultural effects of this 're-feudalisation' lasted long beyond the political purposes it served.

Two such poets were Sir Philip Sidney and Edmund Spenser who were austerely Protestant in their doctrinal views and yet managed to express their principles in the colourful forms of chivalry and pastoral romance; there was a fertile ambiguity in the bringing together of these diverse elements. Sir Philip Sidney was a courtier and diplomat, well connected through his uncle, the Earl of Leicester. He was also at the centre of a group of aristocratic poets. In the 1580s he wrote *Arcadia* which portrayed a land of pastoral allegory and shepherd knights in which Sir Henry Lee would have felt at home. Indeed one of the events in *Arcadia* is a tilt between Philisides and Laelius in the presence of Queen Helen of Corinth – no reader could have failed to see Sidney, Lee and Elizabeth transported as these characters into an ideal world.

Much poetic imagery was given life in chivalric events organised by Lee. For instance, he entertained Elizabeth at Woodstock in 1575 and one of the characters appearing in the entertainment was a Faerie Queene. Edmund Spenser was to take this image and put it at the centre of the greatest epic poem in English. The first three books of Spenser's *The Faerie Queene* were published in 1590 with a dedication to Elizabeth. Spenser's declared intention for his poem was to 'fashion a gentleman or noble person in vertuous and gentle discipline'. But he also wished to portray in allegory the religious and political struggles of his age. His belief was that poetic images could plant virtuous responses in men's minds. In Book One, for instance, there is Una, the one signifying undivided imperial authority as exercised by Elizabeth;

in contrast there is the false Duessa, 'clad in scarlet red', representing the Pope, usurping imperial authority and bringing disorder to the world. Hopes for the triumph of good over evil are pinned on a series of knights but also on various manifestations of Elizabeth. She appears as the fiercely anti-Papal Virgo but also in the neo-Platonic form of Venus. Elizabeth's public virtue is pictured in Gloriana's just government and her private virtue is seen in Belphoebe's chastity. But the character which is the cornerstone of the poem, and of the whole cultural project surrounding the Queen, according to Frances Yates, is Astraea.

In classical myth Astraea was the last of the immortals to leave the earth during the world's decline into the age of iron. She is portrayed as the Just Virgin holding an ear of corn and thus, while barren herself, promotes fertility. In Dante's *Monarchia*, which three hundred years previously had condemned papal usurpation of imperial authority, Astraea was the Imperial Virgin. In restoring the Royal Supremacy, Elizabeth, as Astraea, was restoring a golden age in which peace, justice and all the virtues could flourish once again. One of the poets who dedicated much of his work to Elizabeth as Astraea was Sir John Davies. This is the last verse of an acrostic (which like all the others spelt out *Elisabetha Regina*), written near the end of the reign:

Rudeness itself she doth refine,
E'en like an alchemist divine,
Gross times of iron turning
Into the purest form of gold,
Not to corrupt till heaven wax old,
And be refined with burning.

For all its celebration of the golden age brought by Elizabeth as Astraea, notes of an underlying anxiety can be detected. No taint of corruption could touch Elizabeth but it was still thought to be rife amongst government servants, and while Heaven might be ageless, the Queen herself was not, however much rhetoric there was about her eternal youth. And although political and religious struggles could be seen as a refining fire, that did not promise an easy time ahead.

Visual images of Elizabeth could be seen everywhere. Cut out patterns were issued in the 1570s to serve the needs of provincial painters and she appeared in engravings and woodcuts and on coins and medallions. As her father had been portrayed in the frontispiece to the 'Great Bible' so she became more familiar through the 'Bishops Book'.

The portraits of Elizabeth (*see exercise pages 436–8*) increasingly followed poetry in showing her laden with symbols of justice and all the virtues, a phoenix for renewal or a moon for imperial chastity and dominion over the seas, black for her constancy and white for her purity. The Renaissance theory of the portrait went well beyond the importance of a recognisable likeness; its purpose was to perfect nature and so elicit from the viewer a virtuous response. In studying the portrait of a ruler the viewer, aided by symbols, should see through the individual to the inner, neo-Platonic ideal of a monarch. That theory was known in Elizabethan England, although there was little evidence of Renaissance techniques in Elizabeth's portraits which lacked the subtleties of perspective or the careful modelling in light and shade of contemporary Italian art. This was partly because of the lack of artistic education in England (there were few skilled or distinctive English master painters in the sixteenth century, apart from the miniaturist, Nicholas Hilliard), but it was also related to the purpose of the portraits. They were icons to be revered and therefore little Renaissance naturalism was called for.

As Elizabeth's reign wore on, any attempt at portraying the reality of her changing appearance was abandoned. Instead what was presented was the famous mask of youth established by Nicholas Hilliard. This was not just convention or the Queen's personal vanity (which was considerable) but a matter of political concern given that the war against Spain made the Queen's image ever more important as an enduring national symbol. In 1596 the Serjeant Painter was to order the destruction of unseemly portraits and in 1600 the Privy Council was trying to call in portraits which did not comply with the official pattern. Robert Cecil in particular was co-ordinating the projection of the royal image through the poetry of Sir John Davies and the portraits of Marcus Gheeraerts, the most accomplished painter of the latter years of the reign. (*See the* Ditchley *and the* Rainbow *portraits on pages 409–10.*) In paintings such as Gheeraerts', the mask of youth served its purpose of representing unchanging stability but such symbolism could only paper over the financial and political cracks brought on by the strains of war against Spain, Europe's greatest power, and, although the mask of youth promised eternal stability, it could only have that meaning as long as the Queen lived.

Around the image of the last Tudor monarch clustered a rich array of symbols. The Court poets and painters who employed them transcended mere propaganda in a way that the scholars and artists working for Henry VIII had rarely achieved. The Elizabethans managed to turn their political and religious commitments into a distinctive aesthetic. Perhaps this was made possible because of the creative tensions brought about by England's vulnerable but defiant position, open to European culture and politics but separated off by its national Reformation. Or there were the ideological, as well as personal, tensions in Elizabethan Court politics – for instance, the cult of the Virgin Queen was made more intense by Puritan fears that Elizabeth would marry the Catholic Duke of Alençon. But such tensions and ambiguities could only be held in balance by the person of the Queen. All that could follow her was disappointed expectation, despite some attempts at similar myth making around James I's son, Prince Henry. The Court culture of the Stuarts, especially under Charles I, came to express rather than resolve religious tensions and to promote not unity, but the alienation of Court from country. When Elizabeth died, her image remained like a ghost to haunt her Stuart successors and to taunt them with their inadequacies.

7 AN ELIZABETHAN WORLD PICTURE?

In 1943 E M W Tillyard published his account of the structure of the ideas fundamental to the Elizabethan age, *The Elizabethan World Picture*. Without understanding these ideas, which were the assumptions and commonplaces of the time concerning the universe and mankind, much of the writing of Elizabethan authors, such as Shakespeare, Marlowe or Jonson would remain only partly comprehensible. In particular Tillyard saw in this world picture a belief in a cosmic order and hierarchy 'so taken for granted, so much part of the collective mind of the people, that it is hardly mentioned except in explicitly didactic passages'. Certainly the ideas identified by Tillyard were of importance to the Elizabethans. They derived largely from classical authorities such as Ptolemy (for astronomy), Aristotle (for natural science) and Galen (for the workings of the human body). What remains under debate is whether these ideas were ever so coherent or universally accepted. There were new theories jostling with those of the classical authorities and also political complexities which may have radically affected the idea of cosmic order and hierarchy even during the Elizabethan period.

In Ptolemy's scheme of the cosmos the earth was at the centre surrounded by nine 'spheres' (or ten or eleven according to some versions), each enclosing the other, with the outer sphere as the *'primum mobile'* determining the movement of all that lay within it. The spheres moved in perfect harmony. This was taken literally – the 'music of the spheres' was the ideal which the great Tudor musicians and composers, such as Tallis and Byrd, tried to express. Beneath the outermost sphere was the firmament of fixed stars and then in the lower spheres were the seven planets, each held to its perfect circular motion. Finally, the sphere of the moon divided the incorruptible ether, in which angels lived, from the unstable, sublunar region of earth and mortal man.

The hierarchy of beings which stretched from God down through the spheres to inanimate objects on the earth was the 'Great Chain of Being'. Beneath God were the different orders of the angels: seraphim in the *'primum mobile'*, cherubim in the firmament and the less exalted angels in the sphere of the moon. Next there was mankind which shared rationality with the angels above and material existence with the creatures below. Mankind occupied several subdivisions of the Chain of Being, princes at the top stretching down through nobility and gentry to the most lowly peasant at the bottom. Beneath mankind came the animals, in turn subdivided into those with memory, movement and senses, such as dogs, down to those creatures with only limited senses, such as molluscs. Plants were next, being endowed with life but without senses. Finally there were the inanimate objects which made up the earth.

The material of this hierarchically constructed universe consisted of four elements – fire, air, water and earth. Each class in the Chain of Being had a primate depending on the balance of these four elements. For instance, gold was reckoned to be the finest, most durable metal because it contained fire, air, water and earth in balanced proportion.

Each individual human being was thought to be a microcosm, that is containing in miniature the features of the universe. Mankind was unique in combining features from above and beneath the moon, from the rational command of the mind to the unstable, sublunary desires of the lower body. There was a Chain of Being in the body – the liver produced 'vegetable' spirits for the basic functions of the body, which rose to be 'sensible' spirits (i.e. mobilising the senses) in the heart and finally to the 'vital' spirits of rationality in the brain. The four elements of the universe were represented by the four 'humours' of the body. These were choler (akin to fire), blood (air), phlegm (water) and melancholy (earth). Health, according to Galen, depended on the four humours being held in balance. And someone's temperament was the result of whichever humour was dominant. For instance, if you were of a fiery disposition you were 'choleric'. In this hierarchically ordered universe it seemed everything was inter-related and everything had its place.

The implications of this for the cultural, social and political attitudes of the time were enormous. Spenser, for instance, influenced by neo-Platonic thinking, identified love as the principle of order in the universe. The four elements would be in perpetual conflict except that love 'did place them all in order, and compel to keep themselves within their sundry reigns, together linkt with adamantine chains'.

And the various ranks of society were portrayed as essential links in an ordered universe ordained by God. Where there was rebellion then chaos would surely follow – whether the rebellion was that of Satan against God; or of the stomach against the head in the microcosm, the body, during illness; or a subject against his prince. Richard Hooker, the defender of the Anglican Church against Puritan enthusiasm, put the theory at its most moderate: 'Is it possible that man, being not only the noblest creature in the world but even a very world himself, his transgressing the law of nature should draw no harm after it?'

The place of the prince in the Chain of Being was gradually elaborated by the end of Elizabeth's reign into the 'divine right of kings'. The prince being ordained of God could lay claim to absolute, unchallengeable authority. The development of this doctrine was probably a reaction to threats of Elizabeth's deposition by Roman Catholic forces. She herself, however, made relatively little of 'divine right', stressing her adherence to law and liberties; the first two Stuarts were to push the doctrine further and finally stimulated a dramatic reaction against it.

When ideas are abstracted it is possible to arrange them in a coherent 'world picture'. Although there were undoubtedly common assumptions and intellectual traditions, the ideas outlined above existed in the thinking and writings of individuals – individuals who frequently disagreed with one other, or who were quite happy to hold to contradictory ideas themselves. One leading example was John Dee, Queen Elizabeth's favourite philosopher.

Dee was at the centre of a considerable network of intellectual life. He counted amongst his patrons a wide range of courtiers including the Sidney and Dudley families, and he served Emperor Rudolf II, as well as Queen Elizabeth. He knew or corresponded with most of the leading European scholars of his day. His pupils included those who were to be leading poets, mathematicians and explorers, possibly even Drake. The library at his house in Mortlake represented contemporary learning more completely than any other; and gatherings there brought together some of the finest minds of the period.

At the heart of Dee's thought was mathematics which for him was the key to understanding the universe: 'By Numbers . . . we may both wind and draw ourselves into the deep search and view, of all creatures distinct virtues, natures, properties and Forms; And, also, farther, arise, climb, ascend and mount up (with Speculative Wings) in spirit, to behold in the Glass of Creation, the Form of Forms.' In his *Preface to Euclid* (published in 1570), Dee did not just write of pure mathematics but showed how it lay at the heart of music, painting and architecture. Vital to architecture, for instance, is mathematical proportion and in that it is linked to the microcosm, the human body, which also reflects eternal proportion. This was all in accord with the Elizabethan world picture although it had little immediate application at the time – there were magnificent vernacular buildings, such as Hardwick Hall with its novel expanses of glass, but truly classical proportions were not to be seen in England until the following century.

Where Dee's ideas did make a practical contribution was in the art of navigation. His improved charts enabled captains of the Muscovy Company's ships to leave coastal navigation in favour of more direct oceanic routes. He much influenced Richard Hakluyt whose *The principall Navigations, Voiages and Discoveries of the English nation* was to become the textbook account of English exploration. In 1577 Dee published *General and Rare Memorials pertaining to the Perfect Arte of Navigation* in which he argued for the creation of a navy, along with suggestions as to how it could be financed and how it might spread Elizabeth's sovereignty across large tracts of North America. He saw the emergence of a British Empire (his phrase), both secure and farflung, as certainly as a 'Mathematicall demonstration' (*see the frontispiece on page 407*). Dee's *General and Rare Memorials* were not applied directly as policy but they opened up further the prospect of maritime expansion; this also subtly qualified the fixity of any 'world picture' and drove forward practical scientific enquiry.

Dee also saw practical applications of his knowledge in ways which we would dismiss as being fanciful. Number being the key to the universe, he thought that mathematical language was a means of conjuring angels and gaining universal knowledge. He was much influenced by Hermeticism, derived from the writings of Hermes Trismegistus (thought to be ancient Egyptian, actually from the later Roman period) which were rediscovered during the Renaissance by neo-Platonic philosophers. Hermeticism sought to reveal the 'sympathies' which bound the universe together. Certain colours or plants or stones had 'sympathies' with the stars and could be used by a magus with sufficient occult knowledge to channel and to store the powers of those stars (*the popular version of these beliefs was outlined on pages 388–91*). Such magical beliefs, although at one with the idea of mankind as microcosm, contradicted orthodox Aristotelian thinking and Dee's growing obsession with the occult finally marginalised him. Towards the end of his career he was thought eccentric, if not dangerously heretical, and was to die in extreme poverty in 1608.

What Dee's career showed was that there was no single, settled view of the universe. For instance, he had encountered the writings of Copernicus who earlier in the century had argued that the sun, rather than the earth, as Ptolemy had maintained, was at the centre of the universe. Dee never explicitly agreed with this but some of his astronomical work revealed Copernican assumptions. He also assumed that there was no fixed boundary to the realm of fixed stars. Here again the Elizabethan world picture is shown to be tentative even within one individual's thinking.

Thomas Digges did explicitly embrace the new cosmology of Copernicus in his 1576 work *The Prognostication Everlasting*. He also represented the universe as being infinite rather than enclosed, and in 1577 was to observe a comet which cut across the spheres and orbited the sun. This did not mean Ptolemy's system (Ptolemy was one of the great classical authorities along with Aristotle and Galen) was immediately scrapped but it was brought into doubt. Similarly, the authority of Galen had been brought into question by a Swiss called Paracelsus (who had made his point by burning the standard medical works of the time in Basle in 1527) and by his followers, a number of whom were to be found in Elizabethan England. In place of Galen's view of illness as the imbalance of the four humours, Paracelsus had argued that interacting with the four elements were three 'qualities' which in chemical form were sulphur, salt and mercury. Illness therefore required chemical treatment. This was a branch of alchemy, more usually known for projects such as attempts to turn lead into gold, but it was the beginning of the chemical medicine which is still with us today. Those who read Digges or Paracelsus could not simply see the universe as drawn by Ptolemy, Aristotle and Galen.

By the end of Elizabeth's reign, empiricism, the expansion of knowledge through experiment, was gaining ground. William Gilbert published *De Magnete* in 1600 in which he demonstrated the magnetism of the earth. He had learned much from observing metalworkers and he set little store by the 'probable guesses and opinions of the ordinary professors of philosophy'. Rather than a static, received world picture, he praised a philosophy which had 'grown so much from things diligently observed'.

Elizabethan scientists continually questioned, amended and diversified their world picture. However, in terms of the circulation of ideas in the Elizabethan period, far more importance lies with the creation of theatres such as The Rose or The Globe. Plays had long existed for performance in the courtyards of inns or market places, but now for the first time in England since the Romans there were buildings dedicated to drama, which in the case of large amphitheatres such as The Globe, could seat thousands. The consequent demand for new plays was huge and the golden age of English drama, with playwrights such as Christopher Marlowe, Ben Jonson and pre-eminently, William Shakespeare, had begun. Such dramatists appeared to represent the Chain of Being as a more definite set of ideas than did scientists engaged in subtle debate or private speculation. These ideas were not just natural or traditional. Heywood in his *Apology for Actors* had argued that a purpose of plays was to teach 'subjects obedience to their king' by showing them 'the untimely end of such as have moved tumults, commotions and insurrections'. This shows that people had to be repeatedly shown the virtues of order rather than it just being taken for granted. It might also be the case that Heywood was reassuring patrons, mainly courtiers, and the royal authorities that their plays were not written to be appropriated for subversive causes. After all there was to be considerable alarm that a play about the deposition of Richard II (possibly Shakespeare's) was shown in a number of public places just before the Essex rebellion in 1601.

The 'New Historicists', such as Stephen Greenblatt, have a more subtle account of how Elizabethan and early Stuart drama relates to social order and the powers that be. They find clues in other texts from the period, about the control of prisoners, the sick (especially from the plague) and newly discovered peoples in the New World, to suggest how power operates through drama. Greenblatt argues that 'power defines itself in the relation to that which threatens it'. He means that power only exists when it has something to suppress; it does not exist in a stable, hierarchical Chain of Being. For instance, newly discovered native Americans were studied and their ways recorded and explained so that control could be exercised by their colonial masters. Similarly in the Henry IV plays by Shakespeare, Prince Hal learned about the low life from practical experience in the company of the happily debauched Falstaff and his cronies, a low life which as king he could later condemn and thereby express his power. From this point of view the Chain of Being was evident in the drama only through its being broken. The audience's doubts, in both the Chain of Being and the monarchy it justified, were raised so that they could be contained.

The 'New Historicist' reading of Shakespeare and other Elizabethan dramatists is certainly controversial. More conservative critics complain that such historical reductionism obscures the beauty and universal truths of the drama, whereas those to the left argue that genuinely subversive voices can be heard in many Elizabethan plays, and they were not just called into existence so that they could be controlled. What the debate does make clear is that there is no single reading of Shakespeare or, for that matter, any other aspect of Tudor culture. But a historical reading is always likely to be concerned with the complex, intimate relationship between culture and the power of a Tudor state which was never fully secure and which, from the inauguration of the new dynasty in 1485 through the Reformation to the cult of Gloriana, was ever re-fashioning itself in the minds of the English people.

8 BIBLIOGRAPHY

D Cressy *Literacy and the Social Order: Reading and Writing in Tudor and Stuart England* (Cambridge, 1980).

A Fox & J Guy *Reassessing the Henrician Age: Humanism, Politics and Reform 1500–1550* (Blackwell, 1986).

S Greenblatt *Shakespearean Negotiations: the Circulation of Social Energy in Renaissance England* (Oxford, 1988).

D Loades *The Tudor Court* (Batsford, 1986).

R Porter (ed.) & M Teich *The Renaissance in National Context* (Chapter 8 on England by D Starkey) (Cambridge, 1992).

R Strong *The Cult of Elizabeth: Elizabethan Portraiture and Pageantry* (Thames & Hudson, 1977).

F A Yates *Astraea: the Imperial Theme in the Sixteenth Century* (Penguin, 1978).

9 DISCUSSION POINTS AND EXERCISES

A *This section consists of questions or points that might be used for discussion (or written answers) as a way of expanding on the chapter and testing understanding of it:*

1   Why was English culture changed so profoundly in the Tudor period?

2 What are the problems in assessing literacy in the sixteenth century?

3 What were the social and political effects of printing and of education in the Tudor period?

4 In what ways was education effected by (*a*) humanism?
(*b*) the Reformation?

5 What was the impact of early Tudor politics on humanism?

6 What was the impact of humanism on early Tudor politics?

7 How far reaching were the cultural changes caused by the Reformation in England?

8 Why was the royal image of such importance to the Tudors?

9 What image of himself did Henry VIII seek to propagate?

10 What was the significance of the elaborate cult which developed around Elizabeth I?

11 Was there such a thing as an 'Elizabethan world picture'?

B *Essay questions*

1 What were the principles and what were the consequences of educational change in Tudor England?

2 How far was English culture affected by continental influences in the sixteenth century?

3 Why, and with what result, did humanism and the 'New Learning' develop in England in the reigns of Henry VII and Henry VIII?

4 What was the impact of the Tudor Court on English culture?

5 'A Golden Age'. How far can this description be applied to the arts in England under Elizabeth I?

6 Why, and in what ways, did 'the imperial theme' assume such importance in Tudor culture?

10 SOURCE EXERCISE – ROYAL PORTRAITS

Leaders wishing to consolidate their personal authority, and obscure any opposition, ensure that triumphant visual images of themselves are displayed far and wide. The aim is to impress the popular imagination with their charisma in a way that could never be achieved by words alone. Modern personality cults tend to be associated with totalitarian regimes and the technology of the mass media. However, the Tudors developed what might be thought of as the prototype of the personality cult in England. Its effects are still with us – the earliest royal image that springs to most people's mind is that of Henry VIII.

Turbulence in religion and foreign affairs and an insecure succession gave the Tudors and their supporters sufficient motive to make political capital out of portraiture. The originals could be viewed by quite large numbers (at least of the political nation) at Court or in great houses, but there were also numerous copies sold to be hung in mansions and manor houses up and down the country. The purpose of this exercise is to explore what political messages such portraits were intended to convey.

First review the background to them below and then, having studied the individual portraits, answer the following questions.

A 1 *See page 403, Holbein's cartoon (working drawing) of Henry VIII with Henry VII, 1537. The inscription hailed Henry VII for ending civil discord and Henry VIII for establishing true religion*

In contrast with the figure of Henry VII how does the image of Henry VIII convey so powerful an impression?

2 *See page 404, an anonymous allegorical picture of Edward VI, 1548. Edward sits enthroned next to his father's deathbed with Seymour and the other councillors looking on.*

What is the meaning of the figures and events in the bottom left and the top right of the picture?

What was the political message to be conveyed in surrounding the young King by his councillors, his dying father and the other, allegorical scenes?

3 *See page 405, an anonymous* Coronation portrait of Elizabeth I, *date unknown. The royal insignia borne by the Queen include a crown with closed arches – a symbol of imperial authority.*

Does this portrait project any personal or novel characteristics, or is it purely formal?

4 *See page 406, an allegory of* The Tudor Succession *by Lucas de Heere. This was probably painted to celebrate the Treaty of Blois with France in 1572. Elizabeth brings in Peace trampling down weapons of war.*

Bearing in mind Elizabeth's vulnerability as a female ruler and the recent difficulties created by Mary, Queen of Scots, how might this painting have bolstered Elizabeth's authority?

5 *See page 407, the frontispiece to John Dee's* General and Rare Memorials *pertayning to the Perfect Art of Navigation, 1577. Elizabeth sits, in Dee's words, 'at the Helm of the Imperiall Ship, of the most parte of Christendome: if so, it be her Graces Pleasure'. Kneeling on the shore is 'Brytanica' and the figure standing on a rocky pinnacle is 'Opportunity'.*

In what ways does Dee's frontispiece offer encouragement to Elizabeth to pursue a policy of maritime expansion?

6 *See page 408,* The Sieve Portrait *of Elizabeth I, c.1580. There is debate as to the painter, it is sometimes attributed to Cornelius Kitel and some-*

times Federico Zuccari. Sir Christopher Hatton, the likely patron, stands in the rear. A column may symbolise the chastity of Laura and also refer to the Pillars of Hercules. On the column here is the story of Aeneas abandoning his love, Dido, to found a new empire. (The Tudors claimed descent from Brutus the Trojan.) Note also the globe.

How does this portrait develop Dee's theme?

7 *See page 409, The Ditchley portrait of Elizabeth I by Marcus Gheeraerts, 1592. Ditchley was the Oxfordshire home of Sir Henry Lee who had just retired as the Queen's Champion.*
What is the significance of the map and the weather?

8 *See page 410, The Rainbow portrait of Elizabeth I by Marcus Gheeraerts, c.1600. The rainbow symbolises peace. The serpent and the jewel represent the wisdom in her heart and the armillary sphere (a skeletal globe) her dedication to the universe as supported by the Word of God.*

Why is Elizabeth portrayed with eyes and ears on her golden cloak? What reference might be intended by the chivalric gauntlet on her ruff? What might be the significance of the flowers?

How might this portrait relate to the poetic image of Elizabeth as Astraea?

B Using your analysis of these portraits and having examined the other royal portraits on pages 1, 32, 55, 160, 182 and 208, give an account of the development and significance of royal portraiture under the Tudors.

XV

THE ECONOMY AND SOCIETY OF TUDOR ENGLAND

———

1 INTRODUCTION

NINETEENTH-CENTURY historians such as Macaulay or Maitland saw the Tudor years as marking the beginnings of a national identity, started by Henry VIII with the Break from Rome, and reaching its height in that very embodiment of Englishness, Elizabeth I or 'Gloriana'. However, it was also a time when Parliament, the 'mother' of all its kind, began to flex its muscles in defence of an Englishman's constitutional rights and freedom in the face of a potential royal tyranny supported by the ill-gotten gains of the Dissolution of the Monasteries.

Such a 'Whig' interpretation of the Tudor age was challenged in the 1920s by the Marxist school. This took as its starting point Friedrich Engel's view of the English Civil War as a bourgeois revolution marking the end of feudalism. The roots of the war were sought and found in the sixteenth century. It was seen as a period of embryonic class warfare which pitched an outdated aristocracy against the new dynamic forces of capitalism, the gentry and the mercantile interest of London in particular. Left-wing historians such as Professor R H Tawney and Christopher Hill were leading proponents of this type of interpretation.

The period since 1945 has seen the demise of the Marxist interpretation and a general agreement that more research needs to be undertaken before an accurate pattern can be discerned. The time for fitting history into a predetermined model of political behaviour has passed. Recent research has shown rising and falling fortunes among aristocracy, gentry and yeomenry. Class warfare and tension has now been replaced by an awareness of class consensus among landowners of all types, and a strong sense of social cohesion. Research into the Tudor age has thus far failed to provide sufficient or satisfactory evidence for the long-term social and economic causes of the Civil War.

One trend which has been established is that of a polarisation in late Tudor society between the 'haves' and the 'have nots'. According to Keith Wrightson, those with land and property were able to become wealthier, whilst those with little or no land found themselves worse off owing to the impact of inflation. Debate has ranged over the causes, but the 'monetarist school', who based their views on the impact of the debasement of the coinage and the inward flow of American bullion, have been superseded in importance by the present day adherence to market forces as a cause of economic change in the pre-industrialised society of the sixteenth century. According to Clarkson, factors such as demographic growth, self-interest and a new emphasis on property are now deemed to be the major determinants of Tudor economic growth, capital formation and the resulting social changes which had taken place by 1603.

Like a large jigsaw with a sizable number of pieces missing, the complete picture of the economy and society of Tudor England is impossible to appreciate, but a pattern does emerge. The central problem facing the historian is the difficulty of finding source material which is both continuous over a period, and comprehensive. The problem is a scarcity of good sources, and contemporaries' own inability to understand the diversity of their world. With hindsight, regional and local evidence can be used to suggest a national picture – but it is often tentative and open to huge variations.

2 POPULATION

There are no exact figures for population levels in Tudor England, because no national census existed on which we can rely. Yet a growing amount of evidence provides the basis for a clear pattern in which the Tudor years witnessed a phase of demographic growth starting around 1500, gaining momentum after 1540, and lasting into the mid – seventeenth century.

1450	*c.* 2.1 million	*1545*	*c.* 2.8 million
1525	*c.* 2.3 million	*1603*	*c.* 3.8 million

The impact of this increase in numbers was wide-ranging and central to economic and social developments in the period. A rising population rate averaging 1 per cent p.a. faced a relatively inelastic supply of foodstuffs, causing rising prices, whereas an increasing supply of young labour faced a job market expanding more slowly, with a resulting depression of wage rates. Looking back from 1584, Richard Hakluyt remarked that 'through our long peace and seldom sickness we are grown more populous than ever heretofore'. The rise in population may have been caused by a falling mortality rate and increasing fertility, the result of a long-term trend of prosperity. The population estimates are the result of investigations into other matters. The first comprehensive valuation of lands and personal wealth took place in the 1520s, for a taxation (1522 Subsidy) or military service (the 1524 Muster lists to show all able-bodied men). The densest areas of population were East Anglia, Essex, Devon and Cornwall, with Kent as the most populous. Least dense were the west Midlands, the North-West and West, and over 90 per cent of the population of England and Wales were rural. The population was small compared to that of France at c.15 million, so that a French herald in 1549 concluded that there were 'more labourers of vines in France than people of England of all estates'.

The paramount source is the parish register of births, marriages and deaths required by Thomas Cromwell from 1538 onwards, but few examples survive until the second half of the century, and the records are dependent upon a conscientious minister if they are to be valuable. Enough material does survive to provide us with a rough picture. The average family size was 4–5 members and some 40 per cent of the population were under 16 years old. Life expectancy was about 35 years, though much less in the towns, and higher in the 'healthy' periods between the arrivals of the killer diseases, bubonic or pneumonic plague. They returned regularly (e.g. 1499/1500, 1513), whilst the 'sweat' was severe in 1508.

Continued harvest failure, another regular occurrence, seriously endangered those living close to subsistence level (e.g. in 1527 and 1594–8). A string of poor harvests combined with sickness, as under Mary I, or from 1594–8, dented the population rise by trebling the mortality rate, both locally as in Tamworth, Staffs (1557–8), and nationally. Yet from 1538, existing parish registers do show an excess of births over burials as a general trend. Between 1575–84, in a sample of 400 parishes the ratio between births and deaths was 3:2.

Marriage usually took place when there were sufficient funds to set up a household, around the average age of 26 in the sixteenth century, though the age of women to marry may well have been lower. Certainly, the age of marriage was falling, suggesting growing wealth, and fertility rates were rising, suggesting better, more abundant food and a higher standard of living. However, these figures are tentative and reflect the experience of the 'better off' in Tudor society. By the late 1580s and 1590s the fall in wage rates was leading to later marriage and a decline in the birth rate while wars, famine and plague caused a higher mortality rate. The ratio of births to deaths in the last decade was around 1.2:1.

As a church ceremony for marriage was a legal requirement only from the 1750s onwards, pre-marital sexual relations (or 'bundling' as contemporaries referred to it) may have increased or begun at an earlier age. It was the act of betrothal, rather than marriage itself, which bound the couple together, and it may have been the case that the age of betrothal fell during the Tudors. Illegitimacy rates appeared to have remained low however, possibly because children were later 'legalised' by the marriage ceremony and betrothal, or because the bastardy laws became harsher; or perhaps because marriages were happening earlier, or simply because the records only show relatively few cases.

3 THE PRICE RISE

The Tudor period witnessed a rise in the general price of goods and foodstuffs. It was of such intensity that it has become known as the Price Revolution, and historians have produced various arguments as to its timing within the period and, above all, its causes. The Victorian scholar J E Thorold Rogers saw the decisive change in prices as beginning in the 1540s, whereas Y S Brenner (1962) argued that the price rise could be traced back as far as the 1480s. Professor R B Outhwaite, however, has concluded that inflation before 1510 was gentle and mainly centred on agricultural prices. It was the unusual jump in these prices in the 1520s which sparked the Price Revolution, and with it the end of a long-time stability in wage rates.

The causes of the price phenomenon have been ascribed to either monetary (increasing the money supply) or physical reasons. Contemporaries, who had little to record on the issue before the late 1540s, emphasised the debasement of the coinage (the fall in its precious metal content and subsequent value). Between 1541 and 1551 there does appear to have been a near 50 per cent fall in the exchange rate between London and Antwerp. This monetarist argument held sway until after 1945, bolstered by another group of historians for whom debasement was not the issue. American historians such as Earl J Hamilton (1928) and J U Nef (1941) emphasised instead the impact of New World bullion on the European economy. The switch to seeking the prime cause of the Price Rise in agricultural, industrial and demographic trends (the physical causes) came about in the 1950s in the work of historians such as Phelps-Brown and S V Hopkins in 1957. They saw monetary developments as of secondary importance to the trend towards an imbalance between population and resources under the Tudors. Professor R B Outhwaite and Professor D C Coleman have argued similarly, but have attributed to the monetarist argument the role of a catalyst. Debasement and bullion simply increased the pace of price inflation generated by the 'real' factors.

The evidence for the physical causes of the Price Rise is best seen via the Phelps-Brown Hopkins Index for the period 1450–1600. Here, a basket of consumer goods representing the demands of ordinary people, rather like the Retail Price Index, shows an average six-fold rise in price levels 1450–1600. Under Henry VII and the early years of Henry VIII, prices were virtually stationary, the result of bountiful harvests in the 1490s, and few poor ones in the first two decades. Indeed in 1509–10, wheat prices were at their lowest for two hundred years.

People were full of 'belly-cheer', allowing seed-corn, crucial for the next harvest, to be regularly saved back and not eaten. By the 1520s a rise in commodity prices is discernible, e.g. the doubling of oats and oxen prices (1500–35) and general prices not falling back to old levels. It is possible that such inflation was not serious enough to be noticed until the 1540s, when rumblings among contemporaries do appear to have gathered pace, but by 1550 the average price of all grains was three and a half times that in 1500. Under the later Tudors prices continued to rise with a crescendo reached in the last two decades when corn prices doubled between 1586 and 1596, from 25 shillings per quarter to 50 shillings.

The general price rise was therefore not a steady, continuous rising curve, but included better years and periods of high inflation. Care needs to be taken in using the Phelps-Brown Hopkins Index, but it does suggest that the country as a whole faced a general upward trend. Although it is impossible to establish with certainty how far prices did rise under the Tudors, rise they did, cereals leading the way with a six or sevenfold rise in the average price of all grains.

Three factors, then, help to explain the phenomenon of the Price Rise: the debasement of the coinage, the influx of bullion and the rise in population. The Crown's need for cash to meet the needs of foreign policy and war under Henry VIII and his son increased the need to expand the supply of coin, the equivalent of 'printing money'. A small debasement in 1526–7 was the precursor to the 'Great Debasement' of 1544–51, which perhaps doubled the volume of coin in circulation. The coincidence of poor harvests during the 1550s served to worsen the situation and caused the high price inflation of the 1540–60 period. The influx of foreign bullion began to increase in the second half of the century, to replace coin lost or exported to purchase ornamentation for house or church. Once American bullion began to arrive in sizeable quantities into Seville, it spread quickly throughout Europe by trade and Spanish armies. England's own domestic inflation was probably worsened by importing the European inflation which ensued. Sir Thomas Gresham (1519[?]–79), founder of the royal Exchange, wrote to Queen Elizabeth I:

> It may please your majesty to understand that the first occasion
> of the fall of the exchange did grow by the king's majesty, your
> late father, in abasing his coin from six ounces fine to three
> ounces fine. Whereupon the exchange fell from 25 shillings and
> 8 pence to 13 shillings and 4 pence, which was the occasion that
> all your fine gold was conveyed out of this your realm.
> Secondly, by reason of his wars, the king's majesty fell into
> great debt in Flanders. And for the payment there of they had
> no other device but to pay it by exchange, and to carry over his
> fine gold for the payment of the same. Thirdly, the great

freedom of the Steelyard and granting of licence for the carrying of your wool and other commodities out of your realm . . . it may plainly appear to your highness as the exchange is the thing that eats out all princes, to the whole destruction of their common weal, if it be not substantially looked unto; so likewise the exchange is the chiefest and richest thing only above all other to restore your majesty and your realm to fine gold and silver, and is the means that makes all foreign commodities with all kinds of victuals good cheap, and likewise keeps your fine gold and silver within your realm . . .

1   *What does Gresham argue were the reasons for inflation?*
2   *To what extent does Gresham's argument support a monetarist interpretation of the Price Revolution? Explain your answer.*
3   *What are the problems of this source for the historian?*

Yet it was the steady, constant increase in the population which gave the inflationary period of the sixteenth century its characteristic length, and helps to explain the marked difference between the cost of food and that of manufactured goods, which rose only two or three-fold.

The Price Rise had a vital impact upon Tudor society and was the underlying cause of many of the economic and social developments. To survive inflationary pressures, some extended the cultivation area to include more marginal, less productive land; others were forced to become landless labourers hiring out their services in the locality if it could support them, whilst a third group migrated to the towns. Speedy changes to productivity levels were unlikely, given the basic nature of agricultural technology and the cost of land reclamation or use of marginal land. As the expanding population steadily increased demand for foodstuffs in short supply, the price rise was the inevitable result of such market forces. In manufacturing, the growing labour supply depressed wage rates.

Sustained harvest failure could lead to real hardship, without the insulation of wages inclusive of food and drink, the dual economy (workers doing two jobs) and bartering. By contrast the better off were protected from inflation by income from production, tithes, demesne produce kept for their own consumption, and by rents 'in kind'. Population growth was the driving force then behind the Price Revolution, but debasement of the coinage and the import of bullion provided added momentum, along with natural disasters like harvest failure. It is against this backdrop that the Tudor economy and social policy must be understood.

4 OVERSEAS TRADE

The expansion of overseas trade during the Tudor century marked a significant step forward for England on the international stage. At its outset, the country was a minor player in international commerce; by the close, English ships were to be found engaged in trade war over much of the known world, with London at the centre.

The early part of the sixteenth century was not free of regulation, but the contrast between this and the later period is clear. The 1485 Navigation Act sought to encourage English shipping and seamanship by forbidding the import of wine in foreign vessels, and later fish was to be compulsorily eaten on Wednesdays. The dominating export commodity of the first half of the century was woollen cloth, which boomed under the early Tudors to reach 130 000 cloths p.a. by 1550, some 75 per cent of the value of all exports. Cloth export was regulated by Henry VII in 1485 to include only those unfinished cloths valued at less than 40 shillings, so that finer cloths could be domestically finished by dyeing and fulling. Woollen cloth was the lynchpin for Henry VII's 'Magnus Intercursus' (1496) establishing the London-Antwerp trading axis in unfinished broadcloth and the lighter kerseys. Customs revenue consequently rose from an average of £33 000 p.a. (1485–95) to £50 000 (1518–20), before settling at around £35 000 under Henry VIII whose wars did little to improve trade.

At the hub of activity were the trading companies: the Merchants of the Staple (London and Calais) who had the monopoly of woollen cloth (granted in 1550), and the Merchant Adventurers who dealt in everything else. They became the most powerful English business organisation, controlling entry to trade and pursuing protectionist policies, although foreign merchants (e.g. the Hanseatic League of North German merchants) still controlled a sizeable portion of trade (40–50 per cent).

The importance of cloth for customs revenue clearly became central but there were other commodities involved in early Tudor trade. Wine and wood from France, coal and tin, herring, cod and dried fish from Scandinavia, pilchards exported to Portugal. The Company of Fishmongers had six separate halls in the City and by 1532 were ranked fourth among the livery companies. Wrought iron was brought from Spain, barley and malt sent to Flanders in return for sweet wine, glass, raisins, paper, dyestuffs and manufactured goods. The prospect of new commercial markets encouraged Henry VII to promote the explorations of John and Sebastian Cabot to Newfoundland (1496) and to Hudson's Bay (1506). In the 1530s William Hawkins penetrated Upper Guinea (West Africa) for pepper and ivory, later extending out to Brazil for dyewood in return for slaves.

The London-Antwerp cloth axis which so dominated the years 1485–1550 was much less influential during the latter half of the sixteenth century. Clashes with Spain and the closing of Antwerp's Scheldt river, all contributed to the search for new foreign commercial centres. It is this period which witnessed the growing regulation and intervention of the Crown through the Privy Council. The attack on the privileges afforded to foreign traders such as those of the Hanseatic League, based in the Steelyard area of London, was supported by a Crown needing money from customs revenues and with a vested interest in promoting native trading companies. The switch of the cloth trade to Emden and Middleburg after the 1560s was at Privy Council instigation, the result of native pressure. The development of lighter more, colourful cloth mixtures ('New Draperies') and a growing demand for them in the Mediterranean helped to diversify away from the Netherlands.

New trading companies were established, centred on London, given monopoly control and were government backed. From 1555–87 the Muscovy Company, the first joint-stock company, was founded to trade with Russia and was heavily backed by the Court. In 1579 the Eastland Company was chartered to import goods from the Baltic. While trade with the Mediterranean brought home silk, spices and oils, and the Levant Company was founded to trade with the Ottomans in 1581. Merchant shipping increased quite dramatically under Elizabeth. In 1560 there were some 70 ships between 100–199 tonnes and 6 over 200 tonnes – by 1582 they numbered 155 and 18 respectively. Privateering (licensed piracy) in the Caribbean at the expense of Spain provided a commercial benefit as Drake's exploits at Nombre de Dios testified, as did his circumnavigation of 1578–80. Between 1584–7 there was a failed attempt to settle Roanoke Island off Virginia, to provide raw materials, promote Christianity and to challenge Spain by driving them 'out of trade to idleness' (*Sir Richard Hakluyt*).

The profit motive led English merchants to cut out foreign middlemen wherever possible, whether Italian, Netherlander or Hansa, and to trade directly in finished goods. By 1600, white unfinished Old Draperies were still at the 1540 figure (125 000 cloths p.a.), whereas New Draperies represented 20 per cent of total exports. However, it was growing domestic demand for foreign luxury goods such as Spanish leather, French wine, Portuguese and Levant spices, sugar from Morocco (Barbary Company 1585–97) and fashion, which provided an added incentive since profit margins were high. Martin Frobisher's search for a North-West passage to the East and its spice trade was similarly motivated. English woollen cloth with its small margins was traded with Newfoundland fish and New Draperies, which were in high demand in Southern Europe. By 1603 overseas trade looked to wider horizons than in 1485 and the English presence in world trade was much greater and over longer distances. At the centre of business lay the City of London, grown enormously in size and influence at the expense of the old traditional 'outports' like

Southampton and Hull, whose late medieval 'hey-day', continuing under the early Tudors, had gone.

5 TOWNS

London, alone among English towns and cities, compared favourably with European counterparts, with a population of around 60 000 in 1500. It was ten times wealthier than the second city, Norwich, and fifteen times wealthier than Bristol, the third. At the top of the social scale, the capital was extremely wealthy, creating and supplying a heavy demand for luxuries and basic goods and foodstuffs. Yet it also had areas of deep squalor and poverty in the slums to the north and north-east, and outside the city walls. Some 5 per cent of its population owned about 80 per cent of the total wealth. The richest among the estimated 2000 strong merchant class in 1501 were the mercers, tailors and goldsmiths. According to the 1552 Subsidy assessment the wealthiest was Sir Stephen Jenyns, merchant tailor, assessed at £3500. He used his wealth to build much of the church of St Andrew's Undershaft in the City, and left more than £2500 to various benefactors at his death in 1524. The 1522 assessment shows forty-five London merchants assessed at above £1000, whereas there were only seven others of such wealth throughout the rest of the country.

A significant development was the growth of the capital during the sixteenth century, part of a process which saw its population grow from 2 per cent of the total population in 1520, to 11 per cent by 1700. By 1600 London's populace numbered some 200 000, having doubled its 1570 level. This growth resulted from foreign and native rural immigration in search of employment, plus the greater opportunities for begging, crime and poor relief. London's magnetic attraction was based upon its strengthening position as the country's trading and financial centre. Its very size attracted service industries and the food and fuel distribution trades. Spices, dried fruit and luxuries such as silks and calicoes were sold by a burgeoning number of middlemen. Above all, London was the centre of the cloth trade.

London's rise to pre-eminence did cause its problems. A rising volume of death from starvation or disease, as shown in 1563 when around 20 000 died from the plague, was matched by rising unemployment and house prices. Already, by 1550, Robert Crowley complained of landlords raising rents 'some double, some triple and some four-fold to that they were within these twelve years past'. Religious radicalism was spawned from the prevailing conditions, helped by the capital's role as an educational centre through the Inns of Court, and as a centre for book publication. It was the first town or city to have an organised scheme of Poor Relief (1547), itself a measure of the problems it faced. What is surprising given the extremes of economic and social conditions, is the relative dearth of riot throughout the sixteenth-century boom years for the capital.

Apart from London, towns were small by comparison with Europe. Norwich, Bristol, Newcastle and Coventry numbered some 10 000, Northampton and Leicester perhaps only 3000. Only about 10 per cent of the population were urban dwellers, with country towns often numbering hundreds only. The major urban areas were mainly located in the south and eastern half of the country, thus contributing to the long-term migration from the north and west to the south and east.

Outside the town walls usually lay an area of shacks (the suburbs), whose populace was frequently outside the legal jurisdiction of the town authorities. Within the walls workshops were situated either inside or in front of the houses with rarely more than four or five employees per workshop. Many townspeople had a plot of land as well, and partible inheritance was the norm (wealth and land divided between heirs). Conditions were often dirty and cramped, with a growing number of poor, both able-bodied and 'impotent', seeking alms, work or relief in all early Tudor towns, a problem which was to worsen by the 1590s. Between 1532–42 over 1400 apprentices were attracted into Bristol from the West Country and such an influx of migrants could cause higher house prices. In 1534 the Worcester authorities had to institute a rent freeze.

The eight hundred or so market towns and cities were centres for a wide range of occupations. By 1525 Norwich, admittedly the second city, had over eighty different crafts and trades. Most large towns were similarly structured, though often built around one specialist craft or trade e.g. cloth (Lavenham in Suffolk) or leather (Nottingham). Other common urban occupations were metalwork, building and food distribution, though over 40 per cent of urban workers seem to have worked in textiles in the 1520s, highlighting the centrality of cloth. The guardians of craft traditions and the welfare of their members were the urban gilds, which sought to control entry to the craft or 'mystery', keep an eye on production levels and quality, enforce apprenticeship regulations, and set wages and prices. The gilds were, however, in general decline under the Tudors, the result of changing trading patterns, an increasing labour supply, new industries creating alternative employment, and increasing state regulation. Gilds, however, maintained their role as networks of social privilege. London's 150 gilds included the twelve Livery companies which were all well-trodden paths to power within the City. The ruling urban oligarchies were usually self-perpetuating within the one or two leading families.

Some towns were facing a crisis in the first half of the sixteenth century. Disease, the loss of trade to London, competition from other areas or from outside the town's immediate jurisdiction and even the clothier's 'putting-out' system, all contributed in some part to the urban decline. In his *Discourse of the Common Weal* (1549), Sir Thomas Smith highlighted that 'not only the good towns are decayed sore in their houses, streets and other buildings, but also the country in their highways and bridges'. Old clothing towns suffered (e.g. Lincoln and York), as well as the outports, and some towns were left with little more than the role of a market town. In a letter to Henry VIII in 1538 John Baker wrote:

> I am a poor craftsman who has travelled and gone through the most part of your realm to earn my living. I have been in most of the cities and large towns in England. I have also gone through many little towns and villages, but alas it did pity my heart to see in every place so many monuments where houses have been and now there is nothing but bare walls standing. Which I think is very dishonourous unto your highness and causes much inconvenience among your people. It causes men to lie by the highwayside there to rob and it also causes much murder.
>
> Now if it please your grace to hear what is the cause of such decay and ruin within your Realm, it is this. In every place where your majesty has given estates and lordship to any gentleman, if a poor man comes unto one of them asking that he might have a tenement or farm to rent, the lord answers in this way: 'If you want this tenement from me, you must pay me so much money for a fine'. And he raiseth that fine to a great sum of money and the rest to be paid yearly beside. The poor man then seeing there is no remedy but either to have it or to be destitute of any habitation, sells all that he hath to pay the fine.

1 *What does John Baker suggest were the causes of urban decay and poverty?*

2 *Assess the reliability of this source.*

By the early years of Elizabeth a degree of recovery was visible. In Norwich greater diversification into clothes (hats, tailors, shoemakers and gloves) had begun to take place. Building and allied trades were expanding, as was the supply of imported luxuries. A similar story can be seen in York, Bristol and Exeter as they developed as provincial capitals, with gentlemen building town houses requiring service industries, and new occupations such as vintners and brewers being established. There is evidence then of urban renewal generated by the growing wealth of the local landowners, by the end of the century.

6 THE DOMESTIC ECONOMY

The vast majority of trade during the period was undertaken within the country, perhaps between 90–5 per cent. Much of it travelled by roads suitable for droving cattle or pack-horses, by river and then by creeks to small inland hamlets, and by coastal shipping. Goods made their way to market towns or to ports for shipment to London or abroad; inward cargoes were broken up at main centres and then distributed out across the country to reach small towns and villages.

Coastal trade was massive in volume, comprising both foreign and domestic goods such as grain and coal, and transported via head-ports like Bristol and York. Coal from Newcastle in the 1590s went overwhelmingly for domestic use, as did Cornish tin. This inter-regional trade often ended up in small craft of under 10 tonnes, and a large variety of vessels was used for more localised transportation. To ease transport problems and in typically regulatory fashion, the Tudors passed eight acts to help improve or maintain rivers.

Apart from the Thames, the three other great trading rivers were the Great Ouse, the Severn and the Trent. The Ouse served eight counties, some of them the country's wealthiest and was navigable as far as Bedford for vessels of 15 tonnes. The Severn, navigable to Welshpool was a vital artery for corn, grain and Shropshire coal. Pack horses took Oswestry cloth to London via Shrewsbury, some 140 miles at 20 miles per day, and the first road map of nine long distance routes out of London was published in 1541. These roads were primarily for droving animals, carrying carts and for people, enabling traders to meet at the fairs of many of the market towns in England and Wales.

To compensate for England's backwardness in commerce and industry the early Tudors, especially Henry VII, attracted foreign immigrants to introduce new processes, and to stimulate native production. Many of the foreigners wanted to make profits in a relatively undeveloped commercial nation, or were seeking religious or racial refuge. Before 1550, around 40 per cent of the cloth trade lay in the hands of the Hansa, Flemings, Italians and French, centred on the Blackfriars Liberty and the Steelyard area, both outside the City of London's jurisdiction. The 3000 alien craftsmen of 1500 had risen to 10 000 by 1540, despite restrictions imposed by the Crown whereby no alien was allowed to own land, had to pay twice the amount of tax, and faced restrictions in the exercise of their crafts and trades. Some did seek 'Denization' (naturalisation) which could lead to an easing of the strictures. In 1534 aliens were prohibited from work as pewterers, printers and bookbinders as the Crown sought to protect and stimulate native employment in this area. The revocation of the Hanseatic League's privileges in the 1550s at the request of the trading companies was similarly motivated.

Foreign expertise often lay at the heart of new developments in manufacturing. A Frenchman, Peter Bauck, established an iron-smelting industry in the Sussex Weald, producing bronze cannon in 1533. Window glass production spread across the country after the arrival of French glass-makers, in particular Jean Carre of Arras in 1567. Daniel Hochstetter, a German mining engineer, set up the Mines Royal in Keswick, whilst William Humphrey and Christopher Schutz began the Mineral and Battery Company in Tintern. Foreigners introduced the notion of mixing wool with silk to create the New Draperies, and established paper-milling. What they all had in common was the support of the Crown which protected and regulated the new industries by issuing patents giving a temporary monopoly and, therefore, high profits. It was a crude but quite effective way of stimulating domestic production and employment, advancing native manufacturing and of reducing foreign imports with their detrimental effects on the balance of payments at a time of high inflation.

One notable feature of the Tudor economy was the growing level of government involvement to regulate and stimulate it. There was certainly no really coherent economic policy behind this interventionism, it was much more a series of *ad-hoc* responses to circumstances and problems, and as the Tudor era wore on, examples of government intervention grew in number. Between 1485 and 1603, over three hundred parliamentary statutes were passed to regulate economic affairs. Most of these laid down penalties for stipulated offences, the rest were permissive laws allowing or prompting specific economic behaviour, and a barrage of proclamations was issued by the Tudors. Supervision of laws was patchy and sporadic, however, with local constables sometimes reticent to hand matters over to the Justice of the Peace, and they in turn sometimes reluctant to enforce regulations if unemployment might result. Much of penal enforcement relied heavily upon the testimony of 'promoters and informers', often of the 'meaner sort' who would receive a proportion of the fine upon conviction.

The Crown also used its powers of patronage to control and promote activity through the grants of licences, patents and monopolies. Licences often exempted individuals from statutes or proclamation, such as that which allowed Robert Dudley, Earl of Leicester, to import cloth; or else they were used to appoint agents for the Crown, as with Seler's licence to develop a salt industry. Patents were granted by the Crown to help new industries, providing a temporary monopoly in return for cash. Soap, glass, paper, saltpetre and playing cards were all examples of such, although by the end of the sixteenth century patents were open to corruption, often relating to existing industries, and offering profitable benefits to courtiers. Monopolistic control of goods and processes by courtiers caused much hostility after Robert Bell's protest in the 1571 Parliament. It returned again in 1592, and became the main issue of the 1601 session, calling into question the Queen's prerogative and forcing a measure of retreat by the Crown when the 1602 Darcy vs

Allen case, over the monopoly of playing cards, found against such a use of monopolies, although many continued.

Government intervention was also required to regulate and control the food supply. Good harvest years left the country with a sufficiency, but poor years meant a huge deficit with more mouths to be fed. Statute was used to control the export of grain. Until 1534 a fifteenth-century law setting a threshold price of 6 shillings and 8 pence per quarter, above which export was forbidden, was applicable, and this was raised in 1563 and in 1593. Shrewsbury Council imported 3200 bushels of corn from the Baltic through the Eastland Company in 1596, to provide bread for the poor, and local officials generally were empowered to search for grain supplies in poor harvest. Whilst boroughs regulated their markets for prices, weights and measures, Crown action was required to deal with supply problems in the corn areas, ranging from the hoarding of grain (engrossing) to buying grain before it came to market (forestalling). Corn merchants or 'badgers' were closely monitored and a statute of 1532 required a badger to be licensed by three JPs, and the licence was to be renewed every year from 1563. Crown supervision up to 1563 relied on local JPs, sheriffs and town councils for information, but thereafter detailed supervision was given over to a Commission for grain. Price fixing on a national scale as Henry VIII had attempted on meat, beer, wine and sugar, was not resorted to (except on wine), during the Elizabethan years, when market price and a degree of regulation were preferred.

England's reputation as a key primary producer of raw wool was superseded after 1500 by her status as a supplier of woollen cloth. Cloth was the commodity which kept idle and poor hands busy, becoming the undoubted pillar of the economy. Between the mid-fifteenth and the mid-seventeenth centuries, the value of English textile exports rose 5–6 times in real terms taking inflation into account. The industry employed many thousands of mostly part-time employees, and in 1555 the cloth entrepreneurs (clothiers) were prohibited by the Weavers Act from centralising looms in one place to cut costs at the expense of jobs for the poor outworkers. Central to the industry was the 'putting-out' system, whereby clothiers hired out looms to a large number of families to produce the cloth from wool. Thus agrarian employment was combined with manufacturing. Within the family, children carded the wool, women spun and men wove and did some elementary finishing. Despite this more efficient division of labour, the work force made up 60 per cent of costs.

The main production areas were the West Riding, the West Country and above all East Anglia, which contributed 25 per cent of national production. The core area of south Suffolk and north Essex around Lavenham became the densest area of population in Tudor England, after London. Traditional 'Old Draperies' of white, undressed, woollen cloth comprised the short broadcloth of the North and the less rough 'kerseys' of the South. Success in turn attracted more people to swell the labour supply, causing industrial growth, but a trade depression in cloth, as in the 1550s, or a run of poor harvests, could quickly cause unemployment and starvation, which would ripple back to wool supply areas e.g. Wales or Lincolnshire.

The 'New Draperies' marked a further progression in cloth and were the result of diversification after the depression of the mid-century. Government support for skilled foreign immigrants with new technology attracted Protestant refugees from the Netherlands during the 1560–70s, who settled in east and south-east England. They brought continental techniques and styles, mixing worsted yarns – even silk – with the wool, to produce lighter, more colourful and cheaper cloths such as 'bays and says'. Nor was cloth the only textile commodity; a small linen industry based on Lancashire flax and imported Irish yarn began, whilst the Lake District and the Cotswolds became centres of hosiery.

Mining industries also began to be exploited more intensively. In 1500 the rich mineral resources of tin, lead and coal were hardly scratched. Major sources were the Northumberland and Durham field, centred on the outport of Newcastle, and in north Lancashire and the Forest of Dean. Certainly the income generated strengthened the finances of the Percy family, and of Thomas, Lord Darcy, in Yorkshire. The scant records do suggest a surge in production by the 1590s when Newcastle was shipping over 100 000 tonnes p.a., mostly to London, but also to areas of timber shortage e.g. Cambridge, and to the growing glass and metal industries.

Lead and tin were mined from the Pennines, the Mendips and Cornwall, both goods being in high demand in Europe. Cornish tin production doubled from 1490–1550. Iron-smelting, producing cast-iron in new blast furnaces using charcoal from the Sussex and Kent Wealds, was another notable development to meet the demands of naval dockyards. The three furnaces of the 1530s had grown to twenty-six in thirty years, and the industry spread to the Forest of Dean and to the west Midlands around Dudley, to produce cannon, shot and wrought-iron. Some deforestation, e.g. in the Weald, was caused by the expanding need for timber to make charcoal, itself a growing industry. Craftsmen were not scarce – even remote rural areas such as Myddle in Shropshire contained over 10 per cent of craftsmen in 1550, whilst in Oakham in Rutland, 25 per cent of adult workers had a craft. Clearly some families combined farming with industrial production such as nail-making and mining.

Ship-building and fishing were large employers of labour, especially on the east coast. Henry VII encouraged the building of a merchant fleet by issuing 'bounties' (1488–91), and a dry dock was built at Portsmouth (1495–7). His son established naval dockyards at Deptford (1513) and these gradually grew in importance, owing to the improved navigability of the Thames, and their proximity to London.

One of the liveliest industries under the Tudors was the building trade and allied occupations e.g. quarrying. Evidence from parish churches clearly suggests a great deal of building between 1480–1540, and a growing use of stained glass, mostly funded by wealthy local families. Both Canterbury Cathedral and Bath Abbey contain significant amounts of work from this period, emphasising that monasteries were adding to their buildings and were increasingly important local employers until the 1530s. Furthermore, the houses of the wealthy élite were changing from a primarily defensive role, to one of peaceful, leisured residence, though this was less the case near the Scottish border. The early Tudors witnessed the dawning of the English Country House of two or three storeys. Bradgate (Leicestershire) and Compton Wynyates (Warwickshire) are both good examples. Henry VIII's own expenditure on such buildings as Hampton Court was over £60 000 between 1536–9.

The Tudor governments took responsibility for establishing hours of work, wages and employment conditions. By a statute of 1495, hours of work were regulated into a national pattern. From March to September a 14–15 hour day was worked, at other times dawn until dusk. This pattern was kept constant throughout the Tudor era, maintained by the 1563 Statute of Artificers, and lasted until the nineteenth century. Failure to observe these hours meant a proportionate reduction in wages until 1563. A 65–75 hour week was balanced by the slow pace of work and over fifty holidays in pre-Reformation England, reduced to twenty-seven by the Protestant regime in 1552, who took exception to holidays 'spent miserably in drunkenness, in glossing, in strife, in dancing, dicing, idleness and gluttony' (*Hugh Latimer*).

Under the early Tudors, government and local corporations shared responsibility for setting wages. A 1389 law imposed national wage maxima and JPs were empowered to assess rates within such limits. This was re-enacted in 1514 with some adjustment to the growing disparity between wage levels. Wages varied between trades, and between craftsmen and labourers. Wages could often include meat and drink and the money wage would differ accordingly. In 1519 labourers were to be paid 1 penny per day, with meat and drink, a vital advantage in later years of inflation, whilst master craftsmen were to be paid 6 pence per day, exclusive of food and drink, and semi-skilled labour received 4 pence per day. The average income of the lowest class of wage-earner must have been between £2 and £2 10s. per year for those in continual work, out of which was to be found rent, fuel, light, clothing and food. Inflation ate away at these fixed rates, and by mid-century the wage rates for agricultural labourers had fallen by possibly 40 per cent in real terms.

The great landmark of government regulatory policy for employment and wages, indeed one of the major statutes of the Tudor era, was the Statute of Artificers (1563). It set out to enforce a universal obligation to work and to provide employment for that workforce; it may furthermore have protected 'skilled' artisans from unskilled competition. The background for the Statute was the commercial crisis of the 1550s, particularly the decline in woollen cloth exports which caused unemployment, and the Marian 'sweating sickness', whose virulence created short-term labour shortage and applied an upward pressure on wage rates. Enormously comprehensive in its range of regulation, the Act targeted the young, single and full-time 'servant in husbandry' rather than the casual or part-time labourers (who were not dealt with until a statute of 1598).

Under the Act, all able unemployed persons were required to seek work and had to accept the offer of regular employment: men in husbandry, girls in service. All unmarried persons under the age of 30 were forced to serve any employer who needed them for agriculture and food production at harvest, and they were to be trained and employed in a craft. All males between 12 and 60, and women up to the age of 40, were to work on the land unless gentry born, heirs to lands worth more than £10 p.a. or to goods above £40 p.a., or else involved in occupations such as a skilled craft, education, mining, metalwork, seafaring or the grain market. To restrict migration and vagrancy, binding contracts of service of one year hire minimum were imposed on servant or workman, with testimonials required before leaving the parish and only with 'due cause'.

JPs were empowered to assess local wage rate maxima on an annual basis, thereby creating in theory a sensitivity of response to changing circumstances. It became an offence to give or to receive higher wages. Working hours were regulated as set down in 1495, although the penalty for absence was heavy at 1 penny per hour out of a daily rate of up to 6 pence.

The impact of the Statute was not as profound as the government had hoped. Its creators underestimated the enormous volume of unemployment generated by the economic conditions of the last third of the century; they were reacting to mid-century experiences when price inflation had only recently been grasped. The Act did not provide fair wages much beyond the short-term, but held them down relative to the inflation of the 1560–1600 period. The prohibition of wages 'in kind' in 1566 removed a hedge against inflation and forced the labourer into the full blizzard of the money economy. Furthermore, assessments were generally made in the summer before harvest, thereby condemning wage levels to lag behind prices. Such was the distress caused by the calamities of the 1590s that the authorities in Chester increased its wage assessment by nearly 20 per cent between 1593 and 1597. By holding down wage levels by setting maxima, by introducing a large pool of able-bodied, unskilled labour into the labour market, thus further depressing wage rates, and by expanding the pool of 'cheaper' apprentices, the Act helped the progressive deterioration in standards of living for those wholly, or largely, reliant on wage earning. Nor did it achieve its desired aim of immobilising those able-bodied elements, perhaps 10 per cent of the population p.a., whose unemployment and migration posed such a threat to property. The failure of the Statute of Artificers to effectively address the employment and wage issue in 1563, however understandable, was a direct cause of the government's further interventions in the 1570s and 1590s to provide organised, compulsory relief for the poor.

7 THE STRUCTURE OF RURAL SOCIETY

The source of all social, military and political power and wealth was the ownership of land, and the greatest landowner was the monarch. Henry VII was worth about £10 000 p.a. in 1485 and set out deliberately to increase the gap between himself and potential rivals within the ranks of old medieval barons such as Sir William Stanley, with an income of around £1000 p.a. Only the Crown enjoyed full ownership of land, and therefore all landowners held their land by some form of tenancy, if only from the Crown, in return for military service or as a result of military glory. Landowning contained certain seigneurial rights – e.g. the holding of the manor (leet) court, of fairs and markets, of exploiting mineral wealth and water rights. Tudor England was divided into approximately 50 000 manors, the majority having an absentee landlord and being run by his steward.

At the head of the social structure was the **peerage**. Numbers for the sixteenth century were fairly constant at around 50–60, once the early Tudors had established themselves. There was a wide variation in income, but under the early Tudors the wealthiest were the Duke of Buckingham (£6000 p.a.) until 1521 and the Archbishop of Canterbury (£5400 p.a.), down to just below £1000 p.a. at the bottom, based on the 1523 Assessment. Peers were privileged to enjoy trial by their equals, not to be arrested for debt or petty crime, nor to suffer branding. They sought to keep their ancestral lands intact, to provide for son's patrimony and daughter's dowry, and to avoid the dangers of Attainder of family estates by the Crown. Equally damaging was dying without male heir, which often caused partition, or with young children under the age of majority, which led to wardship. In 1510 and 1533 sumptuary laws regulated what social classes could and could not wear, further distinguishing the peerage. Another distinguishing feature was the right of 'retaining' or wearing of a lord's livery by 'fee'dmen' (men paid a fee).

In 1516 Henry Percy, fifth Earl of Northumberland, had 166 daily servants retained in his Yorkshire household. The early Tudors, especially Henry VII punished open retaining financially, as Lord Burgavenny found to his great cost, and in 1524 Wolsey brought

Thomas Lord Dacre to Star Chamber for similar reasons. The real thrust behind the royal attack on retaining was the need to enforce loyalty to the Tudor rose, and to uphold law and order against 'maintenance', that is, the corrupting of the law by peers to help their retainers.

Knights made up the next stratum of society, again varying in wealth, but according to Professor Hoskins averaging about £200 p.a. in the early Tudor years. In 1600, Thomas Wilson estimated the number of knights at around 500, though around 350 might be more accurate. Knighthood was not a hereditary right but had to be confirmed, usually by the ruler, and was distinguished by the right to use a coat of arms. Also with the right to wear armorial badges were the **squires**, owning at least one manor, if not several, with an income of around £80 p.a., and numbering perhaps 1000 in Henrician times. Along with the squires were the **gentry**, without the right to wear arms, but generally recognised to be landowners of substance, of honest reputation, who were allowed to call themselves 'gent'. Together the squires and gentry made up around 3000 men, many being the younger sons of peers, knights and squires, or of rich merchants and lawyers. Under the Henrician regime, gentry owned lands above £10 p.a. in value. Below the gentlemen were the **yeomen**, difficult to define precisely except that they were solidly wealthy, made a decent living from farming a substantial acreage, but did not have sufficient land or reputation to enter the landowning lists. The **husbandman** of the Henrician era farmed perhaps 10–30 acres held on a variety of leases, with little if any of his own land, whilst the **cottager** farmer had smaller acreage and often undertook some form of extra cottage industry to supplement and regulate income levels. At the bottom of the social scale were the many **landless labourers**, who hired out their labour in return for wage payment, and the **bondmen**, still technically serfs. Their numbers were reducing during the century. In 1500, in Fawcett in Norfolk, there were eight bondmen of the Duke of Norfolk, but by 1575 none existed. That same year Elizabeth I gave 300 of her bondmen to Sir Henry Lee who arranged for them to purchase their freedom.

Relationships within the working structure of rural society were cemented by the system of landholding. Large landowners would hold land as tenants of the Crown 'in capite', in return for a nominal rent but allowing the Crown to maintain its medieval dues and customs such as wardship. Within the manor there existed free tenants, customary tenants and leaseholders. **Free tenants** enjoyed absolute security, paying a token or 'quit rent' to the lord, unchanged since medieval times, and could do what they wanted with the land. **Customary tenants** were the most numerous by far, and in the Henrician period constituted some 60 per cent of the whole tenancy according to Professor R H Tawney. Land was held according to the custom of the manor and a copy of the lease was held in the Manor Court. Those **copyholders** who held land by inheritance were in the strongest position, paying a fixed annual rent and a fixed level of entry fine (i.e. payment equal to a given number of years rental value upon taking possession of the tenancy) at a time of rising income for producers. Other copyholders held land for two or three named lives or for a specified number of years, all with fixed or variable fines payable to the lord on entry to the land. This majority lacked the guarantees and protection afforded by manorial custom and depended ultimately upon the lord's good will and market conditions. Unfixed entry fines or annual rent levels meant a higher price for the tenant to find once the copyhold expired. **Leaseholders** held their lands not through manorial custom but in common law, renting for either the duration of three named lives or for a fixed number of years, usually between 7 and 99, and at full market price. Most leaseholders tried to renew the lease before all three of the named lives died, and many would sub-let at the highest possible prices (rack-rents).

The trend throughout the Tudor period was for an extension of leasehold tenure, with copyholders with weak tenure being forced to convert to leasehold at rack-rent prices. Also, as the population and prices rose, the terms of tenancies became more difficult, entry fines increased, and periods of leases were shortened as landowners exerted more pressure for profit. Higher rental levels themselves were likely to have been price-inflationary over the century. In 1536 the rebels of the Pilgrimage of Grace wanted entry fines (gressons) limited to two years rent and the Council of the North saw fit to investigate rack-renting enclosure and engrossing (amalgamating two farms) in 1537.

Finally, among the tenantry, the **Tenants-at-Will** held their land at the will of the landlord and could be summarily evicted, with no protection in common law or manorial custom. Usually they were made up of the poorest cottagers and over the century faced a rise in rentals with which their income could not keep pace.

8 ENCLOSURE

The vast majority of the Tudor population was involved in some form of farming. In the **fielden** counties of the South and East small nucleated settlements dominated, surrounded by the village 'strips' of land. In forest areas secondary occupations along with farming made full use of the seasons. Farmers sought to provide for their families and to produce enough to sell in the local market for the best profit. The Tudor period did see some diversification from the two main types of farming, arable and livestock, or a mix of these two, but such trends arrived later on between 1560 and 1600. Flax and hemp, woad, sainfoin (a herb grown for fodder), coleseed and rapeseed were some of the common new products. The century did see an expansion of land use to meet the population's growing demand for cereals, or to create sheep pasture, and to this end the fenlands of East Anglia were drained and more marginal difficult land brought into cultivation.

If agriculture remained mainly conservative in its style for most of the period, the dynamics within agriculture were a source of intense controversy for contemporaries and exerted a powerful influence on social developments. The conflict centred upon the issue of enclosure. In 1497 an Italian visitor remarked that English farmers were 'so lazy and slow that they do not bother to sow more wheat than is necessary for their own consumption; they prefer to let the ground be transformed into pasture for the use of the sheep that they breed in large numbers'. A little excessive, perhaps: enclosure was not new, it had been practised long before the Tudors. The loss of up to a third of the population from the Black Death of the mid-fourteenth century, and the slow rate of recovery, had meant that many farmhouses had fallen into ruin in the meantime. Wars and plague made tenants difficult to find and landlords laid grass as the best alternative solution, being less labour intensive, less costly because wages were relatively high, and easier to maintain with sheep cropping and fertilizing the land. Demand, firstly for raw wool and then for woollen cloth for export and home consumption, made pasture farming more profitable than arable, and this provided the incentive for some of the Tudor enclosures.

For its detractors, enclosure was responsible for many of rural society's problems – high prices of grain, depopulation, unemployment and starvation threatening law and order. Much of the criticism lacked accuracy – enclosure took place sometimes after agreement between landlord and tenants. It was not a national phenomenon but caused by localised or regional circumstances. Worse than the Act of Enclosure itself were the other abuses committed by landlords such as the engrossing of farms (amalgamating two farms), the emparking of land to create parkland for country houses, and the encroachment upon common land.

Enclosure was a wide term used to include hedging and cultivating waste ground, consolidating arable strips and dividing common pasture, but it also included the extinction of common rights over a piece of land by hedging or fencing, and this caused problems in times of rising population when the use of ancient common land was at a premium. The particular areas prone to enclosure were those areas of the country of mainly mixed farming (cereals and livestock) in the Midlands and the South-East. Common rights of pasturage were essential to manure arable fields, and to provide grazing opportunities for the livestock of small cottagers or husbandmen. Here lay the battleground between sheep and grain, landlord and tenant. Furthermore, the nature of land tenure in the area was important. Customary tenants were protected by manorial courts, but tenants-at-will and copyhold leaseholders were not. It was they who were more easily evicted or who could not pay the higher rental for a new lease. They had to rely on government action, look to rebellion or add to the swelling number of unemployed and wage labour. Thomas More complained in *Utopia* of that 'covetous and insatiable cormorant' the encloser, and that sheep did 'eat up and swallow down the very men themselves'.

Tudor government tried to control and regulate the excesses. Between 1485 and 1597 eleven statutes were passed against depopulation and enclosure, eight Royal Commissions investigated illegal enclosures, and a welter of proclamation was issued too. Their problem was to balance the profitability of the cloth industry with the need to feed and employ the rising population. As landowners themselves, their interests could conflict. Much illicit enclosure since 1488 was discovered, but the cost of litigation and the threat of eviction caused only one conviction out of twenty-two cases brought to court in Leicestershire, a problem area. Proclamations of the 1520s ordered the destruction of all enclosures made since 1485 unless proved lawful in Chancery (1526).

The Tudor government's response was therefore gradual, and until 1536 relied optimistically upon landowners to monitor their own behaviour and enforce the legislation or proclamation. In the 1533 Sheep and Farms Act, for example, the number of sheep per farmer was limited to a maximum of 2400 and engrossing was restricted – farmers were to occupy only two farms at most. After 1536 prosecution by the Crown became possible, suggesting that earlier efforts to control enclosure based on trust had foundered, and highlighting the central problem of enforcing Tudor proclamation away from the power base of London.

The 'Commonwealth Men' was one important pressure group numbering among them men such as the cleric Hugh Latimer, the pamphleteer Robert Crowley, John Hales, Thomas Smith and William Cecil. Enclosure and depopulation, according to peasants, preachers and pamphleteers, became the cause of uprooting husbandmen, destroying farmhouses and causing a shortage of grain. Sheep became the symbol of such discontent, and the new Protestant regime of the Protector Somerset could not afford economic disturbances to threaten its political and religious policies. Commissions were sent out in June 1548 to gather evidence of enclosure of commons, emparking, engrossing and conversion from tillage to pasture, all perceived sins against the Commonwealth and the causes of grain shortage and rising prices. The only Commission to complete was that of John Hales for the south Midlands, which made a point of principle by having a furrow ploughed across the Earl of Warwick's lands.

To stimulate a return to arable farming a tax on sheep was introduced for a short time from March to November 1549, charged at 1*d.* per sheep over 150, and 8*d.* per £ on every cloth in store. In the same year Thomas Smith argued in his *A Discourse of the Common Weal of this Realm of England* that the government should promote 'every man to set plough in the ground, to husband waste grounds, yea to turn the lands which be enclosed form pasture to arable land; for every man will the gladder follow that wherein they see the more profit and gain'. By the Marian Act of 1555, farmers who kept more than 120 sheep had to keep more than two milch cows and rear one calf to promote dairy farming. However, the mid-century collapse in the cloth market led to a reduction in the controversy and the rising price of cereals made enclosure less attractive under Elizabeth until the disastrously poor harvests of the mid-1590s forced the government's hand once more. Acts of 1595–7 required lands which had been arable for twelve years before conversion to be returned to tillage.

The enclosure controversy was substantially, if not entirely a problem of Norfolk and the south and east Midlands, and although it reached its height in the early sixteenth century, much of the damage was done by the volume of enclosure which took place before 1485. Certainly land was increasingly viewed as an economic investment for profit under the Tudors, rather than as a basis for subsistence and military service. Some half to three-quarters of a million acres were enclosed, of which a large percentage was arable land, but the incidence was both patchy and piecemeal. Evicted arable tenants moved to other local employment or swelled the urban poor and vagrant ranks. Of some three hundred people called before Star Chamber from 1518 to 1529 for enclosure since 1485, seventy-four pleaded guilty, but many were pardoned.

There were also different justifiable motives for enclosure. Sometimes it was to rationalise decayed villages e.g. Holyoak (Leicestershire.) in 1496, or to provide land for cattle to meet growing demand. In the later period the desire for convertible husbandry (land which could be switched between arable and livestock use), stimulated enclosure as arable prices rose to generate higher incomes for producers. Certainly enclosure marked a shift from 'strip'-based communal farming to individual farming, it did facilitate innovation and increase land values, if at the cost of dispossessing vulnerable tenants in high risk areas. For landowners, enclosure had clear benefits, and there were a growing number in the period who sought to consolidate their holdings and maximise their profits from land.

9 THE LAND MARKET

Under the Tudors of the early sixteenth century, the market in land was more active at the level of the tenant farmer, concentration seeming to be on changes of copyhold at the manorial level. The shift to greater activity in the freehold (ownership) market took place between the 1520s and 1540s, when over 1000 transactions took place per year. One cause of the earlier inactivity in the freehold land market may have been the widespread implementation of the 'use'. To avoid having to pay a sum of money to the Crown when an heir succeeded to an estate, and to avoid becoming a ward of the Crown, landowners by knight-service employed a body of trustees ('**feoffees to use**') to look after the lands, whilst reserving for the 'use' of himself and his heirs the annual income. Consequently, no freehold estates passed down upon the owner's death, thus incurring no liability for feudal dues. By the 1536 Statute of Uses such evasion was not prohibited, but liability for the feudal dues fell on the trustees, thus making the process less attractive. By the Statute of Wills (1540), two-thirds of such knight-service land could be handed on to younger sons and this was a likely cause of fragmentation of estates and an impetus to the land market.

A familiar pattern emerges upon investigation of the land market. There were relatively few speculators and profiteers, but the market largely consisted of established landed families of moderate means or their younger sons who, faced with a small patrimony, made their fortune in government, land or commerce in London or the large provincial towns, and then purchased land of their own. Sir Ralph Sadler, Master of the Wardrobe to Henry VIII, was such a man. There were 'new' rich: yeoman stock such as Sir John Gostwick of Willington, who by 1545 owned 15 000 acres, or Nicholas Bacon, who between 1546 and 1578 spent £32 000 on land, a third of it from the Crown. Yeoman farmers themselves often bought single farms or freeholdings between 50 and 100 acres, mostly costing less than £100, and usually these men were heads of families. There was a limited chance of upward mobility for the yeomen. Nicholas Bacon, Robert Phillips of Wispington and the Temple family of Stowe, Buckinghamshire, did provide examples of such social progress. However, during the sixteenth century, more land came into the hands of the knights, squires and 'mere gentry' who owned the medium-sized estates. This constituted a rise of the gentry, both in terms of increased numbers within the ranks, and in the volume of land held.

Landowners however, found that the increasing demand for land from a growing population meant that they could exact larger entry fines for leases, convert tenancies from copyhold to leasehold, shorten the length of leases, and charge much higher rents at full market price (rack-rents). Rents on the Herbert estates in Wiltshire rose from 13*d.* to 20*d.* per acre p.a. between 1535 and 1550 and to 28*d.* by the 1570s. For the landowner, rising income levels, the increased commercial advantage of converting copyhold to leasehold, the restriction on labour costs, and the insulation from market prices afforded by rents in kind and by farming the demesne for home consumption, all meant a growing amount of wealth to be spent on further land acquisitions or on conspicuous consumption.

10 THE RISE OF THE GENTRY

Undoubtedly there were a number of exceptional men during the Tudor period who were of low birth, and who exploited their talents to the full to become wealthy and influential men. Thomas Cromwell, Sir Thomas Smith and William Petre were of such low-born stock, but their stories were untypical. One of the most controversial issues between historians of the period has been the question of whether, and to what extent, the gentry were rising in their fortunes, and whether the aristocracy were in decline. It is a debate which nowadays lacks the heat it once generated, but it marks an interesting historiographical feature.

The fifty peers of 1450 had grown to around sixty by 1560, some rising by land purchase (e.g. the Spencers of Warwickshire), others by office or marriage. William Cecil, Lord Burghley's grandfather, had been a yeoman-gentleman. Henry VIII and Edward VI created or restored nearly fifty peerages, some from gentry backgrounds (e.g. Somerset, Northumberland, Winchester), but the peerage's size became much more static under Elizabeth, whose miserliness over forty years in creating only a handful of peerages frustrated leading wealthy gentlemen and denied them further social advancement.

Professor R H Tawney suggested that generally the gentry were rising as a class at the expense of both the Crown and the peerage, based on a ten counties survey of over 3000 manors (1560–1640). Professor Lawrence Stone supported this view, arguing that there was a shift of landed wealth under Elizabeth, with the peerage selling 28 per cent of their manors, the average manorial holding falling from fifty-four to thirty-nine. This had long-term political effects and was one cause of the English Civil War, as the relationship between the Crown, its natural but increasingly outdated supporters, the peerage, and the gentry, changed. Heavy criticism of this interpretation led to heated academic debate. For example, Professor Trevor-Roper concluded that the gentry as a whole were not rising; indeed the poorer or 'mere' gentry were themselves falling on difficult times. Professor J Hexter also criticised Stone's idea of a crisis of the aristocracy, suggesting instead that only the peerage's military power over the gentry had been weakened.

Since the debate died down, a commonly-held interpretation has emerged. Dr Palliser, for example, has concluded that what happened was 'less a decline of the nobility than an expansion of the gentry, within which the nobles formed a smaller proportion', a process not helped by Elizabeth's famed unwillingness to create peers. Nor were the peers becoming outdated as Tawney, and particularly Stone, suggested. The peerage was deeply involved in the land market, as one might expect, and although the numbers of manors held by the peerage dropped from 3400 (1558) to 2200 (1600), they were purchasing regularly into the 1590s. There is evidence of many of them rationalising their manorial holdings by selling off unwanted manors, and of some embracing the profit motive once thought to be the preserve of the gentry. Income was also sought from sources other than land, such as trade or law, or usually through office and the Court. As a long-term explanation for the Civil War, the rise of the gentry and the crisis of the aristocracy in the later Tudor period will not do. The causes of 1642 must be looked for in the period after 1603.

Monastic lands were not the only source of new land. Chantry, collegiate and episcopal sales or exchanges further stimulated the flourishing land market as people sold on lands and consolidated their holdings. The Crown too provided a stimulus by selling their own royal estates. Between 1536 and 1554 the Tudors raised £1.25 million in this way and Elizabeth liquidated £860 000 in three stages. There seems then to have been a steady rise in land sales (1560–1620), mostly within the landowning classes. The increasingly active land market after the Dissolution and the rising income from producing cereals, cloth, or from trade, did lead to an undoubted expansion in the numbers of gentry.

Yet there is also evidence of people buying into the gentry stratum. In 1577 William Harrison suggested that yeomen were buying up the lands of gents in trouble, and then providing the education necessary for their sons to become recognised as a bona fide gent. Half of Yorkshire's new gentry were yeomen, whilst William Stumpe began as a clothier, his son becoming a knight. Both London commerce and governmental office generated wealth to allow land purchase and movement up the social scale, as the Bacons and Cecils showed, while Elizabeth of Hardwicke, moved in four shrewd marriages from daughter of a minor Derbyshire gent to Countess of Shrewsbury. Nor should it be forgotten that debt, biological fate and bad luck, all contributed to the decline of some gentry; but for the vast majority the late Tudor period was one of rising fortunes. Yet the opposite was true for the humbler folk of the Henrician period.

11 POVERTY

William Harrison, in his social analysis of the Elizabethan years (1588), highlighted the lowest stratum of English society as consisting of 'lay labourers, poor husbandmen and some retailers . . . copyholders and all artificers [who] have neither voice nor authoritie in the Commonwealth but are to be ruled'. Inequality was a traditional and accepted feature of English society, which rested on a large percentage of the population who earned little, rented their houses and had little to fall back on in a bad year. It was this sector which was increasingly subjected to poverty in the Tudor years, who suffered most from plague and hunger when harvests failed, and whose money wages often had to be supplemented by barter after the 1540s.

The causes were demographic in the long-term, as more labour chased employment in a land where opportunities were becoming relatively scarce. Engrossing, emparking and short-term trade depression played a role, as did the demobilization of soldiers and sailors and the growing costs of meeting entry fines and rental levels. It is debatable whether the dissolution of the monasteries further worsened problems by creating unemployment among the estimated 10 000 religious, or by opening up monastic lands to the more grasping demands of the laity, who did not have to keep up the traditional obligations to the poor made by the Church.

The picture which emerges is that of a society gradually polarising under the Tudors, the rich becoming richer, the poor poorer and more numerous. Those with sufficient land to become suppliers to the market, or at least to be self-sufficient, survived and improved their position, whilst those who were merely consumers faced continuing pressure on their finances and were most likely to slide into poverty through eviction, voluntary surrender and migration. Poverty became an increasingly serious urban problem, with pressure placed on town services by non-productive consumers, and causing a worsening of the quality and cost of housing.

The burden of looking after the poor was not readily shouldered by Tudor secular society nor by government. Early Tudor legislation was similar to the medieval laws of Richard II in the twin aims of keeping the poor immobile, and by deterring the able-bodied unemployed from idleness by severe punishment. The central problem was the migrant unemployed who were not homogenous but consisted of different types of people, with differing reasons for migration. Of these 'sturdy beggars', some were rogues, some were honest men and women fallen on hard times, some disbanded soldiery. Widows appear to have made up a large proportion of the urban poor, often running alehouses or brothels, yet there were also families facing temporary hardship.

Until the last quarter of the sixteenth century only those physically unable to work were regarded as deserving of relief. Poverty itself was not a qualification. The population shrinkage caused by the Black Death of the mid-fourteenth century meant that vacancies for employment had exceeded the demands of the labour force, driving up wage levels and preventing widespread poverty. Specific localised poverty was mopped up by the Church, by alms-giving or by individual generosity such as that of Stephen Jenyns, Merchant Taylor, endowing a school for twelve poor boys in his native Wolverhampton. Before the Reformation, bishops used almoners for charitable giving, monks and nuns gave their left-overs ('broken meats') and waste drink to the poor, and hospitals were provided for the care of the sick and destitute. The century did witness a shift in government attitude and policy, from the reliance upon self-help and a non-interventionist approach under much of the Henrician period, to gradual state intervention and regulation, culminating in the major legislation of Elizabeth's last years.

As poverty became an issue under the Tudors, a variety of solutions were tried, many designed to create fear and injury. The major objective of the authorities was to maintain law and order, prevent crime and uphold security. In 1495 a new law required beggars and the idle to be put in the stocks for three days, to be whipped and then returned to their original parish. The demarcation between 'impotent' beggar, those suffering physical disability, and the 'idle', i.e. able-bodied but unemployed, was a central feature of Tudor policy. The legislation suffered from a lack of enforcement, partly due to the difficulties of establishing the original parish, but it did illustrate the simplicity of contemporary attitudes to the poor and the *ad hoc* nature of the government's response. Tudor towns did see an increase in begging. Licences were granted in Gloucester in 1504, and beggars were forced to wear badges in York.

In 1531 a depression in the cloth trade following the severing of relations with the Netherlands, caused a rise in unemployment, despite an order to clothiers to maintain employment levels. The new legislation of 1531 distinguished between the impotent disabled poor, who were allowed to beg officially under licence from the JP in their own community, and the able-bodied, who were given no charity whatsoever. Vagrants, (able-bodied migrants), were to be whipped and returned to their own parish, whilst unlicensed beggars, and those giving alms to them, were to be fined. As a result, able-bodied, unemployed poor were forced to break the law or starve. An enlightened scheme of public works on roads and harbours was suggested by William Marshall in a failed bill of 1535. Significantly the Act of 1536 ordered parishes or town authorities to take responsibility for the impotent poor, and the apprenticeship of children. Defaulting parishes were to be fined 20 shillings per month, with churchwardens given the supervisory role. Able-bodied poor were still lumped together as shirkers, based on the understanding that work was readily available. Here was the first example of Crown intervention, learning from the example of London where the first efforts at providing a continuing, if voluntary, fund for the poor had begun in 1533.

By 1547 the inexorable economic processes of the time, together with political and religious insecurities, led to the infamous legislation of that year. With frightening severity the Edwardian legislation tried to hand out a short, sharp shock to any person likely to cause disruption. A vagrant was defined as an able-bodied person lacking support and unemployed for more than three days. The first conviction for vagrancy meant being branded with a 'V' on the chest and being given to the informant as a slave for two years. The slave was to perform any task, or risk being whipped, chained or imprisoned on a diet of bread and water. The informant was further empowered to sell, lease or bequeath a slave. Runaways were to be enslaved for life and execution followed a second offence. A second conviction for vagrancy led to life-long slavery, an 'S' being branded on the face, whilst a third meant a felon's death on the gibbet. If no informant was involved, a convicted vagrant became a corporate slave of the parish or local authority. Vagrant children could be seized by anyone prepared to teach them a trade, with boys kept until the age of 24 and girls until 20. Parental permission was not needed, and escape could mean enslavement upon capture. Impotent beggars, however, were to be sent back to their original parish, to be provided for by voluntary organised charity in houses for the disabled poor, funded by weekly collections in church. Enforcement fell upon the parish constable, but the draconian measures proved to be too extreme to be effectively enforced and the legislation was repealed in 1550 in favour of a return to the 1531 Act.

Ten proclamations against 'talebearers' or seditious vagabonds (1548–9) further illustrates the fears for stability by the Somerset regime. Legislation in 1552 introduced the registration of impotent poor and ended freelance begging for relief. Pressure was exerted on unwilling contributors to alms by vicars and even by bishops. This marked a shift from purely voluntary giving, and showed that the element of compulsion, a crucial difference between the early and later Tudor periods, was necessary.

Urban authorities had already established compulsory poor rates by mid-century. London (1547), Norwich (1549) and York (1551), met their own specific problems of unemployment and poverty through contributions which varied according to wealth. London acquired St Bartholomew's Hospital from the Crown (1546–7), Bethlehem Hospital (Bedlam) for the insane, and Christ's Hospital for orphans (1552). Bridewell Palace became a house of correction for employing the able-bodied poor.

The Act of Uniformity (1559) saw the first step in the methodical expansion of the state's involvement, when non-attendance at an Anglican church meant a 1 shilling fine per Sunday, the monies going to support the poor, under the supervision of churchwardens. By 1603 this was a crucial factor in coping with rural poverty. Failure to contribute a donation of whatever size led to a summons before JPs at Quarter Sessions and possible imprisonment.

The watershed came in 1572 when legislation based upon the Norwich scheme (1570) was enacted on a national basis, creating a universal statutory obligation for the first time. The Act at last recognised the concept of 'able-bodied unemployed'. Demobilized soldiers and sailors were licensed to return home and were exempted from the penalties of the Act, as were harvest workers and evicted servants. JPs were to assess the cost of relief for the local poor and compulsory weekly contributions were exacted for the aged and impotent, who were forbidden to beg unless the parish could not support them.

Unlicensed begging resulted in burning through the right ear or, if under the age of 14, whipping. Surplus funds were to be used to build houses of correction for rogues and vagabonds. The new office of Overseer of the Poor was unpaid and was appointed annually by the JP from among substantial householders. A further Act of 1576 laid up stocks of hemp, flax, wool and iron for the able-bodied poor to work on, and required at least one house of correction per county. These two Acts signified a major advance; until then only those physically unable to work had been deemed deserving, whereas now the existence of deserving unemployed, fit and willing labour who could find no employment, was recognised. The next two decades were marked by a long series of decent harvests, except for those of 1573 and 1586, and allowed the government to concentrate on expanding the food supply from cereal production at home, importing from abroad and fixing prices. By 1593 the clauses in the 1572 Act requiring ear-boring, whipping and death, had been replaced by whipping and imprisonment.

The last decade of the century saw a large number of able-bodied jobless swelling the ranks of the young, aged and disabled, as urban poverty escalated beyond the expectations of the 1570s, due to the impact of war on trade and the further growth in the population. Between 1593 and 1597 a series of disastrous harvests across Europe meant that wheat was priced at 80 per cent above its norm, leading to famine. Urban authorities faced rising prices for imported grain. In Bristol the cost of a bushel rose from 6 shillings to 20 shillings (1596–8), and riots, caused by dearer bread, broke out in London, Oxfordshire and Norfolk, forcing Parliament to be re-called in October 1597. Of the seventeen Bills introduced, eleven were related to relieving poverty. An act to deal with the 'Professional Poor' in 1598 required vagrants to be arrested, whipped and returned to their own parish: into service if able-bodied, the almshouse if not. The gaols of houses of correction, even galleys and banishment were resorted to, if necessary, for 'dangerous' rogues who refused to work, with execution as a felon as the final sanction.

The Act for the Maintenance of Husbandry and Tillage (1598) tried to freeze the agricultural picture as in 1558 by returning pasture land to arable; but more important was the Act for the Relief of the Poor (1598). It contained little that was new but it codified comprehensively the Tudor regime's attempts to deal with the issue. The duties of the Overseer of the Poor were defined, including the power to set children and those with no assets to work; churchwardens were to help with the assessment and collection of the Poor Rate. Materials were to be provided for the poor to work on, funded from taxation, while children were to be apprenticed – boys until the age of 24, girls until 21. The problems of collecting sufficient funds were also realised. Overseers were to meet monthly and to submit annual accounts to the JP. If a parish was unable to cope with the burden, the rates were to be spread over the local hundred, and other parishes were asked to contribute. Refusal to pay the Rate meant possible imprisonment and that goods could be seized. Begging was henceforth regarded as unnecessary and the equivalent of vagrancy. With minor alterations in 1601, this parish-based legislation remained in force until 1834.

The effectiveness of poor provision is difficult to evaluate. Rural parishes appear to have produced very low levels of subsistence, just enough, along with charity, to survive the shortages of the 1590s crisis years. Informal and *ad hoc* almsgiving continued on a large scale and voluntary private gifts probably exceeded the levels of statutory relief. The causes of poverty were not really understood sufficiently to be addressed and therefore little was done to ease poverty in general. Private endowments for charity were of vital importance, rising according to Professor Jordan from £227 000 (1541–60) to £634 000 (1601–20). This marked a decline in real terms over the period, but together with the Poor Rate it was enough to cope with most conditions. As Dr J Pound has concluded, 'both poverty and vagrancy were fairly well-contained, and to say that either created a dangerous national situation would be to strain the evidence'.

12 CRIME, LAW AND ORDER

Tudor governments relied heavily upon a combination of statutes, proclamations and licensing to maintain law, order and stability. It was in the nature of sixteenth-century states that the writ of central government did not run very far, and depended upon the co-operation and involvement of the local political élites. Economic and social difficulties made the task harder, forcing constant vigilance and a steady stream of legislation and directives. Nevertheless, it was an impossible task to suppress violence completely, especially in times of dearth. An effective legal machinery was yet to appear, and corruption and vested interest were difficult to combat.

Central government, perhaps not surprisingly as representatives of the landowning classes, tended to intervene on those matters which were deemed to be dangerous to the Commonwealth, a threat to landowning interests or to be socially unacceptable. The Tudors were aware that they needed to work with the political nation, and that this relationship needed nurturing. The issue of retaining highlights the point. There was no attempt by the Tudors to destroy retaining, rather they sought to control and contain it, through the use of a Crown licence (1504). There was no great sudden change in behaviour among nobles, who continued to condone the violence of their livery men, but by the mid-sixteenth century there had been a decline in such activity. As late as the last quarter of the century, feuds were alive between retaining nobles in Herefordshire and Wiltshire. It was a similar story with weaponry – essential for protection and social esteem, but a potential threat. Again the Crown tried to control rather than prohibit possession, though gunpowder proved to be a difficult problem. Statutes against guns were issued in 1514 and 1542 to restrict murders, robberies, felonies and riots. Guns were to be a minimum of three feet long to prevent concealment but they could be kept for defence, and the same motive lay behind a 1562 act to prevent rapiers from becoming too long. Yet in 1579 a proclamation complained about the failure to enforce the laws against the carrying of fire-arms.

There was also an attempt to define, clarify and extend felonies (crimes punishable by death), particularly in the Henrician period. Hunting at night, poaching, abducting women (1487), theft from masters, homosexuality (1534), witchcraft (1542) and poisoning (1531) were all defined as felonies, though they tended to be short-term reactions to contemporary events and many were later repealed. 'Benefit of clergy', whereby penalties could be waived for crimes by clerics, was limited. It could only be claimed once, and was only available to the minor orders. Psalm 51, verse 1 (the 'Neck verse') had to be read to qualify, and after 1489 branding on the left thumb with an 'M' (murder), or 'T' (theft and other felonies), was introduced. About 20 per cent of felons obtained benefit, the ability to read at all often being sufficient to escape hanging, and it is important to remember that petty pilfering meant survival for the bottom stratum of society. An increasing number of crimes were steadily excluded from benefit under the Tudors as the Crown sought to strengthen their grip on society and maintain law and order. Often exemptions from claiming benefit were aimed at protecting property. After 1489, highway robbery or theft from a church ceased to be liable to benefit, and burglary in a variety of forms was exempted from Henry VIII through to Elizabeth I.

The core problem for Tudor central government was local particularism. Landowners in the localities were not prepared always to prosecute an offender with the full weight of the law, and there was no police force. Additionally, there were privileged quasi-independent areas where the Crown's writ was limited. These jurisdictions, like Tyndale or St Martin-le-grand, were refuges from full effective prosecutions for felons. Criminals often crossed the River Severn to escape the Crown's jurisdiction, although the Marcher lordships were gradually brought to heel by the early Tudors who abolished all permanent sanctuaries, and in 1536 only allowed a maximum of forty days refuge. Even if a case was brought to court, juries were often made up of the 'poorer sort', open to corruption and frequently ill-educated. The Crown resorted to the quicker and less formal court of Star Chamber, and the Councils of the North and Welsh Marches to enforce laws more speedily. Most capital trials were held at Assizes or Quarter Sessions, the latter's early monopoly to try all felonies being gradually eroded. Grand larceny (theft of goods over 12d. in value) and difficult cases increasingly went to Assizes.

Assize courts were also the usual courts to try witchcraft. Imprisonment was viewed as a lenient sentence, despite the terrible conditions. Hanging sought to strangle slowly rather than to break the neck, and afterwards goods were forfeited to the Crown. Refusing to plead or remaining silent meant being crushed to death, whilst for some crimes physical mutilation provided a public warning – for example, forgery and perjury meant the loss of both ears and being branded on the face.

By the late sixteenth century, disorder still prevailed, worsened by the population pressure and economic privations of the 1590s. The search for food and employment, as well as the presence of disabled soldiers, led to rising violence among the lower classes, with the dagger or staff favoured weapons, so that by 1600 there is evidence of travellers on highways carrying personal weapons in secret to combat mugging. Yet at the same time there was an increase in the number of cases being brought to the courts. While sixty-seven cases came before Star Chamber in 1559, over 700 were dealt with in 1603. Local violence was occasionally condoned by the landowning classes – for example, Sir William Herbert was fined 1000 marks for so doing, seriously damaging his local reputation and standing. Piracy was another violent crime often carried out under landowner protection. An increasing volume of the rising coastal trade was hit, with local coastal villages happy to share in profit and gain. The Crown tried to suppress piracy by statute in 1536, making it a felony, and then by two later commissions (1563 and 1577), but successes were rare and the war with Spain even forced a shift in the Crown's position, royal licences being issued to turn piracy into privateering.

13 CONCLUSION

The years between 1485 and 1603 witnessed remarkable progress in many spheres of economic activity. The era under the Tudors was centrally focused on meeting changing circumstances, often beyond the Crown's control, and on managing those changes. Population growth, the expansion of trade caused by the voyages of discovery of other Europeans, and not least the tensions created between the Reformation and Counter-reformation Churches, were examples of major changes during the sixteenth century which exerted a serious impact upon the country and the Tudor regime. The Crown's response was twofold. Firstly, to take advantage of changing circumstances where it could, and to create further opportunities; secondly, to regulate and control, thereby increasing government intervention. If the growth of London, the expansion of trade at home and abroad, and the increase in consumption and landholding among the political élite, all displayed the fruits of opportunism, the enormous rise in the use of statute, proclamation and licence, coupled with the burgeoning responsibilities of the JP, all testify to the growing involvement of central government. Undoubtedly the English economy of 1603 was more complex and sophisticated when compared with that of 1485.

Yet there was a significant degree of continuity between 1485 and 1603. Land ownership was still the key to power and prestige, with trade and service occupations, such as law, perceived as the means to acquire wealth and then land. Many old families had survived well, although a few casualties had been lost. Government might have grown in size and level of involvement, but it still had a serious problem in exerting effective authority away from the Home Counties. This continuity was symbolised by the Tudors themselves and the England bequeathed peacefully by Elizabeth to James VI of Scotland in 1603, possessed a much more advanced, varied and complex economy and society than existed upon Henry VII's seizure of the throne in 1485. It was this strength which was the achievement of the Tudor years.

14 BIBLIOGRAPHY

A L Beier *The Problem of the Poor in Tudor and Early Stuart England* (Methuen Lancaster pamphlet, 1983).
D C Coleman *The Economy of England 1450–1750* (OUP, 1978).
N Heard *Tudor Economy and Society* (Hodder & Stoughton, Access to History, 1992).
W G Hoskins *The Age of Plunder 1500–1547* (Longman, 1976).
D M Palliser *The Age of Elizabeth* (Longman, 1983).
J Pound *Poverty and Vagrancy in Tudor England* (Longman, 1978 ed).
P Williams *The Tudor Regime* (OUP,1991).
J Youings *Sixteenth Century England* (Penguin, 1984).

15 DISCUSSION POINTS AND EXERCISES

A *This section consists of questions or points that might be used for discussion (or written answers) as a way of expanding on the chapter and testing understanding of it:*

1 How have historians' views of the Tudor society changed in the last seventy years?

2 How fast was the rise in the population of Tudor England? What caused it and what limited it?

3 When in the century was the 'Price Rise' at its steepest and what brought it about?

4 What were the main sources of England's wealth in overseas trade?

5 What were the consequences of the growth of London in the sixteenth century?

6 In what ways did the domestic economy develop in the Tudor period?

7 Which were the most advantageous, and which the most disadvantageous, forms of land tenure for a tenant?

8 Why was enclosure so explosive an issue in the sixteenth century and why was it so difficult to control?

9 Who made the most gains from the Tudor land market?

10 Did the relative status and wealth of nobility and gentry change under the Tudors?

11 How did contemporaries analyse poverty in the sixteenth century, and how effectively did the government cope with it?

12 Why did the Crown find it so difficult to control crime?

B *Essay questions*

1 Analyse the effects of the growth of population in Tudor England.

2 Why, and with what success, did Tudor governments attempt to control enclosure?

3 Who gained and who lost from the Price Rise of the sixteenth century?

4 With what degree of success did the Tudors cope with England's social problems?

5 How and why did the pattern of English trade change 1485–1603?

6 Discuss the reasons for London's rapid growth during the Tudor century.

7 Explain how and why the English economy developed 1550–1603.

16 DOCUMENTARY EXERCISE – THE PROBLEM OF POVERTY

A. Wage Rates and their Purchasing power 1540–1609

Purchasing Power of Agricultural Labourer

Decade	Money wage rate	Cost of living	Purchasing power wage rate
(1450–99	100	100	100)
1540–49	118	167	71
1550–59	160	271	59
1560–69	177	269	66
1570–79	207	298	69
1580–89	203	354	57
1590–99	219	443	49

100 = the base rate

B. Edward Hext (JP) – letter to Burghley 25 September 1596

And I may justly say that the infinite numbers of the idle, wandering people and robbers of the land are the chiefest cause of the dearth, for though they labour not, and yet they spend doubly as much as the labourer does, for they lie idly in the ale houses day and night eating and drinking excessively. And within these three months I took a thief that was executed this last assizes, that confessed unto me that he and two more lay in an ale house three weeks, in which time they ate twenty fat sheep whereof they stole every night one; besides, they break many a poor man's plough by stealing an ox or two from him, and [he] not being able to buy more, leases a great part of his tillage that year. Others lease their sheep out of their folds, by which their grounds are not so fruitful as otherwise they would be . . .

C. Act for the Maintenance of Husbandry and Tillage 1598

Whereas the strength and flourishing estate of this kingdom hath been always and is greatly advanced by the maintenance of the plough and tillage, being the occasion of the increase and multiplying of people both for service in the wars and in times of peace, being also a principal means that people are set on work, and thereby withdrawn from idleness, drunkenness, unlawful games and all other lewd practices and conditions of life; and whereas by the same means of tillage and husbandry the greater part of the subjects are preserved from extreme poverty in a competent estate of maintenance and means to live, and the wealth of the realm is kept dispersed and distributed in many hands, where it is more ready to answer all necessary charges for the service of the realm . . . be it enacted by the authority aforesaid, that if any person or body politic or corporate shall offend against the premises, every such person or body politic or corporate so offending shall lose and forfeit for every acre not restored or not continued as aforesaid, the sum of twenty shillings for every year that he or they so offend; and that the said penalties or forfeitures shall be divided in three equal parts, whereof one third part to be to the Queen's Majesty, her heirs and successors to her and their own use [and] one third part to the Queen's Majesty, her heirs and successors for relief of the poor in the parish where the offence shall be committed . . . and the other third part to such person as will sue for the same in any court of record at Westminster . . .

D. *The Poor Law Act 1598*

Be it enacted . . . that the churchwardens of every parish, and four substantial householders . . . shall be called Overseers of the Poor of the same parish, and they or the greater part of them shall take order from time to time . . . for setting to work of the children of all such whose parents shall not by the same persons be thought able to keep and maintain their children, and also all such persons married or unmarried as having no means to maintain them, use no ordinary and daily trade of life to get their living by: and also to raise weekly or otherwise (by taxation of every inhabitant and every occupier of lands in the same parish in such competent sum and sums of money as they shall think fit) a convenient stock of flax, hemp, wool, thread, iron and other necessary ware and stuff to set the poor on work, and also competent sums of money for and towards the necessary relief of the lame, impotent, old, blind and such other among them being poor and not able to work . . . And . . . it shall be lawful for the said churchwardens and overseers, or the greater part of them, by the assent of any two Justices of the Peace, to bind such children as aforesaid to be apprentices, where they shall see convenient, till such man child shall come to the age of four and twenty years, and such woman child to the age of one and twenty years . . .

E. *Act for the Punishment of Vagabonds 1598*

. . . And it be enacted . . . that every person which is by this present Act declared to be a rogue, vagabond or sturdy beggar, which shall be, at any time after the said feast of Easter next coming, taken begging, vagrant, wandering or misordering themselves in any part of this realm or the dominion of Wales, shall upon their apprehension . . . be stripped naked from the middle upwards and shall be openly whipped until his or her body be bloody and shall be forthwith sent from parish to parish by the officers of every the same the next straight way to the parish where he was born, if the same may be known by the party's confession or otherwise; and if the same be not known, then to the parish where he or she last dwelt before the same punishment by the space of one year, there to put him or her self to labour as a true subject ought to do . . .

1 *Compare sources B and C on the impact of enclosure.*

2 *To what extent does source A help to explain the problems referred to in sources D and E?*

3 *'The threat to law, order and social stability in the 1590s forced the Tudor government to intervene directly in local affairs.' Using the sources and your knowledge, comment on this view.*

XVI

TUDOR REBELLIONS 1485–1603

1 INTRODUCTION

HISTORIANS have identified two main kinds of rebellions (or 'commotions' as contemporaries preferred to call them) during this period in England. (*For discussion of Irish rebellions see Chapter XII.*) In the first sort the leaders tried to seize political power by presenting their own alternative candidate for the throne or by seeking for themselves powerful positions around the monarchy. Examples of this variety are the efforts of the pretenders Lambert Simnel and Perkin Warbeck to usurp the throne from Henry VII, the overthrow of Somerset by Northumberland in 1549, Wyatt's Rebellion of 1554, the Revolt of the Northern Earls in 1569 and Essex's conspiracy of 1601.

The second category was a protest, or demonstration in force, whose aim was simply to obtain redress of grievances by bringing them to the attention of the government. Into this group would fit the 1497 Cornish Rising, the disturbances associated with the 'Amicable Grant' in 1525, the Lincolnshire Rebellion and the Pilgrimage of Grace of 1536–7, the Western Rebellion of 1549 and Kett's Rebellion of the same year.

Nevertheless, neither kind was acceptable in the prevailing intellectual climate. The mystical importance of monarchy was underlined by the coronation ceremony (especially by the anointing ritual), by a dazzling Court life and public displays, tournaments, and pageants. Moreover, such a monarch could dispense patronage, rewarding loyal followers and forging useful chains of obedience with powerful families in the regions. Thus to challenge such a figure was both unwise and treasonable.

Contemporary political theorists agreed that resistance to this lawful authority was to be condemned. Cromwell, Morrison, Starkey, Barnes, Cheke and Nichols all agreed that non-resistance was the only reasonable response to grievances. Nichols railed against the Western Rebels in 1549, accusing them of inviting God's wrath, neglecting their husbandry and families and of rebelling against their natural sovereign. Sir John Cheke had this to say in 1549 when he took the Kett rebels to task in his *The Hurt of Sedition*:

> How can you keep your own if you keep no order? Your wife and children, how can they be defended from other men's violence, if you will in other things break all order; and by what means will you be obeyed of yours as servants if you will not obey the King as subjects?

Such writers tended to see England as a harmonious commonwealth and they likened it to a human body or 'body politic'. A popular way of describing this harmony was as a 'Great Chain of Being', (*see pages 430–1*), as the political thinker Sir John Fortescue makes clear in this extract:

> God created as many different kinds of things as he did creatures, so that there is no creature which does not differ in some respect superior or inferior to all the rest. So that from the highest angel down to the lowest of his kind there is absolutely not found an angel that is not a superior and inferior; nor from man down to the meanest worm is there any creature which is not in some respect superior to one creature and inferior to another so that there is nothing which the bond of order does not embrace.

There were also the teachings of Protestant preachers. Latimer, for example, argued that a sinful man should be prepared to suffer under tyrants:

> If the King should require of thee an unjust request, yet art thou bound to pay it and not to resist and rebel . . . the King indeed is in peril of his soul for asking of an unjust request; and God will in his due time reckon with him for it: but thou must not take upon thee to judge Him . . . And know this, that whensoever there is any unjust exaction laid upon thee it is a plague and punishment for thy sin.

1 *How would you describe the kind of society outlined by Fortescue?*
2 *What comfort is Latimer able to offer to those suffering in this life?*

It is true of course that Calvin put forward a doctrine of limited resistance which was taken further by his successor Beza and Duplessis-Mornay. This remained, however, a minority view. As much for reformed thinkers as for Catholics, the consensus was that religion was the prime cohesive force in society. Life, they argued, was hard for Christians but these hardships were the inescapable result of Adam's fall from grace. For them sinful man must accept strong government; in obeying earthly rulers he obeyed God. As Paget wrote to Protector Somerset at the height of Kett's Rebellion in 1549, 'societie in a realme doth consiste and ys maynteyned by meane of religion and lawe'.

These theoretical objections against rebellion were supported by powerful practical arguments. There was always the threat that rebellion at home might be accompanied by danger from abroad as a contemporary wondered in 1536, 'If Lincolnshire seke to distroye Englande, what wonder is it if Fraunce and Scotlande sometime have fought to offend me?' Fears of invasion, especially of Habsburg domination, intensified as the century wore on. There were rumours that the French were poised to attack the Scilly Isles in 1549, and indeed Somerset's deployment of troops in that year took more account of potential French and Scottish moves than of the rebels.

Such anxieties could, of course, be heightened by reference to history, which could be used to show that rebellions had always failed in the past. Morrison in his *Lamentations* gave a catalogue of failed uprisings from the fourteenth and fifteenth centuries, reminding his readers of how Henry VII had dealt with the Cornishmen at Blackheath in 1496. Cranmer, meanwhile, culled examples from the Old Testament to show the fate of the children of Israel who rebelled against Moses, in his sermon on the 1549 rebellion. He also mentioned the 1525 Peasants' Revolt in Germany, maintaining that over 100 000 rebels had been killed in two months, and the later excesses of Jan of Leyden and the Anabaptists at Münster, the seige of which was followed by terrible carnage.

It was also worth reminding contemporaries of the punishment in store for captured rebels. While it is true that the Tudors had no standing army, they were usually able to rely on loyal forces to suppress disorder. There were in any event existing military obligations on citizens going back to the 1285 Statute of Westminster which obliged all able-bodied men between the ages of 16 and 60 to be equipped and skilled with weapons. There was in fact no real trained militia until at least 1573, and indeed the first rising to be put down by any sort of centralised system was the 1569 Revolt of the Northern Earls.

The scope of the law of treason was gradually extended in the course of the sixteenth century until it covered far more than offences against the person of the King and his family. Under Henry VIII it came to include threats to the King's status as Supreme Head of the Church of England, to his various marriages and to the succession. Further development took place under Elizabeth.

Moreover the authorities could proceed against treason in several ways. Parliament could pass an Act of Attainder against a prominent rebel which entailed the death penalty and the forfeiture of the family's possessions and honour. Judges could be sent on a Commission of Oyer and Terminer to deal with treason, but such a serious charge could not be heard by Quarter Sessions, the Star Chamber or the

Council of the North. However, the Council in the Marches of Wales had had such powers delegated to it. The scales were often weighted against the defendant, for the state of the law was often obscure, and vague gossip and confessions obtained under torture were sometimes admissable. Thus Court factions could occasionally manipulate justice for their own ends. In 1535, for example, Sir Thomas More was entrapped by Sir Richard Rich in private conversation, and in 1554 Sir Nicholas Throckmorton, accused of complicity in Wyatt's Rebellion, was allowed no defence counsel or access to law books. Not surprisingly, therefore, of 883 accused of treason between 1532 and 1540, no less than 38 per cent were executed.

Lesser charges could carry similarly baleful penalties. Arbitrary imprisonment and torture could follow from a charge of sedition, while rumour-mongers were liable to be sent to the galleys in chains, to be mutilated, whipped or pilloried. Indeed the use of torture seems to have become increasingly common after 1536, and the Council was not slow to use its right to commit prisoners to the Fleet. Such was the strength of the authorities' fear of the 'many-headed monster' of social turmoil and anarchy. Even the abortive 'Oxfordshire Rising' of 1596, which involved only a handful of conspirators and which never got beyond the planning stage, provoked a frenzied reaction from the political community.

Yet the Tudor period was marked by a series of rebellions in each of the categories listed above. What were these movements and what conclusions can the historian draw from their occurrence?

2 THE YORKSHIRE REBELLION 1489

Henry VII was bedevilled in the early years of his reign by threats to his throne. The exploits of Lambert Simnel are well known. In 1487 Simnel was presented by dissident Yorkists as 'Edward VI', the son of the Duke of Clarence and Isabel of Warwick, and hence the nephew of Edward IV. Crowned King of Ireland, he crossed the Irish Sea and was defeated in June at the Battle of Stoke, which can be seen as the last battle of the Wars of the Roses. Indeed it was the last occasion when a reigning king had to take the field in person against a rival claimant to the throne (*see page 35*).

The Yorkshire Rebellion, by contrast, can be seen as a classic example of a 'loyal' rebellion. Parliament granted Henry a subsidy of £100 000 to enable him to intervene on Brittany's behalf against the French Crown, and it fell to the fourth Earl of Northumberland to collect it. The population of the northern shires had suffered a poor harvest in 1488, and it was, in any case, unaccustomed to heavy taxation.

On 28 April 1489 Northumberland tried to explain to a mob at Topcliffe, near Thirsk, the need for the tax. Abandoned by his retinue, he was assassinated and the rebels went on to take York. Localised rioting continued and Henry made plans to come North, but the rising was crushed by the Earl of Surrey before the King could arrive.

Surrey hanged several ring-leaders, but Henry never received most of his subsidy and this method of raising money was never tried again. The incident had shown the fragility of public order, but it had never posed a serious danger to the monarchy or to Henry VII in person. The rebels wished to express a localised grievance in a way respectful to the King, if not to all his tax collectors. Henry, however, rated his financial needs and authority above popular consent.

3 THE CORNISH REBELLION 1497

The second popular disorder of Henry VII's reign was a much more serious affair than the Yorkshire Rising and overlapped with the second dynastic threat to his throne, when the Fleming Perkin Warbeck tried to impersonate Edward IV's younger son, Richard, Duke of York and to seize the throne with help from Ireland, France, Flanders and Scotland.

The Cornish Rising stemmed from Henry's need for money to deal with the Warbeck threat, and in 1497 he was granted an unprecedented parliamentary grant of £88 606 consisting of a subsidy, two-fifteenths and one-tenth. While Cornwall's MPs had voted for this exaction in Parliament, the Cornish people felt that a war in Scotland was too remote a cause for them and they began a march to present their grievances to the government. Under the leadership of Flamank, a Bodmin lawyer, and Joseph, a blacksmith from St Keverne in the Lizard, they marched via Exeter, Wells, Salisbury, Winchester and Guildford to Blackheath, a traditional gathering place for aggrieved peasants. On the way they managed to pick up a peer, Lord Audley, long disappointed that the King had not rewarded him better. The Cornishmen were careful to stress that their complaint was not against the King, but against his 'evil counsellors' Morton and Bray. This was not mere rhetoric, but a genuinely felt grievance against unpopular ministers. Henry's reaction was swift and decisive. On 16 June 25 000 royal troops put the Cornishmen to flight, killing up to 1000 of them. Audley, Flamank and Joseph were all executed and their dismembered heads were set up on London Bridge.

The revolt was not, however, in vain, for Henry came to terms with James IV at the Ayton truce and sought to run down his expensive commitments on the continent. The people of Cornwall had shown that they were not yet wholly absorbed into the nation.

4 RESISTANCE TO TAXATION 1513 TO 1525

The third rebellion reverts to the tradition of simple resistance to taxation, of which the Yorkshire Rising had been an example. In 1523 Wolsey tried to raise a substantial sum: this time he asked for £800 000. Despite the opposition of the House of Commons, who offered half that sum, he had collected £136 578 of the subsidy component of £151 215 by the spring of 1525. This represents the largest grant in taxation in the whole period from 1485 to 1543.

At this point, Wolsey decided to push his luck by sending out commissioners to collect the so-called 'Amicable Grant', which was really a non-parliamentary tax based on 1522 valuations. In many ways it most resembled a benevolence, seeking one-sixth of the value of the laity's goods and one-third of the clergy's. Commissions were sent out in late March to nobles and clerics in each county to levy the grant, but in Professor Scarisbrick's words they 'came upon lambs already close shorn'. Archbishop Warham of Canterbury reported the refusal of the Kentish clergy to pay, and the commissioners encountered similar difficulties in Norwich, Ely, Reading, Essex, Huntingdonshire, London, Warwickshire and elsewhere. The opposition seems due, partly to the unpopularity of Wolsey's foreign policy, and partly to a genuine inability to pay.

The most serious opposition to the Grant came, however, from the Lavenham and Sudbury areas of Suffolk from where the Dukes of Norfolk and Suffolk wrote to Henry urging concessions. Wolsey urged strong measures to enforce payment, but he was overruled by Henry who ordered the abandonment of the Grant, claiming that he had been unaware of it. Furthermore, in a carefully stage-managed display of clemency, Henry pardoned the ringleaders of the Suffolk rebels after their appearance in Star Chamber (*see also pages 71–2*).

For once a rebellion had been successful and Wolsey's enemies rejoiced to see his discomfiture at having to save Henry's face by accepting responsibility himself. Henry knew that his kingship rested ultimately on a partnership with the tax-paying classes, and that this vocal extra-parliamentary opinion would make an impact on his foreign policy. Three main factors seem to account for this result: London, usually loyal, was adamant and courageous in its resistance, opposition to the levy was spread widely over several counties and rumours of opposition in one county encouraged refusal elsewhere, and those councillors charged with the collection of the Grant, like Warham, Norfolk and Suffolk were quick to report the opposition to it.

5 THE LINCOLNSHIRE RISING 1536

The fourth major Tudor rebellion introduces, for the first time, an element of opposition to the religious changes being introduced in the course of the Henrician Reformation (*see pages 97–9*).

In September 1536, three sets of government commissioners were at work in Lincolnshire: Vicegerent Cromwell's commissioners to dissolve the smaller monasteries following the 1536 act, royal commissioners assessing and collecting the 1534 subsidy and Bishop Longland of Lincoln's agents enforcing the Ten Articles Act, and Cromwell's First Injunctions enquiring into the fitness and education of the clergy (including monks). It was widely believed that Longland was responsible for Henry VIII's divorce from Catherine of Aragon. Although the Bishop was doctrinally conservative, he was also a strict disciplinarian and the first prelate to implement the Injunctions with vigour.

In this atmosphere rumours abounded: church jewels and plate would be impounded; gold was to return to the mint for testing; taxes would be imposed on horned cattle, baptisms, marriages and burials; no church would be allowed within five miles of another; the eating of white bread, goose or capon was to require a tribute payable to the King. The fears of the beneficed clergy of the diocese were further aroused by fears of the confiscation of glebe (the farm land of a village priest) and tithes and their replacement by fixed stipends.

As the rumours spread the clergy gathered at Louth, Caistor and Horncastle. A rousing sermon preached at Louth on 1 October inflamed the several hundred beneficed clergy gathered there, and on the following day, the Bishop's registrar, arriving to carry out a visitation of the clergy, was seized by townsfolk guarding the church treasure house. Meanwhile, a leader emerged in Nicholas Melton, a shoemaker ('Captain Cobbler'), whose supporters seem to have been paid from church funds; but a more striking development from 4 October was the emerging leadership of at least eighteen local gentry in the rising. Their role was to give the movement an air of legitimacy, turning a plebeian riot into a demonstration against royal policies, and after the murder of Dr Raynes, Longland's hated chancellor, and the distribution of his money and clothes among the crowd, the gentry were able to present their articles of grievance.

Their manifesto included the following demands: the King should abandon the subsidy; the abbeys were to be untouched and their dissolution commissioners Leigh and Layton to be punished for their inquisitorial methods; the Church's 'ancient liberties' to be restored; and 'heretical' bishops like Cranmer and Latimer were to be removed. There were also two secular demands which seem to reflect gentry aspirations: that the Statute of Uses (*see page 462*) be repealed and that 'base-born' councillors, like Cromwell and Rich, be punished. The sheriff had to explain to the commons what the Statute of Uses was. It also seems unlikely that Lincolnshire peasants were familiar with Cromwell or Rich. It is perhaps significant that the rebels apparently accepted the Royal Supremacy; denial of this would after all have been treason.

Armed with this list of grievances 10 000 rebels marched to Lincoln joined by monks from three monasteries which feared dissolution – Barlings, Bardney and Kirkstead. Lord Hussey, the principal noble in the county, defected to them as the host approached the county town, damaging three of Longland's properties on the way and sending a revised set of their articles to London. The royal reply reached Lincoln on 10 October, threatening punishment if the rebels failed to disperse. Indeed, Henry had little good to say for the county and its inhabitants, describing them as: 'the rude commons of one shire, and that one of the most brute and beastly of the whole realm'.

Meanwhile a royal army under the Duke of Suffolk arrived at Stamford, forty miles away and the moment of decision for the eighteen gentry rebels had arrived. They decided that further resistance would be treason and sued for pardon. Clearly when it came to the point, no gentleman would appear in arms against his lawful sovereign. On 11 October Lancaster Herald (bearer of Royal instructions) arrived and persuaded the remaining rebels to go home. By 18 October the rising can be said to be over.

What then was the movement all about? It seems clear that there was a substantial element of religious conservatism articulated by priests and monks and accepted by the commons. Most historians are also convinced that the lead given by the gentry was significant. Substantial gentlemen like Willoughby and Dymoke had had earlier favours from the Tudors, but now they feared the Duke of Suffolk's attempt to create, with royal backing, a powerful Brandon interest in the shire. Charles Brandon, Duke of Suffolk, was after all Henry's brother-in-law and boon companion, who in 1529 had obtained the wardship of Katherine Willoughby, a Lincolnshire heiress, who was intended to marry his son, the Earl of Lincoln. In 1534 Lincoln died and Suffolk married Katherine himself and resisted all claims to the Willoughby inheritance from male members of the family. Hence the Willoughby participation in the rising seems readily explicable.

After the collapse of the rising the expected retribution followed: over a hundred death sentences were handed down for treason of which fifty-seven were carried out. Significantly perhaps the clergy were dealt with especially harshly, and on 14 November 1536, Lincolnshire received a royal pardon. By the end of the reign, however, it could be argued that the rebellion had eventually achieved some success: in 1540 the Statute of Uses was abandoned – to be replaced by the Statute of Wills; and two Lincolnshire gentry families enjoyed some favour, William Willoughby became a peer and Edward Dymoke was appointed treasurer of Boulogne.

6 THE PILGRIMAGE OF GRACE 1536

While the Lincolnshire events were serious, the rising in most of the counties further to the north between October and December 1536, over apparently similar issues, was the greatest expression of opposition that Henry VIII ever faced in England. It began in October when Robert Aske, an astute and successful lawyer, organised musters in the East Riding of Yorkshire on his return from visiting the Lincolnshire rebels at Caistor. On 16 October a force of 10 000 'pilgrims' took the city of York, and both Hull and Pontefract fell soon afterwards. The first version of their demands issued at York bore a close resemblance to those of the Lincolnshire rebels, attacking the dissolution of the monasteries, heretics, base-born royal councillors and the Statute of Uses. For their banner they chose the potent symbol of the Five Wounds of Christ, to which they added a marching song, the word 'pilgrimage' to describe their movement and the following oath:

> Ye shall not enter into this our Pilgrimage of Grace for the Commonwealth, but only for the love that ye do bear unto Almighty God his faith, and the Holy Church militant and the maintenance thereof, to the preservation of the King's person and his issue, to the purifying of the nobility, and to expulse all villein blood and evil councillors against the commonwealth from his Grace and his Privy Council of the same. And that ye shall not enter into our said Pilgrimage for no particular profit to yourself, nor to do any displeasure to any private person, but by counsel of the commonwealth, nor slay nor murder for no envy, but in your hearts put away fear and dread, and take afore you the Cross of Christ, and in your hearts His faith, the Restitution of the Church, the suppression of those Heretics and their opinions, by all the holy contents of this book.

1 *Why did the rebels choose the word 'pilgrimage' for their rising?*
2 *In what ways could the oath be regarded as loyal to the King?*

Meanwhile, rumours similar to those that had circulated in Lincolnshire were spread – perhaps deliberately by the clergy – throughout the North: that there would be taxes on baptisms, marriages and burials, on cows and sheep, and a prohibition on poor men eating dairy products or white bread. Simultaneously, risings appeared elsewhere in the North: in Northumberland and Durham and in areas of Yorkshire. All these areas rose on or around 11 October 1536, usually under noble or gentry leaders: thus Lord Latimer, a Neville and member of the Council of the North, and Sir Christopher Danby, took Barnard Castle, attacked and pillaged Bishop Tunstall of Durham's castle at Bishop Auckland before entering York. In Cumberland musters were held at Kirkby Stephen and Penrith and in Westmorland, but

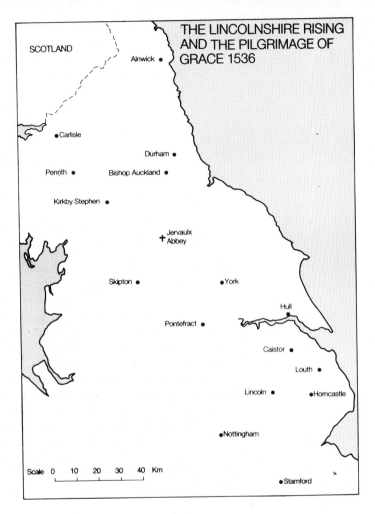

THE LINCOLNSHIRE RISING AND THE PILGRIMAGE OF GRACE 1536

SCOTLAND

Alnwick ●

● Carlisle

Durham ●

Penrith ●   Bishop Auckland ●

Kirkby Stephen ●

✝ Jervaulx Abbey

Skipton ●   ● York

Hull ●

Pontefract ●

Caistor ●

Louth ●

Lincoln ●   ● Horncastle

● Nottingham

Scale 0   10   20   30   40 Km

● Stamford

Lancashire stayed loyal when the Earl of Derby declared for the King and prevented rebellion from spilling over into Cheshire and North Wales. A few pockets of loyalty held out within the main rebel area: Scarborough, Skipton Castle, Berwick and Carlisle.

Such widespread disturbances caught the government unawares. The Duke of Suffolk was preoccupied in Lincolnshire, and the Earl of Shrewsbury awaited Henry's orders at Nottingham. Lord Darcy, holding Pontefract for the King, appealed for assistance but surrendered after a week's siege claiming that he had run out of supplies and gunpowder. As Darcy is known to have felt disgruntled at his exclusion from office, and to have opposed both Henry's divorce and the Royal Supremacy, this may be a thin excuse.

At this stage Aske's intentions seem to have been to overawe the government with a show of force and thus to get them to grant his demands. He had no plan to form an alternative regime or to remove Henry VIII; rather he seems to have wanted a greater say for the North in the nation's affairs, to remove Cromwell and to reverse certain policies of the Henrician Reformation. In order to achieve these aims he would need substantial magnate support, and he spent several days at Pontefract 19–21 October arguing the pilgrims' case to Darcy, Edward Lee, the Archbishop of York, and an assortment of knights and gentlemen. This case was now put forward in the form of the twenty-four Pontefract Articles, which were later put to Henry and which developed those presented at York, to include a demand for the return of a limited papal spiritual supremacy, a list of heretics, complaints about entry fines and enclosures and a demand that Princess Mary be restored her rights to the succession.

The pilgrims presented a petition to Henry at Doncaster. His reply of 2 November was to reject the demands, but promising a pardon for all save ten ringleaders. At this stage Henry seems to have felt that the rebellion would now collapse and he would be able to save face and maintain his prestige without making any concessions.

Henry's reply was regarded with suspicion by the pilgrims, who now proposed a second meeting at Doncaster, having clarified their manifesto, which Henry had found 'general, dark and obscure'. On 3 December Henry instructed Norfolk to grant a general pardon, prolong the truce and promise a Parliament, and on 6 December Norfolk met a delegation of pilgrims, to whom he promised that most of their articles could be discussed in Parliament, and that a compromise could be arrived at on the abbeys, which would surrender to the King's commissioners and then be restored until Parliament met. Aske announced these terms to 3000 commons at Pontefract on 7 December, and on the following day Lancaster Herald formally read the King's pardon to the commons who began to disperse. Aske submitted at Doncaster, kneeling in Norfolk's presence, abandoning the title of 'captain' and removing his badge.

Henry had won: he had stood by Cromwell and the 'heretic' bishops, neither ratifying nor repudiating the terms, which were in any case never written down. Thus ended the largest popular revolt in English history up to that time, or indeed ever, in terms of numbers and geographical range. The King had survived the greatest crisis of his reign by keeping a cool head and playing for time.

The problem remains, however, of establishing the cause or causes of the rising. Was it a popular rebellion of the North as a whole against the Henrician regime? Was it a feudal or neo-feudal phenomenon, a reaction by old-established and overmighty families of the North to Tudor centralisation? Or was it, as Professor Elton has claimed, an attempt by a defeated faction at Court to create a power base in the North to achieve a political victory over the centre? Certainly it is tempting to suggest that most of the grievances of the rebels did not affect the commons, and that the issue of the dissolution of the monasteries may have been exaggerated – after all the pilgrims made little effort to restore dissolved houses, of which, in any event, only the smaller had yet been affected. There is certainly evidence of incitement by gentry who used the same muster techniques as for war against the Scots, and no doubt many leading families, including the Percies, did have genuine complaints. Darcy, Constable and Hussey had a history of opposition at Court, all were religious conservatives and all had been in touch with Chapuys, the Imperial ambassador. Moreover Aske's links, both with this group and with the Lincolnshire rising, are clearly established. Was the Pilgrimage not therefore a pre-planned *coup* by a tightly knit group of disaffected conservative gentry?

To answer this question it will be necessary to examine a number of possible causes of unrest, and to address first the suggestion that there may have been economic grievances affecting the commons. Recent taxation measures had no doubt been unpopular, particularly after two years of dearth, bad weather and poor harvests but there is no evidence that this was a major grievance. Another possible material complaint was enclosures, but these were only resented in certain valleys of the West Riding of Yorkshire, the uplands of the Lake District, the Vale of York and a few other areas. Entry fines or gressums, whereby tenants paid a charge to inherit a tenancy were exacted west of the Pennines by the Cliffords and Nevilles, but they were not a serious problem elsewhere. Tithes were attacked in parts of the North-West, and the Earl of Cumberland's exploitation of the ancient feudal tenure of geld or cornage did arouse opposition on his lands. All told, however, it is hard to see that economic troubles, while no doubt serious, could have been by themselves a sufficient cause of a major rebellion.

Was the Pilgrimage perhaps a popular religious rising? Certainly the mass of the laity do seem to have opposed threats to traditional rituals, practices and beliefs. They cherished local religious festivals and church ornaments, and they were easily alarmed by the kind of rumours that spread so easily in 1536 about imminent confiscations and taxes. Moreover, monasteries were popular institutions, dispensing hospitality and education, maintaining vital public works, distributing alms and offering employment. However, it is worth pointing out that they were also valued by the gentry for lucrative monastic stewardships. Yet the pilgrims only attempted to restore 16 out of 55 dissolved houses in the North, and there is considerable evidence of clerical, rather than popular, pressure to express religious grievances. It would seem reasonable, therefore, to seek for further motives to explain the Pilgrimage as a whole.

Can the movement be seen as a feudal rising by the Percies or other northern magnate families? Henry Percy, sixth Earl of Northumberland, was the head of the most powerful magnate family, with estates in Northumberland itself, Yorkshire and Cumberland. He was, in addition, Warden of both the East and Middle Marches, Lieutenant of Yorkshire and life Sheriff of Northumberland, but he suffered from a serious weakness: the lack of an heir. Accordingly, in an extraordinary gesture, he made Henry VIII himself his sole heir, and thus he was in no position to lead the rising once it had begun. Hence he seems to have remained aloof while other members of his family, his brother Sir Thomas Percy for example, expressed their fears of the extension of royal power into the North-East rather more actively. Indeed Sir Ingram and Sir Thomas Percy fought for their own inheritance rather than for any grandiose 'Percy interest', but there were also many Percy tenants who joined the rising as captains including four members of Northumberland's council such as Aske himself.

It may, therefore, be possible to show that something of the old Percy network remained to figure in the rising, but what of other families? The Duke of Norfolk might have sympathised with the rising as an opponent of Cromwell and the 'heretical' bishops, but expediency and calculation seem to have kept him loyal – after all, this could be a chance for the Howards to spread their power and landholding from East Anglia to the North. The Earl of Shrewsbury was another religious conservative, but he had done well out of Henry VIII and his firm stand stiffened the resolve of others like Rutland and Huntingdon. The Earl of Derby, as we have seen, ensured that all of Lancashire, south of the River Ribble, stayed loyal, while Lord Dacre of Gilsland, acquitted in a treason trial only two years before, and the Neville Earl of Westmorland, lay low throughout the disturbances. The Clifford Earl of Cumberland found that part of the movement was directed against his exacting agrarian policies, so that he lacked an obvious incentive to back the revolt. For all their dislike of the Statute of Uses, therefore, many great nobles either supported the King or did nothing.

Finally, what can we make of the theory that the Pilgrimage was the result of a plot by members of the defeated Aragonese faction at Court? It is true that Hussey had been Mary Tudor's chamberlain and that Darcy, described by C S L Davies as 'a prime example of an enclosing landlord' had long plotted with Chapuys. For such men the chief enemy was perceived to be the upstart Thomas Cromwell, and the chief aim to restore Mary in the succession and to reverse the result of recent faction in-fighting at Court. Of course, if this theory is correct, it becomes easier to make sense of some of the articles in the Pontefract Manifesto, like the third clause about the Second Succession Act and the succession in Scotland. Aske and his associates were determined for Mary Tudor to succeed to avoid a Scottish claim stemming from the marriage of Henry's older sister Margaret to James IV of Scotland.

It is difficult, in the light of recent research, to regard the Pilgrimage as a truly popular or spontaneous rising; that there must have been some form of conspiracy is now beyond doubt. Yet the conspiracy theory is not able to provide a complete explanation of the outbreak of the rising, still less of its subsequent spread.

The North did not settle down with Aske's surrender, for Sir Francis Bigod's rebellion broke out in the East Riding in January 1537. He was captured in Cumberland the following month and suffered execution at Norfolk's hand with 177 of his cronies. Fellow victims included Lord Darcy, Sir Thomas Percy, Sir Stephen Hammerton, Sir Robert Constable, Robert Aske and a clutch of clerics, including the Prior of Bridlington and the Abbot of Jervaux.

Henry also re-organised the Council of the North, choosing first Bishop Tunstall, then Archbishop Holgate as its president, while he appointed a mere gentleman as Warden of the West March in Sir William Eure. The Crown had won a signal victory in the North in the 1530s, but the 1569 rising was to show that it would require more than one success to carry out a permanent change there. The extreme north remained both a military and an administrative problem.

7 THE WESTERN OR 'PRAYER BOOK' REBELLION 1549

It was not until 1549 that the spectre of rebellion arose again in England in two simultaneous, but unconnected risings (*see pages 167–70*).

The writ of Tudor government was always more difficult to enforce in the 'dark corners of the land': the Marches of Wales, the extreme north-west, the north-east and the south-west. The Western Rebellion erupted as a result of the attempts of Protector Somerset to compel all parishes to use the new 1549 Prayer Book, which represented a discernible shift towards Protestantism. On Whit Monday the parishioners of Sampford Courtenay in Devon objected to their priest saying the new service and forced him to say Mass in the old style, describing the new liturgy as 'but like a Christmas game'. By 20 June, a force of rebels from Devon and Cornwall gathered at Crediton where they were promised a general pardon on Somerset's behalf if they would disperse. At the same time the government ordered a Devon gentleman, Sir Peter Carew, to investigate the situation. By 23 June the rebel army had moved to Clyst St Mary, and Carew was on his way to London to report serious disorder.

The Protector's forces were already stretched with enclosure riots breaking out in Somerset, Wiltshire and Hampshire and in parts of the Midlands and the South-East. At the same time danger could always threaten from overseas to embarrass a regime beset by internal difficulties: either or both of the Scots or the French could invade. Nevertheless Somerset, who was later rather unfairly accused of lack of resolution in the 1549 disturbances, sent the Lord Privy Seal, Lord

Russell to put the rebellion down. On 16 August the rebels were annihilated by him at Okehampton, where as many as 4000 may have died on the rebel side.

Does the Prayer Book Rebellion then deserve its title? Certainly of the sixteen demands almost all are religious, demanding: Henry VIII's Six Articles Act, the Latin Mass, and a partial restoration of the monasteries. They must have been written by clerics who believed that no religious changes could legally take place while Edward VI was still a minor – in other words the 1549 Prayer Book was the work of 'evil counsellors'. Only one article is clearly secular, demanding a limit to the size of gentry households, and one is struck by the lack of gentry support for the movement – in contrast, of course, to the Pilgrimage of Grace. Most of the rising's leaders were yeomen or tradesmen; in other words from just outside the gentry class. The western gentry supported the Crown, perhaps aware of a vested interest in the progress of the Reformation stemming from their possession of former monastic lands.

8 KETT'S REBELLION 1549

While the Western Rebellion was at its height, a series of anti-enclosure riots in Norfolk rapidly grew into a major protest. Robert Kett, a well-to-do tanner turned landowner, encouraged disturbances against a neighbouring rival, Sir John Flowerdew, despite Kett's own record as an encloser of common land and a purchaser of former monastic property. By 12 July 16 000 rebels had set up camp on Mousehold Heath, just outside the city of Norwich. Neither the local gentry nor the city authorities were able to compel them to disperse, but on 21 July York Herald offered them a pardon if they would return home.

The rebels' reply was to attack Norwich and to overwhelm its feeble defences. On 30 July, William Parr, Marquis of Northampton, arrived with a force of 14 000 troops, including some Italian mercenaries and Suffolk gentry, but on the next day Northampton was obliged to abandon the city. The rebellion was finally put down by John Dudley, Earl of Warwick, who arrived with 12 000 men on 23 August. Four days later at Dussindale about 3000 rebels were killed and Kett was captured to be condemned to death for treason and hanged with forty-eight of his accomplices in December.

What then were the causes of the Kett Rebellion? Somerset himself has often been blamed for inciting the movement through his social policy, and it is quite true that he had set up a commission on enclosures which was still at work. Some of the rebels do seem to have believed that they were doing no more than anticipating government policy; in other words, that they were doing what the authorities wanted them to. Only one article of grievance refers specifically to enclosures, but there are plenty of references to the burden of rent increases, to wardships, common rights and foldcourse (where landlords could pasture their own flocks on tenants' land or common land). Two articles mention lawyers' seizure of, and speculation in, land, one criticises the local leet court for inequitable distribution of common land, and one urges freedom for bondmen, of which there were still a few in Norfolk on the Howard estates. The religious temper of the rebels was decidedly Protestant and the new 1549 Prayer Book was in daily use, while four of the articles of grievance were on religion: demanding better preaching, condemning non-residence among clergy, asking for clerical teaching of poor children and calling for tithe reform. Time and again the Kett rebels harked back to some golden age during Henry VII's reign. This was a protest of a local community mainly directed against the exactions of landlords, and thus it was difficult for it to evoke a national response.

Somerset's priority was to establish garrisons to deal with the French and Scottish threats before turning to internal disorder which had in any case broken out all over the country. Thus his initial response to Kett was conciliatory, while making clear that he had no time for rebels, 'lewd, seditious and evil disposed persons', as he put it. It was, after all, Somerset who sent Northampton to overawe the rebels and who was stunned by his failure. He now saw that this required a substantial military effort. If Russell had not put down the Western Rebellion, Somerset would probably have sent Warwick to Devon and given himself the Norfolk command. As it was, Warwick was now available to suppress Kett, and Somerset had to face criticism from his enemies on the Council of alleged weakness and hesitation in dealing with the crisis. With the advantage of hindsight Somerset's approach looks eminently reasonable. The Kett rising was serious, but it did not physically threaten the government unlike 1381, 1450 and 1497, for there was no plan to march on London or to release the King from the grip of evil ministers. Indeed, as we have seen, many of the rebels seem to have seen themselves as pro-government, merely pre-empting measures which they expected Somerset to take anyway.

9 THE ACCESSION OF MARY TUDOR AND WYATT'S REBELLION 1554

Mary Tudor's seizure of the throne after her half-brother's death (*see pages 177–8*) has some claim to be seen as the only successful rebellion in the entire Tudor period, leading Dr Loach to call it, 'one of the most surprising events of the sixteenth century'. It certainly contrasts sharply with the failed popular risings of 1549.

However, Wyatt's Rebellion showed that Mary's position on the throne was not immediately secure. With this rebellion we are back on familiar ground, for the early months of 1554 saw the first attempt since the days of Perkin Warbeck to unseat a reigning monarch, when Sir Thomas Wyatt, a Kentish gentleman, tried to mount a rebellion using the issue of Mary's projected marriage to Philip of Spain. Wyatt's plot was part of a wider network of risings planned at the end of 1553, involving Hertfordshire, Devon and Leicestershire, as well as the French ambassador Antoine de Noailles. Eventually only Wyatt managed to raise realistic support and he determined to pose as the rescuer of Mary from foolish advice, stirring up very effective anti-Spanish propaganda over the marriage issue. Little was said at first about more far-reaching aims, but it is fairly clear, at least, that Wyatt kept open the option of replacing Mary by Elizabeth if he could not compel the Queen to abandon her marital plans.

However, owing to his own errors and Mary's courage in remaining in London to rally resistance (*see pages 186–9*) Wyatt was defeated on the outskirts of the capital in February 1554.

Historians have been divided as to the weight which they place upon religious or political motives in Wyatt's Rebellion. Clearly Wyatt tapped a rich vein of anti-Spanish xenophobia and he received support from those who preferred an English bridegroom, Edward Courtenay perhaps, and who feared entanglements in French wars if the links with Spain were further reinforced. There is quite strong evidence that many of the rebels were Protestants, including some of the leaders, although it has not been possible to establish that Wyatt himself was Protestant. What is clear, however, is that a good many of Mary's subjects were sufficiently disgruntled with her policies after the first few months of her reign to contemplate open rebellion and, moreover, that Wyatt came nearer than any other Tudor rebel to removing a monarch from the throne. While Wyatt involved fewer men than in the 1549 rebellions, his proximity to London and his manifest intention to take the capital made him infinitely more dangerous. Its danger was enhanced because it was a quarrel within the ranks of the political community, rather than a threat to the whole social order when the élite would tend to close ranks. It could also be seen as a violent attempt by a section of the political nation to interfere in the formulation of foreign policy, and this may well have been a new trend.

Fortunately for Mary, loyalty to the Tudor dynasty, pure chance and abhorrence of all rebellion came to her aid, and of course it is now clear that Wyatt suffered significant weaknesses from the start. Opposition to the Spanish match may well have been strong, but it was not that strong. Wyatt only managed to involve one important noble – the Duke of Suffolk – and he failed to raise a worthwhile force. Finally, for all the Protestant zeal of some of those who did choose to take part, the orthodox Protestant leadership refused to get involved, fearing perhaps to challenge a legitimate monarch and hoping that Mary's religious policies would turn out to be more moderate than they did. A conventional domestic revolt had little chance of success against a monarch sustained by enough magnates.

10 THE REVOLT OF THE NORTHERN EARLS 1569

There were no further uprisings in Mary's reign, and Elizabeth had a chance to establish her regime before a rebellion emerged once again in a familiar area – the north-east led by the Earls of Northumberland and Westmorland (*see pages 247–8*).

In 1568, Mary Queen of Scots fled to England in the aftermath of her defeat in Scotland, and over the course of the next twenty years she was involved in numerous plots against Elizabeth to restore Catholicism and to place her on the throne. Almost all of these conspiracies were uncovered and the chief plotters dealt with before they could be put into effect: the Ridolfi Plot of 1571, the Parry Plot of 1585 and the Babington Plot of 1586 all ended in this way. The only one which became a rebellion as such was the Northern Rising in 1569.

Mary, of course, was a danger partly because of her Catholicism and partly because of her claim to the English throne – all the more so when Elizabeth remained unmarried and the succession question remained very much alive. At the same time relations with Spain were poor, especially after Cecil's orders to impound a Spanish bullion fleet in English harbours, Cecil was unpopular for other reasons and Protestantism had yet to take a hold.

A plan emerged to marry the Duke of Norfolk to Mary: this would, it was argued, cause the overthrow of Cecil, settle the succession problem and ensure peace with both France and Spain thus ensuring that England would no longer be isolated in Europe. The plan had some appeal to Protestants like Leicester, Pembroke and Throckmorton, who saw it as a way of reducing the potency of Mary's own commitment to Catholicism, as Norfolk was a Protestant himself. It had, of course, rather less appeal to Elizabeth who foresaw that Mary would soon become recognised as her heir, that an ultimate Catholic succession was therefore inevitable and that she would have to dispense with the loyal and able William Cecil.

On 6 September Leicester confessed his involvement and on the 16 September Norfolk left the Court for his estate at Kenninghall in Norfolk and the natural assumption was that he had gone to raise the North. It is doubtful, however, if a coherent plan existed at this stage, partly because papal approval for a Catholic conspiracy in the form of the Bull *Regnans in Excelsis* did not appear until 1570, and partly because of the weak link in the form of the Earl of Northumberland, who sympathised with the outlines of the plan, but urged Mary to marry a Catholic like Philip II of Spain.

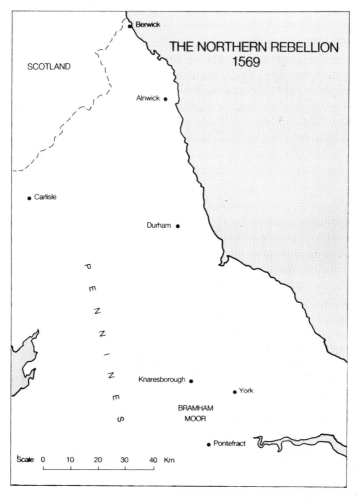

THE NORTHERN REBELLION
1569

SCOTLAND

Berwick

Alnwick ●

● Carlisle

Durham ●

P
E
N
N
I
N
E
S

Knaresborough ●

● York

BRAMHAM
MOOR

● Pontefract

Scale 0   10   20   30   40 Km

The Percy family had been restored to their ancient dignity as Earls
of Northumberland in 1557 and to the Wardenships of the East and
Middle Marches. While their prestige was not what it had been, they
still owned forty townships, two key castles at Alnwick and
Warkworth and 2000 tenants scattered over the far north-east,
Yorkshire, Cumberland and Sussex, but the Earls' doubts were compounded by Norfolk's indecision.

Norfolk was aware that his own gentry and tenantry in East Anglia
would be reluctant to rise, and on 1 October he sent his brother-in-law
Charles, sixth Earl of Westmorland, a message urging him not to rebel.
He then returned to London to throw himself on Elizabeth's mercy,
thus placing the two northern Earls in a dilemma, from which they
tried to extricate themselves by assuring the Earl of Sussex at York on 9
October that they had no part in any plot. Sussex seemed convinced by

495

this for he reported on 13 October, 'all is very quiet here and the time of year will shortly cool hot humours', but Elizabeth summoned the two lords to appear before the Council in London with a fuller explanation. Meanwhile Northumberland hesitated as Mary and the Spanish ambassador, de Spes, urged caution.

Yet during the first week of November both Earls came to the conclusion that they had to rise as all other avenues had failed to change the Queen's policies. Their Catholic followers were urging them to rebel, and the formidable Lady Westmorland reinforced this advice with her own pressure. They were also naturally worried by Elizabeth's insistence that they should come to Court. Thus on 14 November they made their first demonstration at Durham Cathedral when all evidence of Protestantism was removed and Mass celebrated according to the old rite.

Sussex viewed events with concern and on 16 November wrote to the Council about the difficulties in raising troops, and on the same day the Earls issued this proclamation:

Thomas, Earl of Northumberland and Charles, Earl of Westmorland, the Queen's most true and lawful subjects, and to all her highness' people, sends greeting:- Whereas diverse new set up nobles about the Queen's majesty, have and do daily, not only go about to overthrow and put down the ancient nobility of this realm, but also have misused the Queen's majesty's own person, and also have by the space of twelve years now past, set up, and maintained a new found religion and heresy, contrary to God's word. For the amending and redressing whereof, diverse foreign powers do purpose shortly to invade these realms, which will be to our utter destruction, if we do not ourselves speedily forfend the same. Wherefore we are now constrained at this time to go about to amend and redress it ourselves, which if we should not do and foreigners enter upon us we should be all made slaves and bondmen to them. These are therefore to will and require you, and every of you, being above the age of sixteen years and not sixty, as your duty to God doth bind you, for the setting forth of his true and catholic religion; and as you tender the commonwealth of your country, to come and resort unto us with all speed, with all such armour and furniture as you, or any of you have. This fail you not herein, as you will answer the contrary at your perils. God save the Queen.

1 *Comment on the references to the Queen in this passage.*

2 *What arguments are used in the passage to justify rebellion?*

By 22 November the rebels had reached Bramham Moor near Tadcaster with roughly 5400 men while Sussex disposed of less than a tenth of this force. He was therefore surprised to hear that on 24 November the rebels had turned back to Knaresborough. This move was, however, partly to consolidate their strength and partly to await Spanish help in the North, where they believed their strength to lie. Rumours abounded of the approach of fresh royal forces, and the rebels feared the imminent removal of Mary to Coventry in the hands of the loyalist Earl of Shrewsbury. Support from Lancashire and Cheshire was also missing as both the Bishop of Carlisle and the Earl of Derby (Lord-Lieutenant of Lancashire) were popular with local Catholic gentry. Finally they were disappointed by the failure of their appeals to Catholic nobles and by the lack of Spanish help – the Duke of Alva apparently thought that the whole venture was unsound and that he was better occupied in putting down the revolt in the Netherlands.

By December it was clear that the royal forces, using the new militia system, would soon wear down the rising, and by the end of the month both leaders were safely over the border in Scotland. Their rising had failed through its incoherence and aimlessness, its lack of clear articles or demands, its limited geographical support, the failure to mobilise fully the resources of the two Earls and a confusion over their precise religious aims. Moreover, several vital nobles failed to cross the Pennines to assist: Cumberland, despite being a supporter of Mary, lacked vigour, Dacre was involved in litigation, and Lord Scrope, Norfolk's brother-in-law, loyally kept order in Cumberland for the Queen throughout the disturbances. A small group of local nobles and gentry actively contained the rebellion, among them the Vice-President of the Council of the North, Sir Thomas Gargrave, who held Pontefract, Sir John Forster, who held the Berwick area and Sussex himself. Elizabeth sought revenge, but many of the 700 death sentences were commuted. Westmorland died in exile, his lands confiscated and his title abolished, while Northumberland was betrayed into government hands and was executed at York in August 1572.

What caused the Earls to embark on such a desperate adventure? Personal resentment of the encroachments of the Tudor regime must have played a large part: Northumberland had been deprived of the Wardenship of the Middle March in favour of his arch-rival Sir John Forster, and Elizabeth's cousin Lord Hunsdon was given charge of Berwick and the East March. Westmorland's feelings were similar: he felt impoverished, he had recently lost the title 'Lieutenant General of the North' which he had held under Mary Tudor and his wife, Norfolk's sister, exerted pressure of her own, exclaiming of her brother, 'What a simple man the Duke is, to begin a matter and not to go through with it; we and our country were shamed for ever, that now in the end we should seek holes to creep into.' Bastard feudal allegiance still counted for something in the far North: gentry involved in the rebellion were often the Earls' retainers and the largest groups of supporters came from Brancepeth, Raby and Topcliffe all either Neville or Percy seats.

Religion also played a major part: of the four main agitators two, Thomas Markenfeld and Dr Morton, had both just returned from trips abroad fired with enthusiasm for the Counter-reformation and Northumberland himself had converted to Catholicism as recently as 1567. There was also resentment at the apparent influx of militant Protestant clergy into the Durham diocese led by the puritan Bishop Pilkington. Perhaps Professor Lawrence Stone is right when he describes the rising as 'the last episode in 500 years of protest by the Highland Zone against the interference of London'.

The long term settlement of the North does suggest that the traditional autonomy of the region had finally withered. The Earldom of Northumberland passed in 1572 to Sir Henry Percy, who never held office in the North and lacked a clientage network there, preferring to live at Petworth in Sussex. The Council of the North was reconstituted in 1572 under the Puritan third Earl of Huntingdon, the Queen's cousin and an outsider with no local ties, to include Durham, Northumberland, Cumberland and Westmorland in its area of responsibility. Aristocratic territorial power seemed a growing anachronism in Elizabethan England.

11 THE ESSEX REVOLT 1601

The last Tudor rebellion ends the series with a whimper rather than a bang: the almost farcical attempt by a disgruntled and over-mighty subject to seize power.

As the 1590s wore on, the Earl of Essex felt increasingly both that he was thwarted in his own advancement by Burghley, and that his own personal following would melt away if he could not sufficiently reward his own clients. Indeed, when Burghley died in 1598 Essex's worst fears seemed to be realised: Burghley's son Robert Cecil became both Chancellor of the Duchy of Lancaster and Master of the Court of Wards, and one of his protégés, Lord Buckhurst, became Lord Treasurer. Essex found his own position threatened soon after his triumph in 1596 at Cadiz, when he returned to Court in 1599 from Ireland having failed to put down the Earl of Tyrone's rebellion. When Elizabeth destroyed Essex's credit structure in September 1600 by refusing to renew his patents on the import of sweet wines, Essex was faced with two options: retire and retrench or try to seize power by force.

It came as little surprise when Essex went for the second option, gathering an affinity of disgruntled noblemen, all like himself deeply in debt and including three other Earls, Southampton, Bedford and Rutland. Thus Essex assembled a coalition of impecunious, disaffected place-seekers, whose motives were largely personal. There was for example no religious unity in the group, for many Essexians were Catholics – among them Blount, Danvers, Catesby and Tresham – while Essex himself was a Protestant. Foreign policy was perhaps more of a bone of contention, as Essex favoured a more vigorous, daring policy in the Netherlands, in France and at sea, while Cecil was keen to reduce commitments.

The rising itself was all over in the course of a few hours on the streets of London on 8 February 1601. Essex himself was captured and shortly executed. Thus ended ignominiously a struggle for power and influence showing that the technique of palace revolution was no longer feasible as an instrument of Court politics.

12 CONCLUSION

Is it possible to reach any sort of general conclusions from such a disparate set of events?

The historian is struck first perhaps by the refusal of most rebels to challenge the Crown directly. The aura of monarchy and the widespread belief in theories of obligation usually prevented explicit criticism of the monarch. Even Wyatt's Rebellion shows this, for while Wyatt himself had a coherent plan to remove Mary Tudor, many of his supporters saw the main motive as to stop the marriage. Rebels preferred to seek a scapegoat like Cromwell in 1536 or Cecil in 1569 and to protest their loyalty to the Crown. This tactic made it harder, even after 1534, to convict them for treason – even rioting to do damage was only treasonable if at least forty people were present for more than two hours.

Secondly, it is clear that each Tudor monarch faced at least one serious revolt and that they encountered significant military problems in suppressing them. The Duke of Norfolk was nervous about engaging his troops in 1536, and in 1549 Somerset had to resort to foreign mercenaries, when his difficulties were exacerbated by the absence of a leading nobleman in each of the areas of revolt: in 1549 Norfolk was in the Tower and the Earl of Devon was absent from the West Country. Certainly the authorities were worried in 1549 that the harmony of Tudor society was about to collapse: Somerset complained, 'All have conceived a wonderful hate against gentlemen and taketh them all as their enemies' and Cranmer had this to say of the Western Rebels, 'standeth it with any reason to turn upside down the good order of the whole world, that is everywhere and hath been, that is to say the commoners to be governed by the nobles and the servants by their masters?' Mary Tudor could not have survived Wyatt's Rebellion in 1554 without the loyalty of several key nobles and their retainers, and the need was seen for more effective propaganda and some kind of national militia. In the short run Mary enhanced magnate power, at least in the North, by restoring Northumberland to his estates as a bulwark against Scottish incursions in 1557, but in the longer term Elizabeth drove the northern magnates themselves to revolt and began the construction of a northern security system that did not rely on over-mighty nobles.

Thirdly, it is difficult to detect a clear link between poor harvests and outbursts of rebellion. Burghley declared, 'there is nothing will sooner lead men into sedition than dearth of victual', but many historians will agree with Professor Hobsbawm, that people who are hungry are so concerned with finding food to live, that they have no time for anything else. In fact none of the major disorders was directly occasioned by dearth: the 1535 harvest was poor but that in 1536 was good, there was a straight run of good harvests from 1546 to 1548 and the three that preceded the 1569 rebellion were all bountiful too. The worst harvests were from 1555 to 1557 and from 1594 to 1598 when no revolts occurred.

Fourthly, amazingly little violence was inflicted by the rebels, although of course the government's revenge was frequently savage. In 1536 the Lincolnshire rebels only killed two people, and, in general, outbursts of violence and victimisation were isolated incidents in what were essentially movements of peaceful resistance to specific policies of the government. In Kett's Rebellion, Matthew Parker escaped with a bad fright after preaching on disobedience. French peasant upheavals were by contrast much more violent.

Fifthly, the relative lack of resistance to taxation demands, with a few obvious exceptions like 1525, also contrasts markedly with French experience. The principle of tithe-paying was never challenged; indeed a conservative resistance to disturbance in the pattern of traditional Catholic worship looms much larger as an issue. There were, moreover, no extreme radical Protestant sects involved in disorders – unlike in Germany.

Sixthly, one cannot but be struck by the provincialism of most rebellions. Almost every rising was the response of a local community to purely local grievance, and hence co-ordination with other areas hardly ever happened, if it was even tried. Peasants were reluctant to stray far from their fields, especially at harvest time. Only the gentry could have organised a more widespread uprising, and as we have seen, gentry leadership of popular revolts was by no means universal.

Finally, did Tudor rebellions achieve any of their aims, or restrain the actions of either the monarch or the ruling élite? The 1525 reaction to the 'Amicable Grant' was successful in the short run, but it had no permanent effect in restraining Henry VIII's demands for more revenue, and the 1549 rebellions led to Northumberland's triumph over Somerset, uniting the ruling class and ensuring firmer government control. It is true that the Statute of Uses, which featured as an issue in

1536, was partially revoked by the later Statute of Wills, but it could be argued strongly that the sixteenth-century rebellions tended to strengthen, as well as, to restrain the Crown. The Crown had a chance to eliminate, or at least greatly to weaken, some of its main enemies – Neville, Percy and Howard, and to improve military recruitment and installations. Under Elizabeth more draconian treason laws were passed and the landed classes' fears may well have disposed them to greater loyalty to the established order. From the vantage point of 1603, the Crown seemed to have ridden the storms of the previous 120 years very well.

13 BIBLIOGRAPHY

C S L Davies *Peace, Print and Protestantism* (Paladin, 1977).
G R Elton *Reform and Reformation* (Edward Arnold, 1977).
A Fletcher *Tudor Rebellions* (Longman Seminar Studies, 3rd edition 1983).
J Guy *Tudor England* (OUP, 1988).
P Williams *The Tudor Regime* (OUP, 1979).
J Youings *Sixteenth Century England* (Penguin, 1984).

14 DISCUSSION POINTS AND EXERCISES

A *This section consists of questions or points that might be used for discussion (or written answers) as a way of expanding on the chapter and testing understanding of it:*

1 What prevented rebellions happening more often than they did?

2 In what sense was the Yorkshire Rebellion a 'loyal' rebellion?

3 Did the 1497 Cornish Rebellion achieve anything?

4 Why was the 'Amicable Grant' withdrawn?

5 How far was the Lincolnshire uprising of 1536 a 'popular' rebellion?

6 What evidence is there that the Pilgrimage of Grace was a pre-planned conspiracy?

7 Why did the Prayer Book Rebellion of 1549 occur in the West Country?

8 How far is it reasonable to describe Kett's Rebellion as 'conservative'?

9 Can Mary Tudor's accession in 1553 be accurately described as 'the only successful rebellion of the sixteenth century'? Why was it so successful?

10 Why did Wyatt's Rebellion of 1554 come so near to success but ultimately fail?

11 Was the Northern Earls' Rebellion of 1569 doomed from the start? How far was its suppression a turning point?

12 Was Essex's Revolt 'first and foremost a struggle for power and influence, in which issues were of minor significance'?

13 Why was the government wrong to fear popular rebellion after the disastrous harvests of the mid-1590s?

14 Why were Tudor rebellions so limited in their effects?

B *Essay questions*

1 Why did the Tudor dynasty experience so many rebellions?

2 Were the disorders between 1549 and 1554 part of a continuing crisis?

3 Did sixteenth-century rebellions strengthen or weaken the Tudor regime?

4 Were Tudor rebellions 'conservative' or 'radical'?

5 Why were rebellions against the Tudors almost always unsuccessful?

6 'Despite the government's fears, by the end of the sixteenth century the threat of rebellion had much diminished.' Discuss.

15 EXERCISE – TYPES OF REBELLION

Write a brief outline of each rebellion in answer to these questions:

1 What were the motives for rebellion?

2 How did the rebels try to bring pressure to bear on the government?

3 How close did the rebellion come to success?

4 How neatly does this rebellion fit into one of the two types outlined at the beginning of the chapter: (*a*) an attempt to seize power? (*b*) A protest or demonstration in force?

Then answer the following general questions:

1 Which were the protests of most widespread popularity? What made them so popular?

2 What conditions made it more or less likely that there would be an attempt to seize political power?

3 Can you suggest any further types of rebellion beyond the two already identified?

4 Was one type of rebellion more likely to succeed than another?

INDEX

Shrewsbury d. 1538   486, 489
Talbot, Sir John, Earl of Shrewsbury 5, 9
Tawney, Professor R H   457, 463
tenant-at-will   458
Ten Articles (1536)   14ff, 111, 422
Tewkesbury, Battle of (1471)   4, 16
Thirty-nine Articles of the Church of England (1563)   243, 255, 265
Thomas, Keith   378, 388–95 *passim*
Throckmorton, Sir George   137
Throckmorton, Sir Nicholas   306
Throckmorton Plot (1583)   249, 322
Tillyard, E M W   401, 430
Tiptoft, John, 1st Earl of Worcester 344
Tittler, Professor R   185, 188, 196, 202
Towton, Battle of (1461)   4, 13
Treason Act (1534)   95f, 133, 162
Treasons Act (1571)   248, 276
Treatise for Reformation without Tarrying for Any (1571)   258f
Trevor-Roper, Professor Hugh 393, 463
Troyes, Treaty of (1420)   4
Troyes, Treaty of (1564)   306
Tudor, Jasper, Earl of Pembroke, Duke of Bedford   15, 26, 33, 34
tunnage and poundage   20, 44, 51, 69
Tunstall, Cuthbert (Bishop of London, later Bishop of Durham)   164, 174, 194, 351
Turner, Dr William   164, 257
Tyndale, William   85, 89, 420
Tyrell, Anthony   249
Tyrone's Rebellion (1595–1603) 326f, 370ff

Udal, Nicholas   168, 415
Uniformity, Act of (1549)   167, 192
Uniformity, Act of (1552)   175f, 192
Uniformity, Act of (1559)   242f, 245, 253, 260, 285, 467
Union of Utrecht   322
Uses, Satute of (1536)   462, 483f

Valor Ecclesiasticus (1535)   98
Vaucelles, Truce of (1556)   200
Vaughan, Sir Cuthbert   200

Vere, John de, 13th Earl of Oxford 34
Vergil, Polydore   2, 38f, 62, 72f, 417
Vermigli, Peter Martyr   164, 192
Vesey, John (Bishop of Exeter) 165, 174, 341, 349
Vestiarian Controversy (1559) 252f, 263, 264

Wakefield, Battle of (1466)   4, 12
Wales   16, 17f, 26, 43, 130, 335f, 339, 349ff
Walsingham, Sir Francis   211–19 *passim*, 302, 315, 316
Warbeck, Perkin   35, 36f, 345
wardship   21, 44, 45, 228, 232
Warham, William (Archbishop of Canterbury, Lord Chancellor) 58f, 92
Warwick, Earl of *see* Neville, Richard, 1st Earl of Warwick; George, Duke of Clarence, 1st Earl of Warwick; Edward, 2nd Earl of Warwick; Dudley, John, 1st Earl of Warwick
Watson, Thomas (Bishop of Lincoln)   194, 196
Wentworth, Paul, MP   280, 282
Wentworth, Peter, MP   258, 281, 282, 286f, 291
Wernham, R B   41, 188, 305, 307, 312
Western Rebellion *see* Prayer Book Rebellion
Westmorland, Earl of *see* Neville, Henry, 5th Earl of Westmorland; Neville, Charles, 6th Earl of Westmorland
Whig   390, 439
Whitgift, John (Archbishop of Canterbury)   215, 219, 257, 258, 264ff
Williams, Penry   34, 47, 224
Wills, Statute of (1540)   462
Wiltshire, Earl of *see* Boleyn, Sir Thomas, 1st Earl of Wiltshire; Paulet, Sir William, 1st Earl of Wiltshire
Winchester, Marquis of *see* Paulet, Sir William, Marquis of Winchester
witchcraft   392–6